International Business

Third edition

Stuart Wall

Sonal Minocha

Bronwen Rees

**Financial Times
Prentice Hall
is an imprint of**

Harlow, England • London • New York • Boston • San Francisco • Toronto • Sydney • Singapore • Hong Kong
Tokyo • Seoul • Taipei • New Delhi • Cape Town • Madrid • Mexico City • Amsterdam • Munich • Paris • Milan

Pearson Education Limited
Edinburgh Gate
Harlow
Essex CM20 2JE
England
and Associated Companies throughout the world

Visit us on the World Wide Web at:
www.pearsoned.co.uk

First published 2001
Third edition published 2010

ISBN: 978-0-273-72372-1

British Library Cataloguing-in-Publication Data
A catalogue record for this book is available from the British Library

Library of Congress Cataloging-in-Publication Data
Wall, Stuart, 1946–
  International business / Stuart Wall, Sonal Minocha, and Bronwen Rees.
— 3rd ed.
      p. cm.
  Includes bibliographical references and index.
  ISBN 978-0-273-72372-1 (pbk. : alk. paper) 1. International business
enterprises. 2. International economic relations. 3. Globalization.
I. Minocha, Sonal. II. Rees, Bronwen. III. Title.
  HD62.4. W343 2010
  338.8'8

10 9 8 7 6 5 4 3 2
13 12 11 10 09

Typeset in 10/12.5 pt Sabon by 73
Printed and bound by Ashford Color Press, Gosport

The publisher's policy is to use paper manufactured from sustainable forests.

Brief contents

Contents

3 International business: theory and practice   79

8 International human resource management

Supporting resources

Visit **www.pearsoned.co.uk/wall** to find valuable online resources

Companion Website for students
- Self-assessment questions to test your understanding
- Weblinks to useful sources of information
- Short answer questions to develop your skills in analysing and interpreting data

For instructors
- Complete, downloadable Instructor's Manual
- Powerpoint slides that can be downloaded and used for in-class presentations

Also: The Companion Website provides the following features:
- Search tool to help locate specific items of content
- E-mail results and profile tools to send results of quizzes to instructors
- Online help and support to assist with website usage and troubleshooting

For more information please contact your local Pearson Education sales representative or visit **www.pearsoned.co.uk/wall**

Preface: using this book

The inter-connectedness of our global economy has been brought into sharp focus by the worldwide impact of the so-called 'credit crunch', which many see as having its origin in the ('sub prime') housing market of the USA. Problems which began with excessive lending by financial intermediaries to non-creditworthy house purchasers in the USA quickly escalated into a worldwide recession, brought about by 'financial engineering' which created a wide range of derivative assets based on these high risk mortgages. The impacts of holding such 'toxic' assets in the portfolios of financial institutions of many countries have been felt by companies and individuals worldwide, with liquidity shortages reducing global demand, output and employment.

This book is primarily written for students taking modules in *international business* on a range of undergraduate and postgraduate programmes. Any text on international business must, of necessity, span a wide variety of topic areas and embrace a number of different subject disciplines. In that sense it is clearly difficult to locate its boundaries precisely. What we can be sure about is that we are studying a vibrant, ever-changing set of issues and relationships, which will almost certainly have major impacts on all our lives. It could hardly be otherwise when almost one-quarter of the world's recorded output is exported and when changes in business practices or technology in Beijing (China), will have major implications for a workforce as far away as Detroit (USA) or Birmingham (UK)! It has become increasingly clear that a proper understanding of worldwide patterns and trends in international business must draw upon far more than the conventional economic discipline of 'international trade and finance', or the in-depth analysis of 'multinational firm activity', or even the study of key functional areas such as marketing, management, finance and accounting. Important though all these contributions undoubtedly are, attention is increasingly being paid to the often subtle, but highly significant, organisational and cultural characteristics that underpin production and trade in a globalised economy. In fact, today's study of international business draws heavily on disciplines as diverse as law, sociology, anthropology, psychology, politics, history and geography, as well as those previously mentioned.

The first chapter of this book identifies some current patterns and trends, which are of key concern to those engaged in international business, whether from a corporate or national perspective. Chapters 2 to 6 then concentrate on issues that affect most types of international business, whatever their sector of activity, nature of operations or stage reached in the internationalisation process. The principles, practices and institutions underpinning international trading relationships are reviewed, as are a wide variety of external 'environmental factors', which play a key role in determining both the direction and outcome of international business activity. These include political, legal, sociocultural, ethical, ecological, economic and technological factors, all of which shape the environment in which the international business must operate. After considering these 'universal' aspects of international business, the more 'firm-specific' aspects are investigated in Chapters 7 to 10 with an in-depth analysis of the alternative courses of action facing the international business, whether in terms of corporate strategy, human resource management, marketing, accounting and finance, operations management or logistics.

Throughout the book you will find up-to-date case materials to illustrate many of the international issues involved. A number of questions will help direct your thoughts to some of the principles underpinning the facts and events presented in each case study. In a similar vein, you will also find a number of 'pause for thought' sections within the text of each chapter, to which you will find outline responses at the end of the book to self-check your lines of reasoning. A number of 'Boxes' are presented to take further some of the analysis presented in the text. Each chapter concludes with a brief review of further sources of reading and information, including useful websites.

If you turn to the *companion website* to this book, some interactive questions (with solutions) can be found to help you self-check the content of each chapter.

For this third edition all data, empirical and case study materials have been thoroughly updated and revised with a number of entirely new cases integrated within the text. On occasions the text has been further developed to reflect contemporary debate, as with the more detailed scrutiny of the international financial system and associated accounting conventions and standards in Chapter 10.

Acknowledgements

We should like to thank Geoff Black, who has made an important contribution to Chapter 10. We would also like to thank Alan Griffiths for contributing important case materials at various parts of the text and Jonathan Wilson for much helpful advice and useful additional content on China.

We would also like to express our gratitude for all the help received from Eleanor Wall in helping develop case studies and other applied materials for the book. Our thanks also to all those who have given permission for the use of material in the book.

Stuart Wall
Sonal Minocha
Bronwen Rees

Publisher's acknowledgements

We are grateful to the following for permission to reproduce copyright material:

Figures
Figures 2.2 and 3.6 adapted from Healey, N. The Multinational Corporation, in *Applied Economics*, 11th edn (Griffith, A. and Wall, S. (eds) 2007), Pearson Education; Figure 3.3 from Michael E. Porter, *The Competitive Advantage of Nations*, published 1998, Palgrave, reproduced with permission of Palgrave Macmillan also reprinted with the permission of The Free Press, a Division of Simon & Schuster, Inc., from THE COMPETITIVE ADVANTAGE

OF NATIONS by Michael E. Porter. Copyright © 1990, 1998 Michael E. Porter. All rights reserved. Figure 5.1 adapted from *International Business: A Managerial Perspective*, Addison-Wesley (Griffin, R.W. and Pustay, M.W. 1996); Figure 5.2 adapted from *Cultures and Organizations: Software of the Mind*, Revised and Expanded 2nd Edition, McGraw-Hill (Hofstede, G. and Hofstede, G.J. 2005); Figure 7.1(b) adapted with the permission of The Free Press, a Division of Simon & Schuster, Inc., from COMPETITIVE STRATEGY: Techniques for Analyzing Industries and Competitors by Michael E. Porter. Copyright © 1980, 1998 by The Free Press. All rights reserved. Figure 7.2 The BCG Portfolio Matrix from the Product Portfolio Matrix, © 1970, The Boston Consulting Group. Figure 7.3(a) reprinted by permission of *Harvard Business Review*. From 'Strategies of Diversification' by H.I. Ansoff, Sep/Oct 1957. Copyright 1957 by the Harvard Business School Publishing Corporation, all rights reserved. Figure 7.5 adapted with the permission of The Free Press, a Division of Simon & Schuster, Inc. from COMPETITIVE ADVANTAGE: Creating and Sustaining Superior Performance by Michael E. Porter. Copyright © 1985, 1998 by Michael E. Porter. All rights reserved. Figure 7.11 from Horizontal Acquisitions: The Benefits and Risk to Long-term Performance, in *Mastering Strategy*, p. 202 (Capron, L. 1999), Financial Times Prentice Hall; Figure 7.12 adapted from *The Knowledge-Creating Company: How Japanese Companies Create the Dynamics of Innovation*, Oxford University Press (Nonaka, I. and Takeuchi, H. 1995), by permission of Oxford University Press, Inc. Figure 7.13 from Game Theory in the Real World, in *Mastering Strategy* (Gertner, R. and Knez, M. 2000), Financial Times Prentice Hall; Figure 8.1 adapted from *Policy and Practice in European Human Resource Management*, Routledge/Thomson Learning (Brewster, C. and Hegewisch, A. 1994) p. 6; Figure 8.2 from Human Resource Management: An Agenda for the 1990s, *International Journal of Human Resource Management*, vol. 1, no. 1 (Hendry, J. and Pettigrew, A. 1990), reprinted by permission of the publisher (Taylor & Francis Group, http://www.informaworld.com); Figure 9.1 from *International Business: Theories, Policies and Practices*, Financial Times Prentice Hall (Tayeb, M. 2000); Figure 9.6 from The Big Mac: A global-to-local look at pricing, *Federal Reserve Bank of Dallas: Economic Letter*, Vol. 3, No. 9 (Landry, A. 2008).

Tables

Table 1.4 adapted from Michael E. Porter, Klaus Schwab and Xavier Sala-i-Martin, *The Global Competitiveness Report 2007–2008*, published 2007, World Economic Forum reproduced with permission of Palgrave Macmillan.; Table 2.1 reprinted and adapted from *Journal of World Business*, 32(3), Lei, D., Slocum, J. and Pitts, R.A., Building competitive advantage: managing strategic alliances to promote organisational learning. Copyright 1997, with permission from Elsevier. Table 2.3 from *Removing Barriers to SME Access to International Markets*, OECD (OECD 2008) p.31, (Table 1.4 Top ten barriers to SME access to international markets as reported by member economies, pp. 36, Source: *OECD Member Economy Policymaker Survey and SME Survey*, 2006, *reproduced in Removing Barriers to SME Access to International Markets*, OECD 2008); Table 2.4 from *OECD Member Economy Policymaker Survey and SME Survey*, OECD (OECD 2006) p. 35, (Table 1.5. Structure of government support programmes, p. 41, Source: *OECD Member Economy Policymaker Survey and SME Survey*, 2006, *reproduced in Removing Barriers to SME Access to International Markets*, OECD 2008); Table 4.2 adapted from Country Risk Ratings in *Management International Review*, Universität Hohenheim (Dichtl, E. and Koeglmayr, H.G. 1986); Table 5.3 adapted from *Cultures and Organizations: Software of the Mind*, Revised and Expanded 2nd Edition, McGraw-Hill (Hofstede, G. and Hofstede, G.J. 2005); Table 5.4 reprinted and adapted from *Organizational Dynamics*, vol. 24, no. 4, Snow, C.C., Davison, S.C., Snell, S.A. and Hambrik, D.C., Use of Transnational Teams to Globalize your Company, pp. 90–107. Copyright 1996, with permission from Elsevier. Table 5.5 adapted from THE SEVEN CULTURES OF CAPITALISM by Charles Hampden-Turner, Alfons Trompenaars, copyright © 1993 by Charles Hampden-Turner. Used by permission of Doubleday, a division of Random House, Inc. and adapted from *The Seven Cultures of Capitalism* by Charles Hampden-Turner and Fons Trompenaars, published in 1995 by Piatkus Books. Copyright © 1994 by Charles Hampden-Turner and Fons

Trompenaars. Reprinted by permission of the authors; Table 7.5 adapted from *International Business: Theories, Policies and Practices*, Financial Times Prentice Hall (Tayeb, M. 2000); Table 7.6 from *Operations Management*, 2nd ed., Financial Times Prentice Hall (Slack, N., Chambers, S., Harland, C., Harrison, A. and Johnson, R. 1998); Table 9.5 adapted from The Big Mac Index: Sandwiched, *The Economist*, 25 July 2008, p. 82, © The Economist Newspaper Limited, London 2008; Table 9.8 from Euromonitor International; Table 10.4 from *Framework for the Preparation and Presentation of Financial Statements*, International Accounting Standards Board (IASB) (IASB 2001); Tables 10.5, 10.6, 10.7, 10.8 adapted from Tesco plc Annual Report 2008.

Text

Box 1.3 adapted from *Human Development Report* by United Nations Development Programme (1999) by permission of Oxford University Press, Inc.; Case Studies 2.5, 5.1 and 5.4 adapted from Cultural determinants of competitiveness by A. Griffiths, in *Dimensions of International Competitiveness: Issues and Policies* (Lloyd-Reason, L. and Wall, S. (eds.) 2000), Edward Elgar; Case Study 3.1 adapted from *The Economist*, 27 April 2000, © The Economist Newspaper Limited, London 2000; Case Study 3.2 from Healey, N., The Multinational Corporation, in *Applied Economics*, 11th edn (Griffith, A. and Wall, S. (eds) 2007), Pearson Education; Case Study 4.6 from *Inter-Partner Relationships and Performance in UK-Chinese Joint Ventures: An Interaction Approach* (Wilson, Jonathan 2003), unpublished Ph.D. thesis, University of Middlesex; Case Study 5.2 adapted from The modelling of issues and perspectives in MNEs by J. Kidd, J. and Li Xue, in *Dimensions of International Competitiveness: Issues and Policies* (Lloyd-Reason, L. and Wall, S. (eds.) 2000), Edward Elgar; Box 6.1 from Beyer, J. and Nino, D., *Journal of Management Inquiry*, vol. 8, no. 3, copyright © 1999, SAGE Publications. Reprinted by Permission of SAGE Publications. Case Study 7.7 from Game Theory: How to Make It Pay, in *Mastering Global Business* (Garicano, L. 1999), Financial Times Prentice Hall; Case Study 7.8 adapted from Game Theory in the Real World, *Mastering Strategy* (Gertner, R. and Knez, M. 2000), Financial Times Prentice Hall; Box 8.1 adapted from National culture, choice of management and business performance: the case of foreign firms in Greece by Kessapidou, S. and Varsakelis, N., in *Dimensions of International Competitiveness: Issues and Policies* (Lloyd-Reason, L. and Wall, S. (eds.) 2000), Edward Elgar; Case Study 8.3 from Mindset of a Toyota manager revealed, *Financial Times*, 27 November 2008 (Mitchell, A.).

The *Financial Times*

Case Study 1.2 from Happy Birthday, globalisation, *Financial Times*, 6 May 2003 (Tomkins, R.); Case Study 1.3 from How to play the home advantage, *Financial Times*, 27 November 2008 (Marsh, P.); Case Study 1.4 adapted from US companies choose: National, multinational or "a-national", *Financial Times*, 16 August 2007 (Guerrera, F.); Case Study 1.5 adapted from Korean shipbuilders struggle to keep Chinese in their wake, *Financial Times*, 27 March 2007 (Fifield, A.); Case Study 2.6 adapted from Seoul sleepwalk: why an Asian export champion is at risk of losing his way, *Financial Times*, 19 March 2007 (Fifield, A.); Case Study 2.8 from Daewoo to cultivate Madagascar land for free *Financial Times*, 20 November 2008 (Jung-a, S., Olive, C. and Burgis, T.); Case Study 3.3 from Mandelson warns on hidden cost of anti-dumping tariffs, *Financial Times*, 4 September 2007 (Bounds, A.); Case Study 3.4 from Harbours of resentment, *Financial Times*, 1 December 2008, p. 11 (Houlder, V. and Peel, M.); Case Study 3.5 from WTO to rule on US import duties, *Financial Times*, 21 January 2009 (Williams, F.); Box 4.2 from Randall, J. and Treacy, B. (2000) 'Digital Buccaneers Caught in a Legal Web', *Financial Times*, 30 May. In *Mastering Risk* by James Pickford (2001) Financial Times Prentice Hall; Case Study 4.3 from Tougher scrutiny of foreign takeovers, *Financial Times*, 27 July 2007 (Kirchgaessner, S.); Case Study 4.4 adapted from Intellectual Property Rights (IPR) in India: Novartis, *Financial Times*, 7 August 2007 (Cookson, C. and Yee, A.); Case Study 4.8 from China allows direct offshore investments, *Financial Times*, 21 August 2007 (Anderlini, J.); Case Study 4.9 from Finance chiefs take pessimistic view on outlook, *Financial Times*, 10 December 2008, p. 24 (Willman, J.); Case Study 5.3 from Culture of communication breaks through traditional barriers, *Financial Times*, 10 September 2007

(Kwon Young-Soo); Case Study 5.5 from In European countries, there are three or four competitors. In the US, there are 10 or 20, *Financial Times*, 25 February 2003 (Skapinker, M.); Case Study 5.7 from Organisations, too, can be put on the couch, *Financial Times*, 20 June 2003 (Benady, A.); Case Study 6.3 from Bribery has long been used to land international contracts. New laws will make that tougher., *Financial Times*, 8 May 2003 (Catan, T. and Chaffin, J.); Case Study 6.4 from US groups in ethical standards push, *Financial Times*, 8 December 2008 (Guerrera, F. and Birchall, J.); Case Study 6.7 adapted from OECD slams biofuels subsidies for sparking food price inflation, *Financial Times*, 11 September 2007 (Bounds, A.); Case Study 6.8 from Prices too low to promote clean-up, *Financial Times*, 8 December 2008 (Harvey, F.); Table on page 246 from Largest pharmaceuticals M&A deals, *Financial Times*, 24 January 2009; Case Study 7.1 from Takeover would inject much-needed diversity into product portfolio, *Financial Times*, 24 January 2009 (Jack, A.); Case Study 7.2 from Flawed conception, *Financial Times*, 17 January 2009 (Guerrera, F.); Case Study 7.3 from Crossing the Atlantic can end in oblivion, *Financial Times*, 25 February 2003 (Wilman, J.); Figure 7.4 adapted from Prahalad, C.K. (1999) 'Changes in the Competitive Battlefield', *Financial Times*, 4 October. In *Mastering Strategy* (2000) Financial Times Prentice Hall.; Case Study 7.4 from Detroit spinners?, *Financial Times*, 19 November 2008 (Reed, J. and Simon, B.); Case Study 8.5 from Flexible working saves jobs whilst trimming the fat, *Financial Times*, 27 November 2008 (Donkin, R.); Case Study 9.2 from A better burger thanks to data crunching, *Financial Times*, 6 September 2007 (Matthews, R.); Case Study 9.4 from Road of new rich littered with potholes, *Financial Times*, 1 August 2007 (Leahy, J.); Case Study 9.5 from Anti-war sentiment is likely to give fresh impetus to the waning supremacy of US brands, *Financial Times*, 27 March 2003 (Tomkins, R.); Case Study 9.6 from Lessons for marketers who face a hard sell, *Financial Times*, 20 November 2008 (Edgecliffe-Johnson, A. and Bradshaw, T.); Case Study 9.7 from Love in a warm climate, *Financial Times*, 24 July 2003 (Merchant, K.); Case Study 9.8 from Indian stores in search of drama, *Financial Times*, 30 December 2008 (Yee, A.); Case Study 10.1 and Figure 10.2 from SIV managers dig out their manuals, *Financial Times*, 30 August 2007 (Davies, P.); Case Study 10.2 from Seniority brings a false sense of security, *Financial Times*, 7 October 2008 (Tett, G.); Case Study 10.3 from Sum of the parts, *Financial Times*, 17 November 2008, p. 12 (Milne, R.); Case Study 10.4 from Spate of downgrades raises fears that a big economy could be next, *Financial Times*, 23 January 2009 (Johnson, M. and Oakley, D.); Case Study 10.5 from Insight: Risk needs a human touch but models hold the whip hand, *Financial Times*, 23 January 2009 (Davies, P.).

In some instances we have been unable to trace the owners of copyright material, and we would appreciate any information that would enable us to do so.

Abbreviations

APEC	Asia-Pacific Economic Corporation
ART	alternative risk transfer
ASB	Accounting Standards Board (London)
ASEAN	Association of South East Asian Nations
BIT	bilateral investment treaties
B2B	business-to-business
CAP	Common Agricultural Policy
CCFF	Compensatory and Contingency Financing Facility
CDO	collateralised debt obligations
CED	cross elasticity of demand
CFF	Compensatory Financing Facility
CIM	Chartered Institute of Marketing
CIMA	Chartered Institute of Management Accountants (London)
CIS	Commonwealth of Independent States
CJV	cooperative joint venture
DTT	double taxation treaties
EAGGF	European Agricultural Guarantee and Guidance Fund
ECU	European Currency Unit
EER	effective exchange rate
EFF	Extended Fund Facility
EJV	equity joint venture
EPZ	export processing zone
ERM	Exchange Rate Mechanism
ERP	enterprise resource planning
EU	European Union
fdi	foreign direct investment
FSC	foreign sales corporation
GAAP	generally accepted accounting practices
GATT	General Agreement on Tariffs and Trade
GDP	gross domestic product
GM	genetically modified
GNP	gross national product
HICPs	Harmonised Indices of Consumer Prices
HRM	human resource management
IASB	International Accounting Standards Board
IASs	International Accounting Standards
IBRD	International Bank for Reconstruction and Development
IDA	International Development Association
IED	income elasticity of demand
IFC	International Finance Corporation
IHRM	international human resource management
II	internationalisation index

IJV	international joint venture
ILO	International Labour Office
IMF	International Monetary Fund
IMM	International Monetary Market
IPLC	international product life cycle
IPR	intellectual property rights
ISCT	Integrated Social Contract Theory
LDC	less-developed country
LIBOR	London Interbank Offer Rate
LIFFE	London International Finance and Futures Exchange
LRAC	long-run average cost
LSE	London Stock Exchange
MAI	multilateral agreement on investment
M & A	mergers and acquisitions
MES	minimum efficient size
MGQ	Maximum Guaranteed Quantity
MID	modularity-in-design
MIP	modularity-in-production
MIU	modularity-in-use
MNE	multinational enterprise
NAFTA	North American Free Trade Association
NGO	non-governmental organisation
OECD	Organisation for Economic Co-operation and Development
OTC	over the counter
PED	price elasticity of demand
PEST	political, economic, social and technological environmental analysis
PESTEL	political, economic, social, technological, legal and ecological analysis
Plc	public limited company
PPP	purchasing power parity
R & D	research and development
RER	real exchange rate
RPI	Retail Price Index
RTA	regional trading arrangement
RULC	relative unit labour costs
SAF	Structural Adjustment Facility
SAL	Structural Adjustment Lending
SDR	Special Drawing Right
SEC	Securities and Exchange Commission (USA)
SFF	Supplementary Financing Facility
SIV	structured investment vehicle
SKU	stock-keeping unit
SME	small to medium-sized enterprise
SWF	sovereign wealth funds
TNI	transnationality index
UNCTAD	United Nations Conference on Trade, Aid and Development
UNIDO	United Nations Industrial Development Organisation
VER	voluntary export restraint
WIPO	World Intellectual Property Organisation
WOFE	wholly-owned foreign enterprise
WTO	World Trade Organisation

Chapter 1

Introduction to international business

By the end of this chapter you should be able to:

- outline some of the key patterns and trends in international business activity;

- explain the various dimensions of the term 'globalisation';

- examine the role and importance of the multinational enterprise (MNE) in the global economy;

- discuss the contribution of different disciplines to an understanding of international business activity.

Introduction

A useful starting point for a book on international business is to identify some of the more recent patterns and trends in business activity worldwide. Of course, these patterns and trends are in part the *result* of some of the strategic choices taken by firms with an international orientation and in part the *stimulus* for future changes of direction by such firms. We shall examine each of these perspectives in later chapters of this book.

Patterns and trends in international business

Let us first identify some of the more important and measurable trends in international business activity.

Rapid growth in world trade and investment

Figure 1.1 indicates some aspects of the growth in international trade and capital flows using *index numbers* based on 1980 = 1 for exports and foreign direct investment (fdi) respectively. (The term fdi refers to international investment in productive facilities such as plant, machinery and equipment.) Between 1980 and 2007 *world exports* of goods and services have more than doubled in real terms, reaching over $17,000 billion in 2007 and accounting for over 31% of world gross domestic product.

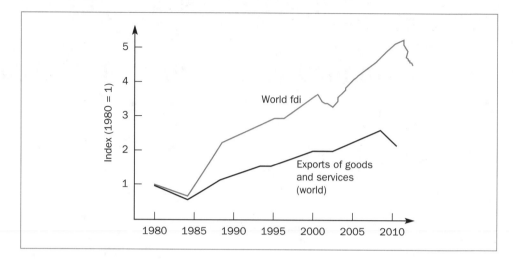

Figure 1.1 Changes in trade and capital flows
Sources: World Bank, UNCTAD (various).

Put another way, global exports of goods and services have increased at the astonishing rate of almost 5% per year in real terms between 1980 and 2007. It is worth noting that, while the 'high-income economies' (GNP of $11,456 per capita or more) have accounted for most of this growth in absolute value of global exports, the 'developing economies' (GNP of $935 or less) have increased their share of global exports, with the developing economies' exports rising at an above average 6% per annum in real terms between 1980 and 2007. This trend has resulted in the *exports–to GDP ratio* of the 'developing economies' rising much faster than that of the 'high income economies'. As a result the export:GDP ratio of developing economies now exceeds that of the high-income economies, with exports accounting for some 25% of GDP in developing economies in 2007, but only some 24% of GDP in high-income economies at that date. The contribution of developing economies to international business is an issue we return to at various points in this book.

Over the same time period flows of *world foreign direct investment* have increased more than fivefold in real terms, reaching around $1800 billion in 2007, some $400 billion above the previous peak year in 2000. Figure 1.2 provides more detail on this rapid growth in world fdi inflows over the period 1980–2007. The developed, developing and transition economies, the latter including South East Europe and the Commonwealth of Independent States (Russia and states of the former Soviet Union), all saw continued growth in inward fdi, following the global dip in inward fdi in the 2000–03 period.

▪ Rapid growth in cross-border mergers and acquisitions

There has been a rapid growth in cross-border mergers and acquisitions (M & A) since 1990, despite a decline over the 2000–03 period. Between 1990 and 2007 the value of global cross-border M & A rose eightfold from around $200 billion per annum in 1990 to over $1600 billion per annum in 2007. Much of this activity has been concentrated in financial services, insurance, life sciences, telecommunications

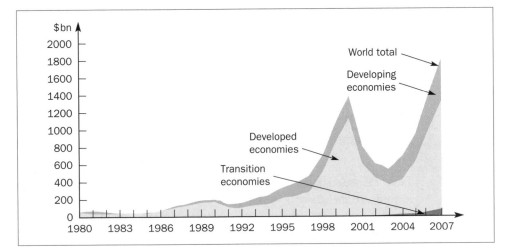

Figure 1.2 **FDI inflows: global and by groups of economies, 1980–2007**
Source: *World Investment Report* (UNCTAD 2008), p. 3.

and the media, with M & A being a key factor in accounting for the rise in fdi noted in Figure 1.2. Largely as a result of cross-border mergers, we can see from Table 1.1 that the 100 largest MNEs increased their foreign assets by almost 11% in 2006 alone, their foreign sales by 9% and their foreign employment by around 7% (*World Development Report*, 2008).

We review the contribution of MNEs to international business activity in much greater detail later in this chapter (pp. 28–36) and in Chapter 7.

More liberalised markets on a global scale

We noted in Figures 1.1 to 1.2 the rapid growth of foreign direct investment (fdi) and its relevance for cross-border mergers and acquisitions by multinational enterprises.

Table 1.1 **Snapshot of the world's 100 largest MNEs, 2006**

Variable	2006	*Percentage change on year earlier*
Assets ($bn)		
Foreign	5245	+10.8%
Total	9239	+6.4%
Foreign to total (%)	57%	2.3%
Sales ($bn)		
Foreign	4078	+9.0%
Total	7088	+7.0%
Foreign to total (%)	58%	+1.0%
Employment (000)		
Foreign	8582	+6.9%
Total	15,388	+1.9%
Foreign to total (%)	56%	+2.7%

Source: *World Development Report* (World Bank 2008).

Table 1.2 **National regulatory changes, 1993–2007**

Item	1993	1995	1997	1999	2001	2003	2005	2007
Number of countries that introduced change	56	63	76	65	71	82	92	58
Number of regulatory changes	100	112	150	139	207	242	203	98
More favourable to fdi	99	106	134	130	193	218	162	74
Less favourable to fdi	1	6	16	9	14	24	41	24

Source: Adapted from *World Investment Report* (UNCTAD 2008).

Table 1.2 uses data from the United Nations Conference on Trade, Aid and Development to indicate the growth in regulatory changes affecting fdi by national governments. We can see that the overwhelming majority of these changes are regarded as being 'more favourable' to fdi flows.

More globally-dispersed value chains

With more market liberalisation comes increased worldwide competition which, together with rapid technological change, has placed increased pressures on large firms to adopt the most efficient and appropriate production and marketing locations if they are to survive and prosper. With improved international communications helping MNEs to coordinate and control geographically-dispersed activities, including service functions, the result has been an increased propensity for MNEs to shift certain production and service activities to low-cost centres overseas. Put another way, MNEs are engaged in an unending search for increased competitive advantage in terms of costs, resources, logistics and markets and are increasingly willing to reconfigure the geographical locations of their activities accordingly.

> **pause for thought 1** Can you give a recent example of an MNE adjusting the geographical location of its production or support activities?

We can, for example, use the so-called transnationality index (TNI) to illustrate the increased international dispersion of production and service activities by multinational enterprises. The TNI is a simple average of three ratios for a multinational enterprise, namely foreign assets : total assets, foreign sales : total sales and foreign employment : total employment. As we note below (Table 1.9) whereas for the world's largest 100 MNEs this average across the three ratios was only 51% in 1990, by 2006 the average had risen sharply to 61.6%, indicating a rapid growth in international orientation by the top 100 global MNEs. We return to this issue in more detail below (pp. 28–36) and in Chapter 7.

Bi-polar to tri-polar (triad)

The old *bi-polar* world economy, which was dominated by North America and Europe, has moved on to a *tri-polar* world economy dominated by the 'triad' of North America, the European Union and South-East Asia. These three regions now account

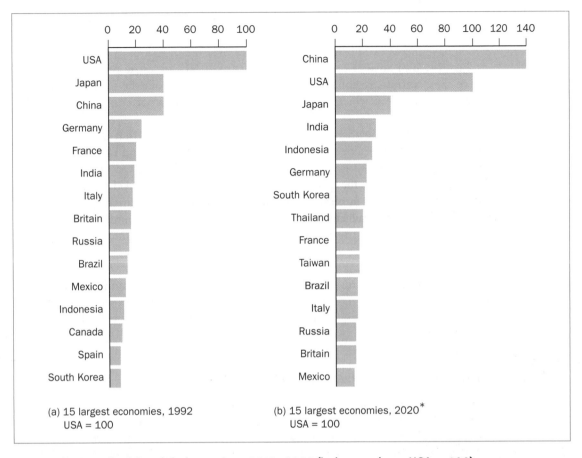

Figure 1.3 Growth of the global economy, 1992–2020 (index numbers, USA = 100)

*Forecasts assume countries grow at regional rates projected in the World Bank's *Global Economic Prospects* report.
Source: World Bank and author's own work.

for around 80% of the total value of world exports and 84% of world manufacturing value added.

The inclusion of the third leg of the triad, namely East and South-East Asia, is further reinforced by projections into the future. Figure 1.3 provides some World Bank projections for changes in national contributions to the world economy over the period 1992–2020. Although in terms of market size the global economy is currently dominated by the rich industrial economies of the USA, Japan, Germany, France, Italy and the UK, it is projected that by 2020 economies such as China, India, Indonesia, South Korea, Thailand and Taiwan will all have moved into the 'top ten'. This is an important pattern, suggesting that the attention of market-orientated companies will be increasingly drawn to these regions.

■ Growth of regional trading arrangements

As we note in Chapter 3, there has been a rapid growth in regional trading blocs and in associated regional trading arrangements (RTAs), which give preferential treatment to trade in goods and services between members of these blocs. Only countries *within* the particular regional trading bloc (e.g. the EU, NAFTA) benefit from these RTAs, which have increased substantially in number over the past decade or so. This has led to the growth of 'insiderisation', i.e. attempts by MNEs to locate productive facilities inside these various regional trading blocs in order to avoid the protective and discriminatory barriers which would otherwise face their exports to countries within these blocs.

Certainly there is evidence to support the belief of MNEs that being inside such blocs confers considerable advantages. For example Roberts and Deichmann (2008) found that spillovers of growth between members of RTAs averaged around 14% in the period 1970–2000. In other words, every 1% increase in the average growth rate of RTA partners brought a 'growth bonus' of 0.14% to other members of the RTA. In Europe and East Asia, where historically regional integration has been strongest, the average growth spillover was even larger at around 0.17% over the period 1970–2000. In a similar vein, as regards the benefits of membership of a regional trading bloc, Frankel (1997) noted that during the early 1990s, intra-regional trade within one such regional trading bloc – the Andean community of Bolivia, Colombia, Ecuador, Peru and Venezuela – was 2.7 times higher than the levels of national income and geographic separation of those economies would have led us to expect.

Growth of bilateral investment and trade treaties

Nor is it only within the broad based regional trading blocs that preferential treatment is available to participating countries and companies. For example there has been a rapid growth in *bilateral (two country) investment and trade treaties*, which can take various forms, the major ones being *bilateral investment treaties* (BITs) and *double taxation treaties* (DTTs). Over 2600 BITs had been notified to the World Trade Organisation (WTO) by 2009 which, while they may encourage foreign direct investment (fdi) flows between the two countries concluding the investment treaty, arguably discriminate against fdi flows involving countries that are *not* signatories to the BIT. Similarly around 2700 DTTs had been notified to the WTO by 2009, again arguably reducing tax rates and stimulating investments and trade between the two countries involved, but creating a complex patchwork of investment and taxation regimes which are difficult to manage on a global scale. We consider the impact of such bilateral treaties in more detail in Chapter 3.

Growth of sovereign wealth funds (SWFs)

Sovereign wealth funds (SWFs) are government owned investment vehicles managed separately from the official reserves of the country. They have usually been accumulated by those governments as the result of high global commodity prices for their exports. High energy (e.g. oil), food and other primary product prices over recent years have meant that an estimated $5000 billion is now available for potential investment by countries such as the United Arab Emirates, Saudi Arabia, Dubai, Kuwait, China, Norway, the Russian Federation and Singapore, amongst others. The SWFs will often be invested in projects with higher risks but higher expected future returns. Professional portfolio management techniques are often adopted with a view to generating a sustainable future income stream via investments in bonds, equities and other assets. In 2009 Barclays Bank raised $7 billion of funds from this source rather than accept UK government funding to help it cope with the liquidity crisis of the 'credit crunch' (see Chapter 10, p. 382). In 2009 there were 70 SWFs in 44 countries with assets ranging in value from $20 million (São Tomé and Príncipe) to more than $500 billion in the United Arab Emirates.

■ Growth of 'defensive techniques' to combat global insecurity

The global growth of foreign direct investment and the increasingly 'footloose' activities of MNEs have already been documented as widely-used indicators of globalisation. Many commentators have also drawn attention to parallels between the rapid growth in formal, legal cross-border relationships and the rapid growth in a wide range of illegal cross-border relationships including, at one extreme, activities more commonly associated with terrorism. Some of the characteristics of globalisation reviewed in Box 1.3 (p. 15) are seen as conducive to such growth, especially the weakening of power and control by nation states and the proliferation of new, less detectable methods of communication.

Whilst a proper investigation of so complex an issue is beyond the scope of this section, we can perhaps draw attention to what many believe is a new global business environment since 11 September 2001 (9/11), which is perhaps the date most closely associated with the advent of global insecurity. The additional insurance premiums required since 9/11 is one important indicator of the costs to international business of such 'defensive techniques'. In the airline industry alone it has been estimated that global insurance premiums rocketed from $1.7 billion in 2001 to over $6 billion just one year later in 2002. When we factor these extra insurance premiums across *all* industries and include monetarised values for the increased time costs to business of additional security-related delays as well as the extra costs associated with more security-related personnel and equipment, then the sums involved rapidly escalate. For example, it has been estimated that the *actual* growth of global GDP has fallen since 9/11 by around one per cent per annum relative to the previously *projected* growth. If so, the impact of 9/11 has cost the global economy some £1750 billion over the period 2001–2008.

pause for thought 2   Can you suggest which sectors/industries have been the main 'losers' with the heightened concerns over global terrorism and which the main 'beneficiaries'?

■ Changing area patterns of international costs

Of particular interest to international business location is the area pattern of *international labour costs*, both wage and non-wage (employers' social security contributions, holiday pay, etc.). Comparable data is notoriously difficult to derive, both within broad geographical regions and between such regions. In any case it is not just overall labour costs that are important but these costs in relation to labour productivity, as can be seen from Table 1.3.

Table 1.3 **Labour costs and labour productivity, 2006**

Country	Total labour costs ($ per hour)	Total labour costs ($ per hour Index: UK = 100)	Labour productivity (Index UK = 100)
Mexico	2.6	21.8	35.2
Korea	13.6	20.9	48.4
France	24.6	95.7	118.1
UK	25.7	100.0	100.0
Japan	21.8	84.8	82.4
US	23.7	92.2	116.2
Germany	33.0	128.4	109.7

Source: Adapted from US Department of Labor (2007) *Hourly Compensation Costs in Manufacturing*; OECD (2007) *Dataset: OECD Estimates of Labour Productivity Levels.*

pause for thought 3

Using the data in Table 1.3 how do France and Germany compare as possible locations for a labour-intensive production process? What other factors might be taken into account?

Table 1.3 indicates considerable variation in overall labour costs per hour worked in 2006, from $2.6 per hour in Mexico to $33.0 per hour in Germany (US Department of Labor 2007). The second column expresses this same data as an index number (UK = 100) and suggests that overall labour costs per hour are 78.2% less in Mexico than in the UK but 28.4% more in Germany than the UK. However, international firms must sometimes be careful not to be unduly influenced by such data alone. For example labour productivity data is also of vital importance to location decisions, and the third column expresses labour productivity data as an index number (UK = 100). Mexico now looks relatively less attractive compared to the UK than if we concentrated on overall labour costs alone. Although it has overall labour costs per hour as low as 21.8% of those in the UK its labour productivity is only 35.2% of that in the UK, so that the advantage of Mexico in terms of overall *labour costs per unit of output* is relatively small. Japan has labour costs per hour which are 15.2% lower than the UK, but its labour productivity is 17.6% lower than in the UK, so that overall *labour costs per unit of output* are arguably higher in Japan than in the UK.

Table 1.4 provides some interesting international comparisons when wage costs are adjusted for productivity differentials and other microeconomic determinants of business competitiveness. The top ten most competitive countries listed in the table are certainly not in the category of the low wage economies! We can therefore see how important the productivity issue and other aspects of the business environment (e.g. access to R & D, to business clusters, to legal protection of property rights, to corruption-free dealings, etc.) really are as regards overall business competitiveness. The USA (1st), Germany (2nd), Finland (3rd), Sweden (4th), Denmark (5th), Switzerland (6th), the Netherlands (7th), Austria (8th) and Japan (10th) are hardly low-wage economies, yet their relatively high levels of productivity and other advantages as regards the business environment in which they operate, give them a ranking in the 'top ten' economies in terms of business cost competitiveness (World Economic Forum 2008).

Table 1.4 Ranking of countries in terms of business competitiveness*

Country	Rank	Country	Rank
USA	1	Malaysia	21
Germany	2	New Zealand	22
Finland	3	Taiwan	23
Sweden	4	Ireland	24
Denmark	5	Tunisia	25
Switzerland	6	Estonia	26
Netherlands	7	Spain	27
Austria	8	UAE	28
Singapore	9	Chile	29
Japan	10	Portugal	30
UK	11	India	31
Hong Kong	12	Czech Republic	32
Norway	13	Qatar	33
Canada	14	South Africa	34
Belgium	15	Slovenia	35
Iceland	16	Indonesia	36
France	17	Thailand	37
Australia	18	Oman	38
Korea	19	Lithuania	39
Israel	20	Malta	40

Note: *Including competitiveness of company operations.

Source: Adapted from Porter, M.E., Schwab, K. and Sala-i-Martin, X. (eds) *The Global Competitiveness Report 2007–2008*, Table 1.

A more complete assessment of true labour costs would use the idea of relative unit labour costs (RULC), which are explored further in Box 1.1 below.

Box 1.1   Relative Unit Labour Costs (RULC)

Labour costs per unit of output (unit labour costs) are determined by both the wages of the workers and the output per worker (labour productivity). International competitiveness, in terms of unit labour costs, is also influenced by exchange rates. For example, depreciation of the currency makes exports cheaper in terms of the foreign currency (see Chapter 3) and therefore can even compensate for low labour productivity and high money wages. When we bring all these three elements together and express each of them relative to a country's main competitors, we can derive the most widely used measure of labour cost competitiveness, namely relative unit labour costs (RULC).

The calculation of RULC is as follows:

$$\frac{\text{Relative labour costs}}{\text{Relative labour productivity}} \times \text{Exchange rate} = \text{RULC}$$

This formula emphasises that lower RULC for, say, the UK could be achieved either by reducing the UK's relative labour costs, or by raising the UK's relative labour productivity, or by lowering the UK's effective exchange rate, or by some combination of all three.

Between 1999 (the launch of the euro) and late 2007 the sterling exchange rate rose significantly relative to the euro, reaching £1 = €1.50 in early 2008. Clearly we can see

▶

> Box 1.1   Continued
>
> from this analysis that the UK's RULC, other things being equal, would then rise as compared to its EU competitors. Only by reducing UK relative labour costs and/or raising UK relative labour productivity could this rise in the sterling exchange rate (relative to the euro) be offset and UK exporters remain competitive with their European rivals. Multinational companies located in the UK have sought to offset the adverse impact of the sharp rise in the sterling exchange rate (relative to the euro) on their cost competitiveness. For example, they have supplied an increasing proportion of their EU market from other overseas plants (rather than from those located in the UK), and have forced suppliers to their UK plants to invoice bills in euros (rather than in sterling), etc.
>
> Since early 2008, however, the sterling exchange rate began to fall rapidly against a stronger euro, bringing renewed hope for UK producers vis-à-vis their EU counterparts. By early 2009 the sterling exchange rate had fallen to £1 = €1.03, reducing the UK's RULC vis-à-vis the Eurozone countries and giving UK producers significant advantages over their European counterparts. Chapters 3 and 10 look in still more detail at the impacts of changes in exchange rates.

Such changes in area patterns of international costs have had a significant impact on the international location of business activity, as is indicated in Case Study 1.1.

CASE 1.1   Dyson relocates production to South-East Asia

In 2006 the Dyson dual cyclone bagless cleaner had outsold Hoover in terms of sales value in its own US 'backyard', despite Hoover being a household name in vacuum cleaner production since 1908. Dyson is now the US market leader, with around 21% of the US cleaner market, ahead of Hoover's 16%. Although Hoover sells more vacuum cleaners by volume, the higher technology Dyson cleaners command a premium price, giving greater sales value from lower volume sales. James Dyson points to some key decisions several years earlier as the foundation for this success.

Dyson had announced that it was moving production of its washing machines from the UK to Malaysia, which followed its earlier decision in 2002 to shift production of its revolutionary dual cyclone bagless vacuum cleaner to Malaysia with the loss of over 800 jobs at the Dyson factory in Malmesbury, Wiltshire, which had produced some 8000 vacuum cleaners per day.

Dyson was keen to point out that since the day the first Dyson dual cyclone vacuum cleaner went on sale in 1993, the company had been operating in a price-cutting market in which its competitors were able to pass on to their customers the lower costs from manufacturing outside the UK. In contrast Dyson has faced the further problems of rises in UK labour costs, land prices, taxation and other overhead costs while still trying to substantially increase its investment in new technology. For example, direct labour costs in Britain had doubled over the previous ten years, partly because of the need to pay high wages in an area around Swindon with almost zero unemployment.

Dyson claimed that the sums no longer added up and it faced going out of business if it continued manufacturing its product in the UK. As of September 2002 all vacuum cleaner production had shifted to Malaysia. The company argued that its production costs will benefit from the much lower wages in Malaysia, equivalent to £1.50 per hour as compared to the then £4.10 per hour in the UK. Indeed the company estimated that lower wages would reduce its unit production costs by around 30%. Further cost savings would also come from now having most of its component suppliers nearby (South-East Asian component suppliers having progressively replaced those from the UK) and being much closer to emerging new markets in Japan, Australia and the Far East. In addition, the Malaysian government had offered various 'subsidies' in the form of grants for setting up the Dyson factories there, as well as lower taxes and other benefits.

While lamenting the loss of UK jobs, the consolation to Dyson in moving his vacuum cleaner manufacturing to Malaysia was that it would now generate enough cash to maintain the company's commitment to reinvesting up to 20% of turnover in research and development (R & D). Dyson believed that it was the technological advantages secured by R & D that would keep the company alive and ensure that 1150 other jobs in Malmesbury were safe, more than 300 of which involved engineers, scientists, designers and testers – the brains that ensure Dyson products remain a step ahead of the rest. Dyson claims to have exported the brawn, keeping the higher-level value-added parts at home since Dyson's comparative advantage lies in researching and designing new products to ensure the company stays two steps ahead of its rivals, most of whom manufacture in the Far East. Indeed he claimed that to have followed the rest of British industry, which invests an average of only 2% of turnover, would have been to neglect Dyson's engineering and technological heritage and to follow in the footsteps of Britain's car, television and other domestic appliances.

As noted above, Dyson's decision to switch production away from the UK was closely related to increasing supply but at lower cost, with labour costs and office rents in Malaysia in 2009 still at a third of the UK level. Production in Asia also meant that the costs of exporting to large markets in this area was minimised, which enabled Dyson to compete globally with such companies as Electrolux of Sweden, Glen Dimplex of Ireland and Candy of Italy. The innovative nature of the company has continued with the introduction in October 2006 of the Dyson 'Airblade', the first hygienic hand dryer which is 83% more energy efficient than its competitors. Dyson, is the 88th largest private company in the UK, and is 25th in the fastest growth of profits league, according to the Sunday Times/PriceWaterhouseCoopers Profit Track 100. This publication tracks the top performing UK private companies, and in 2007 it reported that since 2002 Dyson's operating profits had grown at an average rate of 73% per year. The strategic move to outsource production while keeping the research base in the UK seems to have borne fruit in terms of profits growth.

Questions

1 How can Dyson argue that it is in the interest of his British workforce that he relocates production to Malaysia?

2 Can you suggest any implications of this study for developed and developing countries?

3 Can you apply the idea of relative unit costs (RULCs) in Box 1.1 to this situation?

◼ Other international patterns/trends

As well as the factors already discussed, a number of other patterns and trends are likely to be relevant to different types of international business activity.

- *International communications*. There have been dramatic increases in various modes of international communication. For example, the time spent on international telephone calls has risen from 33 billion minutes in 1990 to over 120 billion minutes by the end of 2008. Internet usage is also rising exponentially, with the 2008 *Human Development Report* (UNDP 2008) noting that the number of Internet hosts per 1000 people worldwide had risen from a mere 1.7 in 1990 to 136 in 2005/06 with cellular mobile phone subscribers per 1000 people worldwide also rising from only 2 in 1990 to 341 in 2005/06 (UNDP 2008). Various studies have found a strong and positive correlation between the extent of the telephone network and Internet usage. From this perspective it is important to note that the number of telephone mainlines per 1000 people has increased around sixfold in *developing countries* over this period from 21 per 1000 people in 1990 to over 132 per 1000 people at present.
- *International travel*. The number of international tourists has more than trebled from 260 million travellers a year in 1980 to over 800 million travellers a year in 2008. The growth of tourism is closely correlated with the growth of world GDP and is an important source of income and employment for many developed and developing countries alike.
- *International growth in leisure pursuits*. In 1880 some 80% of the time left over after necessities such as sleeping and eating were attended to, was used for earning a living. Today that percentage has fallen to below 40% over the average lifetime of an individual in the advanced industrialised economies and is projected to continue falling to around 25% over the next decade. This dramatic increase in leisure-time availability in the higher-income advanced industrialised economies clearly has major implications for consumption patterns and therefore for the deployment of productive resources.
- *International growth in ageing populations*. Between 1950 and 2008 the median age (at which 50% of the population is below it and 50% above) of the world's population rose by only 3 years, from 23.6 years in 1950 to 26.5 years in 2008. However over the next 40 years the UN projects that the median age will rise dramatically to 37 years by 2050, with 17 advanced industrialised economies having a median age of 50 years or above. This has major implications for international business in terms of productive location (e.g. adequate supply of labour of working age) as well as the range of products likely to be in global demand.
- *International growth in currency transactions*. The daily turnover in foreign exchange markets has dramatically increased from $15 billion in the mid-1970s to over $2400 billion in 2008. This has contributed to greater exchange rate volatility, on occasions putting severe pressure on national economies and currencies (e.g. Argentina's peso in 2001/02).
- *International growth in countertrade*. When conventional means of payment for international transactions are difficult, costly or not available, then a range of barter (swap)-type transactions may be used instead. Whereas such 'countertrade' only accounted for 2% of world trade in 1975, by 2008 over 20% of world trade

involved some element of barter, with the former Soviet Union and the Eastern European economies particularly active in using countertrade.

Can you think of any other patterns and trends that might be of interest to a multinational enterprise? Explain your reasoning in each case.

Globalisation

Globalisation is much talked about in the media and is often used to refer to more closely integrated economies worldwide, with products, people and money moving more easily and in greater volume and value throughout the world. Hill (2005) usefully illustrates the realities of globalisation with an example of an American driving a car, designed and produced in Germany, which was assembled in Mexico from components made in Japan, using fabricated steel for the chassis from Korea and rubber for the wheels from Malaysia. The car is filled with petrol refined in the US, from oil extracted by a French oil company from oil reserves off the coast of Africa, and transported to the US refinery by a ship owned by a Greek shipping line.

▣ Globalisation as a multi-dimensional process

Of course the term 'globalisation' is by no means the preserve of economists alone. Indeed it has been approached from the perspective of at least four academic disciplines, within each of which it tends to take on different characteristics:

- *economists* focus on the growth of international trade, the increase in international capital flows and the progressive dominance of the multinational enterprise (MNE) form of business organisation within domestic and global business activity;
- *political scientists* view globalisation as a process that leads to the undermining of the nation state and the emergence of new forms of governance;
- *sociologists* view globalisation in terms of the rise of a global culture and the domination of the media by global companies;
- *international relations experts* tend to focus on the emergence of global conflicts and global institutions.

▣ Different perspectives on globalisation

Certainly the world is seen as becoming increasingly interconnected as the result of economic, political, sociological and cultural forces. A one-dimensional view of globalisation, which thinks purely in terms of market forces, is likely to result in only a partial picture at best. Box 1.2 presents a range of perspectives and definitions of globalisation.

Some argue that globalisation is a long-standing phenomenon and not really anything new, pointing out that world trade and investment, as a proportion of world GDP, is little different today from what it was a century ago and that international borders were as open at that time as they are today with just as many people migrating abroad. Indeed Adam Smith, as long ago as 1787, defined the businessmen of his time as 'men without country'.

Box 1.2 Definitions of globalisation

- '. . . the process of transformation of local phenomena into global ones. It can be described as a process by which the people of the world are unified into a single society and function together. This process is a combination of economic, technological, sociocultural and political forces' (Croucher 2003: 10).
- '. . . a widening, deepening and speeding up of interconnectedness in all aspects of contemporary social life from the cultural to the criminal, the financial to the spiritual' (Held *et al.* 1999: 2).
- '. . . increasing global interconnectedness, so that events in one part of the world are affected by, have to take account of, and also influence, other parts of the world. It also refers to an increasing sense of a single global whole' (Tiplady 2003: 2).
- '. . . the worldwide movement towards economic, financial, trade and communications integration. Globalisation implies opening out beyond local and nationalistic perspectives to a broader outlook of an interconnected and inter-dependent world with the free transfer of capital, goods and services across national frontiers' (Business Dictionary).
- '. . . refers to the shift toward a more integrated and interdependent world economy . . . [through] the merging of historically distinct and separate national markets into one huge global market place' (Hill 2005: 6).
- '. . . process by which the whole world becomes a single market. This means that goods and services, capital and labour are traded on a worldwide basis, and information and the results of research flow readily between countries' (Black 2002).
- '. . . reflects a business orientation based on the belief that the world is becoming more homogenous and that distinctions between national markets are not only fading but, for some products, will eventually disappear' (Czinkota and Ronkainen 1999: 454).

However, those who believe that globalisation really is a new phenomenon tend to agree that at least three key elements are commonly involved.

1 *Shrinking space.* The lives of all individuals are increasingly interconnected by events worldwide. This is not only a matter of fact but one which people increasingly perceive to be the case, recognising that their jobs, income levels, health, and living environment depend on factors outside national and local boundaries.

2 *Shrinking time.* With the rapid developments in communication and information technologies, events occurring in one place have almost instantaneous (real time) impacts worldwide. A fall in share prices in Wall Street can have almost immediate consequences for share prices in London, Frankfurt or Tokyo.

3 *Disappearing borders.* The nation state and its associated borders seem increasingly irrelevant as 'barriers' to international events and influences. Decisions taken by regional trading blocs (e.g. EU, NAFTA) and supranational bodies (e.g. IMF, World Trade Organisation) increasingly override national policy making in economic and business affairs as well as in other areas such as law enforcement and human rights.

pause for thought 5 How might events in the aftermath of 9/11 relate to these three elements? Would this be evidence for or against the view that globalisation really is a new phenomenon?

Box 1.3 attempts to capture some of the features that currently underpin the use of the term 'globalisation' as being something different from what has gone before.

Box 1.3   Globalisation features

New markets

- Growing global markets in services – banking, insurance, transport.
- New financial markets – deregulated, globally linked, working around the clock, with action at a distance in real time, with new instruments such as derivatives.
- Deregulation of antitrust laws and growth of mergers and acquisitions.
- Global consumer markets with global brands.

New tools of communication

- Internet and electronic communications linking many people simultaneously.
- Cellular phones and mobile telephony.
- Fax machines.
- Faster and cheaper transport by air, rail, sea and road.
- Computer-aided design and manufacture.

New actors

- Multinational corporations integrating their production and marketing, dominating world production.
- The World Trade Organisation – the first multilateral organisation with authority to force national governments to comply with trade rules.
- A growing international network of non-governmental organisations (NGOs).
- Regional blocs proliferating and gaining importance – European Union, Association of South-East Asian Nations, Mercosur, North American Free Trade Association, Southern African Development Community, among many others.
- More policy coordination groups: G-7, G-8, OECD, IMF, World Bank.

New rules and norms

- Market economic policies spreading around the world, with greater privatisation and liberalisation than in earlier decades.
- Widespread adoption of democracy as the choice of political regime.
- Human rights conventions and instruments building up in both coverage and number of signatories – and growing awareness among people around the world.
- Consensus goals and action agenda for development.
- Conventions and agreements on the global environment – biodiversity, ozone layer, disposal of hazardous wastes, desertification, climate change.
- Multilateral agreements in trade, taking on such new agendas as environmental and social conditions.
- New multilateral agreements – for services, intellectual property, communications – more binding on national governments than any previous agreements.

Source: Adapted from *Human Development Report* by United Nations Development Programme (1999), by permission of Oxford University Press, Inc.

■ Outcomes of globalisation

Of course there are different schools of thought as to the possible outcomes of globalisation even among those who do accept the reality of globalisation.

- *Hyperglobalists* envisage the global economy as being inhabited by powerless nation states at the mercy of 'footloose' multinational enterprises bestowing jobs and wealth creation opportunities on favoured national clients. National cultural differences are largely seen by these progressively powerful multinationals as merely variations in consumer preferences to be reflected in their international marketing mix.
- *Transformationalists* recognise that globalisation is a powerful force impacting economic, social and political environments, but take a much less prescriptive stance as to what the outcomes of those impacts might be. Predictions as to any end-state of a globalised economy can only be tentative and premature. Rather globalisation involves a complex set of intermittent, uneven processes with unpredictable outcomes rather than a linear progression to a predictable end-state.

It is this more pragmatic transformationalist approach that is most commonly encountered in debates on globalisation. While there may be many theories as to the causes of globalisation, most writers would agree that globalisation is a discontinuous historical process. Its dynamic proceeds in fits and starts and its effects are experienced differentially across the globe. Some regions are more deeply affected by globalisation than others. Even within nation states, some sectors may experience the effects of globalisation more sharply than others. Many have argued that globalisation is tending to reinforce inequalities of power both within and across nation states, resulting in global hierarchies of privilege and control for some, but economic and social exclusion for others.

Giddens subscribes to the 'transformationalists' 'approach:

Globalisation is a complex process which is not necessarily teleological in character – that is to say, it is not necessarily an inexorable historical process with an end in sight. Rather, it is characterised by a set of mutually opposing tendencies (Giddens 1990).

McGrew (1992) has tried to identify a number of these opposing tendencies.

- *Universalisation versus particularisation.* While globalisation may tend to make many aspects of modern social life universal (e.g. assembly-line production, fast food restaurants, consumer fashions), it can also help to point out the differences between what happens in particular places and what happens elsewhere. This focus on differences can foster the resurgence of regional and national identities.
- *Homogenisation versus differentiation.* While globalisation may result in an essential homogeneity ('sameness') in product, process and institutions (e.g. city life, organisational offices and bureaucracies), it may also mean that the general must be assimilated within the local. For example, human rights are interpreted in different ways across the globe, the practice of specific religions such as Christianity or Buddhism may take on different forms in different places, and so on.
- *Integration versus fragmentation.* Globalisation creates new forms of global, regional and transnational communities that unite (integrate) people across territorial boundaries (e.g. the MNE, international trade unions, etc.). However, it also has the potential to divide and fragment communities (e.g. labour becoming divided along sectoral, local, national and ethnic lines).

It may be useful to review globalisation in rather more detail under four separate headings:

1 Globalisation and markets
2 Globalisation and production
3 Globalisation and the role of the nation state
4 Globalisation and new rules and norms.

The rest of the chapter then goes on to discuss globalisation and the multinational enterprise.

■ 1 Globalisation and markets

Case Study 1.2 reviews the suggestion that the forces of globalisation would establish global markets for standardised products purchased in huge volumes by consumers worldwide.

CASE 1.2 **Happy birthday, globalisation** **FT**

Marketing guru Theodore Levitt, a professor at Harvard Business School, was never a man given to understatement. But even by his standards, the prophecy he made on 1 May 1983 was bold. 'The globalisation of markets is at hand,' he declared in a *Harvard Business Review* article, written at a time when the word 'globalisation' was virtually unknown. Prof Levitt's message was simple. As new technology extended the reach of global media and brought down the cost of communications, the world was shrinking. As a result, consumer tastes everywhere were converging, creating global markets for standardised products on a previously unimagined scale.

His theory was colourfully illustrated. 'In Brazil, thousands swarm daily from pre-industrial Bahian darkness into exploding coastal cities, there quickly to install television sets in crowded corrugated huts and, next to battered Volkswagens, make sacrificial offerings of fruit or fresh-killed chickens to Macumban spirits' he wrote. And again 'During Biafra's fratricidal war against the Ibos, daily televised reports showed soldiers carrying bloodstained swords and listening to transistor radios while drinking Coca-Cola.'

Globalisation meant that old-fashioned 'multinational' companies that made different products to suit local tastes were doomed. They would be undercut by 'global corporations' that offered the same products in the same way everywhere, benefiting from 'enormous economies of scale' in production, distribution, marketing and management. 'The world's needs and desires have been irrevocably homogenised,' Prof Levitt proclaimed. 'This makes the multinational corporation obsolete and the global corporation absolute.'

Was he right? He was certainly influential. Sir Martin Sorrell, Chief Executive of WPP, well remembers the day the article appeared. At the time – April 1983 – he was Finance Director of Saatchi & Saatchi, then a relatively small outfit that was briefly to become the world's biggest advertising and marketing conglomerate.

▶

'I read the piece and I remember giving it to Maurice (Saatchi) saying "this is a key article". We distributed it to all our key clients and said "this is the way the world's going and this is the way the Saatchi agency will be positioning itself".' Maurice Saatchi became a passionate believer in Prof Levitt's theory and set about establishing Saatchi as a global operation that would market the new global brands with global advertising campaigns.

Soon after the article appeared the agency put theory into practice with its 'Manhattan' advertisement for British Airways, a science fiction-style spectacular that appeared to show the whole of New York's Manhattan Island coming in to land at London's Heathrow airport. Describing British Airways as 'The world's favourite airline', the same advertisement was dubbed into 20 languages and shown in every country in the world with a developed television network – 35 in all.

Partly as a result of Maurice Saatchi's advocacy, Prof Levitt's prophecy reverberated in boardrooms around the world. Even so, in 1983 it looked a bit of a futuristic fantasy. Many of the world's markets were still closed and nearly a third of its population lived under communism. By the end of the 1980s, however, as the barriers to world trade came down, Prof Levitt was beginning to look more right than he could ever have imagined. People in former communist countries celebrated their freedom by cracking open cans of Coca-Cola, MTV embraced the globe's youth and, in 1990, McDonald's opened in Moscow.

In the 1990s the share prices of global brand-owners such as Coca-Cola, McDonald's and Walt Disney soared as investors savoured the companies' growth prospects. Another sign of the times was the trend for companies to brand or rebrand themselves with global sounding names seemingly plucked from Esperanto, such as Diageo, Novartis and Invensys.

Then, something unexpected happened: a reaction set in. People around the world started demanding more local sovereignty and more protection for their cultural identities. Most worryingly for global brand-owners, consumers in newly opened markets started expressing a desire for local products – which, as local manufacturers adopted western business methods, were simultaneously showing a big improvement in quality.

By the end of the 1990s, most global brand-owners were switching chief executives as their share prices plummeted in response to slowing growth rates. In March 2000 in a signed article in the *Financial Times*, Douglas Daft, Coca-Cola's new chief executive, offered a startling analysis of what had gone wrong. Coca-Cola, Mr Daft wrote, 'had traditionally been a "multi-local" company but as globalisation had gathered pace, it had centralised its decision-making and standardised its practices. We were operating as a big, slow, insulated, sometimes even insensitive "global" company and we were doing it in a new era when nimbleness, speed, transparency and local sensitivity had become absolutely essential to success,' he wrote. But Coca-Cola had learnt its lesson, Mr Daft said. It was that 'the next big evolutionary step of "going global" now has to be "going local". In other words, we have to rediscover our own multi-local heritage.'

Astonishingly, it was almost the opposite of what Prof Levitt had advocated. Yet now it is the almost universally accepted wisdom. The one-size-fits-all approach is out; 'think local, act local' is in. Coca-Cola owns not one brand but more than 200, mostly local; McDonald's varies its menu to suit local tastes; MTV has different pro-gramming to suit different countries and regions.

While homogenisation has affected some product categories – mainly in the tech-nology sector, where there are no cultural barriers to overcome – the paradox of globalisation is that it has led not to a convergence of tastes but to a vast increase in the number of choices available to consumers. People can now buy products from all over the world: global, regional and local.

Another paradox is that technology is aiding the fragmentation. 'Prof Levitt was assuming that the only way to get scale was through standardisation. It was es-sentially the Henry Ford argument,' says Lowell Bryan, a McKinsey director and former student of Prof Levitt. 'But technology has changed the economics of pro-duction. Now, you can have both economies of scale and also deliver very discrete, specialised products.'

Prof Levitt has retired and does not give interviews. But through an intermediary, he indicates that he stands by his story. 'Global consumer products like Coke, Pepsi, McDonald's and Fuji and Kodak film are not fashioned to meet the needs of certain markets. They are simply sold in those markets about the same way they're success-fully sold at home,' he says.

Few would agree that Prof Levitt's prophecy has been entirely borne out. But 20 years after its publication, his article is still widely quoted and read. And you do not have to be right to be interesting. 'Sometimes, even if they are wrong, ideas can set off a chain of debate that results in greater knowledge,' says Richard Tedlow, professor of business administration at Harvard Business School.

Source: Tomkins, R., 'Happy Birthday, globalisation', *Financial Times*, 6 May 2003.

Questions

1 Identify the policy implications for MNEs who fully believe in the globalisation scenario of Professor Levitt.

2 Why do others dispute the validity of this scenario?

3 How does the experience of Coca-Cola support or conflict with the Levitt scenario?

Whilst global markets do indeed exist for some standardised products such as microchips, energy sources (e.g. oil and gas) and other goods and services where little product differentiation is feasible or wanted by users, with other goods and services varying international tastes and preferences mean that product differentiation is vital to appeal to local markets. What Levitt failed to appreciate was that technology would not only provide the mechanisms for large scale, low-cost standardised produc-tion but would also permit customised, bespoke production at reduced cost, using the new methods of batch and modular production now available (see Chapter 10).

Similarly, new techniques for researching and analysing segmented markets (see Chapter 9) would also allow global companies to identify the product differentiation actually needed to meet differing global tastes.

Case Study 1.3 below suggests that businesses may need to consider the 'local' as well as the 'global' when developing market based strategies.

CASE 1.3 How to play the home advantage [FT]

When Enrico Bracalente wants to visit his main suppliers, he does not have to travel far. The 20 factories responsible for the final manufacturing stages of virtually all the 3 million shoes Mr Bracalente's company aims to produce this year (2008) are within 30 km of his head office in Monte San Pietrangeli, southern Italy.

'When we [this company and the suppliers] meet up, it's like a big family,' says Mr Bracalente, who is chief executive of BAG, a shoe company he set up with two others 33 years ago.

Such close-knit relationships might seem quaint in a world of globalised operations. Yet for some companies – even those that face stiff international competition – the difference between success and failure is rooted in a local connection. Four stories illustrate how a local link can help a company stay competitive in the face of more powerful global rivals.

The neighbourhood supplier

The idea that European manufacturers should always seek to reduce costs by moving production out of the Continent is outdated and misguided, says Mr Bracalente. It does not always produce the best result in terms of quality or allow companies to respond to changes in demand, he argues.

BAG, which sells its shoes under the NeroGiardini brand and had sales last year of $155 million, has 200 employees, most in the company's headquarters in southern Italy. Another 1700 people work in BAG's 20 supplier factories in the surrounding region.

BAG and its suppliers concentrate on shoe assembly, a job that is rarely done in Europe. But Mr Bracalente says this gives him a vital source of flexibility and the capacity to make rapid changes in shoe style. Just over half the upper shoe parts are made in low-cost countries such as Serbia and Tunisia. The rest of the uppers and the soles are made locally.

Having such a large part of its shoes made by local suppliers enables Mr Bracalente to make a big play of the 'Made in Italy' label. 'This is a real marketing advantage,' he says. Having suppliers close by means production problems are quickly solved, 'Our technicians can go and visit the suppliers, often in just half an hour,' Mr Bracalente says.

To Mr Bracalente, splitting the assembly functions between BAG and many outside companies is a strength, not a weakness. 'I don't believe you can have an efficient company that employs 2000 people,' he says. 'If you divide the operations into smaller units, you can be productive and flexible while keeping costs down.'

The lure of the market

In the late 1990s Yin Weldon, founder of Sinovac Biotech, spotting an opportunity to become China's first home-grown producer of specialist vaccines.

'I'm both a doctor and a businessman,' says Mr Yin. 'I've always been interested in limiting the spread of illness. But I could also see the chance to exploit a market by making something in China that no one had done before on a large scale.'

What he recognised was that a market for his products – if they could be manu-factured in a reliable way – seemed assured. The Chinese government was keen to promote a local producer of vaccines for hepatitis, if only to reduce the country's dependence on foreign pharmaceutical companies that charged high prices.

Mr Yin used his knowledge of local health agencies – where he had worked dur-ing his earlier career as a scientist – to accelerate the bureaucracy of government cer-tifications for vaccines. Last year Sinovac had sales of $33.5 million, all from the domestic market. Some 85% of the sales came from vaccines for hepatitis A and B, which are sold in China at prices roughly 30% of those of imported vaccines from rivals such as GlaxoSmithKline and Sanofi-Aventis.

Sinovac says it wants to expand its sales into other countries over the next few years. 'Even though right now we get all our sales from China, I'd like to develop the company so that eventually it gains 50% of its revenues from other markets,' says Mr Yin.

A local development base

Farfield, a UK-based maker of novel scientific instruments, also bases its global ac-tivities on a strong local link – a special relationship with the scientists at Durham University in north-east England who came up with the ideas behind the company when they founded it 11 years ago.

'We have a lot of useful exchanges with the physicists and biochemists at Durham who can help us try out our new concepts,' says Gerry Musgrave, chief executive of the Crewe-based company, which had sales last year of about £2 million, of which 80% were exports.

The instruments that Farfield is developing are based on breakthroughs made at Durham in measuring how the wave-like characteristics of laser light are changed when it hits organic molecules. This helps the company come up with ideas for new drug treatment. 'We can see with the instruments what amount to videos of what is going on in the body – with a resolution measured in picometres [thousand billionths of a metre],' says Mr Musgrave. 'This is a type of instrument where we think we have a world lead.'

Know your customer

Hudson Precision Products, a 102 year old company based in Chicago that makes spe-cialist engineering components, has the biggest local market: the whole of the US.

With 85 employees and sales last year of $9 million, the crucial factor driving its operations is its connection with a group of about ten companies in the eastern US, which it has supplied for more than 35 years.

'I often talk to people [among Hudson's customers] who have worked with my father or my grandfather,' says Joan Wrenn, the 72 year old chief executive of the company.

One of Hudson's long-standing US customers is a producer of microphones. It buys tiny components from the Chicago company. '[The customer] has told us they keep buying from us because if they try to get anyone else to make them, the components

▶

cause the microphone to vibrate. For some reason, perhaps because we've done the job for so long, we can make them in just the right way,' Ms Wrenn says.

These relationships have helped the company move into other fields, such as medical equipment. 'The accent on solving problems for these local customers has been something that has given us the expertise and ingenuity necessary to keep in business in a climate that has become increasingly difficult for many of us manufacturers,' Ms Wrenn says.

In a globalised world, having a widely scattered group of customers and suppliers should not be the be-all and end-all. A strong local connection used to build a stronger business is an asset that should never be taken for granted.

Source: Marsh, P., 'How to play the home advantage', *Financial Times*, 27 November 2008.

Question

Consider some of the implications of these examples for business strategy in a globalised economy.

2 Globalisation and production

We have already noted that differences in relative unit labour costs (RULCs) will provide incentives to firms to select particular countries for the production of part or all of a product. In Case Study 1.1 (p. 10) we examined the reasons for Dyson outsourcing parts of its production process to Malaysia. However it may not only be the cost based advantages of alternative production locations which might lead to such outsourcing, but possibly less tangible factors, such as those reviewed in Case Study 1.4.

CASE 1.4 Does a global approach benefit the company?   FT

The suggestion is often made that businesses with a global outlook perform better than those focused on the home market. When Isaac Merritt Singer set up a branch of his sewing machine company in Paris in 1855, he probably did not think he was blazing a trail that US companies would still be following more than 150 years later. Singer's expansion in France turned the New York based company into the first US multinational, pioneering a business model that would be adopted by other icons of American capitalism, from Ford to Standard Oil to General Electric.

But perhaps the most important legacy of Singer's daring move was that it worked: within six years of the French opening, foreign sales had exceeded US revenues. It is a lesson not lost on today's corporate leaders. As the US economy is squeezed by a housing slump, credit turmoil and higher fuel prices, a gap has opened up between companies with large overseas operations and those focused on the domestic market.

In 2007 blue-chips such as General Electric, the conglomerate, IBM, the technology giant, and UPS, the logistics group, hitched a ride on a global economy growing faster than the US. By contrast, companies that depended on domestic consumers such as Wal-Mart, the retail bell-wether, and Home Depot, the do-it-yourself chain, released disappointing results and gloomy predictions.

This dichotomy was reflected in US stock markets, as investors ran for cover from domestic woes. After monitoring more than 40 stock-picking techniques, Merrill Lynch analysts concluded that buying shares in S&P500 with the highest percentage of international sales was the second-best performing investment strategy in 2007. Could the importance of overseas markets destroy the old multinational model whereby companies decentralised manufacturing and sales operations but kept key functions such as the executive office, research and product design in the 'home country'? And if so, are some US companies ready to become truly transnational by scattering their top executives around the world.

Critics of this view suggest there are significant cyclical forces behind the recent rise of US multinationals: forces, in other words, that could change in the near future. First, the dollar has lost nearly a third of its value against America's largest trading partners over the seven years, making it easier for US exporters to sell to the world and boosting the dollar value of overseas earnings. Second, US multinationals have been boosted by global economic growth which has largely been driven by emerging markets hungry for infrastructure and consumer goods – two of America Inc's strongest suits.

But macro-economic and trade factors are only part of the reason overseas profits of US companies are about to register a record 20th consecutive quarter of double-digit growth. US executives argue that they are reaping the benefits of a decade of investment aimed at shifting their companies' centre of gravity away from the domestic market.

For such experts, such radical transformations have been more common among US companies than their foreign rivals for two key reasons; corporate America's constant need to satisfy demanding investors and the presence of fewer regulatory and labour constraints in a country renowned for its free-market spirit.

But even if economic changes and internal revolutions at companies mean, in the words of Steve Mills, head of IBM's global software business, that 'things cannot go back to the way they were', will more companies abandon national allegiance and become truly 'a national'?

'Big Blue' – as IBM is known – claims to be just that, with operations in more than 150 countries and key functions spread around the world. Its head of procurement, for example, is based in Shenzhen, China, half a world away from Mr Palmisano's headquarters in Armonk New York. 'Ours is a boundary-less way of thinking,' says Mr Mills. Halliburton, the oil services group run by Dick Cheney, before he became US vice-president, recently followed the petrodollars trail and moved its chief executive from Houston to Dubai.

However, many US chief executives regard such moves as impractical, if not outright dangerous. They argue that being rooted in the US is not only an insurance policy in case the globalisation tide turns, but also a way of maintaining order and focus in increasingly complex and dispersed enterprises – of letting everybody know where the buck stops and who is in charge.

Jeffrey Immelt, who heads GE, one of the most 'global' companies in the US, recently distilled this view: 'We're an American company but in order to be successful

▶

we've got to win in every corner of the world'. In other words, global aspirations tinged with national pride – which Singer would have understood – is just as recognisable today among US business leaders.

Source: Adapted from Guerrera, F. 'US companies choose: National, multinational or "a-national"', *Financial Times*, 16 August 2007.

Questions

1 Examine the arguments in favour of a global approach to business activity.

2 Examine the arguments against a global approach to business activity.

3 What policy differences might result from this debate?

3 Globalisation and the role of the nation state

It has been argued that one of the major effects of globalisation is to threaten the notion of the territorial nation state, in at least three key respects; its competence, its autonomy and, ultimately, its legitimacy.

- *Loss of competence*. In a global economic system, productive capital, finance and products flow across national boundaries in ever-increasing volumes and values, yet the nation state seems increasingly irrelevant as a 'barrier' to international events and influences. Governments often appear powerless to prevent stock market crashes or recessions in one part of the world having adverse effects on domestic output, employment, interest rates and so on. Attempts to lessen these adverse effects seem, to many citizens, increasingly to reside in *supranational bodies* such as the IMF, World Bank, EU, etc. This inability of nation states to meet the demands of their citizens without international cooperation is seen by many as evidence of the declining *competence* of states, arguably leading to a 'widening and weakening' of the individual nation state.
- *Loss of autonomy*. In such a situation, the *autonomy* and even *legitimacy* of the nation state are also subtly altered. The increased emphasis on international cooperation has brought with it an enormous increase in the number and influence of inter-governmental and non-governmental organisations (NGOs) to such an extent that many writers now argue that national and international policy formulation have become inseparable. For example, whereas in 1909 only 176 international NGOs could be identified, by the year 2008 this number exceeded 30,000 and was still growing! The formerly monolithic national state, with its own independent and broadly coherent policy, is now conceived by many to be a fragmented coalition of bureaucratic agencies each pursuing its own agenda with minimal central direction or control. State autonomy is thereby threatened in economic, financial and ecological areas.
- *Loss of legitimacy*. Of course any loss of competence or autonomy for the nation state is, to many, an implied loss of legitimacy. However, proponents of an alleged 'loss of legitimacy' in the UK often point more directly to the new EU constitutional arrangement proposed in 2003 and earlier adjustments of UK law and practice into conformity with the European Court of Justice and other supranational bodies.

However, as we saw earlier, globalisation consists of a series of conflicting tendencies. While there is some evidence that the relevance of the nation state is declining, other writers claim the alternative view. Some argue that the state retains its positive role in the world through its monopoly of military power which, though rarely used, offers its citizens relative security in a highly dangerous world. Further, it provides a focus for personal and communal identity and finally, in pursuing national interest through cooperation and collaboration, nation states actually empower themselves. The suggestion here is that international cooperation (as opposed to unilateral action) allows states simultaneously to pursue their national interests and at the same time, by collective action, to achieve still more effective control over their national destiny. For example, the international control of exchange rates (e.g. the EU Single Currency) is seen by some as enhancing state *autonomy* rather than diminishing it, since the collective action implicit in a common currency affords more economic security and benefits for nationals than unilateral action.

Globalisation is therefore redefining our understanding of the nation state by introducing a much more complex architecture of political power in which authority is seen as being pluralistic rather than residing solely in the nation state.

Case Study 1.5 would suggest that the nation state, as well as the business itself, may have strategic reasons to support or oppose transnational production activities in globalised economies.

CASE 1.5 Competing in a globalised economy

Emblazoned across the huge blue barns of the Daewoo shipyards on Koje island, off the southern coast of South Korea, are signs of declaring 'No change, no future'. Certainly it is a frequent mantra in Korea, as Hyundai Heavy Industries, Samsung Heavy Industries and Daewoo Shipbuilding and Marine Engineering strive to maintain their positions at the top of the global industry. Right now, the top three are in a sweet spot – orders are rolling in fast, deep hedging means they are insulated against the strong Korean won and their share prices have been sky-rocketing. All are frantically extending their docks and building new quays to allow them to increase capacity.

'Korean shipbuilders are enjoying this very bullish market', says Koh Youngyoul, chief strategy officer at Daewoo, which has a three-year backlog of orders worth $29 billion. But how long will it last? Korean shipbuilders are being threatened by China, which is set to have 23 docks for construction of large ships by 2015, many more than Korea's 15. Meanwhile, Chinese manufacturers, already churning out standard container ships, are trying to make high-tech liquefied natural gas carriers and large containers – the Korean industry's bread and butter.

Korean estimates of the time China will take to close the technological gap range from four years to ten years. Industry operators know they must not be complacent. 'At the moment, China is simply building low-value added ships while Korea is making much more high-technological oriented ships', says Mr Koh of Daewoo, which expected to win orders worth $11 billion this year but had to revise this up to $17 billion after achieving its target in the first half. 'There is no serious competition from China right now but it is only a matter of time until China catches up with Korea like Korea caught up with Japan ten years ago,' says Mr Koh.

Korea came from nowhere to become the world's biggest shipbuilding country and, thanks largely to Hyundai, Samsung and Daewoo, has a global market share of around 40%. The rise of Chinese industry has caused Korean manufacturers to look at Japan's mistakes and make sure that they do not fall into the same trap. 'Japan failed to diversify', says Park Chung-Heum, executive vice-president of project planning at Samsung Heavy, which likewise received $10 billion in orders in the first half and raised its projected orders to $15 billion.

About 90% of all Korean orders are for run-of-the-mill container carriers and tankers but the other 10% is made up of vessels such as floating production storage and offloading oil facilities that Korean shipbuilders hope will be their future. Already Daewoo has built the Agbami FPSO vessel for Chevron, the US oil giant, for a record $1.6 billion offshore oil production facility for Abu Dhabi Marine. Samsung is increasingly concentrating on offshore vessels such as barge-mounted power plants and drilling rigs. It has also built an Arctic tanker for Lukoil and ConocoPhillips that can break 1.5m-thick ice. 'Six years ago the average price of a Samsung ship was $50 million or $80 million at today's prices – but now it is $170 million,' Mr Park says from his office overlooking the Koje shipyards, illustrating both the sophistication of the ships being built and the recent escalation of prices shipyards can command.

But all this new added value carries a risk, namely technology leakage. Korea's National Intelligence Service has been investigating leaks from Korean companies to Chinese competitors and a former Daewoo employee has been arrested for selling drawings to a Chinese company. 'We are very concerned about this sort of leakage' says Mr Park of Samsung. 'Now we are putting watermarks on our drawings and we always print them on paper, not on CD. This is a very critical time and China would like to be able to catch up with Korea.'

Sanjeev Rana, a shipbuilding analyst at Merrill Lynch in Seoul, nevertheless says Korean shipbuilders will be able to remain market leaders in high value ships at least until 2010, although he adds that this is not necessarily a recipe for success.

Korea will maintain their lead in the value added segment but they need to maintain conventional shipbuilding in their portfolio – you can't have everything value added,' Mr Rana says. 'So even if they increase the high-tech component of their portfolio to 65%, they will still be 40 or 35% exposed to China.

Strategy of cheap labour

China might present a threat to Korean shipbuilders, but it also offers significant opportunities. Samsung Heavy Industries and Daewoo Shipbuilding and Marine Engineering, Korea's second and third largest shipbuilders, respectively, have both opened yards across the Yellow Sea. There, Chinese workers construct the blocks that form the basis for Korean ships, which are then transported back to Korea for value-added production. This enables Korean producers to utilise China's cheap labour without – in theory – giving away core technology.

'China is supplying the one-third of the blocks used in our ships, which are put together in the Koje yards', says Park Chung-Heum, executive vice-president of project planning at Samsung Heavy. 'The price of block fabrication in Korea has become very expensive so we are very happy to do this in China.'

Samsung's factory in Ningbo, Zhejiang province, now produces 200,000 tonnes of ship blocks a year, while Daewoo's subsidiary in the north-eastern port city of Yantai, Shandong province, will churn out 220,000 tonnes of ship blocks when it reaches full capacity in 2011. However, Hyundai Heavy, Korea's largest shipbuilder, does not have a joint venture in China and has no plans to open one, says Kevin Chang, a company spokesman. 'Shipbuilding is a very labour-intensive industry and Hyundai Heavy wants to supply jobs for Koreans,' he said.

Source: Adapted from Fifield, A. 'Korean shipbuilders struggle to keep Chinese in their wake', *Financial Times*, 27 March 2007.

Questions

1 Why does Korea look to Japan when reviewing its strategies?

2 Consider the opportunities and threats to Korean shipbuilding from globalisation.

Pro- and anti-globalisation issues

Public announcements of jobs being relocated overseas often help to fuel the impression that globalisation equates with job losses for many countries. It is hardly surprising therefore that many trade union representatives and their members swell the numbers in the broad based coalition sometimes referred to as the 'anti-globalisation movement'. Since this often finds expression in protests against *global institutions* (such as the WTO, World Bank, IMF, Group of 7/8, etc.), the basis of these anti-globalisation protests is considered in more detail in Chapter 3, where these institutions are reviewed – see, for example, discussions of the WTO (pp. 116–22) along with arguments in favour of globalisation.

■ 4 Globalisation and new rules and norms

Not only are new international institutions and trading blocs characteristic of a more globalised economy in which nation states have progressively less influence, but so too are the 'rules and norms' by which they seek to operate (*see* Box 1.3 above). Market-oriented policies, democratic political frameworks, consensus goals involving social and environmental responsibility, and growing multilateral applications of agreed rules were all identified as characteristics of globalisation in Box 1.3. Here we note the importance of good governance and transparency, an absence of corruption and appropriate property rights to the establishment of a sustainable globalised economic environment.

Benefits of good governance

The World Bank (*World Development Report* 2005) has pointed out that *good governance* – including independent agencies, mechanisms for citizens to monitor public behaviour, and rules that constrain corruption – is a key ingredient for growth and prosperity. In an early study Barro (1991) had found a positive correlation between economic growth and measures of political stability for 98 countries surveyed between

1960 and 1985. More recent empirical research points in a similar direction, for example confirming that fdi inflows are *inversely* related to measures of corruption, as with Lipsey (1999) observing a strong negative correlation between corruption and the locational choice of US subsidiaries across Asian countries. Similarly Claugue *et al.* (1999) and Zak (2001) found that productivity and economic growth will improve when governments impartially protect and define property rights. Underpinning these findings is the perception by firms that a non-transparent business environment increases the prevalence of information asymmetries, raises the cost of securing additional information, increases transaction costs (e.g. risk premiums) and creates an uncertain business environment which deters trade and investment. For example Wallsten (2001) found a strong inverse relationship between investment intentions and the threat of asset expropriation, as well as a propensity for firms to charge higher prices to help pay back their initial capital outlays more rapidly when they felt less secure about the intentions of host governments, the higher prices often inhibiting the penetration and growth phase of product life cycles.

Knowledge and information in globalised economies

Management specialist Stephen Kobrin (1994) describes globalisation as driven not by foreign trade and investment but by information flows. It is this latter perspective, which sees globalisation as a process inextricably linked with the creation, distribution and use of knowledge and information, which is the focus here. Many contributors to the globalisation debate regard the technological convergence of information, computer and telecommunications technologies in the late twentieth century as having acted as a key catalyst in the rapid growth of these information-based activities, seen here as the hallmark of the globalised economy (Held *et al.* 1999).

International communications have grown dramatically, as we noted earlier (p. 12). Contemporary discourse often seeks to express globalisation in terms of the exponential growth in the creation, processing and dissemination of knowledge and information. For example, an 'index of globalisation' recently compiled jointly by the Carnegie Foundation and ATKearney (a global consultant) gives considerable weight to the proportion of national populations online as well as to the number of Internet hosts and secure servers per capita. These indicators of access to information technology and associated information flows are seen here as proxy variables for 'global openness', to be used in association with the more conventional indicators of investment, capital flows, foreign income as a proportion of national income and convergence between domestic and international prices when compiling the overall globalisation index (Walker 2001). Singapore often appears as one of the 'most globalised' countries in this index, helped by the fact that it currently has 1010 mobile phones per 1000 people, and 571 Internet users per 1000 people, as well as a recorded outgoing telephone traffic per head per year some four times as much as in the US (UNDP 2008).

The multinational enterprise (MNE)

Put simply, a multinational enterprise (sometimes called a transnational) is a company that has headquarters in one country but has operations in other countries. It is not always obvious that a firm is a multinational. The growth in alliances, joint ventures and mergers and acquisitions, means that consumers tend to recognise the brand, rather than know who the parent company is. Who, for example, now owns Jaguar or Land Rover? The answer in this case is the Indian based Tata Motor Corporation.

> **pause for thought 6** Can you think of brands for three different types of product and identify the multinational company that owns those brands in each case?

Dunning (1993) defines the multinational as a firm 'that engages in foreign direct investment and owns or controls value-adding activities in more than one country'. Typically the multinational would not just own value-adding activities, but might buy resources and create goods and/or services in a variety of countries. While the central strategic planning takes place at the headquarters, considerable latitude will usually be given to affiliates (subsidiaries) to enable them to operate in harmony with their local environments.

Ranking multinationals

Healey (2007) points out that from a statistical point of view, there are two main methods of ranking the world's top multinationals. First, ranking them according to the amount of foreign assets they control and second, ranking them in terms of a 'transnationality index'.

- *Foreign assets*. Table 1.5 ranks the top ten multinationals according to the *value of foreign assets* they control and we can see that four of the top ten are from the USA, three from the UK, two from France, and one from Japan. They are primarily based in the petroleum/energy, telecommunications, and motor vehicle sectors.

Table 1.5 **World's top ten multinationals ranked by foreign assets (and transnationality index), 2006**

Ranking					
Foreign assets	Transnationality index	Company	Country	Industry	Transnationality index (%)
1	71	General Electric	USA	Electrical and Electrical Equipment	53
2	14	British Petroleum	UK	Petroleum	80
3	87	Toyota Motor	Japan	Motor Vehicle	45
4	34	Royal Dutch/Shell	UK/Netherlands	Petroleum	70
5	84	Exxon/Mobil Corporation	USA	Petroleum	68
6	78	Ford Motor Company	USA	Motor Vehicle	60
7	7	Vodafone Group plc	UK	Telecommunications	85
8	26	Total	France	Petroleum	74
9	96	Electricite de France	France	Electricity, Gas and Water	35
10	92	Wal-Mart Stores	USA	Retail	41

Source: Adapted from *World Development Report* (World Bank 2008).

- *Transnationality index*. However, Table 1.5 also provides each company's transnationality index and its transnationality ranking. The *transnationality index* takes a more comprehensive view of a company's global activity and is calculated as the average of the following three ratios:

1 foreign assets/total assets;
2 foreign sales/total sales;
3 and foreign employment/total employment.

For example, we can see that the largest multinational company is General Electric in terms of the foreign assets it owns. However, its transnationality index of 53% means that it is only ranked 71st in terms of this criteria. The reason for this is that even though it has large investments overseas in absolute value, in *percentage* terms most of its assets, sales and employment are still located in the USA. This is in contrast with British Petroleum where 80% of its overall activity in terms of the three ratios is based abroad, and Vodafone where this figure rises to as high as 85%.

If we wanted to find the companies that operate mostly outside their home country, we would have to look at the ten top multinationals in terms of the transnationality index only. These are shown in Table 1.6 and here we see the dominance of EU companies in sectors such as mining, telecommunications, electrics/electronics food/beverages. The companies with the highest transnationality index are often from the smaller countries as a more restricted domestic market creates incentives to operate abroad if they are to maximise their growth in terms of revenue or profits.

Technical definitions of multinationals, however, fail to convey the true scope and diversity of global business, which covers everything from the thousands of medium-sized firms that have overseas operations to the truly gigantic multinationals like IBM, General Motors and Ford. Some multinationals are *vertically integrated*, with different stages of the same productive process taking place in different countries (e.g. British Petroleum). Others are *horizontally integrated*, performing the same

Table 1.6 World's top ten multinationals ranked by the transnationality index (and foreign assets), 2006

Ranking					
Transnationality index	Foreign assets	Company	Country	Industry	Transnationality index (%)
1	92	Barrick Gold Corporation	Canada	Gold/Mining	94
2	37	Xstrata plc	UK	Mining and quarrying	92
3	48	Linde AG	Germany	Industrial trucks/ trailers	89
4	77	Pernard Ricard SA	France	Beverages	87
5	68	WPP Group	UK	Business Services	87
6	67	Liberty Global	USA	Telecommunications	85
7	7	Vodafone Group plc	UK	Telecommunications	85
8	46	Philips Electronics	The Netherlands	Electrical and electronic equipment	85
9	23	Nestlé	Switzerland	Food and beverage	83
10	21	Hutchison Whampoa Limited	Hong Kong/China	Diversified	82

Source: Adapted from *World Development Report* (World Bank 2008).

basic production operations in each of the countries in which they operate (e.g. Marks & Spencer). Many multinationals are household names, marketing global brands (e.g. Rothmans International, IBM, British Airways). Others are holding companies for a portfolio of international companies (e.g. Diageo) or specialise in capital goods that have little name-recognition in the high street (e.g. BTR, Hawker Siddley, GKN).

How important are the multinationals?

In 2007 an estimated 79,000 multinational enterprises, collectively controlled a total of around 800,000 foreign affiliates (subsidiaries), employed almost 82 million people worldwide and accounted for sales revenue of over $31 trillion, some 11% of world GDP. Table 1.7 provides an overview of such multinational activity. Indeed in 2007 the sales of multinationals' foreign affiliates (subsidiaries) far exceeded the total global export of goods and services.

We have already seen in Table 1.1 (p. 3) that the world's 100 largest MNEs alone accounted for over 15.3 million jobs and for annual sales in excess of $7000 billion in value. Only 14 nation states have a GDP that exceeds the turnover of Exxon, Ford or General Motors.

Historically, the bulk of multinational activity has been concentrated in the developed world. Indeed, as recently as the mid-1980s, half of all multinational production took place in only five countries – the United States, Canada, the UK, Germany and the Netherlands. This pattern is now changing rapidly. The rapid industrialisation and economic growth in the so-called 'Bric' economies of Brazil, Russia, India and China and in other newly-industrialising nations of the world has led to a sharp increase in multinational investment in Asia and (to a lesser extent) in South America. Some of these countries, such as Taiwan, South Korea, Hong Kong and Singapore, now have per capita GDP levels that exceed those of most European nations, and indigenous companies from India, China and elsewhere are now beginning to establish production facilities in the 'old world'.

We noted earlier (p. 4) that the old bi-polar world economy has now been replaced by the 'triad' of North America, the European Union and East and South-East Asia, with these three regions accounting for approximately 80% of the world's exports and 84% of world manufacturing output.

Table 1.7 **Multinational activity in a global context**

	2007 ($bn)	Average annual growth rates (%)		
		1986–90	1991–95	1996–2000
Sales of foreign affiliates of MNEs	31,197	19.3	8.8	8.4
Total exports of goods and services	7430	15.8	8.7	4.2
Employment of foreign affiliates (thousands)	81,615	5.3	5.5	11.5
Total assets of foreign affiliates	68,716	17.7	13.7	19.3

Source: Adapted from *World Development Report* (World Bank 2008).

Table 1.8 **Inflows of foreign direct investment ($ billion)**

Region	1990–95 (annual average)	1996–2000	2001	2002	2003	2004	2005	2006	2007
Developed countries	145	581	610	484	364	410	680	920	1248
Developing countries	74	198	206	220	220	265	310	405	495
South East Europe and CIS	6	8	10	11	20	30	31	58	87

Note: Figures are rounded.

Source: Adapted from *World Development Report* (World Bank 2008).

■ Multinationals and fdi

Table 1.8 shows the changing pattern of *foreign direct investment* (fdi) by which domestic companies acquire control over productive facilities overseas. While there is a strong cyclical pattern evident, with foreign direct investment in the rich industrial countries higher during the world boom years of the mid to late 1990s and again in the past few years, as compared to the recessionary years of the early 1990s and the early years of the new millennium, investment in the developing countries shows a sustained increase over the period since 1990, which is less dependent on fluctuations in national income.

Table 1.8 also reflects the reintegration of the former centrally-planned economies of central and eastern Europe into the world economy. These former centrally-planned economies are included in the category 'South East Europe and Commonwealth of Independent States (CIS)'. Although the total volume of inward foreign investment is still relatively low, inflows have increased strongly since the transition process began in 1989. Unsurprisingly, countries that have pushed ahead with market reform and privatisation in particular, have attracted the bulk of the foreign investment, both by creating international confidence in their future economic and political stability and by providing the opportunities for foreign companies to buy local production and distribution facilities. Whilst Eastern European countries such as Poland and the Czech Republic, for example, have been highly successful in attracting multinationals like Ford, Volkswagen and Philip Morris, those that have resisted or delayed market reform, notably many of the states of the former Soviet Union have, in contrast, found foreign companies less willing to risk large-scale inward investment.

■ Multinationals and globalised production

Table 1.9 throws further light on the increasing globalisation of productive activity by showing the progressive growth in the Transnationality Index (TNI) for the world's largest 100 MNEs in their home economies between 1990 and 2006 (UNCTAD 2008). The TNI has been defined above as the average of the three ratios: foreign assets : total assets; foreign sales : total sales; and foreign employment : total employment. A rise in the overall TNI index of 15.5% between 1990 and 2006 suggests still more international involvement of the top 100 MNEs outside their home country.

The European Union (EU) is home to over half of the world's largest MNEs and we can see from Table 1.9 that the average transnationality index (TNI) for the EU has

Table 1.9 Transnationality Index for the world's largest 100 MNEs in their home economies, 1990 and 2006

Economy	Average TNI (%)		Number of MNEs	
	1990	2006	1990	2006
European Union	56.7	74.7	48	52
France	50.9	63.8	14	15
Germany	44.4	54.8	9	14
UK	68.5	72.8	12	13
North America	41.2	60.2	30	25
US	38.5	57.8	28	22
Canada	79.2	78.1	2	3
Japan	35.5	52.1	12	9
Rest of the World	n.a.	n.a.	10	14
All Economies	51.1	61.6	100	100

Source: Adapted from World Investment Report (UNCTAD 2008).

risen from 56.7% to 74.7% over the 1990–2006 period alone. A similar rapid growth in the TNI is indicated for MNEs with North America (41.2% to 60.2%) or Japan (35.5% to 52.1%) as their 'home' base. For 'all economies' the greater internationalisation of production is indicated via the TNI rising from 51.1% to 61.6% in the 1990–2006 time period. Closer scrutiny of this data reveals that the driving forces behind these observed increases in the TNI have been the growth in the foreign sales/total sales and in the foreign employment/total employment components of the TNI. Table 1.9 also indicates the growing importance of multinational activity from companies based outside the European Union, North America and Japan. Whereas only ten multinationals were recorded in the largest 100 from outside these areas in 1990, that number had risen to 14 by 2006.

Multinationals and the developing economies

We noted in Table 1.9 above that an increasing number of MNEs have 'home' economies outside Europe, North America and Japan. Here we review the growing importance of the *developing economies* as the origin of MNE activities.

The foreign assets, foreign sales and foreign employment of the 100 largest MNEs from developing economies are shown in Table 1.10. We can see that they accounted for $571 billion of foreign assets, $605 billion of foreign sales and over 2.1 million foreign employees. Of these largest 100 MNEs from developing countries, the top ten in size accounted for about half of these respective totals, with Hutchinson Whampoa (Hong Kong, China) at the head, followed by Petronas (Malaysia), Samsung Electronics (South Korea), Cernex (Mexico), Hyundai Motor (South Korea) and Singtel (Singapore), respectively.

A further breakdown by region of these largest 100 MNEs from developing economies is provided in Table 1.11, with associated transnationality indices (TNIs).

East and South-East Asia are clearly the major home location of the 100 largest MNEs from developing economies, with 76 MNEs from these areas and transnationality indices (TNIs) well above 50%.

Table 1.10 **Snapshot of the world's 100 largest MNEs from developing economies 2006 (billions of dollars, thousands of employees and per cent)**

Variable	2006
Assets	
Foreign	571
Total	1694
Foreign to total (%)	34%
Sales	
Foreign	605
Total	1304
Foreign to total (%)	46%
Employment	
Foreign	2151
Total	5246
Foreign to total (%)	41%

*In percentage points

Source: Adapted from *World Investment Report* (UNCTAD 2008).

The 100 largest MNEs from developing countries have a smaller overall TNI index than the 100 largest MNEs worldwide (53.9% compared to 61.6%), suggesting a less globally integrated chain of operations. This is also reflected in the fact that they have, on average, only nine affiliates in foreign countries, compared to the average of 41 affiliates in foreign countries for the 100 largest MNEs worldwide.

It may be useful at this point to consider locational aspects of foreign affiliates of MNEs in still more detail.

■ Multinational affiliates and their location

As well as the TNI, we can use measures involving foreign affiliates to indicate the extent to which a company is truly transnational. In Table 1.12 we can see two such indicators.

One relates to the *number of host economies* in which the company has foreign affiliates. Deutsche Post (Germany) leads with foreign affiliates in 111 host economies, with the Royal Dutch/Shell Group (Netherlands/UK) second with foreign affiliates in 98 host economies.

Table 1.11 **Transnationality Index of the 100 largest MNEs from developing economies: by region 2006**

Top 100 MNEs from developing economies	Average TNI	
Region/economy of which	TNI	Number of companies
Africa (South Africa)	45.0	11
South-East Asia	52.3	20
East Asia	58.6	56
West Asia	56.5	3
Latin America and the Caribbean	40.1	10
Total	**53.9**	**100**

Source: Adapted from *World Investment Report* (UNCTAD 2008).

Table 1.12 **Top 15 MNEs, ranked by number of host economies in their affiliates**

Company	Home country	No. of host economies	Internationalisation Index (II)%	Transnationality Index (TNI)%
Deutsche Post AG	Germany	111	83	37
Royal Dutch/ Shell Group	Netherlands/ United Kingdom	98	56	70
Nestlé SA	Switzerland	96	93	83
Siemens AG	Germany	89	75	66
BASF AG	Germany	88	78	57
Proctor & Gamble	United States	75	81	59
GlaxoSmith-Kline	United Kingdom	74	75	54
Linde	Germany	72	91	89
Bayer AG	Germany	71	76	55
Phillips Electronics	Netherlands	68	76	85
Total	France	66	72	74
IBM	United States	66	88	57
WPP Group PLC	United Kingdom	64	65	87
Roche Group	Switzerland	62	89	80
Novaratis	Switzerland	62	92	71

Source: Adapted from *World Investment Report* (UNCTAD 2008).

The *internationalisation index* (II) is another useful indicator of transnational involvement and is the ratio of an MNE's foreign affiliates to its total affiliates, expressed as a percentage. We see that Nestlé has the highest II of 93% of the 15 companies in Table 1.12, followed by Novartis with an II of 92%. Clearly the ranking of companies by number of host economies does not exactly match the ranking by II so that both perspectives can be usefully used, alongside the TNI, when seeking to assess the true transnationality of a company's operations. For example, whilst we can see from Table 1.12 that Deutsche Post AG has foreign affiliates in more overseas (host) economies than any of the other companies, and has 83% of all its affiliate companies overseas, it only has an average of 37% of its total assets, employment and sales located overseas.

◼ Types of MNE

The wide variety of strategies embraced by MNEs has led some writers to distinguish between different types.

- *Global corporations* that view the whole world as their marketplace, with goods and services standardised to meet the needs of consumers worldwide.
- *Multidomestic corporations* that comprise a relatively independent set of subsidiaries, each producing goods and services focused on a particular local market.
- *Transnational corporations* that integrate a geographically dispersed set of specialised activities into a single production process.

For the purposes of this book we will use the term 'multinational enterprise' (MNE) to apply to all three categories discussed above. However, from time to time we will apply terms such as 'market oriented' or 'cost oriented' to different multinationals, but only to indicate the broad strategic thrust behind their activities rather than the 'type' of multinational. The nature of many of today's MNEs will reflect, in part, the methods the company has used in its attempts to internationalise in the past. We discuss these different approaches to internationalisation in more detail in Chapters 2 and 7 respectively.

However, the nature of many of today's MNEs and of their activity in the UK and elsewhere also reflects broader changes in a globalised economy, including changing patterns of consumer behaviour and technological changes.

Useful websites

Now try the self-check questions for this chapter on the companion website at www.pearsoned.co.uk/wall. You will also find further resources as well as useful weblinks.

Many interesting articles can be found in periodicals and newspapers on international business issues. Check the following sites:

www.economist.co.uk
www.ft.com
www.telegraph.co.uk
www.timesonline.co.uk
www.guardian.co.uk
www.Virgin.com
Procter & Gamble's website is at *www.pg.com*
Coca-Cola is *www.cocacola.com*
McDonald's website is *www.mcdonalds.com*

This next site has a wealth of detail about the EU, its institutions and the euro:
www.europa.eu.int
The IMF website is *www.imf.org*
The World Bank website is *www.worldbank.org*
The UN's Food and Agriculture Organisation is at *www.fao.org*

Other websites relevant to international business can be found at the end of each topic-based chapter.

Useful key texts

Daniels, J., Radebaugh, L. and Sullivan, D. (2006) *International Business* (11th edn), Pearson Prentice Hall, especially Part I.

Dicken, P. (2003) *Global Shift: Transforming the World Economy* (4th edn), Paul Chapman Publishing Ltd, especially Chapter 1 and Parts I and II.

Hill, C. (2006) *International Business: Competing in the Global Marketplace* (5th edn), McGraw-Hill Irwin, especially Chapter 1.

Morrison, J. (2006) *The International Business Environment* (2nd edn), Palgrave, especially Chapter 2.

Piggott, J. and Cook, M. (2006) *International Business Economics: A European Perspective*, Palgrave Macmillan, especially Chapters 1 and 6.

Rugman, A. and Collinson, R. (2009) *International Business* (5th edn), FT Prentice Hall, especially Chapter 1.

Tayeb, M. (2000) *International Business: Theories, Policies and Practices*, Financial Times Prentice Hall, especially Chapters 5–8 and 18.

Wild, J., Wild, K. and Han, J. (2006) *International Business: The Challenges of Globalization* (3rd edn), FT Prentice Hall, especially Chapter 1.

Other texts and sources

Barro, R. (1991) 'Economic Growth in a Cross-Section of Countries', *Quarterly Journal of Economics*, 106, 20, pp. 407–43.

Black, J. (2002) *A Dictionary of Economics*, Oxford Business Dictionary, Oxford University Press.

Claugue, C., Keefer, P., Knack, S. and Olson, M. (1999) 'Contract – Intensive Money: Contract Enforcement, Property Rights and Economic Performances', *Journal of Economic Growth*, 4, pp. 185–211.

Corkhill, D. (2000) 'Internationalisation and Competitiveness: the Portuguese Experience', in *Dimensions of International Competitiveness*, Lloyd-Reason, L. and Wall, S. (eds), Edward Elgar.

Croucher, S. (2003) *Globalization and Belonging: The Politics of Identity in a Changing World*, Rowman & Littlefield Publishers.

Czinkota, M. and Ronkainen, I. (1999) *International Marketing* (5th edn), South Western.

Dunning, J.H. (1993) Multinational Enterprises and the Global Economy, Addison-Wesley.

Frankel, J. (1997) *Regional Trading Blocs in the World Economic System*, Institute for International Economics, Washington, DC.

Giddens, A. (1990) *The Consequences of Modernity*, Polity Press.

Healey, N. (2007) 'The Multinational Corporation', in *Applied Economics* (11th edn), Griffiths, A. and Wall, S. (eds), Financial Times Prentice Hall.

Held, D., McGrew, A., Goldblatt, D. and Perraton, J. (1999) *Global Transformations: Politics, Economics and Culture*, Polity Press.

Hill, C. (2005) *International Business: Competing in the Global Marketplace* (5th edn), McGrawHill/Irwin.

Kalwarski, T. (2009) 'International Trade Hits a Wall', *Business Week*, January 26, p. 15.

Kobrin, S.J. (1994) 'Is There a Relationship Between a Geocentric Mind-set and Multinational Strategy?', *Journal of International Business Studies*, 3, pp. 493–511.

Lipsey, R.E. (1999) 'The Location and Characteristics of US Affiliates in Asia', *National Bureau of Economic Research* (NBER) Working Paper, Cambridge, Mass.

McGrew, A. (1992) 'A Global Society', in *Modernity and its Futures*, Hall, S., Held, D. and McGrew, A. (eds), Open University Press.

OECD (2007) *Dataset: OECD Estimates of Labour Productivity Levels*, OECD.

Porter, M.E., Schwab, K. and Sala-i-Martin, X. (eds) (2007) *The Global Competitiveness Report 2007–2008*, World Economic Forum.

Roberts, M. and Deichmann, U. (2008) 'Regional Spillover Estimation' Background paper for the *World Development Report*, 2009.

Tiplady, R. (2003) *One World or Many? The Impact of Globalisation on Mission*, Authentic.

United Nations Conference on Trade and Development (UNCTAD), *World Investment Report* (annual publication).

United Nations Development Programme (UNDP), *Human Development Report* (annual publication), OUP.

US Department of Labor (2007) *Hourly Compensation Costs in Manufacturing*.

Walker, D. (2001) 'Global's Good Side', *Guardian*, 2 May.

Wallsten, S. (2001) 'Ringing in the 20th Century', *World Bank Research Working Paper*, Washington, DC.

World Bank, *World Development Report* (annual publication).

Zak, P. (2001) 'Institutions, Property Rights and Growth', *The Gruter Institute Working Papers*, 2(1): Article 2.

Chapter 2

Internationalisation process

By the end of this chapter you should be able to:

- explain the pressures for internationalisation and why firms move production facilities abroad;

- outline the various methods available to firms seeking to enter foreign markets;

- assess the advantages and disadvantages of each method;

- discuss some of the principles that may contribute to successful international alliances;

- evaluate the different theoretical approaches to internationalisation;

- review the barriers that must be overcome for successful internationalisation.

Introduction

As we note in Chapter 3, there has been a rapid growth in international trade in both goods and services. Such global competition has forced corporations to seek new markets, both at home and abroad, and to speed up the cycle of product development. The costs of entry into these new markets can be formidable. The days of large corporations working solely by themselves would seem to be numbered. Few firms can afford to be sophisticated in all areas of technology or to develop distribution channels and new markets in numerous countries. In addition, rapid technical change and newly emerging patterns and locations of international specialisation place continual pressure on the cost base of the modern corporation. As a means of meeting these challenges, many firms realise that they must find partners to share the risks of expansion. Partnership and collaboration are the order of the day. This in turn creates new and difficult challenges for international managers. The choice of direction is almost infinite. Which markets to expand into? Which products to develop? How much can we afford to invest? Which partners to choose? Which areas of business to keep as core competencies and which to develop with others?

But why and how do firms internationalise? The reasons for going international and the conditions under which firms choose to do so are complex and have been the subject of much debate. In this chapter we examine the history of internationalisation, the reasons firms choose to internationalise, the ways in which this has been done and the theoretical frameworks that seek to explain this process. Chapter 7 looks further into international strategic choice and Chapter 8 considers the types of international organisational structure often adopted by MNEs during the internationalisation process.

Once a firm has decided to go international, this may take place in a wide variety of ways, most of which fall into three broad categories:

1 export-based methods;
2 non-equity methods;
3 equity methods.

Export-based methods for internationalisation

This is the most common way in which a firm begins to go international. It continues to produce its product in the domestic market, but exports a proportion of this output to foreign markets. This may involve physical movements of products by air, sea, road or rail, but it increasingly involves the cross-border transfer of less tangible items such as computer software, graphics, images and the written word.

Exporting is the oldest and most straightforward way of conducting international business. Its growth can be put down to the liberalisation of trade that has taken place globally and within regional trading blocs over recent decades, with the World Trade Organisation significantly reducing tariff rates and quotas imposed on most imports (*see* Chapter 3, p. 116). Other protectionist measures are gradually being phased out or lowered at the *regional* level in free trade areas such as NAFTA (North American Free Trade Association), ASEAN (Association of South East Asian Nations) and the APEC (Asia-Pacific Economic Corporation), and in customs unions such as the Andean Pact and Mercosur, and in economic unions such as the European Union (EU). In addition to these regional arrangements a host of *bilateral* free trade treaties have been concluded, providing further direct exporting opportunities. At the same time, international transportation costs are still falling and cultural barriers to trade are now more readily recognised and overcome than has previously been the case. Governments may further stimulate trade by providing export-promoting initiatives in order to improve the country's balance of payments.

These export-based methods of internationalising are sometimes broken down into 'indirect exporting' and 'direct exporting'.

Indirect exporting

Indirect exporting happens when a firm does not itself undertake any special international activity but rather operates through intermediaries. Under this approach the exporting function is outsourced to other parties, which may prepare the export documentation, take responsibility for the physical distribution of goods and even set up the sales and distribution channels in the foreign market. The role of the intermediary may be played by export houses, confirming houses and buying houses:

■ *an export house* buys products from a domestic firm and sells them abroad on its own account;

- *a confirming house* acts for foreign buyers and is paid on a commission basis, brings sellers and buyers into direct contact (unlike an export house) and guarantees payment will be made to the exporter by the end-user;
- *a buying house* performs similar functions to those of the confirming house but is more active in seeking out sellers to match the buyer's particular needs.

The advantages of such an approach clearly involve the fact that no additional costs need be incurred or expertise acquired in order to access the overseas market. However, there are disadvantages of resorting to indirect exports, which include having little or no control over local marketing issues and little contact with the end-user, so that there is no feedback for product development or marketing.

Such indirect exporting may take different forms. For example, independent export management companies will sometimes handle the export arrangements for a number of clients, providing them with purchasing, shipping, financing and negotiation services (e.g. setting up contracts, providing localised overseas knowledge, etc.) as regards dealing with foreign orders. This is more likely to be the approach adopted by small and medium-sized businesses to indirect exporting. However, larger companies, such as MNEs, will sometimes set up their own subsidiary export management companies to deal with the overseas sales of their entire range of products and brands – as in the case of Unilever, which has established Unilever Export to deal with all its exports from the UK. This enables any scale economies within the exporting function to be gained on behalf of all the products and brands of the MNE.

Indirect exporting sometimes involves unexpected alliances rather than competition between firms. 'Piggybacking', for example, is where different companies share resources in order to access foreign markets more effectively. Here a firm with a compatible product (known as the 'rider') pays to get on board the distribution system already being operated by a firm active in the overseas market (known as the 'carrier'). The 'rider' thereby gains immediate access to the network of outlets operated by the existing 'carrier' while the 'carrier' can reduce various costs by operating closer to full capacity as well as add more value to its activities by offering its clients a greater product range.

■ Direct exporting

Direct exporting would typically involve a firm in distributing and selling its own products to the foreign market. This would generally mean a longer-term commitment to a particular foreign market, with the firm choosing local agents and distributors specific to that market. In-house expertise would need to be developed to keep up these contacts, to conduct market research, prepare the necessary documentation and establish local pricing policies. The advantages of such an approach are that it:

- allows the exporter to closely monitor developments and competition in the host market;
- promotes interaction between producer and end-user;
- involves long-term commitments, such as providing after-sales services to encourage repeat purchases.

You are the managing director of a manufacturing firm, which currently sells all its product on the domestic market. What factors might encourage you to consider exporting abroad (whether directly or indirectly)?

Export processing zones (EPZs)

Direct exporting has been encouraged in recent years by the establishment of export processing zones by countries. These are designated geographical areas within a country that provide appropriate infrastructure and incentives to encourage inward fdi that is focused on direct exporting from the EPZs. The *World Investment Report 2002* noted that most of the countries identified as 'winners' in terms of their export competitiveness within designated product groups, used EPZs or their equivalents to promote the export-oriented inward fdi which has underpinned their subsequent export performance. Successful EPZs can be found, for example, in China, Costa Rica, the Dominican Republic, India, the Philippines and Singapore, all of which provide incentives such as lower (or zero) taxes, less regulation and free or subsidised training. India, for example, removed many of its restrictive labour laws in the 17 Special Economic Zones it created in 2003, to meet the concerns of foreign investors as regards its low labour productivity and highly regulated labour market. However the effective performance of such export processing zones depends not only on the incentives provided but on other policies directed towards enhancing human resources and other aspects of the infrastructure needed to attract and develop export-oriented fdi.

Case Study 2.1 highlights some of the government support programmes in South Africa and Egypt which have been provided to encourage inward investment into these countries.

CASE 2.1 Helping inward fdi

South Africa: Skills Support Programme

As the shortage of skilled labour is a serious constraint on becoming competitive through inward fdi, the South African government has developed several programmes aimed at improving competitive activities in all sectors. The Skills Support Programme (SSP) was introduced in 2005, complementing the previously existing Skills Incentive Programme (SIP) and Small and Medium Enterprises Development Programme (SMEDP).

SSP seeks to encourage greater investment in training, including the introduction of new advanced skills. It provides a cash grant for new projects or the expansion of existing projects, including fdi projects, for up to three years. There are no restrictions on the type of training to be provided. A maximum of 50% of the training costs will be granted to companies whose training programmes are approved. A variety of training activities qualify, including upgrading instructor competence, training in-house assessors, preparing materials and designing programmes. Investors, including foreign direct investors, engaged in manufacturing, high-value agricultural projects, agro-processing, aquaculture, biotechnology, tourism, information and communications technology, recycling, and culture industries, are all eligible.

Egypt: Suppliers Development Programme

The Egyptian government has taken various measures to increase inward fdi, so as to help Egyptian industries become, or remain, globally competitive. In the manufacturing sector in particular, Egyptian producers are struggling to become globally competitive or even competitive in their own markets. The government of Egypt has therefore joined up with the private sector in an initiative known as the National Suppliers Development (NSD) Programme to boost manufacturing growth and stimulate job creation. Through this initiative, the government provides active support to companies, including multinationals, to improve the quality and cost of Egyptian goods and to tailor them to the demands of a globalised world economy.

One hundred multinationals and leading exporters in Egypt have been asked to select up to 20 local suppliers for receiving technical assistance by international consultants to identify efficiency and quality shortfalls, after which they will be able to access bank loans through the NSD Programme to make the necessary improvements. In return, exporters who benefit from the programme agree to expose their Egyptian suppliers to global markets. The NSD Programme has started to yield some results. General Motors, which owns Egypt's largest vehicle assembly plant, has helped pioneer projects under the Programme. Other multinationals involved include DaimlerChrysler, Americana, Cadbury and Hero. The Egyptian government hopes that the NSD Programme will also make Egypt attractive to more multinationals.

Questions

1 Why do countries pay particular attention to export-oriented inward fdi?

2 Suggest how these policies in South Africa and Egypt might help in this respect?

Exporting by either indirect or direct methods is considered less risky than other methods of internationalisation and can be a 'way in' for firms testing out the waters before making the more resource-intensive fdi decision. Of course, some risks are still present when exporting, for example, exchange rates may change unexpectedly, affecting the anticipated profitability of the export transactions. However, the majority of today's international trade (and therefore exporting activity) takes place between firms that are themselves part of a single MNE. In fact, over a half of all world trade takes place *within* the company (*intra-trade*), as we note in Chapter 3. As regards this 'intra-trade', approximately 50% consists of exports by the MNE or its affiliates of *finished products* to its own distribution affiliates for sale in the host country or neighbouring markets. Around a further 50% involves the export of *intermediate products* for final assembly by the MNE's own production affiliates in other countries.

Besides exporting, the firm can internationalise by *investing* in foreign markets. A distinction is often made between *non-equity* and *equity*-based methods of fdi.

Non-equity-based methods for internationalisation

In this form of internationalisation, firms sell technology or know-how under some form of contract, often involving patents, trademarks and copyrights. These are often referred to as *intellectual property rights* and they now form a major part of international transactions, having grown enormously since the 1980s. These non-equity methods of internationalisation often take the form of licensing, franchising or other types of contractual agreement based on these intellectual property rights (*see* Chapter 4, pp. 147–53).

▪ Licensing

At its most simple, *licensing* can mean permission granted by the proprietary owner to a foreign concern (the licensee) in the form of a contract to engage in an activity that would otherwise be legally forbidden. The licensee buys the right to exploit a fairly limited set of technologies and know-how from the licensor, who will usually have protected the intellectual property rights involved by a patent, trademark or copyright. This tends to be a low-cost strategy for internationalisation since the foreign entrant makes little or no resource commitment. The licensor benefits from the licensee's local knowledge and distribution channels, which would otherwise be difficult and time consuming to develop and maintain. Such agreements are often found in industries where R & D and other fixed costs are high, but where aggressive competition is needed at the local level to capture market share. The pharmaceutical and chemical industries provide licensing agreements as do the industrial equipment and defence industries. For example, McDonnell-Douglas and General Dynamics have licensing arrangements with different Japanese and European governments to produce jet fighters.

In *manufacturing industries* the patent is the most common form of protecting intellectual property rights and licensing is often used as a means of controlling industry evolution: for example, Japanese manufacturers have successfully cross-licensed VHS-formatted video recorders to one another as well as to foreign firms that produce them under licence. This helped the VHS standard become dominant worldwide and displaced the competing Sony and Philips' versions. In high-tech industries, where breakthroughs tend to occur discontinuously, licensing helps firms avoid excessive costs from expensive plant and product obsolescence. IBM, for example, has linked up with Motorola Communications and Electronics Inc. to advance the state of X-ray lithography for making superdense chips. Licensing can be costly, however, if a firm transfers its core competencies into those of a competitor. RCS licensed its colour television technologies to Japanese firms during the 1960s only to be leapfrogged by new but related technologies emanating from those competitors. Licensors (the granters of licences) may therefore find themselves under pressure to continuously innovate in order to sustain the licensee's dependence on them in the relationship. Microsoft's various updated Windows systems have been widely criticised as having been introduced primarily as a means of maintaining the dependence of licensees on Microsoft itself, rather than as a source of new capabilities for existing users.

In general, the use of licensing, with its technological associations, has tended to be less readily adopted by the *service industries*, where franchising and other methods of internationalisation are more common. Nevertheless the various intellectual property rights do permit service sector licensing, as in the case of copyright protection (see also Chapter 4, p. 150) of Walt Disney characters. For example, a medium-sized UK stationery company may decide it wishes to produce a range of stationery based on Walt Disney characters. In order to do this, the company would need to approach Disney and discuss the possibility of gaining a licence to sell Disney branded goods in the UK. The licensee (in this case the UK stationery company) pays a fee to Disney in exchange for the rights to use their brand name/logo.

An advantage of licensing to licensors is that they do not have to make a substantial investment in order to gain a presence in overseas markets and they need not acquire the local knowledge which may be so important for success in such markets. Licensing is also an effective way of increasing levels of brand awareness. However, a licensor can be damaged if a licensee produces products of an inferior standard. Licensing is very common in the film and music industry. Products include calendars, videos, books, posters and clothing.

---

pause for thought 2

In 2007 the US alone issued 93,412 patents, more than double the number it issued 20 years ago. Despite the rapid growth of patents worldwide, many observers believe that because of 'global shift' we should pay less attention to this particular indicator of intellectual property rights than we used to. Can you explain their reasoning?

Case Study 2.2 looks at the various arguments for and against using patents as a means of internationalising sales into the EU pharmaceuticals market.

CASE 2.2 Patents and the EU pharmaceuticals market

The arguments for using patent protection for internationalising pharmaceutical products are well known. They include the opportunity for pharmaceutical firms to access global markets to recoup the large expenditures on innovative R & D when only relatively few products eventually pass the rigorous and time-consuming tests to demonstrate both efficacy of treatment as well as meeting health and safety standards. However a recent EU report has criticised aspects of the current operation of patents by international pharmaceutical companies operating in EU markets. On 28 November 2008 the European Commission unveiled the preliminary results of its year-long investigation into the pharmaceutical sector. The report criticised the use of the 'patent cluster', whereby a firm keen to defend a 'blockbuster' drug about to go off-patent files large numbers of new patents for slight modifications to the existing product, allegedly to confuse and intimidate other pharmaceutical firms considering producing generic versions of the previously patented product. The report cites an example of a major pharmaceutical company taking out 1300 new patents across the EU on a single drug about to go off-patent! Such delaying tactics have meant that generic competition in EU pharmaceuticals only begins, on average, some seven months after patent protection has lapsed. As a result the report says EU taxpayers paid about €3 billion more than they would have done had the generics been available immediately the patent expired.

Nor is it merely a matter of time delay! The EU report found that when generics do eventually enter the EU market they do so at a much higher price than in, say, the US market. Generics were found to enter the EU pharmaceutical market at an average price some 25% below that of the branded drug, and drop a further 40% in price after two more years. However in the US pharmaceutical market generic prices were, on average, over 80% below the branded drug price within a year.

Questions

1 Can you suggest reasons for the observed differences in generic drug prices between the EU and US markets?

2 How might the EU seek to tackle the problem? Consider the costs and benefits of any proposed 'solution'?

■ Franchising

In *franchising* the franchisee purchases the right to undertake business activity using the franchisor's name or trademark rather than any patented technology. The scale of this activity varies from so-called 'first-generation franchising' to 'second-generation franchising' in which the franchisor transfers a much more comprehensive business package to the franchisee to help establish a 'start-up position'. This may include detailed guidance on how to operate the franchise, even extending to specialist staff training.

In *first-generation* franchising, the franchisor usually operates at a distance. However, in *second-generation* franchising, the franchisor exerts far more control on the day-to-day running of the local operations. This type of franchising is common in the hotel, fast-food restaurant, and vehicle rental industries, such as Holiday Inn, McDonald's and Avis respectively. Mature domestic service-based industries have chosen franchising as a means of internationalising because:

■ it establishes an immediate presence with relatively little direct investment;
■ it employs a standard marketing approach helping to create a global image;
■ it allows the franchisor a high degree of control.

For instance, Coca-Cola's franchising arrangements with its numerous partners would seem to have given it an advantage over its arch rival PepsiCo. Franchising also helps build up a global brand that can be cultivated and standardised over time. Before opening its first restaurant in Russia, McDonald's flew all key employees to its 'Hamburger University' for a two-week training session. During these sessions, Russian employees learned the McDonald's philosophy and the McDonald's way of addressing customers and maintaining quality standards.

McDonald's and Burger King are perhaps the two best-known examples of international franchises. However, franchising is a very popular method of market entry and is not limited to the fast food industry. Examples include cleaning (Chem-Dry), clothing (Benetton) and childcare (Tiny Tots).

In international franchising, a supplier (*franchiser*) permits a dealer (*franchisee*) the right to market its products and services in that country in exchange for a financial commitment. This commitment usually involves a fee upfront and royalties based on product sales.

- *Advantages for the franchisee* are that they are buying into an existing brand and should receive full support from the franchiser in terms of marketing, training and starting up. When customers walk into a McDonald's restaurant they know exactly what to expect. This is one advantage of global branding.
- *Disadvantages for the franchisee* include restrictions on what they can and cannot do. For example, McDonald's have very strict regulations concerning marketing, pricing, training, etc. A franchisee cannot simply change the staff uniform, alter prices or vary opening hours as the company operates a standardised approach to doing business.
- *Advantages for the franchiser* are that overseas expansion can be much less expensive and that any local adaptations can (with agreement) be made by those well acquainted with cultural issues in that country.
- *Disadvantages for the franchiser* include possible conflict with the franchisee for not following regulations and agreements as well as a threat that the franchisee may opt to 'go it alone' in the future and thus become a direct competitor.

Interestingly McDonald's reacted to more difficult trading conditions by giving franchisees in 2006 more freedom than had previously been the case. It sold some 1500 restaurants to local entrepreneurs across 20 countries, who could invest in running the outlet and in introducing elements of 'customisation' of the product and its delivery to meet local requirements, whilst still retaining McDonald's support in marketing and supply chain provision. These 'developmental licensees' represented a shift by McDonald's in the direction of first generation franchising.

■ Other contractual modes of internationalisation

Besides licensing and franchising, non-equity forms of internationalisation may involve activities such as *management contracting*, where a supplier in one country undertakes to provide to a client in another country certain ongoing management functions, which would otherwise be the responsibility of the client. Other examples include *technical service agreements* that provide for the supply of technical services across borders, as when a company outsources the operation of its computer and telecommunications networks to a foreign firm. India, with its highly educated and inexpensive labour force, is winning many such contracts in many types of teleworking and increasingly in a wide range of 'back office' functions, such as those involving legal and accountancy work (see Case Study 2.3 below). *Contract-based partnerships* may also be formed between firms of different nationalities in order to share the cost of an investment. For example, agreements between pharmaceutical companies, motor vehicle companies and publishing houses may include cooperation, co-research and co-development activities.

CASE 2.3 Legal process outsourcing in India

RSG Consulting analysed the legal market in India in its *RSG India Report* 2008 and noted the rapid development of the legal processing outsourcing (LPO) industry. This initially involved law firms, such as Clifford Chance who in 2006 announced its intention to outsource much of its back office legal work from the UK to India, with potential savings of some £10m per annum. However the *RSG India Report* notes that such outsourcing is spreading beyond legal firms to a wide range of major corporations and financial institutions who are also now outsourcing many of their in-house legal functions to LPO companies. The business case for doing so is extremely strong, as the RSG India Report 2008 notes, since LPO companies employ Indian legal graduates with starting salaries as low as £4700 per annum, compared to the £100,000+ per annum starting salaries of the equivalent legal graduates in major US or UK corporations. Deutsche Bank, BT and Sun Microsystems are just some of the corporations featured in the *RSG India Report* as taking advantage of radically lower labour costs by delivering the more routine and repetitive aspects of legal work from India.

Question

Consider the implications of this contractual mode of internationalisation for (a) UK legal graduates, (b) Indian legal graduates, (c) the UK economy, and (d) the Indian economy.

Equity-based methods for internationalisation

These essentially refer to the use of fdi by the firm as a means of competing internationally in the modern global economy. The major advantage of this method is that the firm secures the greatest level of control over its proprietary information and therefore over any technological advantages it might have. In addition, profits need not be shared with any other parties such as agents, distributors or licensees.

In practice, firms can use different approaches to fdi by acquiring an existing firm, by creating an equity joint venture overseas, by establishing a foreign operation from scratch ('greenfield' investment) or by creating various consortia.

■ Joint ventures

Unlike licensing agreements, *joint ventures* involve creating a new identity in which both the initiating partners take active roles in formulating strategy and making decisions (*see also* Chapter 7). Joint ventures can help:

- to share and lower the costs of high-risk, technology-intensive development projects;
- to gain economies of scale and scope in value-adding activities that can only be justified on a global basis;
- to secure access to a partner's technology, its accumulated learning, proprietary processes or protected market position;
- to create a basis for more effective future competition in the industry involved.

Joint ventures are particularly common in high-technology industries. For instance, Corning Incorporated of the USA has numerous global joint ventures, such as those to produce medical diagnostic equipment with CIBA-Geigy, fibre optics with Cie Financière Optiques and Siemens, colour television tubes with Samsung and Asahi and ceramics for catalytic converters with NGK Insulators of Japan.

Joint ventures usually take one of two forms, namely specialised or shared value-added.

1 *Specialised joint ventures*. Here each partner brings a *specific competency*; for example one might produce and the other market. Such ventures are likely to be organised around *different functions*. One specialised joint venture has involved JVC (Japan) and Thomson (France). JVC contributed the specialised skills involved in the manufacturing technologies needed to produce optical and compact discs, computers and semi-conductors, while Thomson contributed the specific marketing skills needed to compete in fragmented markets such as Europe.

2 *Shared value-added joint ventures*. Here both partners contribute to the *same function* or value-added activity. For example, Fuji-Xerox is a case of a shared value-added joint venture with the design, production and marketing functions all shared.

The major benefits of *specialised joint ventures* include an opportunity to share risks, to learn about a partner's skills and proprietary processes and to gain access to new distribution channels. However, they carry risks as well, perhaps the greatest being that one partner's exposure of its particular competencies may result in the other partner gaining a competitive advantage, which it might subsequently use to become a direct competitor. This happened to GE when it entered into a specialised joint venture with Samsung to produce microwave ovens. Samsung now competes with GE across the whole range of household appliances. Another risk relates to the high co-ordination costs often involved in assimilating the different types of value-added activity of each partner. Sometimes a partner can be relegated to a position of permanent weakness. For example, the GM–Fanuc venture was originally intended to co-design and co-produce robots and flexible automation systems, but GM was unable to learn the critical skills needed from its partner and has ended up as little more than a distributor.

Shared value-added joint ventures pose a slightly different set of risks: partners can more easily lose their competitive advantage since the close working relationships involve the same function. If the venture is not working, it may be more difficult to exit since coordination costs tend to be much higher than they are in specialised joint ventures, with more extensive administrative networks having usually been established.

'Success factors' for joint ventures

Critical success factors for joint ventures might include the following:

■ *Take time to assess the partners*. Extended courtship is often required if a joint venture of either type is to be successful; Corning Incorporated of the USA formed its joint venture with CIBA-Geigy only after two years of courtship. Being too hurried can destroy a venture, as AT & T and Olivetti of Italy discovered when they formed a joint venture to produce personal computers that failed because of an incompatibility in management styles and corporate cultures as well as in objectives.

- *Understand that collaboration is a distinct form of competition.* Competitors as partners must remember that joint ventures are sometimes designed as ways of 'de-skilling' the opposition. Partners must learn from each other's strengths while preserving their own sources of competitive advantage. Many firms enter into joint ventures in the mistaken belief that the other partner is the student rather than the teacher.
- *Learn from partners while limiting unintended information flows.* Companies must carefully design joint ventures so that they do not become 'windows' through which one partner can learn about the other's competencies.
- *Establish specific rules and requirements for joint venture performance at the outset.* For instance, Motorola's transfer of microprocessor technology to Toshiba is explicitly dependent on how much of a market share Motorola gets in Japan.
- *Give managers sufficient autonomy.* Decentralisation of decision making should give managers sufficient autonomy to run the joint venture successfully. Two of the most successful global value-adding joint ventures are those between Fuji-Xerox and Nippon-Otis, which are also among those giving management the greatest autonomy.

It has been found that extensive training and team building is crucial if these joint ventures are to succeed. There are three ways in which effective human resource management (HRM) is critical (*see also* Chapter 8):

1 developing and training managers in negotiation and conflict resolution;
2 acculturation (i.e. cultural awareness) in working with a foreign partner;
3 harmonisation of management styles.

Problems with international joint ventures in China

When the first Sino-foreign joint venture, the Beijing Aviation Food Co., was established in 1980, it led to the beginning of intensive foreign direct investment (fdi) into China, which in turn has contributed to China's continuous growth of 8% every year for the last 15 years. World Trade Organisation (WTO) entry has also boosted inward fdi into China. Combine this with Beijing successfully hosting the Olympics in 2008 and a population of nearly 1.3 billion and it soon becomes evident why so many foreign firms are hurriedly trying to gain a presence in China. With Chinese people having a well-earned reputation for thrift, holding savings of more than US$1 trillion, nowhere is this desire more apparent than in the finance sector. For example, in 2002, Newbridge Capital, the US-based multinational finance corporation sought to tap into this huge savings stockpile and paid US$1.8 billion for nearly 20% of Shenzhen Development Bank, while HSBC paid US$600 million for 10% of Pingan Insurance.

Many foreign companies turn to the *international joint venture* (IJV) as their chosen mode of entry into China. To foreign investors there exist three modes of foreign entry, the first two of which are types of IJV – *equity joint venture* (EJV), *cooperative joint venture* (CJV) and *wholly-owned foreign enterprises* (WOFE). However, IJVs continue to experience high rates of dissolution.

The problems associated with IJVs in China have been well documented (Child 1991; Lu and Bjorkman 1998). Harrigan (1986) states that 'Alliances fail because operating managers do not make them work, not because contracts are poorly written.' One reason for foreign investors to shy away from IJVs is their fear of leaking proprietary technology and know-how to Chinese partners and thus losing long-term competitive advantages (Deng 2001). To the Chinese partner gaining invaluable knowledge is a main strategic objective for entering into an IJV. For the Western partner, the problem is knowing how much of their technical expertise should be shared with their partner. A key factor that allows for sharing information is the establishment of trust between parties. In Chinese culture, trust is very much built on personal relationships and involves socialising and working together in order to build trust. In Western society, trust between business partners is underlined by the contract, therefore there is likely to be less importance placed on building relationships. It is often very difficult to build trust between two companies that originate from very different cultural backgrounds. Lack of cultural understanding and different strategic objectives are two of the main reasons why IJVs continue to experience high failure rates.

China's WTO entry and changes to market entry methods

In recent years *wholly-owned foreign enterprises* (WOFEs) have become a favoured market entry method for some foreign firms entering China. Factors such as Chinese partners competence, joint venture management control, and frustration from IJV failures, have been cited as reasons why the adoption of a WOFE for conducting business in China might be preferable (Yan and Warner 2001). Deng (2001) identifies three key factors driving foreign firms to choose WOFEs: (1) the disappointing performance of too many IJVs, (2) the inherent advantages of WOFEs, and (3) changes in government regulations and a less uncertain environment. Yan and Warner (2001) suggest that as foreign companies keep acquiring practical experience in China, they are increasingly likely to 'go it alone' to pursue success in the Chinese market. However the Chinese government is actively encouraging foreign companies to invest in its western regions, where western cities such as Kunming are far less developed than Shanghai, Guangzhou and Beijing. A major stumbling block for foreign companies entering these western regions is the lack of regional government experience of handling fdi. Given this situation, an IJV may still be the preferred option.

pause for thought 3	How might you expect China's WTO entry to influence the prospects of doing business in China?

Case Study 2.4 suggests a continuous and ongoing search for economically, culturally and politically appropriate means of joint venture development in China.

CASE 2.4   Market entry into China

For well over a decade China has presented itself as an attractive venue for market entry, with over 2.6 billion consumers in a progressively deregulated marketplace experiencing high (if somewhat unverifiable) rates of economic growth. The provisional accession of China into the World Trade Organisation (WTO) in 2000 has provided a still further stimulus to firms seeking market entry as has the rapid diffusion of Internet-related technologies. Nevertheless, the experience of companies seeking to enter the Chinese market in recent years has been less than encouraging. However, these disappointments may have had much to do with Western companies using inappropriate methods in their attempts to internationalise their operations into the Chinese market.

In fact, most Western companies have sought to enter China via the joint-venture route, sharing day-to-day control of the business with a local partner. Having a local partner in a joint venture does provide certain advantages, as in securing contracts that often depend on political linkages and being better able to use guanxi-type relationships (*see* Chapter 5). However, sharing operational control with the local partner can paralyse decision making. Lucent, for example, has seen its share of the market for optical-fibre equipment in China fall from 70% to 30% largely because, in the view of analysts, it has had to negotiate each technological change in its product base with the local partner. Such time delays in rapidly evolving high-technology markets can be extremely adverse.

Worse still, Chinese regulations are often geographically and product specific, forcing Western companies to have separate local partners in different Chinese regions and for different product groups. This restricts the benefits available to joint ventures in terms of economies of scale and scope. For example, Unilever has separate joint ventures in Shanghai for making soap, skin cream and laundry detergent. Adopting a uniform strategy across all these product groups and across different geographic regions has proved difficult to implement as individual partners fear that such coordination may be at the expense of their particular joint venture.

In recognition of these problems, some Western companies have established wholly-owned foreign enterprises (WOFEs). Unfortunately, while this has helped avoid the lengthy decision-making process of joint ventures, it has proved a difficult vehicle for securing contracts and for establishing the local alliances and networks so important in a guanxi business culture.

Vanhonacker (2000) has suggested that a more appropriate vehicle for Chinese market entry than either joint venture or WOFE is the foreign investor shareholding corporation (FISC). In fact, this has many of the characteristics of the Western joint-stock company and Eastman Kodak is currently successfully pioneering an FISC in China. The FISC grants local partners in different geographic regions or product groups, minority stakes in return for their business assets, such as factories, offices and vehicles. Since local partners have lost direct ownership of these assets, they can be removed from day-to-day decisions involving their use. Nevertheless, as part owners of the corporation they have a vested interest in its overall success. They are therefore motivated to help the FISC secure contracts and make best use of local networks and relationships to further its business interests. The FISC can now coordinate activities across many such local partners to exploit any available economies of scale and scope in ways precluded to the joint venture. A further benefit of the FISC is that it has allowed the Chinese political authorities to encourage industrial reform through the back door, with no 'loss of face'. So far Kodak has created two FISCs, Kodak (China) being one of these, in which it holds an 80% share. Kodak (China) has purchased the assets of two domestic photofilm manufacturers (Xiamen Finda and Shantou Era), giving to each of these a 10% shareholding stake and the right to one board member, with Kodak naming the remaining eight board members. Chinese

▶

law requires at least five shareholders, so Kodak (China) has invited two further shareholders to take small stakes in the FISC, namely the Guangdong and Fujian international trust. Kodak itself has made available some $380 million as investment capital for Kodak (China). Similar arrangements are in place for the other Kodak FISC, Kodak (Wuxi), though with different shareholders.

The Chinese authorities have welcomed these Kodak initiatives, and the new FISCs are quoted on the Shanghai and Shenzhen stock exchange making it easier for them to raise capital. Having seen its photo industry almost collapse due to lack of investment and slowness to adopt new high-technology operations, no less than five central government organisations, including three ministries, were willing to cooperate with Kodak in establishing these FISCs. Indeed, Vanhonacker reports that the China State Development Planning Commission, which had been involved in creating Kodak's FISCs, released a research report in 1999 supporting the Kodak model. This is an especially important development since many of China's previously highly protected domestic industries have problems of inefficiency and overcapacity and are in urgent need of investment and modernisation by Western companies willing to transfer technology. For example, in the pharmaceuticals industry alone there are some 1800 domestic manufacturers, 80% of which have sales of less than $1 million with the result that they are internationally inefficient, being currently unable to exploit the large economies of scale and scope typically available in the pharmaceutical industry.

Questions

1 Why are the Chinese authorities receptive to the FISC as a method of internationalisation?

2 What are the benefits to Western companies of using this method rather than the more traditional joint-venture approach?

Alliances

An 'alliance' can take many forms and is much less structured than a joint venture or an acquisition. Jeffrey Reuer (1999) suggests that the 'Four Is' of collaboration (Figure 2.1) will crucially determine whether to enter into an alliance rather than a joint venture or acquisition namely infeasibility, information asymmetry, investment in options and indigestibility.

1 *Infeasibility*. Alliances are more likely when acquisitions contain elements of infeasibility. For example, competition legislation may effectively prevent large corporate acquisitions or may impose conditions deemed unacceptable if they are to go ahead. Restrictions on inward fdi to some industrial/service sectors or countries may have the same effect.

2 *Information asymmetry*. Alliances are more likely the greater the degree of (actual or perceived) information asymmetry. In other words, companies may be more likely to resort to alliances rather than acquisitions when one company knows more than some other company. Even after due diligence, the acquiring company may have reservations as to the true value of the assets to be acquired. In a large-scale

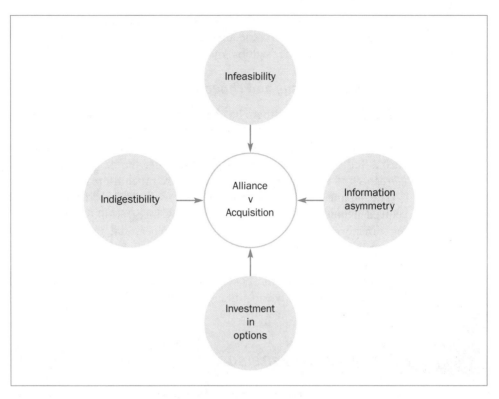

Figure 2.1 **The four 'Is' of collaboration**
Source: Based on Reuer (1999)

analysis of US companies by Reuer and Koza (2000), the announcements of joint ventures and alliances led to higher rises in the stock market prices of the affected companies the greater the degree of information asymmetry perceived as existing between the proposed allies.

3 *Investment in options*. Alliances are more likely the greater the degree of uncertainty as to the future prospects of the combined activity. For example, alliances form a higher proportion of total linkages between companies in uncertain industrial sectors such as biotechnology. An alliance can develop into greater or lesser linkage between two or more companies depending on the degree of success actually achieved by the initial joint activity. This 'staged engagement' can be expressed in terms of *call options*: these confer the right, but not the obligation, for an allied party to expand its equity stake at a pre-specified price at some future date. Put another way, alliances are more likely the greater the perceived need to invest in call options rather than in an immediate equity stake.

4 *Indigestibility*. Alliances are more likely the greater the perceived indigestibility of the potential target for acquisition. (This term arises from the need of an acquiring company to 'digest' the assets of the acquired company.) Such 'indigestibility' raises the anticipated transactions costs of acquisition (i.e. the post-acquisition integration costs). In such circumstances alliances will prove relatively attractive, giving the respective allies greater freedom to link *selected* assets only. As Reuer (1999) points out, Nestlé established a joint venture for breakfast cereals with General Mills in

Europe, but the parties made no attempt to link any of their other businesses. The same happened with Nestlé allying its coffee and tea operations with Coca-Cola to make use of the latter's global distribution system.

■ Consortia, *keiretsus* and *chaebols*

In the USA and Europe there has been little success in building cross-industry consortia, largely as a result of the difficulties involved in getting firms to pool their resources into an integrative organisational design. The one exception in Europe is perhaps the Airbus Industrie. In the Far East, on the other hand, consortia such as the Japanese *keiretsus* and the South Korean *chaebols* are much more commonplace.

The Japanese *keiretsu* is a combination of 20–25 different industrial companies centred around a large traditional company. Integration is achieved through interlocking directorates, bank holdings and close personal ties between senior managers. Group members typically agree not to sell their holdings. Examples include Sumitomo, Mitsubishi, Mitsui and Sanwa. Case Study 2.5 looks at the impact of the *keiretsu* in supporting the post-war Japanese export drive, which has largely been based on the competitive advantages of Japanese firms.

CASE 2.5 The Japanese *keiretsu*

Whereas macro environmental factors have provided the direction and stability needed to underpin Japan's rapid post-war growth in competitiveness, the actual mechanisms underpinning many of its efficiency gains have involved the dynamic behaviour of companies at the corporate level. To understand this process we need to look at the structure of Japanese industry, which consists of two key dimensions. First, there is the large-firm sector dominated by six major groupings of firms (*Kigyo Shudan*). Second, there is the important sector of small and medium-sized firms (*Chusho Kigyo*) whose members often act as sub-contractors to the larger firms.

The six major groupings are Mitsubishi, Mitsui, Sumitomo, Fuyo, Dai-ichi Kangyo (DKB) and Sanwa. The 'core' of each group consists of a number of large enterprises from different sectors of the economy, e.g. metals, oil, electrical, automobiles, etc., together with at least one major bank. Each group maintains its internal cohesiveness through regular meetings of the presidents of the larger companies and by the exchange of shares and directorships between member companies of the group (interlocking directorships). In addition, the various companies within the group would hold each other's shares as a means of affirming their relationship. Such shares would not be actively traded, making it difficult for companies to be taken over under this system as buying sufficient shares to gain control would be extremely difficult. In other words, the corporate governance of Japan was of a type that encouraged stable, long-term relationships between the members of large industrial groupings. However inter-group rivalry was often intense – for example, Mitsubishi motors (Mitsubushi Group) competed actively with Toyota (Mitsui Group) and Isuzu motors (DKB Group) so that the market was often oligopolistic in nature. Surveys in the 1990s that asked Japanese companies for the reasons that motivated them to introduce new technology found that 36% of companies cited domestic competition with other Japanese companies as a major motivating factor.

However, the success of these large exporting firms depends ultimately on the numerous small and medium-sized firms that act as primary, secondary and tertiary sub-contractors to the large firms. Many of the large Japanese companies, such as Toyota, are basically assemblers of parts produced by sub-contractors. For example, Toyota has 158 primary sub-contractors and 4700 secondary sub-contractors and almost 31,600 tertiary sub-contractors – most situated in relatively close proximity to the main parent company. This vertically organised production group or *keiretsu* provides a vital source of competitiveness for Japanese industry. Cost savings derive from the fact that the major firms can save on overheads while, at the same time, also asking the various layers of small companies to trim their costs. As a result, the potential total cost reduction throughout the *keiretsu* can be substantial. The nature of the contractual relationship between companies in Japan is based more on unwritten, long-term contracts based on trust, rather than the more legally framed, one-off 'spot' contracts more prevalent in Europe and the USA.

In terms of production and innovation, Japanese managers began concentrating on the 'focused factory', i.e. on fewer product lines with a view to maximising benefits from economies of scale and scope. Together with these cost benefits, came those based on the learning curve that measured the savings made year after year as a result of increases in cumulative output. For example, between 1984 and 1990 the CD-player market grew very rapidly and Sony, Sharp and Rohm produced their low-powered laser diodes for the CD player. Over this time the costs per unit for the diodes fell from 2000 yen to 200 yen each, showing clearly how cumulative production helps companies to learn how to produce laser diodes more efficiently.

In their continuous quest for lower costs and increased competitiveness, Japanese production managers also concentrated on some basic but important factors:

- First, the Japanese concept of *kaizen* (i.e. the constant search for small incremental improvements in all aspects of company behaviour) was a powerful tool for improving competitive behaviour, especially when economic conditions were relatively difficult and when introducing new technology was expensive. For example, in the 1980s Toyota workers were providing 1.5 million suggestions a year for small improvements in production.
- Second, Japanese production managers, led by those at Toyota Motors, concentrated on the development of the just-in-time or *kanban* system whose aim was to create a continuous process flow both within large firms and also between large assemblers and their various sub-contractors. This meant that each workstation supplied a component to the next station ahead of it on the production line only when needed, saving the costly build up (both purchase and storage) of inventories. The perfection of this process took Toyota over 25 years to achieve.
- Third, the management of quality was also critical for Japanese competitiveness and here the approach was based very much on the ideas of William Edwards Deming who visited Japan in the 1950s and who helped Japan to reverse the usual American approach to quality management by stressing that 85% of the

▶

responsibility for quality should be in the hands of plant workers and only 15% should be dependent on line managers. In other words, the Japanese identified in their approach to *total quality management* that the individual worker was the main quality controller and not the manager, as is often thought to be the case in a high proportion of US and European firms.

It would seem that these approaches by Japanese production managers are continuing to yield productivity gains. For example a study by Oliver *et al.* 2002 showed that Japanese car component makers were still more efficient than their US or European counterparts: over the period 1994–2001, with the average change in labour productivity for car components found to be 20% for Japan, but only 12% for the US and still lower figures for most EU member countries.

However, the strength of such inter-group relationship is subject to change as economics forces pressurise the groups to modify their behaviour. For example, during the period 1990–2007 the tendency for *keiretsu* members to hold each others shares in order to cement their relationship and prevent takeovers (i.e. cross holdings) has decreased from 32% to 12% in terms of the total value of shares held. In addition, there has been a tendency for large parent companies in manufacturing to try to extend their *ownership* of their affiliate companies rather than continue the more traditional relationships with *independent* subcontractors (METI, 2008). In addition, Japanese firm takeovers of foreign firms increased during the 2004–08 period, indicating the greater willingness of such companies to be more aggressive or market driven than before. On the other hand it is also important to understand that *keiretsu* members continue to be prone to over-investment in their financially weak group members (Hiraki and Ito 2008) so that major changes in their 'group habits' will not disappear as rapidly as forecasted by various observers.

Source: Griffiths (2000, 2009).

Questions

1 As well as helping Japanese export performance, what other impacts might you expect the *keiretsu* system to have in the internationalisation process?

2 Can you identify any factors in today's global economy that might put this system under strain?

The South Korean *chaebols* are similar agglomerations, which are also centred around a holding company. These are usually dominated by the founding families. While a *keiretsu* is financed from group banks and run by professional managers, *chaebols* usually get their funding from government and are managed by family members who have been groomed for the job. Prominent examples include Samsung, Daewoo and Sunkyong. Such alliances are usually initiated by merchant and industrialist families and the company keeps the stock in family hands.

Consortia of these types are essentially sophisticated forms of strategic alliances designed to maximise the potential benefits of joint ventures – namely risk sharing, cost reductions, economies of scale, etc. Both in Japan and South Korea governments have played an important role in encouraging such developments. Such consortia tend to have a long-term focus and are uniquely positioned to share the risks of investing in high fixed-cost projects in order to stay at the forefront of technology-based industries. At the same time, risk is diversified because the different companies are involved in many different industries. This encourages investment in the more volatile industries such as satellites, biotechnology, microelectronics and aerospace. The members of the consortia also benefit from strong buyer–supplier relationships, with costs reduced by bulk purchase discounts, etc. It often means extensive resource sharing of components and end products that can produce fast responses to changed consumer requirements, so essential when employing mass customisation techniques.

> **pause for thought 4** Conglomerate mergers have been widely used in Western economies. (a) Give some examples. (b) Suggest the benefits they confer. (c) Consider why they have become less popular in recent times.

It is worth noting that the *keiretsus* and *chaebols* benefit from government in the form of preferential interest rates and capital allocations that, arguably, only a managed economy can deliver. They are also characterised by close ties and shared values leading to mutual understanding and sacrifices that cannot easily be duplicated in the West. These organisations are linked together by networks and personal relationships, so the corporate culture needs to be able to embrace both hierarchical and horizontal integration. Fraternal relationships, mutual long-term commitment and pride in membership are characteristics that are less commonly found in the individualised cultures of the USA or UK (*see* Chapter 5).

Table 2.1 provides a useful summary of some of the benefits and costs of the various types of global alliances or related collaborations previously discussed.

■ Acquisitions and 'greenfield' investment

Some of the problems faced by joint ventures (especially those involving decision making and culture clashes) and by the various kinds of consortia can be avoided by wholly owning the foreign affiliates. This can be achieved through acquisition of, or merger with, an existing firm or through establishing an entirely new foreign operation ('greenfield' investment).

Acquisition of an existing foreign company has a number of advantages compared to 'greenfield' investment; for example, it allows a more rapid market entry, so that there is a quicker return on capital and a ready access to knowledge of the local market. Because of its rapidity, such acquisition can pre-empt a rival's entry into the same market. Further, many of the problems associated with setting up a 'greenfield' site in a foreign country (such as cultural, legal and management issues) can be avoided. By involving a change in ownership, acquisition also avoids costly competitive reactions from the acquired firm. Strategic aspects of acquisitions and mergers policies are considered in more detail in Chapter 7 (pp. 266–76).

Table 2.1 Characteristics of different types of global alliance

Type of global alliance	Benefits	Costs	Critical success factors	Strategic human resources management
Licensing – manufacturing industries	■ Early standardisation of design ■ Ability to capitalise on innovations ■ Access to new technologies ■ Ability to control pace of industry evolution	■ New competitors created ■ Possible eventual exit from industry ■ Possible dependence on licensee	■ Selection of licensee likely to become a competitor ■ Enforcement of patents and licensing agreements	■ Technical knowledge ■ Training of local managers on-site
Licensing – servicing and franchises	■ Fast market entry ■ Low capital cost	■ Quality control ■ Trademark protection	■ Partners compatible in philosophies/values ■ Tight performance standards	■ Socialisation of franchisees and licensees with core values
Joint ventures – specialisation across partners	■ Learning a partner's skills ■ Economies of scale ■ Quasi-vertical integration ■ Faster learning	■ Excessive dependence on partner for skills ■ Deterrent to internal investment	■ Tight and specific performance criteria ■ Entering a venture as 'student' rather than 'teacher' to learn skills from partner ■ Recognising that collaboration is another form of competition to learn new skills	■ Management development and training ■ Negotiation skills ■ Managerial rotation
Joint ventures – shared value-adding	■ Strengths of both partners pooled ■ Faster learning along value chain ■ Fast upgrading of technological skills	■ High switching costs ■ Inability to limit partner's access to information	■ Decentralisation and autonomy from corporate parents ■ Long 'courtship' period ■ Harmonisation of management styles	■ Team-building ■ Acculturation ■ Flexible skills for implicit communication
Consortia, kairetsus, and chaebols	■ Shared risks and costs ■ Building a critical mass in process technologies ■ Fast resource flows and skill transfers	■ Skills and technologies that have no real market worth ■ Bureaucracy ■ Hierarchy	■ Government encouragement ■ Shared values among managers ■ Personal relationships to ensure coordination and priorities ■ Close monitoring of member-company performance	■ 'Clan' cultures ■ Fraternal relationships ■ Extensive mentoring to provide a common vision and mission across member companies

Source: Reprinted and adapted from *Journal of World Business*, 32(3), Lei, D., Slocum, J. and Pitts, R. A. Building competitive advantage: managing strategic alliances to promote organisational learning. Copyright 1997, with permission from Elsevier.

Why invest abroad?

Of course, the 'bottom line' may simply be an estimated higher present value of future profits from establishing a production facility in a foreign country as opposed to the alternatives (e.g. continuing to export to the foreign country). Nevertheless, an fdi decision is a complex process that may be influenced by social relationships within and outside the firm and for which there may be a whole array of other motivating factors. Some approaches seek to classify these *motivating factors* into supply factors, demand factors and political factors.

■ Supply factors

A number of *supply factors* may encourage the firm to resort to foreign direct investment. These may be particularly important for those firms sometimes described as *cost-orientated multinationals*, i.e. those for which the major objective is to reduce costs by internationalising their operations.

Production costs

Foreign locations may be more attractive because of the lower costs of skilled or unskilled labour, lower land prices, tax rates or commercial real-estate rents. We noted earlier (pp. 41–2) the growth of incentives to attract inward fdi, as in the establishment of special economic zones. There has also been a trend to reduce corporate income taxes in both developed and developing countries, as for example the 2007 tax reductions from 15% to 10% in Bulgaria and from 38.5% to 33% in Colombia.

Table 2.2 indicates the growing importance of low and 'flat tax' regimes on individual and corporate income in many countries. Box 2.1 then reviews the case for such 'flat tax' regimes being seen as a mechanism for attracting inward investment.

Table 2.2 **Countries with a flat tax 2007 (percentage tax rate)**

Economy	Individual tax rate (%)	Corporate tax rate (%)
Estonia	22	24
Georgia	12	20
Hong Kong (China)	16	17.5
Iceland	36	18
Kyrgyzstan	10	10
Latvia	25	15
Lithuania	27	15
Mongolia	10	25
Romania	16	16
Russian Federation	13	24
Slovakia	19	19
The FYR of Macedonia	12	10
Ukraine	15	25

Source: World Bank, *World Development Report 2008*.

Box 2.1   **'Flat tax' regimes**

'Supply-side economics' has re-emerged in the taxation debate in recent times with the idea of a 'flat tax'.

The idea of a single, low income tax rate to be paid by all, i.e. a 'flat tax', has been much discussed. For example, the Adam Smith Institute (ASI) has proposed a 'flat tax' of 22% with a personal allowance of £15,000 (three times higher than the current allowance). The cost of setting such a high level of personal allowances – to lift the poorest out of tax – would be £63 billion, but the ASI believes this could be recouped in three years as lower taxes create incentives for us all to work harder and to stop avoiding tax. The suggestion of supporters of the flat tax is that the British tax system has become so complex that few can understand it, unintended disincentives to work frequently occur, and the failure to follow simpler, lower tax regimes in the rest of the world is undermining UK international competitiveness.

However, critics of the 'flat tax' approach point out that it is a myth that the poor will benefit from lower tax rates. For example, Brian Reading of Lombard Street Research noted that 50% of the total income tax revenue is actually paid by the top 10% of income earners, so that 10% (3 million people) would gain the most and the other 90% (27 million people) would lose the most from a move to a 'flat tax' regime which collected the same amount of income tax revenue as is currently collected and kept the same personal allowances (Griffiths and Wall 2007). This would require a flat tax rate of 23% and would potentially result in 24 million losers 'net'.

Source: Griffiths and Wall (2007).

Particular locations can change in terms of their relative popularity as low-cost centres of production. For example, South Korea was once a production centre for low-priced training shoes, but as the country began to prosper, wages rose and this market is now dominated by China (*see also* Case Study 2.6). At the moment Ireland is attractive as a result of its low labour costs, English-speaking population, tax abatement opportunities and an infrastructure containing modern fibre-optic telephone networks. McGraw-Hill publishers moved the maintenance of the circulation files of its 16 magazines to Loughrea, Ireland, while retaining a direct link to its mainframe computers at its New Jersey headquarters.

This type of globalised production decision may often involve *vertical integration*. For example, many US and European companies have integrated forwards by establishing assembly facilities in South-East Asia in order to take account of the relative abundance of cheap, high-quality labour. Companies like America's ITT ship semi-manufactured components to the region, where they are assembled by local labour into finished products, which are then re-exported back to the home market. Such host countries for foreign direct investment are sometimes termed 'production platforms', which underscores their role as providers of a low-cost input into a global, vertically-integrated production process.

Of course, even when looking solely at the factor of labour, we have already noted in Chapter 1 that it is not only labour costs that are important but also labour productivity. Table 1.3 (p. 8) usefully pointed out that sometimes countries with low labour costs may be less attractive because of low labour productivity, and vice versa for high labour-cost countries. In fact, the most revealing overall statistic is relative unit labour costs (RULC) as outlined in Box 1.1 (p. 9).

Case Study 2.6 provides further insights into cost-based influences on internationalisation strategies.

CASE 2.6 China versus South Korea — FT

At Hyundai Motor's noisy factory near Beijing airport, fresh-faced workers are busy attaching bumpers to Sonata sedans or mirrors to Tucson sports utility vehicles and spraying the multi-coloured Elantras that are destined to become taxis for the Chinese capital. In five different models, 68 vehicles roll off the South Korean group's production line every hour. The plant is producing 300,000 cars a year, but output will double with the completion of a second facility next year.

The 4200 Chinese employees – average age 26 – receive a base salary equivalent to $360 (£185, €270) a month and belong to a workers' organisation whose main task seems to be to encourage harder effort rather than push for higher wages. 'The workers here are very flexible – it's the opposite to Korea, where the situation is impossible,' says Noh Jae-man, president of Beijing Hyundai. 'And because we pay our workers better than other companies, they are proud to work at Hyundai and carry out their jobs well.'

By contrast, at Hyundai's main Ulsan plant in South Korea the workers – their age averaging 41 – earn $4580 a month, build only 55 cars an hour, refuse to produce more than three models on each production line, will not allow second shifts (which would eat into their overtime) and are heavily unionised. Last year a 25-day long strike cost Hyundai about 7800 vehicles or Won120 billion ($127 million, £65 million, €95 million) in lost sales.

Like other global manufacturers, Korean companies have flocked to take advantage of China's cheap productive labour and superb infrastructure. LG, the electronics and chemicals conglomerate, has such a huge presence in Nanjing, the capital of Jiangsu province, that Chinese authorities have renamed the main street 'LG Road'.

But while China represents a huge opportunity for manufacturing – dependent South Korea, it also represents a looming danger, as Chinese companies threaten not just to complement but entirely consume Korea's industries. Hyundai may be benefiting in China but it is worried about the aggressive expansion of local car makers such as Chery – and that many Chinese models bear a strong resemblance to the cars made by Korean and other producers. Indeed, South Korea's old economic model of imitation and manufacturing-led growth is now China's model.

Although it underwent radical restructuring and opened its market after the Asian financial crisis struck in 1997, there is a widely held belief that South Korea, one of the worlds' top dozen economies, needs a second wave of reforms if it is to maintain its competitive edge over emerging China and move to the next stage in its remarkable development.

Indeed, with the economy remaining dependent on manufacturing and exports – and, moreover, on just a few types of product, such as mobile phones, semiconductors and cars – concern is growing that Korea is losing its dynamism.

Many economists and business leaders in Seoul say that China is fast moving up the value chain and will soon be making the kinds of computer chips and flat-screen televisions for which Korea has become known. China's export structure, where the proportion made up of electronics and other high-technology products has grown to comprise almost 40 per cent, much more closely resembles that of south Korea than it did a decade ago. Although most technology exports come from foreign-invested companies and the highest-tech components are still imported, the sudden change is giving Korea concern. 'Chinese manufacturing workers earn about 10 per cent of what Korean workers earn but the technology gap between the two countries has rapidly reduced,' Mr Kim says. 'Korea has already lost the personal computer industry and more will follow.'

Lee Kun-hee, the powerful chairman of Samsung Group – which accounts for about 20 per cent of the country's exports – warned that Korea had to 'wake up' or risk 'economic chaos' in five to six years. Samsung might relocate its appliance division, which has posted losses since 2003, to less developed countries, he added. In shipbuilding South Korea has been the world leader for the past decade, but China is closing in so quickly that Seoul's National Intelligence service has launched investigations into technology leaks. Meanwhile, Korea's current four-year lead over Chinese manufacturers of flat-screen televisions is likely to narrow to only one year by 2010, according to the Korea Electronics Association. The Organisation for Economic Co-operation and Development says China has overtaken Japan to become the world's second biggest spender on research and development, investing $136 billion this year.

South Korea's top *chaebols*, the conglomerates such as Samsung and Hyundai, have become global companies and are likely to weather any storm better than the rest of Korea Inc. A much greater concern rests with small and medium-sized enterprises, the mainstay of the economy, which have long supplied components for the big brands but find themselves squeezed by emerging competitors from China. The next problem area Korea will likely face is going to be around the hollowing out of the SME sector.

The sector's problems are worsened by the survival of uncompetitive players. The government gives credit guarantees, under which 85 per cent of the principal is guaranteed, to banks lending to SMEs, which means that poor performers do not go bankrupt. At the same time, Korean companies with bases in China have increasingly localised their procurement of intermediate goods. Korean companies operating in China procured one-quarter of their parts locally in 1996 – but it took less than a decade before half the parts were being sourced there.

Apart from ground being lost in investment and technological advancement, a further erosion in South Korea's competitive position has come from a surge in regulation and economic nationalism. That change in mood came after foreign investors reaped huge profits on the assets they bought at fire-sale prices, following the financial crisis.

Foreign direct investment has fallen to only 7 per cent of GDP, compared with 35 per cent in China. In UNCTAD's 2007 investment report, South Korea ranked 114th out of 141 countries for foreign investment flows. The key to rejuvenating the business environment, economists say, lies in encouraging competition through foreign investment and in embarking on reforms regardless of whether or not they are required by the proposed free trade accord.

'Korea has to allow entrepreneurs to flourish and to allow SMEs to flourish,' says Mr Brilliant from the business council. 'This is not to say that the *chaebol* don't have a role to play but that the business sector must be expanded. If Korea wants job creation, innovation and technology, it has to seek a way to diversify its industrial structure.'

Nevertheless there are several glimmers of hope for the future. Mr Jung points to Korea's obsession with education and the resulting improvements in human capital, and its creativity. 'I think we are at the stage where our future growth will come from technology, design, education, ideas,' he says, adding that Korea filed the second largest number of patent applications with the World Intellectual Property Organisation in 2006. 'The key will be taking advantage of Korea's geographical advantage by producing goods that China cannot make and at a price with which Japan cannot compete.'

Recent OECD data shows labour productivity for South Korea at less than $20 of GDP per hour worked, well below the OECD average of $35 per hour worked and the US $48 per hour worked. Labour market inflexibility is also present, with the cost of firing a South Korean worker at 90 weeks of wages in 2006 compared to the OECD average of only 28 weeks of wages.

Source: Adapted from Fifield, A., 'Seoul sleepwalk: why an Asian export champion is at risk of losing his way', *Financial Times*, 19 March 2007.

Questions

1 Consider some of the implications of this case study for the internationalisation process.

2 Why is it suggested that the South Koreans 'are worried' about developments in China?

Distribution costs

Where transportation costs are a significant proportion of total costs, firms may choose to produce from a foreign location rather than pay the costs of transportation. Heineken, whose products are mainly water-based, finds it cheaper to brew in locations geographically closer to the foreign consumer. International businesses may find it cheaper to establish distribution centres in the foreign location, rather than to send individual consignments directly to sellers. For example, Citrovita, a Brazilian producer of orange concentrate operates a storage and distribution centre in Antwerp, Belgium, so that it can benefit from low shipping rates when transporting in bulk. Mechanisms for minimising distribution costs are considered in more detail in Chapter 10.

Availability of natural resources

This is very important in certain industries such as oil and minerals. Indeed, this reason has often led to *backwards vertical integration* in search of cheaper or more secure inputs into the productive process. Oil companies, such as Exxon, Shell and BP, have provided well-known examples of this approach. In order to secure control of strategic raw materials in oil fields around the world, they established overseas extraction operations in the early years of the twentieth century with the aim of shipping crude oil back to their home markets for refining and sale.

Access to key technology

Many firms find it cheaper to invest in an existing firm rather than put together a new team of research specialists. Many Japanese pharmaceutical manufacturers have invested in small biogenetics companies as an inexpensive means of finding cutting-edge technology. Mitsubishi Electronics took over (and is now profitably running) Apricot in the UK, while Fujitsu is now the second-largest computer corporation in the world, after acquiring ICL, at that point the largest UK computer company.

■ Demand factors

A number of *demand factors* may also encourage the firm to resort to foreign direct investment. These may be particularly important for those firms sometimes described as *market-orientated multinationals*, i.e. those for which the major objective is to internationalise with a view to accessing new markets and greater sales. In this case the internationalisation process is more likely to take the form of *horizontal* (rather than vertical) *integration* into new geographic markets. Figure 2.2 presents a stylised version

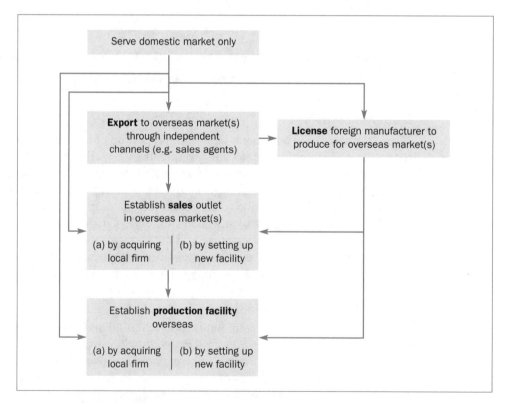

Figure 2.2 **Evolution of a market-orientated multinational**
Source: Adapted from Healey (2007).

of this process with companies gradually switching from exporting (or licensing) to establishing first a sales outlet and finally full production facilities overseas (*see* Healey 2007). Underpinning this process may be a number of identifiable motivating factors of a demand type.

Marketing advantages

There are several types of marketing advantage that may be reaped from investing in overseas enterprises or setting up foreign affiliates. The physical presence of a factory may give a company visibility and the company may also gain from a 'buy-local' attitude, as indicated in Case Study 2.7 below.

CASE 2.7 Toyota wins support for its US operations

In San Antonio, Texas, the heart of America's pick-up truck country, Toyota makes one of the biggest passenger vehicles on the road. At its sixth and newest functioning US vehicle plant, the car company that propelled itself to the top of the global car industry largely by selling American reliable fuel-efficient compact cars, makes nothing but the Tundra large pick-up truck, which gets only about 17 miles to the gallon.

In launching the new Tundra, Toyota is breaching one of the last bastions of America's three struggling Detroit-area carmakers. Toyota's new extra-large version of the truck competes squarely with the Ford F-Series, General Motors' Chevrolet Silverado and Chrysler's Dodge Ram, which are among the respective companies' top-selling and most profitable vehicles.

Roughly one in seven pick-up trucks in the US is sold in Texas, and Toyota has described the new Tundra as one of its most important product launches in 50 years in the US. Its 2.2 million sq foot, $1.28 billion (£630 million, €930 million) plant turns out one vehicle every 73 seconds.

By expanding its US manufacturing footprint to keep up with its growing sales, Toyota has put to rest for now old jibes about taking automotive jobs overseas, which at one point in the 1990s prompted Ford workers to smash Japanese cars with sledgehammers. Local official and employees describe the company as a positive presence in the city and a model employer. 'Toyota gave 4000 of our people jobs,' says Phil Hardberger, San Antonio's mayor, who sold his Ford F150 and bought one of the first Tundra's off the assembly line last year. 'These are not Japanese jobs – these are American, San Antonio jobs.'

Toyota appears to be winning the crucial battle over its status as a good corporate citizen in the US. For example, a December 2006 report by Thomson Datastream identified Toyota as creating 34,675 direct jobs in the US in 2006 via production and supply related activities. However it also identified 386,314 indirect jobs via the spending of the Toyota company in the US on components and supply and via the spending of those employed by Toyota on other goods and services.

Question

As a public relations specialist for Toyota, how might you use the above information to support a 'buy local' attitude towards this Japanese owned company?

Preservation of brand names and trademarks

In order to maintain control over its brands, an established firm may choose to manufacture in the host country rather than merely license its name and run the risk of licensees using inferior materials.

Customer mobility

A firm may be motivated to move its operations close to a business customer if that customer sets up operations elsewhere, in order to reduce the possibility that a host-based competitor might step in and replace it as the supplier. For example, Japanese firms supplying parts to the major Japanese automobile companies have responded to the construction of Japanese automobile assembly plants in the USA and UK by building their own factories, warehouses and research facilities there. This need to move abroad was heightened by the fact that Japanese automobile companies use just-in-time techniques, and it is difficult to be just-in-time when the parts suppliers are thousands of miles away. Of course, subsequently the Japanese car firms have helped to develop the abilities of local firms to supply the quality and frequency of parts and components compatible with their manufacturing practices.

■ Political factors

At least two reasons with a 'political edge' may influence an fdi decision: one is to avoid trade barriers erected by governments (or regional trading blocs) and the other is to take advantage of economic development incentives offered by the government in the host country.

Avoidance of trade barriers

Firms often set up facilities in foreign countries in order to avoid trade barriers (*see also* Chapter 3). For example, US automobile companies have placed consistent pressure on their government to restrict Japanese imports of cars into the USA. At the same time, the Japanese government has itself imposed a voluntary export restraint (VER) on the number of cars exported to the USA. To get around these restrictions, many Japanese companies have set up factories in the USA, not only avoiding the VER but also helping to reduce US consumer opposition to Japanese cars since US jobs are now directly involved.

Taylor (2000) used a measure of 'trade openness' in seeking to estimate the impact of host country government policies on US multinational investment decisions. He found a positive and significant relationship between the two variables, showing that the more 'open' a country's trading regime (e.g. low tariff and other barriers) the more inward fdi from American MNEs it attracted. In actual fact, as Box 2.2 indicates, there are circumstances in which a negative (rather than positive) relationship might be anticipated between trade openness and fdi.

Economic development incentives

Most governments see fdi as creating new employment opportunities, raising the technological base and generally increasing the economic welfare of its citizens. Governments have therefore been ready to offer various incentives to firms to induce them

| Box 2.2 | Government policies, exporting and fdi |

There is a considerable body of evidence (e.g. Markusen 1995) to suggest that imposing higher tariff barriers and other trade restrictions results in MNEs substituting exports to that country by fdi into that country. In other words, in order to overcome these barriers, MNEs invest in production facilities within the country, i.e. 'tariff-jumping' investment. In such circumstances we might expect exports from the multinationals home country to fall and affiliate sales generated by fdi activity in the host country to rise. The suggestion here is there is a *negative* relationship whereby countries with less open trade policies attract more inward fdi from MNEs. Such a negative relationship has indeed been found in a number of studies; for example, Brainard (1997) found that a 1% increase in tariffs resulted in a rise in affiliate sales via fdi of between one-third to one-half of 1%.

Taylor (2000), however, found quite the opposite, namely a *positive* relationship with countries having more open trade policies (less trade restrictions) attracting more rather than less inward fdi from the USA. In this study a 1% increase in tariffs resulted in a fall in affiliate sales via fdi of slightly over 1%. Some of the reasons for these findings may involve the strategy of MNEs in situating their factories wherever the combination of labour, component suppliers and transport is most efficient, then exporting from these 'production platforms' to the rest of the world. In other words, Taylor's findings might be expected where MNEs see fdi as part of a global exporting perspective (see Case Study 2.5) rather than merely as an attempt to sell to a local market protected by tariff barriers. In this sense 'trade openness' would assume a greater importance than 'tariff jumping' in their strategic thinking as regards fdi decisions.

In fact, the most important variable in increasing fdi investment was found to be not 'trade openness' but 'fdi openness'. Here fdi is regarded as being more 'open' the easier it is for the MNE to hire and fire labour, change prices, use the justice system, protect intellectual property, engage in cross-border ventures, understand and comply with regulations, and so on. Taylor (2000) found that a 1% increase in a country's 'fdi openness' leads to a 3% to 4% increase in the flow of fdi to that country.

to locate new facilities in their countries, including tax reductions or tax holidays, free or subsidised access to land or buildings (e.g. zero business rates), specially constructed infrastructure (road, rail, air links) and so on. We noted earlier that in 2003 India joined an increasing number of countries when developing 17 of its own 'export processing zones' (EPZs) providing various incentives to encourage inward fdi that can help India to improve its export competitiveness.

Other factors

The decision to internationalise is complex and the reasons cannot always be neatly contained in the supply, demand and political categories already considered. Other concerns include:

- *The role of management.* The ambitions of management are often crucial in the first stages of the decision to go international. Often a change of chief executive can prompt activity in this area.
- *Motives of the organisation.* Some commentators identify three broad motivations for internationalisation; namely *market seeking* (the lure of additional revenue and

profit from new overseas markets), *efficiency seeking* (the lure of lower production costs) and *resource seeking* (the lure of access to specific types of natural resource).

- *Saturation of the home market.* Restrictions in the size of the home market may mean that further growth requires the firm to gain access to overseas markets.
- *The bandwagon effect.* Intense rivalry can mean that a decision by one firm to enter an overseas market tends to be followed by other firms. The bandwagon effect has doubtless played some part in inducing some firms to enter the Chinese, Eastern European and ex-Soviet markets.
- *International product life cycle.* The internationalisation process may be more than simply an attempt to start new product life cycles elsewhere or to extend the maturity stage of an existing product life cycle. The suggestion here is that there may exist an *international product life cycle* for many products which will govern the geographical location of production in each stage (*see* Chapter 3).

Of course the 'drivers' of internationalisation for a company may involve a mix of conventional supply and demand side factors as well as unconventional strategic objectives, partly corporate and partly governmental, as Case Study 2.8 usefully indicates.

CASE 2.8   Daewoo moves into international agriculture   **FT**

Daewoo Logistics of South Korea said it expected to pay nothing to farm maize and palm oil in an area of Madagascar half the size of Belgium, increasing concerns about the largest farmland investment of this kind. The Indian Ocean island will simply gain employment opportunities from Daewoo's 99-year lease of 1.3 million hectares, officials at the company said. They emphasised that the aim of the investment was to boost Seoul's food security. 'We want to plant corn there to ensure our food security. Food can be a weapon in this world,' said Hong Jong-wan, a manager at Daewoo. 'We can either export the harvests to other countries or ship them back to Korea in case of a food crisis.'

Daewoo said it had agreed with Madagascar's government that it could cultivate 1.3 million hectares of farmland for free when it signed a memorandum of understanding in May 2008. When the company signed the contract in July 2008 it agreed to discuss costs with Madagascar. But Daewoo now believes it will have to pay nothing. 'It is totally undeveloped land which has been left untouched. And we will provide jobs for them by farming it, which is good for Madagascar,' said Mr Hong. The 1.3 million hectares of leased land is more than half the African country's current arable land of 2.5 million hectares.

But Madagascar could also benefit from Daewoo's investment in roads, irrigation and grain storage facilities. However, a European diplomat in southern Africa said: 'We suspect there will be very limited direct benefits [for Madagascar]. Extractive projects have very little spill-over to a broader industrialisation.'

Asian nations have been looking more often in the past five years or so to Africa to meet their resource needs. China has been particularly aggressive in building up stakes in oilfields and mines on the continent, sometimes facing accusations of neo-colonialism. But now the countries are moving from minerals and oil into food. Roelof Horne, who manages Investec Asset Management's Africa fund, said he expected to see more farmland investments on the continent. 'Africa has most of the underutilised fertile land in the world,' he said, though he cautioned that 'land is always an emotive thing'.

Apart from Daewoo, an increasing number of South Korean companies are venturing into Madagascar, investing in projects from nickel mines to power plants. State-run Korea Resources recently signed a preliminary agreement with Madagascar to expand collaboration on resources development including mining projects for other metals.

Daewoo plans to start maize production on 2000 hectares from 2009 and gradually expand it to other parts of the leased land. The company plans to plant maize on 1 million hectares in the western part of Madagascar and oil palm trees on 300,000 hectares in the east.

The company plans to ship the bulk of the harvests back to South Korea and export some supplies to other countries. It is unclear if any of the production will remain in Madagascar, an impoverished nation where the World Food Programme provides food relief to about 600,000 people – about 3.5% of the population. The WFP, the UN agency in charge of emergency food relief, said more than 70% of Madagascar's population lives below the poverty line. 'Some 50% of children under three years of age suffer retarded growth due to a chronically inadequate diet,' it said.

The pursuit of foreign farm investments follows this year's food crisis in 2008, which saw record prices for commodities such as wheat and rice, and food riots in countries from Egypt to Haiti. Prices for agricultural commodities have tumbled in the last six months of 2008 by about half from such levels but nations are concerned about long-term supplies.

Daewoo said it chose Madagascar because it is relatively untouched by Western companies. 'The country could provide bigger opportunities for us as not many Western companies are there,' said Mr Hong. Daewoo plans to develop the arable land in Madagascar over 15 years and intends to provide about half South Korea's maize imports. Heavily populated South Korea is the fourth largest importer of Maize.

Source: Jung-a, S., Olive, C. and Burgis, T. 'Daewoo to cultivate Madagascar land for free', *Financial Times*, 20 November 2008.

Question

Consider the possible advantages and disadvantages to (a) Daewoo, (b) South Korea, (c) Madagascar of adopting this approach to internationalisation.

Theoretical explanations

Attempts have been made to bring together various arguments to form theories or models of the internationalisation process. Some of these theories are taken further in Chapter 3.

■ Ownership-specific advantages

Here the focus is on the assets owned by the firm which might give it a competitive edge vis-à-vis other firms operating in overseas markets. Such ownership-specific advantages might include superior technology, a well-known brand name, economies of scale or scope (*see* Box 7.1, pp. 267–8), managerial or organisational skills, etc.

Internalisation

The focus here is on the costs of entering into a transaction, e.g. the costs of negotiating, monitoring and enforcing a contract. The firm decides whether it is cheaper to own and operate a plant or establishment overseas or to contract with a foreign firm to operate on its behalf through a franchise, licensing or supply agreement. Foreign direct investment is more likely to occur (i.e. the process to be *internalised*) when the costs of negotiating, monitoring and enforcing a contract with a second firm are high. On the other hand, when such transaction costs are low, firms are more likely to contract with outsiders and internationalise by licensing their brand names or franchising their business operations.

Location-specific advantages

These theories have mainly sought to answer the 'where' question involving MNE activity outside the home country as well as the 'why'. The availability and price of natural and human resources in overseas territories, of transport and communications infrastructure, market-size characteristics and other locational attributes are the focus of attempts by these theories to explain the internationalisation process.

Eclectic theory

John Dunning (1993) has sought to bring together all three of these theories, namely ownership, internalisation and locational factors in one combined approach. His so-called 'eclectic paradigm' suggests that firms transfer their *ownership-specific* assets to *locational settings* which offer the most favourable opportunities for their sector of activity while seeking wherever possible to *internalise* these processes in order to retain control of the subsequent revenue generation.

Dunning concluded that companies will only become involved in overseas investment and production (fdi) when the following conditions are all satisfied:

- companies possess an 'ownership-specific' advantage over firms in the host country (e.g. via assets which are internal to the firm, including organisation structure, human capital, financial resources, size and market power);
- it must be more profitable for the multinational to exploit its ownership-specific advantages in an overseas market than in its domestic market. In other words, there must additionally exist 'location-specific' factors which favour overseas production (e.g. special economic or political factors, attractive markets in terms of size, growth or structure, low 'psychic' or 'cultural' distance, etc.); and
- these advantages are best exploited by the firm itself, rather than by selling them to foreign firms. In other words, due to market imperfections (e.g. uncertainty), multi-nationals choose to bypass the market and 'internalise' the use of ownership-specific advantages via vertical and horizontal integration (such internalisation reduces transaction costs in the presence of market imperfections).

The decisions of multinationals to produce abroad are, therefore, determined by a mixture of motives – ownership-specific, locational, and internalisation factors – as noted above.

■ Sequential theory of internationalisation

Adherents of this approach (sometimes called the 'Uppsala model') include Johanson and Widersheim-Paul who examined the internationalisation of Swedish firms. They found a regular process of gradual change involving the firm moving *sequentially* through four discrete stages: (1) intermittent exports; (2) exports via agents; (3) overseas sales via knowledge agreements with local firms, for example by licensing or franchising; (4) foreign direct investment in the overseas market.

This particular sequence is sometimes called the *establishment chain*, the argument being that each of these stages marks a progressive increase in the resource commitment by the firm to the overseas markets involved. There is also a suggestion that as firms move through these sequential stages, the knowledge and information base expands and the 'psychic distance' between themselves and the overseas markets involved contracts, making progression to the next stage that much easier. In this sense the model is dynamic, with the stage already reached by the firm in the internationalisation process helping determine the future course of action likely to be taken. Put another way, the greater the resource commitment to the overseas market and the information and knowledge thereby acquired, the smaller the uncertainty and the perceived risks associated with further internationalisation, leading eventually to foreign direct investment and the establishment of a production affiliate overseas. Firms will move initially to countries that are culturally similar to their own (a close psychic distance) and only later move into culturally diverse geographical areas.

Such a sequential pattern and trajectory has been discernible in Portugal's internationalisation efforts. Typically the first moves were made into the neighbouring economy, Spain. An example of this 'toe in the water' stage was the acquisition by Cimpor, the leading Portuguese cement maker, of Corporación Noroeste, a Spanish cement maker based in Galicia. The next move was for Portuguese firms as diverse as Cenoura, Petrogal, Transportes Luis Simões and Caixa Geral de Depósitos to penetrate the wider Spanish market. As a result of these rapidly expanding two-way flows, an EU regional bloc based in the Iberian peninsula then came into existence during the 1990s as a buoyant new trading area. Using Spain as a springboard, the next natural step for Portugal was into North Africa and the countries that were formerly Portugal's African colonies. The latter were attractive because of language and cultural affinities but also because they were undertaking privatisation programmes, while Brazil became a focal point for economic relations with Mercosur (*see* Chapter 3). The most recent stage has involved investments in the more advanced EU economies. In some cases, a presence has also been established in Eastern Europe, notably Poland, Hungary and Russia.

■ Simultaneous theory of internationalisation

Other writers have put forward a *simultaneous view* of internationalisation, based on global convergence. For example, they suggest that customers' tastes around the world are becoming progressively homogeneous, citing the success of such global products as Coca-Cola or Sony Walkman. This approach contends that the economies of scale and scope available for standardised products in such global markets are so substantial that a gradual, sequential approach to internationalisation is no longer practicable. Proponents of this approach point to studies which suggest that the global awareness of brands has fallen dramatically over time, with less than two years now needed for making consumers worldwide aware of high profile brand images. Critics, however, suggest that there is little evidence for the notion of 'homogenisation' of consumer tastes, indeed quite the opposite with sophisticated customers demanding greater customisation (*See* p. 19). Further, although simultaneous entry into a variety of overseas markets may be possible for highly resourced and established firms, it may be out of the question for smaller or less experienced firms.

■ Network theory

In a network perspective the process of internationalisation is seen as building on existing relationships or creating new relationships in international markets, with the focus shifting from the organisational or economic to that of the social. It is *people* who make the decisions and take the actions.

The series of networks can be considered at three levels.

1 *Macro* – rather than the environment being seen as a set of political, social and economic factors, network theory would see it as a set of diverse interests, powers and characteristics, which may well impinge on national and international business decisions. To enter new markets a firm may have to break old relationships or add new ones. A new entrant may find it difficult to break into a market that already has many stable relationships. Those firms better able to reconfigure their existing networks or which are seeking to enter overseas markets with few existing networked relationships, may be more successful in the internationalisation process.

2 *Inter-organisational* – firms may well stand in different relationships to one another in different markets. They may be competitors in one market, collaborators in another and suppliers and customers to each other in a third. If one firm internationalises, this may draw other firms into the international arena.

3 *Intra-organisational* – relationships within the organisation may well influence the decision-making process. If a multinational has subsidiaries in other countries, decisions may well be taken at the subsidiary level that increases the degree of international involvement of the parent MNE, depending on the degree of decentralisation of decision making permitted by the firm.

The network approach would suggest that internationalisation can be explained, at least in part, by the fact that the other firms and people who are involved in a particular national network themselves internationalise.

■ International product life cycle (IPLC)

The suggestion here is that the pattern and extent of internationalisation achieved by the firm, and future prospects for continuation of that process, will depend in part on the stage in the IPLC reached by the firm. This approach also sees internationalisation as a process and is considered in more detail in Chapter 3 (p. 91).

■ Barriers to internationalisation

Whatever the method of internationalisation proposed or undertaken, there are well documented *barriers* to the internationalisation process. Particular attention has been paid to the barriers faced by small to medium-sized enterprises (SMEs), i.e. companies with less than 500 employees, when attempting to internationalise. Table 2.3 identifies the top ten barriers identified by the OECD (2006) in a large-scale survey within its member economies.

Table 2.3 demonstrates that member economies consider problems which are internal to SMEs to be the main barriers to access to international markets rather than barriers with the external environment, with five out of the top ten citing barriers falling within the *capability* category, and with just one falling within the *business environment* category. A lack of knowledge and scarce internal resources, both financial resources and human resources, feature within the top ten barriers as perceived by SMEs in member economies. External barriers, especially those imposed by governments, score relatively low. 'Unfavourable foreign rules and regulations' is ranked number 22 and 'unfavourable home rules and regulations' is ranked number 44. These findings suggest that knowledge barriers and problems with the development of key capabilities as well as further internal barriers, such as a lack of financial resources and management time and commitment, seem to constitute more serious problems to SMEs trying to internationalise than government imposed or more general regulatory barriers.

Government Support Programmes to overcome barriers

Member economies report a wide range of support programmes, some of which are targeted specially at SMEs, while others are open to all firms, subject to specific conditions, such as those operating within special sectors or those offering high growth

Table 2.3 **Top 10 barriers to SME access to international markets as reported by member economies**

Rank	Classification of barrier	Description of barrier
1	Capabilities	Inadequate quantity of and/or untrained personnel for internationalisation
2	Finance	Shortage of working capital to finance exports
3	Access	Limited information to locate/analyse markets
4	Access	Identifying foreign business opportunities
5	Capabilities	Lack of managerial time to deal with internationalisation
6	Capabilities	Inability to contact potential overseas customers
7	Capabilities	Developing new products for foreign markets
8	Business Environment	Unfamiliar foreign business practices
9	Capabilities	Meeting export product quality/standards/specification
10	Access	Unfamiliar exporting procedures/paperwork

Source: Table 1.4. Top ten barriers to SME access to international markets as reported by member economies, pp. 36, Source: OECD Member Economy Policymaker Survey and SME Survey, 2006, *reproduced in Removing Barriers to SME Access to International Markets*, OECD 2008.

potential. Individual regions within individual member economies offer additional support programmes, which only firms from this specific region can apply for.

Four categories of support programme have been identified (OECD 2006, 2008).

1 *Capabilities support programmes* focus on helping firms to develop internal capabilities which form a critical element of the internationalisation process. This type of programme generally aims at providing firms with the critical resources required for success within their international markets and can be understood theoretically as part of the resource-based view of the firm. Typically, the programmes reported seek to develop the capabilities of the firm and its employees in the following areas: business planning, marketing, training in the area of cultural differences in international markets, language capabilities and knowledge of export procedures. These programmes also support research into specific technologies, such as production processes, logistics and machinery, aimed at providing a competitive edge to the SME receiving the support.

2 *Access to markets support programmes* focus on gaining initial market access to individual markets, either for exporting, sourcing (importing) or local operations. This classification includes the provision of general market information, specific market analysis, the organisation of trade fairs, and off-shore assistance through the foreign consulates of the member economies.

3 *Business environment support programmes* tend to concentrate on seeking to remove international trade barriers and on improving the business environment in the home market to give firms a competitive edge, for example, through improvements in the domestic taxation.

4 *Financial support programmes* provide support to firms in one of three categories: export insurance and loan guarantees, development finance and venture finance, and direct financial support to cover costs of international activities otherwise not possible, such as export promotion, visits to trade fairs and so on.

The four dimensions discussed above may be configured in a number of ways to arrive at a particular government support structure. Table 2.4 provides a useful framework for constructing government support policies for internationalising firms.

Arguments against internationalisation

So far we have reviewed the arguments in favour of an internationalization strategy and the various methods available. It may, however, be useful to caution against the sometimes excessive enthusiasm for such a strategy. Alexander and Korine (2008) outline various reasons why companies should think carefully before embarking on a global strategy. They propose a 'going-global self assessment'.

1 *Are there potential benefits for our company?*
   - Where and when would the benefits of globalisation show up in our financial statements?
   - What is the expected economic value of each benefit?
   - How detailed and solid is our understanding of each one?
   - What is the hard evidence that other companies in similar circumstances have been able to realise these benefits in practice?

Table 2.4 **Model of government support programmes**

Service focus

Access

- General market information
- Specific market analysis
- Trade fairs and trade missions
- Direct support through foreign representation
- Inwards market access

Financial

- Export insurance and loan guarantees
- Development finance and venture finance
- Direct financial support

Capabilities

- Capabilities linked to human capital
- Capabilities linked to process and product technologies
- Capabilities linked to logistics and IT

Business environment

- International trade conditions
- Home market conditions
- Regulatory developments

Mode of international activity

- Exporting
- Importing
- Foreign operations and collaborations

Target group

- Regional v nationwide
- All SMEs v specific segments
- Specific sectors v all sectors

Provision of support

- Government agencies
- Affiliated service providers
- Public institutions
- Private firms
- Independent service providers

Source: Table 1.5. Structure of government support programmes, pp. 41, Source: OECD Member Economy Policymaker Survey and SME Survey, 2006, *reproduced in Removing Barriers to SME Access to International Markets*, OECD 2008.

2 *Do we have the necessary management skills*?
  - What skills are required to realise these benefits?
  - Do we have a clear track record of exhibiting them in the past?
  - Do we know how to further develop them?
3 *Will the costs outweigh the benefits*?
  - What will it cost, in terms of management time and business process investment, to realise the benefits of our globalisation strategy?
  - What would sceptics inside our various business units say about the cost of globalisation and its potential impact on their local performance?
  - What would be the most productive alternative use of all the resources that we plan to devote to our globalisation strategy?

Certainly 'failed' internationalisation strategies have been well documented in recent years (Case Study 2.9) and a stringent self-assessment *prior* to embarking on internationalisation strategies might have helped avoid some of these.

CASE 2.9 Internationalisation may not always deliver!

Royal Ahold is a Dutch supermarket operator which began its international expansion in the 1970s, acquiring related businesses throughout Europe, Asia, Latin America and the US, and eventually becoming the fourth largest retailer in the world in the early years of the millennium. Yet in 2007 the pressure of dissatisfied shareholders had forced the company to abandon its globalisation strategy and sell most of its US and other global operations to private equity firms. Critics point to unrealistic expectations

▶

of global scale economies (see Chapter 7) in food retailing, with purchasing economies available mainly on items provided by global suppliers to all markets – typically no more than 20% of all supermarket items. The need to match cultural differences in food tastes and methods of serving food products is important here. Critics also point to a failure by Royal Ahold to integrate effective management and IT systems across its far flung international operations, for example key suppliers were still able to charge Ahold different prices in different countries as recently as 2007.

Daimler Benz (Germany) merged with Chrysler (US) in 1998 to create a global car company. Karl Benz had constructed the first automobile in 1886 at which time Gottlieb Daimler was active in the same field of business. After years of partnership their businesses were formally integrated in 1926 as the Daimler-Benz Company. In the 1980s Daimler-Benz pursued a strategy of diversification, acquiring MTU, AEG, the aeroplane company Dornier, MBB and Fokker, the latter completing the aviation arm of Daimler-Benz. The vision of the chairman (Mr Reuter) was to transform the firm from a carmaker into an integrated technology group along the lines of General Electric or the Japanese Mitsubishi conglomerate. His vision included generating cross-border synergies between the automobile, the aeroplane and electronics industry, exchanging skills and knowledge, and spreading the company's risks over the many businesses in its portfolio. On 6 May 1998 a new chapter in Daimler's M & A history began: Daimler-Benz AG and Chrysler Corporation announced their merger and the creation of the new DaimlerChrysler AG.

Expected synergies included a more complete product portfolio, with DaimlerChrysler stronger in the high price end of the market and Chrysler in the medium to low price end. Indeed, except in the 'off-road' segment there were no product overlaps – rather the respective product portfolios complemented one another. This was also the case in terms of their geographical markets, with Chrysler a strong player in the NAFTA region, while Daimler-Benz was a leading company in Europe. DaimlerChrysler AG subsequently moved to acquire a third leg in the Asian market to consolidate its position in all regions of the triad. Further synergies were expected in fields such as procurement, common use of parts and sales.

In the event, after years of poor financial returns, Chrysler was sold for $1 to the private equity firm Cerberus in 2007, with cultural dissonance between the German and US arms of the company cited by many as a key underlying factor in this corporate failure.

A similar story can be recounted as regards the Dutch Financial services firm ABN Amro, which acquired banks worldwide but failed to generate the expected return on its global investments. Critics point to unrealistic expectations of the Dutch bank being able to dominate overseas retail banking markets such as Italy and Brazil, when consolidation of local banks with other international banks had already taken place in these countries. ABN Amro was sold off, in 2007, with various parts going to Royal Bank of Scotland, Fortis (Belgium) and Banco Santander (Spain).

Questions

1 Identify some of the factors lying behind these and other 'failures' of internationalisation strategies in recent years.

2 Suggest approaches that might reduce the risks of such 'failures'.

Useful websites

Now try the self-check questions for this chapter on the website at www.pearsoned.co.uk/wall. You will also find further resources as well as useful weblinks.

Sources of information on international trade and payments, international institutions and exchange rates include:

www.wto.org
www.imf.org
www.un.org
www.dti.gov.uk
www.europa.eu.int
www.eubusiness.com

Useful key texts

Daniels, J., Radebaugh, L. and Sullivan, D. (2006) *International Business* (11th edn), Pearson Prentice Hall, especially Chapter 1.

Dicken, P. (2003) *Global Shift: Transforming the World Economy* (4th edn), Paul Chapman Publishing Ltd, especially Chapter 1 and Parts I and II.

Hill, C. (2006) *International Business: Competing in the Global Marketplace* (5th edn), McGraw-Hill Irwin, especially Chapters 14 and 15.

Morrison, J. (2006) *The International Business Environment* (2nd edn), Palgrave, especially Chapter 2 and Chapter 5 (pp. 142–6) and Chapter 11 (pp. 331–6).

Piggott, J. and Cook, M. (2006) *International Business Economics: A European Perspective*, Palgrave Macmillan, especially Chapters 6 and 7.

Rugman, A. and Collinson, R. (2009) *International Business* (5th edn), FT Prentice Hall, especially Chapter 2.

Tayeb, M. (2000) *International Business: Theories, Policies and Practices*, Financial Times Prentice Hall, especially Chapters 5–8 and 18.

Wild, J., Wild, K. and Han, J. (2006) *International Business: The Challenges of Globalization* (3rd edn), FT Prentice Hall, especially Chapter 5.

Other texts and sources

Alexander, M. and Korine, H. (2008) 'Why you shouldn't go global', *Harvard Business Review*, December.

Bennett, R. (1999) *International Business* (2nd edn), Financial Times Pitman Publishing, especially Chapters 1 and 9.

Brainard, S.L. (1997) 'An Empirical Assessment of the Proximity–Concentration Trade-off between Multinational Sales and Trade', *American Economic Review*, 87.

Child, J. (1991) 'A Foreign Perspective on the Management of People in China', *International Journal of Human Resource Management*, 2, pp. 93–107.

Corkhill, D. (2000) 'Internationalisation and Competitiveness: the Portuguese Experience', in *Dimensions of International Competitiveness*, Lloyd-Reason, L. and Wall, S. (eds), Edward Elgar.

Deng, P. (2001) 'WFOEs: the Most Popular Entry Mode into China', *Business Horizons*, July–Aug.

Dunning, J.H. (1993) *Multinational Enterprises and the Global Economy*, Addison-Wesley.

Griffiths, A. (2000) 'Cultural Determinants of Competitiveness: the Japanese Experience', in *Dimensions of International Competitiveness: Issues and Policies*, Lloyd-Reason, L. and Wall, S. (eds), Edward Elgar.

Griffiths, A. and Wall, S. (eds) (2007) *Applied Economics*, Financial Times Prentice Hall.

Harrigan, K.R. (1986) *Managing for Joint Venture Success*, Lexington, MA: Lexington Books.

Healey, N. (2007) 'The Multinational Corporation', in *Applied Economics* (11th edn), Griffiths, A. and Wall, S. (eds), Financial Times Prentice Hall.

Hiraki, T. and Ito, A. (2008) 'Investor biases in Japan: Another pathology of Keiretsu', *Pacific Basin Finance Journal*, Vol 17, (January) pp. 100–124, Elsevier.

Hughes, J. and Weiss, J. (2007) 'Simple rules for making alliances work', *Harvard Business Review*, November, p. 122.

Johanson, J. and Wiedersheim-Paul, F. (1975) 'The Internationalisation of the Firm – Four Swedish Cases', *Journal of Management Studies*, 19, 3.

Lei, D. and Slocum, J. (1996) *Organizational Dynamics*, vol. 24, no. 4.

Lei, D., Slocum, J.W. and Pitts, R.A. (1997) 'Building Cooperative Advantage: Managing Strategic Alliances to Promote Organizational Learning', *Journal of World Business*, 32(3).

Lu, Y. and Bjorkman, I. (1998) 'Human Resource Management in International Joint Ventures in China', *Journal of General Management*, 23, pp. 63–74.

Markusen, J. (1995) 'The Boundaries of Multinational Enterprises and the Theory of International Trade', *Journal of Economic Perspectives*, 9.

METI (2008) 'Summary of the Preliminary Report on the 2007 Basic Survey of Japanese Enterprise Activities', Ministry of Economy, Trade and Industry, Japan.

OECD (2006) *OECD-APEC Keynote Paper on Removing Barriers to SME Access to International Markets*, OECD, Paris.

OECD (2008) *Removing Barriers to SME Access to International Markets*, OECD, Paris.

Oliver, N., Delbridge, R. and Barton, H. (2002) 'Lean Production and Manufacturing, Performance Improvements in Japan', ESRC Centre for Business Research, University of Cambridge, Working Paper No. 232.

Owen, D. (1999) 'Economic Geography Rewritten', *Economic Focus*, January, Dresdner Kleinwort Benson, London, pp. 6–7.

Reisenbeck, H. and Freeling, A. (1991) 'How Global are Global Brands?', *McKinsey Quarterly*, 4.

Reuer, J. (1999) 'The Logic of Alliances', *Financial Times*, 4 October.

Reuer, J. and Koza, M. (2000) 'Asymmetric Information and Joint Venture Performance: Theory and Evidence for Domestic and International Joint Ventures', *Strategic Management Journal*, vol. 1.

Taylor, C.T. (2000) 'The Impact of Host Country Government Policy on US Multinational Investment Decisions', *Harvard Business Review*, March/April.

Teresko, J. (2006) 'Learning from Toyota – Again', *Industry Week*, 1 February.

United Nations Conference on Trade and Development (UNCTAD) *World Investment Report* (annual publication).

United Nations Development Programme (UNDP) *Human Development Report* (annual publication), OUP.

Vanhonacker, W.R. (2000) 'A Better Way to Crack China', *Harvard Business Review*, July/August.

Wilson, J. (2003) 'Inter-Partner Relationships and Performance in UK–Chinese Joint Ventures: an Interaction Approach', unpublished Ph.D. thesis, University of Middlesex.

World Bank, *World Development Report* (annual publication).

Yan, D. and Warner, M. (2001) 'Sino-foreign Joint Ventures versus Wholly Foreign Owned Enterprises in the People's Republic of China', Research Papers in Management Studies, University of Cambridge, October.

Chapter 3

International business: theory and practice

By the end of this chapter you should be able to:

- outline the arguments used to support free trade between nations;

- identify the sources of comparative and competitive advantage between nations;

- discuss the nature and importance of both inter-industry and intra-industry trade in a global economy;

- assess the arguments and practices used to support protectionism;

- examine the impacts of a range of government policies and practices on international business;

- review the role of organisations such as the World Trade Organisation (WTO), World Bank, International Monetary Fund (IMF) and others in the conduct of international business.

Introduction

Most international business is conducted in a context in which the major players believe such business to be of benefit to themselves, to the nation states they represent and even to the broader international community. It would therefore seem appropriate to review the theoretical basis for trade at the outset of this chapter before moving on to discuss some of the issues and practices involving protectionism. The institutions and organisations that underpin the present system of global trade and payments, such as the World Trade Organisation (WTO), World Bank and International Monetary Fund (IMF) are reviewed, together with some recent proposals for reform. Since the European Union (EU) plays such a key role in the UK's international business environment, it is considered in some detail in this chapter.

Gains from trade

■ Absolute advantage

As long ago as 1776, Adam Smith in his *Wealth of Nations* suggested that countries could benefit from specialising in products in which they had an *absolute advantage* over other countries, trading any surpluses with those countries. By 'absolute advantage' Smith meant the ability to produce those products at lower resource cost (e.g. fewer labour and capital inputs) than the other countries.

This was an essentially limited view as to the benefits of international business. For example, in a simple two-country, two-product model, each country would have to demonstrate that it was absolutely more efficient than the other in one of these products if specialisation and trade were to be mutually beneficial.

This can be outlined by reference to Table 3.1, which presents hypothetical data for countries A and B.

Table 3.1 **Absolute advantage**

| | Output from one unit of resource: | |
	Textiles	Steel
Country A	20	40
Country B	80	20

With one unit of resource, country A can produce 20 units of textiles or 40 units of steel. With the same amount of resource country B can produce 80 units of textiles or 20 units of steel.

In terms of steel production one unit of resource in country A can produce twice as much output as one unit of resource in country B. However in terms of textile production, one unit of resource in country B can produce an output which is four times greater than that in country A. In this situation country A is said to have an *absolute advantage* in the production of steel and country B an *absolute advantage* in the production of textiles.

It can be shown that both countries can then gain by specialising in the production of the product in which they have an absolute advantage. This can be seen in Table 3.2, where, by reallocating one unit of resource from textiles to steel in country A and one unit of resource from steel to textiles in country B, world output of *both* products can be increased. This additional world output of both textiles and steel is then traded to the benefit of both countries. There are gains to be made, therefore, from specialisation and trade according to absolute advantage.

Table 3.2 **The gains made from the movement of one unit of resource**

	Textiles	Steel	Movement of one unit of resource from:
Country A	−20	+40	textiles to steel
Country B	+80	−20	steel to textiles
World output	+60	+20	

Comparative advantage

David Ricardo sought, in 1817, to broaden the basis on which trade was seen to be beneficial by developing his theory of *comparative advantage*. Again, we can illustrate by using a simple two-country, two-product model. In this approach even where a country has an absolute advantage (less resource cost) over the other country in *both* products, it can still gain by specialisation and trade in that product in which its *absolute advantage is greatest*, i.e. in which it has a *comparative advantage*. Similarly, the other country that has an absolute disadvantage (higher resource cost) in both products can still gain by specialisation and trade in that product in which its *absolute disadvantage is least*, i.e. in which it also has a *comparative advantage*.

This example is illustrated in Table 3.3 where country A is more efficient in the production of both textiles and steel. The difference between Tables 3.3 and 3.1 is that country A has improved its output of textiles per unit of resource, possibly through technological change in the textile industry. Although country A is better at producing (has an absolute advantage in) both products, there are still gains to be made through specialisation and trade since country A is *relatively* more efficient in the production of textiles.

Table 3.3 **Comparative advantage**

| | Output from one unit of resource: | |
	Textiles	Steel
Country A	320	40
Country B	80	20

This can be seen by referring to Table 3.3 which shows country A is four times better at producing textiles than country B but only two times better at producing steel. In this situation country A is said to have a *comparative advantage* in the production of textiles. Country B is one quarter as good as A at producing textile but half as good as A at producing steel. Whilst B has, therefore, an absolute disadvantage in both products, it is *relatively* least inefficient in the production of steel. In this situation Country B is said to have a *comparative advantage* in the production of steel.

The result of specialisation in the two countries according to comparative advantages means there are gains to be made through trade which can benefit both countries, as illustrated in Table 3.4.

By reallocating resources within the two countries so that each produces more of the product in which it has a comparative advantage (A in textiles, B in steel) it is possible to increase world output, and so there are gains to be made from specialisation and trade. For example by reallocating one unit of resource from steel to textiles in

Table 3.4 **Gains made from the reallocation of resources in a comparative advantage situation**

	Textiles	Steel	Movement of resources:
Country A	+320	−40	1 unit of resource from steel to textiles
Country B	−240	+60	3 units of resource from textiles to steel
World output	+80	+20	

country A and three units of resource from textiles to steel in country B, it is possible to increase world output by 80 units of textiles and 20 units of steel.

Comparative advantage and opportunity cost

In developing the theory of comparative advantage it is possible to use the concept of *opportunity cost*, defined here as the output foregone by producing one more unit of a particular product. Referring back to Table 3.3, if it is assumed that all resources are fully employed then it is only possible to produce one more unit of one commodity if resources are reallocated from the production of the other commodity. In country A, the production of one extra unit of textiles requires one-eighth of a unit of steel to be sacrificed. In country B, the production of one extra unit of textiles requires one-quarter of a unit of steel to be sacrificed. In country A, the production of one extra unit of steel requires eight units of textiles to be sacrificed, whereas in country B the production of one extra unit of steel only requires four units of textiles to be sacrificed. The opportunity cost ratios are summarised in Table 3.5.

Table 3.5 **Opportunity cost ratios**

	Opportunity cost of producing one extra unit of textiles	Opportunity cost of producing one extra unit of steel
Country A	$\frac{1}{8}$ unit of steel	8 units of textiles
Country B	$\frac{1}{4}$ unit of steel	4 units of textiles

Ricardo's theory of comparative advantage for a two-country, two-product model can be re-expressed in terms of *opportunity costs*:

> *A country* has a comparative advantage in that product for which it has a lower opportunity cost than the other country.

In terms of Table 3.5, country A has a comparative advantage in *textiles* ($\frac{1}{8}$ steel sacrificed is lower than $\frac{1}{4}$ steel sacrificed), whereas country B has a comparative advantage in steel (four units of textiles is lower than eight units of textiles sacrificed).

Let us now check whether specialisation and trade according to the comparative advantage we have identified really does provide potential benefits for both countries. Suppose country A produces one extra unit of textiles and country B one less unit of textiles (it specialises in steel). We have the outcome shown in Table 3.6.

In producing one *extra* unit of textiles, A *sacrifices* $\frac{1}{8}$ unit of steel. However in producing one *less* unit of textiles, B *gains* four units of steel. By this marginal reallocation of resources according to our revised definition of comparative advantages (lower opportunity costs), total output of textiles is unchanged but total output of

Table 3.6 **Specialisation according to comparative advantages (lower opportunity costs)**

	Textiles	Steel
Country A	+1	$-\frac{1}{8}$
Country B	−1	+4
	0	$+3\frac{7}{8}$

steel has risen. There is clearly potential for this extra output of steel to be traded to the benefit of *both* countries, provided the terms of trade are appropriate.

Limitations of the theory of comparative advantage

Limitations of the theory can be seen as:

- *Returns to scale.* The theory assumes constant opportunity costs, i.e. constant returns to scale, thus ignoring the possibility that economies or diseconomies of scale can be obtained as output increases.
- *Full employment.* The assumption is made that there is full employment of the factors of production. Thus, as specialisation takes place, those resources freed by one sector are automatically transferred to the sector in which the country is specialising. This assumption means that it is possible to calculate the opportunity costs.
- *Reciprocal demand.* The theory assumes what is known as *double coincidence of wants.* This means that in the example we have used, following specialisation, country A should demand steel from country B, and country B textiles from country A.
- *Transport costs.* Transport costs are not included in the theory of comparative advantage. Transport costs, however, increase production costs and therefore offset some of the potential gains made through specialisation.
- *Factor mobility.* The theory assumes that resources can be reallocated from the production of one product to another. In the real world, however, resources are likely to be immobile. In the example used above, it is unlikely that resources can be freely moved from steel to textile production or from textile to steel production.
- *Free trade.* Free trade is an obvious assumption of the theory of comparative advantage. There are no trade barriers such as tariffs and quotas, for these would limit the scope for specialisation in the two countries. This is unlikely to be the case in the real world.

Ricardo's theory is further developed in Box 3.1, with opportunity costs, terms of trade and diagrammatic representations all used to emphasise the potential benefits from specialisation and trade according to comparative advantages.

Box 3.1 Comparative advantage and opportunity cost

Ricardo's theory can be illustrated using Table 3.7 where, for simplicity, we assume each country to have the same amounts of resources (e.g. labour and capital) available for producing two products, CDs and videos. Initially the analysis will also assume constant returns in producing each product. Table 3.7 shows the production possibilities if each country devotes all its (identical) resources to the production of either CDs or videos.

From Table 3.7 we can see that country A has an absolute advantage in both products (greater output for the same resource input) but a *comparative advantage in videos.* This is because although A is twice as efficient as B in CDs, it is four times as efficient as B in videos. Therefore, according to the principle of comparative advantage, country A should specialise in videos and trade these for the CDs that B produces.

By similar reasoning, from Table 3.7 we can see that country B has an absolute disadvantage in both products (less output for the same resource input) but a *comparative advantage in CDs.* This is because although B is only one-quarter as efficient as A in videos it is one-half

| Box 3.1 | Continued |

Table 3.7 Production possibilities in a two-product, two-country model

Country	Output of CDs	Output of videos
A	2000	800
B	1000	200

as efficient as A in CDs. Therefore, according to the principle of comparative advantage, country B should specialise in CDs and trade these for the videos that A produces.

A country has a *comparative advantage* (in a two-product model) in that product in which its *absolute advantage is greatest* or in which its *absolute disadvantage is least*.

This idea of comparative advantage can be expressed in terms of *opportunity cost* (*see* Table 3.8), defined here as the output foregone by producing one more unit of a particular product. In country A, for example, the production of an extra video has an opportunity cost of only 2.5 CDs whereas for country B the production of an extra video has an opportunity cost of 5 CDs. In other words, country A has a lower opportunity cost in video production than country B, and therefore has a *comparative advantage* in video production, even though it has an *absolute advantage* in both products.

Similarly, country B can produce an extra CD at an opportunity cost of one-fifth (0.2) of a video, whereas country A can only produce an extra CD at an opportunity cost of two-fifths (0.4) of a video. In other words, country B has a lower opportunity cost and therefore *comparative advantage* in CD production even though it has an *absolute disadvantage* in both products.

A country has a *comparative advantage* (in a two-product model) in that product in which it has a *lower opportunity* cost than the other country.

We would conclude that country A has a comparative advantage in videos and country B a comparative advantage in CDs.

Table 3.8 Opportunity costs in a two-product, two-country model

Country	Opportunity cost of 1 extra CD	Opportunity cost of 1 extra video
A	0.4 videos	2.5 CDs
B	0.2 videos	5.0 CDs

■ Gains from specialisation and trade

We can show the potential benefits from specialisation and trade according to comparative advantages in a number of different ways. Clearly a country will benefit if, by specialisation and trade, it can reach a consumption situation better than that which would result from being self-sufficient. Suppose that initially each country tries to be self-sufficient, using half its resources to produce videos and half to produce CDs. This gives us the *self-sufficiency* consumption bundles of C_A (1000 CDs, 400 videos) and C_B (500 CDs, 100 videos) respectively. Provided that the *terms of trade* (i.e. the rate at which videos exchange for CDs) are appropriate, each country can be shown to benefit from specialisation and trade according to comparative advantages.

In Figure 3.1(a), with terms of trade of 1 video : 3 CDs, country A specialises in videos and trades 250 of its 800 videos for 750 CDs (from B), ending at the consumption bundle of C'_A (750 CDs, 550 videos). Since C'_A is *outside* its production possibility frontier, country A could not have achieved this consumption bundle by being self-sufficient.

In Figure 3.1(b), with the same terms of trade of 1 video : 3 CDs, country B specialises in CDs and trades 750 of its 1000 CDs for 250 videos (from A), ending at the consumption bundle of C'_B (250 CDs, 250 videos). Since C'_B is *outside* its production possibility frontier, country B could not have achieved this consumption bundle by being self-sufficient.

If the *terms of trade* are appropriate, both countries can gain from *specialisation and trade according to comparative advantages*.

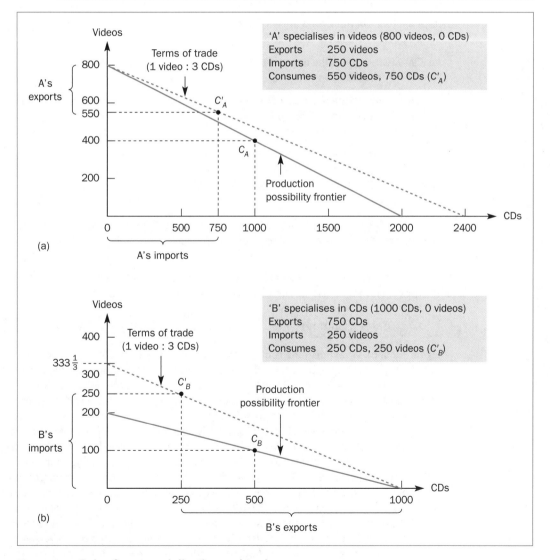

Figure 3.1 **Gains from specialisation and trade**

You should be able to see from Figure 3.1(a) that at terms of trade of *less than* 1 video : 2.5 CDs, country A will be better off by being self-sufficient than by specialising in videos and trading them for CDs. In other words, the slope of A's production possibility frontier represents the 'worst' terms A is prepared to accept if it is to engage in specialisation and trade according to comparative advantages. Similarly, from Figure 3.1(b) we can see that at terms of trade of *less than* 1 CD : 0.2 videos, country B will be better off by being self-sufficient than by specialising in CDs and trading them for videos. In other words, the slope of B's production possibility frontier represents the 'worst' terms B is prepared to accept if it is to engage in specialisation and trade according to comparative advantages.

---

pause for thought 1

(a) If the terms of trade for A are less than 1 video : 2.5 CDs, namely 1 video : 2 CDs, what would be the result of A exporting 250 videos in Figure 3.1?

(b) If the terms of trade for B are less than 1 CD : 0.2 videos, namely 1 CD = 0.1 videos, what would be the result of B exporting 750 CDs in Figure 3.1?

(c) Can you re-express the terms of trade for B of 1 CD : 0.2 videos into a relationship between videos : CDs?

(d) What would be the outcome if the terms of trade for A and for B were exactly as represented by their respective production possibility frontiers?

We can therefore say that the terms of trade which will enable *both* country A and country B to gain from specialisation and trade, must lie between 1 video : 2.5 CDs and 1 video : 5 CDs (i.e. 1 CD : 0.2 videos).

The *terms of trade* which will enable both countries to gain from specialisation and trade must lie between the slopes of their respective production possibility frontiers.

An alternative approach to demonstrating the gains from trade is shown in Box 3.2. This approach makes use of the ideas of consumer and producer surplus.

Box 3.2   Gains from trade

Figure 3.2 shows that free trade could, in theory, bring welfare benefits to an economy previously protected. Suppose the industry is initially completely protected. The domestic price P_D will then be determined solely by the intersection of the domestic supply (S_D-S_D) and domestic demand (D_D-D_D) curves. Suppose that the government now decides to remove these trade barriers and to allow foreign competition. For simplicity, we assume a perfectly elastic 'world' supply curve $P_W - C$, giving a total supply curve (domestic and world) of $S_D AC$. Domestic price will then be forced down to the world level P_W with domestic demand being $0Q_3$ at this price. To meet this domestic demand, $0Q_2$ will be supplied from domestic sources, with Q_2Q_3 supplied from the rest of the world (i.e. imported). The *consumer surplus*, which is the difference between what consumers are prepared to pay and what they have to pay, has risen from $D_D BP_D$ to $D_D CP_W$. The *producer surplus*, which is the difference between the price the producer receives and the minimum necessary to induce production, has fallen from $P_D BS_D$ to $P_W AS_D$. The gain in consumer surplus outweighs the loss in producer surplus by the area ABC, which could then be regarded as the net gain in economic welfare as a result of free trade replacing protectionism.

Box 3.2 **Continued**

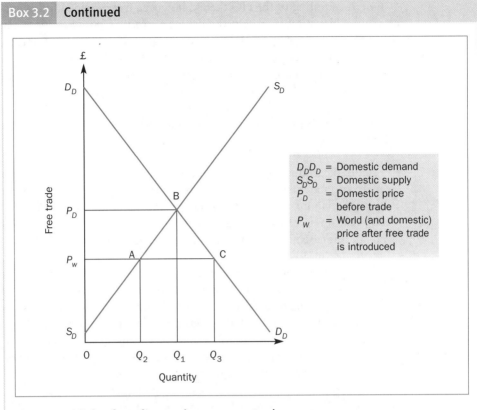

Figure 3.2 **Gains from free trade versus no trade**

pause for thought 2

In the analysis above, what has happened to the area $P_W P_D BA$?

Sources of comparative and competitive advantage

We have seen that countries can gain from trade by specialising in those products in which they have a lower opportunity cost (i.e. a comparative advantage) vis-à-vis other countries and trading surpluses with those countries. An obvious question then presents itself, namely, what is it that gives one country a comparative advantage in certain products over other countries? We briefly review a number of theories that have sought to answer this question.

◼ Factor endowments: Heckscher-Ohlin

Named after two Swedish economists, the Heckscher-Ohlin (HO) theory suggests that *factor endowments* will broadly determine the pattern of trade between nations. The idea here is that those countries with an abundance of certain types of factor (labour, capital, natural resources, etc.) will be able to produce products that embody those abundant factors relatively more cheaply than other, less well endowed, countries. In its simplest form a labour abundant country will be able to produce (and export) labour intensive products relatively more cheaply than a labour scarce country, and so on.

Empirical testing of the HO theory, however, has provided little support for it being a major explanation of observed patterns of trade, even when more complex forms of the theory have been devised. For example, international trade is larger in volume and value terms between the *similar* developed (advanced industrialised) economies rather than between the *dissimilar* (in terms of factor endowments) developed and less developed economies. This is, of course, the opposite to what we might have expected from the HO theory.

Possible reasons for these 'disappointing' empirical results might include the following:

- Factors of production – such as labour, capital, etc. – are hardly homogeneous so aggregate statements such as 'labour abundant' may be relatively meaningless. For example, labour can be broken down into many different skill levels, capital into different levels of technological intensity (e.g. high, medium and low technology), etc. In this case it may make little sense to regard a country as having a comparative advantage in, say, labour-intensive products merely because it is labour abundant vis-à-vis some other country. To compare 'like with like' we may need to disaggregate labour (and any other factor) into its component parts. Only then might we be able to say that a country is labour abundant in, say, highly-skilled labour and might therefore be expected to have a comparative advantage in those products which intensively embody high-skilled labour inputs.

- Products may exhibit *factor intensity reversal* in different countries. For example, producing certain types of car in Japan (with higher real wages) is likely to be a more capital-intensive process than producing the same car in, say, Spain (with lower real wages). The suggestion here is that the higher *relative* price ratio of labour : capital in Japan than in Spain may provide greater incentives to substitute capital for labour in Japan than would be the case in Spain. Where substantial differences in such factor price ratios exist, there might even be factor intensity reversal, with a given product using relatively capital intensive processes in one country but relatively labour-intensive processes in another.

- Factor and product markets must be competitive if differences in factor endowments and therefore factor productivities are to be reflected in differences in product costs. In reality, imperfections in factor markets (existence of unions, large employers, employer confederations, etc.) and in product markets (monopoly or oligopoly, public-sector involvement, etc.) may well result in prices diverging markedly from actual marginal production costs.

- The *terms of trade* between the potential exported and imported products may lie outside the limits which would permit trade to be beneficial to both parties (*see* pp. 84–6). For example, the export : import price ratio may be influenced in arbitrary ways by unexpected fluctuations in relative exchange rates, etc.

- A host of other market imperfections may distort the linkage between factor endowment, actual production costs and the relative prices at which products are exchanged on international markets. Differences between countries in the degree of multinational or governmental involvement in a given sector, in the market structure of production in that sector or in terms of other types of 'market failure', can be expected to break any simple linkage between relative factor endowment and relative product prices.

For all these reasons it may be unsurprising that little empirical evidence exists to suggest that different national factor endowments have played a major part in explaining the observed patterns of international trade flows.

The discussion on increasing *intra-regional* and *inter-regional* trade (pp. 99–100) also has a bearing on why the factor endowment theory appears to be less useful in recent times as an explanation of actual trade patterns.

■ Disaggregated factor endowments

More refined versions of HO have tried to disaggregate the factors of production into units that are more homogeneous for purposes of comparison between countries.

- *Efficiency units.* Here labour and capital inputs are adjusted to take account of productivity differentials. So if American workers are twice as productive in manufacturing as, say, Thai workers, the number of American workers should be multiplied by two when comparing labour factor endowment between the two countries in terms of 'efficiency units'.
- *Human capital.* Workers can be disaggregated by *level* of human capital (e.g. years of education, experience, etc.) and by *type* of human capital (e.g. vocational/non-vocational, marketing/non-marketing, etc.). Again, we can then apply 'weights' to any raw data we might have when comparing labour factor endowment between countries.

■ Revealed comparative advantage

The suggestion here is that the sources of comparative advantage can be determined indirectly by *observing* actual trade flows between countries. For example, it is interesting to note that in the more dynamic sectors of UK industry, there are signs of a shift towards the higher end of the quality market for both UK manufacturing exports and for the production of substitutes for manufacturing imports. In other words, the data arguably suggests a *revealed comparative advantage* for the UK in terms of more technologically intensive manufacturing exports and imports (substitutes).

■ Competitive advantage: Porter

Michael Porter (1990) has attempted to explain the critical factors for success in both national and international production and exchange in terms of *competitive advantages*.

Competitive advantage: corporate

In the *corporate* context, the competitive advantages of a company are defined in terms of the 'marginal' company in that sector of economic activity. In other words, they are the collection of reasons that allow the more successful companies to create positive added-value (profits) in that sector of economic activity as compared to the 'marginal' company, which is just managing to survive. Reasons for such competitive advantages could include some or all of the following:

- *architecture*, benefits to the company from some distinctive aspect of the set of contractual relationships the company has entered into with suppliers and/or customers;
- *innovation*, benefits to the company from being more innovative than rivals (perhaps reinforced by legal structures, e.g. patent laws);

- *incumbency advantages*, benefits to the company from being an early 'player' in that field of activity (reputation, control over scarce resources, etc.).

pause for thought 3 Can you give examples of these sources of competitive advantage using major international businesses?

The essential feature about many of these sources of competitive advantage is that they are usually *temporary*. Distinctive contractual relationships that prove to be successful (e.g. franchising arrangements) can be replicated by other firms, patents that protect innovation eventually expire and even incumbency advantages may not last. New sources of raw materials or other factor inputs may be found, technical change may alter production possibilities and even reputations can be transposed from other fields of economic activity (e.g. Virgin taking its reputation for quality/efficiency in entertainment/transport, etc. into financial services operations). Companies must continually seek new sources of competitive advantage if they are to avoid becoming themselves the 'marginal' firm in any sector of economic activity.

Competitive advantage: national

In the *national* context, Porter has again used this perspective of a dynamic, ever-changing set of competitive advantages as a basis for explaining trade patterns between countries. Porter sees both *product innovation* and *process innovation* as key elements in determining national competitive advantages. In his view these dynamic elements far outweigh the more static elements of 'factor endowments' in determining success in international trading relationships. Still more so when technology is constantly changing the optimal combination of capital/labour/natural resource inputs for a product, when multinationals are so 'footloose' that they can readily relocate across national boundaries and when capital markets provide investment finance on an increasingly global basis.

Porter identifies six key variables as potentially giving a country a competitive advantage over other countries:

1 *demand conditions*: the extent and characteristics of domestic demand;
2 *factor conditions*: transport infrastructure, national resources, human capital endowments, etc.;
3 *firm strategies*: *structures and rivalries*: the organisation and management of companies and the degree of competition in the market structures in which they operate;
4 *related and supporting industries*: quality and extent of supply industries, supporting business services, etc.;
5 *government policies*: nature of the regulatory environment, extent of state intervention in industry and the regions, state support for education and vocational training, etc.;
6 *chance*.

Porter's diamond

The first four of these variables form a *diamond* shape, as shown in Figure 3.3, when mapped as the most important determinants of national competitive advantage.

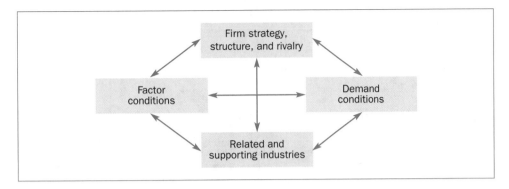

Figure 3.3 Porter's diamond: the determinants of national competitive advantage

Source: Porter, M. (1998) *The Competitive Advantage of Nations*, Palgrave, p. 72.

In Porter's view, the four determinants are interdependent. For example favourable 'demand conditions' will only contribute to national competitive advantage when combined with appropriate 'factor conditions', 'related and supporting industries' and 'firm strategies: structures and rivalries' so that companies are *able* and *willing* to take advantage of the favourable demand conditions. To sustain national competitive advantages in modern, high-technology industries and economies, Porter argues that all four determinants in the 'diamond' must be favourable. However, in less technology intensive industries and economies, one or two of the four determinants being favourable may be sufficient for a national competitive advantage: e.g. natural resource dependent industries may only need favourable 'factor conditions' (presence of an important natural resource) and appropriate infrastructure to extract and transport that resource.

The last two determinants 'government policies' and 'chance' outlined above can interact with the four key determinants of the diamond to open up new opportunities for national competitive advantage. For example government policies in the field of education and training may help create R & D and other knowledge–intensive competitive advantage for a nation. Similarly 'chance' events can play a part, as in the case of Russia supporting a greater US presence in Uzbekistan during the War in Afghanistan in 2001/02, thereby creating new opportunities for US oil companies to exploit the huge oil resources in that country.

pause for thought 4 | Can you identify some possible impacts of 9/11 in terms of national competitive advantage?

■ International product life cycle (IPLC)

The suggestion here (e.g. Vernon and Wells 1991) is that the pattern of products traded between countries will be influenced by the stage of production reached in the international life cycle of a variety of knowledge-intensive products. The *new product stage* (invention/development) will typically occur in the (advanced industrialised) innovating country but then the balance between production and consumption (and therefore between export and import) may shift *geographically* as different

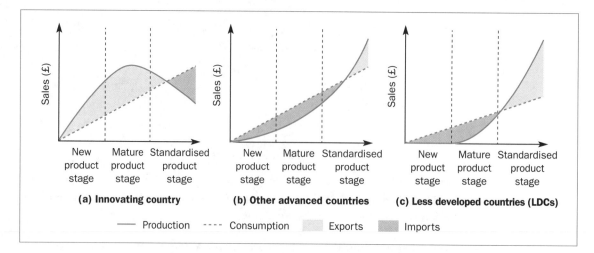

Figure 3.4 The international product life cycle (IPLC) for knowledge-intensive products

stages of the product life cycle are reached. In Figure 3.4 we can see a stylised IPLC for a knowledge-intensive product over three stages of the product life cycle (new product, mature product, standardised product) and for three broad geographical regions (innovating country, other advanced countries, less developed countries – LDCs).

■ *New product stage.* Here production is concentrated in the *innovating country*, as is market demand. A typical scenario for this stage would be where the (initially) relatively low output is sold at premium prices to a price-inelastic domestic market segment (with few, if any, exports). There may be a small amount of production via subsidiaries in 'other advanced countries' but little or none in the LDCs.

■ *Mature product stage.* Both production and consumption typically continue to rise in the *innovating country*, with scale economies beginning to reduce costs and price to a new, more price sensitive mass market segment. Exports to other countries become a higher proportion of total sales. Output of the generic product also rises in the 'other advanced countries', via the output of subsidiaries or of competitors in these countries which have the knowledge-intensive capability of developing close substitutes. These countries typically import a high proportion of their sales from the innovating country, as do the LDCs.

■ *Standardised product stage.* At this stage the technology becomes more widely diffused and is often largely 'embodied' in both capital equipment and process control. Low-cost locations become a more feasible source of quality supply in this stage, often via MNE outsourcing and technology transfer. The LDCs may even become net exporters to the innovating country and to other advanced countries.

Some of the issues previously discussed are raised in Case Study 3.1, which looks at some of the impacts on the US textile and garment industry of moves towards free trade.

| CASE 3.1 | Impacts of freer trade |

The epitaph for America's textile and garment industry was written decades ago. Clothes making is labour intensive, and ten Chinese will work for the price of one American. Everyone knows that sunset industries are best left to developing countries hoping to pull themselves out of poverty; and that only tariffs, quotas and other barriers have sustained America's enormous textile and garments industries, which together employ 1.4 million workers, account for nearly 10% of all American manufacturing, and produce more than $100 billion of goods each year.

Now the end of the free ride is in sight. By 2005 when the trade liberalisation agreements of the World Trade Organisation kick in, most of these barriers will be gone. By then China will also have joined the WTO, bringing its huge textiles and apparel industry to the same open party. An industry that has been protected almost as long as the country has existed (George Washington wore a dark brown domestically made suit to his first inauguration as a 'buy-American' statement) will for the first time be fully exposed to the harsh winds of globalisation.

Each week brings news of another factory closure, the jobs sent to Latin America or Asia where they belong. As go garments, so go textiles – fabric-making tends to 'follow the needle', and over the past few years dozens of American textile makers have moved mills to Mexico to be near to the border-located clothes-making factories, a trend accelerated by the North American Free-Trade Agreement which lowered tariffs.

But despite the defections to Mexico, American textile exports are still rising. And total employment in the garment and textile business is expected to drop just 100,000 or so, to 1.3 million, by 2006, according to industry projections. Trevor Little, a professor at the North Carolina State University college of textiles, reckons that the domestically made share of the American clothing business will fall to about 25%, but stabilise there for the foreseeable future.

Why not zero? Because labour costs do not matter so much in textile making these days. It has become a capital-intensive business, in which a few relatively skilled workers watch over huge mechanical looms. Moreover, America remains the world's second largest grower of cotton (after China), and in many cases it still makes sense to weave near the farms, most of which are in such southern states as North Carolina and Mississippi, rather than to ship cotton abroad.

There is more to garment making, too, than boatloads of cheap T-shirts. At the top end there is high fashion, which is price-insensitive: globalisation has little effect on the designers of Paris, Milan or New York. More broadly there is mainstream style, which changes by the week; speed to market there often counts more than rock-bottom prices. And there is always a demand for high quality, a safe haven for small domestic garment makers from London's Savile Row to New York's Seventh Avenue.

But as strong as these domestic niches may be, they add up to just a few per cent of total sales. To keep a full quarter of the industry at home in the absence of trade barriers will take a lot more. What that will be, reckon the industry bulls, is technology. Those who view the global garment and textile industries through the prism of labour costs see it as an industry dominated by commodities. If the Gap is going to sell a million blue polo shirts year in and year out, Mexico or China is the place to make them. Lead times may be long and the supply chain inflexible, but you can't beat the price.

But today's Internet-driven retail trends go in the opposite direction: mass customisation, 'lots of one', rapid product changes and just-in-time manufacturing. Retailers such as Levi's and Brooks Brothers are already experimenting with the Dell Computer model, where customers order products that are made specially for them. In a black-curtained cube at [TC]² the textile industry's research consortium, technicians show how this future might work. A customer walks in, closes the curtains, strips and dons special disposable undergarments that do not distort her body shape. Then she grabs two ski pole-like handles, presses a button and waits as beams of light trace over her body. Within seconds, a computer generates a 3-D body scan with every possible measurement precisely quantified. The scan booth could be in a clothing store or a stand-alone service. [TC]² even imagines chains of 'tan and scan' parlours in shopping malls.

A body scan is a handy thing. It could be stored on a personal password-protected Website, with temporary access granted to any e-tailer (e-commerce retailer) a customer chooses. Select a Brooks Brothers shirt online, let the site 'measure' your body scan, and get a robot-tailored custom garment by post a week or two later, cut to fit (unless you have put on weight since your last scan). No more size shortages, or settling for standard or idiosyncratic sizes. And, since the garment is custom-made, it can be custom-designed with any combination of material, colours and styles the manufacturer can handle.

This is an extreme view of the future of the clothing industry, and one still years away. There is only a handful of body-scanning booths in use today (the army is using a few to outfit its recruits), and the technology is still too bulky and expensive for all but a few adventurous retailers. But it hints at a day where America can preserve a relatively healthy textile and clothing business without artificial barriers.

In a recent book,[1] Janice Hammond, a Harvard Business School professor, and three co-authors argue that the trend of 'lean retailing' is already having this effect. 'Although it is true that the American apparel industry could have given up in the early 1990s, with only distribution centres and designers remaining in this country, it did not', they write. Instead, companies moved upstream, using technology to help solve the clothing retailer's biggest problem – stocks of garments that are unsold, and, if they go out of style, unsaleable.

American garment makers increasingly offer electronic ordering, automated distribution centres and inventory-management systems tied into those of their customers. The best manufacturers have learned how to deliver orders at a few days' notice, something their offshore competitors cannot match. It is, the authors claim, 'a triumph of information technology, speed and flexibility over low labour rates'.

What this suggests is a natural division of labour: a trouser maker could assemble average-sized khakis in volume in Mexico, but make special sizes such as narrow waists or long inseams in the United States, offering fast turnaround for retailers and

[1]Abernathy, Frederick, Dunlop, John, Hammond, Janice, and Weil, David (1999) *A Stitch in Time: Lean Retailing and the Transformation of Manufacturing – Lessons from the Apparel and Textile Industries*, Oxford University Press.

less risk of overstocking. As the technology advances, the balance between custom and bulk manufacturing may become quite fine. If this comes to pass, the high-tech firms that remain may wonder why they fought so long to keep trade barriers when innovation worked even better.

Source: Adapted from *The Economist*, 27 April 2000. © The Economist Newspaper Limited, London 2000.

Questions

1 What does this case study suggest in terms of the factor endowment theory of international trade?

2 Briefly outline the factors that might permit the USA to retain a sizeable textile and garment industry.

Trade and the world economy

The rapid growth of world trade over the last century reflects, at least in part, the fact that nations have become more interrelated as they have attempted to gain the benefits of freer trade. Table 3.9 compares the *relative growth* of world trade and world output from 1870 to the present day. It shows that the growth rate of world merchandise trade (exports) has exceeded the growth of world output (GDP) in four of the five periods. The only exception to this pattern occurred in the period 1913 to 1950 when two world wars and a major world depression resulted in the widespread adoption of protectionist trade policies. The post-Second World War period (1950–73) saw an unprecedented growth of world trade which far out-stripped the growth of world production. While such data cannot prove causation, we can at least say that growth in world trade is consistent with rising economic prosperity.

It may be useful at this point to consider the *type* of trade flow which underlies the recorded growth in world trade.

■ Type of trade flow

A distinction is frequently made between inter- and intra-industry trade.

- *Inter-industry* trade refers to situations where a country exports products that are fundamentally different in type from those that it imports. The UK exporting computer software to Switzerland but importing precision watches from Switzerland would be an example of inter-industry trade between two countries.

Table 3.9 **Growth in world GDP and merchandise trade 1870–2007 (average annual % change)**

	1870–1900	1900–13	1913–50	1950–73	1973–2007
GDP	2.9	2.5	2.0	5.1	3.0
Trade (exports)	3.8	4.3	0.6	8.2	5.1

Source: Adapted from WTO, International Trade Statistics (various) and Annual Reports (various).

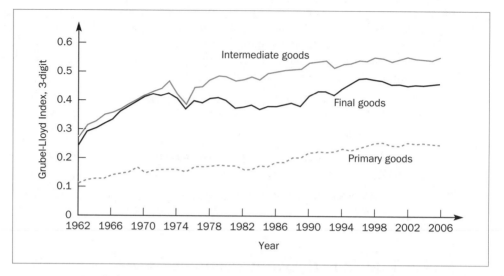

Figure 3.5 **Intra-industry trade has risen for primary, intermediate and final goods**
Source: World Development Report (World Bank 2009), p. 20.

■ *Intra-industry trade* refers to situations where a country exports certain items from a given product range while at the same time importing other items from the same product range. The UK exporting certain types of car to Germany but importing other types of car from Germany would be an example of intra-industry trade. Over half of world trade today is intra-industry trade, which consists of final goods, intermediate goods and primary goods (raw materials, etc.), as can be seen in Figure 3.5.

World *intra-industry* trade in intermediate goods, such as components, semi-finished manufactures, etc. has grown the fastest, more than doubling since 1962, with the growth in intra-industry trade in final goods only narrowly behind.

It is worth noting that intra-industry trade in *intermediate goods* will be more sensitive to changes in transport costs than such trade in *final goods*. For example, if intermediate inputs are two-thirds of the value added for producing a final good, then a 10% increase in transport costs is the equivalent of a 20% increase in VAT on the final product. This heightened sensitivity to transport costs of intermediate goods, which we have seen to be the fastest growing segment of international trade (not least because of progressively geographically dispersed value chains), emphasises the importance of transport costs to the potential growth of global trade.

Clearly the likely explanations for the growth of world trade will be different for each type of trade flow. Factor endowment and other comparative advantage theories are often used in attempts to explain *inter-industry* trade patterns, whereas the activities of multinationals, the international product life cycle and various types of competitive advantage theories are more usually used to account for *intra-industry* trade patterns.

This point is usefully emphasised in the following quotation from the *World Development Report* 2009 (World Bank 2009: 170):

During the first wave [of globalization] from about 1840 to World War 1, transport costs fell enough to make large scale trade possible between places based on their comparative advantage. So Britain traded machinery for Indian tea, Argentine beef and Australian wool; trade increased between *dissimilar countries*. During the second wave [of globalization] after 1950, transport costs fell low enough that small differences in products and tastes fuelled trade between *similar countries*, at least in Europe and North America. Neighbours traded different types of beer and different parts of cars, such as wheels and tyres. Trade in parts and components grew to take advantage of specialization and economies of scale. The first wave of globalization was characterized by 'conventional', *inter-industry* trade that exploited differences in natural endowments, the second by a 'new international trade' driven by economies of scale and product differentiation'.

Most empirical studies suggest, therefore, that it is the growth in *intra-industry* trade flows that have made the greatest contribution to the recorded growth in world trade. The experience of Honda provides a useful case study of the role the multinationals often play in promoting such patterns of trade.

CASE 3.2 Intra-industry trade: Honda

Figure 3.6 shows the Honda motorcycle network in Europe together with its outside supply links. Honda is very much a multinational company with a transnationality index of 82% in 2006 (*World Investment Report*, 2008). In other words, the average of the following ratios exceeds 80% for Honda: foreign assets/total assets, foreign sales/total sales and foreign employment/total employment. Honda began its operations by exporting motorcycles from Japan to Europe, but this was quickly followed by its first European overseas production affiliate in 1962. This affiliate, Honda Benelux NV (Belgium) was set up to provide a 'learning' opportunity before Honda brought its motorcycle and automobile production to Europe. Figure 3.6 shows that, by 2007, Honda's operations had widened significantly, with its affiliates in Germany acting as its main European regional headquarters. Honda Deutschland GmbH coordinates the production and marketing side, while Honda R & D Europe is engaged in research, engineering and designing for all the affiliates in Europe.

Honda's key assembly affiliates are Honda Industriale SpA (Italy), which is wholly owned, and Montessa Honda SA (Spain) which is majority owned (88%). These companies were originally designed to concentrate on the assembly of specific types of motorcycle model appropriate to the different European locations in order to benefit from various economies of scale. At the same time, each assembler exported its own model to the other Honda locations in Europe in order to gain economies in joint production and marketing; in other words, any given model is produced in one location, but a full range of models is offered for sale in all locations. Finally, in the international context, Honda's European models are also exported to subsidiaries in the USA, Brazil and Japan, while its European network imports large and medium-sized motorcycles from its US and Brazilian affiliates.

As far as motorcycle parts are concerned, engines and key parts were initially supplied from Japan. However, in 1985 Honda acquired a 25% stake in Peugeot Motorcycles SA and began producing small engines in France for scooters and mopeds. These engines were then supplied to its Italian and Spanish assemblers of scooters

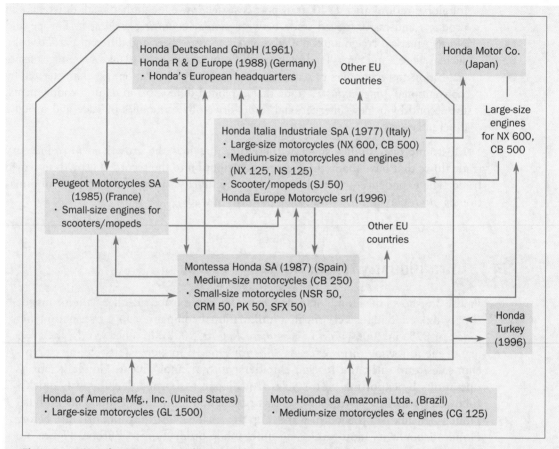

Figure 3.6 Honda: EU motorcycle networks and supply links
Source: Adapted from Healey (2007).

and mopeds. Following this, medium-sized engines began to be produced in Honda Italia Industriale SpA, both for its own models and for Montessa Honda, while the latter began producing frames and other parts locally. Large-sized engines were still, however, supplied from Japan.

This study of Honda illustrates the types of motives underlying multinational activity in a globalised economy and the reasons for the consequent growth in intra-industry trade between countries. The traditional technical economies of scale were exploited to reduce average costs as were the more market-based economies from producing and selling within the EU with its 490 million consumers in 2008. Some non-technical economies of scale have also been exploited with R & D activities concentrated in the UK, Germany and Italy as well as Japan. In addition, the improved communications within the EU and the rise of more sophisticated corporate structures enabled Honda to integrate operations both horizontally, through affiliate specialisation in particular models, and vertically, through specialisation of affiliates in the production of parts. Honda was able to capitalise on its well-known ownership-specific advantages of excellent quality engineering and sound business skills, and to combine this with an intelligent strategy for locating production within the largest consumer market in the world.

The Honda experience helps to illustrate the nature of multinational inter-firm activity within a sophisticated market dominated by product differentiation, which in turn is the basis for much of the growth in the intra-industry trade already noted.

Source: Healey (2007).

Questions

1 How might the Honda case study relate to the various theoretical explanations of the basis for trade?

2 What benefits to Honda might result from integrating its operations both horizontally and vertically?

■ Intra-regional trade

It may be useful to enquire at this stage whether the expanding role of world trade seen in Table 3.9 was accompanied by an increase in the share of that trade conducted on a *regional* basis. It would seem natural that nations would tend to trade more with their immediate neighbours in the first instance, thereby raising the share of world trade occurring between nations within a specific geographical region. This tendency towards *intra-regional* trade can be seen in Table 3.10.

From Table 3.10 it can be seen that the share of intra-regional trade grew most rapidly in Western Europe between 1948 and 2006, while in Asia and North America the share of intra-regional trade also increased but to a lesser degree. Intra-regional trade occurring in other regions remained largely unchanged or even declined (i.e. deregionalisation of trade), as seen in the early and mid-1990s in Central and Eastern Europe, though some renewed growth in intra-regional trade has occurred since 1996. It is also clear from Table 3.10 that intra-regional trading is not a new phenomenon and that geographically adjacent nations in many areas of the world have been trading with each other for many years.

In Chapter 1 we have already noted the growth in preferential terms given to members of regional trading blocs (via regional trading arrangements – RTAs) which has, of course, been a key factor in the growth of intra-regional trade. Box 3.5 considers aspects of both 'trade creation' and 'trade diversion' resulting from regional trading

Table 3.10 **Share of intra-regional trade in total trade 1929–2006 (% of each region's total trade in goods occurring between nations located in that region)**

	1928	1938	1948	1968	1979	1996	2006
Western Europe	50.7	48.8	41.8	63.0	66.2	68.3	73.9
Central/Eastern Europe/USSR	19.0	13.2	46.4	63.5	54.0	18.7	22.8
North America	25.0	22.4	27.1	36.8	29.9	36.0	58.0
Latin America	11.1	17.7	17.7	18.7	20.2	21.2	24.5
Asia	45.5	66.4	38.9	36.6	41.0	51.9	52.6
Africa	10.3	8.9	8.4	9.1	5.6	9.2	9.9
Middle East	5.0	3.6	20.3	8.7	6.4	7.4	7.7

Source: WTO, Annual Reports (various).

arrangements which take the form of a customs union. We also review later in this chapter (p. 116) attempts by the World Trade Organisation (WTO) to remove some of the discriminatory effects (i.e. impacts on non-members) of such regional trading arrangements.

Forecasts suggest continued growth in intra-regional trade, especially should transport costs continue their downward trajectory. This, perhaps somewhat surprising forecast, is supported by the *World Development Report* 2009 (World Bank 2009: 174–6) which notes that international freight costs per ton kilometre have halved since the mid-1970s. Air freight costs fell even more substantially, with air freight prices falling from $3.87 per ton kilometre in 1955 to less than $0.30 per ton kilometre in 2004 (using constant 2000 US dollars). The conclusion of the Report states (World Bank 2009: 21):

> Falling transport costs increase trade more with neighbouring, not distant countries. With a decline in transport costs countries should trade more with countries that are farther away. But trade has become more localized than globalized. Countries trade more with countries that are similar because increasingly the basis of trade is the exploitation of economies of scale [via specialization] . . . falling transport costs make specialization possible.

Barriers to trade

Those involved in international business face a number of methods by which individual countries or regional trading blocs (*see* p. 107) seek to restrict the level of imports into the home market. The World Trade Organisation (WTO) plays an important role in seeking to regulate and remove many of these impediments to trade, as we note below (pp. 116–22).

Tariff

A *tariff* is, in effect, a tax levied on imported goods, usually with the intention of raising the price of imports and thereby discouraging their purchase. Additionally, it is a source of revenue for the government. Tariffs can be of two types: *lump sum* (or *specific*) with the tariff a fixed amount per unit; *ad valorem* (or *percentage*) with the tariff a variable amount per unit. There is a general presumption that tariff barriers will discourage trade and reduce economic welfare. Box 3.3 considers the possible impacts of a tariff in rather more detail.

Box 3.3   Impacts of a tariff

To examine the effect of a tariff, it helps simplify Figure 3.7 if we assume a perfectly elastic world supply of the good S_W at the going world price P_W which implies that any amount of the good can be imported into the UK without there being a change in the world price. In the absence of a tariff, the domestic price would be set by the world price, P_W in Figure 3.7. At this price domestic demand D_D will be $0Q_2$, though domestic supply S_D will only be $0Q_1$. The excess demand, $Q_2 - Q_1$, will be satisfied by importing the good.

If the government now decides to restrict the level of import penetration, it could impose a tariff of, say, $P_W - P'_W$. A tariff always shifts a supply curve vertically upwards by the amount

Box 3.3   Continued

of the tariff, so that in this case the world supply curve shifts vertically upwards from S_W to S'_W. This would raise the domestic price to P'_W which is above the world price P_W. This higher price will reduce the domestic demand for the good to $0Q_4$ while simultaneously encouraging domestic supply to expand from $0Q_1$ to $0Q_3$ and the government will gain tax revenue from the remaining imports which must now pay an import duty (area 3). All these are arguably 'positive' outcomes for governments. However, in terms of resource allocation, the impact of the tariff may be shown to be less favourable. Imports will be reduced from $Q_2 - Q_1$ before the tariff to $Q_4 - Q_3$ after the tariff. Domestic consumer surplus will decline as a result of the tariff by the area $1 + 2 + 3 + 4$, though domestic producer surplus will rise by area 1, and the government will gain tax revenue of $P'_W - P_W \times Q_4 - Q_3$ (i.e. area 3). These gains would be inadequate, however, to compensate consumers for their loss in welfare, yielding a net welfare loss of area $2 + 4$ as a result of imposing a tariff.

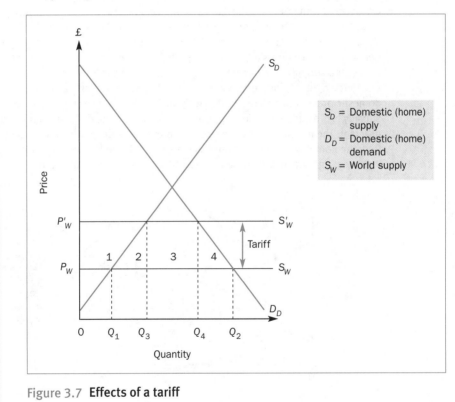

Figure 3.7   **Effects of a tariff**

Non-tariff barriers

In recent years there has also been a considerable increase in trade that is subject to *non-tariff* barriers. The main types of non-tariff barrier in use include the following:

- *Quotas.* A quota is a limit applied to the number of units (or the monetary value) of an imported good that may be sold in a country in a given period.
- *Voluntary export restraints* (VERs). These are arrangements by which an individual exporter or group of exporters agrees with an importing country to limit the

quantity of a specific product to be sold to a particular market over a given period of time. VERs are in effect, quotas. An example of a VER involved the import of cars from Japan into the EU. Until phased out in 2000, there was an understanding that Japanese producers would limit their sales into the UK, France, Spain, Italy and Portugal to a maximum of 1.1 million units in total (the figure excluded output from Japanese plants based in the EU).

■ *Subsidies.* The forms of protection we have described so far have all been designed to restrict the volume of imports directly. An alternative policy is to provide a subsidy to domestic producers so as to improve their competitiveness in both the home and world markets. The effect of subsidies is considered in more detail in Box 3.4.

Box 3.4   Impacts of a subsidy

Once again, with reference to Figure 3.8, we assume that the world supply curve is perfectly elastic at P_W. Under conditions of free trade, the domestic price is set by the world price at P_W. Domestic production is initially $0Q_1$ with imports satisfying the excess level of domestic demand which amounts to $Q_2 - Q_1$. The effect of a general subsidy to an industry would be to shift the supply curve of domestic producers downwards (by the amount of the subsidy) and to the right. The domestic price will remain unchanged at the world price P_W but domestic production will rise to $0Q_3$ with imports reduced to $Q_2 - Q_3$. If, however, the subsidy is provided solely for exporters, the impact on the domestic market could be quite different. The incentive to export may encourage more domestic production to be switched from the home market to the overseas markets, which in turn could result in an increased volume of imports to satisfy the unchanged level of domestic demand.

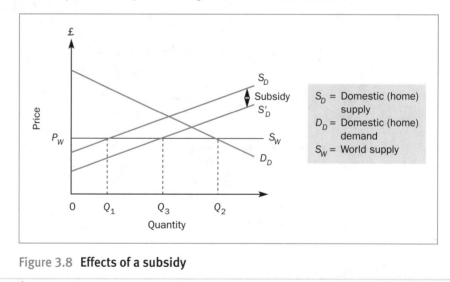

Figure 3.8   **Effects of a subsidy**

■ *Exchange controls.* A system of *exchange controls* was in force in the UK from the outbreak of the Second World War until 1979 when, in order to allow the free flow of capital, they were abolished. They enabled the government to limit the availability of foreign currencies and so curtail excessive imports; for instance, holding a foreign-currency bank account required permission from the Bank of England. Exchange controls could also be employed to discourage speculation and investment abroad.

■ *Safety and technological standards.* These are often imposed in the knowledge that certain imported goods will be unable to meet the specified requirements. The British government used such standards to prevent imports of French turkey and ultra-heat-treated (UHT) milk. Ostensibly the ban on French turkeys was to prevent 'Newcastle disease', a form of fowl pest found in Europe, from reaching the UK. The European Court ruled, however, that the ban was merely an excuse to prevent the free flow of imports.

■ *Time-consuming formalities.* During the 1990s the EU alleged that 'excessive invoicing requirements' required by US importing authorities had hampered exports from member countries to the USA. These problems abound in many parts of the world and often involve considerable administrative and capital costs for many companies. A similar problem in China can lead to a two or three weeks' delay.

■ *Public-sector contracts.* Government often give preference to domestic firms in the issuing of public contracts, despite EU directives requiring member governments to advertise such contracts. A number of Australian states have continued to give price preferences of up to 20% to domestic bidders for public contracts in the latter half of the 1990s. Public contracts are actually placed outside the country of origin in only 1% of cases.

■ *Labour standards.* This bears some resemblance to the point made above concerning safety and technological standards but is rather more controversial. Does the enforcement of minimum labour standards represent a source of support for the poorest workers in the developing world or is it simply a covert form of protection? Low-cost producers, not surprisingly, believe the latter to be the case. The WTO (*see* below) is at present reluctant to go down this route but has come under increasing pressure from governments in the industrialised world to take action on what is perceived as 'unfair' competition by countries which have few, if any, effective minimum labour standards.

Protectionist policies

In this section we briefly review the case for and against protectionist policies. Of course our earlier theoretical arguments supporting free trade (pp. 80–95) are themselves arguments against protectionist policies.

■ The case for protection

Protectionist measures may be applied on a selective or more widespread basis, with most of the measures currently in force falling into the first category. A number of arguments have been used to justify the application of both tariff and non-tariff barriers on a selective basis:

■ to prevent dumping;
■ to protect infant industries;
■ to protect strategically important industries;
■ to maintain employment by preventing the rapid contraction of labour-intensive industries.

Preventing dumping

Dumping occurs where a good is sold in an overseas market at a price below the real cost of production. We note below that under Article 6, the WTO allows retaliatory sanctions to be applied if it can be shown that the dumping materially affected the domestic industry. As well as using the WTO, countries within the EU can refer cases of alleged dumping for investigation by the European Commission. The Commission is then able to recommend the appropriate course of action, which may range from 'no action' where dumping is found not to have taken place, to either obtaining an 'undertaking' of no further dumping, or imposing a tariff.

The prevalence of dumping is indicated by a significant increase in the number of anti-dumping cases initiated by the WTO, as Table 3.11 illustrates, with 2001 seeing a record number in a single year. The US has consistently been one of the main initiators of anti-dumping investigations and has had such success in securing WTO approval for retaliatory tariffs that the current official figures for average US tariffs on manufactured imports of 6% rises to around 23% when these additional retaliatory tariffs are included. Canada, India and the European Union have also initiated numerous actions. The main targets of anti-dumping probes have been the European Union, China, Chinese Taipai and India. The sectors where anti-dumping measures are most widely applied include chemical products and base metals, in particular steel, which is currently a battleground between the US and the EU. The US steel industry has alleged that financial support from European governments has given the EU steel industry an unfair advantage over US producers. In response the US government imposed tariffs of up to 30 per cent on selected steel products in March 2002.

However, as Case Study 3.3 below indicates, an excessive enthusiasm for using 'dumping' as a reason for improving tariffs as a means of discouraging lower priced imports can be counterproductive.

Protecting infant industries

The use of protection in order to *establish new industries* is widely accepted, particularly in the case of developing countries. Article 18 of the WTO explicitly allows such protection. An infant industry is likely to have a relatively high-cost structure in the short run, and in the absence of protective measures may find it difficult to compete with the established overseas industries already benefiting from scale economies. The EU has used this argument to justify protection of its developing high-technological industries.

Protecting strategically important industries

The protection of industries for *strategic reasons* is widely practised both in the UK and the EU, and is not necessarily contrary to the WTO rules (Article 2). The protection of the UK steel industry has in the past been justified on this basis, and the EU has

Table 3.11 **Anti-dumping: cases initiated**

1987	1989	1993	1997	2001	2005
120	96	299	233	348	314

Source: WTO, Annual Reports (various).

used a similar argument to protect agricultural production throughout the Community under the guise of the CAP. In the Uruguay round of the then GATT (now WTO) the developing countries used this argument in seeking to resist calls for the liberalisation of trade in their service sectors. This has been one of the few sectors recording strong growth in recent years and is still a highly 'regulated' sector in most countries.

Maintaining levels of employment

There is a small but growing body of opinion that advocates a degree of protection to maintain levels of employment and that questions the benefits to be derived from international trade and is hostile to the drive by the WTO to liberalise trade. This movement, which is quite diverse, comprises environmentalists, trade unions, charities, third-world activists, among many others, and has manifested itself in WTO/IMF demonstrations in Seattle, Prague and many other locations in recent years. Although not necessarily rejecting the theoretical benefits of free trade, opponents of the WTO contend that the gains are largely expropriated by big business, leaving both workers and developing nations no better off and in many cases actually worse off. Groups such as Global Trade Watch suggest that the WTO has little regard for democracy or for environmental standards and almost always acts against the public interest.

Case against protectionism

A number of arguments are often advanced as reasons for avoiding protectionist policies.

Retaliation

A major drawback to protectionist measures is the prospect of retaliation. The consequences of retaliation could be especially serious for countries increasingly dependent on international trade flows. For example in 2007 German exports of goods and services totalled 38% of GDP, France was 24%, Italy 22% and the UK 19%, with lower percentages for the export : GDP ratio in Japan (14%), and the USA (8%).

Misallocation of resources

Protectionism can erode some of the benefits of free trade. For instance, Box 3.3 showed that a tariff raises domestic supply at the expense of imports. If the domestic producers cannot make such products as cheaply as overseas producers, then one could argue that encouraging high-cost domestic production is a misallocation of international resources.

A related criticism also suggests that protectionism leads to resource misallocation on an international scale, but this time concerns the multinational. Multinationals are the fastest-growing type of business unit in the Western economies, and they are increasingly adopting strategies which locate particular stages of the production process in (to them) appropriate parts of the world. Protectionism may disrupt the flow of goods from one stage of the production process to another, and in this sense inhibit global specialisation.

Case Study 3.3 indicates that imposing tariffs on products derived from globally distributed value chains can have 'unexpected' consequences for multinationals and their 'home' countries.

CASE 3.3 High cost of anti-dumping tariffs FT

Slapping extra tariffs on cheap 'dumped' imports can be counter-productive even when justified, Peter Mandelson, the then EU trade commissioner, told a conference in the Netherlands in 2007. He argued that anti-dumping tariffs and quotas could harm Europe's own manufacturers, which have increasingly outsourced the production of shoes, textiles, light bulbs and other goods, aiming to maintain a competitive edge against cheaper Asian rivals.

'Imposing punitive measures . . . is often both justified and right. But if it is inhibiting companies from pursuing rational production strategies . . . it can also be counter-productive,' he said. While Europe should tackle unfair trade, globalisation meant the definitions of what was European-made had become blurred.

Mr Mandelson said the European Commission had struggled before finally deciding in late 2007 to phase out anti-dumping duties on energy efficient light bulbs made by European companies in China over a year. He had wanted the punitive duties abolished immediately, but fellow commissioners won more time to protect Osram, the German company that is the sole European-based manufacturer. He said: 'If producing cheaply in China helps generate profits and jobs in Europe, how should we treat these companies when disputes over unfair trading arise?'

A further case was leather footwear. The imposition of tariffs on shoes for two years in 2006 led to duties of 16% for China and 10% for Vietnam. A Swedish government report says the duties have caused heavy losses among shoe importers, although these companies may be generating as much as 80% of each shoe's value in the EU through product design. Surveying five typical EU shoemakers, the Swedish government's National Board of Trade says the companies have become 'globalised', creating jobs and investment in the EU.

Even a €20 ($27, £13.50) pair of women's shoes adds value to the European economy. Intermedium, a Dutch company, pays €4.40 to bring the shoes to Europe, then sells them to retailers for €6.65. By that point, €2.45 of the total cost is classified as European value-added. Intermedium and its Chinese supplier make margins of less than 10% each.

For a more expensive €150 pair of shoes, DC of Milan charges retailers €77.80 of which leather accounts for a third. But €40 of €50 value-added is classed as European, mostly going to research and development. 'The European value-added is 79%,' says the report. 'Is this a European or Vietnamese shoe?'

Italy pushed hardest for the duties. Companies still producing entirely in Europe have benefited. Shoe importers, meanwhile, can simply switch their supply source to another low-cost country. 'Globalised' manufacturers, however, could not be so flexible. Since prices were fixed with retailers, most of those EU-based shoemakers had to absorb cost increases.

Source: Bounds, A., 'Mandelson warns on hidden cost of anti-dumping tariffs', *Financial Times*, 4 September 2007.

Question

What does this case study suggest in terms of the 'free trade versus protectionism' debate?

Regional trading arrangements

As we have noted above, the resumption of rapid growth in world trade after the Second World War was tied up with the desire for the resumption of *multilateral trade* under the auspices of the GATT (now WTO). However, this movement towards free trade was accompanied by a parallel movement towards the formation of *regional trading blocs* centred on the EU, North and South America and East Asia. We noted in Table 3.10 that intra-regional trading is not a new phenomenon but one which has been active for at least a century or more. However, there is evidence to suggest that the nations of a given region have begun to create more formal and comprehensive trading and economic links with each other than was previously the case.

There are four broad types of regional trading arrangements (RTAs):

1 *free trade areas*, where member countries reduce or abolish restrictions on trade between each other while maintaining their individual protectionist measures against non-members;
2 *customs unions*, where, as well as liberalising trade among members, a common external tariff is established to protect the group from imports from any non-members;
3 *common markets*, where the customs union is extended to include the free movement of factors of production as well as products within the designated area;
4 *economic unions*, where national economic policies are also harmonised within the common market.

We can usefully review at this point examples of different types of regional trading arrangements across the globe.

■ The European Union (EU) was founded in January 1958 as a *common market* with six member nations. By 2008 the EU included 27 nations with a population of around 490 million, and accounted for some 45% of world trade, with some 68% of EU exports going to other member countries. This group originated as a *common* market, the majority of members effectively progressing into a type of *economic union* with the Maastricht Treaty of 1992 and the advent of the euro and its related financial arrangements on 1 January 1999.
■ In August 1993 the North American Free Trade Agreement (NAFTA) was signed between the US, Canada and Mexico, having grown out of an earlier Canadian–US Free Trade Agreement (CUFTA). NAFTA, as the name implies is a *free trade area* with around 56% of NAFTA exports going to member countries, covering a population of 372 million and accounting for 31% of world output and 17% of world trade.
■ MERCOSUR was established in South America in 1991, evolving out of the Latin American Free Trade Area, with the four initial members being Argentina, Brazil, Paraguay and Uruguay. It developed into a partial *customs union* in 1995 when it imposed a common external tariff covering 85% of total products imported.
■ In Asia and the Pacific, the rather 'loose' Association of South-East Asian Nations (ASEAN) with a population of 300 million was formed in August 1967. In 1991 they agreed to form an ASEAN Free Trade Area (AFTA) by the year 2003. A Common

External Preference Tariff (CEPT) came into force in 1994 as a formal tariff-cutting mechanism for achieving *free trade* in all goods except agricultural products, natural resources and services. In November 1994, the goal of an open trade and investment area was agreed in principle by members of the Asia-Pacific Economic Cooperation Forum (APEC) which includes the members of ASEAN, ANZCERTA (Australia and New Zealand) and NAFTA as well as China, Japan, Korea, Hong Kong, Taiwan, and Papua New Guinea. It is hoped that this arrangement may be realised by 2010 for developed countries and by 2020 for developing countries. This group would account for 38% of the world's population (2.1 billion) and 43% of the world trade in goods.

- On the western side of Latin America, a *free trade area* has been established by Venezuela, Columbia, Ecuador, Peru and Bolivia (ANDEAN PACT).
- In Central and Eastern Europe, a *free trade area* has been established by Poland, the Czech Republic, Slovakia, Hungary, Slovenia, Romania and Bulgaria (CEFTA).

From the above examples it is possible to see that trading blocs have adopted various types of arrangements depending on their specific circumstances.

Three features have characterised post-war regional integration:

1 Post-war regional integration has been primarily centred in Western Europe. Out of 184 agreements notified to GATT/WTO between 1948 and 2002, more than half involved Western European countries, with most of the post-1990 agreements with the EU involving the Central and Eastern European countries.

2 Only a small number of post-war regional agreements have been concluded by developing countries. This is mainly due to continuing competition between these countries involving trade in similar products (e.g. primary products) together with the difficulty of achieving the political stability in some developing countries, which is so vital to trade.

3 The *type* of economic integration between the parties to agreements has varied quite significantly. Most of the notifications made to GATT/WTO have involved free trade areas, with the number of customs unions agreement being much smaller.

In recent years many of these free trade areas have taken the form of *bilateral trade treaties*, often involving the USA (*see* Chapter 1, p. 6).

Those who favour the regional approach argue that the setting up of trading blocs can enable individual countries to purchase products at lower prices because tariff walls between the member countries have been removed; this is the *trade creation effect*. They also argue that regional trading arrangements help to harmonise tax policies and product standards, while also helping to reduce political conflicts. Others argue that where the world is already organised into trading blocs, then negotiations in favour of free trade are more likely to be successful between these large and influential trading blocs than between a large number of individual countries with little power to bargain successfully for tariff reductions.

On the other hand, the critics of regionalism warn that regional trading blocs have, historically, tended to be inward looking, as in the 1930s when discriminatory trade blocs were formed to impose tariffs on non-members. Some also argue that member countries may suffer from being inside a regional bloc because they then have to buy products from within the bloc, when cheaper sources are often available from outside; i.e. the *trade diversion effect*. Further, it is argued that regionalism threatens to erode support for multilateralism in that business groups within a regional bloc will find it easier to obtain protectionist (trade diversionary) deals via preferential pacts than they would in the world of non-discriminatory trade practices favoured by the GATT/ WTO. Finally, it is argued that regionalism will move the world away from free trade due to the increasing tendency for members of a regional group to resort to the use of *non-tariff barriers* (VERs, anti-dumping duties, etc.) when experiencing a surge of imports from other countries inside the group. Such devices can then easily be used by individual countries against non-members from other regional groups.

Box 3.5 looks in more detail at the trade creation and trade diversion elements related to the establishment of a customs union.

Box 3.5   Customs Union: trade creation and trade diversion

As already noted, a customs union is a protected free trade area. Those who favour this approach argue that the setting up of such regional trading blocs can enable individual countries within a broad geographical region to purchase products at lower prices because tariff walls between the member countries have been removed; this is the *trade creation effect*. They also argue that such regional trading arrangements may create opportunities for still deeper integration, such as harmonising tax policies and product standards, while also helping to reduce political conflicts. Supporters also argue that where the world is already organised into trading blocs, then negotiations in favour of free trade are more likely to be successful when individual countries combine to form large and influential trading blocs: a large number of individual countries will, on their own, have little power to bargain successfully with existing trade blocs to secure tariff or subsidy reductions.

On the other hand, the critics of integration warn that regional trading blocs have, historically, tended to be inward looking, as in the 1930s when discriminatory trade blocs were formed to impose tariffs on non-members. Some also argue that member countries may suffer from being inside a regional bloc because they then have to buy products from within the bloc, when cheaper sources are often available from outside; i.e. the *trade diversion effect*. Critics also argue that such regionalism threatens to erode support for multilateralism in that business groups within a regional bloc will find it easier to obtain protectionist (trade diversionary) deals via preferential pacts than they would in the world of non-discriminatory trade practices favoured by the GATT/WTO.

Figure 3.9 looks in more detail at the trade creation versus trade diversion impacts of establishing a regional trading bloc.

We assume that the domestic country initially has a tariff (t) imposed on imports from two separate countries, A and B, both of which are lower (and constant) cost producers, as indicated by their horizontal supply curves S_A and S_B respectively. We assume the tariff (t) imposed on imports from both A and B rules the less efficient country A out from competing in the domestic market altogether but still allows the relatively more efficient country, B to compete.

The 'world' supply curve to the domestic market is therefore $S_d + (S_B + t)$ i.e. *LNK* giving a domestic price of P_d and domestic production of $0q_2$, with imports from country B of q_2q_3, but no trade at all with country A.

Suppose now a regional trading bloc, protected by the common external tariff t, is now formed between the domestic country and country A only. All tariffs between the domestic

▶

Box 3.5   Continued

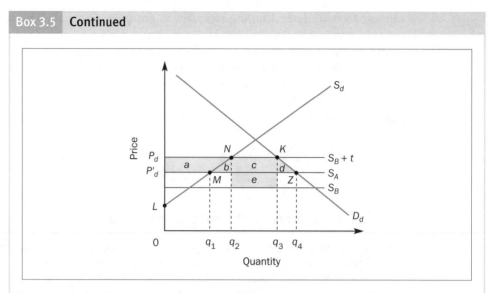

Figure 3.9   Customs Union, trade creation and trade diversion

country and country A are abolished (it is a protected free trade area) so that the 'world' supply curve to the domestic market now becomes *LMZ*. Price in the domestic market falls to P'_d, with imports from country A of q_1q_4 but now no imports from country B.

We have, in this example both trade creation and trade diversion.

- *Trade creation:* The result of removing the tariff *t* on trade with country A has created extra trade (with A) of the magnitude $q_1q_2 + q_3q_4$.
- *Trade diversion:* The result of removing the tariff *t only* on country A (i.e. forming a trading bloc with A) has enabled country A to undercut country B (the more efficient producer) in the domestic market. The volume of trade q_2q_3 previously undertaken with B prior to the trading bloc is now undertaken with the less efficient producer A. Trade has been 'diverted' by the formation of the trading bloc.

Using our earlier ideas of consumer and producer surplus, we can seek to measure gains and losses from trade creation and trade diversion. In Figure 3.9, the reduction in price from P_d to P'_d via creating the trading bloc has increased *consumer surplus* by area $(a + b + c + d)$, but reduced *producer surplus* by area *a*, since domestic production has fallen from q_2 to q_1. The *tariff revenue* $(c + e)$ previously earned on trade with country B is also lost as trade is diverted to tariff free country A.

As long as the *net* benefits $(b + c + d)$ brought about from trade creation exceed the losses $(c + e)$ brought about from trade diversion, then the formation of the economic trading bloc can be regarded as beneficial overall.

Some general observations can be made from this analysis as to when the above condition is most likely to hold and to support the creation of a trading bloc.

- *The greater the degree of overlap in the economies of the countries contemplating the formation of an economic bloc*, the greater the likelihood that the bloc will be a trade-creating one. If economies do not overlap, as in the case when a basically agricultural producing country joins a mainly manufacturing country, then there is little scope for trade creation but a great deal of scope for trade diversion.

Box 3.5	Continued

- *The greater the differences in production costs between the potential members in their overlapping industries*, the greater the potential for trade creation. Conversely if the differences in costs are small, so will be the potential gains.
- *The higher the tariff rates prior to the amalgamation of the economies*, the greater the gains from the associated tariff reductions.

It follows that the greatest gains from the formation of an economic group can be achieved if:

- The economic structure of the economies overlap.
- The industries that are common to both have a wide variation in their costs.
- The level of import tariffs placed by those countries on one another's products is high prior to the formation of the bloc.

Government policies and international business

Government policies can influence international business in a variety of ways, some of which have already been considered in Chapter 2. For example, change in fiscal policies (involving government spending/taxation) or monetary policies (involving money supply/interest rates) will influence the macroeconomic environment in which domestic and international businesses operate. However, sometimes government policies can impact upon international business *indirectly*; for example, changes in interest rates may influence the price of currencies on the foreign exchange markets (*see* Chapter 4), which in turn may exert a strong influence on the prospects for exporting and importing products across national boundaries. It is to this issue of exchange rates that we first turn our attention.

Exchange rates

We note in Chapter 4 that few governments can now influence their exchange rates directly, via unilateral action. More usually they can only influence such rates indirectly whether intentionally or unintentionally. For example, high interest rates used as part of an anti-inflationary monetary policy may make a country's currency relatively attractive on foreign exchange markets, the extra demand then raises the price of that country's currency.

A *rise* in, say, the UK sterling exchange rate makes UK exports dearer abroad in terms of the foreign currency, and UK imports cheaper at home in terms of the domestic currency. Suppose, for example, sterling *appreciates* against the euro from £1 = €1.10 to £1 = €1.40. An item priced at £1000 in the UK would have a euro-zone equivalent price of €1100 prior to the sterling appreciation but €1400 after that appreciation. Not only will exports be dearer abroad but imports will be cheaper at home. An item priced at €1100 in the euro-zone would have a sterling equivalent price of £1000 prior to the sterling appreciation but £785.7 after that appreciation.

The impact of higher export prices and lower import prices on business turnover (and the balance of payments) will depend to some extent on *price elasticities of demand* in the export and import markets respectively.

- If *price elasticity of demand for UK exports is relatively elastic* (greater than one), then any rise in euro-zone prices will reduce total expenditure in euros on those items. Since each euro is now worth less in sterling, this fall in the euro value of UK exports will mean a still more substantial fall in sterling turnover for UK exporters.
- If *price elasticity of demand for UK imports is relatively elastic* (greater than one), then any fall in sterling prices will raise total expenditure in sterling on those items. This is likely to imply a loss of turnover and market share from UK domestic producers to euro-zone producers.

Clearly the more elastic the respective price elasticities of demand for UK exports and UK imports, the greater the disadvantage for businesses located in the UK in trading with the euro-zone after sterling appreciates against the euro, and the greater the advantage for businesses located in the euro-zone in trading with the UK.

For illustrative purposes only we have used an example of sterling rising in value against the euro. In fact (*see* Chapter 10, p. 367) sterling has fallen substantially against both the euro and US dollar in recent times.

pause for thought 5 Can you work through the previous analysis if sterling *depreciates* against the euro? (For example, suppose £1 is now worth €1.00 instead of €1.40.)

Import protection/export support

We have already seen how a variety of *protective trade barriers* (such as tariffs and quotas) can be used to discourage imports into a country, whether imposed unilaterally by a country or collectively as part of a regional trading bloc. An example of the latter would be the Common External Tariff imposed on industrial imports into the EU. Domestic producers can also be helped vis-à-vis overseas producers by a variety of support policies directed towards exporters.

The Common Agricultural Policy (CAP) of the EU provides a useful illustration of government-directed policies involving import protection/export support which exert a strong influence on the operations of farms and agri-businesses, both inside and outside the EU. Box 3.6 considers the operation of the CAP in rather more detail.

Box 3.6 Impacts of EU policies on farms and agri-businesses

The formal title for the executive body of the CAP is the European Agricultural Guarantee and Guidance Fund (EAGGF), often known by its French translation of 'Fonds Européen d'Orientation et de Garantie-Agricole' (FEOGA). As its name implies, one of its key roles is in operating the 'guarantee system' for EU farm incomes.

Different agricultural products are dealt with in slightly different ways, but the basis of the system is the establishment of a 'target price' for each product (Figure 3.10(a)). The target price is not set with reference to world prices, but is based upon the price which producers need to cover costs, including a profit mark-up, in the highest-cost area of production in the

Box 3.6   Continued

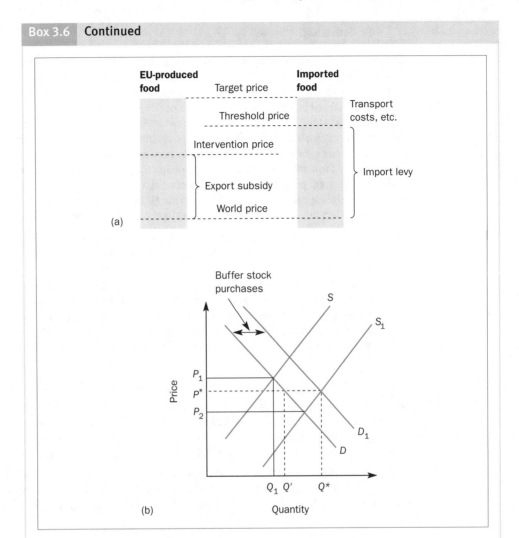

Figure 3.10 (a) CAP system: world price below target price and (b) Guarantee system: maintaining the intervention price (P*)

EU. The EU then sets an 'intervention' or 'guaranteed' price for the product in that area, about 7–10% below the target price. Should the price be in danger of falling below this level, the Commission intervenes to buy up production to keep the price at or above the 'guaranteed' level. The Commission then sets separate target and intervention prices for that product in each area of the Community, related broadly to production costs in that area. As long as the market price in a given area (there are 11 such areas in the UK) is above the intervention price, the producer will sell his produce at prevailing market prices. In effect the intervention price sets a 'floor' below which market price will not be permitted to fall and is therefore the guaranteed minimum price to producers.

In Figure 3.10(b) an increase in supply of agricultural products to S_1 would, if no action were taken, lower the market price from P_1 to P_2 below the intervention or guaranteed price, P^*. At P^* demand is Q' but supply is Q^*. To keep the price at P^*, the EAGGF will buy up the excess $Q^* - Q'$. In terms of Figure 3.10(b), the demand curve is artificially increased to D_1 by the EAGGF purchase.

> **Box 3.6** **Continued**
>
> If this system of guaranteed minimum prices is to work, EU farmers must be protected from low-priced imports from overseas. To this end, levies or tariffs are imposed on imports of agricultural products. If in Figure 3.10(b) the price of imported food were higher than the EU target price then, of course, there would be no need for an import tariff. If, however, the import price is below this, say at the 'world price' in Figure 3.10(a), then an appropriate tariff must be calculated. This need not quite cover the difference between 'target' and 'world' price, since the importer still has to pay transport costs within the EU to get the food to market. The tariff must therefore be large enough to raise the import price at the EU frontier to the target price minus transport costs, i.e. 'threshold price'. This calculation takes place in the highest-cost area of production in the EU, so that the import tariff set will more than protect EU producers in areas with lower target prices (i.e. lower-cost areas).
>
> Should an EU producer wish to export an agricultural product, an export subsidy will be paid to bring his receipts up to the intervention price (*see* Figure 3.10(a)), i.e. the minimum price he would receive in the home market. Problems involving this form of subsidy of oil-seed exports have been a major threat to dealings between the EU and the USA (*see* Chapter 4), with the latter alleging a breach of WTO rules. The system outlined above does not apply to all agricultural products in the EU. About a quarter of these products are covered by different direct subsidy systems, e.g. olive oil and tobacco, and some products such as potatoes, agricultural alcohol, and honey are not covered by EU regulation at all.

Reforms of the CAP over the past decade or so have modified this system which has proved an expensive method of supporting farm incomes. For example, Maximum Guaranteed Quantities (MGQs) have now been set for most agricultural products. If the MGQ is exceeded, the intervention price is cut by 30% in the following year. Further CAP reforms were also agreed in 2003 which came into effect from 2007 onwards. For example 'compulsory modulation' has been introduced whereby payments directly related to agricultural production have been progressively replaced by payments for a wide range of environmental protection activities by EU farmers.

■ Taxation policies

The ability of 'footloose' multinational enterprises to take advantage of tax discrepancies between countries or regions is well known, as in the examples of 'transfer pricing' (*see* Chapter 9, p. 366). Case Study 3.4 shows how the issue of 'tax havens' has risen to greater prominence in an era where governments are seeking greater tax revenues to fund their increased budget deficits from 'bailing out' endangered domestic firms and organisations during the so-called 'credit crunch'.

CASE 3.4 **Harbours of resentment** **FT**

There is growing hostility to the tiny states and islands around the world that harbour an estimated $6,000 billion (£3,895 billion, €4,725 billion) of offshore assets. After months of financial crisis and banking scandals that rocked Liechtenstein and Switzerland, the world's most powerful countries have lost patience.

In Washington in November 2008, finance ministers from the Group of 20 leading industrial and developing nations concluded that tax secrecy 'should be vigorously addressed'. In December 2008 it was the turn of the developing countries. At a United Nations meeting on development in Doha, tax havens came under fire for fuelling capital flight.

'The political climate on the issue of tax havens has changed dramatically over the past three months,' says Jeffrey Owens of the Paris-based Organisation for Economic Co-operation and Development. As the official who has driven the international crackdown on secrecy for more than a decade, he says the new climate could turn the reform promises extracted from many offshore centres into a reality. The financial crisis has intensified the attack on havens. The near-collapse of the West's banking industry has drastically increased governments' need to raise funds, brutally exposed the risks inherent in small countries with large financial sectors, and raised questions about the role of offshore centres in destabilising the system.

Some European finance ministers claim that the 'opaque environment' of offshore finance – particularly hedge funds – contributed to reckless behaviour and, ultimately, the current crisis. President Nicolas Sarkozy of France is among those questioning whether, at a time of taxpayer-funded bail-outs, banks should even be allowed to operate in tax havens.

Onshore businesses in London and New York exploit the offshore benefits offered by the likes of Jersey and the Cayman Islands to optimise the tax efficiency of certain deals, such as the repackaging of debt and cross-border lending. The havens themselves reject claims that they fuelled the crisis. 'It is like blaming a car manufacturer for road crashes,' says an official in one of Britain's overseas territories.

The arrival of Barack Obama in the White House provokes even more anxiety for the havens. As well as launching last year's Stop Tax Haven Abuse Act, the president-elect helped this year to launch the Incorporation Transparency and Law Enforcement Assistance Act. This aims to make it easier for investigators to 'see through opaque corporate ownership structures' and stop the flow of offshore funds to the US from hedge funds and private equity that are 'of unknown origin' but do not have to pass money-laundering checks.

On the campaign trail, Mr Obama also laid bare his hostility to the corporate use of offshore jurisdictions for international tax planning, which analysts estimate accounts for between one-third and a half of the revenues that Washington loses through offshore evasion and avoidance. 'There is a building in the Cayman Islands that houses supposedly 12,000 US-based corporations,' he said. 'That's either the biggest building in the world or the biggest tax scam in the world, and we know which one it is.'

The dangers of focusing solely on small players while ignoring similar shortcomings in some industrialised countries was one lesson of an OECD crackdown on secrecy launched in 1996. Tax havens have exploited this evident hypocrisy to stall reforms pending the introduction of a 'level playing field'.

Delaware is a state in the US which is infamous for allowing corporate financial secrecy of the kind that Barack Obama and many others are seeking to shatter in offshore financial centres. Arguments over Delaware – whose more than 600,000 registered companies compare with an estimated 865,000 inhabitants – are part of a broader fight over what many havens see as rich-country double standards in international action to tackle money laundering and tax evasion. 'The reality of Delaware is not lost on anybody,' says one official involved in efforts to improve financial transparency.

Delaware's corporations are under no obligation to file names of shareholders or beneficial owners, according to a 2006 report by the intergovernmental Financial Action Task Force on money laundering. The state offers a structure known as a limited liability company, which can be registered with not much more than a name and address. The report says Delaware company agents advertise the state as allowing even greater secrecy than offshore tax havens. 'The Delaware LLC provides the anonymity that most international jurisdictions do not offer,' claims one agent website quoted by the task force.

Carl Levin, the senator with whom Mr Obama has campaigned on tax haven reform, is critical of the US failure to heed the task force's calls to lift the confidentiality surrounding companies in Delaware and states such as Nevada and Wyoming.

Source: Houlder, V. and Peel, M., 'Harbours of resentment', *Financial Times*, 1 December 2008, p. 11.

Question

Examine the costs and benefits that might result from government policies to remove 'tax havens'.

International institutions and world trade

Here we pay particular attention to the role of the World Trade Organisation (WTO), as successor to the earlier General Agreement on Tariffs and Trade (GATT). In Chapter 10 we look in more detail at the role of other institutions that also play a key role in underpinning the world trading system, such as the International Monetary Fund (IMF) and the World Bank.

■ General Agreement on Tariffs and Trade (GATT)

The General Agreement on Tariffs and Trade was signed in 1947 by 23 industrialised nations that included the UK, USA, Canada, France and the Benelux countries. The objectives of GATT were to reduce tariffs and other barriers to trade in the belief that freer trade would raise living standards in all participating countries. Since 1947 there have been eight 'rounds' of trade negotiations with the average tariff in the industrialised nations falling from 40% in 1947 to below 5% in 1995 when the GATT was replaced by the World Trade Organisation (WTO). Supporters of the role of GATT point to facts such as the volume of world trade rising by 1500% and world output by 600% over the years of its existence.

■ The World Trade Organisation (WTO)

The World Trade Organisation replaced GATT in 1995 and now has 147 members, with the People's Republic of China, Chinese Taipei and Cambodia being the latest to join. The WTO's members in total account for more than 90% of the value of world trade.

The objectives of the WTO are essentially the same as GATT's, namely to reduce tariffs and other barriers to trade and to eliminate discrimination in trade, and by doing so contribute to rising living standards and a fuller use of world resources.

■ WTO authority

Trade disputes between member states now come under the auspices of the WTO, which has been given more powers than GATT to enforce compliance, using streamlined disputes procedure with provision for appeals and binding arbitration. Whereas under GATT any single member (including the one violating GATT rules) could block a ruling of unfair trade, the findings of the WTO's disputes panels cannot be blocked by a veto of a member state. Countries found to be in violation of a WTO principle must remove the cause of that violation or pay compensation to the injured parties. If the offending party fails to comply with a WTO ruling, the WTO can sanction certain types of retaliation by the aggrieved party.

Since its creation in January 1995, more than 240 cases have been brought before the WTO against only 200 cases brought before GATT in the 47 years of its existence. More than half of these have involved the USA and the EU while around one-quarter have involved developing countries. The WTO also seeks to provide a forum for further multilateral trade negotiations.

■ WTO principles

Both the GATT and its successor the WTO have sought to implement a number of principles:

- *non-discrimination*: the benefits of any trading advantage agreed between two nations (i.e. in bilateral negotiations) must be extended to all nations (i.e. become multilateral). This is sometimes referred to as the 'most-favoured nation' clause;
- *progressive reduction in tariff and non-tariff barriers*: certain exceptions, however, are permitted in specific circumstances. For example, Article 18 allows for the protection of 'infant industries' by the newly industrialising countries, whereas Article 19 permits any country to abstain from a general tariff cut in situations where rising imports might seriously damage domestic production. Similarly, Articles 21–5 allow protection to continue where 'strategic interests' are involved, such as national security;
- *solving trade disputes through consultation rather than retaliation*: again, certain exceptions are permitted. For example, Article 6 permits retaliatory sanctions to be applied if 'dumping' can be proven, i.e. the sale of products at artificially low prices (e.g. below cost). Countries in dispute are expected to negotiate bilaterally, but if these negotiations break down a WTO appointed working-party or panel can investigate the issue and make recommendations. Should any one of the parties refuse to accept this outcome, the WTO can impose fines and/or sanction certain types of retaliation by the aggrieved party.

The WTO has inherited 28 separate accords agreed under the final round of GATT negotiations (the Uruguay round). These accords sought to extend fair trade rules from industrial products to agricultural products, services, textiles, intellectual property rights and investment.

Although the majority of cases heard by the WTO have been brought by the US and EU, there are signs that this is beginning to change. China and other rapidly developing countries are themselves using the WTO to challenge what they see as protectionist policies and actions by the developed economies. Case Study 3.5 provides such an example.

CASE 3.5   WTO to rule on US import duties   FT

The World Trade Organisation agreed on 20 January 2009 to rule on a dispute launched by China over US curbs on imports of steel pipes, tyres and woven sacks.

It is the first case that China has pushed to a dispute panel on its own initiative since it joined the WTO at the end of 2001. The move underscores the growing assertiveness of the world's second-largest exporter in global economic diplomacy.

Before taking office yesterday the administration of Barack Obama pledged to take a tough line against allegedly unfair Chinese trade practices, including undervaluation of its currency. But China has signalled its readiness to challenge actions that may breach WTO rules.

The case involves four sets of parallel anti-dumping and anti-subsidy duties imposed by the US on two types of steel pipe, pneumatic off-road tyres and laminated woven sacks.

China is particularly upset about a US decision in 2007 to change its methodology in subsidy investigations, which has led to the levying of duties against Chinese businesses. Washington, which classifies China as a 'non-market economy', previously confined punitive measures against Chinese imports to anti-dumping duties.

The 'non-market' classification has made it easier for US companies to win anti-dumping actions against Chinese competitors. To claim dumping – selling goods abroad for less than the price at home – US groups can base their price comparisons on data from other countries rather than the Chinese prices. The US has also extended the non-market methodology to investigations involving subsidies.

Beijing argues that imposing two sets of duties on its exports is a 'double remedy' that is illegal and unfair. It notes that Washington has also levied parallel duties on four more products from China and launched parallel dumping and subsidy investigations on a further eight.

China told the WTO's dispute settlement body yesterday that it was 'greatly concerned by the various substantive and procedural problems found in the US anti-dumping and countervailing duty investigations and measures against Chinese products at issue'.

Under WTO rules the panel should issue its decision towards the end of 2009, though procedural delays and subsequent appeals are likely to postpone a final verdict to 2010.

The case is the third China has been involved in against the US in the WTO. The US has brought seven WTO cases against China.

Source: Williams, F., 'WTO to rule on US import duties', *Financial Times*, 21 January 2009.

Question

Examine the reasons for China bringing this WTO case.

■ Perspectives on WTO initiatives

Despite its greater authority, not everyone is convinced that the WTO is using that authority effectively or fairly. It may be useful to briefly review the arguments of both critics and supporters of the WTO.

Critics of the WTO

- *Bias to the 'North'*. Developing countries ('South') exporting to the advanced industrialised countries ('North') face tariffs on their exports that are four to five times higher than those placed on exports from advanced industrialised countries. For example the average tariffs on imports of textiles and garments from developing countries into industrialised countries are 15%–20%, as compared to only 3% on the imports of industrial goods. As a result Bangladesh, one of the world's poorest countries, pays the US $314 million a year in import taxes – about the same as France, the world's fifth richest economy (Walker 2002).

- *Inability to progress the Doha Round of negotiations*. The most recent round of multilateral negotiations by the WTO to reduce trade restrictions began in Doha, Qatar, in 2001. Promises were made to reduce restrictions on trade in textiles and agricultural products (among others) which together account for around 70% of the exports of developing countries. Little progress has been made in either. For example, industrialised countries promised to phase out an elaborate system of quotas applied to textile imports by 2005 but by 2008 many of these quotas still remained. Reducing tariffs on agricultural imports and the subsidies given to agricultural exports was also a key element of the Doha Round. Yet little progress has been made as the powerful agri-businesses in the EU and USA lobby effectively against such measures.

- *Undue pressure on the 'South'*. Critics argue that the WTO is only consistent and effective in pursuing its free trade credentials when it places intense pressures for import liberalisation on the developing ('South') countries. The impact of such pressures can be seen from the fact that indices of 'trade openness' currently place 17 African countries as more accessible to import penetration than either the EU or the US. Yet the most successful developing countries have been those of East Asia which have liberalised slowly and in a staged manner, only lowering trade barriers as domestic productivity rises and home industries become more competitive on world markets.

- *Undue emphasis on protecting trade-related aspects of intellectual property rights*. The 'North' countries account for some 90% of world patents and successfully secured increased protection for intellectual property rights in the WTO 'TRIPS Agreement' (*see* p. 152) in 1995. However, the developing countries insisted before agreeing to the current Doha Round of negotiations, that a declaration be made at Doha confirming their right to 'set aside patents in the interests of public health and to buy or make cheap generic versions of expensive drugs'. While the developing countries see this as applying to any condition which undermines public health, whether diabetes, cancer, asthma, HIV/Aids or whatever the large pharmaceutical companies have sought to limit the list of diseases to which this 'right' applies to malaria, tuberculosis and HIV/Aids, and to give only the poorest countries the opportunity of exercising this 'right'. With no agreement yet reached, critics blame the

WTO for being ineffectual in failing to secure a more broad based application of this 'right' enshrined in the Doha Declaration.

- *Undue emphasis on liberalising trade in services.* Of course many other criticisms have been levelled at the WTO, as for example the suggestion that it is too compliant in seeking to open world markets in *services*, to the benefit of the 'North'. Major proposals for wholesale deregulation of services have been proposed by the EU and US, opening up everything from banking and insurance to energy, water, sanitation and a host of 'public services'.

- *'Localisation' as an alternative doctrine.* Critics of the WTO include adherents of a doctrine opposed to unbridled free trade, namely 'localisation' which proposes that everything that can be produced locally should be produced locally, and to that end nations should protect their economies using trade taxes and legal barriers, though some international trade is still envisaged. The author of the 'localisation' manifesto, Colin Hines, suggests that 'some long-distance trade will still occur for those sectors providing goods and services to other regions of the world that can't provide such items from within their own borders, e.g. certain minerals or cash crops'. However, this is clearly a minimalist world trading environment which, in this view, hardly needs a WTO to regulate and expand it!

---

pause for thought 6   Outline the arguments that could be used both for and against 'localisation'.

Supporters of the WTO may even accept some of these criticisms, yet focus on its role in preventing still greater excesses in a global environment characterised by grossly unequal power relationships between 'North' and 'South'. We now review a number of counter-arguments presented by supporters of the WTO.

■ Supporters of the WTO

- *Unilateralism/bilateralism may be the alternative to multilateralism.* We noted (p. 117) that the WTO embodies a *multilateral* approach to trade negotiations, as in the 'most favoured nation' clause extending benefits to all. We also noted the growth of *bilateral* trade treaties and regional trade arrangements in Chapter 1 (p. 6) which threaten this multilateral approach. In seeking to avoid such discriminatory treaties and arrangements, the WTO has won considerable support. Indeed some see powerful nations (e.g. US) or supranational bodies (e.g. EU) as seeking to impose their own *unilateral* rules on world trading practices and regard the WTO as an indispensable bulwark in the fight against such unilateralism.

- *Absence of rules may be the alternative to imperfect WTO rules.* Even critics of the WTO often hesitate to contemplate a world trading regime with no rules whatsoever. As George Monbiot, a previously strong critic of the WTO has admitted: 'The only thing worse than a world with the wrong international trade rules is a world with no trade rules at all' (Monbiot 2003a).

- *WTO has not distorted trade patterns.* Two working papers for the National Bureau of Economic Research in the US by Richard Rose (2003) suggested that the World Trade Organisation scarcely merits the demonisation it receives. On the basis of extensive research, he finds the WTO members do not display significantly different trading patterns from non-members. Traditional linkages among countries, such as belonging to the same regional trade pact, or sharing languages, borders or colonial histories, appear to be more powerful factors in explaining variations in trade. Membership of WTO and its predecessor organisation, the GATT, appears to have had no strong or consistent impact on policy either, judged by 64 measures of trade policy openness.

■ *WTO is taking more robust action against trade restrictions from the 'North'.* The WTO has, in fact, taken firm action against trade distortions from advanced industrialised economies such as the US, as for example involving its impositions of steel tariffs on imports. The WTO ruled in July 2003 that the US had violated international trading rules when it imposed tariffs of up to 30 per cent on steel imports in 2002. The decision, by a dispute settlement panel of the WTO, was in a case brought by the EU and seven other countries. The US had imposed tariffs of up to 30% in March 2002 on many imported steel products, saying that ailing US steel companies needed protection against a flood of cheap foreign steel. The tariffs particularly hit steelmakers in the EU, Japan and Korea, while excluding most developing countries as well as Mexico and Canada. Brussels had argued that the duties were illegal because they failed to meet the basic test for a safeguard action – a recent surge in imports. Under WTO rules, countries can extend temporary protection to industries hit by import competition, but only under strict conditions. The US had previously lost half a dozen WTO cases concerning safeguard measures, including curbs on steel, wheat, gluten and lamb. The WTO ruled that there was no evidence of such a surge in imports due, as alleged, to 'dumping' by non-US companies of steel in US markets and the WTO gave permission for the disadvantaged countries to retaliate by imposing tariffs themselves on a range of specified US products to the estimated value of the losses they themselves had suffered from the unwarranted tariffs the US had imposed on their exports. (In the event the various countries chose not to exercise this option of retaliation.)

■ *'Localisation'* is viewed by free-traders as diminishing the wealth of poorer nations rather than enhancing it. The World Bank (Dollar and Kraay 2000) has argued that increased openness to trade (the opposite of localisation) raises average incomes and the incomes of the poor; i.e. there is no relationship between increased openness to trade and rising inequality, if anything quite the opposite. Sebastian Edwards of the University of California also concludes in a study of 93 countries that there is a close link between openness to trade and rates of productivity growth. In this view 'localisation' is itself seen as a recipe for increased inequality. George Monbiot, a previous adherent of localisation, observes with some irony that the doctrine itself relies upon enhanced political globalisation.

Colin Hines' model invents a whole new series of global bodies to impose localisation on nation states whether they like it or not. States would be forbidden to pass laws that diminish local control of industry and services. Hines, in other words, prohibits precisely the kind of political autonomy he claims to promote (Monbiot 2003a).

■ *Reformed WTO may have much to commend it.* Even critics of the WTO see the potential for this body undergoing reform to the benefit of the global trading system. Many suggest that greater 'fairness' to the developing countries would result from the WTO placing greater emphasis on the short-term protection of infant-industries and the short-term use of intellectual property rights in the developing countries. Developing countries could then follow the well-trodden path of the now developed countries which, historically, used trade barriers and the acquisition (legally or illegally) of intellectual property to grow themselves. A second 'fairness' might involve extending the rules currently applied by the voluntary 'fair trade' movement to all companies involved in international trade. For example George Monbiot (2003b) suggests that for a company to acquire a (WTO) licence to trade internationally, it would have to demonstrate that it and its suppliers applied certain minimum conditions to the labour force and to environmental protection.

The International Monetary Fund (IMF)

The IMF plays a key role in providing foreign currencies and other sources of world liquidity to support the growth of international trade and payments. It also provides specific packages of financial support for economies in times of need. This latter role involves a variety of 'stabilisation programmes' (*see* p. 125), which provide essential funding but only on condition that the countries receiving funds agree to implement specific programmes of change agreed with the IMF.

■ Foreign currencies and world liquidity

In order to settle balance of payments deficits arising from international trade, theory tells us that deficit countries should be able to run down their foreign exchange reserves or to borrow from surplus countries. Both methods have, in reality, proved next to impossible. The countries most likely to suffer balance of payments deficits are those with low per capita incomes and with few foreign exchange reserves, in other words, countries with low credit ratings on the international banking circuit, making borrowing from surplus countries difficult. It was in order to solve just these sorts of liquidity problems for deficit countries that the IMF was established.

The IMF began in 1946 with just 39 members, but is now a giant international organisation with 171 members. It has an unwieldy board of governors, with one governor from each member country. However, day-to-day decisions are taken by an executive board of twenty-two members, seven of whom are appointed by the USA, Germany, the UK, France, Japan, Saudi Arabia and China, with the remaining 15 elected from geographical constituencies.

Currency quotas

The IMF was originally set up to provide a pool of foreign currencies, which could be used by members to 'finance' temporary balance of payments deficits. This would give deficit countries time to 'adjust' their deficits, i.e. adopt policies which would eventually eliminate them without having to resort to immediate and massive deflations aimed at cutting spending on imports, or to sudden moves towards protectionist measures, or to reductions in the exchange rate to regain price competitiveness. By helping deficit countries to finance their deficits, the IMF was therefore seeking to promote the smooth growth of world income and trade.

Quotas

These have been assigned to each country to determine its access to foreign currency and also its voting rights within the IMF. Critics of the IMF point out that these quotas were allocated *pro rata* to each country's total value of trade, so that in practice the richer countries received much higher quotas than poorer, less trade oriented countries. So for example, in 2006 the US Quota (against which it could access 125%, over 5 years, in foreign currencies) was equivalent to around $40 billion, while that for Tonga and Bhutan was a mere $7 million or so.

Borrowing facilities

There are, however, further facilities for borrowing, with varying degrees of strictness as to the conditions attached. As we shall see, these various facilities and practices, and especially the creation of SDRs (*see* p. 124) have together changed the nature of the IMF. It is no longer the rather conservative institution of its Articles, simply reallocating a *given* pool of world currencies, but one which can intervene actively to find varied sources of finance and even to *create* new world money.

- *Compensatory Financing Facility* (CFF). The CFF was introduced in 1963 to assist primary producing countries in difficulty due to a temporary fall in export earnings (e.g. crop failure or natural disaster).
- *Compensatory and Contingency Financing Facility* (CCFF). This superseded the CFF in August 1988. It has added the possibility of contingency financing to support agreed structural adjustment programmes.
- *Extended Fund Facilities* (EFF). The EFF began in 1974 and was introduced to provide countries with more time to adjust their financial affairs. Most IMF loans had to be repaid in three to five years, but the EFF initially gave up to eight years for repayment, and now even longer.
- *Oil Facilities*. These were temporary facilities established in 1974 to assist countries whose balance of payments had been severely hit by rising oil prices. In theory, the oil facility had an upper limit of 450% of quota (to enable less developed countries with very low quotas to receive significant assistance), but some countries received loans up to 800% of quota. The oil facilities were ended in 1976.
- *Bufferstock Facility*. This was established in June 1969 to finance the building up of bufferstocks by commodity producers at times of falling world prices. Up to 45% of the quota is permitted for this purpose.

In addition to its 'normal' resources, the IMF has a variety of other instruments and facilities at its disposal:

- *Supplementary Financing Facility* (SFF). This is actually a separate trust, established with the IMF as a trustee, in February 1979. It originally borrowed SDR 7.5 billion from the oil producers to assist countries that had exceeded their Credit Tranche borrowing.
- *Enlarged Access Facilities*. Set up in May 1981 after SFF money became fully committed, it allows members to borrow up to 150% of quota in a single year, or up to 450% of quota over a three-year period. The intention is to assist countries with large deficits relative to quota.

- *Structural Adjustment Facility* (SAF). In 1986 a new 'structural adjustment facility' was implemented in order to recycle the loan repayments to some of the Fund's poorer members, the Low Income Developing Countries.
- *Enhanced Structural Adjustment Facility*. At the Venice Summit of 1987 it was agreed to expand the SAF on identical terms but with additional funds. Loans are now determined on need and there is no overall ceiling. However, the IMF operates a policy of 250% of quota as the maximum access unless there are 'exceptional circumstances'. Normal repayments are in ten half-yearly payments, beginning after five-and-a-half years and ending ten years after the date of the loan.
- *Trust Fund Facility*. Between 1976 and 1980 the IMF sold 25 million ounces of gold at market prices. It used most of the revenue to establish a trust fund to assist the lesser developed countries (LDCs). This facility ceased in 1981 when the fund had been exhausted.
- *Systemic Transformation Facility*. Established as a series of initiatives between 1990 and 1993, this facility was designed to channel restructuring funds and support to countries in the former 'Eastern Bloc'.

Intermediation

The role of the IMF does not end with these various facilities. It has been an intermediary in arranging *standby credits* at times when currencies have come under severe strain. These credits have not usually been used, but have helped restore market confidence in a country's ability to withstand speculative pressure, which itself has often eased that pressure. It has also from time to time arranged finance from the Group of Ten leading industrial countries.

Special Drawing Rights (SDRs)

These were introduced by the IMF in 1969, both to raise the total of world official reserves and to serve as a potential replacement for gold and foreign currency in the international monetary system. Special drawing rights were essentially a 'free gift' from the IMF to its members, which could be used to settle debt between countries. The SDR had no separate existence of its own, being simply a book entry with the IMF. It served as international money since it could be transferred to other countries in settlement of debt. The total of SDRs to be created was at the discretion of the IMF, but the allocation of that total was to be strictly in proportion to quotas. To make this new world currency acceptable it was initially valued in gold, with interest rates paid on credit balances. Special Drawing Rights were later valued in terms of a basket of 16 different currencies, the idea being to move away from depending on gold yet to retain confidence in the value of the SDR by avoiding dependence on any single currency. In 1981 this rather unwieldy basket was replaced by a smaller basket of five major currencies.

The fact that SDRs have been given to members in amounts proportional to the size of their quotas has not been without criticism. It is the major trading countries that (as we have seen) have the largest quotas. There have been eight issues of SDRs to date with the most recent (16.0 billion SDR) being in 2002.

The whole matter of SDRs has become much more controversial in recent years as their shortcomings have become more apparent. Although efforts were made to make them more attractive (in 1981 they were denominated in terms of a basket of five currencies – as above – and market rates of interest were allowed), they still only represent 2% of total liquidity and are, essentially, being held by those who least need them (the richer trading countries).

General arrangements to borrow (GAB)

In 1962 the ten largest IMF members plus Switzerland (which is not an IMF member) constructed the GAB. Each of the signatories contributed an amount of its own currency towards a fund which stood at $7 billion in 1982. In January 1983 the fund was increased substantially to $19 billion in order to help alleviate the world banking crisis. Until January 1983 the GAB had been an arrangement available only to signatories, but since then its resources have been available to any country in need.

'Swap' arrangements

In the 1960s the USA instituted a system of currency 'swaps' with other countries, whereby each central bank agrees to lend its own currency, or to acquire currency balances of the other, for a specified time period. Although these are relatively short-term arrangements, there is currently an additional $30 billion to $40 billion that could be added to total reserves under such schemes.

pause for thought 7   Why has the IMF sometimes been termed 'the rich man's club'? Is this criticism fair?

Review of the role of the IMF

The IMF has undoubtedly helped to support the growth of international trade and payments through its various and substantial contributions to world liquidity. Nevertheless, where it has been involved in 'stabilisation programmes' in support of particular LDCs and transition economies at times of financial hardship, it has been the subject of some criticism (*see* Box 3.7).

Box 3.7   IMF stabilisation programmes

IMF stabilisation programmes (*see also* p. 128) seek to address adverse balance of payments situations whilst retaining price stability and encouraging the resumption of economic growth. The main components of typical IMF stabilisation programmes include some or all of the following:

■ *fiscal contraction* – a reduction in the public sector deficit through cuts in public expenditure and/or rises in taxation;

■ *monetary contraction* – restrictions on credit to the public sector and increases in interest rates;

■ *devaluation of the exchange rate* (this is often a pre-condition for the serious negotiation of a stabilisation programme, rather than part of the programme as such);

■ *liberalisation of the economy* – via reduction or elimination of controls, and privatisation of public-sector assets;

> **Box 3.7 Continued**
>
> - *incomes policy* – wage restraint and removal of subsidies and reduction of transfer payments.
>
> Criticisms of the IMF's stabilisation programmes in LDCs and the transition economies can be grouped as follows:
>
> 1 *IMF programmes are inappropriate.* The criticism here is that its approach to policy has been preoccupied with the control of demand, and too little concerned with other weaknesses stemming from problems with the productive system in LDCs and transition economies. By deflating demand, the IMF has imposed large adjustment costs on borrowing countries through losses of output and employment, further impoverishing the poor and even destabilising incumbent governments.
>
> 2 *IMF programmes are inflexible.* The criticism here is that the IMF has imposed its solutions on the country needing to borrow rather than negotiating a more flexible package. This has arguably infringed the sovereignty of states and alienated governments from the measures they are supposed to implement.
>
> 3 *IMF support has been too small, expensive and short term.* The programmes have been criticised for having been too small in magnitude and too short term in duration for economies whose underlying problems are rooted in structural weaknesses and who often face 'adverse' terms of trade (fall in export prices relative to import prices).
>
> 4 *The IMF is dominated by a few major industrial countries.* The criticism here is that the industrial countries have sometimes used their control of the IMF to promote their own interests, as for example in using the IMF to shift a disproportionate amount of the debt burden onto the debtor countries rather than forcing lenders (e.g. banks) to accept some of the debt burden, given their earlier readiness to lend huge funds at high rates of interest to 'risky' ventures.
>
> Box 3.8 on p. 127 looks further at the principles involved in the IMF stabilisation programmes and contrasts those with some of the World Bank's attempts to support the global economic system.

World Bank

The World Bank is, in effect, a grouping of three international institutions, namely the International Bank for Reconstruction and Development (IBRD), the International Development Association (IDA) and the International Finance Corporation (IFC).

International Bank for Reconstruction and Development (IBRD)

The origins of the World Bank lie in the formation of the IBRD in 1946. The IBRD sought to help countries raise the finance needed to reconstruct their war-damaged economies. This often took the form of guaranteeing loans that could then be obtained at lower interest rates than might otherwise have been possible.

International Development Association (IDA)

In 1958 a second international institution was created to operate alongside the IBRD, namely the International Development Association. The main objective of the IDA was to provide development finance for low-income nations which had insufficient resources to pay interest on the IBRD loans.

International Finance Corporation (IFC)

The International Finance Corporation was established in 1959. Unlike the previous two bodies, the IFC concentrates on lending to *private* borrowers involved in development projects.

Initially much of this lending was for specific infrastructure projects such as dams, power facilities, transport links, etc. More recently, the focus of lending has shifted towards improving the efficiency and accountability of the administrative and institutional structures in the recipient countries.

The role of the World Bank has broadened in recent years to include the private sector as well as governments. In June 2003, the International Development Association – the bank's concessional arm, which deals with the world's poorest countries – gave grants of around $100 million (£60 million) to improve the financial services available to small and medium-sized companies. This marked a continued cultural shift away from the bank's traditional public-sector focus.

World Bank 'Structural Adjustment Lending'

Since 1980 the World Bank has been involved in various types of Structural Adjustment Lending (SAL) which accounts for over 20% of the World Bank's lending. These SAL programmes are non-project related, rather they involve lending to support specific programmes or policy which may involve elements of institutional change. These SAL programmes are generally directed towards improving the 'supply side' of the borrowing countries, intending to initiate and fund changes which will ultimately raise productive efficiency in various sectors of their economies.

Box 3.8 provides a rather stereotyped but useful overview of the World Bank's SAL programmes and compares these with the IMF's 'stabilisation programmes' previously discussed (*see* Box 3.7).

Box 3.8	World Bank structural adjustment and stabilisation

Structural adjustment. As noted above, most of the World Bank Structural Adjustment Lending (SAL) programmes have sought to improve the supply side of the economy. Where successful this will result in the downward, to the right, movement of the aggregate supply curve (AS) from AS_1 to AS_2 thus reducing the price level (from P_2 to P_3 with AD_2) and increasing output (from Q_2 to Q_3) – see Figure 3.11. Clearly the remedies involving structural adjustment are rather more palatable than the remedies which involve deflation (see below) in that both output and employment rise, but only after possibly difficult changes to labour and capital market practices and institutions to improve supply-side conditions.

It is also worth noting that the World Bank is seeking to offer progressively 'softer' loans to developing countries.

Stabilisation. As was noted earlier (*see* p. 125) most of the policies in the IMF stabilisation programmes have been of a deflationary nature. This results in the downward movement,

Box 3.8 Continued

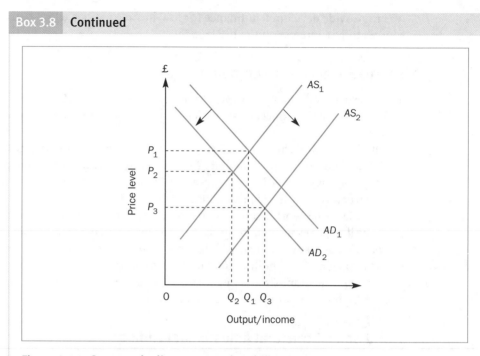

Figure 3.11 **Structural adjustment and stabilisation**

to the left, of the aggregate demand curve (*AD*) from AD_1 to AD_2 thus reducing the price level (from P_1 to P_2 with AS_1) but also reducing output (from Q_1 to Q_2). The debtor country may be made more competitive in its exports and import-substitute sectors, benefiting its balance of payments and reducing its debt, but at the cost of lost output and employment.

Useful websites

Now try the self-check questions for this chapter on the website at www.pearsoned.co.uk/wall. You will also find further resources as well as useful weblinks.

Sources of information on international trade and payments, international institutions and exchange rates include:

www.wto.org
www.imf.org
www.un.org
www.dti.gov.uk
www.europa.eu.int
www.eubusiness.com
Honda website is *www.hondamotorcycle.com*
EU statistics can be found at the Eurostat website at *www.europa.eu.int*

Useful key texts

Daniels, J., Radebaugh, L. and Sullivan, D. (2006) *International Business* (11th edn), Pearson Prentice Hall, especially Chapters 5–7.

Dicken, P. (2003) *Global Shift: Transforming the World Economy* (4th edn), Paul Chapman Publishing Ltd, especially Part II.

Hill, C. (2006) *International Business: Competing in the Global Marketplace* (5th edn), McGraw-Hill Irwin, especially Chapters 4, 5 and 8.

Morrison, J. (2006) *The International Business Environment* (2nd edn), Palgrave, especially Chapter 9.

Piggott, J. and Cook, M. (2006) *International Business Economics: A European Perspective,* Palgrave Macmillan, especially Chapters 2, 3 and 4.

Rugman, A. and Collinson, R. (2009) *International Business* (5th edn), FT Prentice Hall, especially Chapter 6.

Tayeb, M. (2000) *International Business: Theories, Policies and Practices,* Financial Times Prentice Hall, especially Chapters 1 and 11.

Wild, J., Wild, K. and Han, J. (2006) *International Business: The Challenges of Globalization* (3rd edn), FT Prentice Hall, especially Chapter 5.

Other texts and sources

Baldwin, R., Francois, J.F. and Porter, R. (1997) 'The Costs and Benefits of Eastern Enlargement', Centre for Economic Policy Research (CEPR), *Economic Policy*, no. 24.

Dollar, D. and Kraay, A. (2000) 'Growth is good for the Poor', World Bank (unpublished paper), March.

European Commission (2001) 'The Economic Impact of Enlargement', Director General for Economic and Financial Affairs, *Enlargement Papers*, no. 4, June.

Griffiths, A. and Wall, S. (eds) (2007) *Applied Economics* (11th edn), Financial Times Prentice Hall.

Harrison, B. (2007) 'Money and EMU', in *Applied Economics* (11th edn), Griffiths, A. and Wall, S. (eds), Financial Times Prentice Hall.

Healey, N. (2007) 'The Multinational Corporation', in *Applied Economics* (11th edn), Griffiths, A. and Wall, S. (eds), Financial Times Prentice Hall.

McKenzie, G. (1998) 'Financial Regulation and the European Union', *The Economic Review*, April.

Monbiot, G. (2003a) 'I was Wrong about Trade', *The Guardian*, 24 June.

Monbiot, G. (2003b) *The Age of Consent: A Manifesto for a New World Order*, Flamingo.

Porter, M. (1990) *The Competitive Advantage of Nations*, Macmillan.

Rose, R. (2003) 'Companies UK: Unsmash the WTO', *Financial Times*, 26 May.

Rubinsohn, S. (2007) 'Free Trade, Regional Trading Blocs and Protectionism', in *Applied Economics* (11th edn), Griffiths, A. and Wall, S. (eds), Financial Times Prentice Hall.

United Nations Conference on Trade and Development (UNCTAD) *World Investment Report* (annual publication).

United Nations Development Programme (UNDP) *Human Development Report* (annual publication), OUP.

Vernon, R. and Wells, L.T. (1991) *The Manager in the International Economy*, Prentice-Hall, Upper Saddle River, NJ.

Walker, K. (2002) 'Main Development from WTO Talks is a Fine Line in Hypocrisy', *The Guardian*, 26 August.

World Bank, *World Development Report* (annual publication).

Chapter 4

The political, legal, economic and technological environment

By the end of this chapter you should be able to:

- assess the effects of globalisation on world political systems;

- explain the various ways in which political risk can be analysed and minimised;

- discuss the implications of different political and regulatory systems for international business;

- outline the issues that MNEs have to consider in relation to the legal environment, including the increasingly important areas of intellectual property rights and e-commerce legal risks;

- consider the main features of the different types of economic system in which international businesses operate;

- identify and explain some of the key economic variables which influence international businesses in the assessment of their economic environment;

- discuss the opportunities and threats to international business of technological change.

Introduction

In Chapters 1–3, we outlined how the internationalisation of business increasingly transcends national barriers. Nevertheless, the basic unit in which the MNE operates is still the nation state, each one of which has its own method of governance, institutional framework and legal environment. It would be folly indeed for any company thinking of going international to be unaware of these different factors, and to have failed to take them into account before making any significant strategic decisions. In this chapter, we look at the various political and legal elements that make up 'governance', highlight areas of political and legal risk, and suggest ways in which businesses may seek to address such risk.

In the widely-used approach of PESTLE analysis (*see* p. 240) businesses seek to assess the political, economic, social, technological, legal and ecological environments in which they must operate. In this chapter, as well as the political and legal variables, we also pay particular attention to the economic and technological variables that may crucially determine the outcomes for international business of individual investment projects or broad strategic initiatives. Further discussions of the economic and technological issues facing the individual business also take place in Chapters 7–10. For example, Chapter 7 looks at the impacts of new technologies on the supply chain and on other logistical operations.

The following two chapters focus on the sociocultural, environmental and ethical aspects of international business decisions which may also play a part in more sophisticated PEST type analyses.

Political environment

At the heart of governance is the notion of 'sovereignty', which implies the power to rule without constraint and which, for the last three centuries, has been associated with the nation state. We live in a world which is organised as a patchwork of nation states within which different peoples live, with their own systems of government exerting authority over the affairs within their territory. Of course, groupings within those territories may arise from time to time which seek a measure of independence from the central authorities, sometimes claiming nation statehood themselves. Many would also argue that the idea of the nation state has itself been challenged by the growth of globalisation. Before turning to this issue it may be useful to highlight some opposing and arguably contradictory tendencies in globalisation (*see also* Chapter 1).

- *Centralisation versus decentralisation.* Some aspects of globalisation tend to concentrate power, knowledge, information, wealth and decision making. Many believe this to be the case with the rise of the MNE, the growth of regional trading blocs (e.g. the EU), the development of world regulatory bodies such as the WTO, etc. However, such centralising tendencies may conflict with powerful decentralising tendencies as nations, communities and individuals attempt to take greater control over the forces that influence their lives (e.g. the growth of social movements centred on the global environment, peace and gender issues, etc.).
- *Juxtaposition versus syncretisation.* In the globalisation process, time and space become compressed, so that different civilisations, ways of life and social practices become juxtaposed (placed side-by-side). This can create 'shared' cultural and social spaces characterised by an evolving mixture of ideas, knowledge and institutions. Unfortunately this can also stimulate the opposite tendencies, such as a heightened awareness of challenges to the established norms of previously dominant groups, which can result in determined attempts to avoid integration and instead combine against a 'common opponent' (syncretisation).

While there may be many theories as to the causes of globalisation, most writers would agree that globalisation is a discontinuous historical process. Its dynamic proceeds in fits and starts and its effects are experienced differentially across the globe.

Some regions are more deeply affected by globalisation than others. Even within nation states, some communities (e.g. financial) may experience the effects of globalisation more sharply than others (e.g. urban office workers). Many have argued that globalisation is tending to reinforce inequalities of power both within and across nation states, resulting in global hierarchies of privilege and control for some but economic and social exclusion for others.

We have already considered the ways in which globalisation has arguably influenced the notion of the nation state in Chapter 1, suggesting some loss of competence, autonomy, authority and ultimately legitimacy for the nation state (pp. 24–7). We concluded that globalisation is redefining our understanding of the nation state by introducing a much more complex architecture of political power in which authority is seen as being pluralistic rather than residing solely in the nation state.

Political risk

While businesses are largely aware that the political climate in different countries varies enormously, for organisations wishing to go global a far more detailed analysis needs to take place. When considering penetrating or expanding into new markets, organisations need to be able to assess the political risk. Political risk can be defined as: 'uncertainty that stems, in whole or in part, from the exercise of power by governmental and non-governmental actors' (Zonis and Wilkin 2000).

Political risks can be classified into two broad categories, 'macropolitical' and 'micropolitical'.

1 *Macropolitical risks* potentially affect all firms in a country, as in the case of war or sudden changes of government. Such risks may even result in expropriation or confiscation, where governments seize the assets of the firm without compensation. Communist governments in Eastern Europe and China expropriated private firms after the Second World War, with the same happening at different times in the postwar period to private enterprises in Angola, Chile, Ethiopia, Peru and Zambia. Higher general levels of inflation or taxation might adversely affect all firms, as might security risks related to terrorism, etc.

2 *Micropolitical risks* within a country affect only specific firms, industries or types of venture. Such risks may take the form of new regulations or taxes imposed on specific types of businesses in the country. For example, the indebtedness of countries in South America has meant that many have introduced legislation to encourage certain types of exports and discourage certain types of imports. For firms focused on exporting products into these countries, such practices are extremely adverse. However, for MNEs looking for an international location ('platform') from which to produce and export products to other countries, these government policies may appear very attractive.

In globalised economies the political risk to many sectors of an economy may arise from unexpected, and distant political sources, as Case Study 4.1 illustrates.

CASE 4.1 Chinese government and EU milk products

In late 2007, EU producers and consumers of milk products become only too well aware of how political decisions in one part of the world can, with interconnected global markets, transmit market 'shocks' to all corners of the world. A drive by the Chinese government to provide all Chinese children with half a litre of milk a day caused demand for milk to increase dramatically by around 25% a year, with around one-third of all the worldwide production of milk now exported to China. Prices of a litre of milk in the EU rose by over 25% in one week alone in August 2007, with substantial price increase in dairy based products such as cheese, butter and yogurt following closely behind. For example, Kraft raised prices of its cheese based products by 12% in 2007, linking the price rise explicitly to higher milk costs.

However, others blame over-regulation in the EU, rather than globalisation, for milk-based inflation. They argue that it is the excessive milk quotas imposed by the EU in 1984 and due to last until 2015 that has prevented the supply side of the EU market for milk from adjusting to this surge of Chinese demand. Even so some market adjustment is taking place, if only slowly. For example EU dairy farmers are breeding high-performance milk cows and selling these to Chinese farmers, who have little or no tradition of dairy farming. Increased Chinese production of milk is also being helped by Chinese government subsidies for farmers who switch to dairy farming.

Questions

1 In what ways does this case study indicate one or more of the features (discussed in Chapter 1) often associated with globalisation?

2 What aspects of political risk are involved here and how might those political risks have been taken into account?

It may be useful to disaggregate the types of political risk further, as indicated in Table 4.1.

pause for thought 1 You are the MD of a US-based multinational company considering establishing a major affiliate in the UK. Which types of political risk in Table 4.1 are likely to be of major concern?

■ Analysing political risk

Analysing political risk has, in the past, been a rather ad hoc affair, but in more recent times it has become increasingly sophisticated. A common criticism of political risk analysis is that it usually takes place too late, when projects are already underway. More management time and effort is now being directed towards appraising political risk at the initiation stage of projects as companies become more aware of its importance to their future operations. For example, organisations seeking to internationalise typically investigate the following factors in countries

Table 4.1 **Types of political risk and their likely impacts**

Type	Impact on firms
Expropriation/confiscation	Loss of sales Loss of assets Loss of future profits
Campaigns against foreign goods	Loss of sales Increased cost of public relations campaigns to improve public image
Mandatory labour benefits legislation	Increased operating costs
Kidnappings, terrorist threats, and other forms of violence	Disrupted production Increased security costs Increased managerial costs Lower productivity
Civil wars	Destruction of property Lost sales Disruption of production Increased security costs Lower productivity
Inflation	Higher operating costs
Currency devaluations/depreciation	Reduced value of repatriated earnings
Currency revaluations/appreciation	Less competitive in overseas markets and in competing against imports in home market
Increased taxation	Lower after-tax profits

which might become the focus of fdi activity: the system of government, foreign capital controls, industrial regulations, history of civil unrest, diplomatic tensions, and so on.

Managers or their representatives may well visit the countries under investigation, as well as using information and data sources from libraries, the Internet, industry associations, government agencies, banks and insurers. Country-risk reports are also available from risk assessment companies and specialists in particular business activities, often consisting of a country profile and macro-level market/non-market risk assessment. However, such analyses may not include the fine detail that might be vital for particular ventures, and at best provide only an indication of the sociopolitical background.

■ Quantifying political risk

There are more sophisticated ways of analysing political risk, of which one is to identify and then *quantify* the various elements involved. Table 4.2 outlines the criteria that might be used for such an analysis. We can see that some of the criteria in Table 4.2 have a wider minimum to maximum range than others, because that particular risk is perceived as varying more widely between different countries. For example, no country is viewed as having perfect 'stability of the political system', hence the minimum risk assessment is three rather than zero. At the other extreme some countries are viewed as extremely unstable in this respect, receiving the maximum risk assessment, for this criterion, of 14. The respective minimum and maximum scores are

Table 4.2 **Select criteria for evaluating political risk**

Major area	Criteria		Score Minimum	Maximum
Political economic environment	1	Stability of the political system	3	14
	2	Imminent internal conflicts	0	14
	3	External threats to stability	0	12
	4	Degree of control of the economic system	5	9
	5	Reliability of the country as a trading partner	4	12
	6	Constitutional guarantees	2	12
	7	Effectiveness of public administration	3	12
	8	Labour relations and social peace	3	15
Domestic economic conditions	9	Size of the population	4	8
	10	Per capita income	2	10
	11	Economic growth over the last 5 years	2	7
	12	Potential growth over the next 3 years	3	10
	13	Inflation over the past 2 years	2	10
	14	Accessibility of the domestic capital market to outsiders	3	7
	15	Availability of high-quality local labour force	2	8
	16	Possibility of employing foreign nationals	2	8
	17	Availability of energy resources	2	14
	18	Legal requirements regarding environmental pollution	4	8
	19	Infrastructure, including transportation and communication systems	2	14
External economic conditions	20	Import restrictions	2	10
	21	Export restrictions	2	10
	22	Restrictions on foreign investments	3	9
	23	Freedom to set up or engage in partnerships	3	9
	24	Legal protection for brands and products	3	9
	25	Restrictions on monetary transfers	2	8
	26	Revaluation of the currency during the last 5 years	2	7
	27	Balance of payments situation	2	9
	28	Drain on foreign funds through oil and energy imports	3	14
	29	International financial standing	3	8
	30	Restriction on the exchange of local money into foreign currencies	2	8

Source: Adapted from Dichtl and Koeglmayr (1986), p. 6.

indicated for some 30 criteria across three major areas: political economic environment, domestic economic conditions and external economic conditions.

Suppose, for example, that an MNE wishes to evaluate the political risk of pursuing a joint venture in a particular country. If the country scores too highly over the selected criteria deemed appropriate to the joint venture or investment project under consideration, then the MNE will look elsewhere unless there is a way of reducing these risks. For some criteria this may be possible. For example, while the MNE may itself be unable to influence the first criterion in Table 4.2 of 'stability of the political system', it might believe that it can reduce the initial risk score ascribed, say, to the eighth criterion of 'labour relations and social peace'. For example, the MNE may well look at an initial risk score on this criterion for a particular country and then re-evaluate that assessment in the light of its own strategic intentions (e.g. adopting widespread worker consultation procedures, paying above the minimum wage, etc.) and any promises made to it by the authorities of a potential host country (e.g. assurances as to no-strike agreements, etc.). However, should the overall risk-assessment score for a particular project still be higher than that in other countries despite taking into account these planned risk-reduction strategies, this may cause the firm to reconsider its location decision.

Of course, these 'risk scores' for the various criteria will to some extent be subjective, based on management perceptions as to the likelihood (probability) of that risk factor actually occurring. These risk scores must continually be reviewed as events and circumstances (and associated probabilities) are ever-changing. For example, investment in Indonesia facilitated by a close confidant of the then President Suharto before 1997, will have very different political risk scores for the various factors after the fall of President Suharto in 1997, the instability induced by various independence movements (e.g. East Timor in 1999), and recent investigations into state corruption in the pre-1997 period.

pause for thought 2 You are the MD of a US-based MNE specialising in heavy equipment (capital goods) manufacture. You are about to decide whether to establish a production platform in either Italy or Russia. Look at Table 4.2 and identify some of the political risk factors that might influence your decision. What other considerations might be taken into account?

Expected value and political risk

It is not only the probability of a particular political risk factor occurring but the magnitude of its potential impact on the objectives of the company that must also be taken into account. It is worth remembering that the expected value of an event is the sum of the probability of each possible outcome multiplied by the value (impact) of each outcome.

$$EV = \sum_{i=1}^{n} p_i \, x_i$$

where p_i = probability of outcome i (as a decimal)

x_i = value of outcome i

n = number of possible outcomes

So if the firm estimated a 60% probability of a 'strike' labour dispute (criterion 8 'labour relations and social peace' in Table 4.2) occurring so that profits are £10 million and a 40% probability of a 'work to rule' occurring so that profits are £20 million, the expected value (EV) should a labour dispute occur would be:

$$EV \ (£m) = (0.60 \times 10) + (0.40 \times 20)$$

$$= £14 \text{ m}$$

A change in the firm's assessment of the probabilities of these events occurring or the value of their impact should they occur would, of course, influence the expected value calculation.

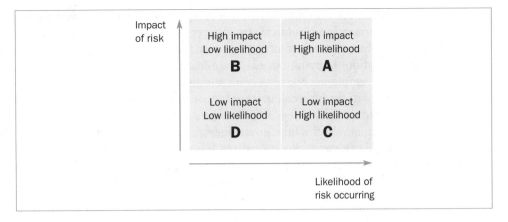

Figure 4.1 **Prioritising (political) risk**

Once identified and assessed, such political risks can be prioritised, as in Figure 4.1. The 'gross risks' (expected values) associated with the various political factors or events are sometimes placed by businesses in a two-by-two diagram, giving four 'boxes'. Box A shows risks (high impact/high likelihood) requiring immediate action, resulting in attempts by the firm to reduce either the probability of their occurrence or the impact should they occur. Perhaps it would also be sensible to have in place contingency plans to cover some of the risks in boxes B and C, but those in D would be of lesser concern.

Responses to political risk

Once the risk has been analysed and assessed, an organisation must decide if there are ways in which such risks can be managed. There are two common responses:

1 improve relative bargaining power;
2 adopt integrative, protective and defensive techniques.

Relative bargaining power

In an attempt to overcome political risk, some MNEs may seek to develop a stronger bargaining position than that of the host country itself. For example, the MNE might attempt to create a situation in which the host country loses more than it gains by taking action against the company. This could be the case when the MNE has proprietary technology that will be lost to the host country if the company is forced to meet certain governmental regulations or where the MNE can credibly threaten to move elsewhere (with significant job losses) to avoid such regulations.

Integrative, protective or defensive techniques

A second approach is to use a set of techniques to prevent the host government interfering with the operations of the MNE.

- *Integrative techniques* ensure that the subsidiary is as fully integrated as possible with the local economy, so that it becomes part of the host country's infrastructure.

Techniques here may include: developing good relations with the host government and other local political groups; producing as much of the product locally as is possible; creating joint ventures and hiring local people to manage and run the operation; carrying out extensive local research and development; and developing good employee relations with the local labour force. These techniques raise the 'costs' to the host country economy of unwelcome interference in MNE activities.

■ *Protective and defensive techniques* seek to limit, in advance, the 'costs' to the MNE should the host government interfere in its activities. Such techniques may include doing as little local manufacturing as possible, locating all research and development outside the country, hiring only those local personnel who are essential, manufacturing the same product in many other different countries, etc.

A risk management strategy involves adopting a comprehensive and systematic approach to dealing with the factors causing political risk. Clearly prioritising the areas of political risk in the manner of Figure 4.1 (above) is one step in such a process. Zonis and Wilkin (2000) suggest that a business might also try to break down the 'drivers' of political risk into three separate categories, namely external, interaction and internal drivers.

1 *External drivers* of political risk involve factors whose probability cannot be influenced by the firm. Examples include political instability (e.g. riots, civil war, coups) and weak public policy (e.g. hyperinflation, currency crisis). Although the company cannot influence these factors itself, it can try to assess accurately their probabilities of occurrence and potential impacts, as a preliminary to taking out appropriate levels of risk insurance.

2 *Interaction drivers* of political risk involve factors that are broadly related to company relationships. Examples include relationships with home-country and host-country governments, regional and local authorities, national and supranational institutions and regulatory bodies, pressure groups, local communities, and so on. Unlike the 'external drivers' the firm *can* influence these 'interaction drivers' by its own actions. It can influence both the probabilities and potential impacts of any breakdown in the various categories of relationship. It can seek to manage such risks by investing resources in fostering those relationships it has given the highest priority in terms of their potential for favourable or unfavourable corporate outcomes. For example, given the importance of *guanxi*-type relationships to business activities in Confucian societies, the politically 'risk averse' firm operating in China or Hong Kong might invest substantial resources in fostering such relationships (*see* Chapter 5).

3 *Internal drivers* of political risk involve factors which are specific to the organisation and *operation* of the company itself. Examples might include the extent to which internal incentive structures are aligned with corporate objectives. An executive remuneration scheme which links bonuses to turnover or market share may be less appropriate where the corporate objective is primarily profit related. The Turnbull Report on corporate governance in 1999 called on the directors of all listed companies in the UK to disclose whether there was an ongoing process for identifying, evaluating and managing significant corporate risks. In particular, it called on company boards regularly to receive and review reports on internal control from line managers and, where appropriate, from specialists in areas such as internal audit.

Case Study 4.2 provides an opportunity to consider political issues and political risk analysis in the context of major decisions involving the future of Rover, then owned by BMW.

CASE 4.2   BMW after Rover

Joachim Milberg took over as chief executive of BMW in 1999. The board had fired his predecessor, Bernd Pischetsrieder, who had made a mess at Rover, the British volume carmaker that he had bought in 1994. The new boss soon came to the conclusion that the German company could turn round the ailing British subsidiary. Mr Milberg held to that view until early March 2000, when he concluded that the worsening situation in Britain had become hopeless, a situation not helped by the continuing strong pound damaging Rover group exports.

Hence the decision to sell Rover for a pittance to Alchemy, a group of British venture capitalists who would have ended up making only a small number of sports cars under the MG label. This decision by BMW to sell Rover caused uproar in the British press and among politicians in the West Midlands who feared large job losses in Rover and in the numerous component suppliers located around the region. The West Midlands has many parliamentary seats, often with only small majorities and which regularly change hands at general elections.

In the event Alchemy eventually withdrew from the bidding process and the bulk of Rover was sold to the Phoenix consortium for the princely sum of £10! Over the previous six years BMW had spent a total of DM9 billion (£34 billion) trying to turn Rover into a car maker with a future, but had posted large losses, as high as £2.5 billion in 1999 as well as writing down Rover assets by £3.2 billion in the same year. The disposal provoked a political storm in Britain, which was still rumbling in April 2000, when BMW bosses were summoned to appear before a parliamentary inquiry.

The British government was furious that it had learnt about the disposal from a leak in the German press. Mr Milberg retorted that the British government had been slow to hear the signals he sent in telephone calls before Christmas as Rover's situation worsened. Even this reply further infuriated the British government as it came under press criticism for failing to 'read' these alleged signals from BMW. BMW had bought Rover because its Board had doubted whether it could survive as a niche firm, then making around 600,000 cars a year. By buying Rover, it secured production of around 400,000 cars, plus the Land Rover business. Having abandoned this strategy, can BMW now survive on its own?

Major losses had resulted from trading Rover group products in the previous years (e.g. £3.2 billion lost in writing down the value of Rover assets in 1999 alone). The strong pound had provided added problems, making Rover group exports progressively less competitive in its major euro-zone markets. One of Rover group's key assets, Land Rover, was to be replaced by an own-brand product, which was much cheaper to produce (fewer basic platforms required). Land Rover could therefore be sold, raising useful revenue. Underlying all this was the conviction that volume car-production will be increasingly in the hands of only a few producers, given the huge scale economies involved. BMW will increasingly focus on niche markets, selling quality cars (e.g. acquisition of Rolls-Royce label from Volkswagen) at premium prices.

Today, giant firms dominate the industry to an even greater extent than they did in 1994. Only Honda, PSA Peugeot Citroen and BMW remain as smaller independents. Of those, BMW is the smallest, at around a third the volume of the others. BMW plans to remain in Britain, moving production of its new Mini from Birmingham to a modernised plant in Oxford. It also has a brand new factory in the Birmingham area producing engines for BMW models produced in the UK and overseas. Continuing good relations with the UK government, workers and consumers would still seem important for BMW.

Questions

1 What political problems were raised by the sale of Rover?

2 How might a more systematic approach to political risk analysis have influenced the outcome for BMW?

The international legal environment

Legal systems vary enormously throughout the world, and these have a significant impact on the ways in which international business is conducted. While many large organisations will employ their own lawyers to advise and settle any disputes, it is important that international managers themselves have some understanding of the likely impacts of legal systems in the countries in which the firm operates.

Types of legal system

The different types of legal system can generally be divided into the following categories: common law; statutory law; code law; religious law; bureaucratic law. These categories need not be mutually exclusive: for example common law can coexist with various types of code law, e.g. civil law.

- *Common law.* This is the foundation of the legal system in the UK and its former colonies, including the USA, Canada, Australia, India, New Zealand, and much of the Caribbean. Common law is essentially unwritten, has developed over long periods of time and is largely founded on the decisions reached by judges over the years on different cases. When a judge makes a particular decision, a *legal precedent* is then established. Such case law has evolved over the centuries, which means that there will obviously be legal variations between countries. For example, manufacturers of defective goods are more liable to litigation in the USA than they are in the UK.
- *Statutory law.* Common law countries depend not only on case law but also on statutory law, i.e. *legislation*, the laws passed by government. This can also be a source of legal variation between countries. For example, the US Freedom of Information Act is more far reaching than similar UK legislation, so that transactions between the government and companies have to be more transparent in the USA than in the UK.

- *Code law*. This is the world's most common system. It is an explicit codification in written terms of what is and what is not permissible. Such laws can be written down in criminal, civil and/or commercial codes, which are then used to determine the outcome of all legal matters. When a legal issue is in dispute, it can then be resolved by reference to the relevant code. Most continental European countries, together with their former colonies, follow this type of legal system.
- *Religious law*. Religious law is based on rules related to the faith and practice of a particular religion. A country that works in this way is called a *theocracy*. Iran is one such example. Here a group of mullahs (holy men) determine what is legal or illegal depending on their interpretation of the Koran, the holy book of Islam. This can pose interesting dilemmas for firms operating in these countries. For example, the Koran says that people should not charge others interest as this is an unfair exploitation of the poor. Thus banks, rather than charging interest, charge up-front fees, and owners of bank deposits are given shares of the bank's profits rather than interest. The emphasis within countries operating under religious laws tends to be on smaller family-owned businesses since the prohibitions we have mentioned often result in less capital being available through national banking systems, forcing a greater emphasis on borrowing from family members. Companies need to be cautious in countries relying on religious laws as there is often an absence of a due process and appeals procedure; for example, companies operating in Saudi Arabia often find that they need a local representative or sponsor to mediate between themselves and the Royal Family in many business disputes.
- *Bureaucratic law*. This occurs in dictatorships and communist countries when bureaucrats largely determine what the laws are, even if these are contrary to the historical laws of the land. MNEs operating in such countries have often found it difficult to manage their affairs as there tends to be a lack of consistency, predictability and appeals procedures.

Effects of national laws on international business

National laws affect international business in a variety of ways. There may be legal rules relating to specific aspects of business operations such as off-shore investment, the environment, ways in which financial accounts are prepared and disclosed, corporate taxation, employee rights and pension provisions. There may even be legal rules as to the amount of assets and shares companies may own and the proportion of profits they are allowed to remit back to their home country. Countries vary enormously in the amount of control they impose in these different areas.

National laws may also affect aspects of the companies' internal organisation such as its human resource management and health and safety policies. These might include factors such as the provision of maternity and paternity leave, payment of a statutory minimum wage, physical working conditions, protection of employees against hazards at work and pollution, pension and medical provisions and childcare facilities.

Of course, the nature of these rules and regulations may, to some extent, reflect the national government's trade and industrial policies. Some governments positively encourage inward investment (such as the current Eastern European countries) while others may create a whole web of red tape and bureaucracy, which may take months or even years to unravel. Certainly the MNE should be aware of national regulations in the following areas.

- *Trade restrictions*: as noted in Chapter 3, various types of regulations may be imposed to restrict trade, even to the extent of imposing sanctions or embargo's on trade with particular countries. Sanctions can take many forms such as restricting access to high-technology goods, withdrawing preferential tariff treatment, boycotting the country's goods or denying new loans.
- *Foreign ownership restrictions*: many governments may limit the foreign ownership of firms for economic or political reasons. This may sometimes be applied to particular industrial sectors, such as air transportation, financial services or telecommunications. For example, Mexico restricts foreign ownership in its energy sector, while the USA limits foreigners to a maximum 25% ownership of US television and radio stations.
- *Environmental restrictions*: sometimes domestic laws in a country can indirectly affect the competitiveness of MNEs. For example, the extensive legislation involving the environmental packaging of goods in Germany means higher costs if products are to meet these environmental restrictions.
- *Exit restrictions*: international businesses also need to take account of the costs of exiting a country, should they need to. Many countries impose legal restraints on the closing of plants in order to protect the rights of employees. For example, in Chinese law, if a partner in a joint venture wishes for any reason to shut down a factory, this would require not only the approval of the entire board, but also the approval of the Chinese government.

Effects of supranational regulations on international business

We have already noted the rapid rise in non-governmental organisations (NGOs) and supranational institutions (e.g. the EU) in Chapter 1. Multinational enterprises must pay careful attention to the regulations imposed by these bodies (and the interpretations placed on them) when devising corporate policy. For example, when companies are offered governmental inducements to retain or initiate production facilities in particular countries within the EU, they must ensure that these inducements are compatible with EU directives on state aid. Otherwise, the aid inducements will be vetoed by the EU, and both the MNE's and host country's policies will be disrupted. An important issue in the initial BMW plan to build new production lines for its Rover Group affiliate in the UK was the 'legality' of a £200 million-plus aid package from the UK government. This part of the 'rescue package' was still being considered by the EU as to its legality when BMW decided instead to dispose of the Rover Group in early 2000 (*see* pp. 139–40). Box 4.1 looks in rather more detail at various EU regulations regarding state aid.

Box 4.1	EU directives and state aid

The EU is carefully scrutinising the 'bail-out' programme of Barak Obama in the US in 2009 to see whether state aid is being provided to US carmakers and others which might be deemed 'unfair' to EU producers. This reflects a long-standing EU concern over 'fair competition'.

The reasoning behind European competition policy is exactly that which created the original European Economic Community (EEC) over 45 years ago. Competition is viewed as

Box 4.1	Continued

bringing consumers greater choice, lower prices and higher-quality goods and services. The European Commission has a set of directives in this area which are designed to underpin 'fair and free' competition. They cover cartels (price fixing, market sharing, etc.), government subsidies (direct or indirect subsidies for inefficient enterprises – state and private), the abuse of dominant market position (differential pricing in different markets, exclusive contracts, predatory pricing, etc.), selective distribution (preventing consumers in one market from buying in another in order to maintain high margins in the first market), and mergers and takeovers. The latter powers were given to the Commission in 1990.

State aid

One of the most active areas of competition policy has involved state aid. The Commission has attempted to restrict the aid paid by member states to their own nationals through Articles 87 and 88 (formerly Articles 92 and 93 of the original Treaty of Rome). These Articles cover various aspects of the distorting effect that subsidies can have on competition between member states. However, it is likely that the progressive implementation of single-market arrangements will result in domestic firms increasing their attempts to obtain state aid from their own governments as a means of helping them meet greater Europe-wide competition. Overall the amount of aid given by member states to their domestic industry had been running at around 1.5% of their respective GDPs during the 1990s but has now been cut back to around 1%, though with considerable variation across member countries.

Currently some €860 billion per year are spent on state aid to EU manufacturing. Germany tops the league of aid recipients as it tries to help its new Länder in the former East Germany to restructure their industry. The main problem with state aid is that the big, industrially powerful countries – Germany, France, UK and Italy – account for some 85% of the total state aid given by EU countries to their domestic industry. This arguably gives such economies considerable advantages over the four 'cohesion' countries – Greece, Portugal, Spain and Ireland – and the 12 countries that joined the EU since 2004.

To counter some of these trends, the European Commission began in the 1990s to scrutinise state aid much more closely – especially where the aid seems to be more than is needed to ensure the ultimate viability of the recipient organisations. For example, in April 1998 the Commission decided that aid paid to the German porcelain firm, Triptis Porzellan GmbH, should be recovered because it believed the aid to be more than was needed to restore the firm's viability, thereby distorting competition in the market.

Article 87 determines all state aid to be illegal, unless it conforms to one or more of a number of exceptions:

- aid to promote improvements of a social character;
- aid to promote economic development in areas with high unemployment or low living standards;
- aid to promote a project of common EU interest;
- aid to the former German Democratic Republic;
- aid to disaster areas;
- sectoral aid to assist in the restructuring of an individual sector in structural decline, e.g. shipbuilding.

In recent years the Commission has also recognised the importance of small and medium-sized enterprises (SMEs) within the EU, so that certain grants and low-interest loans for small businesses are now allowed, as is government support for SME start-ups involving innovation and research and development.

As regards the decision as to whether any governmental support constitutes state aid, the Commission uses the 'market investor principle', i.e. would a rational investor get a reasonable return on the investment undertaken? If the answer is 'no', the state support is regarded as aid rather than as an economic investment. Even when a state aid programme is accepted, the Commission will continually review its implementation.

If a new aid scheme is to be introduced by a member state, the Commission must be informed in advance. The Commission will apply the concept of 'one time – last time' which means that aid for restructuring an industry or rescue aid should only be granted once.

In all these ways it is clear that both MNE and host government must tread carefully through a complex set of legal directives and rules as regards any support via state aid and many other aspects of EU competition policy.

As can be seen from Box 4.2 below, EU directives on data protection can also have an important influence on international business activities.

Box 4.2 EU directives and data protection   **FT**

The Internet may have greatly facilitated global commerce and communication, but differences in national attitudes to data protection are causing legal problems for companies that wish to operate across national borders. In the EU, there is broad agreement that individuals have certain rights over information concerning them and that companies should be prevented from collecting, using, sharing or selling those data without their permission. The EU directive on data protection, passed in October 1998, laid down four basic principles:

1 individuals should be able to obtain and make corrections to information that is held about them by companies or institutions;

2 companies must gain their customers' consent before storing or using information about them;

3 companies must only use data for the original purpose that was expressed at the time of collection, unless the customer agrees otherwise;

4 companies must not obtain more data on individuals than they need to carry out their stated purpose.

Crucially, the directive also provides that data should not be sent to countries that do not follow the same rules. That includes the USA, which has no federal laws governing the 'right to privacy' in commercial transactions and no independent ombudsman for data issues. US attitudes surrounding the use of personal data are generally more relaxed than those of the EU – companies have routinely used transaction records and mailing lists without gaining the permission of the relevant consumers. There are also few restrictions governing the secondary use of data in the USA. Credit-card companies, for instance, are not obliged to ask cardholders if they can use their data for other purposes, nor even to tell them if they have already done so.

These national differences on data privacy have profound consequences for industries that operate in Europe and the USA. When, for example, a European airline wishes to arrange a connecting flight for a passenger via a US airline, compliance with the directive entails that

> ### Box 4.2   Continued
>
> it gains the passenger's permission before using the relevant data to complete the transaction. In theory, any company with subsidiaries in Europe and the USA could face prosecution for exchanging data on individuals without authorisation.
>
> For two years, no agreement could be reached that satisfied both sides. In March 2000, however, EU and US negotiators agreed to recommend a system of self-regulation – the so-called 'safe harbour' principle – under which US companies will sign up to certain standards of privacy on a voluntary basis. These companies would then be deemed to comply with EU privacy rules and would be able to conduct business in Europe. Any violation of the rules would trigger sanctions against the offending company.
>
> *Source*: Randall and Treacy (2000).

Settling international disputes

The cross-border activities of MNEs can create problems in settling international disputes. At least four issues are often involved:

1 Which country's laws apply to the dispute?
2 In which country should the issue be resolved?
3 What techniques should be used to resolve the conflict – litigation, arbitration, mediation or negotiation?
4 How will the settlement be enforced?

The answers to the first two questions may be written into MNE contracts. If not, companies may seek to initiate the legal process in the country most favourable to their own interests (a process known as 'forum shopping'). For example, since monetary rewards for compensation are higher in the USA than elsewhere, many plaintiffs attempt to use USA courts to adjudicate lawsuits involving US companies.

- *Litigation.* The principle of *comity* provides for a country to honour and enforce within its own territory the decisions of foreign courts. 'Comity' requires three conditions to be met:
  1 reciprocity is extended between the countries;
  2 proper notice is given to the defendant;
  3 the foreign court's judgment does not violate domestic statutes or treaty obligations.

- *Arbitration or mediation.* Court cases can be costly and time consuming, so many companies may prefer the process of arbitration whereby the two conflicting parties agree to abide by the decisions of a third party or mediation whereby a third party attempts to bring the positions of the conflicting parties closer together.
- *Governmental disputes.* Sometimes a company may be in dispute with a national government. There is little legal recourse here for companies. For example, the Foreign Sovereign Immunities Act of 1976 in the USA provides that the actions of foreign governments against US firms are beyond the jurisdiction of the US courts. If Germany, say, chose to nationalise IBM's German operation or impose taxes on IBM, there would be no redress for the company. If, however, a government reneges on a commercial agreement, such as repudiating a contract to purchase, then there is the possibility of legal proceedings.

- *Negotiation*. International negotiations bring with them a whole new set of problems over and above those faced when negotiating domestically. The bargaining power of the MNE with host governments or businesses will depend on factors such as the level of technology, nature of the goods or services, importance of its managerial expertise, value of its capital input, etc. The bargaining power of the host country will depend on factors such as the size of the consumer market, the degree of economic and political stability, etc.

The problems facing multinationals in responding to prospective legal disputes involving legal codes inside and outside the home country are well illustrated by Case Study 4.3.

CASE 4.3   Tougher scrutiny of foreign takeovers in US   FT

US takeovers by foreign state-owned companies will now face heightened scrutiny by the inter-agency panel that investigates deals on national security grounds. The Foreign Investment and National Security Act, signed into law in July 2007 by President George W. Bush, requires the Committee on Foreign Investment (Cfius) to conduct a full 90-day investigation of takeovers by government-owned companies, unless the treasury secretary, or another cabinet-level official or deputy, determines they would not impair US national security.

Hank Paulson, treasury secretary, applauded the bill, saying foreign investment was the 'life-blood' of any economy. The new law also intensifies scrutiny of deals involving critical technologies and infrastructure. Mr Paulson, the former Goldman Sachs chief executive, said the new law made clear that the US needed to 'look more closely' at takeovers by state-owned companies, but he was quick to add that the country remained 'very open to investment'.

The bill was signed into law at a crucial time, according to some Washington observers who expect an influx of deals in coming months by government-controlled companies and investment vehicles eager to buy into US equities. In the past, such deals as the proposed takeover of Unocal by CNOOC of China, have bought criticism from some lawmakers in Congress who say they represent a threat to US security and competitiveness.

Mr Paulson said the vast majority of investments in the US by foreign-state owned groups were focused on reaping greater returns and not necessarily assuming control of US assets. He added: 'I'm not saying control is a bad thing.' 'We welcome direct investment, whether it's (for) control or not control. There were a number of them last year that were reviewed by Cfius, that were resolved very quickly and quietly and without controversy,' Mr Paulson said.

Congress began formulating legislation to amend the Cfius process last year after the executive branch panel was lambasted for approving the takeover of port terminals by Dubai Ports World.

Source: Kirchgaessner, S., 'Tougher scrutiny of foreign takeovers', *Financial Times*, 27 July 2007.

Question

Examine the costs and benefits to the various parties resulting from this new legislative approach to takeovers in the US involving government owned overseas companies and/or 'critical technologies and infrastructure.'

Intellectual property rights

The international economy is becoming a 'knowledge-based' economy, so that questions of intellectual copyright are becoming ever more important. The value of intellectual property can quickly be destroyed unless countries enforce rights in this area. Intellectual property rights (IPRs) can take various forms, with patents, trademarks and copyrights being particularly important.

Patents

Patent law confers ownership rights on the *inventor*. To qualify as the subject matter of a patent the invention must be novel, involve an inventive step and be capable of industrial application. 'Novel' seeks to exclude granting monopoly ownership rights to something which already exists; 'inventive' seeks to establish that a step has been taken which would not be obvious to experts in the field; 'industrial application' seeks to avoid the restrictions which would result from ideas and principles being patentable, instead limiting such protection to specific applications of these ideas. Patents depend upon registration for their validity.

- *Paris Convention 1883*. This was the first major attempt to achieve international cooperation in the protection of patents (as well as trademarks and other intellectual property rights). This convention led to the setting up of the International Bureau for the Protection of Industrial Property Rights (BIRPI). One key provision is to grant reciprocity to foreigners whose countries are members of the convention. Another is to grant a 'period of grace' to patents registered in one country before they need to be registered in other countries. After registration a further 'transition period of protection' is granted before the patent holder has to make use of the patent in a particular market; once this transition period is exhausted with no use having been made of the patent, the patent is deemed to expire. The Uruguay Round of GATT agreed a transition period of one year in developed countries, five years in developing countries and 11 years in the least developed countries.
- Two other important treaties allow international recognition of patents granted in member countries:
  1 *European Patent Convention* (EPC);
  2 *Patent Cooperation Treaty* (PCT) of the World Intellectual Property Organisation (WIPO).

These respective treaties allow businesses to make a uniform patent search and application, which is then valid in all signatory countries.

These various methods provide some protection to owners of intellectual property rights, but not all countries have signed them, and enforcement by signatories can be lax. Certainly patents are receiving a much higher profile in terms of international business strategy. For example, the number of patents currently issued in the USA is more than double that of a decade ago. Patents are becoming global in scope with reciprocity agreements and the work of international bodies (e.g. UN, WTO) ensuring that, say, a US patent will restrict attempts to exploit that process or product elsewhere in the world. However, there are international discrepancies, with court decisions in the US making biotechnology and genes (1980), computer software (1981) and business methods

(1998) patentable. At present in the EU only biotechnology and genes of these particular categories are patentable. The whole patenting issue is becoming a key part of MNE international business strategy, as can be seen from Box 4.3.

Box 4.3 Strategic patenting

The USA has permitted more aspects of business activity to be patented than has been the case elsewhere and tends to be more supportive of the rights of patent holders when those patents are challenged. 'Strategic patenting' refers to attempts by MNEs to incorporate their approach to patenting into a more coherent strategic approach, which may be broadly defensive or offensive in its direction. Underlying all this is a general recognition that patents are a valuable 'barrier to entry' in an otherwise more open global economy and that intellectual property protected by patent can be a major factor in stock market evaluations.

■ *Defensive patenting* involves the aggressive defence of established patents by holders. Texas Instruments and National Semiconductors aggressively and successfully defended themselves against perceived patent infringements by Japanese and other chip-makers in the early 1990s. Rivette and Kline (1998) argue that without such defence they would have been bankrupted by lower priced but similar quality chips available from other suppliers in their major markets.

■ *Offensive patenting* involves exploiting patents to increase revenue. For example, IBM boosted its revenue from licensing patents threefold, from $500 million in 1994 to over $1.5 billion in 1999, and is reported as applying for ten new patents every working day. Dell Computers now has around 80 patents for process operations involving manufacture and testing. Biotech and dot.com companies which are currently unprofitable have stock market valuations almost entirely dependent on the patents they possess or have applied for. Companies such as Walker Digital in the USA are now specialising entirely in the holding and development of patents, one of which, Priceline, involves 'reverse auctions' (customers set a price they are willing to pay, companies decide whether they are willing to supply) and is worth over $11 billion.

However, the use of patents as a means of protection of intellectual property rights has become highly politicised and of major importance to the multinational enterprises involved, as can be seen from Case Study 4.4.

CASE 4.4 Intellectual property rights (IPR) in India: Novartis FT

In August 2007 an Indian court dismissed a challenge to the country's patent laws filed by Swiss pharmaceuticals maker Novartis, signalling a victory for health advocates who say they are protecting cheap generic drugs for the developing world. The decision, by Chennai High Court, set back the pharmaceutical industry's hopes of bringing drug patent protection in India up to international standards.

Novartis had sought to revise aspects of India's patent laws, which it said violated World Trade Organisation rules. However public health advocates insisted that India should be allowed to remain the 'pharmacy of the developing world'; 84% of the antiretroviral drugs that Médecins Sans Frontières (MSF) prescribes to HIV/Aids patients come from Indian generic companies.

The dispute tested the bounds of stronger patent laws enacted by Delhi in 2005 and highlighted India's growing importance as a global generic drug-maker. Novartis had disputed a crucial part of Indian law that restricts the patenting of small improvements to drugs, such as a change from tablet to capsule, which can give the maker 20 years more patent protection. It had challenged a decision by India's patent office to reject a patent application for its cancer drug Glivec. Novartis claimed the patent restrictions in the Indian Patents Act were not compliant with WTO rules. Until recently, India did not grant pharmaceutical product patents. As part of WTO negotiations, India enacted a new regime in 2004 with stronger protection of intellectual property rights.

Harvey Bale, director-general of the International Federation of Pharmaceutical Manufacturers, urged Delhi to amend the legislation. 'India has the potential to be a global leader in biomedical R & D, but its current patent legislation condemns it to lag behind.'

Source: Adapted from Jack, A. and Yee, A., 'Intellectual Property Rights (IPR) in India: Novartis', *Financial Times*, 7 August 2007.

Questions

1 Why has Novartis reacted so strongly to the Indian court judgement?

2 What do you consider to be the potential benefits and costs to the Indian pharmaceutical industry of this judgement?

3 How might the WTO TRIPS Agreement be relevant to situations involving intellectual property rights in India?

■ Trademarks

Trademarks have been defined in the Trade Marks Act 1994 as 'any sign capable of being represented graphically which is capable of distinguishing goods or services of one undertaking from those of other undertakings'. This is sometimes referred to as the 'product differentiation' function. Such trademarks require less intellectual activity than patents or copyright to be deemed protectable, with the focus instead being on the commercial activity associated with such trademarks. As with patents, trademarks depend on registration for their validity, which gives the holder the exclusive right to use the mark in the UK for ten years, subject to further renewals in periods of ten years. Infringement occurs where others use the trademark without permission.

Trademarks can be a key element of worldwide 'branding' strategies by companies. Failure to register a brand name can be costly. For example, New Zealand growers of Chinese gooseberries began to market the product as 'kiwifruit' in the 1960s but unfortunately neglected to register a trademark, with the result that growers throughout the world can use this as a generic name for the fruit.

Trademarks are often the context for disputes between rival companies. For example a trademark battle between confectionery giants Nestlé and Mars occurred in

2003 over the 'Have a Break' phrase and became a test-case for the protection of advertising slogans. Swiss-based Nestlé, which makes Kit Kat, has for years had trademark protection over the 'Have a Break, Have a Kit Kat' slogan, as well as over 'Kit Kat' itself. But it wanted to gain similar intellectual property rights over the simpler 'Have a Break' tag-line, in respect of all chocolate products.

Nestlé's initial application to the Trade Mark Registry was turned down in 2002 after Mars, its US-owned rival, objected. However, to bolster its case, the company pointed to consumer research suggesting that use of the phrase 'Have a Break' did elicit the response 'Have a Kit Kat' from consumers. Even so, a High Court judge in the UK was unpersuaded that the public's association meant 'Have a Break' had actually acquired distinctiveness 'as a result of its use as a mark'. Accordingly, he upheld the registry hearing officer's decision.

■ *Trademark Registration Treaty* (Vienna Convention). Once a trademark has been registered, each signatory country must accept it or provide grounds for refusal within 15 months of registration.

■ Copyrights

Copyright law prevents the copying of forms of work (e.g. an article, book, play, poem, music score, etc.) rather than the ideas contained within these forms. However, sometimes the copyright can be extended to the 'structure' underpinning the form actually used (e.g. the plot of a book as well as the book itself).

Copyright (unlike patents and trademarks) applies automatically and does not require registration. For copyright to apply, there must be three key conditions:

1 *a recorded work which is 'original'*, in the sense that the work is different from that of its contemporaries;
2 *of an appropriate description*, i.e. literacy, dramatic, music, artistic, sound recordings, films and broadcasts all qualify. Even business letters can receive protection as 'literacy works';
3 *being sufficiently connected to the country in question*, since copyright is essentially national in character, at least in the first instance. So in the case of the UK, the author (or work) must be connected to the UK by nationality, domicile, source of publication or in some other acceptable way.

The period of copyright in the UK extends to the life of the author +50 years. Copyright protection is not absolute: for example, limited copying of copyright material is permitted for purposes of research or fair journalistic reporting. Breaching copyright beyond any existing provision can result in an injunction to desist and/or the award of damages.

However, there is a continued debate as to what, exactly, should be the appropriate period of time for copyright protection. Case Study 4.5 is a contribution to that debate by a UK government minister.

■ *Berne Convention* and the *Universal Copyright Convention* (UCC) are international agreements which extend the copyright laws of one country to the other signatory countries.

CASE 4.5 Extending copyright

The length of time that sound recordings remain in copyright is a controversial subject and for the past couple of years a debate has raged on whether to extend it from the present 50 years.

Andrew Gowers – who led the Gowers review of intellectual property in the UK – suggested it should remain at 50 years but that this should be reviewed in the light of the European Union commissioner's different view, that it be extended to 95 years.

In the light of that, and in view of the argument about there being a moral case for extending it, the government has been looking at the issue again. The UK ministers responsible felt that 95 years would be disproportionately long, but suggested that there is a case for extending the term to a period of something like 70 years. They advanced the following arguments.

First, there has always been a moral case at the heart of copyright law. If someone produces exceptional work in their 20s that is still being listened to 50 years later, it is right that their earnings from it are not suddenly cut off when they are in their 70s. The suggestion here is that the person who creates a work should be able to enjoy the value of that for the duration of his or her natural life.

A false argument against this suggestion is often made by those who seek to compare musicians with sportspeople or other professionals. No one is going to profit from someone winning the 100 metres decades on from that victory but, in a digital world, ratio stations, mobile phone operators and consumers ensure that music continues to generate revenue far into the future. Why should performers have to watch others profiting from their talent and creativity, especially at the time in their lives when many of them need it most?

The ministers argue that this is not about boosting the wealth of well-known entertainers. Behind those household names is an army of unsung heroes of the music business – the backing singers and session musicians, as well as the large number of featured artists who have never made a vast fortune, whose work continues to be played. Such artists deserve to benefit from others' use of their products during their lifetime.

Second the ministers argue, it should absolutely be the case that the person who creates a work has, within their lifetime, control over how their work is used. Should an artist who is a vegan, for example, have to put up with seeing their music used to promote fast food burgers? Or the music of an environmental campaigner being used to promote cars or airlines? Certainly not, in their view, which justifies their contention that there is a very clear moral case to extend copyright.

The UK has one of the biggest, most successful and most profitable music industries in Europe. But it is faced with serious issues, such as on unlawful file-sharing, and other European countries are looking to the UK to lead the way. The UK government needs a workable system of copyright to underpin the long-term health of UK creative industries. Mr Gower's review was a thorough and thoughtful one and the government took forward his recommendation on illegal file-sharing. But on copyright extension it took a different view.

▶

Getting proper benefits to those who create works is an important part of supporting and maintaining the UK's music industry and it is also the right thing to do. The music industry has a rather chequered past when it comes to ensuring that income from recorded music is fairly distributed to those who create it.

The government needs to find a workable compromise that will balance the interests of musicians, the music business, those using music in the course of their business and the music-buying public.

Source: Burnham, A., 'A moral case for extending copyright', *Financial Times*, 16 December 2008.

Question

Examine the arguments for and against extending copyright protection.

■ Trade-related aspects of intellectual property rights (TRIPS)

The WTO Agreement on *Trade-Related Aspects of Intellectual Property Rights*, the so-called TRIPS Agreement, is based on a recognition that increasingly the value of goods and services entering into international trade resides in the know-how and creativity incorporated into them. The TRIPS Agreement provides for minimum international standards of protection for such know-how and creativity in the areas of copyright and related rights, trademarks, geographical indications, industrial designs, patents, layout-designs of integrated circuits and undisclosed information. It also contains provisions aimed at the effective enforcement of such intellectual property rights, and provides for multilateral dispute settlement. It gives all WTO members transitional periods so that they can meet their obligations under it. Developed-country members have had to comply with all of the provisions of the Agreement since 1 January 1996. For developing countries and certain transition economies, the general transitional period ended on 1 January 2000. For the least-developed countries, the transitional period was 11 years (i.e. until 1 January 2006).

Case Study 4.6 emphasises the growing importance of intellectual property rights to international business and the problems faced by companies that find themselves in breach of those rights.

CASE 4.6 Intellectual property rights in China (IPR): Durex

SSL plc is a major producer of health-related products and is responsible for the famous condom brand 'Durex'. Since its registration as a condom brand in 1929, the name has become well known in many countries. Durex has a 22% global market share, became a premium seller in over 40 countries, and number two in 23 countries. In recent years the company has taken steps to conquer the Chinese market by establishing a 50/50 equity joint venture (EJV) with a Chinese state-owned enterprise. Set up in 1998, the EJV is based in the Chinese coastal city of Qingdao, Shandong Province. The condom market in China is very competitive. Durex's main competitors in China are essentially the other foreign brands. However, one of the company's local competitors is a brand called Jissbon, which in the short term has created a major problem for Durex. The world famous condom producer felt so under threat that it filed a lawsuit against Jissbon on June 24th 2002. Durex accused Jissbon of stealing information from Durex's website and printing it word-for-word to describe its own product.

On its website, Jissbon described itself as 'a British-based world famous condom producer with a 70-year history and 20% of the global market share whose products are sold in more than 140 countries.' The description is very similar to that of Durex.

Durex claims the design of Jissbon's website and even the details it provides are copied from Durex. As a result, Durex accused Jissbon of making claims that Durex alone can genuinely make about its own brand. In response to Durex's accusations, Jissbon admitted that some of the information on its website is false but stressed that the website is not for business purposes but intended to change people's ideas of condoms and safe sex. Durex asked for a formal apology and compensation of 5 million yuan (US$602,410) from Jissbon, saying that Jissbon has caused great loss to Durex's valuable image.

Source: Wilson (2003).

Questions

1 Why did Durex feel it necessary to pursue legal action?

2 What do you consider to be the potential benefits and costs to Durex of this action?

3 How might the WTO TRIPS Agreement be relevant to Durex and to Jissbon and to other situations involving intellectual property rights in China?

Economic systems

■ Free-market economies

Most international business takes place within the context of free-market economies in which the market is the key mechanism for resource allocation. It is here that buyers and sellers interact to determine the prices and quantities of the goods and services exchanged. Of course, the market need not be a particular physical location; for example, foreign exchange is bought and sold worldwide from numerous geographical locations.

Markets yield prices that act as 'signals' to both consumers and producers in resource allocation. For instance, in a situation of excess demand, price will typically rise, acting as a signal to discourage some consumer demand and encourage some additional producer supply, until the quantities bought and sold are once more in balance (equilibrium).

The 'profit motive' is seen as playing a key role here, with higher prices increasing the relative profitability of a product, thereby attracting more resources (labour, capital, land, etc.) into producing that product. In fact profit can be seen as performing at least four key functions:

1 acting as a 'signal' to firms in terms of allocating scarce resources;
2 rewarding risk taking;
3 encouraging productive efficiency (lower costs imply greater profit);
4 providing resources for expansion (e.g. 'ploughed back' profits).

Supporters of such a system see the 'invisible hand' of the free market as the most efficient means of coordinating the innumerable individual decisions which must be taken by consumers and producers every day in global markets. Critics of the free market point to the many examples of 'market failures' which often distort its operation. These can include imperfect information, non-competitive market structures and divergences between private and social costs (externalities), among many other types of market distortion. Occasional periods of economic recession, with declining output and rising unemployment, have helped to temper some of the more excessive claims made by free-market adherents.

> **pause for thought 3**
>
> Choose one of these types of 'market failure' and suggest how it might prevent the market from allocating resources efficiently. Can you repeat your analysis for another type of market failure?

Case Study 4.7 shows how shifts in the demand for and supply of shares in Wellcome, a major pharmaceutical company, influenced the market price of these shares during the early 1990s.

CASE 4.7 Market influences on Wellcome share price

Figure 4.2 uses market analysis to explain some of the observed changes in the Wellcome share price during the early 1990s.

(a) American medical opinion expresses doubts over the effectiveness of Retrovir, a new anti-AIDS drug developed at great expense by Wellcome. There is an increased supply of Wellcome shares as people lose confidence and sell them. Price falls from P_1 to P_2.

(b) A major AIDS conference makes favourable comments on Retrovir. Demand for Wellcome's shares increases (shifts to the right). Price rises from P_1 to P_2.

(c) Enthusiasm for pharmaceutical stocks has been growing; Wellcome had benefited from this, being one of the major drugs companies. Demand had previously risen, but now US investors decide they are over-priced. Supply of Wellcome shares increases. Price falls from P_1 to P_2.

(d) The Wellcome shares provide investors with a high dividend. Demand further increases (shifts to the right). However, the supply of shares to the market decreases (shifts to the left) as shareholders speculate on a further rise in price and sell fewer shares than before. Price rises from P_1 to P_2 (but quantity of shares traded is little affected).

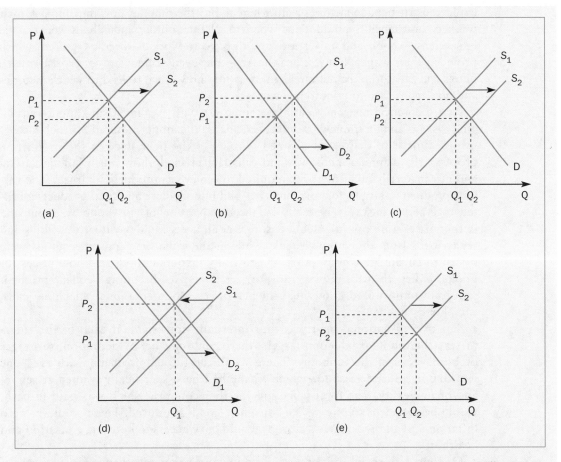

Figure 4.2 Using demand–supply analysis in explanation of specific movements in Wellcome's share price

(e) The Wellcome trust announces its decision to sell 38% of its shares. The market is taken by surprise. The supply curve shifts sharply to the right at a time when share prices are generally depressed. Wellcome's share price falls from P_1 to P_2.

Questions

Consider the likely impact on the Wellcome share price of each of the following:

1 Wellcome announces that it is to begin production of a best-selling ulcer treatment drug, which is currently produced by a rival whose patent is about to expire;

2 Wellcome introduces a rights issue of shares in order to raise new investment capital.

Command economies

Although few examples of a command economy remain, this structure was previously used by many of the so-called 'transition economies' of Central and Eastern Europe. The command economy dominated every aspect of life, often involving the issue of explicit instructions to factories as to where to buy their inputs, how much to pay their workers, how much to produce and where to sell their output; individuals were trained in specialist schools and universities and directed to work at specific factories, which provided their wages, houses, healthcare – and even holidays in enterprise-owned hotels and sanatoria; the national bank was told how much to lend to which factories and how much cash to print to pay wages.

As a theoretical concept, central planning was very elegant. Using 'input–output' analysis (a planning framework which calculated the inputs required for each factory in order for it to deliver its planned outputs to the next stage in the production process), the planning ministry could calculate precisely how much labour, capital and raw materials each enterprise required to achieve its production targets. The various production targets for raw materials and intermediate and final products all fitted together to ensure a perfectly balanced expansion of the economy. Input and output prices were carefully set to ensure that all firms could pay their wage bills and repay loans from the national bank, while at the same time consumer goods were priced to encourage consumption of politically favoured goods (e.g. low prices for books, ballet, theatre, public transport, etc.) and to discourage consumption of politically unfavoured goods (e.g. higher prices for international telephone calls, cars, luxury goods).

The overall national plan was thus internally consistent. If each of the enterprises achieved its production targets, there could not be, by definition, shortages or bottlenecks in the economy. There would be full employment, with everyone working in an enterprise for which he/she had been specifically trained at school and/or university. The total wage bill for the economy, which was paid in cash, would be sufficient to buy all the consumer goods produced. There would be zero inflation and all the country's citizens would have access to housing, education and healthcare.

Of course, in reality this stylised account of a command economy was rarely, if ever, achieved. Plans were devised which were often internally inconsistent, leading to massive shortages or surpluses. Output frequently fell below target as workers saw little incentive to meet productivity targets. Poor-quality products often failed to satisfy either home or overseas consumer demands. The process of economic transformation from central planning to a market economy in Eastern Europe is now well underway, though it has been neither smooth nor uniform. States in the vanguard of reform like Poland, the Czech Republic and Hungary quickly succeeded in creating thriving, dynamic private sectors, which are generating new jobs and contributing to economy recovery; together with Estonia and Slovenia, this group are on the verge of entry to the European Union. In contrast, in the 12 states of the former Soviet Union that now comprise the Commonwealth of Independent States (CIS) the slump in economic activity has been much more prolonged and economic recovery more fragile.

Nevertheless, the direction of movement is towards the market economy, as indeed has largely been the case within the People's Republic of China for more than two decades. This process of transition clearly has implications for both domestic firms within these economies and for multinational enterprises seeking to invest in, or trade with, these economies. Case Study 4.8 raises a number of issues with regard to moving the Chinese economy more firmly in the direction of the market economy.

CASE 4.8   China's capital markets begin to open   FT

China's capital markets took a significant step towards integration with the rest of the world when Beijing announced in August 2007 it would allow individuals directly to buy securities off-shore for the first time. Investors will be able to open accounts at Bank of China branches across the country to trade securities listed in Hong Kong, whose markets, unlike the mainland's, are integrated with the global economy. China's State Administration of Foreign Exchange (Safe) also said these investments, under a pilot scheme, would be exempt from a $50,000 (€37,000, £25,000) limit on the amount of foreign currency Chinese citizens could buy or sell every year. With no restrictions on the amount of foreign currency individuals can buy to invest, Hong Kong's H-share index, which covers mainland Chinese companies listed in the territory, rose almost 9% following the announcement.

Although China has had a stock market since 1990, its infrastructure has trailed that of the Western world in a number of ways, including the maintenance of curbs on investors owning shares overseas and on foreigners buying domestic stocks. Encouraging funds to flow offshore will alleviate some of the pressure. 'Markets are still not fully open because foreigners can't invest directly in the Chinese market and there is no mechanism for shorting stocks (trading in borrowed securities), but these new rules are a big step towards that goal,' said Jerry Lou, equity strategist at Morgan Stanley. Chinese individuals were recently allowed to invest in foreign securities indirectly, through structured products offered by large banks, insurers and fund managers which are themselves constrained by what they can invest in.

Once the proposal secures final approval from the China Banking Regulatory Commission, the programme is due to be expanded to other banks and offshore markets. Initially, however, investors will have to invest through Bank of China, which must conduct all trades through its branch in the northern city of Tianjin's Binhai special economic zone, which enjoys particular favour with the central government.

These reforms continue a process which began in 2000 when a senior Chinese state banker recommended that the country's 'big four' state banks should be floated on the stock market. This may have sounded relatively uncontroversial to outsiders, but in China it was a shocking idea, and not only because making a public proposal of this kind was unprecedented in 50 years of Communist rule. Compelling the big four – which control at least 80% of total banking assets – to obey the diktats of stock market investors rather than government apparatchiks amounted to nothing less than a revolution in China's credit culture.

If credit were one day allocated according to genuine commercial criteria, the wasteful and corrupt state-owned industrial sector that forms the bulwark of the Communist Party's economic power would rapidly become marginalised. In short, the stock market listing of the big four would represent one of the last and largest strides in China's journey from Marxism to market economics. However, 21 years of economic transition have shown that reform is slowest whenever it bumps up against the entrenched interests of the Communist hierarchy.

Among the most compelling reasons for reform is that China can no longer afford to subsidise one of the world's greatest misallocations of credit. Exact statistics are

▶

elusive, but according to senior Chinese government economists, the 300,000 strong state-owned enterprise sector produces only one-third of the country's industrial output but swallows at least two-thirds of its credit resources. Such enterprises, which still employ more than 50% of China's urban workers, are generally poorly managed, overstaffed and unprofitable. Their parlous state finds its most notable expression in the rate of return on assets held by their main creditors – the 'big four': it fell from 1.4% in 1985 to only 0.4% in 2006.

Estimates by Standard and Poor, the credit rating agency, of 'non-performing loans' (NPLs) by the big four banks were as high as 48% of all loans in mid-2003, though official Chinese estimates were lower at 25%. The misallocation of credit to the economy's least profitable sector is sustainable only for as long as Chinese households are willing to keep pouring most of their savings into the state banks, and the finance ministry is willing to keep writing off bad loans by the big four. Now that individuals can buy securities overseas, as noted above, and the Chinese government is taking a harder line on bad debt neither of these assumptions is any longer safe. More and more competition has emerged for the savings of Chinese households, which in 2007 reached Rmb10,000 billion (£740 billion). Not only are several Chinese commercial banks wooing savers in increasingly sophisticated ways, but a new bank regulation installed in 2002 insisted that each of the big four banks reduce its non-performing loan (NPL) ratio by 4% per annum to an official level of no more than 15% of all loans by the end of 2005, which was largely accomplished.

As household savings are funnelled towards more deserving borrowers in the vibrant non-state sector, the effect on China's competitiveness could be dramatic.

Source: Anderlini, J., 'China allows direct offshore investments', *Financial Times*, 21 August 2007.

Questions

1 Consider some of the implications of these changes for Chinese business.

2 What might be the implications for overseas firms seeking to do business with China?

Economic variables and the business environment

Whatever stylised type of economic structure provides the context for international business, a number of key *economic variables* will shape the environment in which such business is conducted. Managers of international businesses must take into account a number of economic indicators in the countries with which they seek to do business if economic opportunities and threats are to be properly assessed.

Real income per head

The gross national product (GNP) is a widely used measure of economic well-being, reflecting the total value of output (or income) attributable to nationals of that country in a given year. To serve as a measure of the *standard of living* this is often expressed 'per head of population' and in 'real terms' (i.e. excluding inflation).

The World Bank and a number of other bodies use annual GNP per head to identify three broad groups of countries, one of which is further subdivided, making four groups in all:

1 *high-income economies*: countries with an annual GDP per head of $11,456 or more (in 2007 values);

2 *middle-income economies*: countries with an annual GNP per head from $936 to $11,455 (in 2007 values).

   Because this group is so broad it has been subdivided into:

   (a) *upper-middle income economies*: annual GNP per head from $3705 to $11,455;

   (b) *lower-middle income economies*: annual GNP per head from $936 to $3704.

3 *low-income economies*: countries with an annual GNP per head of $935 or less (in 2007 values).

Of course, it is not just the *absolute* level of income per head of a country or group of countries that is important in assessing the prospects for business, but *changes* in that level.

Economic growth or recession

This is often expressed in terms of the percentage change in real national income per head and can be a key indicator for future business prospects. For example, where a business is trading in products which have a high *income elasticity of demand* (*see* Box 4.4), such as air travel, then prospective changes in economic growth rates can have a major influence on projected future profitability. As real incomes rise (or fall) by a given percentage, demand for these products increases (or decreases) by more than that percentage. For example, estimates for air travel have suggested income elasticities of demand as high as +4, suggesting that a 1% rise in real income will increase the demand for air travel by over 4%, but equally a 1% fall in real income will decrease the demand for air travel by over 4%.

Box 4.4 Elasticity of demand

Businesses should be aware of at least three types of elasticity of demand if they are to accurately assess prospects for the future.

Income elasticity of demand (IED)

This measures the responsiveness of demand for a product to changes in the real income of consumers.

$$IED = \frac{\% \text{ change in quantity demanded of } X}{\% \text{ change in real income}}$$

For products with high (positive) values for IED, a rise in real income will *shift* the demand curve substantially to the right (*increase*), whereas a fall in real income will *shift* the demand

Box 4.4 **Continued**

curve substantially to the left (*decrease*). Figure 4.3(a) captures these effects of more or less of a product X being demanded at any given price of X due to a change in real income.

Products with a negative value of IED are often called 'inferior goods', with a rise in real income causing demand to shift to the left (*decrease*).

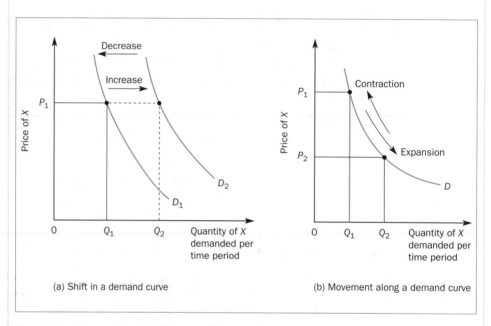

(a) Shift in a demand curve   (b) Movement along a demand curve

Figure 4.3 **Economic conditions and demand**

Price elasticity of demand (PED)

This measures the responsiveness of demand for a product to changes in its own price.

$$PED = \frac{\% \text{ change in quantity demanded of } X}{\% \text{ change in price of } X}$$

When this ratio is greater than 1 (ignoring the sign), we speak of a relatively elastic demand; when smaller than 1, a relatively inelastic demand.

Figure 4.3(b) captures these effects of a movement along the demand curve for X, due to a change in the price of X itself.

Box 9.3 (Chapter 9, p. 362) provides further explanation of the following link between PED and total revenue.

PED > 1 (relatively elastic demand): fall in price raises total revenue, rise in price reduces total revenue.

PED < 1 (relatively inelastic demand): fall in price reduces total revenue, rise in price increases total revenue.

Box 4.4 **Continued**

Cross elasticity of demand (CED)

This measures the responsiveness of demand for a product to changes in the price of some other product.

$$\text{CED} = \frac{\% \text{ change in quantity demanded of } X}{\% \text{ change in price of } Y}$$

Where X and Y are substitutes in consumption, the sign of CED will be positive. A fall in the price of Y, the substitute, will decrease the quantity demanded of X ($-/- = +$)

Where X and Y are complements in consumption (fit together), the sign of CED will be negative. A fall in the price of Y, the complement, will increase the quantity demanded of X ($+/- = -$).

Figure 4.3(a) captures these effects of a shift in the demand curve for X, due to a change in the price of some other product, Y.

For the years 2008–10 the prevailing forecasts have been for a substantial reduction in real national income across developed countries in particular, and a slowing-down of the rate of increase in real national income across developing and emerging economies. The reasons for the so-called 'credit crunch' are considered in more detail in Chapter 10 (pp. 388–95). Here we note that economic recession will create particular problems for products with high income elasticities of demand as, for example, is the case with many leisure and tourism related activities.

Case Study 4.9 indicates how sensitive international business confidence is to economic influences, especially at times of economic recession.

CASE 4.9 Finance chiefs take pessimistic view   **FT**

Confidence in the economic outlook among chief financial officers around the world has collapsed in the last three months of 2008, according to a survey that found the majority expected the recession to last at least another year. Finance chiefs have slashed forecasts for earnings and capital spending in 2009 and have raised their estimates for the number of jobs to be axed next year. The biggest crash in confidence was in the US, with pessimists about the prospects for 2009 outnumbering optimists by nine to one – twice as many as three months ago. More than four in five respondents in Europe and Asia were more pessimistic about the economic outlook.

Weak consumer demand and the turmoil in financial markets were the main concerns for the respondents, with three-quarters saying financial constraints had limited their ability to invest in profitable projects. A similar proportion said they were concerned about the health of the financial institutions they dealt with. Among those using financial derivatives, three out of four said they were worried about the financial prospects for their counterparty.

The quarterly survey of 1275 finance chiefs around the world was conducted by *CFO Europe* magazine, Duke University in the US and Tilburg University in the

▶

Netherlands. The survey has been carried out for 51 consecutive quarters, and asks interviewees about their experiences in the current quarter. The latest results showed confidence about the economy plunging among US, European and Asian respondents, together with their confidence in their own companies' prospects. The numbers they employ were expected to fall by 5% in the US and 6% in Europe in 2009, and earnings to decline by 7–9%. Capital investment was forecast to fall 9–11%. More than half the European finance chiefs forecast the economy would not begin to recover until 2010.

The credit crunch was hitting about half the companies. About a third of the affected companies had difficulty in establishing or renewing bank lines of credit. The cost of credit had soared since summer 2007, with US respondents saying it had risen 177 basis points, compared with 106 basis points in Europe. Among Asian companies, more than half had frozen their headcount while Chinese companies said their top concern was maintaining the morale and productivity of their staff. Only 8% of Chinese respondents said Beijing's stimulus package would boost the economy and 73% said it would provide no more than a cushion.

Source: Willman, J., 'Finance chiefs take pessimistic view on outlook', *Financial Times*, 10 December 2008, p. 24.

Question

How might the survey result affect international business activity? Explain your reasoning.

Exchange rate

When comparing the standard of living (e.g. GNP per head) between different countries it is usual to use a common currency such as the US dollar in the World Bank classification above. Even this may be misleading, since converting the value of GNP expressed in the local currency into a $ equivalent using the *official* exchange rate may misrepresent the actual purchasing power in the local economy. This is because the official exchange rate is influenced by a range of complex forces in the foreign exchange markets and may not accurately reflect the purchasing power of one country's currency in another country. A more accurate picture is given if we use *purchasing power parities* (PPPs) rather than official exchange rates when making this conversion. Purchasing power parities measure how many units of one country's currency are needed to buy *exactly the same basket of goods* as can be bought with a given amount of another country's currency.

Quite apart from the role of the exchange rate in making more accurate international comparisons of GNP, we have seen (Chapter 3) that it is a crucial determinant of export/import competitiveness. Indeed, it is sometimes called an 'expenditure switching' economic variable. For example, a *fall* in the exchange rate will make exports cheaper overseas and imports dearer at home, encouraging consumers in overseas markets to switch from domestic to the now relatively cheaper foreign products and consumers in home markets to switch from the now relatively more expensive foreign products to domestic products. The opposite effects can be expected from a *rise* in the exchange rate, exports becoming relatively more expensive and imports relatively cheaper.

International business must clearly take into account actual and prospective changes in relative exchange rates when evaluating the economic environment in which they are doing business.

pause for thought 4 China has pegged the exchange rate of its own currency the renminbi to the US dollar. How will that influence the EU if the euro continues to weaken against the US dollar?

■ Inflation

Inflation is a persistent tendency for the general level of prices to rise. A modest rate of inflation is often regarded as 'favourable' by business as in such an economic environment any extra costs can more readily be passed on to consumers in the form of higher prices. Of course, excessive rates of inflation can result in instability and rapid increases in costs, often followed by deflationary macroeconomic measures by governments resulting in sharp decreases in consumer demand.

In the UK the Retail Price Index (RPI) is the most widely reported measure of inflation, measuring the change from month to month in the cost of a representative 'basket' of goods and services of the type bought by a typical household. In the EU the Harmonised Index of Consumer Prices (HICP) has been calculated on a standardised basis to allow more accurate comparisons across countries. The HICP uses the geometric mean in its calculation and gives lower recorded rates of inflation for the UK than the RPI, which uses the arithmetic mean and a different 'basket' of goods and services. However, the UK itself adopted the HCIP as its official inflationary measure in 2003.

For a 'cost-orientated' multinational (*see* p. 35), locations with low and stable rates of inflation might prove more attractive in terms of foreign direct investment. (Aspects of strategic policy for a business are considered in more detail in Chapter 7.)

■ Taxes and subsidies

Variations in national tax rates and allowances and in the provision of grants and subsidies can have a major influence on international business decisions. These can obviously include decisions as to where to locate particular elements of the globalised production process. They might also include decisions involving the 'transfer pricing' of internal transactions within the multinational enterprise (*see* p. 366).

This section has dealt with a number of economic variables that might influence the decisions taken by international business. Of course, in reality many of these (and other) variables are changing or are about to change, in different directions at the same time.

Technological environment

Technological change can have important effects on the decisions taken by international business. Technological change can involve *new processes* of production, i.e. new ways of doing things which raise the productivity of factor inputs, as with the use of robotics in car assembly techniques which has dramatically raised output per assembly line worker. Around 80% of technological change has been process innovation. However, technological change can also be embodied in *new products* (goods or services) which were not previously available. Online banking and many new financial services are the direct result of advances in microprocessor based technologies.

■ Technology and employment

One important issue to governments, firms, labour representatives (e.g. unions) and indeed society as a whole has been whether such process innovations have generally resulted in job losses. Each case must, of course, be judged on its separate merits. Box 4.5, however, indicates that there need be no presumption that the continuing technical change that often accompanies inward and outward foreign direct investment by multinational enterprises need necessarily result in job losses. In fact, provided that any cost reductions for productivity gains via the new technologies are passed on to consumers as lower prices and that the demands of consumers are sufficiently responsive (price elastic) to those lower prices, job gains can be anticipated. Of course, whatever the impact on the *volume* of labour required, there may also be changes in the patterns of skills required from those who remain, with the often repeated claim that many craft and intermediate levels of skill have been displaced by automated processes.

Box 4.5   Creating or destroying jobs

New technologies have substantially raised output per unit of labour input (labour productivity) and per unit of factor input, both labour and capital (total factor productivity). There has been much concern that the impact of these productivity gains has been to reduce jobs, i.e. to create technological unemployment. We now consider the principles which will in fact determine whether or not jobs will be lost (or gained) as a result of technological change.

Higher output per unit of factor input reduces costs of production, provided only that wage rates and other factor price increases do not absorb the whole of any productivity gain. Computer-controlled machine tools are a case in point. Data from Renault show that the use of DNC machine tools resulted in machining costs one-third less than those of general-purpose machine tools at the same level of output. Lower costs will cause the profit-maximising firm to lower price and raise output under most market forms, as in Figure 4.4. A downward shift of the average cost curve, via the new technologies, lowers the marginal cost curve from MC_1 to MC_2. The profit-maximising price/output combination ($MC = MR$) now changes from P_1/Q_1 to P_2/Q_2. Price has fallen, output has risen.

The dual effect on employment of higher output per unit of labour (and capital) input can usefully be illustrated from Figure 4.4. The curve $Q = F(N)$ is the familiar production function of economic theory, showing how output (Q) varies with labour input (N), capital and other factors assumed constant. On the one hand the higher labour productivity from technical change shifts the production function outwards to the dashed line $Q' = F(N)$. The original output Q_1 can now be produced with less labour, i.e. with only N_2 labour input instead of N_1 as previously. On the other hand, the cost and price reduction has so raised demand that more output is required. We now move along the new production function Q' until we reach Q_2 output, which requires N_3 labour input. In our example the reduction in labour required per unit output has been more than compensated for by the expansion of output, via lower prices, so that employment has, in fact, risen from N_1 to N_3.

This analysis highlights a number of points on which the final employment outcome for a firm adopting the new techniques will depend:

1 the relationship between new technology and labour productivity, i.e. the extent to which the production function Q shifts outwards;

Box 4.5 **Continued**

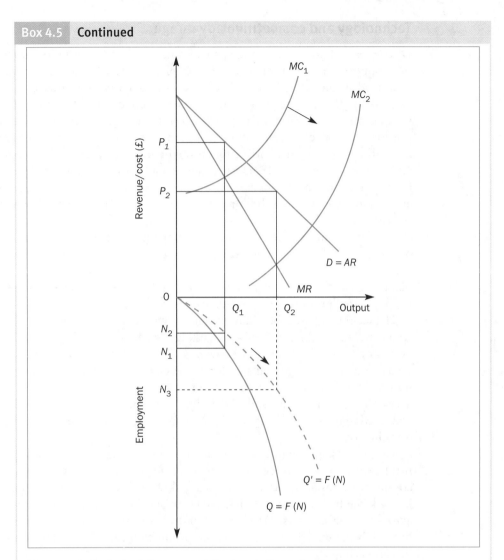

Figure 4.4 **Technical change and the level of employment**

2 the relationship between labour productivity and cost, i.e. the extent to which the marginal cost curve shifts downwards;

3 the relationship between cost and price, i.e. the extent to which cost reductions are passed on to consumers as lower prices;

4 the relationship between lower price and higher demand, i.e. the price elasticity of the demand curve (*see* Box 4.4, p. 159).

Suppose, for instance, that the new process halved labour input per unit output! If this increase in labour productivity (1 above), reduces cost (2 above), and price (3 above), and output doubled (4 above), then the same total labour input would be required. If output more than doubled, then more labour would be employed. The magnitude of the four relationships above will determine whether the firm offers the same, more, or less employment after technical change in the production process.

■ Technology and competitive advantage

Of course, technological change provides national and international businesses with both opportunities and threats. For example, five new broadband wavelengths were auctioned in the UK in early 2000. Access to such wavelengths has been regarded as vital for the new generation of Wireless Application Protocol (WAP) products, making possible the Internet, television and other interactive applications on the third-generation of mobile phones. The British auction of five broadband (third-generation) licences in April 2000 brought in a staggering £22.5 billion, around £20 billion more than Treasury officials had pencilled into their budgets a few months earlier. The German auction of six such licences in August 2000 raised even more, some £30.8 billion. A key question is: can such high expectations be realised?

The impact of technical change on competitive advantages is also considered in other parts of the book. For example new technologies in the manufacture of semiconductors have had a major impact on that industry. The monster chip fabrication plants, or Fabs, can produce more than $8 billion of chips a year, more than several medium-sized producers combined, around 5% of global capacity.

The technology advances have come in two areas, Silicon wafers – the discs from which individual chips are cut – are getting bigger. Plants such as Fishkill in New York State work with dinner-plate sized wafers, 300mm in diameter. At the same time, individual chip sizes are getting smaller. Some elements on the most advanced chips are now only 90 nanometres across, or one-thousandth of the width of a human hair. These changes make it possible to produce nearly three times as many chips from each wafer. Manufacturers using older, 200mm wafers face unit costs that are about 40% higher.

This increasingly challenging production environment has left chipmakers with difficult choices. They can decide to forge ahead with their own 300mm Fabs but face considerable business and technological risks. They can form partnerships with others but risk the high failure rate that comes with joint ventures, particularly those done across national borders. Or they can contract out some or all of their manufacturing but risk being unable to secure enough production capacity during boom times when demand is high.

Technology transfer

It is widely held that multinational activity by more efficient foreign multinationals promotes technology transfer to the benefit of domestic companies. For example, when Nissan established a car plant in north-eastern England, it demanded much higher standards of UK component suppliers than the incumbent national producers such as Ford and Rover. Nissan's engineers assisted these supplying companies to upgrade their production processes in order to meet their requirements. The result was the creation of a strong positive externality: the international competitiveness of the UK car supply industry was strengthened and, as a direct consequence, the quality of the inputs to the existing domestic carmakers improved.

This so-called 'technology transfer' is clearly maximised by such 'direct linkages' with domestic suppliers, which occurs when incoming multinationals like Sony,

Nissan, Honda and Toyota work closely with domestic suppliers to raise the standard of UK-produced inputs. Technology transfer may also bring with it some positive indirect 'demonstration effects' as less efficient local producers seek to imitate the superior processes and organisational advantages of the foreign multinationals.

As Healey (2007) points out there are, however, clear limitations to technology transfer. The inward fdi may, for example, reflect the multinational seeking to exploit an ownership-specific advantage over domestic companies. In such circumstances it is unlikely that the foreign multinational will willingly share the technologically-based sources of its competitive advantage over local rivals. Moreover, in the case of Japanese multinationals, their historical advantage was built upon close relationships with Japanese suppliers. For example, the big four Japanese motorcycle companies (Honda, Yamaha, Suzuki and Kawasaki) rely heavily on a very limited number of domestic suppliers (e.g. Bridgestone for tyres, Nippon Denso for electronic components, etc.). Early dissatisfaction with UK suppliers with regard to quality and reliability of deliveries has led to a number of these Japanese suppliers following their major customers into the European market, thereby reducing the potential scope for technology transfer via linkages with local suppliers.

A further obstacle to technology transfer may involve the issue of cultural dissonance. The psychic distance between US and UK companies is relatively small. Both share a broadly common culture, a common language and they have a reasonably high level of mutual understanding. However, the success of multinationals from, say, Japan or other parts of East and South-East Asia is built on a very different set of social and cultural values, which are not easily transferable to the UK setting (*see* Chapter 5). Companies like Sony, Nissan and Honda have all reported difficulties in establishing Japanese-style work practices, which many economists regard as an integral part of that country's corporate success. The operation of 'just-in-time' production processes and 'quality circles' rely on employee loyalty to his or her company, which in Japan is reinforced by lifetime employment and a shared set of values which emphasises collectivism. Such techniques are much less easily transposed to Western cultures with their stress on individualism and self-determination.

An opposing view points to the potential damage to host country's of technology transfer when it enables foreign affiliates to dominate domestic markets and displace domestic producers. This argument holds still greater weight when such foreign affiliates largely import components and other intermediate inputs rather than using domestic suppliers located in the host country.

■ Types of technology transfer

Technology transfer usually occurs in one of two ways:

1 *internalised transfer* – this takes the form of direct investment by a parent company in its foreign affiliate. Such intra-firm technology transfer may be difficult to measure;
2 *externalised transfer* – this can take a variety of forms: licences, franchises, minority joint ventures, subcontracting, technical assistance, purchase of advanced equipment (embodied technical progress), and so on.

The following factors are widely regarded as increasing the probability of an MNE resorting to 'internalised transfer':

- the more complex and fast moving the technology;
- the larger and more transnational (*see* Chapter 1) the company;
- the more internationally experienced and more technologically specialised the parent company and its affiliates;
- the fewer obstacles placed in the way of fdi by host governments and the more inducements offered;
- the greater the focus of the parent company on utilising advanced technology as rapidly as possible without waiting for host country domestic firms to develop technological capabilities.

Benefits of internalised transfer to host country

The most important benefit to the host country of *internalised technology transfer* is that it gives host country firms access to new, up-to-date and more productive technologies, which are unlikely to be available by any other means. These technologies of the parent company are often based on expensive R & D related to branded products or to complex manufacturing processes, which are part of a globalised pattern of international specialisation. Such technologies would only be shared by the parent company with related parties such as wholly-owned (or majority-stake) affiliates.

Other benefits often follow from access to such technologies, as in the case of the host economy being used by the parent company as a production platform for an export-oriented policy to that region (e.g. Japanese motor vehicle firms using the UK as a production platform to export to the EU). The host country affiliates may also gain access to expensive brand images which further aid overseas sales as well as to substantial financial and other resources owned by the parent company. New operations management and other logistical techniques may be learned by the host country workers, with the general skill base of local labour being raised by exposure to more advanced operations and in-house training methods. In summary, internalised transfer gives the host country, at least in principle, access to the whole range of MNE technological, organisational and skill assets, including those related to tacit knowledge (*see* Chapter 7) as well as explicit knowledge.

Costs of internalised transfer to host country

Local firms may be disadvantaged by being dominated in their home and export markets by the production affiliates of the overseas parent company. This may reduce overall employment and income in the home economy, especially where the parent MNE uses few local resources in component supply or manufacture in its overseas affiliates. Parent companies may, in fact, share little of their tacit or explicit technological, organisational or operational knowledge with the local affiliates, thereby doing little to raise the skill and knowledge base of the local economy.

We consider many other aspects of technological change and their impacts on international business in Chapter 10, especially the impact of Internet-related technologies on business-to-business and business-to-consumer activities.

Useful websites

Now try the self-check questions for this chapter on the website at www.pearsoned.co.uk/wall. You will also find further resources as well as useful weblinks.

Sources of information on international institutions, business and exchange rates include:

www.wto.org
www.imf.org
www.dti.gov.uk
www.europa.eu.int
www.eubusiness.com
www.un.org
The website of the European Central Bank is *www.ecb.int*
The website of the UK Patent Office is *www.patent.gov.uk*
The website for the US Patent and Tradesmark Office is *www.upto.gov*
The European Union's site for intellectual and industrial property is
http://europa.eu.int/comm/internal_market/en/entprop/indprop/index.htm
More information on TRIPS can be found at *www.wto.org/english/tratop*

For information on past decisions of the UK Competition Commission, go to:
www.competition-commission.org

The Business Bureau provides information on legal issues facing business:
www.vianetworks.co.uk

Many interesting articles on labour issues are included in:
www.peoplemanagement.co.uk
www.tomorrowscompany.com
www.croner.co.uk

Pressure group websites include:
www.foe.co.uk
www.greenpeace.org.uk

Useful key texts

Daniels, J., Radebaugh, L. and Sullivan, D. (2006) *International Business* (11th edn), Pearson Prentice Hall, especially Chapters 3 and 4.

Dicken, P. (2003) *Global Shift: Transforming the World Economy* (4th edn), Paul Chapman Publishing Ltd, especially Chapters 4, 5 and 6.

Hill, C. (2006) *International Business: Competing in the Global Marketplace* (5th edn), McGraw-Hill Irwin, especially Chapter 2.

Morrison, J. (2006) *The International Business Environment* (2nd edn), Palgrave, especially Chapters 3, 7, 8 and 10.

Rugman, A. and Collinson, R. (2009) *International Business* (5th edn), FT Prentice Hall, especially Chapters 4 and 13.

Tayeb, M. (2000) *International Business: Theories, Policies and Practices*, Financial Times Prentice Hall, especially Chapters 5, 10 and 12.

Wild, J., Wild, K. and Han, J. (2006) *International Business: The Challenges of Globalization* (3rd edn), FT Prentice Hall, especially Chapters 3, 4 and 6.

Other texts and sources

Dichtl, E. and Koeglmayr, H.G. (1986) 'Country Risk Ratings', *Management International Review*, vol. 26, no. 4.

Griffiths, A. and Wall, S. (2007) 'The European Union', in *Applied Economics* (11th edn), Griffiths, A. and Wall, S. (eds), Financial Times Prentice Hall.

Harrison, B. (2007) 'Money and EMU', in *Applied Economics* (11th edn), Griffiths, A. and Wall, S. (eds), Financial Times Prentice Hall.

Healey, N. (2007) 'The Multinational Corporation' and 'Transition Economies', in *Applied Economics* (11th edn), Griffiths, A. and Wall, S. (eds), Financial Times Prentice Hall.

Heather, K. (1994) 'The Stock Market: a Quick Way to Riches', *Modern Applied Economics*, Harvester Wheatsheaf.

Randall, J. and Treacy, B. (2000) 'Digital Buccaneers Caught in a Legal Web', *Financial Times*, 30 May. In *Mastering Risk* (2001) Financial Times Prentice Hall.

Rivette, K. and Kline, D. (1998) *Rembrandt in the Attic*, Sage.

United Nations Conference on Trade and Development (UNCTAD) *World Investment Report* (annual publication).

United Nations Development Programme (UNDP) *Human Development Report* (annual publication), OUP.

Wilson, J. (2003) 'Inter-Partner Relationships and Performance in UK–Chinese Joint Ventures: An Interaction Approach', unpublished Ph.D. thesis, University of Middlesex.

World Bank, *World Development Report* (annual publication).

Zonis, M. and Wilkin, S. (2000) 'Driving Defensively Through a Minefield of Political Risk', *Financial Times*, 30 May.

Chapter 5

International sociocultural environment

By the end of this chapter you should be able to:

- explain the nature of culture and the differences between national, organisational and occupational culture;

- say why it is important to have an understanding of culture in international business;

- define the different dimensions of culture;

- outline the different ways of analysing national culture in business;

- suggest strategies for developing intercultural competence;

- show an understanding of how to develop multinational teams.

Introduction

Over the ages many philosophers, thinkers, novelists, anthropologists, social scientists and latterly management theorists have grappled with the concept of culture. Definitions have been used to try to capture the all-pervasive scope of cultural influence, as in the following examples.

- We can liken it to the air: it is everywhere, we cannot see it but we know it is there, we breathe it and we cannot exist without it. Culture is not a biological necessity and we will not die if we are deprived of it. But it is rather improbable if not impossible for a person to be devoid of the traces of his or her cultural upbringing and separated from his or her cultural context. (Tayeb 1994)

- Culture should be regarded as the set of distinctive spiritual, material, intellectual and emotional features of society or a social group, and that it encompasses, in addition to art and literature, ways of living together, value systems, traditions and beliefs. (UNESCO 2002)

- Culture . . . is that complex whole which includes knowledge, belief, art, morals, law, custom, and any other capabilities and habits acquired by man as a member of society. (*Encyclopædia Britannica* 2000)

While any definition of culture remains necessarily broad, we can at least see some of the processes by which culture is constructed. As human beings we are social animals and it is from a constant interaction with one another that we learn acceptable ways of being, of behaving, of thinking and of acting. In our day-to-day lives we learn how to act in different circumstances, modelling our behaviour on those around us to build up a coherent set of preferences, beliefs, values and meanings that create our cultural context. At least two features help to distinguish culture from other attributes, such as opinion. The first and most important is that it is enduring and changes very little over time. The second is that it has a social context in that it is expressed as part of a community.

National cultural characteristics

Elias, a famous social scientist and thinker, has made significant contributions to our understanding of culture. He suggested that the development of social institutions and accepted ways of behaving become so closely associated with the groups that historically have dominated particular societies that we can, with reason, speak of national cultural values. In his major work, *The Civilizing Process* (1994), Elias identifies gradual but discernible changes in the expectations of people's interpersonal conduct and in the ways in which they approach their emotions and even bodily functions, as being distinctive between different European states such as Britain, France and Germany. He saw many of these national characteristics arising from variations in the routes by which the different bourgeois and courtly societies evolved. In France, for example, by the eighteenth century the most prominent bourgeois groups and the nobility read, spoke and behaved in roughly the same way, with courtesy, eloquence, respect for hierarchical differences and a sense of honour accepted by a broad strata of French society.

Elias has therefore focused on national cultures as being the outcome of historical power struggles between different groups for dominance in different nation states. The ideas and values associated with the 'successful' groups in such power struggles eventually evolve into 'national' cultures. Of course, other factors may also play a part in this process.

- *Religious background.* While the underlying values and assumptions of all world religions may share some common features, there are arguably some important differences. Weber (1930), for example, argued that individualism, expressed as a preference for personal choice, autonomy and the pursuit of personal goals, was the hallmark of Protestantism, with the result that these characteristics have been incorporated into the 'Protestant' work ethic of many northern European countries. He suggested that this work ethic was in part responsible for the creation of many of the attributes we ascribe to modern Western capitalism. In contrast, Confucianism of East and South-East Asia is characterised by family and group orientation, respect for age and hierarchy, a preference for harmony and the avoidance of conflict and competition, and a set of cultural values quite unlike the acquisitive behaviour of Western capitalism.
- *Ecological factors.* The environment may also play a part in the development of cultural characteristics. It has often been argued that harsh and 'unfriendly' climates and poor agricultural conditions can, over time and across generations, result in people who are hardworking, resilient, patient, tough and aggressive. Tayeb (2000) describes how this can happen using the example of the Arian tribes who, thousands of years ago, migrated from central Asia to India and Iran. Those

Table 5.1 **High context and low context cultures**

High context cultures	Low context cultures
Define personality more in terms of the group than the individual	Are more individualistic than group-orientated
Tend to have a high sensory involvement (low boundaries in terms of personal space)	Tend to have a low sensory involvement (high boundaries in terms of personal space)
Initiate and receive more bodily contact when talking	Convey more information via explicit codes which do not rely so heavily on non-verbal language
Are polychronic, i.e. time does not have a totally linear aspect so that punctuality and scheduling have low priority	Are monochronic, i.e. time is viewed in more linear terms involving punctuality and tight scheduling

who settled in India found a fertile land with plenty of water and rivers and a relatively mild climate. Those who settled in Iran faced harsh variable seasons, salt deserts and very few rivers. Tayeb suggests that it is hardly an accident that Hinduism and Buddhism took root in India, religions noted for their non-violence and passivity. By way of contrast, those from the same ethnic Arian tribes who settled under the harsher ecological conditions of Iran became aggressive, fought other nations and built up the Persian Empire, which ruled over a vast area for centuries.

High and low context cultures

Whatever their origins, attempts have been made to identify some of the differences in national cultural characteristics. For example, early work by Hall (1976) suggested that the various national cultures could be divided into 'high context' and 'low context' cultures in terms of the ways in which people in that culture communicate with one another. Table 5.1 briefly outlines some of the differences between each type. For Hall, the high context cultures include countries or regions such as Japan, China, the Middle East, South America and the southern European countries.

Geert Hofstede (1980) undertook a major research project to identify different national cultures within the same multinational organisation: IBM. Using the responses of some 116,000 IBM employees in 40 countries, Hofstede identified four important dimensions of national culture, namely individualism, power distance, uncertainty avoidance, and masculinity/femininity, to which he later added a fifth dimension: long-term orientation (*see* Figure 5.1).

Individualism

- In *individualist* societies, people tend to put their own interests and those of their immediate family before others. People in such societies would have a high degree of self-respect and independence but a corresponding lack of tolerance for opposing viewpoints. Such people may put their own success through competition over the good of others. Hofstede found that people in the United States, the United Kingdom, Australia, Canada, New Zealand and the Netherlands tend to be relatively individualist in their values.
- In *collectivist* societies there is the belief that the group comes first. Such cultures would contain well-defined social networks in which people are expected to put the

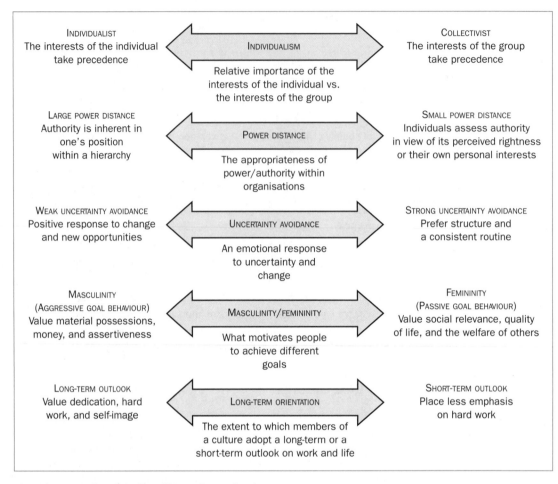

Figure 5.1 Hofstede's five dimensions of culture

Source: Adapted from Griffin and Pustay (1996).

good of the group ahead of their own personal freedom, interests or success. Group members try to fit into their group harmoniously with a minimum of conflict or tension. Hofstede found that people from Mexico, Greece, Hong Kong, Taiwan, Peru, Singapore, Colombia and Pakistan tend to be relatively collectivist in their values.

Power distance

Hofstede refers to power distance as 'the extent to which the less powerful members of institutions and organisations within a country expect and accept that power is distributed unequally'.

■ In *large power distance countries* there is considerable dependence of subordinates on bosses, and a preference for clearly demarcated hierarchy. The emotional distance between hierarchies will tend to be relatively large: subordinates will rarely approach and contradict their bosses. People in such a culture tend to accept the power and authority of their superiors simply on the basis of the superior's position in the hierarchy and to respect the superior's right to that power. Hofstede found that people in the Philippines, Mexico, Venezuela, India, Singapore, France, Spain, Japan and Brazil tend to be relatively power respecting.

■ In *small power distance countries* there is limited dependence of subordinates on bosses, and a preference for consultation. The emotional distance between hierarchies will tend to be relatively small: subordinates will quite readily approach and contradict their bosses. People in such a culture are reluctant to accept the power and authority of their supervisors merely because of their position in the hierarchy. Hofstede found that people in Austria, Israel, Denmark, New Zealand, Ireland, Great Britain, Germany, Australia, Canada and the USA have relatively little power respect.

Uncertainty avoidance

Hofstede defines this as 'the extent to which the members of a culture feel threatened by uncertain or unknown situations. This feeling is, among other things, expressed through nervous stress and in a need for predictability: a need for written and unwritten rules'. An important aspect of the level of uncertainty avoidance in a society is the amount of trust between citizens and authorities.

■ *Weak uncertainty avoidance* (uncertainty accepting) stands for citizen competence; i.e. a belief that ordinary citizens are able to influence their authorities, and that there is some degree of mutual trust among them. People in cultures characterised by weak uncertainty avoidance tend to be positive in their response to change, which is seen more in terms of providing new opportunities rather than as posing considerable threats. Nordic and Anglo-Saxon countries as well as most other Asian and sub-Saharan countries score below average on this dimension (i.e. they exhibit weak uncertainty avoidance).

■ *Strong uncertainty avoidance* implies that decisions should be left to experts; citizens and authorities tend to exhibit mutual distrust for each other. People in cultures characterised by strong uncertainty avoidance will avoid ambiguity whenever possible. These people prefer the structured routine and even bureaucratic way of doing things. Latin, Mediterranean and Central and Eastern European countries tend to score above average on 'uncertainty avoidance', along with Japan, South Korea and Pakistan (i.e. they exhibit strong uncertainty avoidance).

Masculinity/femininity

Hofstede used these labels for a dimension he believed to be the only one on which the scores of men and the women in his sample were consistently and significantly different.

■ *Masculinity* refers to cultures in which the social gender roles are clearly distinct; men are supposed to be more assertive and acquisitive, valuing material possessions and money.

■ *Femininity* refers to cultures in which social gender roles overlap; both men and women are supposed to be modest, tender and concerned with the quality of life.

In some respects the label for this dimension is somewhat confusing. Griffin and Pustay (1996) relabelled it as 'goal orientation', referring it to the way in which people are motivated towards different types of goal. Those people towards the extreme 'masculine' side demonstrate *aggressive goal behaviour*: they place a high premium on material possessions, money and assertiveness. At the other extreme, people on the 'feminine' side who adopt *passive goal behaviour* place a higher value on social relationships, the quality of life and concern for others.

According to Hofstede, in cultures characterised by extremely aggressive goal behaviour, gender roles are rigidly defined: thus men are expected to work and to focus their careers in traditionally male occupations; women are generally expected not to work outside the home and to focus more on families. If they do work outside the home, they are usually expected to pursue work in areas traditionally dominated by women. Many people in Japan tend to exhibit relatively aggressive goal behaviour, whereas many people in Germany, Mexico, Italy and the United States tend to exhibit moderately aggressive goal behaviour. People from the Netherlands, Norway, Sweden, Denmark and Finland tend to exhibit relatively passive goal behaviour.

Table 5.2 gives a rather more detailed account of the impact of these different cultural dimensions.

Table 5.2 Impacts of different cultural dimensions at the workplace

Cultural dimension	Impacts at the workplace
Individualist	Same value standards apply to all: universalism Other people seen as potential resources Task prevails over relationship Calculative model of employer–employee relationship
Collectivist	Value standards differ for in-group and out-groups: particularism Other people seen as members of their group Relationship prevails over task Moral model of employer–employee relationship
Large power distance (power respect)	Hierarchy reflects on existential inequality of roles Subordinates expect to be told what to do Ideal boss is a benevolent autocrat (good father)
Small power distance (power tolerance)	Hierarchy means an inequality of roles, established for convenience Subordinates expect to be consulted Ideal boss is a resourceful democrat
Weak uncertainty avoidance (uncertainty acceptance)	Dislike of rules, written or unwritten Less formalisation and standardisation Readiness to accept change
Strong uncertainty avoidance	Emotional need for rules, written or unwritten More formalisation and standardisation Reluctance to accept change
Masculinity (aggressive goal behaviour)	Assertiveness appreciated Oversell yourself Stress on careers Decisiveness
Femininity (passive goal behaviour)	Assertiveness ridiculed Undersell yourself Stress on life quality Intuition

Table 5.3 **Scores of cultural dimensions (by country)**

Country	Individualism	Power distance	Uncertainty	Masculinity
Argentina	46	49	86	56
Australia	90	36	51	61
Austria	55	11	70	79
Belgium	75	65	94	54
Brazil	38	69	76	49
Canada	80	39	48	52
Chile	23	63	86	28
Colombia	13	67	80	64
Denmark	74	18	23	16
Finland	63	33	59	26
France	71	68	86	43
Germany (FR)	67	35	65	66
Great Britain	89	35	35	66
Greece	35	60	112	57
Hong Kong	25	68	29	57
India	48	77	40	56
Iran	41	58	59	43
Ireland	70	28	35	68
Israel	54	13	81	47
Italy	76	50	75	70
Japan	46	54	92	95
Mexico	30	81	82	69
The Netherlands	80	38	53	14
New Zealand	79	22	49	58
Norway	69	31	50	8
Pakistan	14	55	70	50
Peru	16	64	87	42
Philippines	32	94	44	64
Portugal	27	63	104	31
Singapore	20	74	8	48
South Africa	65	49	49	63
Spain	51	57	86	42
Sweden	71	31	29	5
Switzerland	68	34	58	70
Taiwan	17	58	69	45
Thailand	20	64	64	34
Turkey	37	66	85	45
USA	91	40	46	62
Venezuela	12	81	76	73
Yugoslavia	27	76	88	21

Source: Adapted from Hofstede and Hofstede (2005)

Table 5.3 outlines the original scores obtained by Hofstede (1980) on the first four cultural dimensions across the 40 countries in his initial survey.

pause for thought 1 Look carefully at Table 5.3. Compare and contrast the results for Australia, Denmark, Japan and Singapore. What do these differences imply in terms of business practice?

In later studies Hofstede (1991) added a fifth dimension to his national cultural classification, namely 'long-term orientation'.

Long-term orientation

Hofstede defines this as 'dealing with a society's search for virtue'. Long-term orientation means focusing on the future and implies a cultural trend towards delaying immediate gratification by practising persistence and thriftiness. The top long-term oriented countries were found to be China, Hong Kong, Taiwan, Japan and South Korea in that order. Its opposite, short-term orientation means a greater focus on the present and a more immediate gratification of need, such as spending to support current consumption even if this means borrowing money. The short-term oriented countries in Asia included Pakistan, Philippines and Bangladesh. All Western countries showed a short-term orientation.

Hofstede later extended his survey from 40 to the current total of 74 countries. He also revised the original national scores (shown in Table 5.3) by conducting regular survey updates in each country and extending the sample beyond IBM employees to include students, civil service managers, airline pilots and consumers in subsets of countries for which occupational compatibility could reasonably be answered.

Figure 5.2(a) presents the worldwide average of the five Hofstede dimensions across the 74 countries using the most recent data set, and Figure 5.2(b), (c), (d) and (e) presents these scores for India, China, the UK and the US respectively.

- *Power distance*: China has a much higher power distance score (80) as compared to the world average score of 60, as has India (77), unlike both the UK (35) and the US (40). This suggests much greater respect for position within hierarchies and for receiving direct instructions in China and India as compared to the UK and the US. In fact both China and India score well above the Far East Asian countries' average of 60 on this dimension.
- *Individualism*: China has a much lower individualism score (20) as compared to the world average score of 44, and the Asian average score of 24. The scores in the UK (89) and the US (91) are much higher for this dimension, indicating a much more collectivist outlook in China as compared to greater emphasis on self-reliance, and relatively loose bonds with others in the UK and the US. Interestingly India (48) has an individualism score above the world average, quite different from the situation in China.
- *Masculinity/femininity*: the US has a high masculinity score (62) as has China (66) and the UK (66), compared to the world average of 50. This suggests a greater emphasis on assertiveness, decisiveness and career focus, amongst other 'male characteristics'. The score for India (56), while much lower than those of the UK, China and the US on this dimension, is above the world average for this dimension.
- *Uncertainty avoidance*: the US (46) and the UK (35) have scores for uncertainty avoidance well below the world average of 68. This suggests a high degree of 'acceptance' of uncertainty and ambiguity in these countries, i.e. members of these societies feel comfortable in unstructured situations. Interestingly both India (40) and China (30) also score well below the world average of 68, which suggests a greater acceptance of unstructured situations than one might have expected!
- *Long-term orientation*: China (118) has an exceptionally high score for long-term orientation, with India (61) some distance behind but still well above the world average of 44. The US (29) has a very low score on this dimension, with the UK (25) in a similar position. The emphasis on materialism and immediate gratification in the UK, the US and many other Western countries is in sharp contrast to the greater emphasis on thrift, perseverance and tradition in China, and to a lesser extent India.

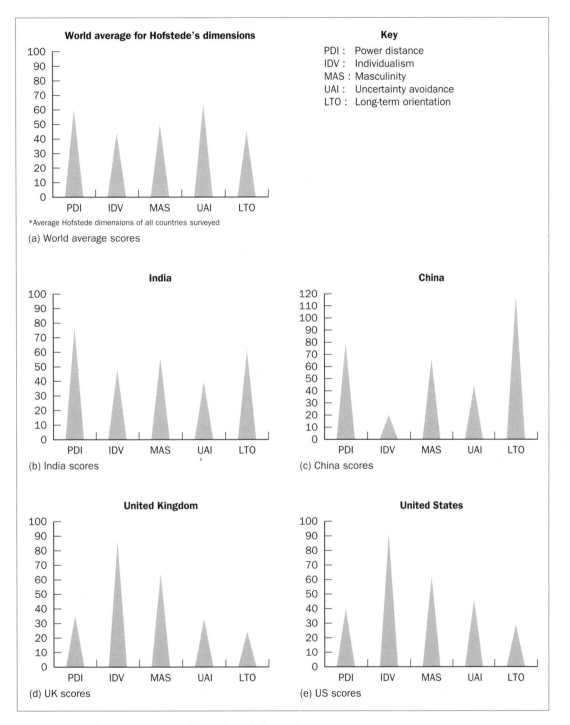

Figure 5.2 **Hofstede scores on five cultural dimensions**

Source: Adapted from Hofstede and Hofstede (2005).

Cultural impacts on international business

In Chapters 1 and 2 we noted the rapid growth in joint ventures, strategic alliances and mergers and acquisitions in a globalised economy. At such times managers and executives often focus on the business needs of the new operations, such as raising finance, acquiring the capital infrastructure, drawing up operational plans and providing technical training. Unfortunately cultural issues at a national or organisational level have often been ignored during these periods of consolidation, as many firms have subsequently found to their cost. Box 5.1 brings this issue into focus.

The situation in Box 5.1 shows 'the clash between American values of individualism, directness and time consciousness and the Japanese interest in face-to-face discussion and consensus building. At the core of the clash are the differing values underlying task-oriented versus process-oriented cultures. Americans typically come to business meetings well informed, focused and expecting an open dialogue. They also expect to take action and assign responsibilities. However, their Asian and Japanese partners place more

---

Box 5.1   A clash of cultures

Mike Burgess is an operations manager from the USA who is in charge of a multicultural team in Indonesia, which includes a number of Japanese experts on production control. At a team meeting beginning at 9.00 a.m. he is surprised to find that at 9.20 a.m. three of the remaining members of the Indonesian team are still arriving, each bringing with them an additional three uninvited participants. The room has to be reorganised and an extra nine chairs brought in. Four members of the Japanese team have reorganised themselves so that they are sitting together. Mr Budi, the senior Indonesian member, is due to deliver the opening formal comments and eventually arrives at 9.45 a.m. He begins his opening address immediately but exceeds his allotted five minutes, taking ten minutes in all. The meeting itself is finally underway at 9.55 a.m.

Mike presents the agenda and outlines the objectives of the meeting and invites questions. To his surprise, no one volunteers with a first question. He then realises that Mr Budi, as senior member, is expecting to be invited to make comments. After he does so the rest of the team joins in. The meeting is going well, but Mike becomes annoyed by side conversations among the Indonesian team members – as a rule he likes his meetings to maintain their focus on achieving the final results and objectives.

Halfway through the meeting, Mike and his marketing director have a disagreement. The openness of the heated debate surprises the Indonesian and Japanese teams. By 10.30 a.m. everyone is irritated and Mike suggests a coffee break, at which point the Indonesians express surprise that Mike has not ordered any snacks. When the meeting reconvenes, Mike wants to reach a decision so he asks Mr Yamaguchi, the senior Japanese team member, to agree to a vote. Mr Yamaguchi replies by asking for a week to consult with his headquarters in Tokyo, which frustrates Mike whose project will now be delayed. Mr Yamaguchi decides this is an opportunity to vent his own frustrations and he questions Mike, who works on the upper floor, about his failure to reply directly to the e-mails he has been sent.

Mr Yamaguchi does not understand why Mike cannot meet with him personally to discuss some of the issues contained in these e-mails.

Source: Adapted from Elashmawi (1998)

emphasis on group harmony, consensus and the need to discuss proposals and actions; they rarely make an immediate decision. Japanese people may come to a meeting, sit as a group, ask ten questions and leave with 20 more in mind. Decisions come later after reaching a consensus. The Indonesian team expects a senior person to open and close important meetings, frequent coffee breaks and snacks and perhaps sufficient time to conduct their daily prayers. Indonesians are used to inviting others to their meetings if they are subject specialists and do not mind side conversations if these are on important points. They also expect seating to be arranged according to seniority, as well as explicit invitations to participate during the course of the meeting. With three sets of competing values, cultural clashes can easily occur and teamwork can be seriously damaged.' (Adapted from Elashmawi, 1998)

It may be useful to briefly review some other possible impacts of Hofstede's analysis of national culture on international business practices.

- *Power distances*: If companies operate with others from nations with different degrees of power distance, misunderstandings can easily arise. For example, a firm from a country with a small power distance, when negotiating in a joint venture, may send a team of experts who are relatively junior. If this team is sent to a large power distance (power-respecting) culture, this may be viewed as an insult. The informality that characterises communication in countries with a small power distance may be misinterpreted by those from a power-respecting culture as an attempt to reduce their authority.
- *Uncertainty avoidance*: Those operating in strong uncertainty avoidance countries tend to adopt more rigid hierarchies and more elaborate rules and procedures for doing business. Risk taking may also be less preferred than in weak uncertainty avoidance (uncertainty accepting) countries such as the United States and Hong Kong. This can affect the way in which certain benefits are received. For example, Japanese firms operating in uncertainty accepting countries such as Canada and the United States have been forced to modify their pay and promotion policies because North American workers are more oriented towards an individualistic 'pay me what I'm worth attitude' and are less worried about job insecurity.

pause for thought 2	What impacts might result in terms of international business practices if two companies involved with one another originate from countries with sharply different scores for 'individualism' and 'long-term orientation'?

Case Study 5.1 provides a useful illustration of national cultural influences on employer/employee engagement practices.

The next section emphasises the types of understanding and awareness that may be needed of national cultural differences if international business negotiations are to be conducted effectively. It emphasises the differences between the collectivist/individualist dimension of national culture, with particular reference to conducting business with Confucian societies, such as China.

A more detailed analysis of management issues for multicultural teams is also presented on pages 188–201 below, including Case Study 5.5. Chapters 8 and 9 also draw heavily on these national cultural characteristics when reviewing international human resource management and international marketing, respectively.

CASE 5.1   National culture and Japanese competitiveness

Among the many factors contributing to Japan's post-war competitiveness has been the sociocultural underpinnings at the national level of its industrial and commercial activities. For example, during most of the post-war era Japan's workers had a strong preference for work over leisure so that as real incomes rose, a high percentage of the additional income was saved. This, coupled with relatively low inflation and low interest rates, helped stimulate investment.

The social framework of Japanese society also played a part, having been influenced by two powerful ideologies, namely Buddhism and Confucianism. Buddhism taught the importance of harmony and respect, reminding people that they should be prepared for change since this was an endemic part of life. Confucianism taught the importance of the individual's position in society and the vital significance of the interaction between a person and his or her immediate superior/inferior. With this background, Japan became a strongly 'vertical' society based on the household or 'ie'. Individuals were subservient to group interest, whether it was within a traditional family framework or in a 'quasi' family-type situation based on the company. This aspect of Japan's nature has been characterised as a society in which work organisation is *gemeinschaft* rather than *gesellschaft* in nature – that is, one based on natural will and close face-to-face relationships rather than one which is based on rational will and which is more utilitarian and goal directed in nature.

Competitiveness also depends to a great extent on how companies manage their most valuable asset – their workers. Japanese corporate strategy on labour management in the large firm sector is very much about creating an efficient internal labour market. First, they hire individuals straight from school or college and employ them as far as possible until retiring age at about 55 to 58 years. On average Japanese companies tend to hire people with 'neyaka', i.e. an optimistic, open minded and wide ranging set of interests as compared to the more specialist hiring policies of many European companies. Second, they mould workers into 'flexible assets' by rotating them between different departments within the company to ensure a broader perspective and a more flexible attitude. Third, they involve workers in in-company training schemes and stress the importance of on-the-job training. Finally, the pay system varies closely with age around the concept of providing workers in large and medium-sized firms with 'lifetime' employment. Japanese managers work hard at creating a stable internal labour market and treat workers as key resources deserving of attention. If workers feel that the company has a commitment to keep them employed, this gives them the confidence to release the 'tacit' knowledge or basic know-how, which often cannot be easily articulated. In other words, workers have the confidence to share any untapped knowledge they may have because they operate within a secure and dynamic environment.

Source: Griffiths (2000, 2009).

Questions

1   How does the discussion above relate to Hofstede's five cultural dimensions?

2   Comment on the scoring for Japan in Hofstede's investigations in Table 5.3. Are there any surprises?

Doing business in Confucian societies: the importance of *guanxi* (connections)

Economists forecast that China will be one of the world's four largest economies by the year 2010. The success has often been attributed to Confucianism, which stresses hard work, thrift and perseverance. Confucius lived from 551–478 BC and societies influenced by his thinking include China, Hong Kong, Taiwan, Japan and Korea, all of which have prospects for sustained economic growth in the new millennium. In these societies 'who you know is more important than what you know'. These connections are known in Chinese as *guanxi*; in Japan they are known as *kankei*; and in Korea as *kwankye*. Here we pay particular attention to *guanxi*.

Under the influence of Confucianism these societies share the following characteristics: disdain for institutional law; strong bonds on the basis of blood, ancestral village and school and military ties; a clear demarcation between members of the in versus out-groups; an ability to grasp the interdependent relationship situations, that may not be obvious to Westerners; and a tendency to view matters from a long-term perspective. These characteristics mean that connections in virtually all social functions, including business, are of the utmost importance. In the West, institutional law and contracts establish what can and should be done and largely overshadow the role of connections.

The word *guanxi* contains two characters that make up the term 'gate/pass' or 'to connect'. Thus *guanxi* refers to the establishment of a connection between independent individuals to enable a bilateral flow of personal or social transactions. Both parties must derive benefits from the transaction to ensure the continuation of such a relationship.

How does this differ from 'networking' in the West? Yeung and Tung (1996) analyse these differences along six dimensions.

1 *Motives: role obligation versus self-interest.* Confucianism emphasises the importance of an individual's place in the hierarchy: individuals are part of a social system, not isolated entities. These include such relationships as ruler–subject, father–son, husband–wife, brother–brother and friend–friend. People have responsibility to the role and not merely to their own self-interest, as in the West.

2 *Reciprocation: self-loss versus self-gain.* In Confucianism everyone is encouraged to become a *yi-ren* (righteous person). To do so, a person must repay favours and increase the value of the favour given. There is a Chinese saying: 'If someone pays you an honour of a linear foot, you should reciprocate by honouring the giver with ten linear feet.'

3 *Time orientation: long-term versus short-term perspective.* In Confucian societies people understand all social interaction within the context of a long-term perspective. Their values are based on an understanding of the interdependence of events and of the relationship between events and time. Every *guanxi* relationship is regarded as 'stock' to be put away in times of abundance and plenty. The 'stock' will then be at their disposal in times of need and trouble. *Guanxi* is maintained through continuous, long-term interactions. Social interactions in the West are usually seen as one-offs with the main emphasis placed on immediate gratification from the situation.

4 *Power differentiation: xia versus power.* In Confucianism everyone striving to become a righteous person becomes a *xia* or knight, attempting to right the wrongs in the world. Those in positions of power and authority must assist the disadvantaged; it is

their obligation to do so. In return, those in positions of power and authority gain face and reputation. While social conscience may be strong in the West, there is no obligation for the powerful to help the disadvantaged.

5 *Nature of power: personal power versus institutional authority.* Governance by ethics is preferred to governance by law. There is a general aversion to law and litigation in Confucian societies. The focus is on personal power and the importance of *guanxi*, since an individual (rather than authority) defines what is permissible in a given context in a given time.

6 *Sanction: shame versus guilt.* The primary sanction in Confucian societies is that of shame. There is great emphasis on face and face-saving. Face implies more than reputation. There is a Chinese saying that 'face is like the bark of a tree; without its bark, the tree dies'. People who lose face in these societies are more than social outcasts; a loss of face brings shame to the person and to his or her family members. Face can be given and taken away only in the broader context of social interactions. To maintain *guanxi*, extra care needs to be taken in acquiring and maintaining 'face' – often known as 'face works'. In the West, probably due to the influence of Judeo-Christianity, sanctions work on the basis of guilt. Thus, if the behaviour deviates from the norm, it is individuals who are required to internalise their understanding of sin.

To many in the West, *guanxi* can appear to resemble nepotism. For example, someone in authority may make decisions based on family ties instead of being based on an objective evaluation of ability. As with any system, it is open to abuse, though defenders of *guanxi* might also point to the arguably adverse impacts of excessive litigation in the USA!

Although *guanxi* may appear undemocratic, it is embedded in a rich cultural heritage which places a strong emphasis on the family and is drawn from the Confucian background in which most of the key relationships already discussed pertain to the family. In fact, the majority of Chinese businesses are family-run concerns. The importance of *guanxi* cannot be overestimated. In their research of 2000 Chinese businesses surveyed in and around Shanghai, Gordon C. Chu and Yanan Ju (1993) found that 92.4% of those polled affirmed the importance of *guanxi* in their daily lives. Also 84.5% indicated that they did not trust strangers until they had had the opportunities to get to know them better, and 71.7% preferred to use *guanxi* connections rather than normal bureaucratic channels.

The following quotation from the chairman of the Lippo group, an Indonesian conglomerate, usefully summarises many of the above points when he stated that he devotes his time exclusively to cultivating relationships while delegating the daily functioning of the group's business to his two sons. In his words, 'I open the door and others walk through.'

■ Effective ways of cultivating *guanxi*

Yeung and Tung (1996) reported the results of their survey of executives who identified the following activities as being crucial for cultivating *guanxi*.

- ■ *Group identification/altercasting.* Kinship and locality are the important bases for *guanxi*. Kinship is based on people's immediate and extended families, while locality refers to the ancestral village or province. Such 'ascribed' relationships are based on common or shared experiences, such as going to the same school, serving in the same military unit or working in the same organisation. As most non-Chinese investors cannot do this, 'altercasting' is an alternative possibility. This means rearranging the social network so that individuals can focus on some element of commonality. The most effective way of doing this is through an intermediary. According to Victor Fung, chairman of Prudential Asia, a Hong Kong investment bank: 'If you are being considered for a new partnership, a personal reference from a respected member of the Chinese business community is worth more than any amount of money you could throw on the table.' As another executive put it: 'The China market is like a pond full of hidden delicious food. A new fish in the pond can starve to death because he doesn't know how to locate the food. Your intermediary is an old fish who knows where every plant and plankton is. He can show you the precise location of this food so you can eat to your heart's satisfaction.'

- *Tendering favours.* Another way of establishing relationships is to offer immediate rewards. Gift-giving, entertainment, overseas trips, sponsoring and support for the children of Chinese officials at universities abroad, are common. When a gift has been received, there is a symbolic breaking down of the boundaries between persons, although these cannot be the basis for long-term *guanxi*.
- *Nurturing long-term mutual benefits.* The intent of this approach is to create an interdependence between two parties in the relationship so that there will be a great cost to either side in severing such ties.
- *Cultivating personal relationships. Guanxi* relations that are based exclusively on material benefits are fragile; many respondents felt that it was important to develop a personal relationship with the partner that cannot be readily imitated by others. 'Personal' means sharing inner feelings or secrets for which, in Chinese society, sincerity and frankness are absolutely essential. To do this you would need to acquire an in-depth knowledge of the Chinese business associate and know what appeals to his or her needs.
- *Cultivating trust.* Finally, cultivating trust is crucial. Around 85% of the companies interviewed indicated that this was an essential condition for cultivating *guanxi*. For many this was based on two factors: 'Deliver what you promise' and 'Don't cheat'. Another way is to learn all you can about the Chinese culture, including its language.

Case Study 5.2 casts further light on the relevance of *guanxi* relationships.

CASE 5.2   East meets West

When East meets West there are clashes with respect to their management practices. For example, in the context of strong global fdi and M & A activity, great demands are placed on joint-venture firms having all their subsidiaries working within a common form of governance, and conforming to the transparency of accounting practices that result from the adoption of GAAP (generally accepted accounting practices). This commonality allows the global management team to

▶

measure, contrast and control their operations in a straightforward way – but such operations are anathema to most Eastern managers. In fairness, we should note that opaqueness is not a unique East/West issue since the Channel Islands, Belgium, Spain and Switzerland all practise low levels of financial disclosure. However, research as to the Oriental concept of probability and risk taking indicates that Asian cultures tend to be more 'fate-oriented' and less willing (than Occidentals) to take a probabilistic view of the world. The inclination towards a lack of disclosure in Asian accounting together with a reluctance to adopt management accounting poses serious problems for those seeking goal congruence in joint operations. It may be useful at this stage to consider in more detail some of the key differences between Western and Eastern practices as they may impinge upon international business activity.

- *Rules versus relationships*. In advanced economies, companies do business within a 'rules-based' system, with business generally conducted by using contracts under laws that are widely known and consistently enforced. Although it may not be apparent to those operating in a rules-based system that has grown up over decades or even centuries, such a system carries large fixed costs. These include the establishment of the legislation and the judiciary, the drafting and interpretation of laws, and the implementation of contracts, all of which involve high sunk costs. On the other hand, once such a system is in place, the incremental cost of enforcing an additional contract is minimal.

  China's is not a rules-based economy, at least not yet; it is still an economy based on relationships. Business transactions are made on the strength not of contracts but of personal agreements. Transactions are purely private, and are neither verifiable nor enforceable in the public sphere. However, the marginal costs of finding, screening and monitoring a potential partner are extremely high. For instance, the relationships have to be managed personally: you cannot afford to delegate the task. A telling difference with the West is that executives in China tend to answer their own phones. Given this marginal cost of cultivating new relationships, it makes sense to do business with close family, then with the extended family, then neighbours from your home town, then former classmates, and only then, reluctantly, with strangers.

- *Ethical norms*. In Western literature it has only been in relatively recent times that business ethics have impinged explicitly on decision-making techniques and structures. In China, however, there has always been a debate about *yi* and *li* – where *yi* is ethical value (justice) and *li* is economic value (profit). Indeed, both *yi* and *li* have been central concepts within Chinese Confucianism. It is said that one cannot 'have both fish and a bear's paw at the same time'. So man will favour *yi* and discard *li*, and thus it is to be understood that '*xiao-ren* (a mean person) is pushed by *li*, whereas *jun-zi* (a gentleman) is delighted by *yi*'. Of course, such attitudes are being increasingly challenged in an age of globalism as the world is effectively reduced to a single market economy.

- *Guanxi*. As already noted, Asians tend to deploy rather opaque accounting practices and to adopt 'gift giving' on a scale that seems to many Westerners as little short of bribery though in many cases this may be a misconception. In China there is the universal practice of *guanxi*, the maintenance of which will involve gift giving. In Chinese society the exchanges of favours involving *guanxi* are not strictly commercial, they are also social – involving *renqing* (social or humanised obligation) and the giving of *mianzi* (the notion of 'face'). More recently, as China opens up, *guanxi* has become known as 'social capital' and has been seen in the West as an important element in securing commercial contracts between corporations. Although 'gift giving' and 'banqueting' are both normal facets of Chinese *guanxi*, many Western firms' operations arguably go too far and operate too close to bribery. Western individuals can become known as 'eat and wine friends', defeating the object of true *guanxi* – which is the offering of favours during the development of a personal relationship. Confucianism is sometimes (many would argue unfairly!) accused of promoting corruption in East Asia given that its teachings call for individuals to improve and maintain relationships among relatives and friends through influence and contacts. The World Bank and the International Monetary Fund now seem more vigilant in acting as 'whistle blowers' whenever they detect funding diversions. Similarly, the United States seems more ready to implement its 1977 laws, which declare acts as criminal if national personnel offer commercial payoffs to public servants abroad. Corporations themselves also seem more ready to tackle perceived corruption. For example, the Royal Dutch/Shell Group in its April 1998 annual report said it had fired 23 of its staff and had terminated contracts with 95 firms on ethical grounds. In China, there is a strong history of *guandao*, or official corruption that is more pervasive than in Japan.

In terms of the management of projects and of joint ventures, there have clearly been examples of attempts by negotiators to ask for bribes in some form. From the Western ethical perspective, giving bribes should be resisted. In an attempt to tackle this issue, the OECD Council adopted in 1996 the 'Recommendation on Bribery of Foreign Public Officials in International Business Transactions' which calls on member countries to act to combat illicit payments in international trade and investment. As part of that recommendation, reference was made to the need 'to take concrete and meaningful steps including examining tax legislation, regulations, and practices insofar as they may indirectly favour bribery' (OECD 1996, C (94) 75). Following this, the OECD Committee on Fiscal Affairs undertook an in-depth review of tax measures that may influence the willingness to make or accept bribes. The committee concluded that bribes paid to foreign public officials should no longer be deductible for tax purposes. They noted that many member countries would have to change their current practices.

Source: Adapted from Kidd and Xue (2000).

Questions

1 Consider some of the differences between a 'rules-based' system and a 'relationship-based' system.

2 How might *guanxi* relationships influence international business activity?

National, organisational and occupational cultures

As well as his major study on differences in national cultures within a given organisation (IBM), Hofstede (1991) undertook a study on variations in organisational culture within the same nation. He compared otherwise similar people in different organisations within the same countries (Denmark and the Netherlands). His results suggested that at the organisational level 'culture' differences consisted mostly of different practices rather than different values (this emphasis was reversed at the national level). Using the word 'culture' for both levels suggested that the two kinds of culture were identical phenomena, but to Hofstede this was clearly false. A nation is not an organisation and the two types of 'culture' are of a different kind.

This conclusion contradicts a popular notion about 'corporate culture' derived from Peters and Waterman's (1982) classic work, *In Search of Excellence*, which assumed that *shared values* represented the core of a corporate culture. Hofstede's work showed that while the values of founders and key leaders may undoubtedly shape organisational cultures, the ways in which these 'cultures' affect ordinary members is through *shared practices*. The fact that organisational cultures are shaped by management practices and not by values explains why such cultures can, to some extent, be managed. As Hofstede points out, values are shaped early in our lives, through family, school and peers so that employers cannot readily change the values of their employees. The only way in which they can affect them is through selecting and promoting employees with the 'desired' values, where appropriate candidates are available. If, in order to change organisational cultures, employers had to change their employees' values, it would arguably be a hopeless task. However, because organisational cultures reside mainly in the more superficial arena of practices rather than values, they are somewhat more manageable.

Table 5.4 provides a brief outline of some aspects of national, corporate (organisational) and occupational cultures. Many of the terms presented are considered further in Box 5.2.

pause for thought 3	Think of any particular company with which you are familiar. Can you identify any distinctive elements in its corporate culture? Can you trace the origin of any of these elements?

Table 5.4 Aspects of national, corporate and occupational cultures

National culture	Corporate culture	Occupational culture
An individual's orientation towards:	A particular company's:	A given occupation's:
■ universalism v particularism	■ values	■ analytical paradigm
	■ rituals	■ work norms and practices
	■ heroes	■ code of ethics
	■ symbols	■ jargon
■ analysing v integrating	NB: Corporate culture can also refer to the values, systems and practices which influence the corporate behaviour of all firms in a country.	
■ individualism v communitarianism		
■ Inner-directedness v outer-directedness		
■ time as sequence v time as synchronisation		
■ achieved status v ascribed status		
■ equality v hierarchy		

Source: Reprinted and adapted from *Organizational Dynamics*, vol. 24, no. 4, Snow, C.C., Davison, S.C., Snell, S.A. and Hambrik, D.C., Use of Transnational Teams to Globalize your Company, pp. 90–107. Copyright 1996, with permission from Elsevier.

Box 5.2 **National and organisational cultural dimensions**

As well as Hofstede's seminal work, Trompenaars (1993) set out a cultural model consisting of seven dimensions, five of which are grouped under 'relationships with people' and the other two are concerned with time and the environment.

1 *Universalism v particularism.* In universal cultures 'rules' are favoured over 'relationships'. Contractual agreements are considered of the utmost importance, and logical, rational analytical thinking and professionalism are of great importance. In particularist cultures there are greater obligations to friendship and kinship and these are maintained through personalism, saving 'face' and paternalism.

2 *Individualism v communitarianism.* This is almost identical to Hofstede's dimension (*see* p. 173), with cultures towards the former end of the spectrum seen as reinforcing the role of the individual and those towards the communitarianism end of the spectrum seen as emphasing the role of groups and larger systems.

3 *Achieving or ascribing.* In achieving societies the emphasis is on esteem related to past achievements. In ascribing societies achievement is a more collective affair and organisations in these societies often justify a high power distance so that things get done. Power here does not need to be legitimised by title or qualification, with esteem often related more to position and age.

4 *Relating to nature.* This concerns beliefs about nature's ability to be controlled. 'Inner-directed' cultures want to overcome nature and depend a great deal on one's own control, while 'outer-directed' cultures see themselves more as a product of the outside world and external environment.

5 *Perceptions of time.* This reflects different attitudes to time: synchronic and circular attitudes allow parallel activities and are less concerned with punctuality. In a 'sequential culture' the focus is on rational efficiency and time is viewed in a more linear fashion.

The scores on four of these dimensions are shown in Table 5.5, following the work of Hampden-Turner and Trompenaars (1994).

pause for thought 4

How do the Trompenaars cultural dimensions in Table 5.5 compare with the cultural dimension scores of Hofstede in Table 5.3. What are the similarities in cultural awareness and are there any implied differences?

Table 5.5 **Scores on four of Trompenaars cultural dimensions**

Country	Universalism (%)	Individualism (%)	Achieved status (%)	Inner-directedness (%)
Australia	40	75	93	61
Belgium	37	61	n.a.	48
Canada	75	80	93	64
France	26	68	94	60
Germany	31	67	96	65
Italy	28	69	81	49
Japan	34	50	86	41
Netherlands	38	n.a.	96	55
Singapore	21	38	79	42
Sweden	n.a.	84	96	45
UK	42	74	94	51
US	77	79	90	68

Source: Adapted from THE SEVEN CULTURES OF CAPITALISM by Charles Hampden-Turner, Alfons Trompenaars, copyright © 1993 by Charles Hampden-Turner. Used by permission of Doubleday, a division of Random House, Inc.

As noted in Table 5.4, corporate culture can refer both to the individual company's values, rituals, heroes and symbols or to the values, systems and practices which are generally accepted by *all home-country companies* within a given nation. Sometimes the national and corporate culture can overlap, as Case Study 5.3 indicates.

CASE 5.3 **Culture of communication breaks through traditional barriers** **FT**

Mr Kwon has a reputation as a trailblazer in corporate Korea in terms of his efforts to change the authoritarian corporate culture. Although LG Philips LCD is a joint venture between LG and Philips, its culture, like that of many other Korean companies, was based on strict hierarchical structures influenced by Confucian traditions.

Mr Kwon has overhauled the company with his mantra of 'horizontal communication'. After a career of rising through the ranks, he became acutely aware of the importance of internet communication. He is convinced that Korean companies will become more competitive if they break down the authoritarian culture, where bosses are to be obeyed and never questioned, to a more creative one. 'The era for authoritarian management is gone. When I make a proposal, I want my staff to say no when they think it does not make sense.'

His bid to encourage greater openness has even stretched to the furniture – the V-shaped meeting room table has been replaced by a U-shaped one. And the walls of his executives' rooms have been replaced by glass.

Source: Kwon Young-Soo, 'Culture of communication breaks through traditional barriers', *Financial Times*, 10 September 2007.

Question

Examine the national and corporate cultural influences that would seem to be involved in this case study.

Case Study 5.4 looks at the second of these aspects of *corporate culture*, taking further the material on Japan presented in Case Study 5.1.

CASE 5.4 **Corporate culture and Japanese competitiveness**

Another important area of debate has been the nature and perceived weaknesses in the much vaunted industrial groupings either of the *Kigyo-Shudan* or *keiretsu* types. The typical corporate governance system in Japan included such attributes as the long-term supply of funds to industry at low interest rates; the monitoring of industry by the main group bank; the extensive cross-holding of shares; the lack of non-corporate shareholders; and the absence of mergers and acquisitions as a means of extracting value from poorly-performing firms. All these attributes arguably created a corporate culture which aided Japan's catch-up process.

However, weaknesses in such a corporate culture began to emerge during the rapidly changing environment of the 1980s, which began to erode the traditional corporate governance system. For example, banks found that large firms began to rely more on the capital market for funds so that a greater proportion of their lending had to be directed to the small and medium-sized companies whose performance was more difficult to monitor. There was also an increasing realisation that the 'old' corporate culture of the *Kigyo-Shudan* form of industrial organisation based on six major industrial groupings (*see* Case Study 2.5) would have to change. Under this system company shares were mostly held by other companies in order to consolidate a relationship rather than as an active form of investment. This would have to change in a globalised environment in which cross-border mergers and acquisitions are increasingly the norm rather than the exception. Further, the changes brought about by financial deregulation will bring new investors into the equity market (pension funds, insurance companies) which are likely to be more active traders of shares.

The other main form of industrial organisation, the *keiretsu* system of parent company and vertically organised subcontracting suppliers, is also changing. For example, the Renault 'revival plan' for Nissan involved a reduction in its capacity by 25% together with the selling of its shareholdings in its affiliated companies where it owns less than 20% of those shares. This inevitably weakens the vertical *keiretsu* 'relationship' based on long-term 'family' type bonds between large firms and their subcontractors who lie below them in the production 'pyramid'. In fact 36% of subcontractors surveyed in 2001 stated an intention of reducing their dependence on specific parent companies. The unwinding of cross-holdings also continues, with a survey by Toyo Keizai estimating that cross-holdings have decreased by 10% between 1992 and 2000 with most of those acquiring the released shares being foreigners who are more interested in profits than the previous holders.

If shares become more easily traded as cross-holdings decrease, then the ownership of Japanese companies may change and restructuring through mergers and acquisitions may eventually become more prevalent. In the past, the importance of creating shareholder value has been relatively unimportant in Japan since managers were mostly recruited from the pool of workers within the company so that there was a lack of a pure profit motive. However, the changing industrial system and the banking reorganisation underway will inevitably shift Japanese corporations in the direction of a greater emphasis on raising short-term profits and increasing shareholder value. For example in the past each *keiretsu* group would have its own 'main' bank, but now those banks have themselves been involved in large amalgamations in attempts to rationalise operations, such as the Mitsubishi-Tokyo Financial Group (MTFG), the Sumitomo-Mitsui Financial Group (SMFG), or the Mizuho Financial Group (MFG). These *keiretsu* groups therefore now include banks from different *keiretsu* and this could, of course, change the nature of individual groups identity and funding.

Japanese firms are meeting the challenges of the new millennium by increasingly redeploying their assets, with the numbers of companies announcing restructuring plans increasing from an average of 42 per month in 1998 to 91 per month in 2001. Many firms are also placing relatively less emphasis on sales and total profits and more emphasis on returns on equity and the efficiency of capital use. The much vaunted Japanese car industry is a classical case of the restructuring process, with

Toyota creating much closer links with Hino Motors and the Yamaha Motor company, while in March 2000 the German-American company Daimler-Chrysler secured control of 34% of Mitsubishi Motors' equity as a means of combining the companies more effectively in order to cut marketing and production costs. Indeed by 2003, Renault owned 37% of Nissan, Daimler-Chrysler owned 34% of Mitsubishi Motors and Ford owned 33% of Mazda Motors. Corporate restructuring in Japan is being led by dynamic companies such as Toyota, which have begun diversifying into auto insurance and consumer finance and Sony, which is in the process of transforming itself into a fully networked corporation by opening an online store.

On the human resource front, the basic pillars of the Japanese employment system have included employment for life, wages according to age/length of service and company-based unions. These have helped Japan to develop an 'internal' labour market where workers in large companies were 'grown' within the organisation in which they were trained. However, the pressures of competition have begun to slowly modify this system. There has been a lowering of the age of retirement for permanent employees in order to decrease wage bills while at the same time there has been a decrease in yearly hirings. Also the number of mid-term employees (i.e. those who change job in mid-career) has increased as companies try to 'poach' good workers. In addition, wages are now being increasingly determined by merit rather than by age, although it should be remembered that only some 20% of Japanese workers are paid according to merit. Finally, more Japanese companies have been resorting to temporary workers as a way of cutting labour costs. In other words, a number of features more reminiscent of the 'external' labour markets familiar in the West are now gradually developing within large Japanese companies.

Some of these points have been reinforced by recent survey evidence. For example a survey from the Japan Ministry of Health and Labour in 2003 showed that in 2002 only 48.6% of employers attached great importance to the lifetime employment system when hiring employees. The same survey also showed that in 2002 some 55.9% of Japanese employers attached greater importance to the merit system of payment when deciding on employees pay.

The period from 2000 to 2007 has seen changes in Japan's corporate culture as companies have looked to restructure their operations. During this period, the importance of mergers and acquisitions have accelerated with the number of M&A deals involving at least one Japanese company surging to 2775 in 2006 as compared to only 621 in 1996. In addition, the new Company law (*Kaisha Ho*) of 2006 has made it easier for foreign firms to buy Japanese firms so that overseas ownership of Japanese firms may rise in the future. However, this does not necessarily mean that there will be *rapid* changes in Japan since it is still a stakeholder environment as opposed to a shareholder one. For example, even though the number of attempts at hostile takeover had increased to 3% of the total of all takeover attempts by 2005, no hostile attempt at takeover in Japan had ever been successful up to that date. Similarly, the widespread practice of mutually holding shares in friendly companies (cross shareholding) actually increased in 2006, after the custom had declined after the collapse of the bubble economy in the early 1990s. Therefore, although a number of changes in Japan's corporate environment are certainly affecting Japan's corporate culture, the pace of such change is difficult to predict.

Source: Griffiths (2000, 2009).

Questions

1 Identify some of the corporate cultural changes underway in Japan and comment on their likely impacts.

2 What factors have been 'driving' these changes in corporate culture?

The linkages between national and corporate/organisational cultures prevalent across the majority of home-country companies is taken further in the next section, using investigatory material from a number of countries.

Interaction of national with organisational cultures

Hofstede has suggested that while management practices differ between organisations and societies they remain remarkably similar within each society. D'Iribane (1996) adopts a similar view and researched this area by carrying out in-depth interviews in the 1980s in three production plants of a French-owned aluminium company, one in France, one in the USA (Maryland) and one in the Netherlands. The plants were technically identical, but interpersonal interactions on the shop floor differed dramatically between them. D'Iribane identified three different 'logics' that controlled the interpersonal interactions at the sites: honour in France; fair contract in the USA; and consensus in the Netherlands. These philosophies represent patterns of thinking, feeling and acting which can be traced back to the national histories of these three societies over the centuries.

In France, for example, D'Iribane argues that the most important feature is that it still is largely a 'class-based' society. Within the plant the different 'classes' coexist on at least three levels: the cadres (managers and professionals), the maitrise (first-line supervisors) and the non-cadres (levels below maitrise). The relationships between these 'classes' are governed by antagonism, yet a sense of respect prevails, for the types of orders a supervisor can give are constrained by a need to respect the honour of the subordinates. In the USA on the other hand, everybody is supposed to be equal and the relationship between management and workers is contractual. While this is less hierarchical than in France, American managers can get away with demanding things from their workers that in France would be impossible. In practice, some people in the USA would seem to be still more equal than others. D'Iribane attributes the US practices to the country's immigrant past: the heritage of the Pilgrim Fathers and other seventeenth- and eighteenth-century white settlers. Since there was no traditional aristocracy as in France, immigrants developed a middle-class society, with relationships governed by contractual agreements. D'Iribane calls them 'pious merchants'. In the Netherlands, while they have pious merchant ancestors, relationships have historically been based on compromise rather than contract. The Republic was borne from a revolt against their Spanish overlords and in order to survive, the former rebels learned to cooperate across religious and ideological lines. The Dutch tradition leaves room for contracts, but negotiations may be re-opened the day after conclusion if new facts emerge. D'Iribane is struck by everybody's respect for facts, which he finds stronger than in either France or in the USA. In France, status and power often prevail over facts; in the USA, moral principles are often seen as superseding facts. Dutch consensus is based on concern as to the individuals' quality of life, which should not be harmed by avoidable conflicts.

However, too simplistic and stereotyped a perspective can sometimes lead to false assumptions as to the national characteristics most closely aligned with 'business success', as Case Study 5.5 suggests.

CASE 5.5   Management gurus might rethink the Dutch approach   FT

In 2002, a group of consultants published a book examining 'the extraordinary successes of Dutch companies acquiring abroad, most especially in the USA'. The book, *Leading Cross-Border Mergers*, by Spencer Stuart, the headhunters and the Trompenaars Hampden-Turner, the Amsterdam-based specialists in inter-cultural management, said that if your company was going to be taken over by foreigners, you should pray they came from the Netherlands.

Dutch owners offered 'autonomy, understanding, respect, collegiality, friendship and complementarity, with no nationalistic agendas', the book says. 'It is a very attractive approach.' Among the chief executives interviewed for the book was Cees van der Hoeven, chief executive of Ahold, the Dutch retailer. Mr van der Hoeven boasted that Ahold was a 'real champion' when it came to making the acquisitions that had turned it into the second largest food retailer in the US. 'In all modesty, we can say that we are by far the best integrators in our sector,' he said.

In 2003, Mr van der Hoeven and Michael Meurs, the chief financial officer, resigned after revealing a $500 million overstatement in earnings at Ahold's US unit. Ahold is not the only Dutch company to have run into difficulties since appearing in the book. Others extolled for their skill in integrating foreign acquisitions included Akzo Nobel, the drugs and chemicals group, Buhrmann, the supplier of office products, and information technology company Getronics – all of which have since been hit by trouble at US subsidiaries.

None of this is likely to lead to immediate changes in the way the Netherlands views management and business. Indeed, the Dutch are considered experienced international managers. They are also successful at forging international partnerships; the Anglo-Dutch groups Unilever and Royal Dutch/Shell are the world's longest-standing cross-border companies.

Dutch managers pride themselves, too, on having an outlook that is far removed from the US obsession with shareholder value and quarterly financial reports. 'The Dutch way of management is different from [other countries],' says Karel Waagenaar, chief executive of Dutch-based W&S, an international firm that provides companies with temporary managers.

'The French like dictating. The Germans look to their superiors and are very obedient. The Americans are no-nonsense – if the boss says "we're going ahead" then you go ahead. The Dutch always try to compromise.'

It is a popular portrayal. The authors of *Leading Cross-Border Mergers* cite foreign observers' admiration of the way the Dutch deal with paradox. 'They are a monarchy, but think and behave like republicans. They are thrifts yet generous, blunt yet caring, protesting yet tolerant,' the book says.

Above all, the Dutch encourage the long-term view in business. The US focus on shareholder returns is seen as damaging to a company's future. 'We have a deep reluctance to accept the Anglo-Saxon framework of "shareholders first". Shareholders are people who never share. Holland is the country of the stakeholder. It should not be the analysts who decide how you run a company. We say: "Forget about the analysts. They kill our long-term thinking",' says one Dutch management consultant.

Ahold's financial problems were widely known so there was little shock at yesterday's resignations. But management observers are waiting to see what drove the US operation to behave as it did before drawing conclusions about the need for Dutch managers to change their approach. Some suspect the affair will confirm what happens when you press managers to produce financial performance beyond what the business can manage. Others wonder whether Dutch companies will have to allow foreign subsidiaries less autonomy. All agree that Dutch companies will think harder before buying US companies in future. And there will probably be less bragging about how good the Dutch are at managing them.

Source: Skapinker, M., 'In European countries, there are three or four competitors. In the US, there are 10 or 20', *Financial Times*, 25 February 2003.

Questions

1 What are believed to be effective Dutch characteristics for managing cross-border mergers and takeovers?

2 How does the Dutch approach differ from that perceived to be followed by other nationalities?

3 What evidence is there in the Case Study for questioning whether these national cultural assumptions will, or will not, bring international business 'success'?

Strategies for developing intercultural competence

Having established the importance of cultural sensitivities to international business operations, how can managers develop their own intercultural competences as well as those of their subordinates? Research Studies such as Brett *et al.* (2006) and Snow *et al.* (1996) has shown that the development of a healthy group process must take into account at least five major factors reflecting different elements of national and corporate cultures:

1 the degree of similarity among the cultural norms of the individuals on the team;
2 the extent to which such norms are manifested in the group;
3 the level of fluency in the common language used by the team;
4 the communication styles and expectations of what constitutes effective group behaviour;
5 the management style of the team leader.

Case Study 5.6 examines various challenges encountered by cross-cultural teams.

CASE 5.6 Challenges to cross-cultural team management

The dangers of imposing single-culture-based approaches when managing multicultural teams was highlighted in the results of a major study of global multicultural teams by Brett, Behfar and Kern (2006). They noted that the cultural differences which can create major problems for effective teamwork are often subtle and unrecognised until damage has actually been inflicted. Awareness of the challenges facing such teams from the outset can, however, help senior management resolve many of the problems before they become irreversible. Four types of challenge were identified as of particular importance in the study.

1 Direct versus indirect communication

In Western cultures communication is usually direct and explicit, whereas in many other cultures communication is indirect and implicit, often embedded in the means chosen to deliver the message and nuanced rather than communicated explicitly.

An example is cited of an American manager leading a project to build an interface for a US and Japanese customer data system. 'When the American manager discovered that several flaws in the system would significantly disrupt company operations, she pointed that out in an e-mail to her American boss and the Japanese team members. Her boss appreciated the direct warnings; her Japanese colleagues were embarrassed, because she had violated their norms for uncovering and discussing problems. Their reaction was to provide her with less access to the people and information she needed to monitor progress. They would probably have responded better if she had pointed out the problems indirectly – for example by asking them what would happen if a certain part of the system was not functioning properly, even though she knew full well that it was malfunctioning and also what the implications were' (Brett *et al.* 2006: 86). The result of 'inappropriate multicultural communication' was, in this case, for the American manager to be denied access to information by the Japanese members of the team, with those identified as violating accepted norms of behaviour typically isolated in Japanese culture.

Table 5.6 **Interpreting high-context communications**

What the British say	What they really mean
Not bad	Good, or very good
Quite good	A bit disappointing
Interesting	That *is* interesting, or It is interesting that you think it is interesting – it seems rather boring to me!
Oh, by the way, ...	I am about to get to the primary purpose of our discussion
I hear what you say	I disagree and do not wish to discuss it any further
With the greatest respect . . .	I think that you are wrong (or a fool)
Perhaps we could consider some other opinions	I don't like your ideas

Source: Brewster, Sparrow and Vernon (2007), p. 20.

2 Differing attitudes towards hierarchy and authority

Whereas teams may often have 'flat' structures, this may create problems for members from cultures which place considerable respect on the posts held rather than the qualities of the post-holder. They may then still exhibit characteristics within the team which would typically be used by them in more hierarchic organisational structures. For example in the Mexican culture knowledge and information may be conveyed to other team members indirectly in the form of an open-ended question, rather than a statement, which may well be interpreted as a lack of knowledge and conviction by other team members from cultures with a large power distance (*see* p. 174).

3 Conflicting norms for decision making

The approach to time and to the openness of the process involved in decision making can vary significantly between cultures. In the study by Brett *et al.* (2006) it was noted that the US members of a US–Indian project team were much more optimistic (2/3 weeks compared to 2/3 months) as to the likely delivery date and much more willing to share setbacks encountered with other team members, than was the case with the Indian team members. A major frustration being that US team members would only find out about problems when work was received, rather than being alerted earlier when the problems were encountered – thereby delaying resolution of such problems. Similarly a frustrated Brazilian manager from a US company purchasing Korean products thought that agreement on three of the four points at issue had been made on day one, only to find that whilst the US team members wanted to proceed to point 4 on day two, the Korean team members wanted to review and re-discuss points 1 to 3.

4 Problems with accents and fluency

Native English speakers were found on occasions wrongly to attribute a lack of fluency in English with a lack of expertise by team members on the problems at issue, creating frustrations all round and inefficiencies in the failure to exploit team expertise to the full.

Questions

1 To what extent might the various cross-cultural issues encountered here have been predicted from the Hofstede 'scores' in Table 5.3?

2 What suggestions might you make for resolving each of the 'challenges' above for a multicultural team you are managing?

Fedor and Werther (1996) have outlined an eight-stage process that can help to create a culturally responsive joint-venture alliance, assuming, of course, that those involved have already accepted the strategic imperatives of such an alliance. By following this multi-step process, decision makers can systematically consider the organisational dynamics of both firms by adding the cultural dimension to the normal strategic, financial and legal considerations. Working through these issues should mean that deeply rooted values are brought to the surface before they damage the prospects of the alliance.

■ Eight-stage process for cultural compatibility

1 *Corporate cultural profiles.* You can't create cultural compatibility unless you first realise where you are coming from. For this reason, it is important to have an idea of the original corporate culture for each of the partners before working out cultural compatibility. There are, of course, many different ways of carrying out cultural audits. Fedor and Werther suggest that the corporate culture can be defined by the unique set of beliefs and methods of problem-solving which underpin each company's activities.

2 *Cultural incompatibility identification.* At this stage, teams can compare profiles and identify problem areas. Such exercises usually reveal ambiguities and inconsistencies that should not be ignored. It could also reveal areas of mutuality that may have gone unnoticed.

3 *Development of a joint business purpose.* Teams need to agree on the nature of their purpose by reaching consensus about business objectives – such as desired rates of return, market shares, salaries, growth and time targets. This should uncover areas where there is any divergence. Reconciling such divergences early might help avoid future misunderstandings.

4 *Operational independence.* Both parties need to agree the degree of operational independence they are hoping to achieve. The degree of independence will depend on how much each party is prepared to reveal about their working practices without making their partners more formidable competitors.

5 *Structural choice.* The legal structure chosen for the alliance must take into account the desired culture. The variety of structures are wide: from open-ended joint ventures with varying ownership splits, through to time-specific technology sharing contracts. The choice is likely to be driven by deep-seated cultural preferences. For example, American-based partners often gain operational control by choosing a structure that gives them the final say in significant decisions, typically secured through majority ownership. This may, however, create obstacles in the design of an international alliance.

6 *Management systems agreement.* It is vital that these factors be taken into consideration. Management systems reflect deeply embedded ways of working that are often manifested in working practices. For example, in the failure of the Colgate–Palmolive/Kao joint venture in shampoo production, it was the Colgate marketing force that set up the marketing and distribution programme. Even the Colgate people questioned whether the market perspectives and practices successful for toothpaste would work for shampoo. In this way, the culture of the joint venture emerged unconsciously from Colgate's desire to maintain control. These were the driving forces creating the international alliance, rather than the unique needs of the shampoo business.

7 *Staffing the international alliance.* Care needs to be taken in selecting the managing director and key senior officers, since corporate cultures tend to be embodied in the values and beliefs of the people who work in them. Careful discussion will also be needed as to the job specifications and responsibilities, which may reveal deep-seated values about how organisations should be run.

8 *Assessing the international alliance's demands on parent company culture.* It is equally important to have a clear picture of what changes may be required in the parent company's culture. How will those changes be made? By whom? These questions may yield further insights into the cultural expectations and capabilities of the respective companies.

Fedor and Werther suggest that assessing the cultural compatibility of international alliances is critical if failure is to be avoided. This is the fourth dimension, after the financial, legal and strategic deal has been struck. Knowing the cultural match between the partners helps define the type of deal most likely to succeed once the deal makers have gone.

Brett *et al.* (2006) compress this eight-stage process into four key 'strategies' team managers might use to enhance the effectiveness of multicultural teams.

1 *Adaptation*: team members adapt practices or attitudes themselves, without changing the team membership or the tasks allocated.
2 *Structural intervention*: removing sources of conflict or inter-personal frictions by formally re-organising the team or redistributing tasks.
3 *Managerial intervention*: leader(s) intervene to establish norms of behaviour and decision making that take account of the multicultural characteristics of the team and/or establish networks of communication that are tailored to suit the different subgroups in the team.
4 *Exit*: removing one or more members from the team.

---

pause for thought 5   Under which situations might you advocate each of the four strategies identified above?

Case Study 5.7 highlights the increasing emphasis being placed on the corporate/organisational culture, even to the extent of adapting psychologically-based personality tests for individuals to the corporate culture. Since, as we note in Chapters 2 and 7, many mergers and acquisitions, joint ventures and alliances fail as much because of *organisational* cultural incompatibility as *international* cultural incompatibility, this new emphasis is receiving much attention by the potential acquirers and acquired.

CASE 5.7   **Corporate 'personality' has a big impact on business success**   **FT**

According to a study by the Chartered Institute of Personnel and Development, 30% of the difference in performance between companies can be attributed to differences in culture. That compares with just 5% that can be attributed to differences in strategy. Other studies have repeatedly found that as many as 75% of mergers and acquisitions fail primarily because of cultural clashes.

The idea that organisational culture or personality exists, and profoundly affects performance, raises no eyebrows these days. But can you go one step further and improve performance by analysing corporate personality in the same way as you might analyse that of an individual?

That is the question raised by Cognosis, a management consultancy that has adapted the Myers-Briggs Type Indicator (MBTI), a personality test widely used in the recruitment and personal development of individuals, and is now applying it to organisations. 'It seems bizarre that, given the critical importance of culture to corporate performance, its management isn't taken more seriously,' says Richard Brown, managing partner of Cognosis.

Methods of measuring personality and motivation

MBTI (Myers-Briggs Type Indicator) is a personality questionnaire used worldwide for individual, team and organisational development. Based on more than 50 years of research, the MBTI promotes understanding of an individual's personality, their motivation and their preferred behaviours and an appreciation of differences between people. It has many applications, including team-building and management and leadership development.

Using the averaged responses to a 15-minute paper containing 30 questions, given to as few as a dozen executives, Cognosis claims to be able to use MBTI to identify four organisational character types. The organisation is then profiled on a number of characteristics, such as its approach to problem solving, how it deals with change, innovation and internal communications and how it will react to stress. 'The resulting insights can be used to allow us to make fairly detailed recommendations about a range of development needs,' says Mr Brown.

What sort of person is your company?

The Cognosis method of analysing company personality sorts companies into four types:

1 Rational – logical and ingenious, e.g. Diageo
2 Sympathetic harmoniser, e.g. EasyJet
3 Pragmatic – focused on the here and now, e.g. Nestlé
4 Idealistic – enthusiastic and insightful, e.g. Interbrew

While no type is better than any other, some organisational character types are better suited to the markets in which they compete and each character type has its own particular development needs, he says.

So drinks company Allied Domecq is a pragmatic 'fixer' organisation, he says. Fixers are action-oriented, resourceful and realistic but tend to value action over strategy. As a consequence they reorganise constantly and achieve inconsistent results.

'The fixer organisation needs to stop and think. It needs to broaden its perspective, look further into the future and articulate its long-term goals. It needs to introduce some structure into its planning and some discipline into its performance management. It also needs to connect with and articulate its values,' says Mr Brown.

Cognosis' approach has met a mixed reception among organisational psychologists and academics. The idea of a simple way of identifying profound truths about a company sounds attractive. But it also raises suspicions that Cognosis may be selling 'snake oil'.

That is certainly the concern of Angela Baron, an organisational psychologist who advises the Chartered Institute of Personnel and Development. 'I agree that corporations have individual cultures but I am not sure I would describe it as a personality. Myers-Briggs is a useful tool for dealing with individuals but it could be enormously dangerous to use it in a way it wasn't designed for,' she says.

Others are concerned that the Cognosis approach may be too glib. 'You can't just flash a questionnaire to understand a culture. You have to immerse yourself in it and get under the skin. This may be a useful way into complex organisational issues but I wonder whether these are the most appropriate dimensions to assess corporate culture. I suspect there are better tools available than this,' says Nigel Nicholson, professor of organisational behaviour at London Business School.

Nevertheless the Open University, which has been remodelling itself to deal with changes in the distance learning market, says its insights have been invaluable. 'We have been engaged in a major change programme. We used Cognosis' approach to culture mapping to look more deeply inside our organisation, identifying the behaviour and attitude changes needed to improve our customer focus and service. It provided new insights into the underlying character of our organisation, and its constituent parts, and identified specific areas for change,' says Professor Geoff Peters, pro-vice-chancellor for strategy and planning.

Sports and leisure conglomerate The Pentland Group is also sold on the idea. 'We plan to use it to understand our own culture in reference to the culture of any takeover target. Think of it as cultural due diligence,' says Tim Hockings, corporate development director.

Source: Benady, A., 'Organisations, too, can be put on the couch', *Financial Times*, 20 June 2003.

Questions

1 Why is such emphasis being placed on cultural aspects of organisational behaviour?

2 If companies could be categorised according to the MBTI test, what benefits might result and to whom?

3 Consider the arguments for and against this organisational approach.

Useful websites

Now try the self-check questions for this chapter on the website at www.pearsoned.co.uk/wall. You will also find further resources as well as useful weblinks.

Many interesting articles on labour issues are included in:

www.peoplemanagement.co.uk
www.tomorrowscompany.com
www.croner.co.uk

For aspects of Asian culture check *www.apmforum.com*
Also *http://english.china.com*
www.japanecho.com
The Commission for Racial Equality is found at *www.cre.gov.uk*

Useful key texts

Daniels, J., Radebaugh, L. and Sullivan, D. (2006) *International Business* (11th edn), Pearson Prentice Hall, especially Chapter 2.

Dicken, P. (2003) *Global Shift: Transforming the World Economy* (4th edn), Paul Chapman Publishing Ltd, especially Chapter 5.

Hill, C. (2006) *International Business: Competing in the Global Marketplace* (5th edn), McGraw-Hill Irwin, especially Chapter 3.

Morrison, J. (2006) *The International Business Environment* (2nd edn), Palgrave, especially Chapter 5.

Rugman, A. and Collinson, R. (2009) *International Business* (5th edn), FT Prentice Hall, especially Chapter 5.

Wild, J., Wild, K. and Han, J. (2006) *International Business: The Challenges of Globalization* (3rd edn), FT Prentice Hall, especially Chapter 2.

Other texts and sources

Brett, J., Behfar, K. and Kern, C. (2006) 'Managing Cultural Teams', *Harvard Business Review*, Nov.

Brewster, C., Sparrow, P. and Vernon, G. (2007) *International Human Resource Management* (2nd edn), Chartered Institute of Personnel and Development.

Chu, G.C. and Ju, Y. (1993) *The Grand Wall in Ruins*, State University of New York Press.

D'Iribane, I., cited in Hofstede, G. (1996) 'Problems Remain but Theories will Change: the Universal and the Specific in 21st Century Global Management', *Organizational Dynamics*, vol. 1, pp. 34–43.

Elashmawi, F. (1998) 'Overcoming Multicultural Clashes in Global Joint Ventures', *European Business Review*, vol. 98, no. 4, pp. 211–16.

Elias, N. (1994) *The Civilizing Process*, Blackwell.

Encyclopædia Britannica (2000), Encyclopædia Britannica (UK) Ltd, London.

Fedor, K.J. and Werther, W.B. Jr (1996) 'The Fourth Dimension: Creating Culturally Responsive International Alliances', *Organizational Dynamics*, vol. 1.

Griffin, R.W. and Pustay, M.W. (1996) *International Business: A Managerial Perspective*, Addison-Wesley.

Griffiths, A. (2000) 'Cultural Determinants of Competitiveness: The Japanese Experience', in *Dimensions of International Competitiveness: Issues and Policies*, Lloyd-Reason, L. and Wall, S. (eds), Edward Elgar.

Hall, E.T. (1976) *Beyond Culture*, Anchor Press.

Hampden-Turner, C. and Trompenaars, F. (1994) *The Seven Cultures of Capitalism*, Piatkus.

Hofstede, G. (1980) *Culture's Consequences*, Sage.

Hofstede, G. (1991) *Cultures and Organizations: Software of the Mind*, McGraw-Hill.

Hofstede, G. and Hofstede, G.J. (2005) *Cultures and Organisations: Software of the Mind*, McGraw Hill.

Hofstede, G., Neuijen, B. and Ohavy, D. (1990) 'Measuring Organisational Cultures: A Qualitative and Quantitative Case Study across Twenty Cases', *Administrative Science Quarterly*, 35.

International Herald Tribune (2007) 'Japan merger culture: an investors' guide', 4 May (http://iht.com/articles/2007/05/04yourmoney/mjapan.php).

Kidd, J. and Xue, Li (2000) 'The Modelling of Issues and Perspectives in MNEs', in *Dimensions of International Competitiveness*, Lloyd-Reason, L. and Wall, S. (eds), Edward Elgar.

Mouer, R. and Kawanishi H. (2005) *A Sociology of Work in Japan*, Cambridge University Press.

Peters, T. and Waterman, R.H. (1982) *In Search of Excellence*, Harper & Row, New York.

Snow, C.C., Davison, S.C., Snell, S.A. and Hambrik, D.C. (1996) 'Use of Transnational Teams to Globalize your Company', *Organizational Dynamics*, vol. 24, no. 4, pp. 90–107.

Tayeb, M. (1994) 'Japanese Managers and British Culture: a Comparative Case Study', *International Journal of Human Resource Management*, 5.

Tayeb, M. (2000) *International Business: Theories, Policies and Practices*, Financial Times Prentice Hall, especially Chapters 4, 13 and 19.

The Japan Times Online (2007) 'Cross-shareholding sees first rise since 90s', 7 September (http://search.japantimes.co.jp/cgi-bin/nb20070902a1.html).

Trompenaars, H. (1993) *Riding the Waves of Culture: Understanding Cultural Diversity in Business*, The Economist Books.

UNESCO (2002) *Universal Declaration on Cultural Diversity* (Adopted by the 31st Session of the General Conference of UNESCO), Paris, 2 November 2001, p. 11.

United Nations Conference on Trade and Development (UNCTAD) *World Investment Report* (annual publication).

United Nations Development Programme (UNDP) *Human Development Report* (annual publication), OUP.

Weber, M. (1930) *The Protestant Ethic and the Spirit of Capitalism*, Allen and Unwin.

World Bank, *World Development Report* (annual publication).

Yeung, I.Y.M. and Tung, K.L. (1996) 'Achieving Business Success in Confucian Societies: the Importance of Guanxi (Connections)', *Organizational Dynamics*, vol. 1.

Chapter 6

International ethical and ecological environment

By the end of this chapter you should be able to:

- explain why an awareness of ethical issues can be important for international business;

- outline the different ethical positions that can be adopted;

- discuss the different ethical approaches that multinationals have taken when trading abroad;

- examine some of the national/international agreements and regulations that have been adopted in an attempt to instill an ethical awareness into business practices, with particular reference to MNE activity;

- assess the importance of managing the ecological environment, for both individuals and companies;

- evaluate the impacts of sustainability related issues on international business activities.

Introduction

What is an organisation for? Why does it exist? How are decisions taken within it? People often assume that organisations exist in order to make a profit or to provide a service in the most cost-effective way. In the West businesses have developed under the capitalist ethic, which focuses on the creation of surplus value (profit) and its distribution to shareholders in the form of dividends. Over time, national governments have increasingly sought to remedy aspects of 'market failure' in such economies, by providing minimum levels of public services in education or health or by seeking to prevent private businesses from abusing their market power. As societies become ever more complex, businesses are beginning to exert still more influence over the ways in which the economy is run, so that even social institutions are becoming more intimately linked with economic patterns. In the UK, for example, the powerful lobby of the supermarkets has exerted considerable influence on transport policies, on the types of goods we consume, on trading relationships with domestic and international suppliers and on the ways in which we define our leisure hours. Thus business organisations are carrying more and more responsibility for the ways in which wealth is both created and distributed and the ways in which we organise ourselves. In these various ways the ethical responsibilities of business are arguably growing. But what do we mean by business ethics?

Ethical standards are generally regarded as those ways of acting or being that are deemed acceptable by some reference group at a particular time and place. These standards can be implicit to the group or explicit, as in the case of a 'code of practice'. The objective of making such standards explicit usually involves an attempt to avoid an excess of self-interest that might mitigate against the 'good of all'. Of course, the key question is, what is the good of all? One man's meat may be another man's poison! Further, even if a code of ethics were to be agreed by a reference group it must be flexible and capable of change, otherwise it can easily become institutionalised, dogmatic and ultimately self-defeating.

Business ethics

Too often, in the past, business ethics have been taken for an 'oxymoron' (a contradiction in terms). At the level of business the prevailing view has often seemed to be that as long as the business is profitable, then 'anything goes'. Somewhere along the line business and ethics have become separated out; no one in business talks about ethics and no one in the moral field of actions talks about business.

And yet, if we can define ethics or morality as the 'set of organising principles by which people live together', ethics must surely play a large part in organisational and business activities – based, as they are, on group dynamics and individual interactions. The reason that the process of applying ethical standards to business or management seems to be difficult may be because it might appear to contradict economic perspectives such as 'competition', which sets organisations (communities of beings) against one another.

This is, of course, a misperception: ethics are as much an integral part of business and commerce as they are of specialised functions, such as financing, accountancy, legal practices, etc. The fundamental issue here is that of choice – and in business choices are made each and every moment. Business decisions are choices in which the decision makers could have acted otherwise. Every decision or action affects people or relationships between people such that an alternative action or inaction would affect them differently. What criteria are these decisions based upon? Are they criteria of profit or of 'well-being'? It is far better for everyone concerned if managers are aware of the ethical significance of their actions and decisions and thus consciously, rather than inadvertently, lead and shape their corporate cultures.

A study by Collins and Porras (1994) cited a number of companies that survived major changes in management, new product development and the impacts of various business cycles. The companies that flourished over a long period were found to be companies that pursued a stable core mission, which provided the basis for all corporate activities and drove decision making through all the business changes encountered. According to Collins and Porras, the 'best' (longest lasting and most profitable) business organisations are those that do not focus on profitability as their primary mission. In their rankings, the highest performing corporations tended to be those that were governed by core beliefs, which transcended purely economic pursuits, seeking rather to produce the finest products in the marketplace, to win customer satisfaction, to serve employees, and so on. Such findings are contrary to much of the theory taught in our business schools.

The authors cited a number of international businesses that have thrived through the creation of ethical cultures. For example, Patagonia Inc. has created a strong corporate culture that values its employees and the social and natural environments in which it conducts business. Patagonia gives 1% of its annual sales revenue to environmental groups and grants employees up to two months off with full compensation to work for non-profit environmental groups. Independent human rights organisations have been invited to audit any of their facilities on request. In response to the 1996 public dialogue on 'sweatshops', Patagonia implemented a corporate policy not to contract with any supplier engaging in such practices.

The Body Shop has also adopted overtly 'ethical' aims, which are explained further in Case Study 6.1.

CASE 6.1 The Body Shop

The Body Shop is a publicly quoted manufacturer and retailer of health and beauty products. It began in 1976 with the opening of the first shop in Brighton and is now an international company rapidly expanding throughout the world. Today The Body Shop has over 2500 shops, operates in 60 countries and trades in 23 languages with over 3000 staff directly employed and a similar number of staff working in franchised retail outlets. Its founder was the late Anita Roddick, a charismatic woman with very firm ideas, particularly about the values involved in business trading. Unlike other companies in this area, they do not use direct marketing or pay for advertising and believe that what differentiates them is not so much the product but, as stated by a previous Head of Corporate Services, 'what they represent as a company'.

They are a known brand retailer who manufactures their own products, which means that, unlike other retailers, they do not work on short cycles. Traditional problems such as branding and design appear less important since the labels have tended to stay the same and the bottles in which the products are sold have also been largely unchanged. They have often been the top sellers in their markets with many new products simply being extensions of existing ones. For much of the time their competitors have had only a marginal impact on their market since their customer profile is that of 20–35-year-old females who have an interest in the environmental and social issues on behalf of which this organisation campaigns.

The Body Shop claims that its values are fundamentally very simple, and represent the initial values of the founders, namely that people, in relating to each other, should act with honesty, care, integrity and respect.

In previous mission statements the Body Shop has emphasised its dedication to the pursuit of social and environmental 'justice' and to furthering the interests of all its stakeholders, whether employees, customers, franchisees, suppliers or shareholders.

It has also emphasised its commitment to ecological sustainability, especially as regards the protection of the environment and thereby safeguarding the interests of future generations who depend on that environment.

In more recent mission statements similar commitments have been made, including the pursuit of 'fair wages', the use of natural materials and ingredients, and support for campaigns to end the needless suffering of animals.

However, as the general manager for corporate culture at Body Shop noted, though these basic values appear superficially quite straightforward, they are notoriously difficult to implement. Indeed, disappointing results from attempts to expand into the US and other acquisitions resulted in financial difficulties which have placed considerable pressure on the ethical focus of the company. Since 1985 The Body Shop has been a public company, quoted on the Stock Exchange and with a growing number of shareholders. Only 18% of shares were in the hands of the founder herself by the time of the takeover of the Body Shop by L'Oréal, the French cosmetics giant, in 2006. It was pointed out by critics that L'Oréal was in the bottom three companies as regards ethical rating from the *Ethical Consumer Magazine*, with particular concern being expressed as regards L'Oréal's animal testing policy and the use of chemicals in its cosmetics.

Questions

1 Can you suggest any hypothetical (or actual) ethical problems which The Body Shop might face (or has faced) in implementing its core values?

2 Consider the implications of the L'Oréal merger in terms of the ethical principles guiding the Body Shop.

Ethics and the corporate culture

In all organisations the same principles arguably apply. Organisations need certain 'ways of acting or being' (which can be either explicit or implicit) as a guide to 'acceptable' behaviour by members of the organisation. In the current business press two things stand out. One is the issue of global competitiveness and the other is a list of alleged wrongdoings by business leaders in virtually all countries. For Beyer and Nino (1999):

> It seems likely that the two are related, that the ethical and cultural fabrics of our business communities and whole societies are being weakened, virtually torn apart by the struggles inherent in unprecedented levels of economic competition. Clearly it is time for management scholars and academics everywhere to begin to address the ethical issues associated with the all-out economic war being waged throughout the world.

Beyer and Nino go on to tell a story which, in their view, has a number of parallels with modern international business practice (*see* Box 6.1).

Box 6.1   An ethical dilemma

McCoy was in the mountains of Nepal on his way to a village considered a holy place with an American anthropologist named Stephen, a Sherpa guide and a group of porters. To get to the village they had to climb across a mountain pass at 18,000 feet (about 5500 metres). The night before the planned climb they camped at around 15,000 feet, near several other groups; four young men from New Zealand, two Swiss couples and a Japanese hiking club.

At 3.30 a.m. the next morning the New Zealanders got the first start up the mountain. The American party left next, followed by the Swiss, while the Japanese lingered in their camp. When the Americans reached about 15,500 feet, Stephen began to feel ill and they stopped to rest. Soon thereafter one of the New Zealanders appeared with a body slung over his back. It was a *sadhu* (old man) he had found on the mountain – almost naked and unconscious, clearly suffering from hypothermia, but still alive. The New Zealander suggested that the porters travelling with the Americans take the old man down the mountain and then went back to join his group. Stephen and the Swiss couples attended to the *sadhu*, stripping off his wet clothes, wrapping him in clothing from their packs and giving him food and drink when he revived.

Meanwhile the businessman McCoy was growing anxious about the delay because he feared that if he waited any longer to resume his climb, the sun would melt the steps carved in the snow that he needed to help him cross the mountain pass. Adding to his worry was the fact that previously he had suffered quite severe altitude sickness even at a lower altitude. Neither of these concerns led him to abandon his goal. He was still determined to cross the mountain pass and reach the sacred village. So he left to catch up with some of the porters who had gone ahead to prepare the way. His friend Stephen, who was still not feeling well, and the Swiss couples stayed behind with the *sadhu*.

An hour or so later, after climbing most of the way, McCoy himself became dizzy and stopped to rest, allowing the Swiss to catch up with him. He asked them about the *sadhu* and was told he was fine and that his friend Stephen was on the way. When Stephen finally arrived he was suffering from altitude sickness and could only walk 15 steps at a time before resting. He was also very angry and accosted McCoy saying, 'How do you feel about contributing to the death of a fellow man?' McCoy was stunned and asked if the *sadhu* had died. 'No', Stephen replied, 'But he will.' He then explained that the Swiss had departed not long after McCoy and that the Japanese, when asked, refused to lend a horse they had with them to carry the man down the mountain to the nearest village. The Japanese then went on their way taking the horse with them. When Stephen asked the Sherpa and the remaining porters if they would take the *sadhu* they also refused, saying they would not have the strength or time to get across the pass if they first carried him down the mountain. Instead, the porters took the old man a short distance down the mountain, where they laid him on a large rock in the sun, and left him there, awake, but weak. No one in the four groups of climbers ever found out whether the *sadhu* lived or died but all got over the pass and on to the holy village that was their goal.

Source: Beyer and Nino (1999). Copyright 1999 by Sage Publications, Inc. Reprinted by permission of Sage Publications.

We can usefully use this account to derive a number of ethical implications, which have some parallels in international business. Beyer and Nino pick out the following parallels.

- First, no one assumed ultimate responsibility for the *sadhu*. By focusing on reaching a holy place, they ignored their ethical responsibilities. Trying to reach the mountain top can be compared with the unremitting competition of global business with its elements of social Darwinism, namely the idea of the survival of the fittest. This modern business 'ethic' would see it as natural that others get left behind. 'Doing unto others as you would have them do unto you' would be suicidal in business. Such attitudes encourage people to set for themselves self-interested (organisational goals) and to pursue them relentlessly with little concern for their effects on others. Some forms of winning in business (getting a new product to market, achieving assigned targets, taking over another firm) can overwhelm broader based ethical principles and impulses.

- Second, the groups involved had no prior experience or model for jointly arriving at a consensus about what to do. They came from four different cultures and lacked a commonality of mutually accepted values that would give them guidance as to what to do. Each group passed the problem on to the other group. There was no strong culture to glue their actions together. This 'buck-passing' between departments and multinational divisions is hardly uncommon.

- Third, there was a failure to act which then itself became the decision. This can often happen in business, especially when something has been going on for some time. The lack of guidance given to Nick Leeson, an inexperienced trader in Singapore in 1996, is arguably one such example.

- Fourth, the decision makers were physically and mentally stressed and under time pressures. It is precisely under these conditions in a hyper-competitive world that personal and corporate values are most severely tested.

- The final parallel is that even though one of the people saw through all of these considerations as regards his ethical responsibility, he did not get the support he needed from the others present to rescue the *sadhu*. It was beyond his individual capacity, a circumstance that often occurs in business. Many ethical decisions require the support of the corporate community. Ethically sensitive and courageous individuals cannot often perform ethically without the support of others.

The lesson here is that it is up to management to provide such support as part of the corporate culture. The ethical dilemma previously described was heightened by the fact that people of different cultures were attempting (or not attempting) to reach a decision. With increasing globalisation, such issues are becoming increasingly common as multinational teams attempt to work together.

pause for thought 1   Can you suggest how two MNEs from different national cultures, which are collaborating on a joint venture, may adopt different ethical positions on certain issues?

Different ethical positions

We have already noted that our actions as individuals are determined in part by the values we hold, which can be influenced by our surroundings and our experiences. But what happens in an organisation?

Corporate agency and responsibility

An organisation is neither an individual nor a total social system. It is comprised of individuals in various roles which may be authorised by the larger 'society' to function for specific, often narrowly defined, purposes. The actions of an organisation are often the result of collective, rather than individual decision making. We saw in Box 6.1 how the *sadhu* was left to die because no single group or person was prepared to take responsibility. This can be true within organisations, even more so when that organisation is trading internationally.

But who is acting in an organisation? Can we reduce the group action down to the level of each individual? Or do we treat an organisation as if the organisation itself was an individual directing the activity of its constituents? Ethically and academically many thinkers have sought to understand the nature of corporate responsibility.

The Nobel Prize economist Milton Friedman declared: 'There is only one social responsibility of business – to use its resources and engage in activities designed to increase its profits so long as it stays within the rules of the game, which is to say, engages in open and free competition without deception or fraud' (Friedman 1970: 126).

This does not mean that 'anything goes': law and common morality should guide action. However, there is an assumption here that profit maximisation is the main responsibility of business. This is based on the so-called 'rational actor' theory. In this view when an individual acts rationally, he/she is seeking to maximise his/her own long-term self-interest. In Friedman's view, that self-interest will be allied to making an overt contribution to enhancing corporate profitability.

However, the idea of such a 'unity of purpose' impacting on the values of those who act on behalf of an organisation has been challenged in various ways.

The principal–agent problem

In the case of a sole trader, the principal (owner) and the agent (manager) are one and the same. However, to assume that it is the owners who control the firm neglects the fact that today the dominant form of industrial organisation is the public limited company (plc), which is usually run by managers rather than by owners. This may lead to conflict between the owners (shareholders) and the managers whenever the managers pursue goals which differ from those of the owners. This conflict is referred to as a type of *principal–agent* problem and emerges when the shareholders (principals) contract a second party, the managers (agents), to perform some tasks on their behalf. In return, the principals offer their agents some compensation (wage payments). However, because the principals are divorced from the day-to-day running of the business, the agents may be able to act as they themselves see fit. This independence of action may be due to their superior knowledge of the company as well as their ability to disguise their actions from the principals. Agents, therefore, may not always act in the manner desired by the principals. Indeed, it may be the agents' goals which predominate. This has led to a number of managerial theories on the behaviour of business organisations, such as sales revenue maximisation and growth maximisation, which see the salary and status of managers being more closely related to turnover and company size rather than to its pure profit performance.

Social contract theory

Thomas Hobbes suggested that human beings tacitly agree to laws and regulations on their behaviour so that they can live in harmony and achieve their own ends in relation to others. Donaldson and Dunfee (1999) take this argument further in their 'Integrated Social Contract Theory', by suggesting that there are basic moral minimums (or 'hypernorms') that govern all social relationships on the macro level. These are subject to debate, can be explicit or tacit, but might include:

- not causing gratuitous harm;
- honouring contracts;
- respecting human rights;
- treating people and organisations fairly.

On a micro level, however, there may be a moral 'free space' dictated by the community in question. Here communities can spell out the specific norms deemed acceptable among themselves as long as these are compatible with the hypernorms. These 'consistent norms' tend to be tacit. Figure 6.1 shows a global model of the Integrated Social Contract Theory (ISCT).

- *Hypernorms* – these moral minima include, for example, fundamental human rights or basic prescriptions common to most major religions. The values they represent are, by definition, acceptable to all cultures and organisations.
- *Consistent norms* – these values are more culturally specific than those at the centre, but are consistent both with hypernorms and other legitimate norms. The ethical codes and vision value statements of companies would fall within this circle.

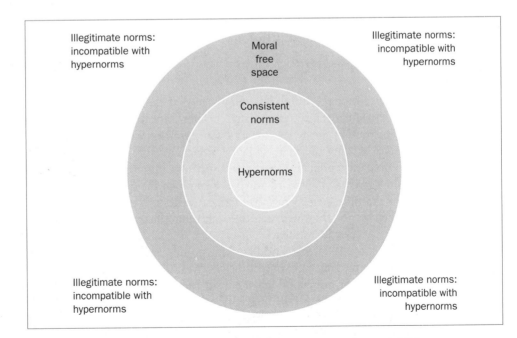

Figure 6.1 **Global norms in the Integrated Social Contract Theory (ISCT)**

- *Moral-free space* – as one moves away from the centre of the circle one finds norms that are inconsistent with at least some of the other legitimate norms existing in other cultures. Such norms often reflect strongly held cultural beliefs, whether at the national, corporate or occupational level (*see* Chapter 5).
- *Illegitimate norms* – these are norms that are incompatible with hypernorms. When values or practices reach a point where they transgress permissible limits (as specified, say, by fundamental human rights) they fall outside the circle and into the 'incompatible' zone. Exposing workers, for instance, to unreasonable levels of carcinogens (e.g. asbestos) is an expression of a value falling outside the circle.

The ISCT model has proved helpful for evaluating ethical behaviour in organisations, especially at the international level (*see* p. 214).

■ Stakeholder theory

There is an increasing focus by leading organisations on their obligation to *stakeholders*, i.e. the internal and external individuals and groups which relate to that organisation. Stakeholders can be defined as any individual or group which can affect or be affected by the achievement of the organisation's objectives. Such stakeholders might include employees, customers, suppliers, consumers, etc.

While the stakeholder perspective may simply appear to be a way of describing an organisation, in fact it also moves away from the moral assumptions that are made in the 'rational actor' theory. Stakeholder theory challenges the position that the primary purpose of a firm is to maximise the welfare of its stockholders (e.g. dividends), arguing instead that the goal of any firm should be to satisfy the aspirations of all its primary stakeholders. In addition to moral obligations to employees, there are additional responsibilities because of the unique and specifically defined relationships between a particular organisation and its stakeholders.

CASE 6.2   Ethics and profits

The conventional wisdom has long been that the more ethical the stance of a company, the lower the returns to shareholders. Socially Responsible Investing (SRI) is an organisation in the UK which challenges this view and insists that its members take into account the environmental, ethical and social impacts of their investments. SRI companies point to their share portfolio outperforming the market average. It would seem that events are moving strongly in the direction of these companies.

For example, since 3 July 2000 all pension funds in the UK must, by law, disclose whether or not they will take into account the environmental, ethical and social impacts of their investments.

Indeed, the 10 largest world banking groups (including Barclays and Royal Bank of Scotland in the UK, Citigroup in the US, West LB in Germany) agreed in 2003 to abide by the 'equator principles' when considering future investments. These principles are based on the policies of the International Finance Corporation (p. 127) which advises the banks on major development projects. Banks agreeing to these 'equator principles' will now grant loans only to projects whose promoters can demonstrate their willingness and ability to conduct the projects in a 'socially responsible manner' and according to 'sound environmental management practices'. Environmental impact anlayses will be required of projects regarded as high and medium risk in this context, including the impact on involuntary resettlement of local people.

Campaign groups, such as Friends of the Earth, while welcoming such initiatives, are cautious as to what they will mean in practice. For example, the banks have refused to say whether they would have regarded the controversial Three Gorges Dam in China (now nearing completion) as having been in breach of the principle and therefore ineligible for the loans actually made.

The growing corporate acceptance of a need to be more socially responsible is reflected in the launch of a new FTSE 4 Good Index in July 2001 in the UK, using social and ethical criteria to rank corporate performance. All companies in three sectors were excluded, namely tobacco, weapons and nuclear power (representing 10% of all FTSE companies). Of the remaining companies, three criteria were applied for ranking purposes: environment, human rights and social issues. If a company 'fails' in any one of these criteria, it is again excluded. Of the 757 companies in the FTSE All-Share Index, only 288 companies have actually made it into the index.

The FTSE itself has produced figures showing that if this new FTSE 4 Good Index had existed over the five years prior to its launch, it would actively have outperformed the more conventional stock exchange indices. The same has been found to be true for the Dow Jones Sustainability Group Index in the USA. This is a similar ethical index introduced in the USA in 1999. When backdated to 1993 it was found to have outperformed the Dow Jones Global Index by 46%.

It was reported in 2008 that annual sales of Fairtrade food and drink in Britain have reached over £350 million, having grown at over 40% per year over the past decade. It has expanded from one brand of coffee ten years ago to around 1000 foodstuffs, including chocolate, fruit, vegetables, juices, snacks, wine, tea, sugar, honey and nuts. A Mori poll found that two-thirds of UK consumers claim to be green or ethical and actively look to purchase products with an environmental/ethical association.

Questions

1 Why is it suggested that the more ethically and environmentally conscious firms might actually be more profitable than those which pay little heed to the environment?

2 For what reasons might we expect UK companies to become more ethically and environmentally aware in the future?

International business ethics

So far we have seen that each organisation, and indeed individual within it, has a role to play in ensuring that decisions have a conscious ethical content. However, how do people deal with one another when the ethical content varies at a cultural level? The cultural differences explored in Chapter 5 have their counterparts in ethical differences. How can managers manoeuvre through the grey areas that exist within and between organisations and cultures. Take, for example, the following illustration. As a director of a joint venture in Hungary you become aware that many of the employees are working long hours on jobs outside the company to supplement their work for the joint venture. You deem this to be not only inefficient but also possibly unethical. When you confront senior managers in the joint venture they defend their workers vigorously. They argue that the wages are not high enough to support families and that there is a tradition of 'moonlighting' which has historically been considered to be ethical. Hungarians, having suffered over 500 years of living with 'oppressors' – the Turks, the Austro-Hungarians and the Russians – typically do not confine their loyalties to any single entity. Clearly, as a director, you have been presented with what is both an efficiency and an ethical dilemma.

Similar dilemmas were highlighted by the work of Turner and Trompenaars (1993) who asked thousands of managers around the world the following question:

> While you are talking and sharing a bottle of beer with a friend who is officially on duty as a safety inspector in the company you both work for, an accident occurs, injuring a shift worker. The National Safety Commission launches an investigation and you are asked for your evidence. There are other witnesses. What right has your friend to expect you to protect him?

The choices offered were these:

1 a definite right;
2 some right;
3 no right.

Fundamental to this question is the ethical tension between a 'right' and the implicit notion of the 'duties' of friendship. The results of the survey were very revealing. To cite only a few figures, approximately 94% of US managers and 91% of Austrian managers answered 3, 'no right', whereas only 53% of French and 59% of Singaporean managers considered there to be 'no right'.

Other studies show striking differences among ethical attitudes towards everyday business problems. One study (Macdonald 1988) revealed that Hong Kong managers considered taking credit for another's work as being at the top of a list of unethical activities; in contrast to their Western counterparts, they considered this to be more unethical than bribery or the gaining of competitor information. The same study showed that 82% of Hong Kong managers thought that additional government regulation would improve ethical conduct in business, whereas only 27% of US managers believed it would.

How then do organisations deal with such ethical and cultural variations? The first step, of course, is to understand that they exist. Many multinationals fail to even acknowledge the ethical implications of cultural differences.

■ Approaches to ethical issues

Enderle (1995) has identified four broad types of approach which international business might take to ethical issues, each of which can be compared to a posture taken historically by nation states as follows:

1 *Foreign country type.* This does not apply its own ethical norms to the foreign country but conforms to the local customs, taking its direction from what prevails

as morality in the host country. The Swiss are often identified with this approach to business.

2 *Empire type.* This resembles the approach of Great Britain in India and elsewhere before 1947. This type of company applies domestic ethical concepts without making any serious modifications to local customs. Empire-type companies export their values in a wholesale fashion, and often do so regardless of the consequences to the host company or its stakeholders.

3 *Interconnection type.* This regards the international sphere as differing from the domestic sphere. Companies here do not necessarily see themselves as protecting a national identity or ethical framework. The notion of national interest becomes blurred with that of the supranational (e.g. the EU).

4 *Global type.* This abstracts from all national or regional differences, viewing the domestic sphere as entirely irrelevant; citizens of all nations need to become more cosmopolitan. Only global citizenry makes sense from this perspective.

In terms of Integrated Social Contract Theory (*see* p. 211) the danger with the 'foreign country' type is that there is nothing to limit the moral-free space of the host country culture. If government corruption and environmental pollution are accepted in the host country, then the 'foreign country' type of approach to ethical issues might be regarded as colluding with this unethical framework.

The 'empire' and 'global' types fall into the opposite trap. Each acts from a fixed idea of what is right or wrong, and so will suffocate the moral-free space of the host country. The 'empire' type sees itself as the bearer of moral truth. In the same way, though perhaps more subtly, the 'global' type seeks to impose moral truth – namely that since only global citizenry makes sense, the company can be impervious to ethical differences that mark a culture's distinctiveness. The opportunity for host cultures to define their own versions of moral and economic truth is lost.

The 'interconnection' type is consistent with the ISCT approach by acknowledging both universal moral limits at the macro level (hypernorms) and also ethical consideration at the micro level. While the notion of national interest is blurred, it does manage to balance moral principles with moral free space in a way that makes it somewhat more convincing than its three counterparts.

So what are the implications of these findings for the international manager? How can they negotiate the stormy sea of differing ethical values and behaviours? It may be instructive to attempt to use the ISCT global values (Figure 6.1) to consider the ethical problems involved with bribery or sensitive payments.

■ Bribery and corruption

Bribery is a major source of concern to many companies trading globally. Are such payments examples of legitimate norms or are such payments invariably a direct violation of hypernorms and other legitimate norms and hence located outside the circle and in the 'illegitimate' area? Not only does the incidence of bribery vary across nations, so too do perceptions as to its being unethical. Studies have shown Hong Kong and Greek managers to be less critical of bribery in certain scenarios than their American counterparts. An interesting question is whether bribery or 'sensitive' payments are more likely to be considered as an acceptable way of conducting international business (hence a legitimate norm) in countries where such practices are commonplace?

Donaldson and Dunfee (1999) do not think so, arguing that it is a myth to believe that bribery is accepted wherever it flourishes. In fact, there is a surprising amount of agreement to the contention that bribery is unethical. We can suggest at least three reasons for this ethical perspective on bribery using the ISCT approach.

1 Acceptance of a bribe usually violates a microsocial contract specifying the duties of the agent (the bribe recipient) to the principal (the employing body), whether the government or a private company.

2 Bribery is typically not a legitimate norm. All countries have laws against the practice. Some countries, even where the practice is flourishing, have draconian penalties. In China in 1994 the president of the Great Wall Machinery and Electronic High-Technology Industrial group, Mr Shen Haifu, was executed for bribery and embezzlement offences, despite the recorded prevalence of such practices in China. The OECD has increased its efforts to reduce bribery by launching, in March 1994, a campaign aimed at reducing the incidence of bribery in international trade transactions.

3 Bribery may violate the hypernorms of political participation and efficiency. When, in the 1970s, Japan bought planes from the American aircraft manufacturer, Lockheed, Prime Minister Tanaka was subsequently found to have accepted tens of millions of dollars in bribes. The Japanese press and other sources questioned whether he was discharging his duties correctly in the context of established norms of political participation; he resigned shortly after the bribery revelation was made public. Another hypernorm, that of efficiency, may also be brought into this arena. Bribery interferes with the market mechanisms role of using 'price' alone as a signal for efficient resource allocation (*see* Chapter 5). Interviews with Indian CEOs have borne this out as they explicitly recognised that inefficiencies grow as decisions are made on the basis of how much money people receive under the table rather than on the basis of price and quality.

Box 6.2 looks in more detail at some of these issues involving bribery and corruption.

Paying bribes carries with it the risk of damaging the company's reputation, both within the country in which the bribes are paid and at home. There is also the risk that the corporate culture of the company itself will become more tolerant of a range of

Box 6.2 TI Corruption Perception Index

Transparency International (TI) is a non-governmental organisation founded in 1993 and based in Berlin. It has developed one of the more comprehensive databases on corruption which it defines as an abuse of public office for private gain. The 'TI Corruption Perception Index' correlates a number of surveys, polls and country studies involving the number of bribe requests which those conducting business in some 180 separate countries perceive to have been made to them. A score of 10 indicates a perception that bribe requests are never made in that country, while a score of 0 indicates a perception that bribe requests are always made. A score of 5.0 indicates a perception that there is an equal chance of a bribe being made as not being made. Of the 180 countries included in the 2008 index, 129 scored 5.0 or below; in other words, businessmen perceive that in well-over two-thirds of these 180 countries in the index it is more likely than not that a bribe request will be made in any given transaction. In 2008 Denmark had the highest score at 9.3, UK 7.7, USA 7.3, China 3.6, India 3.4, Russia 2.1 and Venezuela 1.9.

other practices at the margins of legality. There is also evidence to suggest that those host nations with a reputation for bribery and corruption damage themselves. For example, a direct link between high levels of corruption and low levels of fdi has been found, while high levels of corruption resulted in low rates of economic growth.

Case Study 6.3 considers some recent moves to tighten legal restrictions on bribery and their impacts on international business.

CASE 6.3 Bribery and international business   **FT**

As Mobil Corporation negotiated for a slice of Kazakhstan's prize oil field in 1996, executives probably did not worry too much about paying a $51 million 'success' fee to the government's adviser. The field – Tengiz – was thought to hold more than 6 billion barrels of oil, making it one of the biggest finds in decades. The deal itself was valued at more than $1 billion.

In 2003 that comparatively meagre fee is starting to look a lot more costly. James Giffen, the US consultant who received the money and represented the Kazakh government, has been arrested and charged in what could be the largest ever violation of the Foreign Corrupt Practices Act (FCPA), the US law banning bribery of foreign officials.

In total, authorities have accused him of taking more than $78 million in commissions and fees from Mobil and other western oil companies and then illegally funnelling them to senior Kazakh officials. More ominously for the company, today known as ExxonMobil, US prosecutors have also filed charges against J. Bryan Williams, the former executive who negotiated the deal.

At Mr Giffen's arraignment last month, prosecutors spelt out their intent, stating that ExxonMobil itself was now the subject of their investigation. If prosecutors charge ExxonMobil and it is found guilty of violating the FCPA, the company could be fined tens of millions of dollars. Individual executives could be sentenced to up to five years in prison. In theory, the US government could also bar ExxonMobil from public contracts, withdraw export privileges and suspend investment protection abroad. Just as damaging, such sanctions would almost certainly encourage Kazakh officials to re-examine the terms of the Tengiz deal.

The legal noose is tightening around companies suspected of bribery. Under new legislation in the UK and around the world, companies could face stiff penalties if they do not look carefully at what their executives are doing to win business abroad. Thirty-five nations have now adopted the anti-bribery convention drawn up by the Organisation for Economic Co-operation and Development, under which they undertake to make foreign bribery illegal in their countries. After much foot-dragging, Britain complied with the convention by inserting some last-minute wording into the Anti-Terrorism, Crime and Security Act rushed through parliament in the aftermath of the September 11 attacks. A new UK Corruption Bill, expected to become law in 2004, will formalise the UK law's international grasp.

To complement the OECD convention, other international institutions – including the Organisation of American States, the European Union, the Council of Europe and the United Nations – have passed or are negotiating rules against bribery in

▶

business transactions. The change in attitudes toward bribery of foreign officials has come about largely as a result of US diplomatic pressure. Since the FCPA was passed in the aftermath of the Watergate scandal, US companies have complained that it places them at a disadvantage against companies from other countries that pay bribes to win contracts. The US Commerce Department estimates that between May 1994 and April 2002, the outcome of 474 contracts worth $237 billion may have been affected by bribery. It claims US companies lost 110 of these contracts worth $36 billion.

Despite the US protestations, some claim that the rules simply force US companies to bribe more dexterously. A survey last year by Transparency International, the anti-corruption compaign, found that senior international business executives ranked US companies ahead of rivals from France and Germany in their propensity to bribe. Fifty-eight per cent of respondents also said that US companies gained an unfair advantage by enlisting diplomatic or financial pressure, including the tying of foreign aid to a successful result.

The World Bank has identified corruption as 'the single greatest obstacle to economic and social development', hitting the poor and least-politically connected the hardest. Other international financial institutions such as the International Monetary Fund have blamed corruption for economic crises from Asia to Argentina.

Bribes can add substantially to the cost of public works programmes in developing countries. Businesspeople often speak of 10 per cent as a standard 'commission', but a survey by Control Risks, the consultancy, found that more than a third of business managers thought it was higher. Bribes also result in major projects being awarded to contractors that are unable or unwilling to do the job properly, at even greater cost to the public purse. Across the developing world, crumbling motorways, malfunctioning power stations and other sub-standard infrastructure projects stand as testaments to the damage wrought by such corrupt bidding processes. Such white elephants are paid for with public debt – one of the contributing factors to the collapse of many economies in recent years.

Despite this evidence, there has been far less focus on the international companies that fuel corruption by paying officials to win business. The talk has been of bribe-takers rather than bribe-payers. In part, that is because catching companies in the act of bribing is extremely difficult – both sides in the transaction have a powerful incentive to cover it up. And even if a suspect payment can be identified, it is often difficult to prove that there had been a quid pro quo.

Mr Giffen's case could send the clearest signal yet to companies about the importance of vetting consultants and other intermediaries that help broker deals in foreign countries. ExxonMobil has denied knowledge that any improper payments were made. There are, however, at least two features of Mr Giffen's contract with Mobil that raise questions about the purpose of the transaction. For one, the company agreed to pay Mr Giffen's $51 million success fee on top of the agreed purchase price even though he was nominally representing the government in the transaction. Secondly, the criminal indictment against Mr Giffen claims that Mobil paid him £10 million of the fee months before the Tengiz deal was even completed. 'It is only a matter of time before there is a similar case in Europe,' says Brian Stapleton, managing director for Kroll in northern Europe. 'Companies need to take action to ensure it isn't them.'

Source: Catan, T. and Chaffin, J., 'Bribery has long been used to land international contracts. New laws will make that tougher', *Financial Times*, 8 May 2003.

Questions

1 What are the reasons for taking a firm line against bribery and similar practices?

2 Why do businesses sometimes criticise their governments for acting against such practices?

3 Why do some regard this particular case against Mr Giffen as being of particular importance?

The next section looks at some of the national and international measures adopted in an attempt to combat bribery, corruption and other unethical practices.

International efforts to improve business ethics

Clearly the global economy is presenting new ethical challenges as traditional ways in which societies have controlled corporate behaviour are breaking down. While we have seen that being ethical may, in the long-run, produce good business results, managers may not necessarily be motivated by what happens in the long run!

pause for thought 2   Consider some of the problems involved in devising international codes of ethical conduct.

■ International agreements

A number of international bodies have sought to address ethical issues in international business activities.

United Nations Code of Conduct for Transnational Corporations (1983)

This has its origins in earlier UN recommendations and codes of behaviour:

- 1948 Havana Declaration of the UN, calling for host countries to provide security for foreign investments;
- 1952 UN Resolution that nations have permanent sovereignty over their natural resources;
- 1971 Developing Countries Statement of UN members, whereby 77 developing countries stated that fdi in poorer nations should seek to generate inflows and to avoid outflows of foreign exchange, stimulate aggregate investment and result in 'appropriate technology' being adopted;
- 1974 Commission on Transnational Corporations. These recommendations and codes eventually culminated in the 1983 UN Code of Conduct for MNEs, whereby MNEs should seek to:
  - respect the national sovereignty of host countries, and observe their domestic laws, regulations and administrative practices;

- respect human rights;
- adhere to the objectives of host nations as regards economic and development goals and sociocultural values;
- avoid interfering in internal politics or inter-governmental relations;
- avoid engaging in corrupt practices;
- disclose relevant information to host country governments.

Organisation for Economic Co-operation and Development Guidelines for MNEs (1976)

The 1976 declaration embodies some of the elements outlined above, while recognising the importance of MNEs in the international economy and as a source of investment. It also declared that 'every state has the right to prescribe the conditions under which multinational enterprises operate within its national jurisdiction, subject to international law and the international agreements to which it has subscribed'.

International Labour Office Tripartite Declaration of Principles Concerning MNEs and Social Policy (1977)

This code was drafted on a tripartite basis involving governments, employers' organisations and trade unions. MNE managers are requested to provide worker representatives in individual countries with all the information needed to pursue meaningful negotiations. Governments are requested to actively promote 'full employment'.

The ILO's international labour code also seeks to standardise conditions of employment and sets out minimum rights and standards in various Conventions. For example, Conventions 87 (freedom of association), 98 (right to organise and collective bargaining), 5 and 138 (minimum age for employment of children), 29 and 105 (prohibition of forced labour), 111 (prohibition of discrimination in employment on the basis of race, sex, religion, political affiliation), etc.

UNCTAD Code on Restrictive Business Practices (1980)

The main aim is to prevent and eliminate restrictive business agreements and practices, with the focus on action at the regional and international levels as well as national. Some of the international aspects of the code involve the responsibilities and rights of both host country government and the MNEs. For example, MNEs should conform to the laws on restrictive practices in the host country as well as avoiding engaging in specified activities listed in the code (e.g. those involving cartels, restrictive pricing practices, etc.).

At least four shortcomings of such agreements have been identified:

1 they are largely agreements between national governments and not between corporations or business leaders;
2 they rely on the voluntary compliance of the signatories;
3 the values represented by these codes may not fit with those of all countries;
4 the agreements are often so broad as to be operationally impractical.

The Multilateral Agreement on Investment (MAI)

The MAI might also be mentioned at this point. This was an attempt to make certain investment rules and associated practices legally binding, some of which had clearly ethical and social implications. The negotiations began in 1995 but were abandoned in 1998.

Although these negotiations may be revived under the auspices of the OECD, what has happened in practice has been a wide range of bilateral investment treaties (BITs) between individual countries setting out the rules governing fdi between themselves. A revived MAI would be an attempt to move back to a *multilateral* approach to fdi.

■ Industry-specific agreements

A number of industries have sought to develop codes of conduct for international business practice in specific industries.

- *International Code of Marketing of Breast-Milk Substitutes (1981).* This sought to prevent misleading information as to the merits of their product being explicitly or implicitly given by manufacturers of breast-milk substitutes.
- *Code of Marketing Practices of the International Federation of Pharmaceutical Manufacturers Associations (1984).* This seeks to ensure accurate rather than misleading marketing of a broad range of pharmaceutical products.
- *Rugmark Initiative.* This establishes a code of labour practices for producing rugs. This is an attempt to improve labour conditions in this industry, especially to restrict the use of child labour. Manufacturers who comply with this scheme's criteria can use the rugmark label for their products.
- *World Federation of Sporting Goods Industry.* This also has sought to develop a code of practice with regards to the manufacture of sportswear and equipment.

pause for thought 3	Can you identify and list any other industry-based agreements involving codes of conduct?

As well as these and other industry-specific codes of practice, various individual companies have sought to adopt more ethical practices.

■ Company-specific agreements

A number of individual companies have drawn up codes of conduct that are meant to apply throughout their organisation. Levi Strauss and Co. has been one of the pioneers in setting out the labour practices that contracting firms are expected to follow, with contracts risking being terminated for breaches of these standards. Reebok and Nike have responded in this way after adverse publicity on labour market practices by suppliers. Mattel Inc., one of the world's largest toy manufacturers, announced its 'Global Manufacturing Principles' in 1997 to establish minimum labour standards in its own plants and those of its major subcontractors. It has even established a Monitoring Council to audit each plant in order to check compliance.

pause for thought 4	Can you identify and list any other company-based agreements involving codes of conduct?

Nor are these company-specific agreements necessarily related to a single company. Case Study 6.4 examines a group of major US companies signing up to four key ethical principles in December 2008.

CASE 6.4   US groups in ethical standards push   **FT**

Some of the largest companies in the US, including General Electric, Wal-Mart and PepsiCo launched a drive to improve ethical standards in business in December 2008 in an attempt to stem the decline in corporate America's public standing.

The move by 17 companies, with nearly $1,000 billion in sales, to commit to key principles of good business conduct comes as the financial crisis and recession are fuelling a political backlash against the corporate world.

The huge problems faced by companies, such as banks and carmakers, that are run by highly paid executives have exacerbated anger among ordinary Americans who have seen their living standards deteriorate due to the economic slowdown.

'In these challenging economic times, it is important that the public have confidence in all of business and not just select companies. We take this very seriously', says Larry Thompson, PepsiCo's general counsel and a former deputy US attorney-general.

Under the agreement, from the Ethisphere Institute, companies will sign up to four principles of ethical behaviour: legal compliance, including not paying bribes; transparency; avoiding conflict of interests and increasing accountability.

The organisers admit that the initiative, called the Business Ethics Leadership Alliance, is partly driven by companies' desire to burnish ethical credentials and curry favour with Barack Obama's Democratic administration.

But although the principles are vague and most companies should be able to comply with them, the 17 signatories, which also include United Airlines, Dell and Accenture, have agreed to periodic examinations by independent auditors.

The founding members have also pledged to try to get other companies to join. Gary Hill, chief ethics officer at Wal-Mart, said the retail group would encourage its huge supplier base to sign up to the principles. Mr Hill said that unethical behaviour was on the rise in corporate America, reversing a trend sparked by the regulatory clean-up that followed the Enron collapse.

Some of the companies involved in the pact have faced their own ethical challenges. In 2006 Sempra Energy agreed to pay more than $377 million to settle accusations that it manipulated natural gas prices during the 2001 California energy crisis. Sempra could not be reached. In 2005 Wal-Mart paid $11 million to the Department of Justice to settle an investigation into the use of illegal immigrants by cleaning contractors at its US stores.

Three employees of CACI International, the defence services company, were cited in a 2004 report by the Pentagon into the abuses at Abu Ghraib prison in Baghdad. CACI could not be reached but said at the time: 'Nothing in the . . . report can be construed as CACI employees directing, participating in or even observing [the abuses].'

Source: Guerrera, F. and Birchall, J., 'US groups in ethical standards push', *Financial Times*, 8 December 2008.

Question

Examine the reasons behind this collaboration over ethical standards by the companies concerned.

■ The role of social activists

Social activists have formed various organisations to campaign against particular practices of multinationals.

- *Infant Feeding Action Coalition (INFACT).* This has sought to boycott the Nestlé Corporation as a result of its practice of selling baby formula containing little objective nourishment to underdeveloped countries. After 15 years of lobbying, Nestlé signed an agreement to stop these practices and an independent audit commission was created to monitor its compliance.
- *Coalition for Environmentally Responsible Economies (CERES).* This seeks to engage with investors to promote corporate activities for a 'safe and sustainable future for our planet'. Organisations such as Greenpeace are affiliated to CERES and pays particular attention to the fishing industry.
- *Sullivan Principles.* These principles were devised by the Reverend Leon Sullivan, a Philadelphia minister, a black civil-rights activist and board member of General Motors. In 1977 he devised a set of principles that requested companies to improve workplace and social conditions for blacks in South Africa during the apartheid era. At its peak, over 180 companies were signed up to these principles before the programme ceased in 1994.

■ Bribery and corruption

Following our earlier discussion (*see* pp. 215–19) it may be useful to consider in more detail some of the national/international attempts to reduce this problem. Two important international conventions and a US Act have required member countries to criminalise transnational bribery:

- Organization of American States Inter-American Convention against corruption (1994);
- OECD *Convention on Combating Bribery of Foreign Public Officials (1999).* By mid-2000 some 20 countries had already adopted such laws with another 14 close to enacting them. Countries with laws that outlaw the payment of bribes to foreign officials include Austria, Belgium, Canada, Germany, Japan, Korea, the UK and the USA. In fact, the USA was the first country to pass laws to this effect;
- *US Foreign Corrupt Practices Act 1977.* This made certain payments to foreign officials illegal even when these officials are located abroad, with penalties including prison, fines and disqualification from doing business with the US government.

Although attempts to reduce corruption and bribery in these ways have been broadly welcomed, some criticisms still remain. For example while business ventures may be prosecuted for bribing foreign officials, a wide variety of government inducements are still permissible, some of which are arguably akin to bribes. For example, governments may give substantial sums in aid on the understanding that the recipient country will grant economic and political concessions to the donor country and its companies in return.

Ecological/environmental issues

Ecological and environmental issues are of obvious concern to individuals, governments and the global community, as they are to international business. In an era of increasing governmental and popular concern with issues such as global warming and sustainability, international business must pay careful attention to the ecological and environmental perspectives with regard to all aspects of their operations.

National and global issues

The environment has become an increasingly important focus of national and international policy-makers as global warming, the erosion of the ozone layer and other environmental threats are increasingly linked to worldwide growth in the emissions of harmful substances (e.g. CO_2, chlorofluorocarbons, etc.).

Role of the environment

At a more conceptual level, there is an increasing acceptance of the key role of the environment in business/economic activity in at least three respects:

- *Amenity services*: the natural environment provides consumer services to domestic households in the form of living and recreational space, natural beauty, and so on.
- *Natural resources*: the natural environment is also the source of various inputs into the production process such as mineral deposits, forests, water resources, animal populations, and so on.
- *Waste products*: both production and consumption are activities that generate waste products or residuals. For example, many productive activities generate harmful by-products, which are discharged into the atmosphere or watercourses. Similarly, sewage, litter and other waste products result from many consumption activities. The key point here is that the natural environment is the ultimate dumping place or 'sink' for all these waste products or residuals.

Sustainable development

It is when the environment is regarded as being unable to efficiently fulfil all three functions as the economy grows over a period of time that we use the term 'unsustainable development'. In this view, the earth is a closed system in which a finite set of resources is available for current and future growth. In other words, the capacity of the economy to produce still more products is constrained or limited by the availability of natural resources. Even if resources are sufficient to permit economic growth, the extra production will simply 'draw through' more materials and energy in products, which the environment must ultimately assimilate, since matter and energy cannot be destroyed (Newton's first law of thermodynamics).

Wherever possible, materials must therefore be recycled, renewable energy sources must be used in preference to non-renewable sources, and waste emissions must be limited to the extent that the earth can safely absorb these 'residuals'. This approach has led many economists to propose limiting our demand for goods and services in order to attain a level of economic growth that can be 'sustained' over future generations.

As long ago as 1987, a United Nations report entitled *Our Common Future* provided the most widely used definition of sustainable development: 'development which meets the needs of the present without compromising the ability of future generations to meet their own needs'. Of course, there have been many different views as to how this definition should affect individual, corporate and government actions, though one theme that has been constant in most views is that of 'intergenerational equity'. This is generally understood to involve taking actions to ensure that the development process minimises any adverse impacts on future generations. *Achieving intergenerational equity* includes avoiding adverse environmental impacts such as excessive resource depletion today causing a reduction in the stock of resources available for future use, or levels of pollution emission and waste disposal today proving to be beyond the ability of the environment to absorb them, thereby imposing long-term damage on future generations.

▪ Business issues

In this section our main concern will be with the impact of these environmental issues and concerns at the level of national and international business. In today's global economy a number of driving forces are arguably raising environmental concerns to the forefront of corporate policy debate.

▪ *Environmentally conscious consumers.* Consumer awareness of environmental issues is creating a market for 'green products'. 'Sustainable' and 'sustainability' are now key trigger words in the world of advertising for positive, emotive images associated with words such as 'green', 'wholesome', 'goodness', 'justice' and 'environment', amongst others. They are used sophisticatedly to sell cars, nappies, holidays and even lifestyles. Sustainability sells – how has this come about and what exactly are we being encouraged to buy? We have already noted the growth in sales of *Fairtrade* products in the UK (Case Study 6.2, p. 212). Similarly, in the US Patagonia, a California-based producer of recreational clothing, has developed a loyal base of high-income customers partly because its brand identity includes a commitment to conservation. As already noted (see Case Study 6.1) a similar successful approach has been used by The Body Shop. Starbucks published its first Corporate Social Responsibility Annual Report in 2002, aware of the linkages between consumer satisfaction in its stores and ethical association.

However, even when core activities and products have few direct environmental effects, consumer demand may be significantly influenced by the environmental implications of backward or forward linkages. For instance, Shell petrol sales were adversely affected in 1996 when Greenpeace alleged that the proposed disposal of the Brent Spar oil platform (backward linkages) at sea posed a serious threat to the marine environment. Similarly, Asea Brown Boveri, a Swiss-based multinational received extremely adverse publicity around the same time from environmental groups protesting at its alleged destruction of the Malaysian rainforest. Concern for their 'environmental footprint' is now widespread among MNEs engaged in international business.

Reinhardt (1999) suggested that three key conditions are required for success with 'environmental product differentiation', i.e. segmenting the market so that consumers will pay higher prices for overtly 'environmentally-friendly' products:

1 the company must have identified a distinctive market segment consisting of consumers who really are willing to pay more for environmentally-friendly products;
2 the branding/corporate image must clearly and credibly convey the environmental benefits related to the products;
3 the company must be able to protect itself from imitations for long enough to profit from its 'investment' in the previous two conditions.

■ *Environmentally- and cost-conscious producers.* Producers are increasingly aware that adherence to high environmental standards need not be at the expense of their cost base. In other words, they can be environmentally friendly at the same time as reducing (rather than raising) their cost base. For example, between 1975 and 1996 the multinational, 3M, reduced its waste released to the environment by 1.4 billion pounds in weight and at the same time saved over $750 million in costs. Similarly, between 1992 and 1998 the multinational, S.C. Johnson, reduced its waste output by 420 million pounds in weight while saving over $125 million.

Rank Xerox adopted an 'Environmental Leadership Programme' as early as in 1990 in an attempt both to regain market share lost in the 1980s and to restore profit margins. This programme included waste reduction efforts, product 'return' schemes (when existing products are overtaken by technologically superior alternatives) and design-for-environment initiatives. Substantial cost savings were reported (several hundred million dollars between 1990–95) together with revenue increases, and by the mid-1990s Xerox executives were hailing the programme as a major success. Case Study 6.4 (p. 222) also considers some of the benefits of environmental association.

■ *Environmentally- and risk-conscious producers.* Multinational enterprises are increasingly aware that failure to manage environmental risk factors effectively can lead to adverse publicity, lost revenue and profit and perhaps even more seriously a reduction in their official credit rating, making it more difficult and costly (e.g. higher interest rates) to finance future investment plants. Tesco, the UK's leading supermarket chain, has in the past received negative publicity as a result of a TV documentary about the conditions for workers growing foodstuffs, such as mangetout in Africa, which are exported to the supermarket chain. It has therefore established its own code of conduct and set up a 70-strong team of ethical advisers to help monitor the goods it sells in its stores. The advisers check foodstuffs and other products the chain sells so that its new code of conduct, designed to ensure that its Third World suppliers do not exploit child or forced labour, is adhered to.

■ *Environmentally-conscious governments.* Businesses have a further reason for considering the environmental impacts of their activities, namely the scrutiny of host governments. Where production of a product causes environmental damage, it is likely that this will result in the imposition of taxes or regulations by government. The reasons for this are considered further in Box 6.3.

Case Study 6.5 examines the impact of higher taxes and stricter anti-smoking regulations on tobacco companies. It points out that global businesses may have strategic options which, for better or worse, allow them to mitigate the impacts of governmental attempts to control them.

| Box 6.3 | Environmental impacts, taxes and regulations |

If the production process results in environmental damage that the producer does not (at least initially) have to pay for, then marginal social cost (*MSC*) will be greater than marginal private cost (*MPC*). This is the case in Figure 6.2. The private cost to the firm of producing one more unit of output (*MPC*) is rising, due to extra labour, raw material or capital costs. However, the cost to society of producing that extra unit of output (*MSC*) is rising by more than the cost to the firm (*MSC* > *MPC*). This is because of the environmental damage (e.g. emission of CO_2) caused by producing the last unit, which is a cost to society (e.g. ill health), even if not to the firm. The true cost to society of producing the last unit of output does include the cost to the firm (*MPC*) of using factor input (since these scarce factors are thereby denied to other firms). However, the true cost to society also includes any environmental damage caused by producing the last unit of output. We call any such damage the marginal external cost (*MEC*). We can therefore state that:

Marginal Social Cost = Marginal Private Cost + Marginal External Cost

$$MSC = MPC + MEC$$

In Figure 6.2 a profit-maximising firm will equate *MPC* with *MR*, producing output 0Q and selling this at price 0P. However, the government may realise that from society's point of view the appropriate output is that which equates *MSC* with *MR* (here we assume *MR* to represent both marginal private benefit and marginal social benefit), producing output $0Q_S$ and selling this at price $0P_S$.

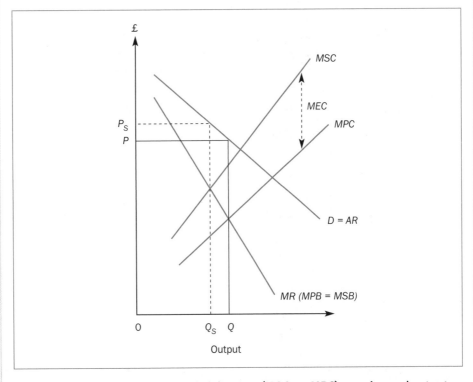

Figure 6.2 **Impact of environmental damage (MSC > MPC) on price and output**

> ### Box 6.3 Continued
>
> To achieve this 'social optimum' solution, the government may try to tax the product (e.g. by raising MPC to MSC). This would be an attempt to 'internalise the externality' by making the producer pay for any damage the producer causes. If MPC is now raised by the tax so that it is equal to MSC, then the profit-maximising firm would itself choose to produce output $0Q_S$ and sell it at price $0P_S$ (at this output and price, $MPC = MSC = MR$ and profits are a maximum). Alternatively, the government might seek to regulate the firm by preventing it producing more than output $0Q_S$. Whatever policy instruments are chosen, business must be aware that production activities that damage the environment are likely to result in adverse impacts on themselves from host governments.

CASE 6.5 Taxing and regulating smoking

The then French President Chirac called for 2004 to be a 'year of results' in terms of fulfilling his pledge to French electors in 2002 to cut smoking by 30% among young people and by 20% among adults within five years. To the delight of campaigners, cigarettes sales in France were estimated to have fallen 12–13% in 2003, following a 3.5% fall in 2002. The cumulative impact of tax rises, i.e. 8.6% in 2002, 11% in January 2003, 20% in October 2003 and 8–10% in January 2004, was starting to bite. Studies consistently show that taxation and pregnancy are the two most effective ways of stopping smoking.

The chairman of the French Alliance Versus Tobacco, an umbrella organisation for 29 anti-smoking helplines, Gerard Dubois, said that it was unprecedented and that calls to quit-smoking helplines had risen seven-fold in the previous year. Also, sales of nicotine gum and patches, made by pharmaceutical giants such as GSK and Pfizer, had increased 89% in the year to September, while turnover of Zyban, an anti-depressant taken by many people giving up smoking, had risen by 20%.

Campaigners regretted, however, that the government was not pressing its advantage further. The political clout of France's 32,000 tobacconists, furious that French cigarettes were now the most expensive in the EU after those sold in the UK, had prompted Jean-Pierre Raffarin, prime minister, to promise a four-year freeze on cigarette duties.

The concession to powerful *buralistes* was the latest measure to pacify this group of opinion formers ahead of the 2004 elections. As many of France's 11 million smokers pass through their local *tobac* on a regular basis, their owners, who often run bars and small bistros on the side, were in a position to bend the ear of a large proportion of the electorate.

After the January 2004 8–10% increase in cigarette taxes, the average pack of 20 cost around €5 ($5.85, £3.50) in France, compared with just €2.50 in neighbouring Spain and €2.90 in Luxembourg.

The French government estimates that more than a third of French adults smoke, of whom half want to stop. France also has the highest proportion of young smokers in Europe, with 53% of 15–24-year-olds counting themselves as regular smokers, compared with an EU average of 41%.

Questions

1 What does the case study tell us about the price elasticity of demand for cigarettes in France?

2 Consider some of the implications for other products of raising taxes sharply on French cigarettes.

3 Can you identify any constraints for the French government in seeking to raise cigarette taxes still further?

Environmental codes and regulations

A number of the national/international codes and regulations involving ethical issues already considered (*see* pp. 219–21), have elements dealing with the environment. There are, in addition, some important environment-specific codes and regulations, which are important to international business.

- *ISO 14001.* The International Organization for Standardization has developed ISO 14001 as a means of certifying companies that adopt certain minimum standards of environmental management.
- *Regional Agreements.* Bilateral investment agreements between nations (e.g. Bolivia – USA bilateral investment treaty) often contain minimum environmental standards as do broader based 'regional' treaties such as NAFTA (North American Free Trade Agreement).
- *Multilateral Agreements.* Various *protocols* have been agreed (e.g. Montreal, Kyoto) as to reductions in greenhouse gas emissions, etc. We explain the issues of global warming, sustainability and 'carbon footprints' and their impacts on international business in more detail below (pp. 231–6).

Use of private standards

This approach has been particularly successful in the US chemical industry. In 1984, toxic gas escaped from the plant of a Union Carbide subsidiary in Bhopal, India, and killed more than 2000 people. The image of the chemical industry was damaged and it faced the threat of punitive government regulation. The industry recognised that it had to act – to forestall government regulations and improve its safety record. As a result, the leading companies in the Chemical Manufacturers Association (CMA) in the USA created an initiative called 'Responsible Care' and developed a set of private regulations that the association's members adopted in 1988.

The US companies that make up the CMA must comply with six management codes that cover such areas as pollution prevention, process safety, and emergency response. If they cannot show good faith efforts to comply, their membership will be terminated. The initiative has enhanced the association's environmental reputation by producing results. Between 1988 and 1994, for example, US chemical companies reduced their environmental releases of toxic materials by almost 50%. Although other industries were also achieving significant reductions during this period, the chemical industry's reductions were steeper than the national average.

The big companies that organised 'Responsible Care' have improved their competitive positions. They spend a lower percentage of their revenues to improve their safety record than smaller competitors in the CMA; similarly, they spend a lower percentage of revenues on the monitoring, reporting, and administrative costs of the regulations.

The problem with non-binding private agreements or voluntary protocols is that they depend on decisions by organisations themselves as to whether compliance is in their own self-interest.

■ Supporting 'environmentally-friendly' activities

We have already seen how negative environmental activities can be taxed or regulated in Box 6.3. Here we look at how positive environmental activities can be nurtured and supported. Case Study 6.6 looks at some of these issues in the context of organic food.

CASE 6.6   Organic farming

Recent studies show that the organic food sector has great potential for expansion. Surveys show nearly 80% of consumers, traumatised by a series of food-contamination scandals, would buy organic produce if it cost the same as conventional food. British production falls well short of meeting that demand. Britain lies in tenth place in terms of land given over to organic production, with less than 2%, compared with Liechtenstein's 17%, Austria's 8.4% and Switzerland's 7.8%.

As a result, Britain imported about 75% of the £550 million of organic food it consumed last year; much of that – humiliatingly – was root crops, cereals and dairy produce, all ideally suited to the British climate and soil. With the annual 40% growth rate in British sales of organic foods likely to continue, and every supermarket now offering a range of products, local farmers have, belatedly, been queuing up to fill that vacuum.

Nevertheless, organic farmers are worried that recent attempts by supermarkets to drastically reduce the 25% premium on prices currently charged for organic products will be passed down the line to themselves. Many believe that if the price premium over non-organic products disappears, then it will be uneconomic for the many small organic farmers to continue production. The pity is that in the long term, organic producers argue, organic farming could supply the mass market relatively cheaply. Yields will gradually increase as the size of organic farms increases, crop rotation kicks in and soil fertility rises. The gradual transformation of what is, in effect, a cottage industry into a serious commercial concern will allow economies of scale, both technical and non-technical. Steady government support, including aid that recognises the rural 'stewardship' provided by organic farmers, would narrow the cost differences with conventional farming.

Only when a certain critical mass has been attained – and many organic advocates believe it must wait until 30% of British land (currently 2%) and 20% of British food is organic – can organic farm prices be expected to fall of their own accord. Until that point, their message will be: please buy organic, but be prepared to pay for it.

Question

Why might the small scale organic farmer seek to grow larger? What opportunities and threats are posed to the organic farmer by large retailers reducing the prices of organic food?

However, sometimes policies directed towards supporting an allegedly 'eco-friendly' activity may not always bring about the outcomes intended. This is the issue discussed in Case Study 6.7 on the continued use of biofuel subsidies.

CASE 6.7   Biofuels subsidies criticised   FT

Governments need to scrap subsidies for biofuels as the current rush to support alternative energy sources will lead to surging food prices and the potential destruction of natural habitats, the Organisation for Economic Co-operation and Development warned in September 2007. The OECD report argued that politicians are rigging the market in favour of an untried technology that will have only limited impact on climate change.

The current push to expand the use of biofuels is creating unsustainable tensions that will disrupt markets without generating significant environmental benefits, say the authors of the report. The report also says that biofuels would cut energy-related emissions by 3% at most. This benefit would come at a huge cost, which would swiftly make biofuels unpopular among taxpayers.

The study estimates the US alone spends $7 billion (£3.4 billion) a year helping make ethanol, with each tonne of CO_2 avoided costing more than $500. In the European Union, it can be almost ten times that. The study states that biofuels could lead to some damage to the environment: 'As long as environmental values are not adequately priced in the market, there will be powerful incentives to replace natural eco-systems such as forests, wetlands and pasture with dedicated bio-energy crops.'

The report recommends governments phase out biofuel subsidies, using 'technology-neutral' carbon taxes to allow the market to find the most efficient ways of reducing greenhouse gases. The survey puts a question market over the EU's plans to derive 10% of transport fuel from plants by 2020. It states that money saved from phasing out subsidies should fund research into so-called second-generation fuels, which are being developed to use waste products and so emit less CO_2 when they are made.

Adrian Bebb, biofuels campaigner with Friends of the Earth said, 'The OECD is right to warn against throwing ourselves head-first down the agro fuels path.' Wheat costs actually doubled in 2007, not only because of a poor harvest but also because farmland previously used for cereals had been converted to growing biofuel energy crops such as rapeseed – the increased demand for biofuels having raised the price of such crops.

Source: Adapted from Bounds, A., 'OECD slams biofuels subsidies for sparking food price inflation', *Financial Times*, 11 September 2007.

Question

Why might subsidising biofuels actually damage the environment?

Global warming, 'carbon footprint' and tradable permits

Global warming refers to the trapping of heat between the earth's surface and gases in the atmosphere, especially carbon dioxide (CO_2). Currently some six billion tones of carbon dioxide are released into the atmosphere each year, largely as a result of burning fossil fuels. In fact carbon dioxide constitutes some 56% of these 'greenhouse gases', with chlorofluorocarbons (CFCs), used mainly in refrigerators, aerosols and air-conditioning systems, accounting for a further 23% of such gases, the rest being methane (14%) and nitrous oxide (7%). By trapping the sun's heat these gases are in turn raising global temperature (global warming). On present estimates, temperatures are expected to increase by a further 1°C in the next two decades, when an increase of merely half a degree in world temperature over the past century is believed to have contributed to a rise of 10cm in sea levels. Higher sea levels (resulting from melting ice caps), flooding and various climatic changes causing increased desertification and drought, have all been widely linked to global warming.

The importance of global warming and its association with CO_2 emission has become increasingly high profile in recent years. The increasing occurrence of extreme weather conditions across many continents, and the overwhelming collection of scientific evidence on the reality of global warming, has convinced all but a few diehard sceptics of the reality of global warming. This has led to increasing pressures on individuals and organisations to reduce their 'carbon footprint' and demonstrate a responsible attitude to the environment.

The Stern Report (Stern 2007) was regarded as a major factor in encouraging governmental policy-makers to make still greater efforts to reduce CO_2 emissions. Box 6.4 outlines the main points raised in the Stern Report.

Box 6.4   Stern Report and global warming

The Stern Report on climate change was published in late 2006, and is widely regarded as the most authoritative of its kind.

Key findings include the following.

- CO_2 in the atmosphere around 1780, i.e. just before the Industrial Revolution, has been estimated at around 280 ppm (parts per million).
- CO_2 in 2006 had risen as high as 382 ppm.
- Greenhouse gases (CO_2, methane, nitrous oxide, etc.) in 2006 were recorded at 430 ppm in CO_2 equivalents.

Do nothing scenario

This will result in the following:

- a temperature rise of 2°C by 2050;
- a temperature rise of 5°C or more by 2100;
- the damage to the global economy of such climate change is an estimated reduction in global GDP per head (i.e. consumption per head) of between 5% and 20% over the next two centuries. This occurs via rising temperatures, droughts, floods, water shortages and extreme weather events.

Intervene scenario

- The Stern Report advocates measures to stabilise greenhouse gas emissions at 550 ppm CO_2 equivalents by 2050.
- This requires global emissions of CO_2 to peak in the next 10–20 years, then fall at a rate of at least 1% to 3% per year.

Box 6.4	Continued

- By 2050 global emissions must be around 25% below current levels.
- Since global GDP should be around three times as high as today in 2050, the CO_2 emissions *per unit* of global GDP must be less than one third of today's level (and sufficiently less to give the 25% reduction on today's levels).
- The Stern Report estimated the cost of stabilisation at 550 ppm CO_2 equivalents to be around 1% of current global GDP (i.e. around £200bn). This expenditure will be required every year, rising to £600 billion per annum in 2050 if global GDP is three times higher.
- Stabilisation would limit temperature rises by 2050 to 2°C, not prevent them. Otherwise temperature rises well in excess of 2°C are predicted – possibly as much as 5°C by 2100.

■ Tradable permits

Tradable permits are a market-based solution to the problem of pollution. With this policy option the polluter is issued with a number of permits to emit a specified amount of pollution. The total number of permits in existence places a limit on the total amount of emissions allowed. Polluters can buy and sell the permits to each other, at a price agreed between the two polluters. In other words the permits are *transferable*.

The underlying principle of tradable permits is that those firms which can achieve a lower level of pollution can benefit by selling permits to those firms which at present find it either too difficult or too expensive to meet the standard set.

The market for permits can be illustrated by Figure 6.3. In order to achieve an optimum level of pollution, the agency responsible for permits may issue Q_s permits. With demand for permits at D_1 the price will be set at P_1. If new polluters enter the market, the demand for permits will increase, as with D_2 in the figure. As such, the permit price will increase to P_2.

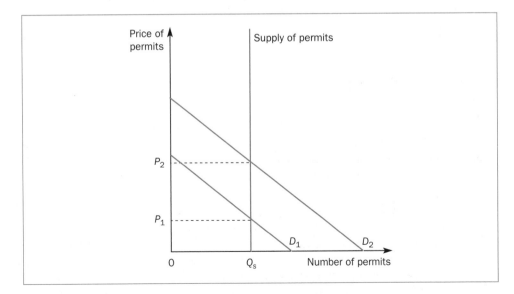

Figure 6.3 **Using permits to control pollution**

If for any reason the agency wishes to relax the standard set then more permits will be issued and the supply curve for permits will shift to the right. Alternatively, the standard could be tightened, by the agency purchasing permits on the open market from polluters, which would have the effect of shifting the supply curve to the left.

The EU Emissions Trading Scheme uses the idea of tradable permits to reduce greenhouse gas emissions, and this is outlined in Box 6.5. Many industries, sectors and nations are developing similar schemes using tradable permits.

Box 6.5   The EU Emissions Trading Scheme

In the EU an Emissions Trading Scheme (ETS) is being seen as a key economic instrument in a move to reduce greenhouse gas emissions. The ETS is to aid the EU in meeting its commitments as part of the Kyoto Protocol. The EU took upon itself as part of the Protocol to reduce greenhouse gas emissions by 8% (from 1990 levels) by 2008–12. The idea behind the ETS is to ensure that those companies within certain sectors responsible for greenhouse gas emissions keep within specific limits by either reducing their emissions or by buying *allowances* from other organisations with lower emissions. The ETS is essentially aimed at placing a cap on emissions.

Background

The emission of greenhouse gases is seen as a major cause of climate change, which has environmental and economic implications, not least in terms of floods and drought. In October 2001 the European Commission proposed that an ETS should be established in the EU in order to deal with greenhouse gas emissions. The result is that an ETS, in the first instance covering only CO_2 (carbon dioxide) emissions, commenced on 1 January 2005, and represented the world's largest market in emission allowances. In the first phase, which ran from 2005–07, the ETS covered companies of a certain size in sectors such as energy, production and processing of ferrous metals, the mineral industrial sectors and factories making cement, glass, lime, brick, ceramics, pulp and paper.

To implement the ETS an electronic registry system has been developed such that when a change in the ownership of allowances takes place there is a transfer of allowances in terms of the registry system accounts. This registry is similar to a banking clearing system that tracks accounts in terms of the ownership of money. In order to buy and sell the allowances each company involved in the scheme will require an account.

How emissions trading works?

This section details a hypothetical situation that will aid in understanding of how emissions trading will operate. In the following analysis we assume there are two companies A and B each emitting 60 million and 45 million tonnes of CO_2 per annum respectively. Each company is illustrated in Figure 6.4. The marginal abatement cost (MAC) curves refer to the extra cost to the firm of *avoiding* emitting the last unit of pollution. The MAC for Company A (MAC_A) increases more slowly than for Company B (MAC_B) indicating that the cost of abatement is more costly for Company B when compared with A.

With no controls on the level of emissions then the total level of CO_2 emissions will be 210 million tonnes (120 million tonnes from company A and 90 million tonnes from company B). If we now assume that the authorities want to reduce CO_2 emissions by 50% (so that 105 million tonnes is the maximum) then this can be achieved by issuing 105 million tonnes of emission allowances. If they are issued on the basis of previous emission levels then company A would receive 60 million emission allowances (or tradable permits) and company B 45 million, based on one allowance representing the right to emit one tonne of CO_2. If this were the case then company A would have to reduce its emissions to 60 million tonnes and company B to 45 million tonnes. Based

Box 6.5 **Continued**

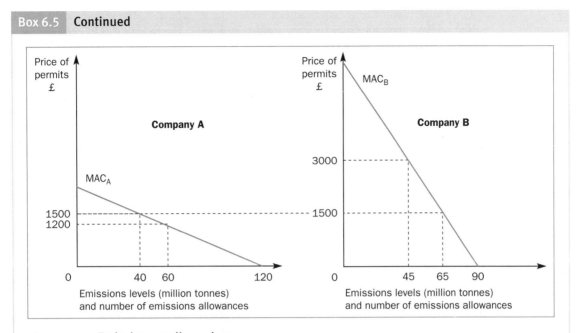

Figure 6.4   **Emissions trading schemes**

on this company A would have a MAC of £1200 and company B £3000. Given this situation company B would buy permits if it could pay less than £3000 and company A would sell them for a price greater than £1200. Company A would sell them since the revenue earned from the sale would be greater than the additional abatement cost incurred by reducing emissions. There is thus a basis for trade in emission allowances and this will continue until the MAC's are identical. In Figure 6.4 this can be seen as £1500 with 40 million tonnes of CO_2 emitted by company A and 65 million tonnes by company B, with company A selling 20 million emission allowances to company B. Overall the price of the allowances will be determined by supply and demand.

Case Study 6.8 looks at the business related impacts of the growing use of carbon trading schemes.

CASE 6.8   **Prices 'no incentive' for a clean-up**   **FT**

Carbon prices have fallen precipitously in the past six months, reflecting the financial crisis and recession. The cost of a permit to produce a tonne of carbon dioxide under the European Union's emissions trading scheme topped €30 ($38) over the summer, but since then has halved, and now hovers near €15–€16.

This is good news for companies needing to buy emissions permits to cover their greenhouse gas output, but bad news for the working of the scheme, which is supposed to encourage companies to cut their emissions. Paul Newman, managing director at Icap brokerage, said: 'At this price there is no incentive for companies to clean up.'

But will the price fall further as the outlook worsens? The price is based on the difference between the number of permits made available to companies and their expected greenhouse gas emissions.

▶

Before the financial crisis this autumn, companies covered by the EU emissions trading scheme were forecast to produce about 1 billion tonnes of carbon dioxide more than they had permits for, over the five years of the scheme's current phase, from 2008–12. But since the situation has deteriorated, analysts have revised their forecasts. Point Carbon, a market analyst, initially estimated a permit shortage of 700 million tonnes in the present phase.

A complicating factor, however, is that EU companies can top up their quota of permits by buying carbon credits from abroad. These credits, issued by the UN under the Kyoto protocol to projects that cut emissions in the developing world, sell for about 25% less than EU permits.

During the present phase of the EU scheme, companies will be allowed to buy a maximum of 1.4 billion of the UN credits. If this full allocation were taken up, there would be a surplus of permits in the EU scheme and carbon prices could fall to near zero.

But Pjersti Ulset, of Point Carbon, said this was unlikely, as companies would keep UN credits for use in the third phase of the scheme, from 2013 to 2020, when prices were likely to be higher. Companies can also bank for use from 2013 to 2020, when they will be given fewer permits, and this would also prop up prices, she said. Finally, she forecast prices would rise to €22 next year and reach €37 in 2012.

Mark Lewis at Deutsche Bank predicted emissions would 'fall off a cliff' next year, owing to the recession.

Businesses covered by the European Union's emissions trading scheme are following talks among member states on the scheme's future operation. At stake is the extent to which they will have to buy carbon permits at auction rather than get them free, as most have until now. The European Commission wants to phase in auctions between 2013 and 2020 with the idea that most companies would pay for all or almost all their permits by 2020. But business lobby groups are pressing for concessions to reflect the economic downturn and some are likely to be granted. They want more free permits, particularly for industries judged at risk from international competition.

Companies making steel, cement and paper, among others, have been pressing for special treatment. But the extent of the threat of 'carbon leakage' – the closure of operations in regions with strict emissions regimes and migration to more lax jurisdictions – is hotly disputed.

The Commission is not expected to rule on which sectors are most at risk of carbon leakage until 2010.

Ten sectors are expected to be covered by the scheme in 2013: electricity generation; oil refining; iron and steel production; cement clinker and lime production; glassmaking; brick and tile manufacturing; pulp and paper production; aluminium; ammonia production and petrochemicals; and aviation.

Source: Harvey, F., 'Prices too low to promote clean-up', *Financial Times*, 8 December 2008.

Questions

1 Consider the causes and impacts of a fall in the price of a permit for carbon.

2 Why are companies following the debate on the future direction of the European Union's Emission Trading Scheme?

Useful websites

Now try the self-check questions for this chapter on the website at www.pearsoned.co.uk/wall. You will also find further resources as well as useful weblinks.

Pressure group websites include:

www.foe.co.uk
www.greenpeace.org.uk
www.panda.org
The National Environmental Trust is at *www.environet.policy.net/*
The issue of sustainability can be considered at: *www.sustainability.co.uk*
Visit The Body Shop website for material on human rights and environmental issues: *www.bodyshop.co.uk*
The Business Owners' Toolkit has a section on pricing and elasticity: *www.toolkit.cch.com*
KPMG has a section devoted to business ethics: *www.kpmg.com/ethics*
Also for cultural specific resources check *www.itp.berkeley.edu/-thorne/HumanResources.html*

Useful key texts

Daniels, J., Radebaugh, L. and Sullivan, D. (2006), *International Business* (11th edn), Pearson Prentice Hall, especially Chapters 3–7.

Dicken, P. (2003) *Global Shift: Transforming the World Economy* (4th edn), Paul Chapman Publishing Ltd, especially Chapter 8.

Hill, C. (2006) *International Business: Competing in the Global Marketplace* (5th edn), McGraw-Hill Irwin, especially Chapters 1 and 2.

Morrison, J. (2006) *The International Business Environment* (2nd edn), Palgrave, especially Chapter 12.

Rugman, A. and Collinson, R. (2009) *International Business* (5th edn), FT Prentice Hall, especially Chapter 5.

Tayeb, M. (2000) *International Business: Theories, Policies and Practices*, Financial Times Prentice Hall, especially Chapters 4 and 19.

Wild, J., Wild, K. and Han, J. (2006) *International Business: The Challenges of Globalization* (3rd edn), FT Prentice Hall, especially Chapter 6.

Other texts and sources

Beyer, J. and Nino, D. (1999) 'Ethics and Cultures in International Business', *Journal of Management Inquiry*, vol. 8, no. 3.

Collins, J.C. and Porras, J.L. (1994) *Built to Last*, Harper Business.

Donaldson, T. and Dunfee, T.W. (1999) 'When Ethics Travel: The Promise and Peril of Global Business Ethics', *California Management Review*, vol. 41, no. 4.

Enderle, G. (1995) 'What is International? A Topology of International Spheres and its Relevance for Business Ethics', Paper presented at the Annual Meeting of the International Association of Business and Society, Vienna, Austria.

Friedman, M. (1970) 'The Social Responsibility of Business', *New York Times Magazine*, 13 September.

Gerson, B. (2006) 'The Reign of Zero Tolerance', *Harvard Business Review*, November, p. 39.

Hasson, R. (2007) 'Why Didn't We Know', *Harvard Business Review*, April, p. 33.

Healey, N. (2007) 'The Multinational Corporation', in *Applied Economics* (11th edn), Griffiths, A. and Wall, S. (eds), Financial Times Prentice Hall.

Heineman, B. (2007) 'Avoiding Integrity Land Mines', *Harvard Business Review*, April, p. 100.

Hornby, W., Gammie, B. and Wall, S. (2001) *Business Economics* (2nd edn), Longman, especially Chapters 10–11.

Lash, J. and Wellington, F. (2007) 'Competitive Advantage on a Warming Planet', *Harvard Business Review*, March, p. 94.

Macdonald, G.M. (1988) 'Ethical Perceptions of Hong Kong Chinese Business Managers', *Journal of Business Ethics*, 7.

Reinhardt, F.L. (1999) *Down to Earth: Applying Business Principles to Environmental Management*, Harvard Business School Press, Boston, MA.

Stern, N. (2007) *Stern Review on the Economics of Climate Change*, Office of Climate Change, London.

Stone, M. (2000) 'Scourges that Strike at the Heart of Global Business', *Financial Times*, 30 May.

Turner, C.H. and Trompenaars, A. (1993) *The Seven Cultures of Capitalism*, Doubleday.

United Nations Conference on Trade and Development (UNCTAD), *World Investment Report* (annual publication).

United Nations Development Programme (UNDP), *Human Development Report* (annual publication), OUP.

Wall, S. (2007) 'Economics of the Environment', in *Applied Economics* (11th edn), Griffiths, A. and Wall, S. (eds), Financial Times Prentice Hall.

World Bank, *World Development Report* (annual publication).

Chapter 7

International strategic issues

By the end of this chapter you should be able to:

- examine the meaning and relevance of business strategy in today's corporate, national and international environment;

- discuss those strategic issues of particular relevance in a globalised economy;

- explain some of the techniques used by international business in developing and reviewing strategic initiatives;

- evaluate the impacts of strategic responses on the structure of the value chain, including operational, logistical and supply chain strategies;

- consider in some detail the strategic issues involved in discrete areas of international business such as mergers, acquisitions and alliances, and knowledge management, technology and innovation.

Introduction

Many definitions have been applied to business strategy which, while differing in detail, broadly agree that it involves devising the guiding rules or principles which influence the direction and scope of the organisations activities over the long term. Kenneth Andrews of the Harvard Business School defined corporate strategy as: 'the pattern of decisions in a company that determines and reveals its objectives, purposes or goals, produces the principal policies and plans for achieving those goals, and defines the range of business the company is to pursue'. We have already considered the contribution of the multinational enterprise (MNE) to the growth of international business activity (Chapter 1, pp. 28–36). Here we review the strategic approaches available to the MNE and the implications of those approaches for the value chain.

Before considering the evolution of business strategy within a global marketplace, it may be useful to briefly review the more conventional ideas and concepts that have dominated business strategy over the past two decades. Many of these ideas originated during the 1970s and 1980s when industrial structures were relatively stable and technical change largely incremental. After reviewing the seminal works of Michael Porter of Harvard University (1980; 1985) which helped to give a more coherent analytical structure to a broad range of managerial practices, we assess the contribution of more recent strategic approaches to international business activity.

Business strategy – ideas and concepts

Techniques such as the following were widely applied to strategic thinking during much of the 1980s and 1990s.

■ SWOT and PESTLE analysis

During the 1970s Kenneth Andrews (the academic writer) proposed a framework for strategy formulation based on the premise that the final strategy adopted by a company should achieve a 'fit' between its internal capabilities (strengths and weaknesses) and the external situation (opportunities and threats). This is commonly known as SWOT analysis (*see* Figure 7.1(a)) and involves undertaking (1) an analysis of the external environment within which the firm operates and (2) an objective appraisal of the organisation's current position in order to determine factors that might influence their ability to compete effectively within a particular market.

1 An *external analysis* should highlight the general environmental influences that a firm must cope with, for example, the political, economic, social, technological, legal and ecological factors (PESTLE) already considered in Chapters 4–6. This analysis of the external environment will lead to the identification of a number of *opportunities* and *threats*.

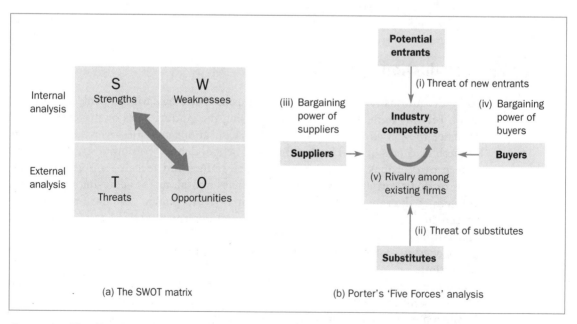

(a) The SWOT matrix   (b) Porter's 'Five Forces' analysis

Figure 7.1 The SWOT Matrix and Porter's 'Five Forces' analysis

Source: Figure 7.1(b) Adapted with the permission of The Free Press, a Division of Simon & Schuster, Inc., from COMPETITIVE STRATEGY: Techniques for Analyzing Industries and Competitors by Michael E. Porter. Copyright © 1980, 1998 by The Free Press. All rights reserved.

2 An *internal analysis* of a firm should identify those things that the organisation does particularly well (strengths) and those features that inhibit its ability to fulfil its purposes (weaknesses). The features to be assessed may include the organisation, personnel, marketing and financial features which are considered further in Chapters 8–10.

Strategic alternatives arise from matching current strengths to environmental opportunities at an acceptable level of risk. This framework was further developed during the 1980s by Michael Porter who proposed a more analytical approach to strategy formulation.

■ Porter's Five Forces analysis

Porter argued that 'the essence of strategy formulation is coping with competition' and that in addition to undertaking a PEST analysis, it is also necessary to undertake a structural analysis of the industry to gauge the strengths and weaknesses of the opposition and also determine the competitive structure of a given market. The key elements in Porter's Five Forces analysis (*see* Figure 7.1(b)) can be identified as the threat of (1) potential entrants and (2) substitutes, as well as the power of (3) suppliers and (4) buyers, together with an exploration of (5) the degree of competitive rivalry.

(1) Threat of potential entrants

The threat of new entrants into an industry depends on the barriers that exist in the market and the expected reaction of existing competitors to the entrant. Porter identified six possible sources of barriers to entry, namely economies of scale, differentiation of the product, capital requirements of entry, cost advantages, access to distribution channels and legislative intervention.

(2) Threat of substitute products

The threat of substitute products can alter the competitive environment within which the firm operates. A new process or product may render an existing product useless. For an individual firm the main issue is the extent to which there is a danger that substitutes may encroach on its activities. The firm may be able to minimise the risks from substitutes by a policy of product differentiation or by achieving a low-cost position in the industry.

(3) Bargaining power of suppliers

Suppliers have the ability to squeeze industry profits by raising prices or reducing the quality of their products. Porter states that a supplier is powerful if few suppliers exist in a particular market, there are no substitute products available, the industry is not an important customer of the supplier, or the supplier's product is an important input to the buyer's business. Japanese firms have shown the importance of establishing a strong relationship with suppliers so that they 'become an extension of the firm itself', as in the *keiretsu* approach to industrial organisation (*see* Chapter 5).

(4) Bargaining power of buyers

In general, the greater the bargaining power of buyers, the greater is their ability to depress industry profitability. Porter identified a number of determinants of bargaining power including; the concentration and size of buyers, the importance of purchases to the buyer in cost terms, the costs of switching between suppliers, and the degree of standardisation of products. Buyers should be treated as rivals but should have a 'friendly relationship based on performance and integrity'.

(5) Rivalry among existing firms

Finally, the extent of rivalry between firms can influence the competitive environment within which the firm operates. Rivalry is influenced by the above forces but also depends on the concentration of firms in the marketplace and their relative market shares, the rate of industry growth, the degree of product differentiation, and the height of exit barriers. Porter refers to the tactics used by firms to seek an advantage over their competitors as 'jockeying for position'. This usually takes the form of policies towards pricing, promotion, product innovation and service level.

According to Porter, strategy formulation requires that each of the above forces be carefully analysed in order to successfully:

- *position the company* so that its capabilities provide the best defence against the competitive forces;
- *influence the balance* of the forces through strategic moves, thereby improving the company's position;
- *anticipate changes* in the factors underlying the forces and respond to them.

■ Portfolio analysis

The Boston Consulting Group's portfolio matrix (see Figure 7.2) provides a useful framework for examining an organisation's own competitive position. The organisation's portfolio of products is subjected to a detailed analysis according to market share, growth rate and cash flow. The four alternative categories of company (or product) that emerge from the model are given the labels of 'stars', 'cash cows', 'dogs' and 'problem children' (or 'question marks').

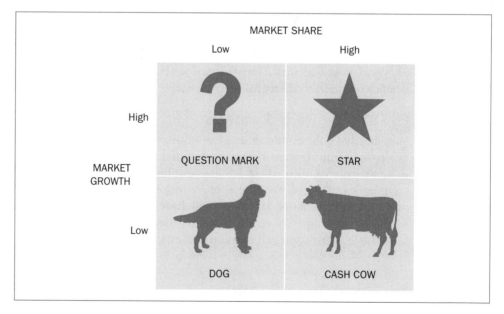

Figure 7.2 The Boston Consulting Group growth-share matrix

Source: The BCG Portfolio Matrix from the Product Portfolio Matrix, © 1970, The Boston Consulting Group.

- *Stars* have high market share, high growth, but limited cash flow due to the substantial amount of investment required to maintain growth. Successful *stars* go on to become *cash cows*.
- *Cash cows* have a high market share but slow growth. They tend to generate a very positive cash flow that can be used to develop other products.
- *Dogs* have a low share of a slow-growth market. They may be profitable, but only at the expense of cash reinvestment, and thus generate little for other products.
- *Problem children* have a low share of a fast-growing market and need more cash than they can generate themselves in order to keep up with the market.

The growth–share matrix is useful in providing a visual display of the strengths of a portfolio and therefore can be helpful in guiding the strategic direction of each business. However, there have been several criticisms aimed at the Boston Portfolio, namely that it is prone to oversimplification and that it takes no account of other key variables such as differentiation and market structure.

Choice of strategy

There have been several theoretical models of strategic choice, each of which seeks to identify the main strategic options open to the business in pursuit of its objectives. The following three approaches to strategic choice are often referred to.

- *product–market strategies* – which determine where the organisation competes and the direction of growth (e.g. Ansoff);
- *competitive strategies* – which influence the action/reaction patterns an organisation will pursue for competitive advantage (e.g. Porter);
- *institutional strategies* – which involve a variety of formal and informal relationships with other firms usually directed towards the method of growth (e.g. acquisition v. organic).

Product–market strategies

Igor Ansoff (1968) presented the various strategic options in the form of a matrix (*see* Figure 7.3(a)).

- *Market penetration* strategy refers to gaining a larger share of the market by exploiting the firm's existing products. Unless the particular market is growing, this will involve taking business away from competitors, perhaps using one or more of the 4 Ps (*see* Chapter 9) in a national or international context.
- *Market development* strategy involves taking present products into new markets, and thus focusing activities on market opportunities and competitor situations.
- *Product development* strategy is where new products are introduced into existing markets, with the focus moving towards developing, launching and supporting additions to the product range.
- *Diversification* strategy involves the company branching out into both new products and new markets. This strategy can be further subdivided into horizontal, vertical, concentric and conglomerate diversification.

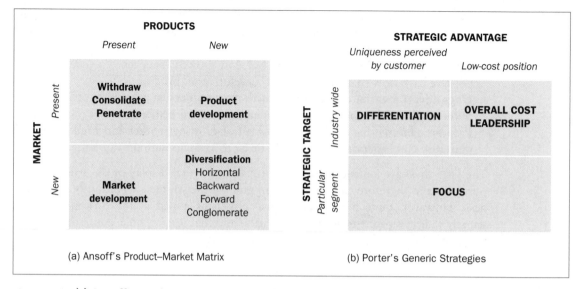

Figure 7.3 (a) Ansoff's product–market matrix; (b) Porter's generic strategies

Source: Figure 7.3(a) Reprinted by permission of *Harvard Business Review*. From 'Strategies of Diversification' by H.I. Ansoff, Sep/Oct 1957. Copyright 1957 by the Harvard Business School Publishing Corporation, all rights reserved.

> **pause for thought 1**   Can you define and give examples of each of these four types of diversification strategy?

Competitive strategies

Porter (1980) and later writers emphasised the contribution of strategic decisions to achieving some *competitive advantage* over the competition.

Such competitive advantages were often expressed in terms of the additional 'added value' the more successful firms in an industry were able to generate vis-à-vis the most marginal firm in that industry.

> Where no explicit comparator is stated, the relevant benchmark is the marginal firm in the industry. The weakest firm which still finds it worthwhile to serve the market provides the baseline against which the competitive advantage of all other firms can be set. (Kay 1993)

These competitive advantages could be attributed to a host of potential factors:

- *architecture* (a more effective set of contractual relationships with suppliers/ customers);
- *incumbency advantages* (reputation, branding, scale economies, etc.);
- *access to strategic assets* (raw materials, wavebands, scarce labour inputs, etc.);
- *innovation* (product or process, protected by patents, licences, etc.);
- *operational efficiencies* (quality circles, just-in-time techniques, re-engineering, etc.).

Our discussion here is primarily in terms of *organisations*. Aspects of *national* competitive advantage (e.g. Porter's diamond) have already been considered in Chapter 3 (pp. 90–91).

Generic strategies

Writing in 1980 in his pioneering book, *Competitive Strategy*, Porter identifies three *generic* strategies open to firms, which may help position the firm to achieve such competitive advantages. These are overall cost leadership, differentiation and focus.

- *Overall cost leadership strategy* requires the business to achieve lower costs than other competitors in the industry while maintaining product quality. This strategy requires aggressive investment in efficient plant and machinery, tight cost controls and cost minimisation in functional areas. An organisation must understand the critical activities in the business' value chain that are the sources for cost advantage and endeavour to excel in one or more of them.
- *Differentiation strategy* is based on creating 'something unique, unmatched by its competitors' which is 'valued by its buyers beyond offering simply a lower price' (Porter 1985). This entails achieving industry-wide recognition of different and superior products compared to competitors, which might result from using superior technology or providing superior customer service.
- *Focus strategy* involves selecting 'a particular buyer group, segment of the product line, or geographic market' as the basis for competition rather than the whole industry. This strategy is 'built around serving a particular target very well' in order to achieve better results. Within the targeted segment the business may attempt to compete on a low cost or differentiation basis.

Mintzberg (Mintzberg and Quinn 1991) examined both Ansoff's and Porter's models of strategic choice and suggested an alternative view of generic strategies. Mintzberg sees such strategies as being divided into five groupings, which can be summarised as locating, distinguishing, elaborating, extending and reconceiving the core business.

Case Study 7.1 reviews some strategic thinking in the pharmaceutical and drink sectors, which usefully illustrates some of the approaches already encountered.

CASE 7.1   Strategies in practice   FT

The pharmaceutical sector

Pfizer's proposed takeover of Wyeth could help strengthen and diversify its portfolio of products and defer a medium-term fall in revenues, without redressing the longer term problems with its pipeline of experimental medicines. The world's largest drugs company, created through large-scale mergers, has felt growing investor pressure to act as leading medicines approach patent expiry. None is more significant than the 2011 deadline for its blockbuster cholesterol-lowering treatment Lipitor.

Jeffrey Kindler, chief executive, has put in place a series of measures to tackle the coming gap, with a series of smaller deals and licensing arrangements; cost cutting; expansion and diversification; and efforts to create a more entrepreneurial culture. Yet many remain sceptical these initiatives will fully compensate for pressures ahead. 'Most of us speculated Pfizer has to do something to deal with the huge gap of Lipitor,' said one investment banker. 'Can you engineer yourself out of that hole on your own?'

▶

Target	Acquirer	Deal value ($bn)
Warner-Lambert	Pfizer	111.8
SmithKline Beecham	Glaxo Wellcome	79.6
Aventis	Sanofi-Synthelabo	71.3
Pharmacia Corp	Pfizer	59.8
Genentech (44.1%)	Roche	42.6
Astra	Zeneca	39.9
Hoechst	Rhone-Poulenc	33.8
Pharmacia & Upjohn	Monsanto	31.9
Ciba-Geigy	Sandoz	27.0
Schering (92.4%)	Bayer	19.3

Source: 'Largest pharmaceuticals M&A deals', *Financial Times*, 24 January 2009

Wyeth provides a range of other products to help boost revenues, including Prevnar, a pneumococcal vaccine that generated a little under $3 billion last year. The 'mega-merger' could distract the two companies' managements and force the abandonment of a possible takeover of Crucell, the Dutch vaccines company that in early 2009 said it was in talks with Wyeth.

If that deal goes ahead, Pfizer would gain further market share and extra potential in vaccines. The combination with Wyeth would also allow Pfizer to recover some consumer healthcare activities. Finally, a merger would allow further restructuring and cost-cutting in sales, marketing and even potentially in research and development operations, helping reduce pressure on margins.

Analysts argued that with the two companies' drugs there were few significant overlaps to trigger demands from regulators to divest products on competition grounds. But the biggest concern could be whether the deal – which could cost more than $60 billion – would so distract Pfizer's management that there would be little time for it to consider other smaller deals with fledgling biotech companies essential to renewing its pipeline.

Fintan Walton, head of consultancy PharmaVentures, said: 'If it's a live deal, it's a bad deal. It doesn't overcome the patent losses, and a merger will lock them into dormancy for a year. They could live to regret it even if there is a short-term cost-cutting appeal.'

Other large pharmaceuticals companies have been holding back from big deals, partly to see what Pfizer would do, otherwise fearing a bidding war. While the giant consumes its prey, others could snap up smaller promising companies before Pfizer is again able to hunt.

Source: Jack, A., 'Takeover would inject much needed diversity into product portfolio', *Financial Times*, 24 January 2009.

Brewing

SABMiller, the world's second largest brewer, can claim that few emerging markets are too difficult for its 'all-terrain' brewing and distribution. For the London listed group, even war-ravaged southern Sudan is not off limits. The skills SABMiller developed across Africa have served it well in expanding its business in eastern

Europe, Latin America and Asia from its home market of South Africa over the past 15 years. But success in the fastest growing beer market in Asia is elusive. 'Beer is expensive in India. The reason is that it's taxed heavily,' says Jean-Marc Delpon de Vaux, managing director of SABMiller India. 'At Rs34 [70 cents] a bottle, a man has to work for a beer [for] over an hour.' A beer costs the equivalent of a quarter of a clothing factory worker's daily earnings – out of the reach of many of the country's 1.2 billion people.

Nevertheless, the Indian market has great potential. Beer volumes are growing 14% a year in an emerging market famed for its hot summers as much as for rising middle class incomes. Most analysts agree that alcohol consumption has plenty of room to expand. Indians consume barely one litre of beer per person a year. The average Chinese by comparison, consumes 23 litres a year, a little over the world average of 22 litres.

Bangalore-based Mr Delpon de Vauz forecasts rapid growth. From a low base, beer consumption in India will multiply upwards of five times in the next five years. A stunted market poised for high growth has whetted the appetite of beverages groups. United Breweries, the Indian group headed by Vijay Mallya, is the leader in the 12 million hectolitre a year market with its Kingfisher brand. SABMiller is second with 38% market share from its ten local breweries, Diageo and Heineken are in talks with UB while Anheuser-Busch plans to launch its Budweiser brand.

Standing between drinks groups and improved profits are high taxes and a low number of retail outlets. On a $350 million turnover, SABMiller makes a slender 2.3% operating profit margin. A state-by-state system taxes alcohol by volume and not alcohol content. Taxes are 49% of beer's retail price compared with a global average of 34%. Brewers, after distribution and retail costs, receive only 35% of the retail price. The global average is 55%.

'In China our biggest challenge is that the selling price to consumers is so low it's extremely difficult to turn a profit, despite huge volumes,' says Nigel Fairbrass, of SABMiller in London. 'In India the challenge is that the price to consumers is far too high because of the regulatory and tax environment, and that keeps volumes low.'

Availability is a challenge. The Indian drinker has to travel many miles to find a bottle of beer. India has one point of sales for every 21,000 people compared with one for every 3000 in Indonesia. Beer drinking in India retains the stigma of the illicit. Advertising is banned. Brewers lend their brands to mineral water, soda and, in the case of Kingfisher, an airline, to gain recognition. For many Indians, drinking has yet to evolve from oblivion seeking. Knock Out, one of SABMiller's local brands, bears a name redolent of an era before responsible drinking took hold in more developed markets. The group makes no effort to market its products to women.

Oddities abound. Power cuts top the list. Executives complain the country's best barley eludes breweries to feed Saudi race horses. SABMiller's brewery in Rajasthan is held to ransom by a recycled bottle suppliers' cartel and must negotiate complex labelling requirements for the different states across India's north east. One encouraging factor is the vast quantity of spirits that Indians consume. A more benign tax regime has helped push consumption of hard liquor near the global average. Brewers expect beer to catch up, once the regulatory environment eases.

SABMiller has bet heavily on this change since acquiring its first brewery in India eight years ago. An array of local, international and newly launched brands are aimed at chipping away at Kingfisher's dominance. Foster's, Peroni and Indus Pride target the wealthier drinker. Mr Delpon de Vaux is leading a $500 million investment programme and a multi-brand assault on Kingfisher. 'At some time, affluent customers in five-star hotels will not be seen drinking the beer of the auto-rickshaw driver down the road,' he says.

Source: Lamont, J., 'SABMiller in battle to take lid off India's beer market', *Financial Times*, 30 December 2008.

Question

How might the various strategic approaches outlined above apply to these case studies?

Institutional strategies

The focus here is on possible relationships with other firms and organisations. An initial decision for a firm seeking growth is whether to do so using its own endeavours (e.g. *organic growth*) or to short-cut the growth process by some kind of institutional tie-up with other firms. These can, of course, take many forms, including the franchise, joint venture, alliances and mergers and acquisitions considered in Chapter 2. We return to consider mergers and acquisitions in more detail later in this chapter after briefly reviewing what many believe to be the new competitive landscape of a globalised economy within which all strategic choices must now take place.

To the above we can, of course, add many other conventional techniques of business analysis which are well covered elsewhere (e.g. Hornby *et al.* 2001, Chapter 9), such as product life cycle, strategic clock, value chain analysis, barriers to entry and contestable market theory, and so on. However, our main concern here is with international business strategies in a far less stable context than pertained in the 1970s and 1980s when many of these techniques were devised and applied.

Corporate strategy in a global economy

Prahalad (1999) paints a vivid picture of a 'discontinuous competitive landscape' as characterising much of the 1990s and early years of the millennium. Industries are no longer the stable entities they once were:

- rapid technology changes and the convergence of technologies (e.g. computer and telecommunications) are constantly redefining industrial 'boundaries' so that the 'old' industrial structures become barely recognisable;
- privatisation and deregulation have become global trends within industrial sectors (e.g. telecommunications, power, water, healthcare, financial services) and even within nations themselves (e.g. transition economies, China);
- Internet-related technologies are beginning to have major impacts on business-to-business and business-to-customer relationships;
- pressure groups based around environmental and ecological sensitivities are progressively well organised and influential;
- new forms of institutional arrangements and liaisons are exerting greater influences on organisational structures than hitherto (e.g. strategic alliances, franchising).

In a progressively less stable environment dominated by such discontinuities, there will arguably be a shift in perspective away from the previous strategic focus of Porter and his contemporaries in which companies are seen as seeking to identify and exploit competitive advantages within stable industrial structures.

pause for thought 2
Think of the marginal (just surviving) firm in an industry with which you are familiar. Can you identify some of the competitive advantages of the market leader in that industry over the marginal firm?

Strategy in the new competitive environment

The more conventional strategic models focused on securing competitive advantages by better utilising one or more of the five factors mentioned above. However, the discontinuities outlined previously have changed the setting in which much of the strategic discussion must now take place. Prahalad (1999) goes on to suggest four key 'transformations' which must now be registered.

1   *Recognising changes in strategic space.* Deregulation and privatisation of previously government-controlled industries, access to new market opportunities in large developing countries (e.g. China, India, Brazil) and in the transitional economies of Central and Eastern Europe, together with the rapidly changing technological environment, are creating entirely new strategic opportunities. Take the case of the large energy utilities. They must now decide on the extent of integration (power generation, power transmission within industrial and/or consumer sectors), the geographical reach of their operations (domestic/overseas), the extent of diversification (other types of energy, non-energy fields), and so on. Powergen in the UK is a good example of a traditional utility with its historical base in electricity generation which, in a decade or so, has transformed itself into a global provider of electricity services (generation and transmission), water and other infrastructure services. Clearly the strategic 'space' available to companies is ever expanding, creating entirely new possibilities in the modern global economy.

2   *Recognising globalisation impacts.* As we discuss in more detail below, globalisation of business activity is itself opening up new strategic opportunities and threats. Arguably the distinction between local and global business will itself become increasingly irrelevant. The local businesses must devise their own strategic response to the impact of globalised players. Nirula, the Indian fast-food chain, raising standards of hygiene and restaurant ambience in response to competition from McDonald's, is one type of local response and McDonald's providing more lamb and vegetarian produce in its Indian stores is another. Mass customisation and quick-response strategies (*see* p. 298) require global businesses to be increasingly responsive to local consumers. Additionally, globalisation opens up new strategic initiatives in terms of geographical locations, modes of transnational collaboration, financial accountability, and logistical provision.

3   *Recognising the importance of timely responses.* Even annual planning cycles are arguably becoming progressively obsolete as the speed of corporate response becomes a still more critical success factor, both to seize opportunities and to repel threats.

4 *Recognising the enhanced importance of innovation.* Although innovation has long been recognised as a critical success factor, its role is still further enhanced in an environment dominated by the 'discontinuities' previously mentioned. Successful companies must still innovate in terms of new products and processes but now such innovation must also be directed towards providing the company with faster and more reliable information on customers as part of mass customisation, quick response and personalised product business philosophies.

These factors are arguably changing the context for business strategy from positioning the company within a clear-cut industrial structure, to stretching and shaping that structure by its own strategic initiatives. It may no longer be sensible or efficient to devise strategic blueprints over a protracted planning timeframe and then seek to apply the blueprints mechanically given that events and circumstances are changing so rapidly. The direction of broad strategic thrust can be determined as a route map, but tactical and operational adjustments must be continually appraised and modified along the way.

Nor can the traditional strategy hierarchies continue unchallenged – i.e. top management creating strategy and middle management implementing it. Those who are closest to the product and market are becoming increasingly important as well-informed sources for identifying opportunities to exploit or threats to repel. Arguably the roles of middle and lower management in the strategic process are being considerably enhanced by the 'discontinuities' previously observed. Top managers are finding themselves progressively removed from competitive reality in an era of discontinuous

The emerging view of strategy contrasts dramatically with the traditional view. The difference is shown below:

Traditional view	**Emerging view**
· Strategy as *fit* with resources	· Strategy as *stretch and leverage*
· Strategy as *positioning in existing* industry space	· Strategy as *creating new industry* space
· Strategy as *top management* activity	· Strategy as *total organisational* process
· Strategy as an *analytical* exercise	· Strategy as an *analytical and organisational* exercise
· Strategy as *extrapolating* the past	· Strategy as *creating the future*

Figure 7.4 The new view of strategy
Source: Adapted from Prahalad (1999).

change. Their role is rather to set a broad course, to ensure that effective and responsive middle and lower management are in place to exercise delegated strategic responsibilities, and to provide an appropriate infrastructure for strategic delivery. For example, a key role of top managers in various media-related activities may be to secure access to an appropriate broadband wavelength by successfully competing in the UK or German waveband auctions. Such access is likely to be a prerequisite for competitive involvement in a whole raft of Internet-related products for home and business consumption via mobile telephony.

Figure 7.4 provides a useful summary of the traditional and emerging views of international business strategy.

Case Study 7.2 on the rise and fall of the Citigroup Conglomerate provides a useful context for reviewing some of the ideas in Figure 7.4.

CASE 7.2   Strategic mistakes at Citigroup   **FT**

By the morning of 6 April 1998 when Sandy Weill and John Reed entered the Waldorf Astoria sporting matching ties dotted with umbrellas to face the press corps, their deal had entered the annals of business history. As flashes exploded on the faces of Mr Weill, then chief executive of Travelers, and Mr Reed, his counterpart at Citicorp, their $83 billion merger was already being described as the deal of the century.

The union of the insurance, brokerage and securities businesses assembled by Mr Weill through a frenzy of acquisitions over the previous decade and Citicorp's international consumer and commercial lending operations was supposed to change the banking world forever. As Mr Reed told the *Financial Times* after welcoming more than 100 million savers and thousands of companies in over 100 countries under Citigroup's big red umbrella: 'This was a deal you simply had to do.'

A decade later, the dream of an all-purpose global financial conglomerate capable of selling insurance to New Jersey housewives and stocks to Thai investors lies in tatters. Weakened by years of in-fighting, poor management, misguided strategies and lax oversight by regulators and its board, Citigroup has been dealt a near mortal blow by the most virulent financial crisis in generations.

After yesterday's news of an $8 billion (£5.6 billion, €6.3 billion) loss in the last three months of 2008, its fifth straight quarter in the red, Citigroup's market value hovers around $20 billion – a fraction of its $155 billion capitalisation on the day of the merger. As Citi fights for survival and the US government considers whether to take it out of its misery and nationalise it, the financial world has reacted with shock and disbelief to the dramatic unravelling of a once-mighty banking giant.

Even if Citi escapes collapse after $50 billion plus in credit losses, a $300 billion government bail-out and a catastrophic plunge in its shares, the bank's earnings power, reach and credibility with customers and investors will be compromised for years to come.

Yet, for all the drama of the past few months, which culminated in this week's plan to sell or spin off $600 billion worth of unwanted assets or businesses – a third of Citi – the roots of the company's demise stretch back to that April morning ten years ago.

▶

As Mr Pandit has said, the merger between Citicorp and Travelers was never fully completed. Legend has it that Citi's beginnings were undermined by the lack of personal chemistry between Mr Weill, the Brooklynite upstart with a voracious appetite for acquisitions and Mr Reed, the patrician banker with a world vision.

But although the two co-chief executives had a tempestuous relationship that led to a bitter clash and Mr Reed's ousting in 2000, the original sin of Citi's conception was that its diverse businesses were not properly integrated. 'It was a marriage of convenience in some sense,' recalls an executive who worked on the merger. 'Citicorp had a great franchise and needed good management and Travelers had good management and needed a franchise.'

The result was an uncomfortable agglomeration of businesses and management teams that lacked a common strategy, ranging from the street-smart traders of Salomon Brothers to the ambassadorial bankers that flew Citicorp's flag in foreign lands.

One former executive recalls that the first organisational structure had so many co-heads of units that the new company was quickly dubbed 'the Noah's Ark'.

Mr Weill and Mr Reed tried to instill a sense of mission in the disparate provinces of their empire by touting the idea of cross-selling products to its huge client base. As Mr Weill said in the aftermath of the merger: 'It's about cross-marketing and providing better products to clients.'

At its simplest, the concept was that Citicorp's savers would flock to Travelers' insurance and brokerage offerings while companies borrowing from Citicorp would seek the advice and capital market services of Salomon. That, in turn, spawned the oft-repeated idea of a 'financial supermarket' – a one-stop shop with the product breadth and the geographical reach to satisfy companies' and consumers' every need.

Mr Weill's lieutenants say that cross-selling was only part of the plan and was quietly ditched in Citi's early years when it became apparent that customers and companies liked to shop around for financial services.

Bob Willumstad, who joined Mr Weill when he headed the small firm Commercial Credit in the late 1980s and was his consumer banking supremo throughout the Citi years, describes the company as more like a 'financial mall' than a supermarket. 'These businesses were never integrated by design, at least on the consumer side,' he says. 'There was never a major effort to teach branch tellers to sell annuities, mortgages and credit cards.

Instead, the advantage of having so many businesses side-by-side was to provide the combined group with such unrivalled scale and geographical presence as to impress investors and crush rivals active in just one product or region. 'Each business had to strive to be number one in its sector, while the sheer size benefited the group through lower funding costs and other economies of scale, recalls another member of Mr Weill's inner circle. 'It was the same model as General Electric.'

For several years, it appeared to work. Investors, enthralled by Mr Weill's charismatic, bullish personality and ability to drive earnings growth, propelled Citi's shares higher. After a dip during the Russian crisis and the implosion of Long Term Capital Management in 1998, the company's stock began a long period of outperformance, peaking at $56 in 2006.

But critics say that unlike GE, whose sprawling portfolio of businesses is held together by internal disciplines honed over decades, the financial giant lacked a coherent management philosophy. Mr Weill was brilliant at striking deals and convincing investors of their merits, but putting in place a succession plan and ensuring that Citi had a structure that would survive in the long-term was never top of his agenda.

Even Mr Weill's friends say that the flip side of his charisma was an overbearing, controlling personality epitomised by a neon sign on his desk proclaiming either 'The Chairman is Happy' or, more menacingly, 'the Chairman is Not Happy' – that worked against Citi's long-term interests.

Mr Weill could not be reached for comment.

Former executives say Citi was a devolved institution where divisional leaders were free to run their businesses and to build fiefdoms, provided they sent profits back to the headquarters where Mr Weill ruled with an iron fist. The desire to please Citi's voluble leader prompted frequent infighting – a former manager describes Citi as a 'loose collection of warring tribes' – that led to the departures of senior executives.

The brain drain hurt Citi's businesses and deprived it of talented managers who could, one day, have aspired to the top job.

To many observers, Citi's repeated brushes with regulators over the years – including a large fine for predatory lending in the US, the temporary closure of its operations in Japan for violations of banking laws and a £14 million penalty in the UK for its co-called 'Dr Evil' trade, after a Citi bet on euro bonds caused a major disruption in fixed income markets across Europe – were a symptom of its disjointed, dysfunctional structure.

It was regulatory pressure – from the crusade of Eliot Spitzer, the then New York State attorney-general, against conflicts of interests on Wall Street – that contributed to Mr Weill's decision to step down as chief executive in 2003. (He remained chairman until 2006.)

His successor was Chuck Prince, the company's legal counsel, who was seen as a safe pair of hands who could steer the company through rough regulatory waters.

Mr Prince did that but little else. The reality was that succeeding Mr Weill in leading Citi's loose collection of business would have been tough for most executives. For Mr Prince, who had little experience of running an operating unit, it proved impossible.

Mr Prince's tenure, which ended with his ousting in December 2007, was marked by two mistakes that could yet prove fatal for Citi: a deep dive into risky mortgage assets in an effort to replicate the stellar returns being reaped by the likes of Goldman; and a sharp increase in expenses and costs that hobbled Citi's profits and put its balance sheet under severe strain.

Crucially Citi's pliant board – mainly comprised of other chief executives – did little to correct the shortcomings of the novice chief. Now, as Citi slides into the abyss, its flawed past weighs heavily on its future.

Source: Guerrera, F., 'Flawed conception', *Financial Times*, 17 January 2009.

Question

Use Figure 7.4 to evaluate the strategic decision making of this global financial intermediary.

International business and the value chain

We noted in Chapter 1 that international production is dominated by MNEs that are increasingly transnational in operation, including horizontally and vertically integrated activities more widely dispersed on a geographical basis. This brings into focus the *value chain* in Figure 7.5, which breaks down the full collection of activities that companies perform into 'primary' and 'secondary' activities.

- *Primary activities* are those required to create the product (good or service, including inbound raw materials, components and other inputs), sell the product and distribute it to the marketplace.
- *Secondary activities* include a variety of functions such as human resource management, technological development, management information systems, finance for procurement, etc. These secondary activities are required to support the primary activities.

It is useful to remember that an effective international business strategy must encompass *all* parts of the value chain configuration, wherever their geographical location. Later chapters of this book consider the international dimension of these various activities in their own right. Here we concentrate on international strategic approaches that might help the firm maximise the sum of these individual activities. International strategies that yield *global synergies* for the firm over its entire value chain are likely to be of particular interest, where synergies refer to the so-called '2 + 2 > 4 effect' whereby the whole becomes greater than the sum of the individual parts.

A number of sources can be identified as contributing to these global synergies.

Sources of global synergies

Expanding internationally may allow firms to reconfigure their value chains and raise overall corporate profitability in ways that would not otherwise be available within a

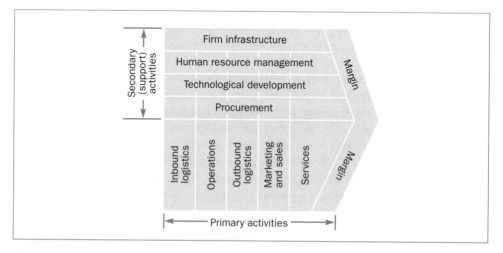

Figure 7.5 **Value chain**

wholly domestic context. International businesses may be able to develop these 'global synergies' from a variety of sources.

- *Localisation on a global scale* where only the international business can disperse individual value-creating activities (both 'primary' and 'secondary') around the world to locations where they can be undertaken most efficiently (at least cost) and effectively. For example we saw in Chapter 1 (p. 8) how labour costs and productivities varied markedly between different geographical locations.
- *Economies of scale* where it is only by becoming an international business that the firm can operate at such a size that all available economies of scale (technical and non-technical) are achieved for a particular activity within the value chain. This is especially important when the 'minimum efficient size' for an activity within the firm's value chain exceeds the maximum level of output achievable within the domestic economy (*see* Box 7.1, p. 267).
- *Economies of scope and experience* where only the international business can configure the most appropriate *mix* of activities (*economies of scope*) within the value chain consistent with efficient and effective production. Or where only by becoming an international business can the firm secure the *economies of experience* essential to minimising (cumulative) average costs (*see* p. 299).
- *Non-organic growth on an international scale* where the international business recognises that organic growth is insufficient to meet its key objectives and where some form of *institutional arrangement* with one or more overseas firm(s) is seen as the way ahead. The various institutional mechanism's available have already been touched on in Chapter 2 and are considered in more detail in the international context below. Of course these institutional linkages may themselves be a means to achieving one or more of the global synergies already identified.
- *Increase in geographical reach of core competencies* where the international business seeks to earn a still higher return from its distinctive core competencies by applying those competencies to new geographic markets.

International business strategies

The enormous variety of operations embraced by the term 'multinational' has led some writers to distinguish between four key strategies when competing in the international business environment: a global strategy, a transnational strategy, a multidomestic strategy and an international strategy. The appropriateness of the particular strategy selected will depend to a considerable extent on the pressures faced by the international business in terms of both cost and local responsiveness, as indicated in Figure 7.6. These will become clearer as we discuss the nature of these various strategies and their associated advantages and disadvantages.

■ Global strategy

This is particularly appropriate when the firm faces high pressures in terms of cost competitiveness but low pressures in terms of being responsive to local market conditions. Firms adopting a global strategy focus on being cost competitive by securing the various economies of scale and scope outlined in Box 7.1 (p. 267) and economies of

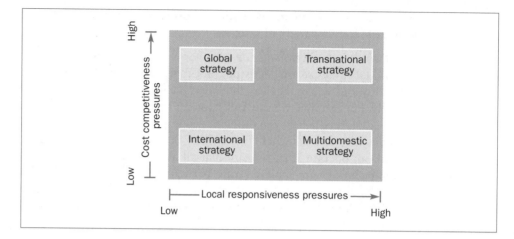

Figure 7.6 **Four international strategies**

experience (p. 299). Production, marketing and R & D activities tend to be concentrated in a few (and in extreme cases a single) favourable geographical locations rather than being widely dispersed. The emphasis of the global firm is on a homogenous, standardised product to maximise these various technical and non-technical economies. Of course such a low-cost strategy is only possible where few pressures exist to localise either production or marketing. If localisation pressures were high, then shorter production runs of a locally-differentiated product would invariably raise both technical (production) and non-technical (function/support services) costs.

The global strategy is best suited to industrial products for which there are high pressures for cost reductions but relatively low pressures for the product to be differentiated to meet local market requirements. The semiconductor industry is widely regarded as suitable for this strategy, with global standards placing a premium on firms such as Intel, Motorola and Texas Instruments producing standardised products at minimum cost. A global strategy does not suit many consumer goods markets where product differentiation is a key to local/cultural acceptability.

■ Transnational strategy

This is particularly appropriate when the firm faces pressures in terms of both cost competitiveness and responsiveness to local conditions. Of course such local responsiveness may involve more than the 'local' market acceptability of a differentiated product. It might, for example, also reflect entry barriers which effectively protect the local market from the import of a standardised product, however locally acceptable to consumers.

Firms adopting the transnational strategy cannot depend on cost reductions via scale economies from producing a standardised product in a few selected geographical locations. Rather, they must seek cost reductions by exploiting *location economies* appropriate to a particular element of the value chain; for example, locating labour-intensive component production in countries where relative unit labour costs (RULCs – *see* p. 9) are low. Another cost reduction mechanism open to a transnational strategy might involve benefiting from *experience economies* (*see* p. 299) related to cumulative production across a larger number of geographical locations. *Global learning* may be a further mechanism yielding cost reductions, as when foreign subsidiaries themselves add value to any core competencies transferred from the parent company. The foreign subsidiaries may go on to develop the expertise to become the primary centres for further, initially unforeseen, value added activities, thereby increasing global efficiency. Foreign subsidiaries may then be able to use this 'global learning' to transfer their own (newly acquired) core competencies to other foreign subsidiaries or back to the parent company itself.

These cost reduction outcomes via a transnational strategy must, of course, remain consistent with the high pressure towards local responsiveness. For example, local responsiveness may require product differentiation and non-standardised marketing and HRM approaches appropriate to local sociocultural sensitivities.

Implementing a transnational strategy is likely to require a high degree of complex organisational coordination across geographically-dispersed primary and secondary activities within the global value chain. There is also likely to be an element of conflict between cost reductions via the various mechanisms outlined above and cost increases resulting from an increased local responsiveness which inhibits scale economies of both a technical and non-technical nature. How then can the international business implement a transnational strategy?

There are of course many variants, but a widely-used method for implementing this strategy involves the idea of 'modularity' in both design and production (*see* p. 301). This approach is currently being widely used in the car industry as part of a transnational strategy, whereby production activities are progressively broken down into a number of large but separate elements that can be carried out independently in different international locations, chosen according to the optimum mix of factor inputs (cost and quality) for each element. Final assembly, characterised by local responsiveness in terms of product differentiation involving design and other features, often takes place at, or near to, the intended market.

Ford is following this approach, making many different models but using the same 'platform' – the basic chassis and other standardised internal parts. Design and technological breakthroughs of this kind permit even the transnational strategy to benefit from scale economies, as in the production of the basic platform. However, Ford plans to produce ten different vehicles from this common platform, with differentiated features reflecting the need to respond to localised consumer preferences.

■ Multidomestic strategy

This is particularly appropriate when the firm faces low pressures in terms of cost competitiveness but high pressures in terms of local responsiveness. This strategy tends to involve establishing relatively independent subsidiaries, each providing a full range of value chain activities (primary and secondary) within each national market. The subsidiary is broadly free to customise its products, focus its marketing and select and recruit its personnel, all in keeping with the local culture and the expressed preferences of its customers in each local market.

Such a strategy is more likely to occur when economies of scale in production and marketing are low, and when there are high coordination costs between parent and subsidiary. A disadvantage of such local 'independence' may also be an inability to realise potential experience economies. A further disadvantage may manifest itself in the autonomous actions of subsidiaries, sometimes paying little regard to broader-based corporate objectives. A classic example in this respect is the decision by the US subsidiary of Philips NV in the late 1970s to purchase the Matsushita VHS-format video-cassette recorders (VCRs) and put its own label on them, when the parent company was seeking to establish its own V2000 VCRs as the industry standard.

International strategy

This is particularly appropriate when the firm faces low pressures as regards both cost competitiveness and local responsiveness. The international strategy places the main focus on establishing the 'core architecture' (e.g. product development and R & D) underpinning the value chain at the home base of the MNE and seeking to translate this more or less intact to the national market overseas. Some localised production and marketing activities may be permitted, but these will be limited in scope. McDonald's, IBM, Microsoft, Wal Mart, Kelloggs and Procter & Gamble are often cited as companies pursuing an international strategy in which head office keeps a tight rein over product strategy and marketing initiatives.

Table 7.1 Characteristics of four international strategies

Strategy	Advantages	Disadvantages
Global	Standardised products become highly cost competitive Economies of scale Economies of experience Emphasise home country core competencies	Less responsive to local conditions Loss of market share if consumer behaviour becomes more responsive to localised characteristics Few opportunities for global learning
Transnational	Economies of location via a geographically-dispersed value chain Economies of experience Global learning stemming from the sharing of core competencies Product differentiation, with production and marketing responsive to local conditions	Complex coordination to implement strategy Possible conflicts between cost competitiveness and local responsiveness
Multidomestic	Highly customised production and marketing, emphasising local responsiveness Most appropriate where the minimum efficient size (MES) is relatively low for key elements of the value chain and strong local/cultural preferences exist.	Loss of location economies (which require a geographically-dispersed value chain) Loss of experience economies Little global learning where core competencies are not transferred between foreign companies Lack of corporate group cohesion
International	Core competencies transferred to foreign markets Economies of scale for centralised markets in 'core architecture' (e.g. product development, R & D)	Less responsive to local conditions Less location economies available, via retention of 'core architecture' Less global learning as few core competencies transferred Less experience economies available

Over time some additional local customisation of product and marketing has tended to accompany the international strategy. Not least because of some well publicised failures from an overly strict adherence to the 'core architecture' at head offices. For example IKEA, the Swedish furniture retailer, transferred its retailing formula developed in Sweden into other nations. While such a transfer has proved successful in the UK and elsewhere, it most certainly failed in the USA, with product ranges proving inappropriate to both the larger American physiques (e.g. beds and sofas were too small), the American preferences for larger storage spaces (drawers, bedroom chests and other containers too confined), and European-sized curtains proving incompatible with the sizes of American windows. After entering the US market in 1985, IKEA had realised by the early 1990s that it would need to customise its product range to the American market if it was going to succeed there, which it has duly done to considerable success.

Such celebrated failures, together with a growing awareness of the benefits of at least a limited amount of local responsiveness, have somewhat diluted the international strategy, though it still remains one in which a centralised core architecture persists. It is most appropriate to situations where the parent firm possesses core competencies, which are unmatched by indigenous competitors in foreign markets, and where the key characteristics of the product are broadly welcomed by consumers in those markets.

Table 7.1 reviews the advantages and disadvantages of these four international strategies.

Case Study 7.3 investigates the strategies behind a number of the mechanisms adopted for market entry to the US.

CASE 7.3   MNE strategies in the US market   **FT**

Management theorists have a special rule for companies expanding outside their home markets; never underestimate the liability of foreigners. Ambitious executives, operating on unfamiliar turf, fail to recognise cultural differences. European companies moving into the US are no exception, says Julian Birkinshaw, of the London Business School. 'Too often they say "Oh I know America. This should be straightforward." In more distant countries, they know there are cultural factors to overcome and work hard to overcome them. In the US they are deceived by the cultural proximity.'

In recent decades, the US has proved attractive to many European businesses. Some have prospered but others have been scarred by the process. And for some, crossing the Atlantic has ended in disaster – even oblivion. All went with high hopes. For some, entering the world's largest market is part of a strategy of global acquisitions. Deutsche Telekom, for example, bought Voicestream, the US mobile operator, as part of a portfolio of international telecommunications businesses. France's Vivendi paid $34 billion in 2000 for Universal Studios to build a global media giant. Marks and Spencer bought Brooks Brothers, the upmarket clothing retailer, and King's Supermarkets in 1988 as part of its expansion plans outside the UK.

Some believed a US acquisition alone could turn them into a global business. When Farnell, the UK component distributor, bought Premier Consolidated of the US for $2.8 billion in 1996, Farnell's market value was less than £1 billion ($1.5 billion at the time).

▶

Howard Poulson, then chief executive, said the deal was a once-in-a-lifetime opportunity. 'With one move, we have transformed ourselves into a truly global company.' The hubris at what became Premier Farnell was shortlived. Two years later, Mr Poulson had departed after two profit warnings and a slashed dividend. Like many other chief executives, he had underestimated the challenge of a US acquisition. One of his mistakes was to pay too much. His reasoning was that unless Farnell snapped up Premier, a US rival would act and squeeze it out of important markets. This is a common error for European companies entering the US, says Marco Becht of the European Corporate Governance Institute in Brussels – particularly during the stock market euphoria of the 1990s. 'It was hard to resist – everyone was doing it. If you didn't want to look like "old Europe", you did it like the Americans.'

This reflects the difficulty many European executives have in understanding just how competitive the US market is. 'In most European countries, there are three or four significant players,' says Prof Birkinshaw, 'There are often 10–20 competitors in the US in sectors such as retailing.'

Dixons, the UK electronics retailer, discovered this when it bought Silo, a US chain in 1987. A recession followed and Silo, which had over-expanded, was unable to compete with bigger rivals. Eventually Dixons sold the US chain and took write-offs of more than £200 million.

Renault also found it had misunderstood the US consumer after it had attempted to enter the US in the 1970s through a partnership with American Motors. But it chose to launch its assault in small cars, one of the most competitive segments and one with weak profit margins. It also made technical errors, including under-powering its models in the wrong expectation that the energy crisis would end the American love affair with gas-guzzlers. The strategy was supposed to be cheaper than building a presence in the US from scratch, which Renault estimated would have cost at least $1.5 billion. By the time it managed to pull out by selling AMC to Chrysler, the venture had cost it an estimated $730 million – with little to show for it. Indeed, it almost brought the French carmaker to bankruptcy. Renault has yet to return to the US, except through Nissan Motor, its Japanese arm.

Given the competitive intensity of the US market, it is essential to have a clear strategy. But the European companies that fail in the US often lack a clear strategy, says Subi Rangan of Insead, the French management school. 'Global strategy is never a substitute for a good business strategy. International expansion is one of the things companies do to conceal a lack of strategy. The activity gives shareholders the impression that something is being achieved,' says Prof Rangan.

Retail groups can find it particularly hard to stand out in such a competitive market. But that is only one of the problems faced by businesses that are close to consumers. 'They have to capture the local zeitgeist,' says Joanna Waterous, who heads the European retail practice of McKinsey, the consultants. This is not easy when head office is thousands of miles away and may not grasp the subtle cultural differences of the US market.

Whether they can overcome this distance will depend on the skill with which the US businesss is managed, says LBS's Prof Birkinshaw. When Ericsson bought a California company called Raynet, a fibre optics group, in 1996, it adopted its standard integration approach and soon found it had driven out most of the staff whose skills were essential to the business. In subsequent acquisitions, the Swedish group was much more hands-off.

But leaving too much to US management can also be risky, as several European companies have found. When Midland Bank bought a majority stake in Crocker National Corporation of California in 1981, it promised the regulators it would not take control of management. The last UK bank to expand overseas, Midland, was catapulted into the world's top 10 banks by the deal. But within a year, Crocker's local managers had authorised an expansion in the California property market and racked up levels of debt that almost brought Midland to collapse before it sold its US subsidiary to Wells Fargo.

BP is another European company that found its US activities weighing heavily when it took a majority stake in Sohio. It eventually took full control of the US oil group after a series of moves by local managers that weakened Sohio's position. Sohio had squandered much of the cash from its Alaskan field in an unsuccessful effort to build up reserves in the lower 48 US states. And it bought Kennecott, a copper mining company, just as the metal's price was beginning to collapse.

Such failures in management reflect cultural differences, says Marco Becht of the European Corporate Governance Institute. But these gaps can impinge in other ways, including American legal traditions and the liabilities these impose on companies. 'Litigation can begin as soon as the deal is done,' he says. He cites the case launched against DaimlerChrysler by Kirk Kerkorian, who claims that the German company failed to pay enough for control of Chrysler in 1998.

Prof Birkinshaw says that these legal differences penetrate day-to-day management in the US. 'Swedes put trust in the handshake, but the US relies on legal documents.'

Some of the companies that do well are the truly multinational companies such as Unilever and Nestlé that have grown much bigger outside their home countries over long periods. They have little difficulty building their operations in the US, though they often prefer to start from scratch and make acquisitions later.

And whatever the difficulties about entering the US, most observers expect there to be no shortage of candidates to follow where others have gone. On the day that Ahold announced its problems, Egg, the UK-based internet bank said it was exploring venturing into the US market.

Ms Waterous says the answer to why companies still go to the US is the same that Willie Sutton gave for why he robbed banks, 'It's where the money is!'

Source: Wilman, J., 'Crossing the Atlantic can end in oblivian', *Financial Times*, 25 February 2003.

Questions

1 Using the four international strategies shown in Figure 7.6, suggest which companies would appear to have followed one of these strategies in their approach to the US.

2 What can we learn in a strategic context from the successes and failures in the Case Study?

3 Apart from strategic issues, what other factors determine success or failure in approaching the US market?

4 What is meant by the suggestion that 'global strategy is never a good substitute for business strategy'?

International business strategies and political perspectives

The broad framework discussed in the last section has been adapted to give further insights into strategic decision making by MNEs. In particular there has been a focus on the alleged trade-off between the need for MNEs to be responsive to the *national* concerns of host countries (or regional groupings) on the one hand, and to be *economically integrated* (globally or regionally) on the other. Following Rugman and Collinson (2009) we can use Figure 7.7 to illustrate this so-called *integration–responsiveness* framework.

Economic integration–national responsiveness framework

■ *National responsiveness.* The horizontal axis of Figure 7.7 corresponds to an essentially political dimension, namely 'national responsiveness'. It refers to the pressures on MNEs to respond to different national or regional (e.g. EU) standards imposed by governments and agencies and to different consumer tastes in segmented national (or regional) markets.

■ *Economic integration.* The vertical axis of Figure 7.7 corresponds to an index of 'economic integration' worldwide (i.e. globalisation), or more regionally focused as in the case of increased integration within the EU. It refers to the pressures on MNEs to develop economies of scale, to develop location economies (via global specialisation for appropriate activities within the value chain), to develop experience economies and to seek to benefit from other efficiency advantages from increased coordination and control of geographically-dispersed activities.

Strategies appropriate to the MNE will then depend on the quadrant they inhabit or seek to inhabit.

■ *Quadrant 1* (high economic integration, low national responsiveness). Here the MNE operates in a market characterised by high economic integration pressures and

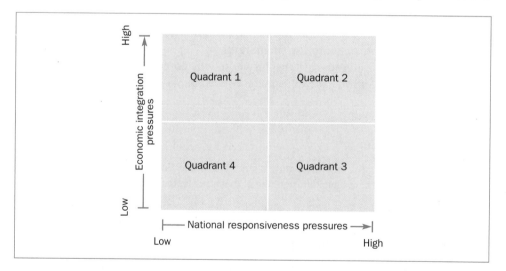

Figure 7.7 **Integration–responsiveness framework**

its strategy must therefore incorporate a drive for cost and price competitiveness. Typically MNEs in this quadrant will be centralised in structure, often using mergers and acquisitions to achieve economies of scale, scope and experience (Box 7.1 p. 267). However, the MNE in this quadrant need not be unduly concerned with responding to host country national (political, regulatory and cultural) concerns as these are deemed to have a 'low' impact on its operation.

■ *Quadrant 2* (high economic integration, high national responsiveness). Here the MNE operates in a market characterised by strong international cost and price competitiveness pressures but it must meet such challenges while paying due regard to the high political sensitivities of host national/regional governments and agencies. The MNE in this quadrant will face a variety of policy options which seek a compromise between these two, somewhat opposing tendencies. The co-ordination of a variety of flexible responses (*see also* p. 298) may be challenging for the MNE. Rugman and Hodgetts suggest that many MNEs based in one or other of the triad regional groupings face these compromises, and the most adaptive and innovative in terms of policy/organisation are the ones which tend to thrive.

■ *Quadrant 3* (low economic integration, high national responsiveness). Here economic integration is less important to the MNE than national responsiveness. Production practices, product specification and support activities (e.g. marketing) must be carefully adapted to the consumer characteristics, standards and regulation of the national/regional grouping. Economic integration is much less important (less cost and price competitive pressures) than a decentralised strategy responsive to national (regional) characteristics. In practice segmented strategies appealing to niche and target groups within the national/regional economies are likely, as in the case of food products and higher-quality (designer) clothes.

■ *Quadrant 4* (low economic integration, low national responsiveness). Few scale economies or location economies via a more geographically-dispersed value chain are likely in this quadrant so price competition will tend to be less fierce. Nor are there many benefits from seeking close alignment with national (regional) regulations, standards and consumer characteristics. A broadly standardised product can, however, be sold by MNEs in this quadrant and there may be benefits from a centralised transfer of core competencies to overseas national (regional) subsidiaries.

The high population (380 million rising to over 450 million with enlargement) and high income base of the EU will then permit substantial scale economies for products conforming to clearly demarcated EU specifications. In other words high economic integration within the EU will serve EU 'home' MNEs well in competition with their triad (*see* p. 4) counterparts. By using more stringent directives and other regulations re product specifications, the EU is placing less focus on member state national responsiveness but more focus on EU supranational (regional) responsiveness. To support EU 'winners' the EU competition policy is seen by many as increasingly directed towards supporting cross-border merger activities, strategic partnerships and the achievement of scale economies.

Case Study 7.4 looks at integration-responsiveness issues.

CASE 7.4 US carmaking: political and economic imperatives **FT**

The plant that assembles Chrysler's Jeep Wrangler near Toledo, Ohio, sprawls across four buildings, but Chrysler occupies only one of them. The others house three of the troubled carmaker's suppliers. South Korea's Hyundai Mobis builds the Wrangler's chassis, while Kuka, a German maker of robots and welding machines, puts together the body. The facility's paint shop is operated by Magna international of Canada, with Chrysler responsible only for the vehicles' final assembly.

The plant, opened in 2005, illustrates the interdependence of Detroit's troubled carmakers and their myriad suppliers in the US and overseas. Relationships like these lie at the heart of the intense lobbying effort by Chrysler and its two bigger Detroit-based rivals – General Motors and Ford – to persuade US lawmakers to approve a $25 billion (€20 billion, £17 billion) rescue package.

Congress began hearings yesterday on the plan, aimed at averting the collapse of an industry that accounts for about 4% of gross domestic product but is quickly running out of cash. Were either GM or Ford to go bankrupt, it would mark the biggest business failure in US history. The Detroit carmakers operate 105 US assembly and component plants, with close to 240,000 employees. They provide healthcare benefits for 2 million Americans and pensions for almost three-quarters of a million people.

Proponents of the bail-out claim that the damage would spread much further. Carmaking, they argue, has one of the largest 'multiplier' effects of any industry: for every job, at least seven more people are employed indirectly. Manufacturers, parts suppliers and dealers say the impact of a collapse on the real economy would dwarf that of this year's bank failures. Nearly all the jobs lost would be blue-collar, with the pain felt largely in Michigan, Ohio and Indiana. Michigan already has unemployment of almost 9%, the highest of any state.

According to CSM Worldwide, the automotive consultancy, three-quarters of suppliers of 68 of the key components and modules that go into cars derive 20% or more of their business from the Detroit companies. About 37% of suppliers generate more than half their business from GM, Ford or Chrysler. Many are already unprofitable and the loss of a single big customer – a Ford or a GM – could push them over the edge, disrupting the supply chain of other customers.

Advocates of a bail-out say, therefore, that the failure of one large Detroit company could cause the other two to collapse. 'Everything is so intimately connected that if one of these guys goes down, it would probably take the entire industry down,' says David Cole of the University of Michigan's Centre for Automotive Research.

Other large US companies – notably airlines – have filed for Chapter 11 protection and continued doing business for years. But carmakers and industry analysts say that a bankruptcy filing for an automaker would cause a collapse of sales as consumers baulked at buying a car whose warranty might not be honoured or for which they might have trouble getting parts.

Past industry experience suggests that the failure of the three carmakers, while widely felt, might in fact come at a cost lower than the sum of their lost parts. At least some of the Detroit companies' operations would probably survive and employ workers under new owners. Daewoo Motors failed in 2001 at a heavy short-term cost to employment and its local and overseas plants. Ten years later, five of the former carmakers' plants in Korea have been busy turning out Chevrolets and other cars for none other than GM under its GM DAT joint venture with Daewoo's creditors and others.

When US suppliers such as Delphi or Collins & Aikman filed for bankruptcy in 2005, their European units carried on doing business after being sold or ring-fenced from their parents. The Detroit companies would have a harder time selling their unionised Midwestern car plants but some of their suppliers would probably survive, picking up business from Japanese carmakers and emerging leaner from the process.

Indeed, there are signs that Detroit's overseas arms are preparing themselves for all eventualities, including failure of their owners. Opel, GM's German subsidiary, is in talks with federal and state governments about lining up €1 billion in guarantees to keep it going in case its owner's troubles deepen.

Nor is the past record on state-led rescues of 'national champion' carmakers encouraging. Chrysler secured a $1.5 billion in loan guarantees in 1979 – a bailout seen today as having addressed the symptoms of Chrysler's problems rather than their root cause. The UK government poured millions of pounds into trying to save MG Rover, only to see it fail in 2005 at an estimated cost to taxpayers and business of £870 million. China's Shanghai Automotive owns some remnants of the business.

Yet politics rather than economics is likely to prevail in Washington. Organised labour is a key Democratic constituency and jobs in several 'swing' states that voted Democratic in the presidential election are on the line. 'We are determined to pass legislation that will save the jobs of millions of workers whose livelihoods are on the line,' Senate majority leader Harry Reid said last week. 'They deserve no less.'

GM and Ford, as publicly traded companies, may prove more politically palatable candidates for aid than Chrysler, owned by Gerberus, the private equity firm. Industry insiders say the company is the only one in Detroit that could fail without taking its two rivals down with it. The impact on suppliers would also be comparatively muted.

But the reckoning will be costly to Detroit in any scenario. Whatever happens, tens of thousands will lose their jobs in the months ahead. According to S&P, even with financial aid, 'US automakers are unlikely to avoid further sweeping changes to their product lines, market focus, or possibly their status as independent entities.'

Source: Reed, J. and Simon, B., 'Detroit spinners', *Financial Times*, 19 November 2008.

Questions

1 Examine the reasons for and against a rescue by the US government of the 'big 3' US carmakers.

2 Evaluate the strategies, using Figure 7.7, appropriate to existing 'big 3' carmakers, GM, Ford and Chrysler.

3 Evaluate the strategies, using Figure 7.7, appropriate to new entrants to the industry.

Institutional strategies and international business

To a greater or lesser extent, all four strategies discussed in the previous two sections may involve the firm in devising new *institutional arrangements*, especially where 'green field' foreign direct investment (*see* p. 57) overseas is deemed inappropriate. Mergers and acquisitions and strategic alliances were seen, in Chapter 1, to be an increasingly prominent aspect of international business. In this section we consider these institutional arrangements within the international business environment in rather more detail.

■ Mergers and acquisitions (M & A)

We have already noted (*see* Chapter 2) how globalisation has influenced MNE perspectives of horizontal and vertical integration, with the former particularly relevant to cost-oriented MNEs and the latter to market-oriented MNEs. Laurence Capron (1999) expressed similar views in her assertion that two types of synergy (sometimes described as the '2 + 2 > 4 effect') are typically used to justify mergers and acquisitions, namely cost and revenue based synergies:

- *cost-based synergies* – horizontal acquisitions have traditionally been considered an effective means of achieving economies of scale in production, in R & D and in administrative, logistical and sales functions;
- *revenue-based synergies* – horizontal or vertical acquisitions enable companies to develop new competencies, which may in turn enable them to command a price premium (via increased market power, higher innovation capabilities) or to increase sales volume (via increased market leverage – both geographic and product-line extension).

Figure 7.8 provides a still broader classification of the potential synergies from M & A activity, breaking them down this time into 'real term' and 'financial' issues. Box 7.1 looks in rather more detail at some of the synergies commonly ascribed to M & A.

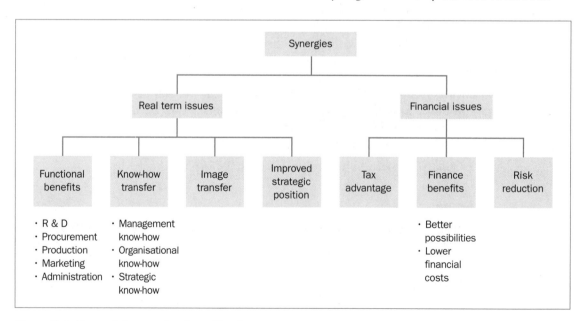

Figure 7.8 **Potential synergies from M & A**

Box 7.1   Mergers and acquisitions incentives

Mergers and acquisitions constitute the main vehicle by which firms grow in size (accounts for around 60% of the increase in industrial concentration in the UK) and provide a more rapid alternative to organic growth via 'ploughed-back' profits. Of course, it also offers benefits in terms of cost efficiencies, risk reduction and market power.

Cost efficiencies

The suggestion here is that growth in firm size can provide economies of scale, i.e. a fall in long-run average costs (see Figure 7.9). These can be of a technical or a non-technical variety.

1 **Technical economies.** These are related to an increase in size of the plant or production unit and are most common in horizontal M & As. Reasons include:

   ■ *specialisation of labour or capital*, which becomes more possible as output increases. Specialisation raises productivity per unit of labour/capital input, so that average variable costs fall as output increases;

   ■ *the 'engineers rule'* whereby material costs increase as the square but volume (capacity) increases as the cube, so that material costs per unit of capacity fall as output increases;

   ■ *dovetailing of processes*, which may only be feasible at high levels of output. For example, if the finished product needs processes A, B and C respectively producing 10, 20, 30 items per hour, then only at 60 units per hour can all processes 'dovetail' and avoid incurring the unnecessary cost of spare (unused) capacity.

2 **Non-technical (enterprise) economies.** These are related to an increase in size of the enterprise as a whole and are valid for both horizontal and vertical M & As. Reasons include:

   ■ *financial economies* – larger enterprises can raise financial capital more cheaply (lower interest rates, access to share and rights issues via Stock Exchange listings, etc.);

   ■ *administrative, marketing and other functional economies* – existing functional departments can often increase throughput without a pro-rata increase in their establishment;

   ■ *distributive economies* – more efficient distributional and supply-chain operations become feasible with greater size (lorries, ships and other containers can be dispatched with loads nearer to capacity, etc.);

   ■ *purchasing economies* – bulk buying discounts are available for larger enterprises. Also, vertical integration (e.g. backwards) means that components can be purchased at cost from the now internal supplier rather than at cost plus profit.

As can be seen from Figure 7.9, where economies of scale exist for these various reasons, the long-run average cost ($LRAC$) curve will fall as output rises over the range $0-Q_1$. The more substantial these economies of scale, the steeper the fall in the $LRAC$ curve, which then means that any firm producing less output than Q_1 is at a considerable cost disadvantage vis-à-vis its competitors. This output (Q_1) at which $LRAC$ is a minimum is often called the 'minimum efficient size' (MES). The larger Q_1 is relative to total industry output, the fewer efficient firms the industry can sustain. For example, if Q_1 is 50% of the usual UK output of glass, then arguably the UK can only sustain two efficient glass producers.

▶

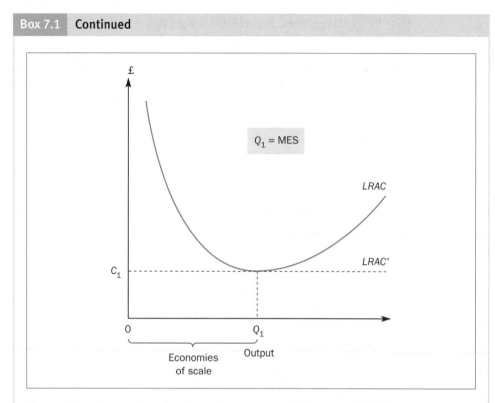

Figure 7.9   Economies of scale and minimum efficient size (MES)

Some surveys suggest that if a firm attempts to produce beyond the MES (Q_1), average costs then begin to rise. These are called diseconomies of scale, and are usually attributed to managerial problems in handling output growth efficiently. However, other surveys suggest that while *LRAC* ceases to fall, there is little evidence that it actually rises for levels of output beyond Q_1 (i.e. *LRAC'* in Figure 7.9).

Other cost efficiencies can result from economies of scope via M & A (*see also* p. 308). Here the suggestion is that a more appropriate mix of products or activities in the company's portfolio can help reduce average costs. The joint production of two or more products by the firm or its engagement in two or more activities can bring complementarities which may yield overall cost savings (e.g. heat from energy production by the firm may be available as a by-product to support its other activities).

- *Risk reduction.* This applies particularly to conglomerate M & As, which involve diversifying the firm's existing portfolio of products or activities. Such diversification helps cushion the firm against any damaging movements which are restricted to particular product groups or particular countries.
- *Market power.* The enlarged firm can use its higher market share or capitalised value to exert greater influence on price or on competitor actions/reactions in 'game' playing situations (*see* p. 279). Enhanced market power can be deployed to raise corporate profit or to achieve other corporate objectives.

A merger takes place with the mutual agreement of the management of both companies, usually through an exchange of shares of the merging firms with shares of the new legal entity. Additional funds are not usually required for the act of merging, and the new venture often reflects the name of both the companies concerned.

An acquisition (or takeover) occurs when the management of Firm A makes a direct offer to the shareholders of Firm B and acquires a controlling interest. Usually the price offered to Firm B shareholders is substantially higher than the current share price on the stock market. In other words, a takeover involves a direct transaction between the management of the acquiring firm and the stockholders of the acquired firm. Takeovers usually require additional funds to be raised by the acquiring firm (Firm A) for the acquisition of the other firm (Firm B), and the identity of the acquired company is often subsumed within that of the purchaser.

While it has been widely accepted that successful mergers and acquisitions can create value and add growth, the outcome of such integration has often proved disappointing. Indeed, this has to some extent been anticipated by the short-run stock market return to acquiring companies, which for some time has been approximately zero. Robert Gertner (2000) suggests that at least three reasons underlie these disappointing outcomes: unpredictability, agency problems and managerial error.

- *Unpredictability.* The 'discontinuities' already outlined (*see* pp. 248–51) give ample reasons why linear predictions of the future are unlikely to be realised. Nevertheless, this may not be the whole story. Mitchell and Lehn (1990) found that for acquisitions where the stock market reacts negatively to the merger announcement, the subsequent break-up (divestment) of the new entity was more likely to occur. This suggests that the stock market does in fact have some ability to identify those mergers and acquisitions that are more likely to fail in the future.
- *Agency problems.* Where the principal–agent problem occurs (*see* p. 210), there may well be a separation of interests between those of shareholders (principals) and managers (agents). It may then follow that a merger/acquisition viewed as favourable by one may actually be unfavourable to the other. Buckingham and Atkinson (1999) note that only 17% of mergers and acquisitions produced any value for shareholders while 53% of them actually destroyed shareholder value. However, there is ample evidence (Fuller 2007) that managers remuneration and perquisites may be more closely related to variables such as corporate turnover and growth rates than to corporate profitability. This misalignment of incentives (agency problem) may be an important factor in the continued drive towards M&A as a strategic focus.
- *Managerial errors.* Lack of knowledge, errors of judgement and managerial hubris (overconfidence) can manifest themselves in all three phases of M & A activity, i.e. the planning, implementation and operational phases. For example, in the *planning phase* imagined synergy is far more common than actual synergy, as is indicated in Case Study 7.5 using the Daimler-Benz and Chrysler merger. Often the actual estimates of merger benefits prove too optimistic and in reality the enhanced resource base of the company may not add value in the ways planned. In the *implementation phase* culture clashes at corporate or national levels may also occur, preventing potential synergies being realised (*see* Chapter 5). For example, at the corporate level, acquisitions involving a traditional bureaucratic company with an innovative entrepreneurial company will invariably bring conflicts, with the result that for some

employees there will be a loss of identification with, and motivation by, the new employer. High-quality human resources are extremely mobile and key knowledge, skills, contacts and capabilities are embedded in these employees, whose loss as a result of the M & A activity will seriously diminish the prospects of the new corporate entity. Finally, in the *operational phase* the hoped for economies of scale and scope outlined in Box 7.1 may fail to materialise, for a variety of logistical reasons.

Case Study 7.5 on the Daimler-Benz and Chrysler merger usefully illustrates some of these aspects of a cross-border merger.

CASE 7.5 Daimler-Benz AG and Chrysler

Karl Benz constructed the first automobile in 1886 at which time Gottlieb Daimler was active in the same field of business. After years of partnership their businesses were formally integrated in 1926 as the Daimler-Benz Company. In the 1980s Daimler-Benz pursued a strategy of diversification, acquiring MTU, AEG, the aeroplane company Dornier, MBB and Fokker, the latter completing the aviation arm of Daimler-Benz. The vision of the chairman (Mr Reuter) was to transform the firm from a car maker into an integrated technology group along the lines of General Electric or the Japanese Mitsubishi conglomerate. His vision included generating cross-border synergies between the automobile, the aeroplane and electronics industry, exchanging skills and knowledge, and spreading the company's risks over the many businesses in its portfolio.

Daimler's first acquisition round

This round of acquisitions soon ran into trouble. The electronics industry was being pressurised by cheap components from Asia, the civil aviation industry was badly affected by the recession of the late 1980s early 1990s and the market for military aeroplanes collapsed after the end of the cold war. Further, many of the acquired businesses had needed restructuring to make them internationally cost competitive. Few of the newly acquired firms had proved to be cash cows for Daimler, quite the opposite, absorbing profits as the company invested heavily in them during restructuring. In terms of Porter's 'parenting advantage' concept it would seem that Daimler provided neither benefits to its acquired businesses nor gained competitive advantages or other benefits from them. For example Daimler proved unable to provide readily transferable skills from its core automobile business to units like AEG or Fokker. The outcome was that AEG – one of the best-known and established German companies – was broken up, with the brand sold to Electrolux, some parts integrated into other Daimler businesses and most others closed. With Fokker (aeroplanes) the outcome was similar – Fokker was on the edge of bankruptcy after Daimler withdrew financial support in 1996. Arguably Daimler not only destroyed shareholder value, but also destroyed whole companies with its attempt to build a conglomerate based on unrealistic expectations of planned synergies.

Daimler's first round of acquisitions ended with the highest loss since its foundation (DM5.8 billion) being announced in 1995, mainly due to restructuring charges.

Applying M & A success measurements it would seem that the strategy had failed. Many of the acquired firms had been sold off or closed and in terms of stock market figures the market value of Daimler had plunged during the diversification period from DM53 billion in 1986 to DM35 billion in 1995.

Daimler's merger with Chrysler

On 6 May 1998 a new chapter in Daimler's M & A history began: Daimler-Benz AG and Chrysler Corporation announced their merger and the creation of the new DaimlerChrysler AG. To understand this merger one must first consider all the environmental factors. The automobile industry is becoming increasingly mature, with only certain regions (especially Asia) offering higher than average growth opportunities. If a car maker wants to survive, it must have a global reach and be established in all markets of the triad (for example, the number of independent car producers has halved in the last 30 years). A second factor involves the time dimension. Those who wish to sustain their position must react very quickly to changing demands and must renew their product portfolio more frequently. As a result, they are forced to share expensive fixed overheads (e.g. gain synergies in research and development) and use economies of scale and scope to keep variable costs down. Arguably only large, globalised companies can fulfil these criteria.

The Daimler–Chrysler management engaged international merger experts to assist in all the vital steps of the pre- and post-merger phases. The merger with Chrysler was undertaken with a view to capitalising on core competencies. Both companies, as car producers, sought to keep their core business in the automobile sector. Other expressed reasons involved increasing market power and sharing infrastructure, identified in Figure 7.8 as 'real term' issues. Figure 7.10 outlines some

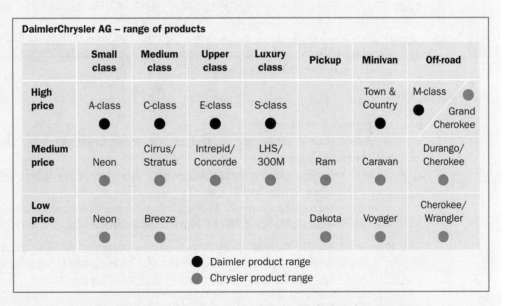

DaimlerChrysler AG – range of products

	Small class	Medium class	Upper class	Luxury class	Pickup	Minivan	Off-road
High price	A-class ●	C-class ●	E-class ●	S-class ●		Town & Country ●	M-class ● / Grand Cherokee ●
Medium price	Neon ●	Cirrus/ Stratus ●	Intrepid/ Concorde ●	LHS/ 300M ●	Ram ●	Caravan ●	Durango/ Cherokee ●
Low price	Neon ●	Breeze ●			Dakota ●	Voyager ●	Cherokee/ Wrangler ●

● Daimler product range
● Chrysler product range

Figure 7.10 **Product range synergies in the Daimler and Chrysler merger**

of the product range synergies stated by the participants as relevant to this particular merger.

As can be seen in Figure 7.10, except in the 'off-road' segment there were no product overlaps – rather the respective product portfolios complemented one another. This was also the case in terms of their geographical markets, with Chrysler a strong player in the NAFTA region, while Daimler-Benz was a leading company in Europe. DaimlerChrysler AG subsequently moved to acquire a third leg in the Asian market to consolidate its position in all regions of the triad.

Further synergies were identified in fields such as procurement, common use of parts and sales. Synergies totalling DM2.5 billion were stated as having already been obtained in those fields within one year of the merger. Going forward, more synergies were targeted in sales, production, research and development and sales. For example, Chrysler brands were expected to gain entry into the European market by using the market knowledge acquired by the established Daimler sales network and some of its distribution outlets. Pilot plants in South America were already being used as test beds for combining production of Daimler and Chrysler vehicles with standardised parts to be used across the different models wherever possible. Common efforts in R & D were also undertaken in the field of future drive concepts. Further synergies of DM6.4 billion were expected by 2001. When these projected savings were compared with the estimated merger costs of DM550 million, then the advantages became obvious.

A number of critical success factors were highlighted by the chairman, Mr Barnevik.

- In the pre-merger phase
  - *Act quickly and keep it secret.* The company tried to limit the number of people involved and to act rapidly to achieve surprise and momentum. It is better to concentrate on essentials rather than be distracted by less important details.
  - *Approach M & A as a project.* The whole merger and subsequent integration should be done in the form of a series of mini-projects. Therefore, strong project managers are necessary.
  - *Negotiation team to be kept as small as possible.* This helps to keep the negotiations secret and to make decisions more quickly.

- In the post-merger phase
  - *Find key people.* They are important for accelerating projects, integrating people and cultures.
  - *Walk to talk.* Top management must engage directly with people to make sure they participate in the overall vision.
  - *Maintain centralised control.* The use of a centralised control system made information available faster and facilitated quick decisions.

The Daimler–Chrysler merger seemed to incorporate many of these factors. The merger was undertaken in a record time, with only six months elapsing between the announcement and the actual flotation of Daimler–Chrysler shares. The whole preparation took place without any leaks from the negotiation team, with the global auto industry caught unawares by the announcement of this transatlantic alliance. Key people were found and more than 90 projects for integration defined.

Daimler–Chrysler installed special post-merger integration (PMI) teams and a PMI network by which all participants had 24-hour worldwide access to an information base, obtaining details on the various integration projects. As well as the PMI teams, issue resolution teams (IRT) were installed. Their objectives included supervising and coordinating the PMI projects. Speed, accuracy, reliable communication, transparency and clear goals were the objectives of these developments. The achievement of synergy potential was monitored all the time. Accordingly the PMI teams encouraged the sharing of existing resources and, if necessary, the raising of new resource allocations. Synergies to the value of more than DM2.5 billion were stated as being achieved overall in the first year of operation.

Daimler–Chrysler also introduced a new Integrated Controlling System (ICS) using common concepts and data to help compare the different businesses. This approach helped to eliminate contradictory rules as regards definition and to foster rationalisation and integration. A vital element for a successful cross-border integration, and arguably the most difficult was recognised as being the creation of one common culture and corporate identity, especially where the new business involves different national as well as corporate cultures. Chrysler perceived German companies as being too comfortable, less innovative and less project-orientated than US companies. On the other hand, Daimler-Benz thought its American partner was too capitalistic and insensitive towards the German social security system.

In an attempt to combine these different cultures and mentalities, a conscious effort was made to create a culture of discussion. A senior management figure was appointed to communicate the goals company-wide, to field e-mails and to respond to the enquiries of worried employees. Interchange programmes took place to make intercultural understanding easier, involving brief information visits, shared projects, seminars or even longer stays abroad. Daimler–Chrysler sought to clarify from the outset that this was a genuine merger of 'equals'. It kept two bases: one in Auburn Hills, USA, and one in Stuttgart, Germany, and the respective CEOs, Robert Eaton and Jurgen Schrempp, led the company together. Both companies were equally represented at board level with equal rights and so avoided the victor/vanquished syndrome.

Of course, there were some negative aspects. Several high-profile former Chrysler executives left the new company. With those departures went valuable skills and personal knowledge. Nevertheless, many of the critical factors for a successful merger would seem to have been applied.

Yet many of these initial expectations for the merger ultimately proved excessively optimistic. Daimler and Chrysler demerged in mid-2007 and, for many years prior to this, problems within the merged company had become increasingly apparent. Many of the German executives and workers resented the loss of 'Benz' in the new corporate name. Although the mantra throughout the merger process was of a 'merger of equals', most people thought this a ploy to gain acceptance of the merger by the US government and Chrysler employees, rather than reflecting reality! It was noted at

▶

the time of the demerger in 2007 that the Daimler Chrysler Board had changed from the equal number of 1998 to a ten to one ratio in favour of Daimler. Cultural differences in business practices began to emerge in many aspects of the new company, not least as regards employee reward structures. The 'Chrysler' element venture saw the need to increase employee incentives to match those in rivals GM and Ford, including a range of bonus and health care payments, estimated at as much as $2000 per vehicle produced in the years subsequent to the merger.

Sources: Various, including Guenther (2000).

Questions

1 What lessons might be learned about M & A from Daimler-Benz's first round of acquisitions?

2 What lessons might be learned about M & A from the Daimler–Chrysler merger?

As already noted, a key strategic goal used to support M & A activity is that the combined entity creates positive net value (i.e. creates potential synergies). Of course, the *realisation* of any potential synergies will crucially depend on whether the *post-integration phase* really does permit the transfer of core competencies, from acquirer to target or vice versa. A study by Laurence Capron (1999) has examined this very issue and identified a number of strategic implications. In a survey of 253 companies in the manufacturing sector which merged horizontally between 1988 and 1992 across Europe and North America, some interesting results were obtained, as shown in Figure 7.11.

Figure 7.11(a) would suggest that the *potential* for synergies via M & A activity is considerable, as such integration is commonly followed by a transfer of competencies both to and from the target. For example, as regards 'sales networks', some 43% of respondents recognised that the *acquirer's* sales network was used to a substantial extent to distribute the target's products and 35% of respondents recognised that the target's sales network was used to distribute the acquirer's products.

Figure 7.11(b) is particularly relevant to the post-acquisition phase, with respondents asked to assess the extent to which the acquisition improved the performance of both the target and the acquirer. Four performance measures were used: general performance, cost savings (cost-based synergies), innovation capabilities (revenue-based synergies) and market coverage (revenue-based synergies). Only 49% of the respondents considered that the effect of the M & A activity has been to create positive net value (overall outcome) in terms of combined value though over half indicated a positive combined outcome in terms of specific objectives such as market share (56%), sales revenue (59%) and profitability (53%).

Interestingly, even for these horizontal acquisitions, less than half identified cost-based synergies as being realised in terms of either production costs (46%) or input costs (40%). However, from the perspective of revenue-based synergies, the results were more encouraging, with 64% of respondents acknowledging that acquisitions broaden their product line and 70% reporting increased geographic market coverage. In similar vein, some 49% of respondents reported improved R & D capabilities, 47% improved product quality and 34% reduced time to market.

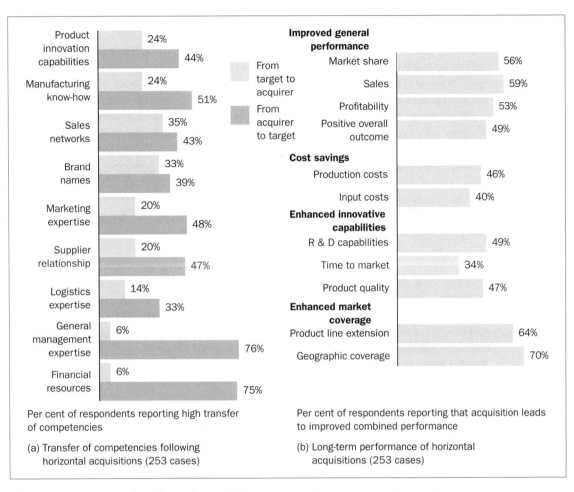

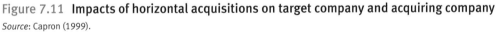

Figure 7.11 **Impacts of horizontal acquisitions on target company and acquiring company**
Source: Capron (1999).

From a strategic perspective there would therefore seem to be a widely recognised potential for achieving synergies involving the transfer of competencies via M & A activity. However, the outcomes would seem to suggest that this potential has often failed to be realised, with net value actually falling and competencies lost. This would seem especially so as regards cost-based synergies, though the evidence is more favourable as regards revenue-based synergies. Particular attention should be paid to the post-merger phase to ensure that the identified potential is translated into reality.

Technological change and strategic choice

Case Study 7.6 below usefully reminds us that strategic choices are never made in a static environment but in dynamic, ever-changing environments. One of the key catalysts for such change is technology itself, which may then force a rapid re-examination of previous strategic directions.

CASE 7.6 Telematics and strategic choices

Many technological advances involve information and communication techniques (ICT) of one type or another. Telematics provides a useful example of new opportunities resulting from ICT developments.

Telematics adapts ICT technologies to create vehicle management systems, thereby helping resolve many logistical problems. Tracking systems that can pinpoint a vehicle's location down to a few metres with the help of global positioning system (GPS) satellites are now commonplace, and can help suppliers monitor the progress of deliveries and increase efficiency in the supply chain. New automated monitoring systems, which are much like the black-box recorders found in aircraft, go one step further. As well as delivering a constant stream of data detailing each vehicle's speed and location, they can provide diagnostic information on engine and driving performance, which can then be transmitted wirelessly to engineers working remotely.

According to telematics providers, the benefits of these systems are not restricted to greater visibility and efficiency. They also point out that an important factor driving demand in telematics is the need to comply with new legislation. MobilAria, a subsidiary of the world's largest automotive parts maker Delphi, recently marketed its FleetOutlook system on the grounds that it would help companies comply with forthcoming regulations from the US Department of Transportation. The company claims that its system will track, record and automate everything from driver work logs to fuel tax accounts.

Again on the legislative side, the aforementioned black box from IBM and SIS got a public relations boost when the Irish government officially welcomed its introduction. Data collected by the boxes would help the country achieve European road safety targets, said the Irish transport minister.

UPS, the logistics group, estimates that a forthcoming upgrade to its own in-house fleet management system will cut about 100 million miles a year from the routes covered by its delivery trucks, saving approximately 14 million gallons of fuel. Managers can work out much more efficient routes when they know exactly how many parcels are coming through the system on a given day.

And customers benefit as well, says Ken Lacy, UPS chief information officer. 'When you have got the ability to have a total view of everything that is moving through your channels, you can imagine the reduction in inventory that you have to carry.' UPS's system currently tracks smart labels attached to about 90% of the packages it delivers every year, he adds, many of them along the same routes used by the Pony Express riders of old.

Question

Consider some of the new strategic initiatives which might be available to firms from technological advances in telematics.

Knowledge management

Before addressing this issue it will be helpful to begin with a definition of 'knowledge' itself. Knowledge is certainly not data, which are objective facts available to users without judgement. Nor is knowledge the same as information, which is merely data which have been categorised, analysed and summarised in order to give the data a context, i.e. a relevance and purpose. The following definition does, however, tell us something about what knowledge actually is.

> Information therefore is data endowed with relevance and purpose. Information develops into knowledge when it is used to make comparison, assess consequences, establish connections, and engage in a dialogue. Knowledge can, therefore, be seen as information that comes laden with experience, judgement, intuition and values. (Empson 1999)

Definitions such as this would question whether many IT-based 'knowledge management systems' are anything more than sophisticated information filing and disseminating systems. Figure 7.12 would, in this view, provide a more relevant breakdown of the key ingredients of a knowledge management system.

It may be useful to first consider the four knowledge 'labels' used in Figure 7.12:

1 *explicit knowledge*: codified knowledge available in books, reports, online, etc.;
2 *tacit knowledge*: knowledge embodied in human experience and practice;
3 *individual knowledge*: the source of much tacit and explicit knowledge;
4 *collective knowledge*: the outcome of corporate structures and processes for converting tacit and individual knowledge into explicit knowledge available for corporate use in process or product innovation.

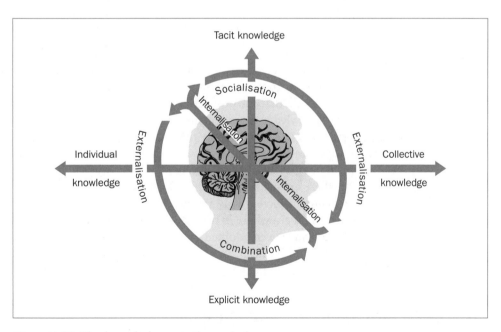

Figure 7.12 **The knowledge-creating spiral**

Source: Adapted from *The Knowledge Creating Company: How Japanese Companies Create the Dynamics of Innovation* by Ikujiro Nonaka and Hirotaka Takeuchi, © 1995 by Oxford University Press, Inc.

Nonaka and Takeuchi (1995) identify four interrelated processes *(see* Figure 7.12) by which knowledge flows around the organisation and is converted into different forms:

1 *socialisation*: the process of communicating the tacit knowledge that resides within the individual human resource base of companies throughout the organisation;
2 *externalisation*: the process of converting tacit knowledge into an explicit codified form accessible to others in the organisation both individually and collectively;
3 *combination*: the process of analysing, classifying and integrating the explicit knowledge within the organisation into forms which can more readily be used in pursuing that organisation's objectives. Arguably these more usable 'forms' themselves constitute new explicit knowledge;
4 *internalisation*: the process by which individuals absorb explicit knowledge so that it becomes a foundation from which new forms of tacit and explicit knowledge may subsequently emerge.

Nonaka and Takeuchi suggest five key mechanisms by which knowledge creation (seen from this perspective) can be encouraged.

1 *Intention.* Senior management must be committed to accumulating, exploiting and renewing the knowledge base within their organisations and to creating management systems compatible with this intention.
2 *Autonomy.* Individuals are the major source of new knowledge and they must be given organisational support to explore and develop new ideas.
3 *Creative chaos.* An internal 'culture' must be established which is willing to use new knowledge to challenge existing orthodoxies.
4 *Redundancy.* Knowledge should not be allowed to become 'redundant' via it being rationed to selected individuals only within the organisation. Instead knowledge exchange must be encouraged and supported throughout the organisation.
5 *Requisite variety.* The internal diversity within the organisation must at least match that of the external environment within which it operates.

Husenan and Goodman (1999) report that 78% of the major US companies surveyed claim to be 'moving towards becoming knowledge-based'. However, the authors themselves concluded that most of these companies are confusing 'information management' with 'knowledge management' and in their words, are 'nowhere near' devising a strategic framework to promote the agenda illustrated in Figure 7.12. A strategic imperative would seem to be to make as many as possible of the five conditions outlined above an integral part of the organisation's knowledge management system.

Of course, there are many other discrete areas of business activity in which strategic issues are playing an increasingly important part in a globalised economy. Some of these are touched on elsewhere in this book. Here we move on to consider some of the techniques which have been adopted by international businesses in an attempt to evaluate the external environment in which they operate and to devise specific strategies and counter-strategies to further their own objectives vis-à-vis those of their rivals.

Techniques for strategic analysis

Again, we must be selective. We consider in detail some of the more widely-used techniques for strategic analysis.

Game-based techniques

This approach has been widely used in highly-concentrated industries and markets dominated by a few large firms. The idea is to estimate for each proposed strategy the firm might adopt, the likely counter-strategies of the rival (or rivals). A variety of assumptions can be made as to how a firm views the likely counter-strategies to be adopted by the rival.

Decision rules

These assumptions are built into 'decision rules', two of which are widely adopted:

1 *maxi-min decision rule* – assumes that the rival (Firm B) reacts in the worst (for Firm A) way possible for each A strategy. Firm A then selects the best (maxi) of these worst (mini) possible outcomes.
2 *mini-max decision rule* – assumes that the rival (Firm B) reacts in the best (for Firm A) way possible for each A strategy. Firm A then selects the worst (mini) of these best (maxi) possible outcomes.

Of course, many other decision rules can be devised for such games. Box 7.2 shows an example of a market share game using the maxi-min decision rule.

Box 7.2 Two-firm zero-sum game

We might usefully illustrate the principles involved in game theory by a simple two-firm (duopoly) game, involving market share. By its very nature, a market share game must be 'zero sum', in that any gain by one player must be offset exactly by the loss of the other(s).

Suppose Firm A is considering two possible strategies to raise its market share, either a 20% price cut or a 10% increase in advertising expenditure (note that here each strategy involves only a single-policy variable). Whatever initial strategy Firm A adopts, it anticipates that its rival, Firm B, will react by using either a price cut or extra advertising to defend its market share. Firm A now evaluates the market share that it can expect for each initial strategy and each possible counter-strategy by Firm B. The outcomes expected by A are summarised in the pay-off matrix of Table 7.2.

If A cuts price, and B responds with a price cut, A receives 60% of the market. However, if B responds with extra advertising, A receives 70% of the market. The 'worst' outcome for A (60% of the market) will occur if B responds with a price cut. If A adopts the strategy of extra advertising, then the 'worst' outcome for A (50% of the market) will again occur if B responds with a price cut rather than extra advertising (55% of the market).

Table 7.2 **Firm A's pay-off matrix: market share game (%)**

		Firm B's strategies	
		Price cut	Extra advertising
Firm A's strategies	Price cut	60*†	70†
	Extra advertising	50*	55

* 'Worst' outcome for A of each A strategy.

† 'Worst' outcome for B of each B strategy.

> **Box 7.2   Continued**
>
> If A expects B to play the game astutely, i.e. choose the counter-strategy best for itself (worst for A), then A will choose the price-cut strategy, as this gives it 60% of the market rather than 50%. If A plays the game in this way, selecting the best of the worst possible outcomes for each initial strategy, it is said to be adopting a 'maxi-min' decision rule or approach to the game.
>
> If B adopts the same maxi-min approach as A, and has made the same evaluation of outcomes as A, it also will adopt a price-cut strategy. For instance, if B adopts a price-cut strategy, its 'worst' outcome will occur if A responds with a price cut; B then gets 40% of the market (100% minus 60%) rather than 50% as would be the case if A responds with extra advertising. If B adopts extra advertising, its 'worst' outcome will again occur if A responds with a price cut; B then receives 30% (100% minus 70%) instead of 45% (100% minus 55%) if A responds with extra advertising. The best of the 'worst possible' outcomes for B occurs if B adopts a price cut, which gives it 40% of the market rather than 30%.
>
> In this particular game we have a stable equilibrium (a 'Nash' equilibrium – *see below*), without any resort to collusion. Both firms initially cut price, then accept the respective market shares which fulfil their maxi-min targets 60% to A, 40% to B. There could then follow the price stability which has been seen to be a feature of some oligopoly situations. In some games the optimal strategy for each firm may not even have been an initial price cut, but rather non-price competition (such as advertising). Game theory can predict both price stability and extensive non-price competition.
>
> The problem with game theory is that it can equally predict unstable solutions, with extensive price as well as non-price competition. An unstable solution might follow if each firm, faced with the pay-off matrix of Table 7.2 adopts entirely different strategies. Firm B might not use the maxi-min approach of A, but take more risk. Instead of the price cut it might adopt the 'extra advertising' strategy, hoping to induce an advertising response from firm A and gain 45% of the market, but risk getting only 30% if A responds with a price cut. Suppose this is what happens. Firm A now receives 70% of the market, but B only receives 30%, which is below its initial expectation of 45%. This may provoke B into alternative strategy formulation, setting off a further chain reaction. The game may then fail to settle down quickly, if at all, to a stable solution, i.e. one in which each firm receives a market share which meets its overall expectation. An unstable solution might also follow if each firm evaluates the pay-off matrix differently from the other. Even if they then adopt the same approach to the game, one firm at least will be 'disappointed', possibly provoking action and counteraction.

A number of other ideas are widely presented in game theory approaches.

- *Dominant strategy.* In this approach the firm seeks to do the best it can (in terms of the objectives set) irrespective of the possible actions/reactions of any rival(s).
- *Nash equilibrium.* This occurs when each firm is doing the best that it can in terms of its own objective(s), given the strategies chosen by the other firms in the market.
- *Prisoner's dilemma.* This is an outcome where the equilibrium for the game involves both firms doing worse than they would have done had they colluded, and is sometimes called a 'cartel game' because the obvious implication is that the firms would be better off by colluding.

There are different types of game to which these ideas might be applied.

One-shot game

The suggestion here is that the decision to be made by each firm is 'once for all'. We can illustrate this type of game using Table 7.3, which is a pay-off matrix that expresses the net gains for each of two firms in terms of daily profit, the first value being that for Firm A and the second value that for Firm B. The single policy variable shown here is output level, which can be set high or low, with the pay-off dependent on the rival's reaction. Clearly this is a non-zero sum game since the total daily profit for each combination of policies varies rather than remains constant (for example, total profit is £3000 in the bottom right quadrant but £6000 elsewhere).

Table 7.3 Pay-off matrix (daily profits)

| | | Firm B | |
		Low output	High output
Firm A	Low output	£3000; £3000	£2000; £4000
	High output	£4000; £2000	£1500; £1500

Suppose, initially, that we treat this situation as a one-shot game.

- 'High output' would be the dominant strategy for each firm, giving both Firm A and Firm B £4000 in daily profit should the other firm select 'low output'. However, if both firms follow this dominant strategy and select 'high output', they each receive only £1500 daily profit.
- If each firm follows a maxi-min decision rule, then Firm A selects 'low output' as the best of the worst possible outcomes (£2000 > £1500), as does Firm B (£2000 > £1500). The combination (low output, low output) will then be a Nash equilibrium, with each firm satisfied that it is doing the best that it can in terms of its own objective, given the strategy chosen by the other firm (each actually receives £3000).
- If each firm follows a mini-max decision rule, you should be able to show that both Firm A and Firm B will still select 'low output' as the worst of the best possible outcomes (£3000 < £4000 for each firm). The combination (low output/low output) remains a Nash equilibrium.

Even if one firm follows a maxi-min and the other a mini-max decision rule, the combination (low output/low output) will remain a Nash equilibrium in this particular game. We could reasonably describe this output combination (low/low) as a stable, Nash-type equilibrium.

Repeated game

However, should we view the pay-off matrix in Table 7.3 as part of a repeated game, then the situation so far described might be subject to considerable change. We might expect the respective firms to alter the strategies they pursue and the game to have a different outcome.

Suppose the firms initially establish the low output/low output 'solution' to the game, whether as the result of a 'Nash equilibrium' or by some form of agreement between the firms. Unlike the one-shot game, a firm in a repeated game can modify its strategy from one period to the next, and can also respond to any changes in strategy by the other firm.

■ *Cheating.* If Table 7.3 is now viewed as the pay-off matrix for a repeated game, there would seem to be a possible incentive for either firm to depart from its initial 'low output' policy in the next period. Had the initial 'low output' policy been mutually agreed by the two firms in an attempt to avoid the mutually damaging high output/high output combination should each firm have followed its 'dominant strategy', we might regard such a departure as *cheating* on an agreement. By unexpectedly switching to high output, either firm could benefit by raising daily profit (from £3000 to £4000), though the loss of profit (from £3000 to £2000) by the other firm might provoke an eventual retaliation in some future time period, resulting in the mutually damaging high output/high output combination.

■ *Tit-for-tat strategy.* Whether or not any 'cheating' is likely to benefit a firm will depend on a number of factors, not least the rapidity with which any rival responds to a breach of the agreement: the more rapid the response of the rival, the smaller any net benefits from cheating will be. Suppose, in our example, it takes the other firm five days to respond with higher output: then on each of these days the cheating firm gains a first-mover advantage (*see also* p. 283) of an extra £1000 in profit from breaching the agreement as compared with upholding the agreement. If the response of the rival were to be more rapid, say, in three days, then only £3000 rather than £5000 benefit would accrue as a first-mover advantage. Of course, once the rival has responded, both firms are damaged in Table 7.3 compared with the pre-cheating situation, losing £1500 profit per day from the high output/high output combination. This may, of course, induce both firms to restore the initial agreement.

If it becomes known that rivals are likely to respond rapidly to any cheating on agreements (or even departures from Nash-type equilibriums) by adopting *tit-for-tat* strategies, then this may itself deter attempts by either firm to cheat. Provided that each firm believes the rival is sufficiently well informed to be aware of any change in its strategy, it will anticipate a tit-for-tat response that will ensure that any benefits from cheating are of shorter duration. When factored into the decision-making process, the anticipation of a lower profit stream may deter any attempt by either firm to cheat.

Sequential games

In the games considered so far, each firm has been able to make decisions at the same time (i.e. simultaneously). However, in a sequential game the moves and countermoves take place in a defined order: one firm makes a move and only then does the rival decide how to react to that move. Table 7.4 is a pay-off matrix showing net gains

Table 7.4 **Pay-off matrix (profit per period)**

		Firm B	
		Low price	High price
Firm A	Low price	£1000; £1000	£3000; £2000
	High price	£2000; £3000	£500; £500

as profit per period for each of two firms. The individual pay-offs depend on the price (low or high) selected by one firm and the price response of the rival, in this non-zero sum game.

The dominant strategy for both firm A and firm B is to set a low price (£3000 profit), but if they both follow this strategy the outcome is mutually damaging (£1000 profit each). You should be able to see that a maxi-min decision rule followed by each firm would lead to a low price/low price outcome in which the expectations of each firm are fulfilled given that they have adopted this decision rule.

pause for thought 3   What would the outcome have been had each firm adopted a mini-max decision rule?

First-mover advantages

If decisions can only be taken in sequence, an important issue is whether the firm making the first move can secure any advantage!

- *Suppose firm A is in a position to move first.* It can choose 'low price', forcing firm B to choose between 'low price' (£1000) and 'high price' (£2000). Firm A might now anticipate that firm B will attempt to maximise its own return given the constrained situation (via A's first move) in which B finds itself. In this case firm B selects 'high price', and firm A receives £3000 profit per period. The first move by A has given a net profit advantage to A of £2000 (£3000–£1000) as compared to the previous low price/low price outcome.
- *Suppose firm B is in a position to move first.* It can now choose 'low price' in the expectation that firm A will respond with 'high price' (£2000 > £1000) as firm A now seeks to maximise its own return given the constrained situation (via B's first move) in which it finds itself. In this case, firm B receives a pay-off of £3000 profit per period and a net profit advantage of £2000 via the first move.

Clearly this game does contain first-mover advantages, which lie in first anticipating the likely responses of the rival and then channelling those responses in a particular direction as a result of making the first move.

Case Study 7.7 indicates the use of game theory in designing the US airwaves auction. These ideas were instrumental in encouraging both the UK and German governments to use auctions in the allocation of broadband licences in 2000.

CASE 7.7   Game theory in action: designing the US airwaves auction

In 1993 the US Congress decided to auction off licences to use the electromagnetic spectrum for personal communication services. This involved selling off thousands of licences with different geographic coverage and at different spectrum locations.

Auctioning off the licences was a break with the tradition of direct licence allocation to those with a bigger 'need'. It required the Federal Communications Commission (FCC) to set up a mechanism capable of efficiently allocating licences to the bidder most valuing it. Game theory (and game theorists) played an important role

▶

in both the design of the actual auction mechanism used and in advising bidders on optimal bidding strategies.

Auctions are, a priori, an ideal method for allocating goods to those who place a higher value on them, as these people are likely to make the highest bid. However, research by game theorists has shown that the design of the auction matters, both for the efficiency of the allocation – does the good go to the person who values it most? – and the revenues earned for the seller. In this particular instance, Congress had asked the FCC to ensure that the spectrum was used in an efficient and intensive way, rather than simply to maximise auction income for the Federal government.

According to an account in the *Journal of Economics Perspectives*, by two of the economists involved in the design (Preston McAfee of Texas A & M and John McMillan of University of California, San Diego), the designers considered the existence of complementarities between the licences as the most important threat to efficiency in this particular context.

For the bidder, the value of each individual licence depends to a large extent on whether another licence has been obtained so that several licences can be grouped together to form a coherent region. The auction design needed to allow for the coherent aggregation of licences, so that a bidder would not find himself bidding for a licence as a part of a whole to discover that he is in fact awarded an incoherent entity of much smaller value to him or her.

Following the advice of several economic theorists employed by the bidders, including Stanford economists Paul Milgrom and Robert Wilson, plus McAfee and McMillan, the FCC opted for a novel design: a simultaneous ascending auction, in which the bidding for all the licences remained open as long as bidding in any of the licences remained active. The aggregation of licences was facilitated by the fact that bidding and the observation of the bids, were simultaneous.

For all its advantages, the simultaneous ascending auctions involved an important risk of implicit collusion between rival bidders. To avoid this problem, the identity of the bidder would remain hidden until the auction concluded. But it was still possible for a bidder to find ways to signal their intention in order to ensure allocation of the preferred licence at a low cost. In fact, as subsequent portions of the spectrum were auctioned off, complaints about this type of behaviour increased. For example, Mercury PCS, a US telecom operator, was accused of highlighting its interest in winning a specific licence by ending the bid amount in January 1997 with the postal codes of the particular city in which it was interested.

On the bidders side, the consultants to the bidders have not made public their recommendations. We can only speculate that game theory was used by bidders both to enhance the rationality of their bidding and to understand and influence the bidding behaviour of the rival bidders.

First, game theory could introduce a higher degree of rationality in the bidding process by helping to design optimal bidding strategies. For example, game theorists have long understood that in auction settings bidding as much as one would be actually willing to pay for a good could lead to what is known as the winner's curse: imagine that a licence will be in fact equally valuable to any firm, but that each firm has a different opinion about how valuable it is likely to be. Clearly the winning bid is most likely to be from the most optimistic firm. But the most optimistic firm's estimate of the value of the audio waves will be biased upwards – it will be too high. In fact, if the highest bidder wins without taking into account this effect, he will overpay, and winning will be a curse. Developing an algorithm for bidding that takes into account this curse requires the use of game theory.

Game theory could also be used by a bidder to understand the incentives of rival bidders and formulate strategies capable of altering their behaviour. In particular, if one could credibly commit to winning a licence, one could win the licence at zero cost, as the incentives for the rivals to bid when they know they are not going to win the licence, are likely to be low. An actual example of this could be the allocation in the April 1997 sale of wireless data frequencies, of the licences for several cities like Minneapolis, for $1.

To sum up, by identifying the individual incentives of each player in each auction design, game theory helped the designers and consultants in understanding the impact of the rules of the game on the behaviour of the actors. As McAfee and McMillan put it in their account: 'The role of theory is to show how people behave in various circumstances, and to identify the trade-offs involved in altering those circumstances.'

Source: Garicano (1999).

Questions

1 Briefly summarise the benefits to bidders of being familiar with game theory.

2 Does it help the sellers (here the government) to be aware of the principles underlying game theory?

Garicano (1999) counsels against using game theory to 'solve' the game in terms of some type of equilibrium solution with a precise numerical answer. His arguments are that the possible solutions to the games are often too sensitive to the assumptions the modeller makes. These assumptions might involve:

- the timing of the moves;
- the information available to the players;
- the rationality of the decisions taken;
- the consequences of playing the game under changing 'decision rules'.

The major benefit of game theory analysis is arguably to focus attention on competitor behaviour and consequent implications for policy. For example, if British Airways understands that price warfare on Atlantic routes with Virgin is a 'prisoners dilemma' outcome, with both parties doing worse than need be the case, then remedial action can be sought. This may involve changing the 'rules of the game' (e.g. some kind of tacit collusion) in order to remove the incentives which induced both British Airways and Virgin to engage in such price warfare. It is guidance as to an appropriate type of strategic response that is arguably more important than any hypothetical (and unrealistic) numerical solution.

Strategic scenario analysis

Scenario analysis is another approach that is widely used to evaluate possible future outcomes of different courses of action (e.g. high, medium, low profitability scenarios). In more sophisticated treatments probabilities may be assigned to each outcome and expected values calculated. Arguably scenario analysis takes a broader perspective in terms of strategic direction than does game theory, the latter confining itself to competitor actions/reactions. Put another way, scenario analysis is more useful in dealing with broad based structural uncertainties, i.e. those stemming from changes in macroeconomic or industry-wide factors, whereas game theory is more useful in dealing with the strategic uncertainties related to rival reactions.

A scenario can be defined as an internally consistent view of the future, which often reflects a situation in which a large number of variables are seen as moving in a particular direction. (This is quite unlike 'sensitivity analysis', which often involves allowing a single variable to change and then assessing the impact of this single variable change on the whole system.) Gertner and Knez (2000) argue that the combination of scenario analysis with game theoretic approaches can create a still more effective technique for modelling the business environment. They term this technique 'strategic scenario analysis' and argue that it can help capture both structural and strategic uncertainties as a guide to policy formation. Case Study 7.8 outlines this approach in the context of new product development.

CASE 7.8 Strategic scenario analysis: AMD versus Intel

In 1997 Advanced Micro Devices (AMD) introduced its K6 microprocessor. Its aim was to capture leadership of the market for fast microprocessors, a position held at the time by Intel. The primary risk to AMD was that Intel would quickly introduce a comparable or superior chip and, with its brand equity, drive AMD out of the high-end chip segment.

The emerging cheap PC market dampened this risk for AMD, and is the focus of this case study. While the K6 chip was aimed at the high-end market, alternative versions (made in the same plant) could be sold in the low-end market. However, this low-end 'hedge' depended on Intel staying out of the low-end segment. Our strategic scenario analysis will focus on the low-end PC market and on the uncertainty surrounding Intel's decision as to whether or not to enter the low-end segment.

The key to strategic reasoning in general, and the application of strategic scenario analysis in particular, is for the decision-maker to take the perspective of other players in an effort to predict how they will behave. In this case, decision-makers at AMD needed to take Intel's perspective into account. So in what follows we develop a simple scenario game which seeks to capture the trade-offs Intel had to make when deciding whether to enter the low-end segment. The results of that analysis in turn provide a foundation for the judgements AMD had to make about the likelihood of significant low-end market share.

In our game, Intel has to decide whether to bide its time as regards the low-end segment (i.e. 'wait'), with the option of introducing its low price Celeron chip at some later time, or to bring the Celeron chip into play without delay (i.e. 'introduce'). Besides Intel, there are two other sets of players: the competition (i.e. other chip makers) – AMD and National Semiconductor (NS), which will surely introduce low-end chips immediately; and the major PC manufacturers who purchase the chips – NEC, Compaq, IBM, Toshiba, DEC and others.

Intel faces many critical uncertainties in making its 'wait/introduce' decision. The most important are: (i) the demand for cheap PCs (and therefore the derived demand for low-end chips); (ii) the quality of its competitors' low-end chips; (iii) whether Intel's brand equity is strong enough to overcome its second-mover disadvantage if it waits.

Intel's uncertainties are linked to those faced by the PC manufacturers and the rival chip makers. The PC manufacturers will have to decide whether to buy the AMD/NS chips or Intel's. AMD and NS face capacity and pricing decisions that will depend on whether Intel has entered the low-end market.

For simplicity we focus on a single structural uncertainty – cheap PC demand – and a single strategic uncertainty – PC manufacturers' purchase decisions. The next step in any scenario analysis is to determine the minimum number of states that each scenario variable can assume. The idea is to choose as many states (scenarios) as will lead to qualitatively different outcomes. In many situations two or three states will suffice; 'average', 'more successful than expected', and 'failure' may capture the essence of the uncertainty.

So, while there is a continuum of alternative demand outcomes for cheap PCs, here we assume there are only two: 'high' or 'low'. Similarly, for the PC makers we assume a 40/60 versus a 60/40 split, where Intel retains either 40% or 60% of the market respectively. Note that the PC manufacturers have mixed motives in their purchase decisions. The demand for their product is likely to be higher if they use an Intel chip, but the price of competitors' chips is likely to be lower. The decision will come down to the price/performance trade-offs and the strength of Intel's brand equity.

The simplified description of the game generates eight initial scenarios, four under each of the two possible Intel actions – 'introduce' or 'wait' (Figure 7.13). The next step is to eliminate scenarios that are either implausible or internally inconsistent.

Beginning with those that arise under the Intel 'introduce' decision, scenarios 1 and 3 are relatively implausible. If Intel enters with a low-end chip that is comparable to the competition's low-end chip, Intel should be able to capture at least 60% of the market, whether demand is high or low. Hence, we can regard the 40/60 (Intel/other chip makers) scenarios 1 and 3 as implausible and we are left with two scenarios under 'introduce', whereby Intel gets 60% of either a large or small market for cheap PCs.

Under the 'wait' decision, all four scenarios are plausible, depending on how long Intel actually waits before introducing its low-end chip after observing the level of demand for cheap PCs. However, it will not be optimal for Intel to introduce its low-end chips if demand for cheap PCs turns out to be low. Hence scenarios 7 and 8 are not internally consistent from a game theoretical perspective. This leaves us with two scenarios to consider under 'wait', whereby Intel gets either 40% or 60% of the low-end PC market under conditions of high demand.

▶

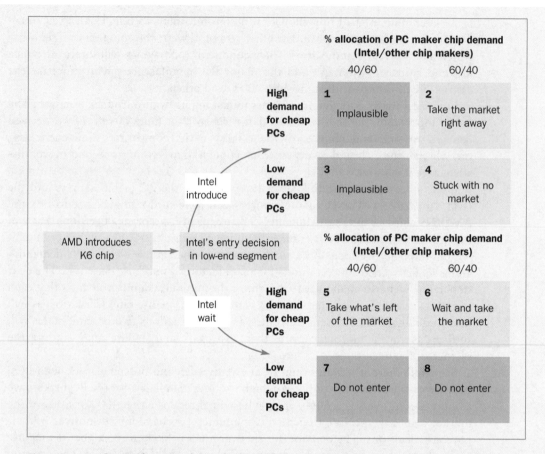

Figure 7.13 **Strategic scenario analysis of the low-end PC market by Intel after AMD introduced its K6 chip, % allocations (Intel/other chip makers)**
Source: Gertner and Knez (2000).

Clearly this approach has eliminated scenarios 1, 3, 7 and 8 leaving scenarios 2, 4, 5 and 6 still in play.

From this simple scenario analysis we see that Intel's downside risk from an 'introduce' strategy is simply that the market for cheap PCs does not materialise – the 'stuck with no market' scenario. Of course, the upside is that the market does materialise – the 'take the market right away' scenario. If Intel follows the 'wait' strategy, the risk is that demand will be high and the PC manufacturers will commit to buying from the competition, which will give Intel a second-mover disadvantage – the 'take what's left' scenario. Alternatively, many PC manufacturers may switch to Intel as soon as it enters because of its brand equity – the 'wait and take the market' scenario.

As in most entry decisions, the benefit of waiting is the option value of observing whether demand is high or low before committing assets to enter. The value of this option depends on the degree of second-mover disadvantage. In Intel's case, that disadvantage is relatively low. It knows it will be able to capture significant market share with its brand equity (provided it has a price competitive chip). The question is to what extent profits will be dissipated through price competition.

The next step is to take the model beyond its role of explaining the strategic structure of the competitive environment and to use it to provide insights into the decision itself. The way to do this is to analyse each scenario in detail and determine pay-offs for each player. This can then be used to predict competitors' behaviour and to determine which course of action is most profitable.

In 1997 Intel in fact decided not to introduce a low-end chip for the emerging cheap PC market. Subsequently, the demand for cheap PCs grew rapidly. Intel was forced to introduce an underperforming chip in early 1998, leaving 80% of the low-end chip market to its competitors (mostly AMD). Andy Grove, the company's chairman, commented that the cheap PC boom was 'broader and more profound' than he had anticipated the previous autumn.

From AMD's perspective, Intel's delayed entry opened a critical window of opportunity. AMD had time to establish a strong position in the low-end market that could support its attempts to enter the more lucrative high end – Intel's dominant market. Ignoring the obvious criticism of hindsight bias, our simple strategic scenario analysis suggests that AMD had good reason to bet that Intel would delay, increasing AMD's expected pay-offs from introducing the K6 chip.

Source: Adapted from Gertner and Knez (2000).

Questions

1 Comment further on why this Case Study suggests that 'AMD had good reason to bet that Intel would delay'.

2 What might Intel be expected to learn from this experience? Consider any implications this might have for AMD's future use of strategic scenario analysis.

International operations management and logistical strategies

Both international operations management and international logistics involve the coordination of a set of interrelated activities directed towards the efficient production and supply of goods and services. Although there is some overlap between them, for the purposes of this chapter we deal with each approach separately.

International operations management

Operations management can be regarded as one of the key managerial roles within any organisation and has been defined as 'the management of a system which provides goods or services to or for a customer, and involves the design, planning and control of the system' (Harris 1989). The systems theory approach to operations management is based on the view that an organisation can be seen as a network of interconnected components, each performing a role or function. Each component within this system is influential to the extent that if one component were absent or ineffective in some way, then the behaviour of the whole system would change. These basic relationships involved in systems theory can be expressed diagrammatically in terms of inputs and outputs, as in Figure 7.14.

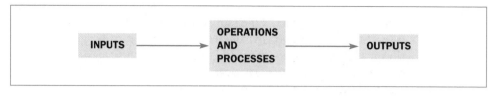

Figure 7.14 **The operations management system approach**

Although this systems approach is commonly applied to manufacturing, it can equally be used in the context of distributive activities, such as transport operations or warehousing. However, for purposes of illustration we first illustrate a 'traditional' approach to operations management within manufacturing before extending the scope of the discussion to consider its changing role within a globalised economy.

Operations management: a manufacturing perspective

Operations management is concerned with managing the transformation process whereby input resources are converted into outputs. Five general approaches can be used for managing the transformation process within manufacturing, namely project processes, jobbing processes, batch processes, mass processes and continuous processes. Each of these methods involves utilising different approaches to organising and managing the manufacturing activities, depending on the different volume and variety of products required, as can be seen from Figure 7.15.

- *Project processes*. These are traditionally used to produce highly customised, one-off items such as the construction of a new building, the production of a cinema film or the installation of a computer system (i.e. low-volume, high-variety products).

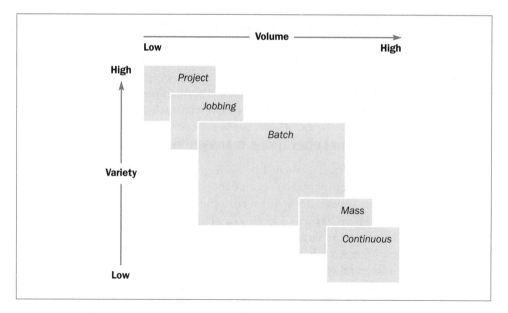

Figure 7.15 **Characteristics of some traditional methods of manufacture**

There is a sequence of operations, but this sequence can be uncertain, may require alteration during the production process itself and is not usually repeated. With this type of process, the resources necessary for transformation will usually be allocated in a manner specific to each product.

■ *Jobbing processes.* These involve the manufacture of a unique item from beginning to end as a result of an individual order. Products subjected to jobbing processes are usually of a smaller stature than those subjected to project processes and may include handmade shoes, restored furniture and individualised computer systems. As with project processes, this type of process is also characterised by low volume, high variety and low repetition, but the transforming resources involved in job processes are typically shared between several products. The main features of jobbing processes are the high set-up costs, flexible multi-use equipment required, skilled and versatile labour required, high worker motivation and a high-priced product. Advantages include creating a unique product to the exact specifications of the customer, for which a premium price might be charged. Disadvantages include the limited opportunities for economies of scale.

■ *Batch processes.* These involve the manufacture of a number of similar items whereby a batch of products is processed through a given stage before the entire batch is moved on to the next stage in a well-defined sequence. Examples of batch production include car components, machine tool manufacturing and the production of clothes. Batch processes are typically characterised by larger volumes but a narrower variety of products than are produced by project or jobbing processes. The larger output provides some opportunity for scale economies, resulting in lower costs per unit than jobbing processes. The main features of batch processes are less skilled labour required, use of more specialised but flexible machinery, the possibility of repeat orders, some standardisation of product and the ability to supply a larger market.

■ *Mass processes.* These involve the use of a mass-production line whereby the product moves continuously from one operation to another without stopping. Mass processes typically produce goods in larger volumes but are less varied in terms of their design characteristics. Examples of mass processes include motor vehicle manufacturing, food preparation in fast-food restaurants and the production of compact discs. The operations involved in mass production processes are largely repetitive, highly predictable, very efficient but rather inflexible.

■ *Continuous processes.* These can be considered as a variation of mass processes in that goods are produced in even larger volumes and are often highly standardised in their design, such as petrochemical refineries, beer, paper and electricity production. The operations involved in continuous processes are usually more automated and standardised than mass processes and are often literally produced in an endless flow. The main features of mass or continuous (flow) processes are high capital investment, a greater proportion of unskilled and semi-skilled labour; specialised plant and equipment with little flexibility; highly automated production and the huge economies of scale which are available.

Some mass production manufacturing systems have adopted the 'just-in-time' (JIT) philosophy that aims to minimise stock-holding costs by planning the arrival of raw materials and components just as they are needed. This requires a highly efficient ordering system, normally computerised, that is linked directly to the suppliers, who, in turn, must be highly reliable. Customers orders 'pull' production and stocks through the manufacturing process, thus eliminating the need for large stock holdings and driving down the costs of production. Although this can reduce significantly the stock-holding costs, it also increases the danger of production disruption due to non-arrival of stock supplies.

pause for thought 4	Why, historically, have mass and continuous processes become a predominant form of manufacture in the past few decades?

In more recent times there has been considerable focus on slimming down 'mass production' processes into more flexible or 'lean production' approaches to manufacturing (*see* Box 7.3).

Box 7.3 Lean production

The Japanese have adopted a 'total approach' to removing anything that does not add value to the final product. The term lean production has been applied to this approach which aims to produce more by using less, and is to be achieved by:

- involving both management and workers in the decision-making and suggestion-making process;
- minimising the use of key resources such as materials, manpower, floor space, capacity and time;
- introducing just-in-time (JIT) materials handling in order to lower stock-holding costs and to minimise the need for buffer stocks;
- encouraging worker participation in quality circles where improvements can be suggested and discussed;
- introducing preventative maintenance;
- using multiple purpose machines for flexible production;
- employing and training multi-skilled operatives;
- encouraging teamwork.

This approach slimmed down 'mass' production into a flexible or 'lean' production system. Advantages claimed for this approach include:

- an increase in quality of product and after-sales service;
- shorter product development time;
- faster reaction to changes in consumer preferences;
- a reduction in unit costs of production without sacrificing quality;
- a better trained and more motivated workforce.

■ Operations management: a non-manufacturing perspective

In addition to the manufacture of goods, operations management is also concerned with the provision of services. Processes are equally relevant in both manufacturing and service delivery systems but the technologies for delivering services are clearly quite different from those used in manufacturing. As a result of this distinction, Slack *et al.* (1998) identified three process types specific to service operations namely, professional service, service shops and mass services, ranging from low volume/high variety to high volume/low variety respectively. Some writers argue that the five general process types applied to manufacturing are also appropriate to service operations.

Case Study 7.9 looks at the use of operations management techniques to an essentially non-manufacturing operation. This involves the marketing of handicraft products in the context of new, global opportunities.

CASE 7.9   Operations management system: Khan Handicrafts

Some of the key operations management issues can be illustrated in the context of Khan Handicrafts, which is a medium-sized co-operative located in Dhaka, Bangladesh. Khan Handicrafts currently serves three different segments of the market, namely foreign tourists (who buy 10% of products at a premium price), local 'expatriates' (who buy 40% of products at an above average price), and middle/upper class Bangladeshi's (who buy 50% of products at a lower 'local' price). The higher profit margin derived from the first two of these market segments has prompted Khan to concentrate on the tourist and ex-patriate markets, although this has involved increased amounts of quality control and design input. However, Khan is currently experiencing both a declining home market (reductions in aid agencies) and greater competition within that market. As a result, the organisation is reconsidering its strategic plan for the next decade. One option under active consideration involves moving into the export business.

Figure 7.16 summarises the current system in terms of systems theory. The co-operative's major systems input can be considered to be the workers within its 53 member societies. These societies are made up of poor rural men and women who utilise their woodwork, pottery, sewing, weaving and basket-work skills. Further inputs to the system include finance/capital, storage facilities, raw materials (e.g. dye, wood, clay, etc.) and the equipment necessary to produce the goods. There is also an element of design input, whereby products are produced in accordance with specific customer requirements. Design might be subsumed within the 'information' heading,

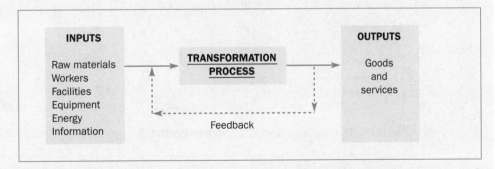

Figure 7.16 **The operations management system of Khan Handicrafts**

which might also include advice given by Khan to its member societies to remain solvent in terms of cash flow management.

The transformation stage of the system takes these inputs and uses them, together with the skills of the workers, to produce the desired outputs. The major output of the Khan organisation is obviously not only the goods produced but also their successful marketing. In other words, the outputs are both goods produced and a range of services which include distribution of the goods directly through Khan's own outlets and as an intermediary in using the outlets of others. In some ways the transformation process for Khan involves acting as an intermediary between producers (its member societies) and the consumers (currently foreign tourists, local expatriates and middle/upper-class Bangladeshis).

A more detailed systems diagram (Figure 7.17) can be used to express the operations of the Khan organisation incorporating the fact that its primary activity is to market the goods produced by the member societies of the co-operative. These goods are marketed either directly through one of Khan Handicraft's own marketing outlets or, more usually, through other outlets. At the central warehouse, the

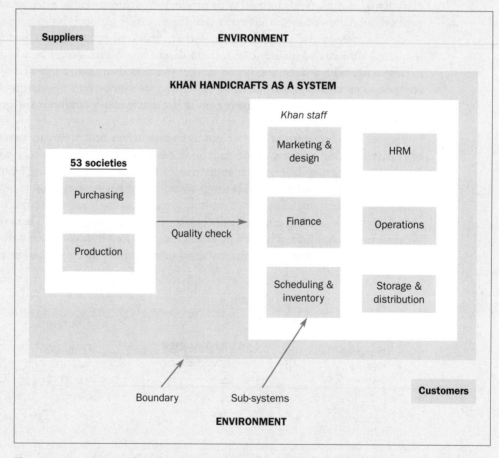

Figure 7.17   A more detailed systems diagram of Khan Handicrafts

products are subjected to a rapid quality check, labelled with a Khan tag and securely stored until they are dispatched in batches to retail outlets. Khan also uses its extensive market knowledge to influence the design process of individual societies.

The influence of the environment on the transformation process is of particular importance when using the systems theory approach to operations management. It is important to understand that the organisation is embedded in its external environment and any changes in these factors, such as political, economic, social or technological changes, may result in changes in the system or one of its components. For example, it can already be seen in the case of Khan that the restrictions on aid missions imposed by the government is affecting a key market segment, namely the demand for its products by home-based expatriates. In attempting to develop existing and new market segments (e.g. export) in response to this environmental change, Khan will need to factor into its operations management system appropriate mechanisms for dealing with the new requirements for quality, flexibility, timeliness, capacity, etc. An important element in dealing with the environment involves the introduction of physical or organisational 'buffering' techniques wherever possible as a means of minimising the impacts of unforeseeable 'environmental' disruptions, whether on the side of supply or demand.

One of the problems of the systems approach involves precisely delineating the boundaries between the operation function and other functions involved in the production of goods and services. A broad approach is adopted for the Khan systems analysis. A further problem involves modelling the hierarchy of operations appropriately, in particular the treatment given to internal customers and suppliers as compared to external customers and suppliers. Indeed, a network of micro operations, each involved in transforming inputs into outputs, are often key components of the overall macro operation. The fulfilment of customer needs will require the successful integration of all these operations.

Current operations management issues

If the organisation is to successfully achieve its objective of moving into the export business, there are various operations management issues that must be considered.

- *Design*. The current design system utilised by Khan involves little input from its constituent societies. The Khan staff control the design activity as they feel they are more aware of the needs of customers within the market and therefore more able to design products that will satisfy those needs. As competition increases within the current market and Khan seeks to become established in the export market, the design element of the products will become increasingly important. It will be vital for Khan to identify exactly what its customers require from the product in terms of features, colour, fashion, etc. so it can meet, if not exceed, these requirements in order to gain a competitive edge. Changes to the traditional design specifications of products may require the workers to be retrained so that they have the skills to produce exactly what is required to a high standard. Khan may also need to alert workers to the fact that in export markets

▶

product design will often supersede functional aspects in terms of buyer behaviour. The company may also consider revising its current policy and encourage design input from the workers who may be able to contribute new ideas, thereby improving the quality of products and the efficiency of the system as a whole. If Khan is to succeed in breaking into the export market, it may also consider consulting its clients to request their input in terms of design features and technical aspects of the products.

- *Manufacture.* The manufacture of the products can continue to take place locally but a stronger emphasis must now be placed on improving the quality of the goods produced for a more discriminating export market. Obviously, if the possibility of entering the export market is to be a realistic option, Khan is going to have to seriously rethink its quality control procedures. Given the problems it currently experiences in producing goods of the standard needed by the foreign tourists segment of its market, dramatic improvements will be required. To achieve a higher quality of output, a better and more standardised quality of input (e.g. dyes) will be required. This could be done by introducing a degree of centralisation in supplying raw materials to the individual groups for the manufacturing process. There will also need to be greater quality control at various stages of manufacture, not least to control costs, e.g. if dyeing of spotted or cracked wax occurs in the batik work, this expensive process will have been wasted. It will be important for workers to inspect their own work for errors at each phase of the production process. This may involve additional training but should significantly reduce the need for quality inspections when the finished goods arrive at the central warehouse.
- *Distribution.* This will be a key component of the operations management system. Orders may be made in bulk by foreign purchasers and will often involve an element of product modification. Khan will need to ensure that these features are embodied in the design of sufficient numbers of products supplied to the central warehouse. Khan may also have to oversee the incorporation of higher quality raw materials (sometimes provided by customers themselves) into the manufacturing process, replacing previous sources of domestic supply. Flexibility will be an important element in such adjustments as, for example, in having to meet specialised and higher quality bulk orders, as compared to simply providing products, as made, in smaller batches to customers imposing less onerous time requirements.
- *Capacity.* Khan may need to expand capacity in order to cope with demand from both home and export markets, especially when the latter may involve bulk ordering. This is likely to involve larger warehousing facilities and more careful attention to demand estimation and production possibilities in order to ensure that orders are met and capacity is not exceeded. Even though, at present, some spare capacity is available, implementation of the new strategy is likely to require the purchase or leasing of additional storage space. The location of this warehousing capacity may need to be reviewed, e.g. ease of access to ports or airports may now become an important factor. Associated with enhanced capacity may be an extra requirement for labour input, as, for example, in support of additional quality control and stock-handling activities.

- *Stock (inventory).* Stock levels must be more carefully monitored in order to avoid 'stock-out' costs and resulting lost orders. Systems will be needed to handle the warehouse dispatch and location within the warehouse of the more differentiated products required by the export market. While sufficient stock must be held to meet urgent orders and provide adequate numbers of sample items on request, too much stock can result in excessive stock-handling costs. Improvements in inventory management will be an important component of any move into the export market.

- *Purchasing.* The current policy regarding purchasing is that the individual societies purchase their own raw materials as required. Central purchasing may be an important element in ensuring the higher quality based products required by the export market. In fact bulk purchase of such inputs at discounts may also lead to the benefit of reducing the cost of purchasing for both domestic and overseas markets, thereby raising profit margins. However, the need for extra storage space already mentioned may absorb part of any additional profit. Some purchasing may now be undertaken under the direction of the clients themselves as they seek to ensure a better quality product.

- *Scheduling.* This will also be a key component of the operations management system. Any delay in receipt or dispatch of stock may endanger future orders, by adding to movement and delivery time. Efficient scheduling of inputs and outputs will also help reduce average stock levels and associated stock holding costs.

- *Employees.* A further operations management issue that will need consideration is that of the workers and the effect any changes made to current procedures will have on them. Khan may experience resistance from the workers in trying to implement the changes necessary to successfully enter the export market. For example, the majority of rural workers are only part-time and will have difficulty displaying the flexibility required to meet delivery dates due to their other commitments. The special training required might also cause problems as it will involve trying to change ingrained concepts (as to quality and design features for example) which may take years to modify and standardise.

It is important to understand that all of these elements are interrelated; for example, the decision to enter the export market will affect the production process selected, the skills and training requirements of the labour force, the layout of facilities, the warehousing capacity required, etc. These linkages highlight the need for a feedback loop within the overall system so that the elements can be monitored, controlled and any necessary changes made. The combination and interaction of these elements clearly have important implications for the organisation's overall operations management strategy.

Question

If Khan is to broaden its market base (for example, by moving into the export market segment), what strategic issues might be involved?

■ Flexible specialisation

The growth of world markets and the increasing and more rapid availability of detailed information on consumer characteristics and behaviour patterns in segmented markets are posing strategic challenges for operations management, for instance in choosing whether and to what extent to adopt a flexible specialisation approach to manufacture.

Flexible specialisation is a term that is often applied to new methods of manufacturing that attempt to produce 'an expandable range of highly specialised products' (Lowson *et al.* 1999). The strategy of flexible specialisation has emerged as a result of the globalised and information intensive environment within which firms operate and the increase in demand for products that are custom-made and more varied in nature.

This method of manufacturing has been considered as representing a departure from the more traditional approaches outlined above, and its principles have even been described as the reverse of those of mass production (or 'Fordism') which relies on producing large quantities of products as cheaply as possible in an attempt to maximise the return on investment. Mass production processes typically have very low unit costs because of the increased scale of production, the use of highly specialised machinery and the use of low-skilled, easily trained labour. However, the demand for such standardised goods is limited and the inflexibility of the mass production process means that it cannot efficiently adapt to situations where demand is more turbulent, as in the case of changes in fashion or design requirements.

This lack of flexibility experienced by the traditional manufacturing methods has led to the emergence of a more flexible process whereby 'the new flexible firms, reacting to rapidly changing market demand, seek to generalise the skills of workers so that they can adapt to a wide range of tasks' (Lowson *et al.* 1999). Attempts to achieve such generality in employees' skills arguably conflicts with the central aim of Fordism, namely to achieve maximum economies of scale and specialisation among the workforce in order to produce highly uniform products. It has even been suggested that the term 'flexible specialisation' implies a return to the fundamentals of the system of craft production whereby the output is unique and very variable. The flexibility that craft producers can achieve and their ability to modify their ideas to suit customer requirements are the main aims of a strategy of flexible specialisation.

At least for larger enterprises, the more traditional methods of operation have tended to be 'scale-based' and 'focused', involving the mass production of standardised goods using capital-intensive processes with low levels of mainly unskilled labour, and consequently high levels of recorded labour productivity. Costs are typically low, giving successful companies the opportunity to reduce prices and capture substantial market share of mature markets. Of course, this rather stylised approach has already undergone considerable change, with techniques such as 'continuous improvement' being adopted in many large-scale processes to raise quality. For example, tightly knit cross-functional groups have been established within many volume-manufacturing processes to improve performance, raise quality, reduce waste, etc. However, this is not the same as flexible specialisation, which in its more modern guise can be seen as underpinning 'flexible-scope-based' and especially 'quick response' approaches to meeting changes in consumer demand. Perhaps the 'mass customisation' approach best captures the key ingredients of flexible specialisation, namely an approach, which emphasises the primacy of carefully utilising selected packages of short-run processes ('modules') to meet specific customer requirements.

Implications of flexible specialisation

One implication of the flexible specialisation approach is to render less useful the idea of the learning or experience curve in contributing to productive efficiency, whether for the provision of goods or services. As indicated in Figure 7.18, costs per unit are regarded as varying inversely and exponentially with *cumulative output*, reflecting the importance of learning by experience. Such a relationship had been identified as early as the 1930s when studies suggested that a doubling of the cumulative production of airframes was accomplished by a 20% reduction in unit labour costs (Griffiths and Wall 2000). Initially such decreases in costs were related to the ability of workers to improve performance of a task through repetition and of workers and management discovering more effective methods of undertaking such tasks through experience. Arguably some of the benefits from continuous improvement techniques can be attributed to such factors. However, such experience curve relationships depend on product and process standardisation, which are characteristics conspicuously absent from flexible specialisation approaches.

In a similar way, flexible specialisation shifts the focus away from various internal economies of scale as a major source of competitive advantage. Conventionally,

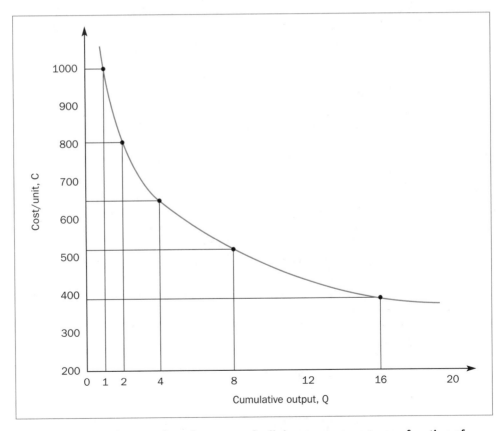

Figure 7.18 **Experience or learning curve: declining average costs as a function of cumulative output**

increased efficiencies become available to the firm from higher volumes of output, as for example via the technical economies of higher productivity resulting from increased specialisation of labour and capital inputs. These, together with economies from increased dimensions (material inputs increase as the square, capacity as the cube) and linked processes (lowest common multiple for dovetailing separate processes being a high volume of output), combine to generate substantial reductions in technical costs of production from higher output. Under flexible specialisation such considerations become largely redundant. Instead the focus shifts towards the external economies of scale available from siting clusters or networks of small-scale producers and suppliers in geographically adjacent areas. Of course, the more recent developments of information technology may allow such networks to develop at greater geographical distance.

The focus under flexible specialisation shifts rather to issues such as economies of scope, whereby the product mix becomes an important aspect of cost reduction. Here firms may benefit from the joint use of inputs such as management, administration, marketing or storage facilities across two or more products, bringing cost savings for all the products produced.

It has been suggested that flexible specialisation and mass customisation techniques can only be successfully implemented by radically overhauling the organisational and cultural context in which goods and services are provided. For example, the tightly knit, cross-functional teams so appropriate to continuous improvement must become more loosely organised 'dynamic networks of relatively autonomous operating units' (Pine 1993). These groups or 'process modules' must continuously strive to increase their capability of performing an ever-expanding set of tasks, giving greater scope for the company to incorporate them into the provision of a wide array of customised goods and services. This is rather different from the situation under continuous improvement, where the assumption is that the objective of the group is to better achieve a specified task which has a well-defined role in developing the overall product. With flexible specialisation the overall product is continually changing at the behest of consumer demand and the key ingredient is to develop multi-faceted process 'modules' which can readily adapt to a wide variety of demand configurations. Of course, a prerequisite for the success of such a 'quick response' approach is that some 'architecture' exists which is capable of rapidly converting specialised customer requirements into an appropriate combination of process modules capable of meeting those requirements. This is likely to involve sophisticated but reliable information-technology systems. For example, in the USA, Bally Engineering Structures Inc. uses a computer-driven intelligence network (CDIN) whereby sales personnel can directly input design specifications that have been agreed with customers for industrial refrigeration units and the system can, in real time, devise a combination of process modules capable of delivering the desired output. Case Study 7.6 above looks at some recent information technology based developments which are supporting the application of 'quick response' techniques.

■ Integration versus modularity

An important contemporary debate involving aspects of operations management is whether to remain integrated in the sense of retaining centralised control of the entire design and production processes, or whether to move in a modular direction. A 'modular product' has been defined as 'a complex product whose individual elements have each been designed independently and yet function together as a seamless whole'

(Sako and Murray 1999). As we shall see, the role of 'enterprise resource planning' has played a part in this debate.

Enterprise resource planning (ERP)

This term refers to the wide variety of company-wide information systems that are increasingly replacing the more fragmented, stand-alone IT systems in many companies. Such ERP systems provide centralised real time data on all elements of an organisations operations, no matter how globalised they might be. Manufacturing strategy ceases to involve a sequence of discrete decisions which 'lock' the enterprise into a certain mode of manufacture or operation. Rather it involves the continuous application of intelligence to operational processes which at the same time may open up new product and service opportunities. The increased availability of data may permit the introduction of new and more efficient operational processes (e.g. the introduction of worldwide benchmarking standards) as well as refined and enhanced products more closely attuned to customer requirements.

Modular strategies

Globalisation has been a driving force for modular strategies, since these can help companies engage in large worldwide investments without a huge increase in fixed costs and with fewer of the problems typically associated with managing complex global operations. Modular strategies can embrace production, design and/or use (Figure 7.19).

■ *Modularity-in-production (MIP).* This provided the initial impetus to adopt modules in the car industry. Here production activities are broken down into a number of large but separate elements that can be carried out independently, with the finished vehicle then being assembled from these large sub-assemblies. Such modular

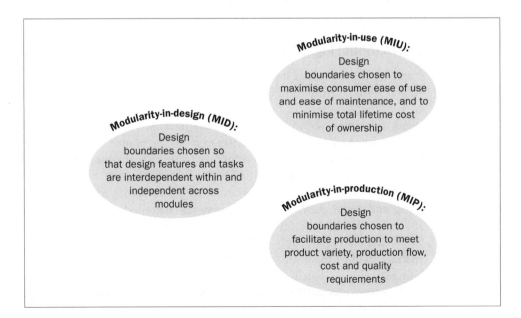

Figure 7.19 **Three arenas of modularisation**

production systems can help reduce the fixed capital overhead required for production, especially where selected modules are outsourced. Specialisation of labour and management on smaller, independent modules can also result in productivity gains and lower variable costs.

■ *Modularity-in-design (MID)*. There may be more problems in establishing modularity in the design process. This will be particularly true where the finished product embodies systems as well as sub-assembly components. For example, a finished vehicle offers climate control and vehicle safety 'systems' which, to be provided effectively, require design input into a whole range of sub-assembly module operations. Modularity-in-design may therefore require that boundaries be carefully drawn so as to capture as many interdependencies as possible within the modular groupings.

■ *Modularity-in-use (MIU)*. This was the main reason for the introduction of modularity in the computer industry. It became increasingly obvious that consumers required computer-related products that were both compatible and upgradeable. Much effort was therefore expended in standardising interfaces between different elements of the product architecture to give these desired user attributes. The then leader, IBM, found that the electro-mechanical system could be disaggregated without adversely affecting performance.

Of course, creating a modular product in any or all of these ways may have organisational consequences, not all of which may be foreseen. For example, a module product architecture may result in modular business organisation. This has certainly been the case in the computer industry. It can also stimulate certain types of organisational practice, such as outsourcing and shift power relationships between companies. For example, IBM's decision to outsource the development and production of its operating system to Microsoft and of its chip components to Intel was an important factor in shifting power away from the overall product architecture to these designers and producers of modular systems elements.

■ International logistics

Logistics is a term that has long been associated with military activities, and in particular with coordinating the movements of troops, armaments and other supplies to specified locations in the most efficient ways technically feasible. When first applied to business some 30 years ago the term was mainly used to refer to the total flow of finished products downstream from the plant to the customers. In more recent times it has been extended further to include the major part of the total flows of materials (finished and unfinished) and information both downstream and upstream. Activities such as transport, storage, inventory management, materials handling and order processing are commonly included within the 'logistics' heading. Indeed, over the last decade the term 'supply chain management' has sometimes been used interchangeably with 'logistics'. This still broader perspective includes the management of the entire chain from supply of raw materials through manufacture and assembly to distribution to the end consumer. As we shall see, when logistics is viewed from this broad perspective it increasingly becomes a strategic as well as an operational issue.

Logistical principles

Before turning to some specific areas of logistical concern for international business, it may be useful to review a number of logistical principles which are of general relevance. Many of these principles touch on the costs associated with holding stock (inventory), which are briefly reviewed in Box 7.4.

Box 7.4 Inventory (stock) costs and control

There are three broad categories of costs involving inventories. The cost of holding stock (carrying costs), costs of obtaining stock (ordering costs) and the costs of failing to have adequate stock (stock-out costs).

Inventory costs include the following:

- *Holding or carrying costs.* These might include insurance, storage costs (staff, equipment, handling, deterioration, obsolescence, security). These might also include opportunity costs, i.e. the financial cost in terms of alternatives foregone (e.g. interest) through having capital tied up.
- *Order costs.* These occur when obtaining stock and might include the costs of clerical and administrative work in raising an order, any associated transport costs and inspection of stock on arrival, etc.
- *Stock-out costs.* These are difficult to quantify but might include the following:

  Stock-out of raw materials and work-in-progress, which may result in machine and operator idle time and possibly the need for overtime payments to catch up on missed production.

  Stock-out of finished goods, which may result in:

  (i)   missed orders from occasional customers;

  (ii) missed delivery dates resulting in a deterioration in customer/supplier relations;

  (iii) penalty clauses incurred for late delivery.

  Stock-out of tools and spares, which may result in an increase in downtime of machinery and loss of production.

Stock carrying costs can be expected to rise as the order size increases, for reasons already discussed. However stock ordering costs can be expected to fall as the order size increases (*see* Figure 7.20).

If we ignore stock-out costs which are notoriously difficult to quantify, then total (inventory) costs can be regarded as the sum of the carrying and ordering costs. These will be at a minimum for the following value of Q (output).

Economic order quantity

$$Q = \sqrt{\frac{2 \cdot CoD}{Cc}}$$

Where Q = economic order quantity
Co = ordering costs for one order
D = annual demand for stock
Cc = carrying cost for one item p.a.

A firm uses 100,000 components per annum in its manufacturing process each of which cost the firm £10 to purchase from its supplier. The carrying costs of stocking these

▶

Box 7.4   Continued

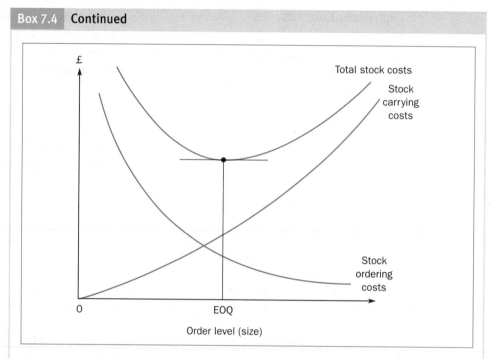

Figure 7.20   Finding the economic order quantity (EOQ)

components is estimated as 15% per annum of the purchase price. The ordering costs are estimated at £10 per order. Find the economic order quantity.

Solution

$$EOQ = \sqrt{\frac{2 \cdot CoD}{Cc}}$$

Where Co = £10 per order
D = 100,000 units p.a.
Cc = £10 × 0.15 = £1.50 per item per annum.

i.e. EOQ $= \sqrt{\dfrac{2 \cdot (10) \cdot (100,000)}{1.50}}$

i.e. EOQ = 1155 units

Of course, more complex inventory control situations with variable usage rates, variable lead times and gradual (rather than instantaneous) replenishment may be encountered by firms.

- *Square root law.* The amount of safety stock required will decline by a fraction whose denominator is the square root of the reduction in number of stock-holding points in the logistical system. For example, a reduction from 17 separate warehouses to a single separate warehouse will lead to an approximate reduction of $1/\sqrt{16} = 0.25$ or 25% in the safety stock required, which in turn implies an approximately pro rata reduction in stock-holding cost.

- *Logistical cost trade-offs.* It will often be the case that logistical changes will reduce certain specified costs but only at the expense of raising other costs. Such changes will only be applied where the net outcome is positive, i.e. the logistical cost trade-off is 'favourable'. For example, while the reduction in number of separate warehouses reduces stock-holding costs it may well have other impacts. On the positive side, the larger scale of warehousing operations may further reduce inventory and associated materials handling costs. On the negative side there may be additional transport costs incurred by distributions from a fewer number of larger warehouses to local customers. Only if the overall reduction in inventory and material handling costs more than compensates for any increases in transport related costs will this logistical trade-off be deemed 'favourable' to the enterprise. More generally MNEs must address such logistical trade-offs whenever they consider centralising production in factories/plants to create scale economies and reduced average production costs while simultaneously incurring additional transportation costs and lengthened lead time to customers.
- *Time compression.* This refers to the various attempts to accelerate the flows of materials and information in logistical systems. It is sometimes extended to cover a variety of techniques and approaches, such as just-in-time (*see* p. 292), quick response (*see* p. 298), lead-time management, lean logistics, process mapping techniques, and so on. The idea behind many of these techniques has been to reduce the expenditure of time within various aspects of the supply chain, with particular attention paid to eliminating slack time and time used in non-value adding activities. Even here, however, the logistical trade-offs will often apply. For example, saving time within large, highly automated and synchronised centralised warehousing systems may be at the expense of incurring more time by lengthening the geographical supply chain to the final customer.
- *Postponement principle.* The company will benefit by postponing decisions as to the precise configuration of customised product until as late a stage as possible within the supply chain. This implies that companies should hold stock in generic form for as long as possible before deciding how to extend the product range by reconfiguring that stock into the separate 'stock-keeping units' (SKUs) which correspond to customised products. The application of this 'postponement principle' reduces the volume of inventory in the global supply chain and the costs associated with under-supplying (stock-out costs) or over-supplying (stock handling costs) a particular market with a customised product. However, the logistical cost trade-off principle can be expected to apply yet again, since the reduction in overall inventory costs may be at the expense of incurring additional costs associated with extending the global supply chain (e.g. transport/distribution costs).

■ International distribution systems

International business might, at one extreme, pay little heed to the logistical aspects of delivery by exporting on an ex-works basis. The responsibility in this case would be on the overseas purchaser to arrange for the collection of the goods and to bear all the insurance and freight costs. This rarely happens in practice, with the result that sellers and buyers must make an agreement as to their respective responsibilities and duties in trade, with the range of possibilities often referred to as 'incoterms'.

Incoterms

The International Chamber of Commerce has drafted standard definitions of export delivery terms to clarify these issues:

- ex works (EXW): customers collect goods from the exporters premises;
- free on board (FOB): customers only take responsibility after the goods are loaded onto the ship in the exporters country;
- free carrier (FRC): as for FOB, but applies to any form of carrier, ship or otherwise;
- cost, insurance and freight (CIF): customers only take responsibility after the goods have reached a named foreign destination (i.e. exporter bears all transport and insurance costs to that point);
- delivered at frontier (DAF): customers only take responsibility after the goods have passed through a named frontier;
- delivered duty paid (DDP): customers only take responsibility after the goods have reached their premises. This is increasingly becoming the standard approach for export sales.

Types of distribution channel

'Distribution channel' refers to the route the product takes from producer to the final consumer. Such channels must fulfil a number of functions, including the physical movement of the products, their storage prior to transit or sale, the transfer of title to the products and their presentation to the customer.

Four main types of channel are commonly identified:

1 *direct system*: no intermediaries involved, with orders sent directly from a factory or warehouse in the home country to the overseas purchaser;
2 *transit system*: exports sent to a transit (or 'satellite') warehouse/depot in another country. This then acts as a 'break bulk' point, with some items despatched in bulk over long distances and others in smaller units to more local destinations;
3 *classical system*: here each foreign country has its own separate warehouse/depot. Exports are sent to these and then distributed within that national market. Such warehouses/depots both 'break bulk' and perform a stock-holding function, with nationals of that country being served by locally held inventories;
4 *multicountry system*: as for the classical system, except that the separate warehouses/depots may serve several adjoining countries rather than one country only.

Table 7.5 summarises some of the advantages/disadvantages of each of the four types of distributional channel.

Choice of distributional channel

In practice a few key factors will determine the choice of distributional channel:

- *foreign customer base*: the direct system is more likely to be used where a small number of large overseas purchasers are involved;
- *export volumes*: the use of 'break-bulk' or stockholding warehouses/depots will only be economically viable when export volumes exceed certain 'threshold' levels;

Table 7.5 **International distribution systems**

Types of system	Advantages	Disadvantages
1 Direct	■ No need for foreign warehouse ■ Greater inventory centralisation/ Lower inventory level	■ Longer order lead time ■ Less load consolidation/ higher transport costs
2 Transit	■ Permits breaking of bulk ■ Greater load consolidation, so lower transport costs ■ Less packaging and administration	■ Extra handling costs in foreign markets
3 Classical	■ Permits breaking of bulk ■ Greater load consolidation, so lower transport costs ■ Less packaging and administration ■ Shorter order lead times ■ Local stock availability ■ Lower import dues	■ Incurs full warehousing cost ■ Decentralisation of inventory increases total stockholding
4 Multicountry	■ Higher degree of inventory centralisation and lower unit warehousing costs than 3	■ Longer lead times to customers ■ Higher delivery costs ■ Difficult to coordinate with nationally based sales organisation

Source: Adapted from Tayeb (2000).

■ *value density of product*: those products with a high ratio of value to weight/volume (i.e. high value density) are more suited to direct systems since they can more easily absorb the higher associated transport costs;

■ *order lead times*: where direct systems are inappropriate (e.g. low value density) yet where customers required rapid and reliable delivery, stock may have to be held locally (i.e. classical or multicountry systems).

Recent evidence suggests a rise in *direct, transit* and *multicountry systems*. The rise of e-commerce is increasing direct systems use with international and personalised delivery via parcel networks (e.g. 'just for you', J4U delivery). Transit and multi-country systems have also been increasing, with many MNEs consolidating warehousing in a few large 'pan-European' distribution centres. Sony, Rank Xerox, Philips, Kellogg's, Nike and IBM have moved in this direction and away from the classical system previously adopted. Some of these choices of distribution channels may be influenced by opportunities for 'economies of scope' (*see* p. 268).

Transport

Transport issues are implicit in the choice of distributional channels and in other locational decisions for the multinational organisation. In traditional heavy industries the location chosen will often depend on whether the operation is 'bulk forming' or 'bulk reducing'. Bulk-forming operations, such as in furniture manufacture, need to be close

Table 7.6 **The relative performance of each mode of transport**

Operation's performance objective	Mode of transport				
	Road	Rail	Air	Water	Pipeline
Delivery speed	2	3	1	5	4
Delivery dependability	2	3	4	5	1
Quality	2	3	4	5	1
Cost	3	4	5	2	1
Route flexibility	1	2	3	4	5

Source: Slack *et al.* (1998).

to their markets in order to cut transport costs. However, for bulk-reducing operations, such as in the steel industry, the main need is to be close to the heavy raw materials used as inputs. Modern industries increasingly use lighter raw materials so that they, together with the service industries, tend to be more 'footloose'.

For any firm, access to rail, road, sea and air links is important, both for the inward movement of inputs and the outward movement of outputs (goods and services). New electronic technologies are reducing the importance of distance in some product areas such as books, CDs and software but in many other areas of economic activity transport costs still increase with distance.

Of course, the transport mode chosen will depend not only on cost but on the relative importance for that product or service of: speed of delivery, dependability of delivery, quality deterioration issues, transport costs, route flexibility. As shown in Table 7.6, Slack *et al.* (1998) suggest the ranking of the different modes of transport as regards these factors.

We noted in Chapter 2 that transport costs can be a factor in influencing MNE decisions as to whether to export or to produce abroad. However, transport issues can also influence other organisational and strategic decisions in international business, as indicated in Box 7.5.

Box 7.5   Economies of scope and the transport sector

Economies of scope refer to cost benefits from changing the mix of production, as, for instance, when a number of related commodities or services are produced using common processing facilities. The potential for such economies of scope can be found in the transport industry. For example, the deregulation of the aircraft industry in the USA after 1978 resulted in significant changes in the structure of carrier operations. Instead of a large number of individual routes between various cities, the carriers redesigned the route system into a hub and spoke system reminiscent of a bicycle wheel. Travel was routed from, say, a city positioned at the end of one 'spoke' through a 'hub' or central airport, then out again to another city at the end of another spoke.

For example, in Figure 7.21(a) we have five point-to-point direct links from cities A to B, C to D, E to F, G to H and I to J respectively. If these are replaced by ten services from each of the cities to a hub airport, as in Figure 7.21(b), the number of city pairs that can be served rises sharply from five to 55. The total number of city pairs that can be served is given by the formula $n(n+1)/2$, where n is the number of spokes (cities served) emanating from the hub airport. It follows that if the number of spokes from the hub rises to 50, then the number of city pairs that can be linked rises to 1275. This system has advantages, because

Box 7.5 **Continued**

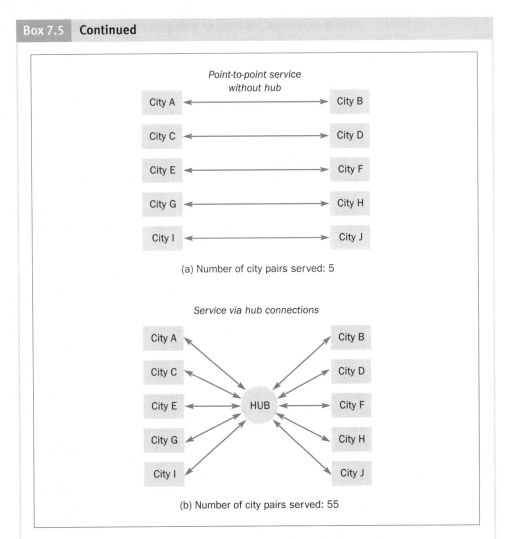

*Point-to-point service
without hub*

City A ←——————————→ City B

City C ←——————————→ City D

City E ←——————————→ City F

City G ←——————————→ City H

City I ←——————————→ City J

(a) Number of city pairs served: 5

Service via hub connections

City A

City C

City E ←——→ HUB ←——→ City F

City G

City I

City B

City D

City H

City J

(b) Number of city pairs served: 55

Figure 7.21 **Economies of scope and US aircraft routing operations**

all the passengers destined for a city at the end of one spoke will be collected at the hub airport from all the other cities at the end of the other spokes. This means that there will be many more passengers per flight, allowing definite economies of density: i.e. larger aircraft can be used, with associated savings in costs. On the marketing side, the hub system also facilitates more departures to a larger number of cities, making the marketing of a more integrated service network a more attractive proposition.

In this way economies of scope are realised. By serving a large number of city-pair markets through the hub, a carrier also provides many different products or combinations of products not previously available. These lead on to further economies as, for instance, airlines are now able to meet travel demands that have different characteristics from those previously met. In this case business and vacation travel can use a single network of flights instead of a variety of interconnecting networks of flights. The hub might permit still further 'common carriage' and cost reductions: for example, business-oriented routes might become still more cost-effective now that there is a greater chance (with a larger number of spokes) that vacation visitors might also wish to use these business-oriented routes.

Of course, the siting and location of depots/warehouses can provide similar benefits in terms of economies of scope.

Centralisation versus decentralisation

There has been much debate over the years of the logistical benefits and costs of centralised versus decentralised distributive systems. Certainly the predominant trend in logistics has been towards the centralisation of inventory holding in both national and international business, taking advantage of the 'square root law' previously discussed (*see* p. 304). We saw that moving from a decentralised system of 17 warehouses to a completely centralised system of one warehouse would cut the required amount of safety stock by one-quarter. It has generally been perceived that the resulting savings in stock-holding costs outweigh any increases in transport and related costs resulting from a geographically extended distribution system. Certainly Buck (1992) provided case study support of this 'favourable' logistical cost trade-off for a Dutch manufacturing company. By closing one warehouse in each of the UK, Germany, the Netherlands, Denmark, France, Belgium, Switzerland, Italy and Spain (nine closures in total), and completely centralising warehousing in Rotterdam, the company reported an overall distribution cost saving of over $4 million per annum. Some $3 million of this annualised cost saving being attributed to savings in 'inventory costs' and much of the remaining cost savings to 'inbound freight' ($0.66 million) and 'labour' ($0.30 million) savings. The only rise in costs being attributed to 'outbound delivery' ($0.26 million) as transport linkages to the markets in the respective nine countries became geographically extended, but this rise being overwhelmed by the cost savings elsewhere.

There has been a similar tendency towards centralisation in productive systems as MNEs operate on an increasingly global scale and seek to achieve scale economies wherever possible, even if some parts of other overall productive processes are geographically located in different international countries. This again places greater strain on the logistical system in terms of delivering rapidly and efficiently to the final consumer. Christopher (1998) has pointed to the fact that the presumption in this case of a 'favourable' logistical trade-off (i.e. cost-reducing benefits of large-scale production outweighing the cost-increasing impacts of a more transport intensive and slower distribution system) may be over-optimistic in many cases.

Useful websites

Now try the self-check questions for this chapter on the website at www.pearsoned.co.uk/wall. You will also find further resources as well as useful weblinks.

Interesting material on global marketing and segmentation strategies can be obtained from:

www.marketingweek.co.uk
www.globalweb.co.uk
www.Virgin.com
Procter & Gamble's website is *www.pg.com*
Coca-Cola's website is *www.cocacola.com*
McDonald's website is *www.mcdonalds.com*

Useful key texts

Daniels, J., Radebaugh, L. and Sullivan, D. (2006) *International Business* (11th edn), Pearson Prentice Hall, especially Chapter 6.

Dicken, P. (2003) *Global Shift: Transforming the World Economy* (4th edn), Paul Chapman Publishing Ltd, especially Chapters 7 and 8.

Hill, C. (2006) *International Business: Competing in the Global Marketplace* (5th edn), McGraw-Hill Irwin, especially Part 5.

Morrison, J. (2006) *The International Business Environment* (2nd edn), Palgrave, especially Chapters 2 and 4.

Piggott, J. and Cook, M. (2006) *International Business Economics: A European Perspective*, Palgrave Macmillan, especially Chapter 7.

Wild, J., Wild, K. and Han, J. (2006) *International Business: The Challenges of Globalization* (3rd edn), FT Prentice Hall, especially Chapter 11 and 15.

Other texts and sources

Ansoff, H.I. (1968) *Corporate Strategy*, Penguin.

Buck, R. (1992) 'Choosing a distribution strategy', *Site Selection Europe* 9: 60–3.

Buckingham, L. and Atkinson, D. (1999) 'Whisper it . . . Takeovers Don't Pay', *Guardian*, 30 November.

Capron, L. (1999) 'Horizontal Acquisitions: the Benefits and Risk to Long-term Performance', *Mastering Strategy*, p. 202, Financial Times Prentice Hall.

Christopher, M. (1998) *Logistics and Supply Chain Management*, FT Prentice Hall.

Empson, L. (1999) 'Lessons from Professional Services Firms', *Financial Times*, 8 November.

Fuller, E. (2007) 'Mergers and Acquisitions in the Growth of the Firm', in *Applied Economics* (11th edn), Griffiths, A. and Wall, S. (eds), Financial Times Prentice Hall.

Garicano, L. (1999) 'Game Theory: How to Make It Pay', *Mastering Global Business*, Financial Times Prentice Hall.

Gertner, R. (2000) 'How Boards Can Say No to M&A', *Mastering Strategy*, Financial Times Prentice Hall.

Gertner, R. and Knez, M. (2000) 'Game Theory in the Real World', *Mastering Strategy*, Financial Times Prentice Hall.

Ghemawat, P. (2007) 'Managing Differences: The Central Challenge of Global Strategy', *Harvard Business Review*, March p. 58.

Griffiths, A. and Wall, S. (2000) *Intermediate Microeconomics: Theory and Applications* (2nd edn), FT Prentice Hall.

Guenther, F. (2000) 'Critical Factors in M & A', Ashcroft International School of Management, APU.

Harris, N. (1989) *Service Operations Management*, Cassell.

Healey, N. (2007) 'The Multinational Corporation', in *Applied Economics* (11th edn), Griffiths, A. and Wall, S. (eds), Financial Times Prentice Hall.

Hornby, W., Gammie, B. and Wall, S. (2001) *Business Economics* (2nd edn), Longman, especially Chapters 10–11.

Husenan, R. and Goodman, J. (1999) *Leading the Knowledge: The Nature of Competition in the 21st Century*, Sage.

Kanter, R. (2006) 'Innovation: The Classic Traps', *Harvard Business Review*, November p. 72.

Kay, J. (1993) 'Economics in Business', *Economics and Business Education*, vol. 1, part 1, no. 2.

Lowson, B., King, R. and Hunter, A. (1999) *Quick Response: Managing the Supply Chain to Meet Consumer Demand*, John Wiley & Sons.

Mauboussin, M. (2006) 'Ten Ways to Create Shareholder Value', *Harvard Business Review*, September p. 66.

Mintzberg, H. and Quinn, J.B. (1991) *Strategy Process: Concepts, Contexts, Cases*, Prentice Hall.

Mitchell, M. and Lehn, K. (1990) 'Do Bad Bidders Become Good Targets?', *Journal of Political Economy*, vol. 98.

Nonaka, I. and Takeuchi, H. (1995) *The Knowledge-Creating Company: How Japanese Companies Create the Dynamics of Innovation*, OUP.

Pine, B.J. (1993) *Mass Customisation: The New Frontier in Business Competition*, Harvard Business School Press.

Porter, M.E. (1980) *Competitive Strategy*, Free Press, Collier Macmillan, New York.

Porter, M.E. (1985) *Competitive Advantage*, Free Press, New York.

Porter, M.E. (1986) *Competition in Global Industries*, Harvard Business School Press.

Prahalad, C.K. (1999) 'Changes in the Competitive Battlefield', *Financial Times*, 4 October. In *Mastering Strategy* (2000) Financial Times Prentice Hall.

Roberto, M., Bohmer, R. and Edmondson, A. (2006) 'Facing Ambiguous Threats', *Harvard Business Review*, November p. 106.

Rugman, A. and Collinson, R. (2009) *International Business* (5th edn), FT Prentice Hall, especially Chapters 8, 9 and 10.

Sako, M. and Murray F. (1999) 'Modular Strategies in Cars and Computers', *Financial Times*, 6 December.

Slack, N., Chambers, S., Harland, C., Harrison, A. and Johnson, R. (1998) *Operations Management* (2nd edn), FT Prentice Hall.

Stalk, G. (2006) 'Curveball: Strategies to Fool the Competition', *Harvard Business Review*, September p. 114.

Tayeb, M. (2000) *International Business: Theories, Policies and Practices*, Financial Times Prentice Hall, especially Chapters 5–8 and 14–15.

Thomas, A. and Fritz, L. (2006) 'Disaster Relief, Inc.' *Harvard Business Review*, November p. 114.

United Nations Conference on Trade and Development (UNCTAD), *World Investment Report* (annual publication).

United Nations Development Programme (UNDP), *Human Development Report* (annual publication), OUP.

World Bank, *World Development Report* (annual publication).

Zook, C. (2007) 'Finding your Next Core Business', *Harvard Business Review*, April, p. 66.

Chapter 8

International human resource management

By the end of this chapter you should be able to:

- explain why it is so important to manage people effectively;

- outline the key issues involved in international aspects of HRM;

- describe the methods used and the particular problems faced by MNEs in managing human resources;

- evaluate some strategic issues in international human resource management (IHRM).

Introduction

In order to create and distribute products (goods or services) every organisation needs people. Over time and in different places the ways in which people are being managed are constantly changing, though a general consensus has emerged that people are an organisation's greatest asset. This has led to an increasing interest in the way in which people are managed and how they are rewarded. After briefly reviewing the human resource management (HRM) function the emphasis shifts to defining the *international* context of that function and the problems and opportunities associated with it.

Human resource management function

Human resource management (HRM) is a concept that first emerged in the 1980s and concerns those aspects of management that deal with the human side of organisations. Armstrong (1999) defines HRM as: 'a strategic and coherent approach to the management of an organisation's most valued assets – the people working there who individually and collectively contribute to the achievement of its goals'.

A broader definition is given by Boxall and Purcell:

'Human resource management includes the firm's work systems and its employment practices. It embraces both individual and collective aspects of people management. It is not restricted to any one style or ideology. It engages the energies of both line and specialist managers (where the latter exists) and typically entails a range of messages for a variety of workforce groups' (2008: 28).

Managing human resources is a central function within an organisation and its effective implementation involves combining the skills and knowledge of the human resource department with the expertise of line managers in other departments. The human resource function is a wide-ranging subject that covers, among other things: management/worker communications; elements of work psychology; employee relations, training and motivation; organisation of the physical and social conditions of work; and personnel management. In contrast with 'personnel management' – which deals purely with the practical aspects of recruitment, staff appraisal, training, job evaluation, etc. – HRM has a strategic dimension and involves the total deployment of all the human resources available to the firm, including the integration of personnel and other HRM considerations into the firm's overall corporate planning and strategy formulation procedures. It is proactive, seeking to continuously discover new ways of utilising the labour force in a more productive manner, thus giving the business a competitive edge.

For the purposes of this chapter, we shall adopt Brewster's and Hegewisch's (1994) model of HRM (Figure 8.1) which shows that the corporate strategies, HRM strategies and HRM practices are located within both an *internal environment* (which includes organisational features such as size, structure and corporate culture) and an *external environment* (which includes national culture, power systems, legislation, education and employee representation). The model shows how the human resource

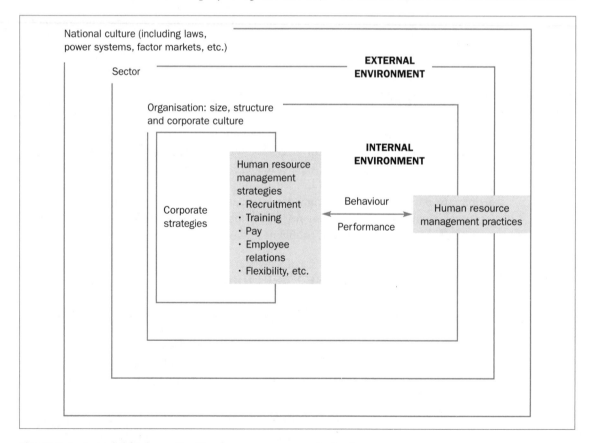

Figure 8.1 **A model for investigating human resource strategies**
Source: Adapted from Brewster and Hegewisch (1994).

strategies and practices interact with, and are part of, the broader environment in which the company operates. The model may also serve as a reminder to practitioners that their human resource strategies must reflect the organisational and national cultures in which they are operating.

Human resource management has grown in importance over the past decades largely in response to the impacts of increasing internationalisation in fragmenting product and labour markets and creating the need for ever more strategic ways of managing people competitively. In the UK, prior to the 1980s, managing the workforce was largely the responsibility of the personnel department and focused on trade unions, the collective bargaining process and the handling of grievances and disputes. As a concept, HRM has arguably been imported into Europe from the United States. Its major differences with the former personnel departments being that it is more strategic, that management speaks more directly to employees rather than through the unions, and that it is underpinned by more scientific methods of measuring people's performance. Nevertheless, although more strategic in focus, HRM issues still involve functions and aspects such as recruitment, training, pay, employee relations, and workforce flexibility.

Oechsler (2000) drew up a useful framework (*see* Table 8.1) for examining how the HRM function and its aims and practices have changed over time.

As we can see, changes in the type of environment in which businesses operate have led to increasing diversity in the role of HRM. Innovation and flexibility are now key elements of that role, as are issues of diversity, teamwork, and partnerships. Increasing globalisation, as we shall see, has further increased the challenges faced by HRM managers.

Table 8.1 **Changing aspects of the HRM function**

	1950s–1960s	*1970s–early 1980s*	*Mid-1980s–1990s*
Management metaphor	**Structuring (providing order)**	**Fit, matching, Consistency**	**Dynamic balance between dualities**
Nature of the environment	Relatively orderly and stable	Incrementally changing with increasing competition	Turbulent, complex, highly competitive
Focus of management attention	Structure and systems	Strategy and management processes	Innovation, flexibility, and organisational capabilities
	Planning systems	Strategic management: *matching* environmental threats and opportunities to internal strengths and weaknesses	Channelling entrepreneurship
	Budgeting systems	Organisation:	Focusing diversity
	Organisational structure	ensuring consistency between the 7 Ss	Integrating decentralised subsidiaries/business units
	Information systems	Human resource management:	Creating teamwork among strong individuals
	Job evaluation	*fitting* jobs to people	Planning opportunism
		Job design: matching technical and task specifications to social needs	Partnerships between competitors

In an attempt to investigate HRM issues in a wider environmental context, including that of internationalisation, a model of human resource management was developed by Beer *et al.* (1984) at Harvard University. According to this Harvard model, HRM strategies should develop from an in-depth analysis of (i) the demands of the various stakeholders in a business (e.g. shareholders, employees, the government, etc.) and (ii) a number of situational factors (e.g. the state of the labour market, the skills and motivation of the workforce, management styles, etc.). According to the Harvard researchers, both stakeholder expectations and situational factors need to be considered when formulating human resource strategies and the effectiveness of the outcomes should be evaluated under four headings: commitment (i.e. employees' loyalty), competence (i.e. employees' skills), congruence (i.e. shared vision of workers and management) and cost efficiencies (i.e. operational efficiency). The Harvard model suggests that human resource policies should be directed towards raising attainment levels for each of these four categories; for example, competence could be increased through the provision of extra training, adjustments to recruitment policy, different incentivisation schemes, and so on.

Hendry and Pettigrew (1990) offer an adaptation of the Harvard model (Figure 8.2) that attempts to integrate HRM issues with a still broader range of external societal

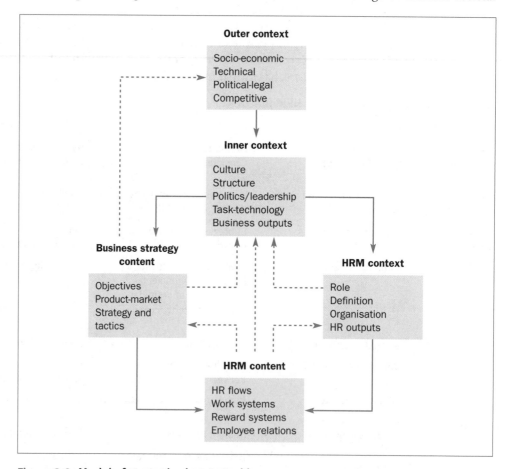

Figure 8.2 **Model of strategic change and human resource management**

Source: Human Resource Management: An Agenda for the 1990s, *International Journal of Human Resource Management*, vol. 1, no. 1 (Hendry, J. and Pettigrew, A. 1990), reprinted by permission of the publisher (Taylor & Francis Group, http://www.informaworld.com)

influences (such as socio-economic, technical, political, legal and competitive issues) which may vary considerably in different international situations. These 'outer context' issues will influence HRM strategies and practices, as will a variety of 'inner context' and business strategic issues.

Before turning to the more obviously international aspects of HRM, it will be useful to see how both the internal and external environment impact on the human resource function in a specific firm. Case Study 8.1 below looks at this issue in the context of the Royal Bank of Scotland.

CASE 8.1 HRM and the external environment

A thorough understanding of the components of the *external environment* and their dynamic nature is crucial if an organisation such as the Royal Bank of Scotland (RBS) is to achieve long-term success, as has been well illustrated by the seismic impacts of the 'credit crunch' on RBS and other financial institutions. RBS was 'bailed out' in late 2008 by the government with the results that 57% of the company is now government owned. Before that overwhelming event (see below) the emphasis had been on devising HRM strategies to respond to the prevailing belief that the most important characteristic of today's business environment – and therefore the yardstick against which management techniques must be measured – is increasing competition within both the domestic and international financial market. Increasing levels of competition within the financial services industry compel organisations in this sector to strive to improve productivity, with a key way of achieving this improvement being to manage human resources more effectively. The HRM department of the RBS could achieve this by empowering employees (i.e. allowing workers to have more influence over job-related decisions thereby increasing staff involvement), encouraging teamwork (in order to improve quality and efficiency) and introducing clear and consistently applied communication and assessment mechanisms (to enhance staff performance and increase awareness).

By introducing these initiatives into the workforce RBS has been seeking to encourage employee involvement, thereby maximising the contribution made by employees. The direct effect of involvement in the organisation is expected to be an increase in the individual employee's commitment to the workplace or the job (one of the four important categories under the Harvard model), reflected in increased productivity, lower labour turnover and reduced absenteeism. For the RBS this empowerment of employees may also call for new skills on the part of both the managers and employees and it will be the role of the HRM function to try to successfully implement these changes. The HRM department will be involved in designing policies and procedures to encourage employee involvement in line with the overall strategic plan of the RBS. For example, managers may need training in the techniques of participative management if they have been used to a control management style, and employees may require confidence-building sessions and training in decision-making. This departure from a control culture which focuses upon close supervision can also have an impact on organisational structures; for example, the tall hierarchies with numerous reporting levels traditionally associated with companies like the RBS, may need to be replaced by the more modern, flatter structures which better facilitate empowerment.

A further component of the external environment that the RBS needs to consider involves the workforce and the changes that are occurring within it. For example, the British labour force is projected to increase by 1.8 million people between 1995 and 2010 (i.e. from 27.8 million to 29.6 million), with an estimated 1.4 million of this increase being women so that by 2006 women will represent 46% of the entire British labour force. These statistics arguably highlight the importance to the HRM department of the RBS of effectively utilising programmes for managing diversity among its workforce, whereby women and other minority employees receive support, recognition and the same opportunities as non-minority workers. The increasing proportion of women in the workforce may be attributed in part to socio-economic influences such as the social acceptability of women in employment and the growing availability of part-time work. These factors may oblige the RBS to adopt more open approaches to recruitment and to consider the necessity of providing more extensive training. It will be the role of the HRM department to proactively implement strategies to successfully manage diversity among the workforce. This may involve addressing stereotypes to ensure that a job does not become 'sex-typed' (i.e. deemed appropriate only for one gender) and developing gender-neutral job titles to encourage both male and female applicants. The HRM department might, for example, suggest that the RBS becomes involved in government-supported national projects, specifically aimed at increasing the proportion of women in management.

The HRM department of the RBS must also undertake a thorough analysis of the *internal environment* in order for the organisation to retain its competitive edge. These internal influences may include: the company's strategy, objectives, and values; the leadership styles and goals of top management; the organisational structure, size, and culture; and the nature of the business.

An organisation's vision or mission statement is a brief explanation of its fundamental purpose and objectives and what it is striving to achieve. For example, the mission statement of the RBS includes: 'to provide financial services of the highest quality'. Organisations then develop objectives and strategies in an attempt to provide more focus and guidance for employees in seeking to achieve the company's mission. The role of the HRM department here will be to support the process of sharing an understanding about what needs to be achieved, and then managing and developing people in a way which will facilitate the achievement of these objectives. For example, in common with other companies in the financial services sector, the RBS has been seeking to change from a culture that rewards performance using a 'slow' incremental pay system, into one that more closely relates pay to personal performance and achievement. The HRM department has therefore been involved in introducing new performance appraisal systems and incentive schemes in an attempt to help the company achieve its long-term strategic objectives. By introducing more beneficial bonus and profit sharing schemes, whereby pay is more closely related to individual and corporate performance, employees will arguably become more motivated to contribute to the achievement of the overall goals of the RBS.

A further internal factor that will influence the HRM function is the merger of the RBS with National Westminster Group. This merger will, of course, be of potential benefit to many employees by creating new opportunities and offering enhanced career prospects in the new, larger business. It will also place greater emphasis on the HRM function of the company and may even involve an expansion of the existing department and its operations. It will certainly be necessary to review the current HRM practices of the new and enlarged business and perhaps revise these in order to bring them into line with the objectives of the RBS. As well as increasing the activity of the HRM department in areas such as recruitment, selection, training and development, this expansion will inevitably also require the clear communication of the RBS's culture, values and strategy across a wider and more disparate cohort of employees. It is essential that the HRM functions of both businesses be closely integrated so that there is a well-defined, common goal for the new, expanded business.

Of course internal HRM goals and strategies must be constantly reviewed when external realities change. The emphasis in 2009 for RBS is in managing 'downsizing' and of changing HRM strategies in response to a realisation that arguably reward structures have moved too far in incentivising a short term outlook by RBS managers as opposed to the longer term outlook required for a sustainable business in the financial services sector.

Questions

1 Can you identify HRM policies for RBS which might support the four outcomes identified in the Harvard model, namely commitment, competence, congruence and cost efficiencies?

2 Examine the ways in which the 'credit crunch' might have an impact on specific HRM policies within RBS.

3 Outline the strategic implications of this Case Study for the HRM function within an organisation.

International human resource management (IHRM)

The growth of business at an international level has led to an increase in the number of publications about international human resource management. However, what do we mean by this phrase? Boxhall defines IHRM as being:

> concerned with the human resource problems of multinational firms in foreign subsidiaries (such as expatriate management) or more broadly, with the unfolding HRM issues that are associated with the various stages of the internationalisation process (Boxall 1992).

Mark Mendenhall (2000) sought to be more specific by outlining a number of criteria relevant to a definition of IHRM.

1 IHRM is concerned with HRM issues that cross national boundaries or are conducted in locations other than the home country headquarters of the organisations within the study.

2 IHRM is concerned with the relationships between the HRM activities of organisations and the foreign environments in which the organisations operate.

3 IHRM includes comparative HRM studies; for example how companies in Japan, Thailand, Austria and Switzerland plan for increased employee commitment, upgrading of employee skills and so on.

4 IHRM does *not* include studies that are focused on issues outside the traditional activities inherent in the HRM function. In other words, topics such as leadership style, unless specifically linked to an HRM function (e.g. developing a selection programme to measure and select global leaders) do not qualify to be in the domain of IHRM. Such studies would arguably lie within the domain of *organisational behaviour*.

5 IHRM does *not* include studies of HRM activities in single countries. A study of personnel selection practices in Saudi Arabia, whether undertaken by an English, German or Canadian researcher, is still a study about domestic HRM in Saudi Arabia. Though such studies may have interest to those who work in international HRM issues, they are essentially examples of domestic HRM research.

■ IHRM and organisational structure

The type of international organisational structure adopted by the MNE will provide the context for many of the IHRM issues faced by the company. There are at least five widely recognised types of international organisational structures available to MNEs. There is no 'standard model' in this respect. A multinational enterprise may change from one type to another at different stages of the internationalisation process or as senior management perceives that emerging corporate needs are better served by one particular type.

The five readily identified 'types' of organisational structure include:

1 international division structure;
2 international geographic/regional structure;
3 international product structure;
4 international functional structure;
5 matrix or mixed structure.

Figure 8.3 outlines the first four of these types.

1 *The international division structure* is often used in the early stage of internationalisation with an 'international division' merely added to the existing divisional structures. As the activity within the international division grows (e.g. sales volume/ value, number of overseas markets, etc.) then this division may itself need to be reorganised according to function, product or geographic area.

2 *The international geographic/regional structure* involves separating out the different geographical/regional areas in which the MNE operates. Each geographic area may be given its own division with its own functional departments; MNEs with a wide variety of products in their portfolio sold across many geographic areas often adopt this organisational structure.

3 *The international product structure* is where an MNE's divisions are established on the basis of related product lines rather than geographical area. Each product division is responsible for all functions relating to those items in that particular product portfolio – e.g. production, marking, finance and personnel relating to chocolate products for an MNE with confectionery interests. This structure is often adopted by MNEs with a variety of unrelated product lines (e.g. conglomerate MNEs).

4 *The international functional structure* gives each functional department of the MNE (production, marketing, finance, etc.) responsibility for the international operations of that function.

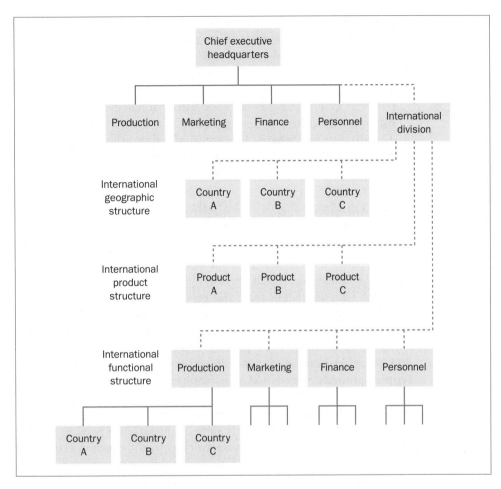

Figure 8.3 **International organisational structures**

Matrix (or mixed) structures bring together the functional, geographical and product structures and combine them in an attempt to meet the needs of a *specific activity or project*. Once that activity or project is completed, the 'team' is often disbanded and return to their original position within the divisional or other structures of the MNE.

International HRM approaches

When conducting business globally, organisations will also need to integrate HRM into their international strategy. How they do this will depend on the approach they adopt as regards HRM policies. Four approaches are often used to describe the ways in which MNEs might conduct their international HRM policies.

1 *The ethnocentric approach*. In the ethnocentric approach, all key positions in the host country subsidiary are filled by nationals of the parent company. This approach offers the most direct control by the parent company over the host country subsidiary, and is often adopted when there is felt to be a need to maintain good communications

between the headquarters of the MNE and the subsidiary. This ethnocentric approach is often followed in the early stages of internationalisation when the MNE is seeking to establish a new business or product in another country.

2 *The polycentric approach.* Here, host country nationals are recruited to manage the subsidiaries in their own country. This allows the MNE to take a lower profile in sensitive economic and political situations and helps to avoid intercultural management problems.

3 *The geocentric approach.* This approach utilises the best people for all the key jobs throughout the organisation, whatever their nationality or whatever the geographical location of the post to be filled. In this way an international executive team can be developed.

4 *The regiocentric approach.* Here the MNE divides its operations into geographic regions and moves staff within particular regions, e.g. Europe, America, Asia, rather than between regions.

Choices between these different approaches will depend on the culture, philosophy and the local conditions in which the firm operates. Vodafone has adopted the ethnocentric approach with its UK HR team and processes used as a benchmark in its ethnocentric and global model for people management. The model will see the firm's local HR teams across 25 countries adopting a standardised structure with four key areas: HR services, including administrative and process support; business partnering; centres of expertise; and 'other functions', such as health and safety. Addidas, however, uses a mainly regiocentric approach, with HRM staff familiar with the cultural context of the region of operation responsible for leading the HRM functions of the subsidiaries located within the international region and country in question. Some international companies may adopt an ethnocentric approach in some countries and a polycentric approach in others. However a key element in this choice will involve the question as to how an international firm can manage a dispersed and diverse workforce responsively and effectively, retaining a measure of overall cohesion while being sensitive to local conditions.

Some firms have sought to resolve this dilemma by maintaining an international group of HRM managers with an ethnocentric orientation at the centre, who can be moved in and out of the worldwide operations, yet at the same time devolving HRM responsibility down the line so that the firm can remain responsive to local developments. This approach is followed by BMW, as indicated in its annual report:

'(BMW) guidelines are defined and steered centrally and lived and implemented by the human resources departments and executives across the globe . . . once a management board is set up in a foreign subsidiary, the local HRM takes responsibility for management of middle management and operative levels. This includes aspects such as recruitment, training and employee relations. The key is that the (central) IHR management provides guidance and supervises the application of BMW's HR policies. Cultural issues and differences may be a challenge, and IHRM should provide means to analyse these and adjust the local HR approach accordingly' (BMW Group, Annual Report 2007).

Finding the right balance between integration and decentralisation for IHRM is complex, and the mix will depend on the following factors.

■ *Degree and type of internationalisation.* We have seen (*see* Chapter 2) that there is a range of options for international firms as to how they may expand, from exporting through to using wholly-owned subsidiaries. In general an integrated and more ethnocentric approach to HRM is often adopted for the wholly-owned subsidiary, with the MNE retaining centralised control over the way in which its employees are managed.

- *Type of industry and markets served.* Porter (1986) distinguishes the multidomestic industry, in which competition within each country is largely internal (retailing, distribution and insurance), from the global industry in which competition is worldwide (electronic equipment, branded food, defence products). Porter suggests that strategies for the global industry are more likely to involve the firm in integrating its activities worldwide, especially where strong brand images are involved. For the global industry, therefore, IHRM is more likely to be ethnocentric while for the multidomestic industry IHRM is more likely to be polycentric and to resemble that typically used in the particular country in which the subsidiary operates.
- *Characteristics of staff.* The types of employees may well influence the degree to which the IHRM function is decentralised. For example, if the employees of a subsidiary consist of highly skilled, experienced and fully committed staff, the IHRM function may be decentralised. Where, however, the employees mainly consist of unskilled and temporary staff (perhaps where the MNE has bought into a cheap labour market) then headquarters will usually wish to exercise a greater degree of control over the corporate foreign subsidiary.
- *Cultural preferences.* The degree of integration or decentralisation will also depend on the cultural preferences towards either of these approaches to management in both the organisation and in the country in which the subsidiary operates. The latter reflects Hofstede's idea of national 'cultural distance' (*see* Chapter 5), and is considered further in the context of Greece in Box 8.1.

Box 8.1 Greek national culture and decentralisation of the IHRM function

While the global nature of multinational activity may call for increased consistency, the variety of cultural environments in which the MNE operates may call for differentiation. Workplace values and behaviours are widely regarded as being influenced by national as well as corporate cultural characteristics. As Laurent (1986) claims, 'if we accept the view that human resource management (HRM) approaches are cultural artefacts reflecting the basic assumptions and values of the national culture in which organisations are embedded, international HRM becomes one of the most challenging corporate tasks in multinational organisations'.

Greece is clustered in the 'Mediterranean culture' sector of managerial models; native managers are assumed to be less individualistic and more comfortable with highly bureaucratic organisational structures in order to achieve their objectives. In Hofstede's terms, Greece is characterised by large power distance and strong uncertainty avoidance (*see* Figure 5.1, p. 174). Since the early 1960s, Greece has been the host country for many foreign firms, initially in manufacturing and more recently in services.

It is broadly accepted that management practices which reinforce national cultural values are more likely to yield better outcomes in terms of performance, with a mismatch between work unit management practices and national culture likely to reduce performance. The

Box 8.1 Continued

suggestion here is that multinationals, which have established their affiliates in Greece, will be more efficient if their management practices are better adapted to the national culture of Greece. Theory suggests that this adaptation will be better achieved where the national culture of the home country of the MNE is close to that of Greece. In other words, MNEs from collectivist, large power distance and strong uncertainty avoidance countries will be at a small cultural distance from Greece and will better integrate into the organisational culture of the Greek affiliate. The following hypothesis is therefore suggested by Kessapidou and Varsakelis (2000).

Hypothesis: MNEs from home countries at a large cultural distance from Greece will prefer to employ local managers and permit more decentralised IHRM practices.

This hypothesis would then predict that MNEs from home countries with national cultural characteristics of the individualist, small power distance and weak uncertainty avoidance variety (i.e. the opposites to Greece) will prefer to employ local managers and permit more decentralised IHRM practices.

In their analysis of the operations of 485 foreign affiliates in Greece over the years 1994–96, Kessapidou and Varsakelis found considerable evidence to support this hypothesis. MNEs from home countries at a large cultural distance from Greece (e.g. UK, the Netherlands and USA, with cultural distance factors of 4.27, 4.03 and 3.47 respectively) were much more likely to employ local managers and adopt a decentralised approach to IHRM than countries at a small cultural distance from Greece (e.g. Italy, France and Spain, with cultural distance factors of 1.46, 0.99 and 0.58 respectively).

Source: Adapted from Kessapidou and Varsakelis (2000).

pause for thought 1 Look back to Table 5.3 in Chapter 5. Which of these four approaches to IHRM might you expect an MNE which has Great Britain as its headquarters to adopt as regards an overseas affiliate in (a) Japan, (b) Canada?

Table 8.2 outlines some advantages and disadvantages of a decentralised approach to IHRM.

Figure 8.4 outlines a number of internal organisational influences which will influence the extent of integration or decentralisation of the IHRM function by MNEs.

Box 8.1 above has looked in more detail at the suggestion that national cultural attributes may also play a key role in an MNE's choice of a centralised or decentralised approach to IHRM.

Table 8.2 **Advantages and disadvantages of a 'decentralised' approach to IHRM**

Advantages	Disadvantages
Groups within the subsidiary can gain in status	Tendency to become 'exclusive'
Groups within the subsidiary become more cohesive, fostering group identity	Loss of central control, higher administrative costs as HRM function is sent 'down the line'
IHRM takes place within a culture appropriate to the local workforce and customers	Loss of organisational control and organisational identity

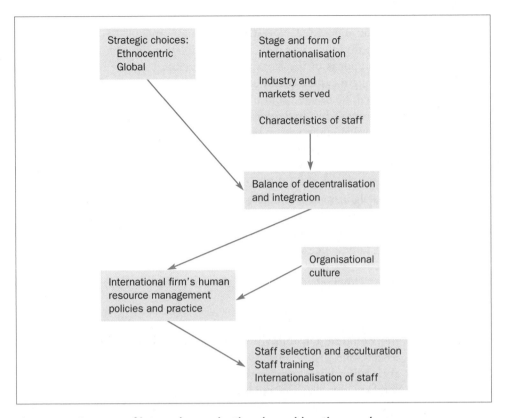

Figure 8.4 Impacts of internal organisational considerations on human resource management

Of course, corporate culture and national culture can exert separate, and sometimes opposing, influences. Morosini *et al.* (1998) suggest that specific absorptive mechanisms (such as job rotation, incentives, internal reporting systems and global coordination functions) involving people from different national backgrounds sharing a strong corporate culture can help to facilitate the cross-border transfer of routines and repertoires. Nevertheless, when national cultural characteristics are particularly strong and diverse these may dominate these internal absorptive mechanisms which seek to reinforce aspects of corporate culture irrespective of national identity. This would certainly seem to be indicated by Case Study 8.2, which considers the impacts on IHRM of theocratic (religious-based) cultures within Islamic countries.

CASE 8.2 Islamic culture and IHRM

Islam has grown enormously over the past three decades. In the countries where it is prevalent, from West Africa to the Lebanon, Malaysia to Indonesia, Muslims are returning to Islamic traditions, as a way of rediscovering their identity and as an alternative to the materialism and tensions of the twentieth century.

Islam is an all-encompassing creed, governing every aspect of public and private life. The Koran is regarded as containing the revealed words of God which can act as a guide and a steer. Nevertheless, humans are able to choose and intervene in their own destiny, and must be held responsible for the consequences of their deeds. The economic ideas of the Koran are quite close to those of the West, with the Koran advocating a system based on individual enterprise and reward. As for the Muslim individual, he or she should be guided by his/her conscience to treat employees and others responsibly. Individuals should pay a reasonable wage, charge a fair price and be restrained in the way in which they use any profits. They also have a responsibility for protecting the environment.

However, the way in which Islam is manifest is very different across nations. At the extreme end, the Taliban regime in Afghanistan does not allow women to work outside their homes, and girls do not attend schools or colleges. In Iran, however, while women have to follow a strict dress code at work and there is a policy of segregation on public occasions such as prayers, Iranian women are doing relatively well in public life. Women can go into most jobs and professions, and unlike their peers in Saudi, they can drive cars and vote.

The following work-related values of Islamic culture in Iran have been identified by Latifi (1997):

- equality before God;
- individual responsibility within a framework of cooperation with others;
- a view that people in positions of power should treat subordinates kindly, as if their subordinates are brothers or sisters;
- fatalism, but also a recognition of personal choice;
- encouragement of consultation at all levels of decision making, from family to the wider community.

Latifi closely observed a sample of Iranian managers and found traces of Islamic values in the HRM style. Iranian employees thought of their managers as sympathetic brothers and sisters or compassionate fathers and mothers. The family-like relationship seemed to have been extended to include social and teacher roles for the managers, and they were frequently involved in their subordinates' private lives and family matters. A high proportion of managers were willing to make their time and organisations available for high-school and university students who might wish to conduct a research project or acquire work experience as part of their courses. They viewed this as part of their responsibility to society and to the next generation of managers.

In Malaysia, Endot (1995) also found that Islam had filtered down to the HRM practices. One of the companies offers its employees interest-free loans for vehicle or house purchase, or for preparation for a wedding ceremony. Another organises Islamic study circles for managers. These are segregated, but help create cohesiveness of relationships among the members. Another company sends its employees on short courses in Islamic teachings, in order that the employees understand Islam and its values. Yet another organisation recruits individuals who have graduated in Islamic studies, only later exposing them to techniques of modern management.

In a study carried out in the Arab Middle East, decision-making and management–employee relationships were found to be characterised by a process of consultation, rooted in Islamic traditions. For example, the Koran asserts that those who conduct their affairs by consultation will receive favour. However, this does not take the form of the Western model of consultative decision-making. Rather consultation is used to avoid potential conflicts between executives and their subordinates: to please, placate or win over people who may be potential obstacles. It is also an information-gathering mechanism. So while consultation may occur, it usually involves only a few selected people and is not part of a hierarchical decision-making structure.

Questions

1 What type of approach to IHRM would you expect to be adopted if a Western MNE acquires an Iranian-based company which has been operating successfully for some time?

2 What results might you expect if the MNE were to use the Harvard model to evaluate the outcomes of the current HRM function within the Iranian firm? (Use commitment, competence, congruence and cost efficiencies.)

IHRM policies and practices

At this point it may be useful to consider in rather more detail some of the key elements within an IHRM programme.

■ Training and development in an international context

Obviously, training and development increases in complexity as MNEs move abroad. The type of training that takes place would usually depend on a number of factors:

■ the degree to which management is centralised;
■ the types of workers employed in subsidiaries or joint ventures;
■ the importance of branding, and the extent to which employees are expected to reflect the brand;
■ the cultural expectations of training.

In a global company, the training may well be centralised so that suppliers, employees and distributors are aware of the brand image that needs to be communicated. In Ford, for example, training programmes are set up centrally, and then translated and delivered to all main suppliers, subsidiaries and distributors. If, however, a more polycentric approach is taken, then the training may well be far more local, and more in line with the local culture.

Other problems may arise with teamworking. There has been a great deal of work done over the past three decades on how to train teams, and how to ensure that there is synergy in teamwork. Business psychologists such as Belbin, for example, have drawn up the types of characters that would make an ideal team, and have devised methods for testing the personalities of the team members in order that teams could be composed of a balance of types. In a cross-cultural context, it is not only the personality types that have to be taken into account, but also the very real cultural differences and approaches between team members. Attempts at cross-cultural team training are becoming increasingly prominent in MNEs.

A further problem for MNEs is how to ensure that employees sent abroad (expatriates) are fully immersed in the foreign culture. Many MNEs run extensive training programmes for employees going overseas, designed to provide individuals with information and experience related to local customs, cultures and work habits so that they can interact and work more effectively with local colleagues. Indeed, such programmes may also be run for spouses and children.

Research shows that the following are the most popular:

- environmental briefings used to provide information about such things as geography, climate, housing and schools;
- cultural orientation designed to familiarise the individual with cultural institutions and value systems of the host country;
- cultural assimilations to provide participants with intercultural encounters;
- language training;
- sensitivity training designed to help develop attitudinal flexibility;
- field experience which sends the participant to the country of assignment to get them used to the emotional stress of living and working with people of a different culture.

The following case study looks at the implications for IHRM within Toyota subsidiaries operating outside Japan.

CASE 8.3 Mindset of a Toyota manager revealed FT

In 1983 John Shook became the first westerner to work at Toyota's headquarters in Japan. His job was to help the Japanese carmaker transfer production to the US, which involved interpreting and explaining Toyota's legendary 'lean' manufacturing to people who had never heard of it. While even Toyota cannot escape the effects of the current recession – Fitch, the ratings agency, has just lowered its credit rating – it remains the case that since the mid-1980s, Toyota has overtaken Ford to become the US's second biggest carmaker. Every gain in its market share has come at the expense of the big three – Ford, GM and Chrysler – and it is a real possibility that they will not survive this recession in their current form.

Toyota's rise generated a flood of books, starting with *The Machine That Changed the World*, about its many tools, techniques and practices, broadening recently to a growing interest in its approach to management. Somehow, however, its 'secret' of success has remained elusive. In *Managing to Learn*, Shook, now director of the Japan technology programme at the University of Michigan, distils lessons from decades of experience of Toyota, which he tries to present in a way westerners can not only understand but also apply for themselves. Although written mainly for lean 'converts' and published by a lean specialist, this may be the first book that actually helps outsiders connect the dots and get a glimpse into how Toyota ticks. It does so using an extended invented story about how a young middle manager and his boss set about tackling a problem with the translation of technical documents from Japanese to English.

Ostensibly, it is all about their application of a single Toyota management tool – 'A3 decision making' – which forces managers to put on a single piece of paper everything anyone needs to know about a problem: why it matters, what is causing it, what we want to achieve, how to achieve it and how we will know we have been successful. The book charts the young manager's journey. He starts out jumping to a conclusion and investing his ego in promoting and defending it, only to discover he is wrong. Thanks to his boss's coaching, he realises that his real contribution lies in researching the facts and letting them speak for themselves. He must leave ego behind to become a detective who gets to the root of the problem. Then he must learn another lesson: how to build consensus around the answer and promote it entrepreneurially to the rest of the organisation.

As the story unfolds, Shook peels away Toyota's thinking and management philosophy layer by layer. Western managers think their job is to get results. Toyota thinks a manager's job is to design and sustain processes that generate these results as a matter of course. Western managers think they employ workers to do a job. Toyota employs workers to learn how to do the job better – to keep improving that process, and therefore the results. Western managers think management is about knowing the answers and telling other people what to do. Toyota disagrees again: if managers tell staff what to do they take responsibility away.

The manager's job is to help staff learn problem-solving skills and work out what they need to do for themselves. Real organisational leadership is about doing both – improving operations and developing people – at the same time in such a way that they are mutually supporting. As Shook shows, Toyota embeds the philosophy in day-to-day decision making and management tools such as the A3 so that staff have no choice but to learn it in a way they never forget.

Source: Mitchell A., 'Mindset of a Toyota manager revealed', *Financial Times*, 27 November 2008.

Questions

1 Identify some of the differences between Japanese and Western approaches to the HRM function.

2 Examine the IHRM strategies that might help to embed the Toyota management philosophy within a Western organisation.

■ Pay and international employee relations

The way in which an organisation seeks to reward its employees may be critical to its success. As Hegewisch points out:

> the pay package is one of the most obvious and visible expressions of the employment relationship; it is the main issue in the exchange between employer and employee, expressing the connection between the labour market, the individual's work and the performance of the employing organisation itself (1991: 28).

As a result of competitive pressures, organisations are constantly looking to increase the 'added value' of their employees by encouraging them to increase their efforts beyond any minimal standard. The theoretical understanding of pay and other reward structures stems from theories of motivation.

Table 8.3 Indian employment legislation and reward mechanisms

Labour law	Content
Minimum Wages Act 1948	Prescribes minimum wages for all employees in all establishments or working at home in certain employment specified in the schedule of the Act
Payment of Wages Act 1936	Regulates issues relating to time limits within which wages shall be distributed to employees and that no deductions other than those authorised by the law are made by the employers
Child Labour (Prohibition & Regulation) Act 1986	Prohibits the engagement of children in certain employments and to regulate the conditions of work of children in certain other employments
Apprentices Act 1961	Provides regulation and control of training of apprentices
Payment of Bonus Act 1965	Provides for the payment of bonuses to persons employed in certain establishments on the basis of profits or on the basis of production or productivity. The Act is applicable to establishments employing 20 or more people
Payment of Gratuity Act 1972	Provides for a scheme for the payment of gratuity to all employees in all establishments employing ten or more employees
Maternity Benefit Act 1961	Regulates the employment of women in certain establishments for a prescribed period before and after child birth and provides certain other benefits
Workmen's Compensation Act 1923	Compensation shall be provided to a workman for any injury suffered during the course of his employment or to his dependants in the case of his death

Source: Various including www.citehr.com/80534-labour-laws-india.html

To design an appropriate reward strategy for employees taking up an international position, may require a number of factors to be considered. These include a knowledge of the laws, customs, environment, and employment practices of the foreign countries; familiarity with currency relationships and the effect of inflation on compensation; an understanding of the allowances appropriate to particular countries, and so on. For example awareness of employment related legislation in the country of operation is vital to an appropriate international reward structure. India has as many as 45 labour laws at national level and close to four times that at the level of state governments (Kaushik 2006). Table 8.3 outlines some of these most important laws a human resource department in India needs to consider as regards a proposed reward structure.

The main method of drawing up a compensation package is known as the 'balance sheet' approach. This approach is, according to Reynolds (1986): 'a system designed to equalise the purchasing power of employees at comparable position levels living overseas and in the home country, and to provide incentives to offset qualitative differences between assignment locations'.

In order to achieve such 'balance', the organisation must take into account a number of factors when sending employees to a different country:

- income taxes incurred in both home and host country;
- housing allowances (which might range from financial assistance to employees to providing company housing);

- cost-of-living allowances (to make up any differences in prices between home and foreign country);
- contributions to savings, pension schemes, etc. while abroad;
- relocation allowances (including the moving, shipping and storage of personal and household items and temporary living expenses);
- education allowances for expatriate's children (e.g. language tuition and enrolment fees in the host country or boarding school fees in the home country);
- medical, emergency and security cover.

However there is arguably much more to identifying appropriate international pay and remuneration packages than merely being aware of legal pay-related requirements and equalising global purchasing power at similar positions in the organisations, as Case Study 8.4 indicates.

CASE 8.4 Reward mechanisms in cross-cultural contexts

Both India and the UK have minimum wages, but they differ a great deal from one another. The UK minimum wage *per hour* is £5.73 in 2009, whereas the Indian minimum wage *per day* is less than half of that: £2.11. A multinational operating in India must consider those laws, but also take care that its wages are competitive in the market. If it fails to do so, the skilled people will work for other companies.

Another aspect needing thought is the payment of bonuses. The UK is a short-term orientated country, whereas India is much more long-term orientated (*see* Chapter 5, p. 179). As bonuses are mostly performance-related and paid when achieving a set goal for the year, they are arguably more suitable for employees based in short-term orientated countries, such as the UK, but might offend or not be appreciated by Indian employees.

China has different priorities compared to Western societies and current motivation methods/rewards such as flexible hours, health services and pension funds need to be reconsidered. In the context of BMW, using Trompenaars model (*see* Chapter 5, p. 189) Germany is an achieving culture whereas China has an ascribing one, meaning its focus is on collectivism and moral responsibilities. Using Hofstede's model (Chapter 5, p. 174) China is a long-term orientated country compared to Germany and so dedication is valued and delayed gratification is acceptable. For instance, pay, although significant, is less appreciated in comparison to other rewards: 'pay is less important than the range of benefits (housing, food, childcare, etc.) typically provided for employees' (Harris *et al.* 2003: 96). Although Western countries are likely to be motivated by economic gains, in China this is not enough to ensure commitment. Pay should be fair but offering incentives with a higher value attached are recommended such as contributory housing payments or childcare facilities which would help maintain BMW's reputation for having the industry's largest female workforce. China is a collectivist society where 'group interests prevail over individual interests and the individual derives his/her social identity from the groups of which he/she is a member – including family, school class, work unit' (Mead 2005: 44). Therefore group rewards, such as the corporate profit-sharing scheme currently run by BMW are suitable as everyone is equally rewarded and such group

▶

rewards could be more appropriate compared to an individual focus on reward structures.

Jackson (2002) concurs with this approach, suggesting that as China is a particularistic-ascribing country, reward and promotion should be based on group performance or seniority criteria, rather than individual achievement. Further, not only financial rewards, such as pay and bonuses, should be integrated into the reward package, but also social benefits, such as 'lifetime' employment, housing allowances and insurance. Even though there are some discrepancies, awareness is needed of the new labour law and the rising bargaining power of trade unions.

New labour laws may also influence the reward mechanisms proposed, as for example the change in 2008 in labour laws in China. A new labour contract law came into effect on 1 January 2008 requiring that every employee in China must be employed based on a written contract. Oral contracts are not permitted, and the contract must include the contents of work, labour protection and working conditions, labour remuneration and conditions for the termination of a labour contract.

Article 36 limits the working time per week to 44 hours on average. This restricts work to not more than eight hours per day on five days per week plus Saturday as a half work day with four hours. Working hours may be extended due to requirements but should not exceed one hour per day. If the extension is due to special reasons, overtime should not exceed three hours per day. It is illegal to work more than nine hours overtime per week or more than 36 hours overtime per month. Thus, the longest legal workweek is set at 49 hours. Overtime is to be paid at least 150% of the normal wages. Employers are required to guarantee that staff have one day off in a week. The minimum age for employment is 16, and probationary periods may be agreed upon in the contract, yet they shall not exceed six months. Article 7 states that workers have the right to participate and organise trade unions.

Questions

1 Using the content in this Case Study and in Table 5.3 (p. 177) and Figure 5.2 (p. 179) consider how the cultural factors might influence an organisation's rewards policies.

2 How might the new 2008 Labour Laws in China influence reward related policies?

■ Appraisal

A formalised and systematic appraisal scheme will enable a regular assessment of an individual's performance, highlight potential, and identify training and development needs. A comprehensive appraisal system can provide the basis for key managerial decisions, such as those relating to the allocation of duties and responsibilities, pay, levels of supervision or delegation, promotion, training and development, and so on.

The benefits of a comprehensive appraisal system include the following:

- it can identify an individual's strengths and weaknesses, and show how these can be overcome;
- it can reveal organisational obstacles blocking progress;
- it can provide useful feedback to help improve human resource planning;
- it can improve communications by giving staff a chance to talk about expectations.

According to James (1988), performance appraisal has its roots in three key principles. People learn/work/achieve more when they are given:

1 adequate feedback as to how they are performing;
2 clear and attainable goals;
3 involvement in the setting of tasks and goals.

Again, there are cultural factors which need to be taken into account when drawing up appraisal schemes for workers in foreign countries.

Performance appraisal is, for example, less emphasised in India where there is relatively low coverage of employees under formal performance appraisal. India is very seniority based, so that the older a person, the more respectful and rewarding the work is expected to become, arguably restricting the perceived relevance of performance appraisal to career progression (Chatterjee, 2007). The 'reservation system', which seeks to allocate employment opportunities to specific social groups (e.g. 15% of jobs must go to scheduled casts) may be another factor restricting career planning within Indian organisations.

Table 8.4 highlights the cultural influences on appraisal systems with a key aspect being whether the country is regarded as 'low context' or 'high context' (*see* Chapter 5, Table 5.1).

Table 8.4 **Cultural variations: performance appraisals**

Dimension General	USA Low context	Saudi Arabia High context	Japan High context
Objective of performance appraisal.	Fairness, employee development.	Placement.	Direction of company/ employee development.
Who does appraisal?	Supervisor.	Manager several levels up. Appraiser has to know employee well.	Mentor and supervisor. Appraiser has to know employee well.
Authority of appraiser.	Presumed in supervisory role or position. Supervisor takes slight lead.	Reputation important (prestige is determined by nationality, sex, family, tribe, title, education). Authority of appraiser important.	Respect accorded by employee to supervisor or appraiser. Done co-equally.
How often?	Once a year.	Once a year.	Developmental or periodically once a month. Evaluation appraisal after first 12 years.
Assumptions.	Objective appraiser is fair.	Subjective appraiser more important than objective. Connections are more important.	Objective and subjective. Japanese can be trained in anything.
Manner of communication and feedback.	Criticism direct. Criticism may be in writing. Objective, authentic.	Criticism subtle. Older more likely to be direct. Criticism not given.	Criticism subtle. Criticism given verbally. Observe formalities in writing.
Rebuttals.	American will rebut appraisal.	Saudi Arabian will rebut appraisal.	Japanese would rarely rebut appraisal.
Praise.	Given individually.	Given individually.	Given to entire group.
Motivators.	Money and position. Career development.	Loyalty to supervisor.	Internal excellence.

Source: Adapted from Harris and Moran (1991).

Work practice in an international context

Flexible working is an increasingly sought after approach within many countries. The strategic IHRM director may have to evaluate the impacts of adopting flexible working on the organization as a whole, especially in times of global recession. Case Study 8.5 suggests some positive potential from using this approach, especially in times of global downturn.

CASE 8.5   Flexible working and IHRM   **FT**

Joe Macri, a senior marketing manager at Microsoft, holds regular meetings with his European management team from his office in Dublin. Until a few months ago, they used to meet at Amsterdam airport, the easiest venue for face-to-face meetings. Now they get together just once or twice a year. All other meetings are 'virtual', using a multi-camera system that allows everyone in the meeting to see everyone else at the same time. 'Now, if anyone falls asleep – and it has been known in past phone conferences – we can all see who it is,' says Mr Macri, Europe general manager for business marketing. 'It saves money, increases productivity and reduces our carbon footprint as a company,' he says. 'And I no longer have to get up at some awful hour to catch my flight to the Netherlands.'

This is just one way in which companies are economising during the downturn. Where once managers would have been sizing up headcounts from the first hint of recession, now there is evidence – even among the string of job cuts announced recently – that companies are trying to hold on to employees in the knowledge that competition for good people will be fiercer than ever in the upturn.

So what practical choices are available to managers in a recession, short of cutting jobs? One option is to investigate possibilities for flexible working. Some companies already use a proportion of temporary and contract workers. Most of these employees understand that they are in the vanguard of corporate job reductions since their work and pay reflects fluctuations in supply and demand more acutely than that of full-time staff. BT, the UK telecommunications group, announced a week ago that it had cut 4000 mainly temporary and contract jobs and planned to shed another 6000 before the end of the financial year.

Within the contract market, however, the news was received with a sense of pragmatism. The Professional Contractors Group, representing more than 18,000 freelance workers in the UK, described the cutback as 'real flexible labour at work in a downturn'. John Brazier, managing director of PCG, said: 'BT's announcement is not good news for any contractor who may be affected by the cuts. However, when you choose to go freelance, you opt for the benefits, such as being your own boss, making more money and having the freedom and variety, as well as the pitfalls, which include less security and less certainty.'

As John Philpott, chief economist at the Chartered Institute for Personnel and Development, points out, temporary staff usually bear the brunt of an economic downturn. 'But contract staff will also be first in line to be hired when the economy eventually recovers since employers will at first be reluctant to recruit people on permanent contracts,' he says.

Meantime, some companies are trying to use their full-time staff more flexibly. BT has some 14,500 employees who work solely from home and 80,000 who have the choice to work part of the time from home. The company says that homeworking has increased productivity, reducing overheads and improving staff retention. 'We can see the difference now at BT centre,' says Bill Murphy, managing director of BT Business. 'Mondays and Fridays are quiet but on Tuesdays, Wednesdays and Thursdays the building is packed. That's a classic example of people working elsewhere on Monday and Friday.' This has led to new challenges in management, he says. Employees need to be assessed on their output and the quality of their work rather than on time spent doing a job.

Work Wise UK, a not-for-profit organisation set up by the IT Forum foundation, has calculated that the average cost of running a desk in a UK office is £7000 a year. In central London it is something approaching £10,000 because of higher overheads. 'If you employ 100 people and can withdraw 20 desks in a "hot-desking" arrangement, that's a saving of £140,000 a year,' says Phil Flaxton, Work Wise chief executive. Some start-ups eschew the fixed costs of offices altogether. David Lennan, managing director of Business HR, a consultancy without offices that employs 30 home-based consultants, says: 'The business is visible through our website while our consultants are based all over the country, accessible through a reception number. We meet together a lot, often on clients' premises but also in hotels and coffee shops so everyone knows what is happening.'

While the business is often consulted on alternative ways of working Lennan has noticed an increase recently in clients seeking more information on redundancy procedures. Interim managers, flexible workers by definition, are sometimes brought in to make the hard decisions in restructuring, including job cutting, admits Paul Botting, chairman of the Interim Management Association. 'They bring an independence and objectivity to the workplace. An experienced interim will have worked in many different sectors and is familiar with the kind of restructuring that happens in a recession.

Flexible working seems here to stay but there is little room for sentiment in the employment of contract and temporary staff. Wolfgang Clement, chairman of the Adecco Institute, a research body established by the Adecco staffing group, says that, while qualified employees remain in demand, temporary work prospects for semi-skilled workers are declining. 'Flexible labour markets help get over a crisis more quickly,' he says. 'But, in this kind of market, people shouldn't be in doubt that qualifications and skills are the best protection for the worker and the most reliable guarantees for job security.

Source: Donkin, R., 'Flexible working saves jobs whilst trimming the fat', *Financial Times*, 27 November 2008.

Question

Examine the advantages and disadvantages of flexible working within the IHRM portfolio.

Useful websites

Now try the self-check questions for this chapter on the website at www.pearsoned.co.uk/wall. You will also find further resources as well as useful weblinks.

The human resource network has a number of brief guides on HRM issues: *www.hnetwork.co.uk*

Many human resources issues are covered at: *www.lpd.co.uk*
A wide range of motivational theorists are considered at: *www.westrek.hypermart.net*

Useful key texts

Chatterjee, P. (2007) www.inter-asia.net/conferences/2007-inter-asia-cultural-studies-society-shanghai-conference/speakers/

Daniels, J., Radebaugh, L. and Sullivan, D. (2006) *International Business* (11th edn), Pearson Prentice Hall, especially Chapter 21.

Harris, H., Brewster, C. and Sparrow, P. (2003) *International Human Resource Management*, CIPD.

Hill, C. (2006) *International Business: Competing in the Global Marketplace* (5th edn), McGraw-Hill Irwin, especially Chapter 18.

Jackson, J. (2002) 'Reticence in second language case discussions: anxiety and aspirations', *System*, 30, 65–84.

Mead, W.R. (2005) www.articles.latimes.com/writers/walter-russell-mead

Morrison, J. (2006) *The International Business Environment* (2nd edn), Palgrave, especially Chapters 1 and 5.

Rugman, A. and Collinson, R. (2009) *International Business* (5th edn), FT Prentice Hall, especially Chapter 12.

Tayeb, M. (2000) *International Business: Theories, Policies and Practices*, Financial Times Prentice Hall, especially Chapters 19 and Part VI.

Wild, J., Wild, K. and Han, J. (2006) *International Business: The Challenges of Globalization* (3rd edn), FT Prentice Hall, especially Chapter 16.

Other texts and sources

Armstrong, M. (1999) *A Handbook of Human Resource Management* (7th edn), Kogan Page.

Bassi, L. and McMurrer, D. (2007) 'Maximising your Return on People', *Harvard Business Review*, March p. 115.

Beer, M., Spector, B., Lawrence, P.R., Quinn Mills, D. and Walton, R.E. (1984) *Managing Human Assets*, Free Press.

Bossidy, L. (2007) 'What your leader expects of you', *Harvard Business Review*, April p. 58.

Boxall, P. (1992) 'Strategic HRM: Beginnings of a New Theoretical Sophistication', *Human Resource Management Journal*, vol. 2, no. 3, pp. 60–79.

Boxall, P. and Purcell, J. (2008) *Strategy and Human Resource Management*, Palgrave Macmillan.

Brett, J., Behfar, K. and Kern, M. (2006) 'Managing Multicultural Teams', *Harvard Business Review*, November p. 84.

Brewster, C. and Hegewisch, A. (1994) *Policy and Practice in European Human Resource Management*, Routledge/Thomson Learning, p. 6.

Dowling, P. and Schuler, R. (1990) *International Dimensions of Human Resource Management*, PWS-Kent.

Endot, S. (1995) 'The Islamisation Process in Malaysia', Ph.D. thesis, University of Bradford.

Erickson, T. and Gratton, L. (2007) 'What it Means to Work Here', *Harvard Business Review*, March p. 104.

Foot, M. and Hook, C. (2003) *Introducing Human Resource Management* (3rd edn), Longman.

Goffee, R. and Jones, G. (2007) 'Leading Clever People', *Harvard Business Review*, March p. 72.

Harding, D. and Rouse, T. (2007) 'Human Due Diligence', *Harvard Business Review*, April p. 124.

Harris, P.R. and Moran, R.T. (1991) *Managing Cultural Differences*, Gulf Publishing.

Hegewisch, A. (1991) 'The Decentralisation of Pay Bargaining: European Comparisons', *Personnel Review*, vol. 20, no. 6.

Hendry, J. and Pettigrew, A. (1990) 'Human Resource Management: An Agenda for the 1990s', *International Journal of Human Resource Management*, vol. 1, no. 1.

James, G. (1988) *Performance Appraisal*, Occasional Paper 40, ACAS Work Research Unit.

Kaushik, B. (2006) 'Teacher Truancy in India: The Role of Cultural Norms and Economic Incentives', Working Paper, Centre for Analytic Economics, Cornell University.

Kessapidou, S. and Varsakelis, N. (2000) 'National Culture, Choice of Management and Business Performance: The Case of Foreign Firms in Greece', in *Dimensions of International Competitiveness: Issues and Policies*, Lloyd Reason, L. and Wall, S. (eds), Edward Elgar.

Latifi, F. (1997) 'Management Learning in Natural Context', Ph.D. thesis, Henley Management College, cited in Tayeb, M. (2000).

Laurent, A. (1986) 'The Cross-cultural Puzzle of International Human Resource Management', *Human Resource Management*, 25.

McDonald, F. (2000) 'E-commerce: The Challenge for Human Resource Management', *British Economy Survey*, vol. 29, no. 2.

Mendenhall, M. (2000) *Mapping the Terrain of IHRM: A Call for Ongoing Dialogue*, Paper presented at 15th Workshop on Strategic HRM, Fontainebleau, France, 30 March–1 April.

Miles, S. and Watkins, M. (2007) 'The Leadership Team: Complementary Strengths or Conflicting Agendas?', *Harvard Business Review*, April p. 90.

Morosini, P., Scott, S. and Harbir, S. (1998) 'National Cultural Distance and Cross-border Acquisition Performance', *Journal of International Business*, vol. 29, no. 1.

OECD (1998) *The Economic Impact of Electronic Commerce*, OECD, Paris.

Oechsler, W.A. (2000) *Strategic Human Resource Management in an Age of Flexible Employment*, Paper presented at 15th Workshop on Strategic HRM, Fontainebleau, France, 30 March–1 April.

Parsons, G. and Pascale, R. (2007) 'Crisis at the Summit', *Harvard Business Review*, March, p. 80.

Poole, M. (1990) 'Human Resource Management in an International Perspective', *International Journal of Human Resource Management*, vol. 1, no. 1.

Porter, M.E. (1986) *Competition in Global Industries*, Harvard Business School Press.

Reynolds, C. (1986) 'Compensation of Overseas Personnel', in *Handbooks of Human Resource Administration* (2nd edn), Farnularo, J. (ed.), McGraw-Hill.

Segalla, M. (1999) 'National Cultures, International Business', in *Mastering Global Business*, Financial Times Prentice Hall.

Sull, D. and Spinosa, C. (2007) 'Promise-based Management: The Essence of Execution', *Harvard Business Review*, April p. 78.

United Nations Conference on Trade and Development (UNCTAD), *World Investment Report* (annual publication).

United Nations Development Programme (UNDP), *Human Development Report* (annual publication), OUP.

World Bank, *World Development Report* (annual publication).

Chapter 9

International marketing

By the end of this chapter you should be able to:

- outline the principal activities of marketing;
- differentiate between international marketing and domestic marketing;
- conduct some basic international market research;
- outline the key stages in international marketing;
- specify the key elements in the international marketing mix and discuss how to balance them.

Introduction

Many people see marketing in terms of the advertising that accompanies products – such as that seen on advertising hoardings scattered throughout the world, or encountered on television, radio and the Internet. In fact, marketing is a far more sophisticated and complex activity and for many organisations can mean the difference between success and failure.

The Chartered Institute of Marketing (CIM) defines marketing as 'the management process responsible for identifying and satisfying customer needs profitably'.

The American Marketing Association's definition is: 'The process of planning and executing the conception, pricing, promotion and distribution of ideas, goods and services to create exchanges that satisfy individual and organisational goals.'

Hill and O'Sullivan (2003) describe marketing as: 'a business philosophy that regards customer satisfaction as the key to successful trading and advocates the use of management practices that help identify and respond to customer needs'.

Arguably at least three major elements are involved in the marketing role.

1 *Customer orientation.* This sounds obvious, but in practice many organisations can become so preoccupied with manufacturing processes or technology, that they lose sight of what the customer wants, leaving themselves vulnerable to the activities of competitors who have a keener eye for customer needs.

2 *Integrated effort.* A key role of marketers is to build bridges between the requirements of the customer and the capabilities of the organisation. For example, senior

managers may not have a marketing orientation; they might focus on keeping costs down, as the route to success, when what is actually required might be more investment in research and design, or more stock on the shelves. 'Integrated effort' means a focus on marketing throughout the organisation.

3 *Goal focus.* Many business activities can be focused on achieving short-term profit, rather than looking to the longer-term strategic aims of the organisation. Marketers may play a part in keeping these longer-term strategic aims in focus.

The principal activities of marketing

We have seen that marketing is an integrated activity that takes place throughout the organisation and seeks to align customer needs with the capabilities and goals of the organisation. We can therefore break marketing down into the following activities.

■ Analysis

Market analysis can itself be broken down into at least three elements.

1 *Environmental analysis.* This may involve scanning the environment for risks and opportunities, and seeking to identify factors outside the firm's control (*see also* Chapters 4–6).

2 *Buyer behaviour.* Firms need to have a profile of their existing and potential customer base, and to know how and why their customers purchase. Marketing seeks to identify the buyers, their potential motivation for purchase, their educational levels, income, class, age and many other factors which might influence the decision to purchase.

3 *Market research.* This is the process by which much of the information about the firm's customers and its environment is collected. Without such market research, organisations would have to make guesses about their customers. Such research may involve using data which already exist (secondary data) or using surveys and other methods to collect entirely new data (primary data).

■ Strategy

Once the environment has been scanned, then the organisation must develop a marketing strategy to give a sense of direction for marketing activity. The concepts of market segmentation and marketing mix invariably appear in such strategies.

Market segmentation

Major decisions need to be taken as to which *market segments* to target. A market segment is a group of potential customers who have certain characteristics in common, for example being within a certain age range, income range or occupational profile (*see* Box 9.1). Some of these market segments may be identified as more likely to purchase that product than others. When these segments have been identified, the organisation needs to decide whether one segment or a number of segments are to be targeted. Once that strategic decision is made, then the product can be positioned to meet the particular needs or wants which characterise that segment. The task here is to ensure that the product has a particular set of characteristics which make it competitive with other products in the market.

Box 9.1   Market segmentation

Producers tend to define markets broadly, but within these markets are groups of people who have more specific requirements. Market segmentation is the process by which a total market is broken down into separate groups of customers having identifiably different product needs, using characteristics such as income, age, sex, ethnicity and so on.

Occupational profile

There are many different methods of segmenting a market. One widely-used technique is to classify people according to the occupation of the head of the household as shown in Table 9.1 below, since market research suggests that consumer buying behaviour changes as individuals move from one such group or 'class' to another.

Table 9.1 Occupation of head of household

Group	Description	% of population
A	Higher managerial and professional	3
B	Middle management	11
C_1	Supervisory and clerical	22
C_2	Skilled manual	32
D	Semi-skilled and manual workers	23
E	Pensioners, unemployed	9

VALS framework

Originally developed by Arnold Mitchell in the US in the 1960s, this framework has been much refined and is increasingly used by national and international marketers. It focuses on psychological, demographic and life-style factors to segment consumer groups.

The latest version of VALS segments the English-speaking population aged 18 or older into eight consumer groups.

- *Innovators* – High self-esteem, take charge, sophisticated, curious. Purchases reflect cultivated tastes for up-market, niche products and services.
- *Thinkers* – Motivated by ideals, mature, well educated and reflective. Purchases favour durability, functionality and value.
- *Believers* – Strongly traditional and respect authority. Choose familiar products and established brands.
- *Achievers* – Goal-oriented lifestyles centred on family and career. Purchase premium products that demonstrate success to their peers.
- *Strivers* – Trendy and fun-loving. Purchase stylish products that emulate the purchasers of higher income groups.
- *Experiencers* – Unconventional, active and impulsive. Purchase fashionable products and those related to socialising and entertainment.
- *Makers* – Practical, responsible and self-sufficient. Purchase basic products, reflecting value rather than luxury.
- *Survivors* – Lead narrowly-focused lives with few resources, seek safety and security. Purchase low-cost, well-known brands (i.e. exhibit brand loyalty) and seek out available discounted products.

Segmentation has allowed the growth of small specialist or 'niche' markets. As people have become more affluent, they have been prepared to pay the higher price for a product that meets their precise requirements. The growth of niche markets has also been important in supporting the existence of small firms. In many cases the large firm has found many of these segments to be too small to service profitably.

pause for thought 1	Explain what is meant by the following terms: benefit segmentation; behaviour segmentation; geodemographic segmentation; lifestyle segmentation.

Marketing mix

Strategy will also involve selecting a suitable *marketing mix*, which will take into account the following factors:

- the product itself (what particular defining characteristics should the product have?);
- price (what pricing strategies might be pursued?);
- promotional activity (how do we make consumers aware of this product?);
- place (is it available to key customers?).

These four elements are often referred to as the '4 Ps' and are considered in more detail in the context of international marketing strategies (*see below*). However, they can also play a part in the shorter-term action/reaction patterns ('tactics') of firms in the context of marketing responses to the product life cycle (Table 9.2).

Table 9.2 **Marketing responses to the product life cycle**

	Introduction	*Growth*	*Maturity*	*Decline*
Marketing emphasis	Create product awareness Encourage product trial	Establish high-market share	Fight off competition; generate profits	Minimise marketing expenditure
Product strategy	Introduce basic products	Improve features of basic products	Design product versions for different segments	Rationalise the product range
Pricing strategy	Price skimming or price penetration	Reduce prices enough to expand the market and establish market share	Match or beat the competition	Reduce prices further
Promotional strategy	Advertising and sales promotional to end-users and dealers	Mass media advertising to establish brand image	Emphasise brand strengths to different segments	Minimal level to retain loyal customers
Distribution strategy (Place)	Build selective distribution outlets	Increase the number of outlets	Maintain intensive distribution	Rationalise outlets to minimise distribution costs

Tactics

The tactics to be used are a shorter-term and more detailed extension of the marketing strategy. Many of these 'tactics' can involve individual elements of the '4 Ps'.

- *Product tactics* may involve attempts to utilise or modify the various stages (introduction, growth, maturity, decline) of the 'product life cycle'. For example, attempts may be made to extend the 'maturity stage' by finding new markets for existing products, new uses for the products and/or modifying the product.
- *Price tactics* may involve selecting particular pricing approaches for the product. For instance, 'price skimming' may be adopted whereby the price is initially set at a high level to 'skim' as much revenue and profit out of the product as possible. Alternatively, 'price penetration' may be used whereby a low price is set in order to reach as large a market as possible in a short period of time. 'Discriminatory pricing' may also be considered where the same product is priced lower in some markets than in others (e.g. lower price in those market segments with a higher price elasticity of demand – *see* Box 9.2, pp. 361–2).
- *Promotion tactics* may involve the degree of emphasis given to personal selling, advertising, public relations, sales promotion, etc. 'Push' tactics might focus on the producer offering incentives to key players in each distributional 'channel' to promote their products (e.g. the firm may offer incentives to wholesalers so that they 'push' the firm's products to retailers, etc.). 'Pull' tactics focus on the final consumer, the idea being to stimulate consumer demands which will then stimulate ('pull') retailers/wholesalers into stocking the firm's products.
- *Place tactics* might involve placing a particular emphasis on one or more *distributional channels* for the products in question. For example pre-eminence in distributional policy might be given to distributional channels such as direct selling, producer to retailer, producer to wholesaler or franchising.

■ Planning and management

These various marketing activities need to be integrated throughout the organisation, and this can only be done through careful planning and managing of the whole process.

Planning is the process of assessing market opportunities and matching them with the resources and capabilities of the organisation in order to achieve its objectives. However, planning is not just a one-off exercise. It needs to be integrated into the ever-shifting environment of the firm so that new issues are constantly addressed and met. Forecasts made at this stage will have a major effect on production, financial decisions, research and development and human resource planning.

Managing the process can involve many aspects. For example, in order for the planning to be ongoing, the whole process needs to be monitored to ensure that customer needs are being met effectively. This may involve measuring the outcomes of marketing strategies against objectives that may have been set at the strategic stage, for example, checking whether specific targets have been met for individual products. Customer surveys may also be used to audit the quality of the services delivered. Whatever the method, it is important that monitoring is built into the plan, so that major or minor adjustments can be made. Managing may also involve *organising* the marketing function, for example allocating different tasks to different individuals or different departments.

International marketing

We have outlined the general activities of the marketing process, but how do these apply to international markets? While the basic activities remain the same, the picture is far more complex. International marketing can simply be defined as involving marketing activities that cross national borders. However, such marketing activities can take place at different levels.

- Firms exporting to international markets but which have the majority of their sales in the domestic market. Here the international market is considered secondary to the domestic market.
- Multinational enterprises which have operations and sales worldwide and which regard the home or host country as but one of many equally important market environments.
- Firms (usually MNEs) which seek to adopt global marketing strategies. The basis of global marketing is to identify products or services for which similarities across several markets enable a single, global, marketing strategy to be pursued. Examples today might include Coca-Cola, Heinz, Kellogg's, McDonald's, Marlboro, etc. All the examples given are of consumer products but the potential for globalisation in industrial markets is also great, in particular where there is little or no need to adapt a product to local needs. Thus, a global market exists in areas such as telecommunications, computers, pharmaceuticals, construction machinery, bio-engineering, etc.

pause for thought 2   Can you list some of the differences between domestic marketing and international marketing?

A global branding approach may even be adopted by the firm itself on behalf of all its product portfolio. Case Study 9.1 looks at the global rebranding of British Petroleum (BP), an initiative which first began as far back as 2000 and continues today.

CASE 9.1   Global rebranding of BP

In recent times the image of oil-based products has hardly been positive. Fossil fuels have been linked to CO_2 emissions and therefore to problems such as global warming and the emission of other hazardous substances. This is one of the factors which led BP Amoco to try to differentiate itself from the rest of the oil sector by looking for more environmentally-friendly solutions to providing energy, such as cleaner fuels, solar power and hydrogen cell technology. In addition, the company has changed dramatically over recent years through a series of mergers and acquisitions, which brought together the former British Petroleum, Amoco Corporation, Atlantic Richfield Corporation (ARCO) and Burmah Castrol. The then Chief Executive Sir John Browne spent over £100 million in the two years following the launch of the rebranding initiative in 2000 on a new unified global brand – including a new logo – a makeover for its petrol stations and a media advertising blitz. The new logo has been named the Helios mark after the Greek sun god and is designed to signify dynamic

▶

energy from oil to gas and solar and its initial advertising campaign carried the slogan 'Beyond Petroleum'.

Although these were the official reasons for this rebranding given by the company's Britannic House headquarters, it was widely believed that BP had ambitions outside of the energy field, and that the new logo would aptly cover a growing product portfolio as much as a hydrocarbon group. In fact, a mini supermarket chain did materialise because BP opened up convenience outlets at all its major petrol stations as part of ambitions to increase retail revenues by 10%. The BP Connect stores have featured in-store e-kiosks where customers can check weather and traffic conditions and shop online and in-store cafés offering freshly-made pastries, made-to-order hot snacks and freshly-ground gourmet coffee. Even solar panels have been embedded in the transparent canopies above the pumps to generate clean electricity directly from light to power the pumps and lights.

Many believe the most important reason for BP rebranding itself globally is an acceptance that the traditional image of the oil company has become a negative one in the hearts and minds of the consumer. Petrol prices have been extremely high in recent years (only falling in late 2008) and are meeting consumer resistance and there is also a growing demand throughout the business sector for a social and ethical dimension in all that is done.

Further, customers believe that one petrol is much the same as another, making it almost impossible to build brand loyalty, as indicated by the fact that BP was 58th in a recent survey by consultant Interbrand on globally-recognised product names.

Such rebranding is good business practice, and is being done by every truly successful brand around the world, in the view of consultancy group Wolff Olins. Brands such as Starbucks, Disney or Virgin are despised by a few but liked by millions. In a market filled with coffee bars, Starbucks stands for sociability as well as beverages. Disney stands for much more than cartoons and theme parks. It stands for fun – while Sir Richard Branson's Virgin is nothing if not youthful and irreverent. It can sell anything its founder comes up with – records, airlines, financial services, mobile phones and even energy.

BP argues that it is not mistaken in spending all that cash on rebranding, but it does raise the question of whether the 'Beyond Petroleum' line it included in the initial advertising was correct. It points people in an interesting direction but does not explain what BP stands for, says Mr Jones. The challenge over the next few years will be to fine tune the message so that consumers understand what idea they are buying into – and, having set a new standard delivering on that, consumers do not like to be let down. Nike is seen as a brand that represents more than shoes; it represents winning. Allegations that it was using low-cost labour from poor countries damaged the company's name.

BP is engaged in some of the most politically sensitive countries in the world, such as Colombia, where it has been accused by charities of not doing enough to halt human rights abuses. The possibility that BP might drill in environmentally sensitive areas such as the Arctic National Wildlife Refuge, were it opened up for exploration, have also led to protest at its annual general meeting from green-fingered shareholders. BP is seeking to walk the tightrope between making spectacular financial gains and being seen by the wider community as a company that cares for both customers and employees. Although it has made large numbers of redundancies after taking over first Amoco, then Arco and then Burmah Castrol, it did so by awarding generous financial packages.

Questions

1 Why has BP undertaken such global rebranding?

2 Comment on the prospects for the success of this strategy.

We return to issues of brand value later in the chapter (p. 355).

■ Reasons for international marketing

Obviously international marketing activities at all these levels involve additional risks and uncertainties as compared to selling in a domestic market only. It may be worth briefly reviewing the reasons why firms commonly seek to extend the geographical scale of their marketing activities.

■ *Increasing the size of the market.* Developing new markets abroad may permit the firm to fully exploit scale economies (*see* Chapter 7), which is particularly important when these are substantial for that product. In some cases the minimum efficient size for a firm's production may be greater than the total sales potential of the domestic market. In this case the firm's average costs can only be reduced to their lowest level by finding extra sales in overseas markets.

■ *Extending the product life cycle.* Finding new markets abroad may help extend the maturity stage of the product life cycle. This can be particularly important when domestic markets have reached 'saturation point' for a product.

■ *Supporting international specialisation.* In an attempt to reduce overall production costs, separate elements of an overall product may be produced in large scale in different geographical locations worldwide. For example, labour-intensive components will often be produced in low-cost labour locations, whereas capital-intensive components are more likely to be produced in high-technology locations. The final product, once assembled, must by definition be marketed internationally to achieve the huge sales volumes which are a pre-requisite for international specialisation.

■ *Establishing first-mover advantages.* From a less cost and more market-oriented perspective, being the first entrant within an overseas market may be an advantage. By becoming a 'first mover' a firm may make it difficult for new entrants to compete. For example, advantages include established customer loyalty, greater choice in terms of suppliers and the experience that comes with being the first entrant. The UK cider producer HP Bulmer, became a first mover when they decided to produce cider in Qufu, China. The company established a joint venture with the Chinese firm San Kong Brewery in the knowledge that they would be the first foreign company to produce cider in China.

■ *Helping reduce investment pay-back periods.* Finding overseas markets helps achieve high volume sales early in the product life cycle, thereby reducing the payback period needed to return the initial capital outlay and making many investment projects more attractive. This may help to compensate for modern trends towards shorter product life cycles which are tending to inhibit investment expenditure.

■ *Reducing stock-holding costs.* Overseas markets may provide new sales outlets for surplus stocks (inventories), thereby reducing warehousing and other stock-holding costs.

Decision making and international marketing

It is often said that at least five decisions must potentially be made by those involved in the international marketing process (*see* Figure 9.1), namely:

1 whether to internationalise;
2 which foreign market(s) to enter;
3 how to enter these foreign markets (market-entry strategies);
4 what international marketing mix to adopt (the 4 Ps);
5 how to implement, coordinate and control the international marketing programme.

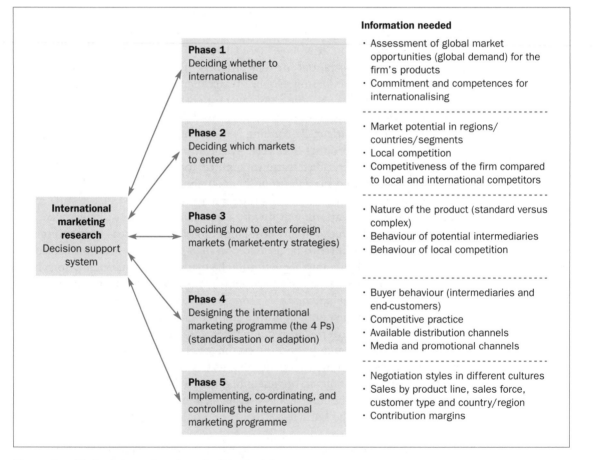

Figure 9.1 **Major international marketing decisions**
Source: Tayeb (2000).

International marketing research can be regarded as a support activity, providing evidence and analysis of patterns and trends to support these five key decisions. We might usefully review each of these decisions and support mechanisms, some of which are considered in rather more detail elsewhere in this book.

■ International marketing research

This function supports all five 'phases' outlined in Figure 9.1 providing vital information and analysis to underpin the decisions associated with each phase. A key aim of market research is to reduce the risk involved in taking effective decisions in these five phases. This is particularly important where the environment in which the firm is operating is unfamiliar. Market research can be divided into two types: desk research which means using information which has already been gathered for another purpose (secondary data), and field research, which involves obtaining information specifically directed towards a particular marketing issue and which is usually original (primary data).

From Figure 9.1 we can see from the 'Information needed' column that data will be required on both a macro level (e.g. GNP, demographic changes, inflation, exchange rates, etc.) and a micro level (e.g. firm sizes, productivities, cost structures, competitor reactions, consumer buying patterns, distribution channels available, etc.).

Desk research

There are numerous sources of secondary information available to the international marketer.

- *International organisations.* The OECD, UN, EU, IMF and World Bank all collect large volumes of mainly macro data on an annual basis for both developed and developing countries. For example, the EU, apart from its many statistical publications, has established over 300 'European Documentation Centres' around the UK (and similar centres in other member countries). These centres are regularly updated with documents (often originating from the European Commission and Parliament) which impact on the single market.
- *National publications.* In the UK National Statistics (formerly the Office for National Statistics (ONS)) publishes detailed annual (sometimes monthly or quarterly) data on most types of economic and socio-economic indicator. Similar information is available in most advanced industrialised economies.
- *National Trade Associations and Chambers of Commerce* (or equivalents). These business agencies in the various countries can be invaluable in providing up-to-date market information.
- *Trade journals.* These often provide up-to-the-minute profiles of various aspects of industries, countries or specific market sectors.
- *Financial Press.* The various FT indices and ratios (and their equivalents elsewhere) provide an invaluable source of up-to-date information on firms and industrial sectors.
- *Internet.* Finally, of course, there is the Internet, though information found here is only as good as the researcher who is using it. Remember that many of the Web pages are commercially-based, and companies will not reveal any secrets that they feel might be useful to their competitors.

The major problems with secondary data are that it is available to competitors, it may be of limited value in terms of comparability between countries, and there may be large gaps in statistical coverage in certain countries. However, it is quick, easy to access, and may save valuable time as compared to field research.

Field research

Primary data may be obtained from a variety of sources. The main advantage of field research is that it is customised to the firm and is unavailable to competitors. However, it is expensive and time consuming and may present particular problems, such as collecting data in some national cultures which have little experience of using scientifically-based research methods. Survey methods that assume a high level of literacy, certain education levels, access to telephones, or a willingness to respond by those surveyed, may need to be reassessed in some international situations.

- *Research agencies.* In most countries there are many enterprises that are specialists in research. Companies can specify the type of data they are interested in and the agency will carry out the research on their behalf.
- *Company networks/personnel.* Original data may be obtained from company networks (e.g. suppliers who also work for rival firms). Sometimes members of a company are sent to investigate the nature of specified markets through 'shopping trips' which, while not rigorously scientific, can help the organisation 'get a feel' for the types of markets they may enter.

Case Study 9.2 reviews some of the benefits from data collection and data analysis in market research.

CASE 9.2   A better burger thanks to data crunching   FT

HG Wells foresaw a time when what he called 'statistical thinking' would play a key role in the running of society. Those who think of statistics as a way of keeping tabs on Albanian coal output will see this as one of his less inspirational predictions. But for anyone who believes in the power of data to create a better world where evidence reigns supreme, the good news is that the future is already here. Or at least the foundations are, in the form of data mining: the extraction of insight from data gathering during the operation of everything from airlines and bookstores to supermarkets and schools.

This was all but impossible before machine-readable records and computing power to crunch the staff. But now we have both, and it is starting to transform our lives, as Yale Law School econometrician Ian Ayres suggests in his book *Super Crunchers* (2007). Two statistical techniques lie at the heart of the revolution: regression and randomisation. The use of regression analysis uncovers connections between say, the chances of people defaulting on their mortgage and factors influencing that risk, such as age, income and type of work.

Airlines, supermarkets, car hire companies and even dating agencies all run computerised 'regression analysis' on their raw data to identify the key factors behind everything from sales of dog food to success in love. The effects can be felt by consumers, says Ayres, in subtle changes in the way they are treated. For example, when airlines cancel flights, some no longer woo faithful frequent fliers, but focus instead on the customers that regression analysis reveals are most likely never to fly with the airline again. Similarly, credit card users wanting to close accounts are assessed using regression methods – only those predicted to be profitable get the sweet-talk.

To reveal the influence of a single factor – say, some new education policy – in the presence of lots of extraneous effects, data miners turn to *randomisation*. People are randomly allocated to two groups: those who will and those who won't be exposed to the new policy. Differences between the two groups can then be put down to the effect on the policy change, as all the other factors have been evenly distributed between them. Medical scientists have used the technique for decades to identify life-saving new therapies, via patients recruited into randomised controlled trials (RCTs). Now its power is being seized on by business. Ads, mail-shot campaigns, even book titles, are tested before launch in colossal RCTs involving hundreds of thousands of people. National policy programmes are starting to be based on RCT results. Ayres cites Mexico's Progresa programme, which targets grants and nutritional supplements on families whose kids stay at school.

Ayres balances his infectious enthusiasm with tales of where data mining can and has gone wrong. Correlation is not causation and 'garbage in' still means 'garbage out' – as demonstrated by the salutary story of how honest mistakes led to a spurious correlation between wider gun ownership and lower crime rates – and to several US states changing their law in line with the 'evidence'.

As Ayres points out, some people have a visceral loathing of the suggestion that the quality of a wine, a movie script or a relationship can be reduced to mere numbers. Yet those seeking a better world, or just a better burger, may have to get used to the idea that, to paraphrase Churchill on democracy, data mining is the worst possible basis for big decisions – apart from all the others.

Source: Matthews, R., 'A better burger thanks to data crunching', *Financial Times*, 6 September 2007.

Question

What does this case study suggest are the benefits of a quantitative approach to market research?

Market selection

The first two of the five phases for the international marketer in Figure 9.1 involve the decision on whether or not to internationalise and the decision on which markets to enter. The first of these decisions has already been considered in some detail in Chapter 2 of this book. Here we focus on the market selection decision (Phase 2 in Figure 9.1).

Segmentation and targeting

As in domestic marketing, once the larger market has been identified, the potential market has to be segmented as the firm's products are unlikely to appeal to the entire market. Segmentation, as we have seen, is the grouping together of customers with similar needs and characteristics. In international marketing, this means grouping countries with similar wants together or looking for similarities between specific groups of customers in different countries.

Shampoo provides a useful example of market segmentation. Shampoo was once considered one market, but new product development, branding and packaging have segmented this market in many ways. Shampoo products can be segmented into medicated hair products (Head & Shoulders), two-in-one (Wash & Go), children's shampoos (L'Oréal Kids), 'balanced' shampoos (Organics, Fructis) and environmentally sensitive shampoos (The Body Shop range). Such strategies permit manufacturers such as Unilever and Procter & Gamble to place a premium price on many of their shampoo products. These forms of lifestyle segmentation are now used by many firms in preference to the social class distinctions of the previous four decades.

Accessibility/actionability

The viability of a particular market segment is determined to a large extent by issues of 'accessibility' and 'actionability' which arguably are even more important in the international context.

- *Accessibility.* This refers to the ability of the firm to reach the potential foreign customers with promotional and distributional techniques and channels. Market segmentation involves identifying groups of customers with common characteristics, but even where such groups exist they may be particularly difficult to access when they cross national borders. For example, finding a media source to host a promotional campaign that is equally effective in reaching high-income female professionals in London, Frankfurt and Milan may prove difficult, as indeed it may in finding a distribution channel to actually supply product to this market segment. It may be that adjustments will have to be made (e.g. narrowing down the intended market segment) because of such accessibility problems for the international marketer.
- *Actionability.* This refers to the ability of the firm to increase its scale of operations to match (with no diminution in efficiency) the now enlarged total market. All too often firms encounter logistical problems in raising capacity which, in effect, prevent the firm from realising the benefits of these new market opportunities. For example, various diseconomies of scale (*see* Chapter 7) may raise average costs or adversely affect product quality. One of the methods firms often use in seeking to overcome this problem of 'actionability' is to seek out alliances and collaborative agreements with existing players in overseas markets (*see* Chapter 7).

PEST analysis

The whole external environment is particularly important when selecting viable overseas markets. Firms often resort to PEST analysis to broadly evaluate the potential of markets for entry. Of course, these various political, economic, sociocultural and technological (and some would add ecological/environmental and legal) factors may be still more uncertain in an international context. Chapters 4–6 have already looked at these factors in some detail.

Targeting strategies

Having selected some potentially attractive international market segments, the firm will often adopt one of three possible targeting strategies: concentration, undifferentiated (or mass) marketing, differentiated marketing.

■ *Concentration.* This refers to targeting a single market segment and developing an appropriate marketing mix for it. In international terms, this means concentrating marketing efforts on one or a small number of market segments to maximise the use of resources. For example, Rolls-Royce has targeted the luxury segment of the car market. Brand value may be crucial to successfully using concentration targeting strategies.

■ *Mass (global) marketing.* This is where a single marketing mix is used worldwide. Very few companies attempt this because enormous resources are required to exploit world markets. It also assumes that markets are relatively homogeneous and that customers will respond to promotions in uniform ways.

■ *Differentiated marketing.* This involves developing a different marketing mix for each of the market segments identified. Here, there is an assumption that the market is heterogeneous with consumers likely to respond in different ways and to different types of products.

Segmentation and targeting take place within a dynamic, ever-changing world business environment. No longer can organisations assume that things will stay the same for any significant period. Segmentation decisions often seek to identify sectors with high and growing levels of demand, but they must also focus on the trading environment that prevails. Any attempts at overt or covert protectionism by individual countries or regional trading blocs can have major impacts on market selection decisions. Indeed, the growth of regional trading blocs has led to 'insiderisation' with companies seeking a presence within a protected market through joint ventures with domestic firms or through founding a subsidiary company providing jobs and tax revenues within the host country. The strength of the competition also needs to be taken into account when deciding which markets to target. Organisations do not want to be crowded out by existing competitors who already have entrenched positions in terms of price, quality or consumer allegiance.

Market-entry strategies

The third decision phase in Figure 9.1 involves deciding how to enter the foreign market. Figure 9.2 outlines a number of possible methods which might be chosen.

These methods are by no means mutually exclusive: firms may be using one or more of these methods for market entry. Figure 9.2 suggests a broad spectrum ranging from minimum risk/minimum reward methods (e.g. indirect exporting) to maximum risk/maximum reward methods (e.g. foreign direct investment). These have already been discussed in some detail in Chapter 2. However, Figure 9.3 shows how Starbucks has tended to use a variety of joint ventures and licensing arrangements with local partners to move into new overseas markets as well as increasing its penetration within these markets. Its 'capital light' market entry strategy is clearly towards the minimum risk/minimum reward end of the spectrum of Figure 9.2.

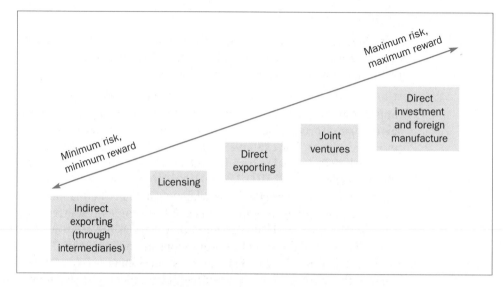

Figure 9.2 **Market-entry methods**

	Where/what	Partners
New channels (exclusive supply arrangements)	· Airlines · Airports · Bookstores · Cruise lines · Department stores · Hotels · Supermarkets	· United, Canadian · Host International · Barnes & Noble · Holland America · Nordstrom · ITT Sheraton, Westin Hotels · Kraft Foods
New markets (through licences with retailers)	· Japan · Malaysia · Philippines · Singapore · South Korea · Taiwan · Thailand	· Sazaby (joint venture) · Berjaya Coffee (licensee) · Restaurant Brands (licensee) · Rustan Coffee (licensee) · Bonvest Holdings (licensee) · ESCO (licensee) · President Group (joint venture) · Coffee Partners (licensee)
New products	· Ice cream · Bottled Frappuccino · Coffee-enhanced dark beer · Online catalogue	· Dreyer's · PepsiCo · Red Hook Brewery · America Online

Starbucks Coffee

Key success factors
· Starbucks invests very little capital in international expansion (< 5% of revenue)
· Local partners bear all business risk
· Licensing allows stricter control over all operations than does franchising – e.g. parent-company consultants visit each store once a month
· Local partners contribute regulatory and cultural expertise – e.g. on product adaptations

Figure 9.3 **Starbucks: capital-light expansion through partnerships**

International marketing mix

The fourth decision phase in Figure 9.1 involves the international marketing mix. The marketing mix of the 4 Ps can take on additional characteristics when viewed from an international perspective. This point is illustrated by Case Study 9.3 which shows how the importance of the various elements in the international marketing mix can vary between countries and regions.

CASE 9.3 Variations in the international marketing mix

International businesses are increasingly aware of consumer differences between countries and regions, even when these consumers otherwise have similar profiles (e.g. in terms of age, income, occupation). As a result, businesses which aspire to a global marketplace, are devoting more resources to identifying these differences before selecting the appropriate international marketing mix for that country or region.

Regina Maruca (2000) has reported on some research led by Dawn Lacobucci of Northwestern University's Kellogg Graduate School of Management. This research tries to get behind the cultural differences that might skew consumer responses to identical surveys in different countries. In other words, the research seeks to identify differences in consumer behaviour that are 'real' rather than 'apparent' as between nations and regions. In a recent test of their model, the researchers found important differences between consumers in four major geographical market segments (namely Asia, Latin America, northern Europe and southern Europe) in rating the products and services of a given company:

- price was seen as a key indicator of quality in Asia, northern Europe and southern Europe, but not in Latin America;
- product quality was seen as driving a company's repeat purchases in Asia, northern Europe and Latin America, but not in southern Europe;
- product after-sales service was seen as influencing repeat purchases in Asia, Latin America and southern Europe, but not in northern Europe;
- product 'value for money' was only seen as driving repeat purchases in Latin America;
- promotion was seen to have most impact on repeat purchases in Latin America and Asia, and least impact in northern Europe and southern Europe. (Here the number of sales representatives was used as a proxy variable for promotion in the sales of a given product in the different areas.)

Lacobucci concluded that 'companies that probe deeper to figure out what their global customers are thinking and feeling stand to create smarter branding strategies'.

Questions

1 If you were devising a marketing mix for selling the company's products used in the survey in northern Europe, where might you place the emphasis?

2 What other factors might play a part in adjusting the marketing mix between different nations and regions?

■ Product

This is the fundamental component of the marketing mix, since price, promotion and place are usually related in various ways to the characteristics which the product itself offers consumers. A key issue in international marketing is the extent to which a standard or differentiated product should be provided.

Standardised or differentiated?

There are good business reasons for trying to make a standard product acceptable to as many customers as possible – for example, it can help reduce average costs in design, production, promotion and distribution. Theodore Levitt of the Harvard Business School contends that tastes and preferences in many cultures are becoming more homogeneous due to the increased frequency of world travel and improved worldwide telecommunications. He claims that when marketers appreciate the fact that consumers share basic interests they can market the same product worldwide and achieve economies of scale. A global marketing strategy is one that maintains a single marketing plan across all countries and yields global name recognition. Coca-Cola and McDonald's are examples of companies that use a global approach to market their products in different countries. Even when arguments for standardisation are strong, those who follow this path may still make subtle variations – for example, McDonald's uses chilli sauce in Mexico instead of ketchup, while in India it serves the 'Maharaja Mac' which features two mutton patties. The motto 'Think global, and act local' symbolises a patterned standardisation strategy which involves developing global product-related marketing strategies while allowing for a degree of adaptation to local market conditions. Some product types would appear more suitable for standardisation than others. Office and industrial equipment, toys, computer games, sporting goods, soft drinks are usually standardised across national borders.

On the other hand, arguments can also be advanced in favour of *product differentiation*. Where international market segments differ from one another, even when some group characteristics are held in common, then a more differentiated product strategy may be advisable. For example, if high-income households in Spain display different wants and needs from high-income households in Germany, products may have to be adapted in an attempt to sell to both groups of consumers simultaneously. Where products are highly culturally conditioned (as with many types of food, some types of drink, clothing, etc.), differentiated products and marketing strategies are commonplace.

Table 9.3 outlines some of the factors supporting internationally standardised products and some of the factors supporting differentiated products.

Ariel washing powder has used nine different formulae throughout Europe, reflecting country-to-country differences in a wide range of factors, such as in water softness, types of washing machine, consumer preferences and legal restrictions on ingredients.

McDonald's has moved further along the product differentiation path in recent years in its various international operations, for a number of reasons.

■ *Reason*: Meeting different consumer tastes. *Examples*: US portion sizes larger; French menu includes traditional snacks such as Croque Monsieur, French pastries,

Table 9.3 Factors supporting product standardisation or product differentiation

Factors supporting standardisation	Factors supporting product differentiation
Rapid technological change, reducing product life cycles (places a premium on rapid global penetration)	Slow technological change, lengthening product life cycles
Substantial scale economies	Few scale economies
International product standards	Local product standards
Short cultural distance to overseas market	Large cultural distance to overseas market
Strong and favourable brand image	Weak and/or unfavourable brand image
Homogeneous consumer preferences (within a given group characteristic, e.g. high income)	Heterogeneous consumer preferences (within a given group characteristic, e.g. high income)
Global competition	Local competition
Centralised management of MNE operations	Decentralised management of MNE operations

stronger coffee; Chinese New Year menu includes authentic cultural dishes and packages; 'McCafe's' used in mature markets such as Australia, the US and the UK, with lattes, cappuccinos and other speciality drinks.

■ *Reason*: Religion. *Examples*: lamb based 'Maharajah Mac' to meet Hindu aversion to beef and Muslim aversion to pork.

■ *Reason*: Local commitment. *Examples*: emphasis on British beef in the UK and on local rice in China.

■ *Reason*: Demographics. *Examples*: 20% of all sales are to children so 'Happy Meal', food with toys themed with popular films, etc. for children up to nine years; 'Mighty Kids meal', for children over nine years who have grown out of the ('fun food with a toy') Happy Meal; 'Giant burger' (40% bigger) to appeal to young men in the 15–32 year age group, identified as important but with poor market penetration by McDonald's.

As most companies are looking for some standardisation, they will often use a *modular product* design that allows the company to adapt to local needs while still achieving economies of scale. Carmakers are beginning to adopt this form of production, with a basic body shape forming the shell around which different features are built (e.g. windscreen designs, sun roofs – see Chapter 7, p. 301).

Branding

Establishing product characteristics which are different from those of the firm's main competitors may be important in helping the firm establish a brand image. Of course, brand image may depend not so much on *actual* product differences but on consumer *perceptions* of product differences, created and reinforced by extensive advertising.

Certainly the potential benefits of brand image may influence the product characteristics sought at the introduction stage of the product life cycle or the modifications considered during the growth or maturity stages of that life cycle. For example, a product may be modified in order to reposition it and/or extend the reach of the brand at the maturity stage of the product life cycle. Such 'brand extension strategies' often appeal to larger companies who are well aware of the value to sales and profits resulting from past investment in brands.

A brand is an element or group of elements that help distinguish the product of a particular supplier or (as we saw in Case Study 9.1) the image of the supplier itself. When attempting to set up brands, organisations need to consider whether the brand should be local (developed for a specific market), regional or global. Branding can sometimes extend into a communication that is separate from the product itself. Kotler and Armstrong (1994) make a distinction between the *utterable brand* (a name like Persil or Guinness) and the *unutterable brand* (a symbol, logo, colour scheme, or even typeface in which the name of the brand appears – such as Coca-Cola). Because of the difficulties of translation into words, the unutterable brand often works best at international level.

When brands are developed successfully, they may allow higher prices to be charged, over and above those charged for non-branded, generic products. These higher prices help create what is often called 'brand value'.

Calculations of brand value involve comparing the prices of similar generic (own-brand) products with the higher price of the branded product. Data from *Interbrand* in 2008 ranked the top five global brands and their associated brand values as follows:

Coca-Cola	$66.67bn
IBM	$59.03bn
Microsoft	$59.01bn
General Electric	$53.09bn
Nokia	$35.94bn

Many brand names do not travel well. There are a large number of examples of companies that have adopted a standardised approach to their branding, but have not researched the implications of translation when launching a brand into another country. For example, Coca-Cola when they first launched in China realised the name translated as 'bite the wax tadpole'. Fortunately, Estée Lauder was quick to notice their proposed export of Country Mist make-up to Germany could experience problems. This is because 'mist' in Germany is slang for 'manure'. Subsequently the product became Country Moist in Germany.

Very often brand names are changed in order to follow a standardisation strategy. For example, in the UK the following products have changed names to fall in-line with the same product in other countries. Starburst was formerly Opal Fruits, Cif formerly Jif, and Snickers formerly Marathon. Mars (the manufacturers of Snickers and Starburst) decided the sweets should be called the same name in the UK as they are in the rest of the world. Reasons for having one universal brand name can be attributed to cost savings by producing a single global advertising and marketing campaign for all countries. Also, with increased travel, consumers are able to recognise a brand abroad. Usually companies adopt expensive advertising campaigns advising of the name change. This needs to be done in a positive way to ensure the brand image maintains its current position in the mind of the consumer.

Case Study 9.4 reviews the rise of luxury brands in India.

CASE 9.4 India's new affluent consumers   FT

To see signs of the increasing spending power of India's affluent classes, a visitor need only drive along the main western road in to Mumbai. After passing the 'Auto Hangar' selling Mercedes cars, the visitor will see the Rolls-Royce dealership and then, further on, a showroom that is still under construction but above which the word 'Porsche' is already clearly visible.

The sudden emergence in India of Porsche, the ultimate symbol of brazen consumption, is raising eyebrows in a country in which, not so long ago, the elite drove the indigenous Hindustan Ambassador. 'People have had the money for a very long time but it is only now that they are starting to feel more comfortable spending it locally rather than abroad,' says Ashish Chordia, chief executive of Porsche Centre India. The showroom, part of a push by Porsche into India's four biggest cities, is one example of the invasion of the country by high-end car-makers and luxury retailers.

Leather goods maker Louis Vuitton and a variety of other LVMH brands are already present in India and a flood of others, such as elite Italian suit maker Brioni, are setting up shop in the country. Capgemini and Merrill Lynch estimated in their annual World Wealth Report that the number of people with net assets of $1 million or more in India is now over 100,000, up 20.5% from a year earlier. It was the second fastest rate of growth in the world, after Singapore's 21.5%. As long as India's economy grows at rates of more than 9% a year, the country is expected to continue generating wealth on this scale, analysts say.

Alex Kuruvilla, managing director of Condé Nast India, which is launching a domestic edition of its flagship magazine Vogue in September, says that during market research, the magazine discovered two types of luxury consumer. There is the 'old money', the people who for decades have shopped and holidayed overseas. They tend to be as discerning as their counterparts anywhere. Then there are the *nouveau riche* – the new industrialists, professionals, entrepreneurs and others – who are not as familiar with luxury goods but have the cash to experiment. Describing the average, *nouveau riche* consumer, Mr Kuruvilla says 'She's got the money. She can come into Delhi and pick up half a dozen of those $2000 bags and that makes her a very important person as far as the market's concerned.' He envisages introducing more niche magazines as the market develops, such as *Brides*. India's wedding market is worth $10 billion and is growing at a rate of 25% a year.

The industry faces a number of challenges, however. Duties on luxury products, such as watches, can be as high as 60% plus state taxes and value added tax, making them uncompetitive against overseas prices, according to research by retail advisory firm Savigny Partners. There is also a paucity of quality retail space outside the luxury hotels. Ermenegildo Zegna, the luxury menswear retailer, discovered this when it opened its first store in India in 2000 in one of Mumbai's leading malls. It was later forced to close because of the 'deteriorating brand environment', which included a McDonald's opening next door, according to Savigny. It reopened this year in Mumbai's Taj Mahal Hotel.

New luxury developments are on the way. DLF, India's largest property developer, is building the Emporio luxury shopping mall in new Delhi. Meanwhile, the ▶

Wadia Group is planning to create a 25-acre development in Mumbai aimed at high-end retailing. But life for the conspicuous consumer remains challenging in India. Mumbai, for instance, lacks the necessary infrastructure for sports cars. While Mr Chordia says the company's sales have increased from about 40 units a year after it opened in 2004 to over 200 today, about 60% of these are of the Cayenne sports utility vehicle. Selling for up to Rs11 million ($275,000), this is more practical than the Porsche sports cars which cost up to Rs14 million and are more vulnerable to abuse on Mumbai's potholed streets, where traffic often moves at walking pace and cars bump each other jostling for space. In addition, the lack of parking often forces car owners to have their driver follow behind in a back-up vehicle to take care of the Porsche when it is not being driven.

Source: Leahy, J., 'Road of new rich littered with potholes', *Financial Times*, 1 August 2007.

Questions

1 Consider the attractiveness of India for luxury products.

2 What problems are often encountered by producers of luxury products?

Corporate branding

Traditionally new drugs in the pharmaceutical sector are given new names to indicate a departure from previous alternatives available. The downside of this strategy is that large corporate investment in branding previous drug products is disassociated from the new products and may be regarded as largely wasted. Corstjens and Carpenter (2000) suggest that pharmaceutical companies might be well advised to consider *corporate branding* as a replacement for individual drug branding. In this way they suggest that company loyalty embedded in consumer allegiance to earlier products can then be transferred to successor products. They suggest that 'a customer looking for a treatment of allergies, for example, would not look for Claritin but for the latest Shering-Plough medicine'.

Positive marketing may even help turn disadvantages of individual drugs into brand benefits. For example, it was noted that Zyrtec, an anti-histamine drug developed by Pfizer induced rather more sleepiness in users than alternative therapies. Rather than allow rivals to use this as a negative, Pfizer sought to stress the positive benefits of drowsiness in increasing the likelihood of a good night's sleep and in reducing the itchiness which often accompanies the use of such drugs.

Successful branding can help to bind consumers to particular products for reasons other than price. This will cause the demand curve to pivot, becoming less steep (i.e. less price elastic – *see* Chapter 4, p. 160). This in turn gives greater opportunities for considering a price raising policy, since less consumers will be lost when there is a conviction that the branded product is of a higher quality than the now lower priced rivals. The linkage between price elasticity of demand and revenue is explored below in Box 9.3.

Case Study 9.5 reviews the debate on whether consumer tastes are consolidating, to the benefits of global brands, or fragmenting, requiring a more segmented approach by marketers.

CASE 9.5 Global brands FT

The manifesto for global brands appeared in 1983 when the *Harvard Business Review* published an essay by Theodore Levitt, 'The Globalisation of Markets'. It was a hymn to homogenisation. Technology, by spreading mass transport and communication, was creating a world in which different cultural preferences and national tastes would disappear, Prof Levitt declared. The result was 'a new commercial reality – the emergence of global markets for standardised consumer products on a previously unimagined scale'. It was goodbye to the multinational and hello to the global company. 'The multinational corporation operates in a number of countries and adjusts its products and practices in each – at high relative cost – whereas the global company operates as if the entire world (or major regions of it) were a single entity: it sells the same things in the same way everywhere.'

When the Berlin Wall fell in 1989, Prof Levitt's theory was put into practice. And for at least two reasons, American companies were best placed to lead the way. One was that they had deep pockets. John Quelch, professor of business administration at Harvard Business School, says: 'The decade following the fall of the Berlin Wall was extraordinarily favourable for American muscle to go anywhere and everywhere in the world faster than their smaller competitors.' Another was that the principal brand attribute of America was freedom, a concept that had a magic resonance for those previously denied it.

Sure enough, once the trade barriers had gone, US brands poured into the world's newly opened markets and consumers lapped them up. The brand owners' share prices soared as investors savoured the prospects for seemingly limitless growth. In 1997 Procter & Gamble boasted that the number of consumers within its reach had shot up from 1 billion to 4.5 billion in a decade, saying its growth opportunities were 'literally unprecedented'.

Even before the decade had ended, however, the brand bubble had begun to burst. People in once-closed markets were happy to celebrate their freedom by tasting the forbidden fruits of American brands. But once the novelty wore off, a backlash set in. Consumers developed a pride in their national identity and started expressing a preference for local products, which, thanks to the introduction of western business methods, were simultaneously showing a big improvement in quality.

It turned out that Theodore Levitt's thesis was just plain wrong. Far from consolidating, consumer markets were in fact fragmenting. People did not want to become part of a homogenous mass, deprived of choice and force-fed standardised products. They wanted to be individuals expressing preferences and proclaiming their identity through what Sigmund Freud once called 'the narcissism of small differences'. In one of those 180-degree turns that periodically make a mockery of management theory, the big US brand owners realised the global approach was doomed and set about returning to the old multinational model in which local managements met local preferences with local products.

Fragmenting consumer tastes have made life much more challenging for global brand-owners. Before it launched Diet Coke in 1982, Coca-Cola had been a

▶

one-product company for nearly a century. Now it manages a portfolio of more than 200 brands, most of them local, and the number increases each year. Even so, its net profits have yet to regain their 1997 peak. McDonald's too, is varying its menus to suit national tastes. It has also experimented with diversification by investing in other food retailing chains such as Chipotle Mexican Grill in the US and Britain's Pret A Manger. Yet in 2002 it recorded the first net loss in its 37 year history as a stock market listed company.

'For many years in many of the most valuable product sectors, you really only had to say that something was American and life was unfairly easy for you,' says Simon Anholt, an adviser to government bodies on country branding. Many products around the world, such as Italy's Brooklyn chewing gum, adopted US-sounding names even though they had no connection with America. Views about America are now becoming more contradictory and ambivalent: some remain positive but, as the Pew research shows, uneasiness or outright hostility to America's position as sole superpower and global hegemon is creating more negative perceptions.

Big American brands such as Coca-Cola and McDonald's are not about to disappear but, to the extent that America's brand equity declines, they may lose some of the advantage they once enjoyed over products from other countries. And as that equity turns negative, they may have to work harder than other countries' brands just to stand still. Already, it is becoming difficult to imagine a new supplier of products or services adopting an American-sounding name in the hope that it will confer an automatic advantage. Of the 200-plus brands invented or acquired by Coca-Cola – from almdudler and Bibo to Tian Yu Di and Youki – hardly any have American associations and their ultimate ownership is often disguised by omitting Coca-Cola's name from the can or bottle.

Like Coca-Cola, other big US brand-owners may hope to counter the effects of declining American brand equity by acquiring local brands. But the trend also opens up an opportunity to China, India, Mexico and other emerging markets, many of which are hoping to follow the example of Japan, Taiwan and South Korea by transforming the image of their products and getting them on to the world stage.

'Emerging countries are now getting very serious about creating brands that are not just domestic but global; and you will increasingly see them sharing the same space as, and competing with, American brands,' says Jagdish Sheth, professor of marketing at Emory University's Goizueta Business School in Atlanta. (The school is named after Roberto Goizueta, the late Coca-Cola chairman and chief executive.)

Amid a shift in tastes and fashions towards the ethnic and the authentic, western consumers are attracted as never before to the cultures and products of distant lands: 'The directions in which culture flows are multiplying and becoming more complex and other voices are beginning to be heard,' says Mr Anholt. 'People want exotic products with unusual stories to tell, partly because they're sick of brand America and partly because these products are just more interesting. The days when it was briefly fashionable to appear as global or monocultural as possible are well and truly over.'

Source: Tomkins, R., 'Anti-war sentiment is likely to give fresh impetus to the waning supremacy of US brands', *Financial Times*, 27 March 2003.

The new cola war: one symptom of the anti-US consumer backlash is the appearance of a range of new soft drink brands catering for Muslims and others who no longer want to drink Coke or Pepsi. In the past few months, France has seen the launch of at least three brands: Mecca-Cola, Arab Cola and Muslim-Up. In Britain, a company has launched Qibla-Cola with plans to expand it overseas. Iran has increased exports of its Zam Zam Cola drink to the Middle East and Europe.

These drinks are not aimed solely at Muslims. 'The feeling against the American administration is not just a Muslim feeling: it's a world feeling,' says Mawfik Mathlouthi, founder of Mecca-Cola. The drink is now sold in 22 countries, mainly in Europe, and Mr Mathlouthi is preparing to launch a chain of fast-food restaurants in Europe and North Africa called Halal Fried Chicken or HFC, to take on the US-based KFC (formerly Kentucky Fried Chicken) chain.

Questions

1 Examine the case for suggesting that consumer tastes are fragmenting rather than consolidating.

2 What are the strategic implications of the trends identified for both marketers and the companies they work for?

3 How might marketers respond to the growing anti-American sentiment alleged in the case study?

■ Price

Price in any marketing context is governed by competition, production costs and company objectives. Box 9.2 reviews some commonly used strategic pricing initiatives.

Box 9.2 Strategic pricing initiatives

- **Penetration pricing** Here price for a new product may even be set below average cost in order to capture market share. The expectation is that prices can be raised and profit margins restored later on in the growth/maturity stages, helped by the fact that average costs may themselves be falling in those stages via the various economies of scale.

- **'Price-skimming'** Here a high price is set for a new product in the introduction/early growth stages which 'skims off' a small but lucrative part of the market. Producers of fashion products, which have a short life and high innovative value as long as only a few people own them, often adopt a skimming strategy. Companies such as IBM, Polaroid and Bosch have operated such price-skimming systems over time. Bosch used a successful skimming policy, supported by patents, in its launch of fuel injection and antilock braking systems.

- **Loss leader (bait) pricing** Where a limited number of products are priced at or below cost to entice customers who may then pay full price on other purchases (e.g. for selected products in supermarkets).

▶

Box 9.2   Continued

- **Clearance pricing** Where rock-bottom prices are charged to clear stock and make resources available for alternative uses.
- **Transfer pricing** (see below, p. 366) Here the price (at least notionally) of a product or part of a product is set with regard to the tax regimes which exist in different countries.
- **Parallel pricing** Where several firms change prices in the same direction and by broadly the same amount.
- **Product line pricing** Where the pricing of one item is related to that of complementary items, with a view to maximising the return on the whole product line. For example, the price of a 'core' product might be set at a low level to encourage sales and then the 'accessories' priced at high levels.
- **Prestige pricing** Where higher prices are associated with higher quality ('Veblen effect').
- **Competitor pricing** As, for example, where the firm follows the prices set by the market leader or engages in price warfare under oligopoly market structures (see Chapter 7).
- **Price discrimination** (see below, p. 364) If demand for a given product can be broken down into market segments, some being more price sensitive than others, then revenue and profits can be increased by charging a different price in each market segment.

International pricing decisions will reflect these aspects and will also need to take into account market differences between countries, exchange rates, difficulties of invoicing and collecting payment across borders, the effects of tariffs and purchase taxes on competitiveness, governmental regulations of the host country and the long-term strategic plan of the company in the different markets in which it operates.

We now review some of the major issues faced by those setting prices in different countries.

Price elasticity of demand (PED) (Box 4.4, p. 160) has already been identified as a key element in the pricing decision, with the decision on whether to raise or lower price crucially dependent on how 'sensitive' consumers are expected to be in responding to that price change. Box 9.3 considers the revenue linkage with PED in rather more detail.

Box 9.3   Price elasticity of demand (PED) and revenue

We have already considered aspects of PED in Box 4.4 (p. 160). For a business to make sensible decisions as to the price it should charge, it will help to be aware of the linkage between PED and total revenue (turnover), where:

$$PED = \frac{\% \text{ change in quantity demanded of } X}{\% \text{ change in price of } X}$$

The 'box' diagram shown in Figure 9.4 helps explain this linkage using a straight line (linear) demand curve (DD).

We can see that with the initial price at OP, total revenue (price × quantity) is shown by area $OPVQ$. A rise in price to OP_1 will lead to a contraction of demand to OQ_1 and a new total revenue indicated by area $OP_1V_1Q_1$. Clearly Area 1 is common to both total revenue situations, but here Area 3 is lost and Area 2 gained. The loss of Area 3 is due to consumers

Box 9.3 Continued

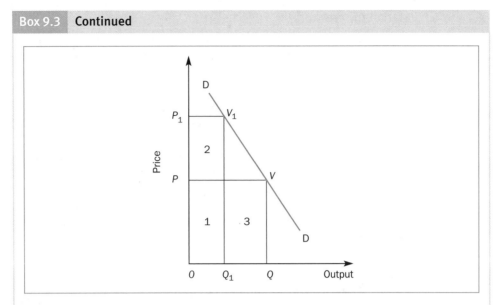

Figure 9.4 **Box diagram to show how revenue varies with price and output**

no longer buying the $Q_1 - Q$ units because of the higher price; the gain of Area 2 is due to the higher price being paid by the Q_1 consumers who still buy the product.

The relationships listed in Table 9.4 will hold true for the box diagram.

We can now use these relationships to make a number of predictions involving price changes and total revenue.

Price changes and total revenue

■ For price rises along a unit elastic demand curve (PED = 1) or segment of a demand curve, there will be no change in total revenue (Area 2 = Area 3).

■ For price rises along a relatively elastic demand curve (PED > 1) or segment of a demand curve, total revenue will decrease as there is a more than proportionate response of lost consumers to the now higher price (Area 2 < Area 3).

■ For price rises along a relatively inelastic demand curve (PED < 1) or segment of a demand curve, total revenue will increase as there is a less than proportionate response of lost consumers to the now higher price (Area 2 > Area 3).

Table 9.4 **PED and revenue**

Numerical value of PED	Relationship between Area 2 and Area 3
1	Area 3 = Area 2
>1	Area 3 > Area 2
<1	Area 3 < Area 2

pause for thought 3 Now rework these predictions for a price decrease in each of the three situations.

Market differences

Clearly some overseas markets are more attractive for a particular product than others in terms of population size, standard of living (e.g. real GNP per head), age profile, purchasing patterns, etc. Of particular interest in terms of international price setting is the possibility and profitability of setting different prices in different geographical markets. When the same product is priced higher in one (international) market than another, this is termed price discrimination.

For this to be possible, there must be barriers preventing purchase in one country at the lower price and resale in another country at the higher price (transport costs, tariff barriers, etc.). For this to be profitable, there must be different 'price elasticities of demand' in the different geographical markets. Where consumers in one country are more responsive to changes in price (i.e. have a higher price elasticity of demand), it can be shown that a firm can earn higher profits by charging a lower price in that country (*see* Box 9.4).

Box 9.4   Price discrimination

This involves charging different prices for an identical product.

In Figure 9.5 the firm faces two international markets, Market A with a relatively inelastic demand and Market B with a relatively elastic demand. To maximise profit the marginal cost of total firm output to both markets (MC_{A+B}) must equal aggregate marginal revenue from both markets (MR_{A+B}). This occurs at output Q_I, giving overall marginal cost of C. Now the conditions for maximum total profit is that the marginal cost of total firm output (C) must equal marginal revenue in each separate market.

i.e. $MC_{A+B} = MR_A = MR_B$ i.e. Q_A and Q_B respectively

No other allocation of output Q_I can raise total profit for the firm.

e.g. 1 more unit sold in market A, 1 less unit sold in market B.

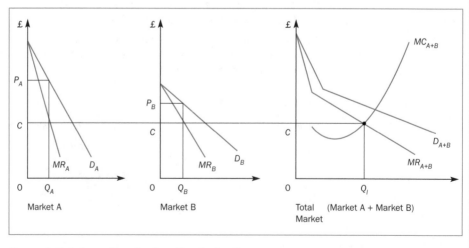

Figure 9.5 **International price discrimination**

| Box 9.4 | Continued |

Q_l unchanged, therefore TC unchanged (ignoring distributional costs).

TR rises by $< C$ in market A TR falls by C in market B

i.e. TR falls net so that $TP (= TR - TC)$ also falls

OR

1 less unit sold in market A, 1 more unit sold in market B.

Same outcome, TR falls net and with TC unchanged, $TP (= TR - TC)$ also falls.

The implication then must be that the profit-maximising price is lower in market B for which demand is more price elastic than in market A for which demand is less price elastic.

That price discrimination occurs in practice is well illustrated by Table 9.5, which shows considerable differences in the US$ price of the 'Big Mac' across a range of countries using current exchange rates.

Table 9.5 **Variations in the US$ price of 'Big Macs'**

Country	Price	Country	Price
Malaysia	$1.70	US	$3.57
Hong Kong	$1.71	New Zealand	$3.72
China	$1.83	Canada	$4.08
Thailand	$1.86	Turkey	$4.32
Indonesia	$2.04	UK	$4.57
South Africa	$2.24	Hungary	$4.64
Egypt	$2.45	Brazil	$4.73
Taiwan	$2.47	Euro Zone area	$5.34
Russia	$2.54	Denmark	$5.34
Japan	$2.62	Switzerland	$6.36
Saudi Arabia	$2.67	Sweden	$6.37
Mexico	$3.15	Norway	$7.88

Source: Adapted from The Big Mac Index: Sandwiched, *The Economist*, 25 July 2008, p. 82 © The Economist Newspaper Limited, London 2008.

pause for thought 4   Can you suggest reasons for the price differences observed in Table 9.5?

Variations in real national income per head (living standards) are another market difference which may result in price variations for a given product across different countries. Figure 9.6 usefully illustrates this relationship. Since only some 6% of the cost of a 'Big Mac' can be attributed to the cost of the ingredients, the clearly positive relationship between the dollar price of a 'Big Mac' and real national income per head (capital) has little to do with different cost factors in the various locations.

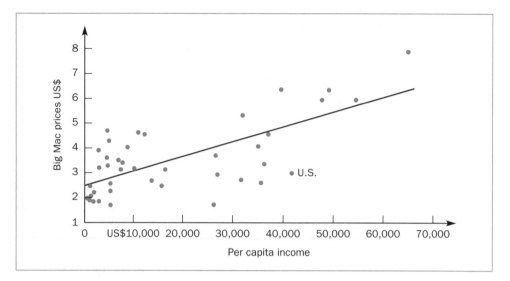

Figure 9.6 Rich countries pay more for Big Macs

Source: Landry, A. (2008) 'The Big Mac: A global-to-local look at pricing', *Federal Reserve Bank of Dallas: Economic Letter*, Vol. 3, No. 9.

■ Transfer pricing

We have already noted in Chapter 4 that multinational enterprises are well placed to take advantage of any differences in national tax and subsidy regimes. One particularly important aspect which might influence pricing policy involves attempts to reduce the corporate tax burden by 'transfer pricing', that is by adjusting the pricing of internal transactions between international subsidiaries of the multinational enterprise.

Multinationals are widely accused by governments of arranging intra-company transactions in order to minimise their tax liabilities, effectively forcing countries to compete to provide the lowest tax regime. Here we consider a simplified example in which a multinational's production is vertically integrated, with operations in two countries. Basic manufacture takes place in country A and final assembly and sale in country B (*see* Table 9.6). In country A, the corporate tax rate is 25%, while in country B it is 50%. Suppose the company's costs (inputs, labour, etc.) in country A are $40 million and it produces intermediate products with a market value of $50 million; if it were to sell these intermediate products on the open market, it would declare a profit of $10 million in country A, incurring a tax liability of $2.5 million in that country.

Table 9.6 Multinational tax avoidances

$m	Scenario 1		Scenario 2	
	Country A	Country B	Country A	Country B
Costs	40	90	40	100
Sales	50	100	60	100
Profit	10	10	20	0
Tax liability	2.5	5	5	0
Total tax	7.5		5	

However, suppose the products are actually intended for the parent company's subsidiary in country B. In Scenario 1, the 'transfer price' (i.e. the internal price used by the company to calculate profits in different countries) is set at the market price of $50 million in country A for the intermediate products which are now to be 'shipped' to country B for $100 million, thus the subsidiary will declare a profit of $10 million and incur a tax liability of $5 million. The company as a whole will face a total tax liability of $7.5 million in countries A and B taken together.

Consider an alternative scenario (Scenario 2), in which the company sets a transfer price above the market price for the intermediate products manufactured in the low-tax country, A. With a transfer price of $60 million rather than $50 million and the same costs of $40 million the subsidiary in country A incurs a higher tax liability (25% of $20 million), but this is more than offset by the lower (in fact, zero) tax liability incurred by the subsidiary in country B. Because the latter is now recording its total costs (including the cost of the intermediate products 'bought' from the subsidiary in country A) as being $100 million rather than $90 million, its profits and tax liability fall to zero. As a result, the total tax liability faced by the company on its international operations is only $5 million, rather than $7.5 million.

The basic issue is that the multinational has earned a total profit of $20 million on its vertically integrated operation, i.e. $100 million actual sales revenue in B minus $80 million costs in A + B. However, by setting transfer prices on intra-company sales and purchases of intermediate products appropriately, the company can 'move' this profit to the lowest tax country, thereby denying the higher tax country (in this case, country B) the tax revenue to which it is entitled. Such transfer pricing can, of course, only succeed when there is no active market for the intermediate products being traded. If the tax authorities in country B can refer to an open market price for the intermediate product, the inflated transfer price being paid can be identified. However, to the extent that many multinationals internalise cross-border operations because they have ownership-specific advantages (e.g. control of a specific raw material or technology), it may be that comparable intermediate products are not available on the open market. For this reason, high-tax countries may find they lose tax revenues to lower-tax centres as business becomes increasingly globalised. This creates, in turn, an incentive for countries to 'compete' for multinational tax revenues by offering low tax rates; the result of such competition is a transfer of income from national governments to the shareholders of multinational companies.

Exchange rates

When exchange rates fluctuate this can change the potential profitability of international contracts. For example, marketers must be alert as to any potential movements in the exchange rate between the date of quotation/invoicing and the date of payment so that the profit margin is not eroded. Price may have to be adjusted to cover adverse exchange rate movements. To reduce the impact of such problems currencies may be purchased on futures markets (*see* p. 397), or products may be priced in 'harder', more stable currencies. Of course, when both parties have a single currency, such as the euro, these problems will be avoided.

When the pound plunged in value against the euro, falling from £1: €1.44 in 2007 to £1: €1.03 in late 2008, this made a significant difference to the pricing of the same products expressed in sterling between the two time periods, as indicated in Table 9.7.

Table 9.7 Impact of falling pound: euro exchange rate on sterling price of specified products, 2007–8

Product	2007	2008
Meal for two in a Paris bistro (€80)	£58.40	£72.27
Beer in a Spanish bar (€3)	£2.19	£2.71
Admission to Van Gogh Museum, Amsterdam (€12.50)	£9.13	£11.74
Two tickets to watch AC Milan (€140)	£102.20	£126.47
Hotel room in Berlin (€100)	£73	£90.33
Danube cruise in Vienna (€25)	£18.25	£22.58

Cross-border payments

In contracts for internationally traded products it is important to specify exactly what a price covers. For example, does it cover cost, insurance and freight?

Tariffs and other taxes

Increases in tariffs (purchase taxes) or raw materials used in production or on overseas sales can force a firm to raise the quoted price of its exports in order to retain its profit margin. In 2008 L'Oréal was faced with a rise in costs of its raw materials when the EU imposed a 7.8% duty on a chemical (dihydromurcenol) imported from India and used in several of its cosmetics lines. Whether the firm will be able to pass these taxes on to the consumer as a higher price will, of course, depend on the price elasticity of demand for the product. The less price elastic the demand, the more of any tax increase can be passed on to the overseas consumer. Tariffs and taxes can have other impacts on trade issues. In an attempt to avoid such tariffs (and sometimes to overcome currency problems) there has been a growth in countertrade, namely the barter of goods and services between countries. Some 5% of all international trade has been estimated as being of this type. Further, any increases (or differences between countries) in *profit related taxes* (e.g. corporation tax) can result in MNEs adopting a policy of 'transfer pricing'. Here firms sell products on to subsidiaries within another country at prices which bear little relation to the true costs incurred at that stage of the overall production process (*see* p. 366).

Government regulations

As well as taxes, overseas governments may influence the firm's price-setting policies by regulations, perhaps setting maximum or minimum prices of products or minimum quality standards for particular products. Regulations may also inhibit other promotional techniques; for example L'Oréal could not use the successful UK free samples promotion of mascara in Norway or Germany, where such free offers are prohibited.

Strategic objectives

Overseas price setting may, of course, be influenced by the strategic objectives of the firm. For example, where market share or revenue maximisation are primary objectives, then prices will tend to be lower (e.g. penetration pricing) than they might be under, say, a profit-maximising objective.

■ Promotion

The objective of promotional campaigns is often expressed as being both to increase the commitment of existing consumers to the product and to capture new consumers. Box 9.5 looks at these objectives in more detail.

Box 9.5 Promotion/advertising and demand

The intention of a promotional strategy which emphasises the superior quality or characteristics of your product is often twofold.

First, to shift the demand curve to the right, so that more of product X is purchased at any given price. This is shown as an increase in demand from DD to $D'D'$ in Figure 9.7, with Q_1 now demanded at price OP. The promotional campaign seeks to change the tastes/preferences of consumers in favour of your product X, either by capturing new consumers for that product or attracting existing consumers away from a competitor product.

Second, to cause the demand curve to pivot and become steeper ($D''D''$ in Figure 9.7), i.e. become less price elastic (see p. 362). A successful promotion will bind consumers to your product for reasons other than price, convincing them that your product really does have an extra 'edge' on rival products in the marketplace. The benefit of this is that a less price elastic demand curve will allow you to raise the price of your product X above OP without losing as many customers as previously, thereby increasing revenue from the product (see Box 9.3).

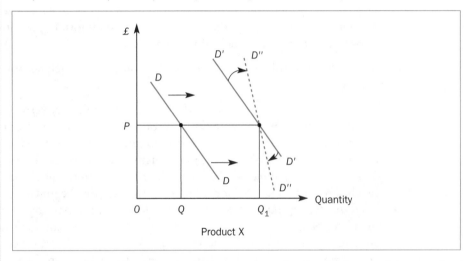

Figure 9.7 **Demand increases and becomes less elastic with successful promotion/advertising campaign**

Box 9.6 UK internet trends in 2007/08

- Britons are the most active Web users in Europe and spent an average 36 minutes each online every day in 2007, up from 14 minutes in 2002.
- Three-quarters of 11 year olds have their own TV, games console and mobile phone.
- Two-thirds of children do not believe they could easily live without a mobile phone and the Internet.
- Some 15% of UK households have a digital video recorder and 78% use it to fast-forward through advertisements.
- Some 16% of over-65s use the Web. They surf for 42 hours every month, more than any other age group. One-quarter of UK Web users are over 50.
- Two-thirds of phone owners use its alarm function instead of a clock.

This is one of the most challenging areas of international marketing, since it is particularly affected by technological, sociocultural and regulatory factors. Promotion may involve press and media campaigns, direct mail, exhibitions or direct selling. When planning international campaigns, companies will need to ask the following questions:

■ *What is the technological infrastructure of the country?* This will influence the prospects for reaching the final consumer. For example, in most industrialised countries over 90% of households own a TV, but this is often only a minority in the developing countries. If using direct selling by telesales, what proportion of the target market in that country possesses a telephone? If planning a poster campaign, what are the panel sizes available in different countries? Panel sizes are different, for example, in France and the UK, which can be important given the high costs of preparing and printing panels of varying sizes.

Table 9.8 takes this issue further in the context of reaching South Korean and Slovakian consumers.

■ *What appeals culturally in the advertisement?* English advertisements quite frequently use humour; French ones use erotic imagery, while in Germany the advertisements tend to be very factual. Great attention therefore needs to be paid to style and content in terms of the cultural impact of the campaign. If using direct selling, what type of sales force will be acceptable? For example, should we use local salespeople, an expatriate sales force or nationals from third countries?

■ *What are the regulations on advertising in this particular country?* The UK, Belgium, the Netherlands and Denmark ban TV commercials for tobacco products but allow press adverts. In the UK any advertisement for tobacco products must carry a health warning. Are there any legal restrictions on the use of direct marketing (such as the use of information stored on computer databases)? Are there any legal restrictions on sales promotions? (Some countries do not allow certain types of free offers to be made; for example, money-off coupons are not allowed in Norway.)

Table 9.8 **Percentage of household ownership 2007**

	South Korea	Slovakia
Possession of black and white TV set	0.9	2.8
Possession of cable TV	69.8	39.8
Possession of colour TV set	99.3	98.3
Possession of personal computer	79.8	46.4
Possession of internet enabled computer	76	35.2
Possession of satellite TV system	12.6	53.5
Possession of telephone	94	41.4

Source: Euromonitor International.

- *What are the different media habits of the country?* For example, the current circulation figures per 1000 of population of women's weekly magazines is around 29 in Germany, compared to 15 for the UK and five for Spain. Similar figures for TV guides are 37 for Germany, ten for the UK and seven for Spain.
- *What type of packaging do we use to retain the brand image yet meet country requirements* (e.g. ecological requirements demanded in Germany)? Do we need special types of labels? How much information needs to be presented about the content of the product?

We can see from these questions that international marketing is not an easy proposition. It requires an intimate knowledge of the market in each country. As market segmentation analysis becomes ever more sophisticated, this too can impact on promotion/advertising strategies.

pause for thought 6

Table 9.8 shows the differences in household ownership of a range of items that may be relevant to a company seeking to engage with consumers.

If an MNE operates in both countries, what implications might these differences in household ownership have for its promotional campaign aiming to reach consumers?

Psychographic factors and promotion

Attempts are being made to segment markets in terms of psychographic factors, i.e. in attitudinal and behavioural characteristics resulting from cultural differences. For example, Roper Starch Worldwide (a leading market research company) claimed to identify four distinct shopping styles worldwide after surveying around 38,000 consumers in 40 countries, namely 'deal makers', 'price seekers', 'brand loyalists' and 'luxury innovators' (Shermach 1995). To the extent that such psychographic segmentation is shown to be reliable, companies can only adopt global promotion/advertising campaigns to clearly defined groupings across various countries. Cultural differences will prevent a more comprehensive advertising approach.

The FCB (Foote, Cone and Belding) two-by-two grid can be used to categorise a product in terms of its consumer orientation, using two key dimensions (*see* Figure 9.8):

1 an 'involvement' spectrum, with the *higher involvement* products reflecting those which are generally believed by consumers to further their personal objectives or have important personal consequences, as opposed to the *lower involvement* products;
2 a 'think-feel' spectrum, where *think products* possess characteristics which are primarily associated with functional outcomes and *feel products* with emotional outcomes.

Only where a product falls in a clearly defined quadrant in all its international markets can a global promotion campaign be applied with any confidence.

Ethnographic factors and promotion

Companies are increasingly sending their market researchers to live in consumers' homes to understand better their consumption patterns and perceptions of products. This practice, known as *ethnography* is based on the study of anthropology and the idea that you get more detailed and accurate information by immersing yourself with

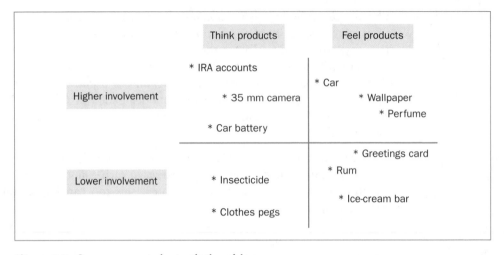

Figure 9.8 **Consumer–product relationships**

the subject (here the consumer). It is an attempt to overcome the known distortions that regularly occur when consumers fill in diaries or questionnaires, where subconsciously respondents often write what they think the researchers want to read. Brewers, for example, have found that men typically overstate how much they actually drank whereas women understate the true quantities. More accurate figures, arguably require researchers to live alongside the consumer and record what, and how often, they actually do drink.

The *Octagon Study* was conducted in 2002 by using an in-depth ethnographic survey of 11 households. Commissioned by Orange, Virgin and Pace, it sought to identify the behaviour of those households in responding to and using various new and established technologies, including mobile phones, the Internet and television. Orange's marketing research manager noted that the main beneficiaries of the study were the new product development team, the brand team and the advertising team as they gained rare and valuable insights into the responses and perceptions of actual users. In a separate ethnographic study, BT, Unilever, Cadbury, Centrica and Vodafone commissioned the 'Moby Study' to investigate the behaviour that makes consumers respond positively to certain brands, products and services and to certain types of advertising.

'Buzz' marketing and promotion

In some ways this is an attempt to promote with minimal expenditure on conventional promotional media. 'Buzz' marketing involves getting the trendsetters in any community themselves to convey the key message of the brand, creating interest in the product with little overt promotion or advertising. The message may be conveyed physically (the avant garde seen with the product), verbally (spoken about in conversation) or virtually (via the Internet). Ford used this approach to promote its new Focus. Having identified 120 people in six core markets as trendsetters (e.g. local DJs), each was given a Focus to drive for six months and promotional materials to distribute to interested acquaintances. Red Bull has also used this approach. For example in its eight US sales areas, representatives identify the bars and clubs visited by trendsetters and offer the owners branded refrigerators and other free goods along with their first order.

Case Study 9.6 reviews some promotional strategies for marketers, especially in times of recession.

CASE 9.6	Lessons for marketers who face a hard sell	**FT**

Ask a dozen advertising agencies for advice on marketing in a downturn and the chances are they each will begin with a lecture on the dangers of cutting budgets. Since the start of the year, industry associations around the world have been marshalling case studies from past slowdowns to persuade marketing directors that those who keep up their spending while rivals back away will emerge strongest. 'What I advise companies is, don't panic,' says Dr. Daniel Howard, professor of marketing at Cox School of Business at Southern Methodist University, Dallas. 'The companies that maintain or increase their marketing expenditure actually gain market share. It is one of the most effective ways of beating your competitors.'

There is plenty of truth in this, but the speed and severity of the current downturn means that few marketers will have the luxury of maintaining their spending, let alone increasing it to outspend their competitors. 'Budgets will go down: they won't go up,' says Barry Judge, chief marketing officer of Best Buy. As the US electronics retailer experiences a steep fall in demand – the company this month warned of a 'seismic' drop in sales – 'you don't have any choice but to spend less on marketing,' he says.

Even for those having to do more with less, however, there are lessons to be learned about how to return stronger. With smaller budgets, 'dollars need to multi-task', says Laura Lang, chief executive of Digitas, the interactive agency owned by the French marketing group Publicis. Everything a company does needs to build its brand, she says.

Many are going back to the lessons of the dotcom crash at the beginning of the decade, which slammed the nascent digital marketing industry into reverse. 'One of the biggest mistakes I saw then was to cut everything a little bit,' recalls Clark Kokich, Chief executive of Razorfish, a Seattle-based digital marketing agency. It's much better to be relentless about setting priorities and do a few things extraordinary well'. Knowing what to focus on is not easy, however. 'We're in the middle of the biggest marketing transformation we've ever seen. People are engaging and interacting differently,' Ms Lang notes. Simply going back to methods that worked in past downturns may not be the wisest choice.

Diageo, whose Johnnie Walker whisky brand won the grand prix at this year's Institute of Practitioners in Advertising Effectiveness Award for its 'keep walking' campaign, intends to keep spending, says David Gates, global brand director for Johnnie Walker. 'The key is making it locally relevant and making it relevant to the times,' he says. He adds that a recession 'doubles the necessity to be really focused' on three or four tactics that can provide a return on investment, such as sponsorship of Lewis Hamilton, the British world champion Formula One driver.

'The ultimate truth of a recession is that it amplifies what a brand stands for,' says Sir John Hegarty, chairman and creative director at advertising agency BBH, now on

▶

his fifth recession. 'When the chips are down, you really do have to think about what it is I like or think about this brand . . . You have to be absolute in what you stand for.' According to Mr Judge, however, the first things to go will be 'image kind of things', intangible brand-building activities where the return on investment is hard to measure. What will take their place, he says, are tried and trusted tools such as coupons. Best Buy has stayed loyal to a traditional marketing tool: the Sunday insert that drops out of 50m US newspapers each weekend. 'That thing always goes out,' Mr Judge says. 'We see a big sales jump from it.' Best Buy is using coupons carefully, wary in an environment where demand is falling of making less from those people who would be coming in to the store anyway.

Customer loyalty programmes and simple customer service measures such as improving your website can produce a better return than flashy digital campaigns. 'If you give people a simple and unchallenged reward for playing with or viewing your ad, they come back for more,' says Ian Hutchinson, global media director at Reckitt Benskiser, one consumer goods company that is increasing its marketing spending. 'Even if you have Sky Plus, you will not fast forward through the commercials if they are fun.'

While revenues from most advertising media are shrinking, online and search marketing (the use of search engines to drive customers to products) is still growing, in part because spending can be changed at a moment's notice based on response rates. Television advertisements have to be booked weeks ahead.

Using public relations teams to seed clips on video sites or get bloggers talking about a new product can be a lot cheaper than buying TV spots. Dove's Campaign for Real Beauty was 'enormously less expensive than other Dove campaigns', says Alessandro Manfredi, Dove's global brand vice president at Unilever. 'We launched the Dove Self Esteem Fund at the Superbowl in the US. It was expensive, but if you only air the ad once in a year, rather than two months of 30 second spots, with the right PR it is more efficient.'

Dove uses up to 15% of its budget on public relations. But only a few viral campaigns, such as Dove's or the Cadbury Gorilla, succeed and the approach remains difficult to measure. Some marketers have concluded the answer is to empathise with cash-strapped consumers. Denny's, the US restaurant chain, launched a 'Who's bailing you out?' campaign in October to tap into anger at the Wall Street rescue by Congress. And Procter & Gamble, the biggest marketing spender of them all, is playing up the value message in ads for nappies, detergent and shaving foam. In-store promotions are becoming a more prominent part of the mix, AG Lafley, P&G's chief executive, noted on a conference call. '[In] a more recessionary type of environment, more decisions are made in the store and we have to be competitive in the store.' 'Those very accountable and measurable media are, in tough times, more resilient,' says Hamish Pringle, chief executive of the IPA.

But Sir John Hegarty warns against over-reliance on market research. 'My criticism of the research industry is that I am seeing less good advertising than I saw 15 to 20 years ago and I have seen the rise of research. Research is proving a disservice to the quality of what we can do. A daring idea doesn't research well.' 'Advertisers should fight the urge to avoid taking risks, developing campaigns that can cut through the economic gloom,' Sir John says. The advice applies even more for companies that have spent years building up a high-end brand. 'The last thing a luxury brand must do is panic and say, "We are cheap". People don't want to be reminded they are in a recession. We are selling optimism.'

Advert advisory

- *Hamish Pringle, Chief Executive, IPA*: 'Sophisticated marketers with the resources and power to gain market share see recessions as the best chance to do so.' IPA studies show that if your ad spending is 10% above the sector average, it will deliver a 1% market share rise.
- *Richard Pinder, Chief Operating Officer, Publicis Worldwide*: 'What an ill brand needs is a virus – a contagious idea that people will want to pass on and share with each other. Track the spread of the virus by measuring online "buzz" about your brand on social networks,' he says.
- *Sir John Hegarty, Creative Director, BBH*: 'To sustain and maintain a brand, we think you need fame . . . The only way to grow is by broadcasting to people who are not necessarily going to buy your products.'
- *Alessandro Manfredi, Global Brand Vice-President, Dove*: 'Most companies still feel the default media is a 30-second TV ad. TV is best for explaining new products, but emotional concepts might be better expressed through outdoor and public relations,' he says.

Source: Edgecliffe-Johnson, A. and Bradshaw, T., 'Lessons for marketers who face a hard sell', *Financial Times*, 20 November 2008.

Questions

1 Consider some promotional lessons that might be drawn from this case study.

2 How might promoting in a recession influence the marketer's approach?

■ Place (distribution)

This is one of the major challenges for the international marketer, and mastery of this aspect can give the firm an edge over its competitors. A common problem in international marketing is for the firm to concentrate too much on the channels closest to the producer rather than channels closest to the customer. Some of these logistical issues involving type of channel selected are considered in more detail in Chapter 7.

The following aspects will influence the type of channel selected:

- the value and type of product;
- the cost and speed of alternative types of transport;
- the ease with which a channel can be managed;
- what the competitors are doing.

It is more difficult to control these channels from outside the overseas country itself. The type of distribution channel selected will also depend on the type of market entry a company has pursued. If it is operating from subsidiaries in that country (internalisation) then the subsidiary itself will often handle the distribution. If, however, products are simply being imported, then a third party such as a local agent may be employed to ensure that the quickest, cheapest and safest method is used. The company must adapt itself to local conditions, using strategies such as employing local distributors or buying such distributors and using them as part of the firm's internal operations, as appropriate to each circumstance.

Case Study 9.7 emphasises the importance of matching the distribution network to the characteristics of both the product and the intended market.

CASE 9.7 Love in a warm climate   FT

Nestlé's early chocolate experiences in India melted before its eyes. The Swiss manufacturer did not reckon on India's heat and poor distribution. Its chocolates were suitable for Europe, not India, where they were sold in tiny shops, sitting in direct sunlight without air-conditioning. Traders joked that Nestlé's chocolate ended up being sold as a drink. 'I told colleagues "if our chocolates become liquid why don't we sell them as liquid",' says Mr Carol Donati, Nestlé's boss in India.

Nestlé launched Chocostick, a liquid chocolate somewhere between a chocolate bar and a drink. Two years later, Chocostick and Chocki, a rival from Cadbury, are the fastest-growing chocolate brands, with a tenth of India's Rs7.2 billion (£97 million) chocolate market. Although demand for the innovative liquid product is slipping, Mr Bharat Puri, head of Cadbury in India, says: 'Ultimately, liquid chocolate is the product that can overcome our biggest barriers – weather and the related problem of distribution, and affordability.'

Liquid chocolates may have expanded the market, but they still only form a small share of the total. Most sales by value and volume come from old, solid, chewy favourites such as Cadburys Dairy Milk and Nestlé's Kit Kat. So while Coca-Cola hotfoots to communities of fewer than 10,000 people, Cadbury which has a two-thirds share of the market, and its closest rival Nestlé, will continue to target cities and small towns with its old favourite chocolate bars – and will continue to be at the mercy of weather, distribution and affordability.

Average summertime temperatures reach 43 degrees Celsius in India. Chocolate melts at body temperature of 36 degrees. India does not have controlled, refrigerated distribution. Air-conditioned supermarkets are rare. This is the environment in which chocolate is transported and sold, and the cost is high. Cadbury loses 1.5% of annual sales of Ra6.85 billion to heat damage; Nestlé loses 0.3–0.5% of Ra5 billion sales each year.

Both revise ingredients to make chocolate withstand heat. European chocolate makers use more vegetable fat, which produces a smoother chocolate. Indian manufacturers are banned from using vegetable fat by law and use less milk fat to produce a heat-resilient chocolate. Sugar is crystallised for long periods to make it harder. Indian chocolates are more resilient to heat than European chocolate by a factor of 2 degrees.

But the long-term answer to heat is a cold chain network. Its absence is a drag on growth. Ferrero Rocher sells a small quantity of its premium European brand to urban Indians each year, and wants to, but cannot, expand because non-refrigerated distribution would ruin its brand equity. It takes three to five years to build up a successful distribution system, a challenge that scares many foreign companies.

India's retailers are skilful improvisers. In north-west India one favoured cooling method is to place chocolates on a wet towel over a sales dispenser that is cooled by evaporation. These days, such techniques are used alongside coolers or fridges. Nestlé and Cadbury either supply coolers or loan small sums to retailers to buy fridges. But the result can be disappointing. To hold down power costs, distributors and retailers switch off air conditioning or fridges at night. When the cooling is switched on in the morning, the cocoa fat solidifies and turns white, presenting a bizarre, unsellable white on black form.

Nestlé has 350,000 mostly small retailers. Cadbury's 475,000 retailers are expanding by 48,000 a year. Even if distributors and retailers behave responsibly, chocolate companies face another hurdle: pricing. Chocki and Chocostick, for example, may be the right product, but even at Rs2 (less than 5 pence) they need to come down by 75% to win rural consumers. More than half Cadbury's sales come from products that cost less than Rs5 each, an indication of how much more acute pricing will become if and when the company penetrates rural India.

For millions of poor rural (and poor urban) Indians, a typical transaction means buying one boiled sweet at a time. Each year Cadbury sells 895 million Eclairs (a sweet confectionery) in 895 million individual transactions at Rs1 each. The challenge is how far can manufacturers lower prices for a market that is not just vast, but where consumers regard anything brown, sweet and chewy like toffee as a chocolate surrogate.

Source: Merchant, K., 'Love in a warm climate', *Financial Times*, 24 July 2003.

Questions

1 What are the problems for marketers of chocolate products reaching the vast, largely untapped Indian market outside the major towns and cities?

2 What possible solutions might there be to these problems? How feasible are these solutions?

3 What aspects of the marketing mix other than 'place' are highlighted by this study?

Case Study 9.8 emphasises the importance of a distribution approach and infrastructure which must be compatible with the cultural behaviour of consumers in the host country.

CASE 9.8   Indian stores in search of drama   FT

When Kishore Biyani tried a 'clean Italian look' of glass and minimalist lines in one of his Big Bazaar stores, he was surprised by the effect on his customers – it drove them away. The sleek section of the store remained empty while the rest of the store bustled. Mr Biyani, head of the Future Group, India's largest retailer, realised the decor was intimidating and alienating the middle-class Indian consumers who were more used to crowded bazaars and shops. 'You need hustle and bustle', says Mr Biyani. 'The Indian model of shopping is theatrical – there is buzz and haggling. If you have wide aisles you have a problem.'

Mr Biyani's Big Bazaar 'hypermarket' stores, which are India's closest equivalent to Wal-Mart, are clean air-conditioned and well lit. But they have deliberately narrow aisles and overflowing display bins that simulate the feel of open-air markets common in India. Drama and theatre are important elements in Mr Biyani's stores, which also include the Pantaloons and Food Bazaar chains. At one store in a Mumbai shopping mall, dance music popular in Indian nightclubs blasts from loudspeakers while customers jostle to reach the best goods.

Modern retail stores are relatively new to India, so Mr Biyani and other retailers are having to adapt to the evolving shopping habits of Indians. The biggest mistake that retailers make is thinking that 'just because you have set something up people will come', says Anirudha Mukhedkar, chief executive of Restore Solutions, a retail consultancy in Bangalore. Shopping in so-called organised stores accounts for only 4% of India's $322 billion (£218 billion) retail industry but this share is expected to grow to 22% or $427 billion by 2010, according to the Federation of Indian Chambers of Commerce and Industry.

Unlike their struggling counterparts in the west, India's retailers are looking at an attractive growth market. But getting it right will be tricky, given the country's diverse population and distinct regional cultures. Understanding India's wide diversity – socio-economic, religious, regional and linguistic – is key to that strategy. 'When you say Indian consumers, there are at least ten Indias,' says Mr Mukhedkar. Cultural preferences vary widely between regions. For example types of rice and how people buy it differs in the north and south, says Harminder Sahni, managing director of Technopak, a retail consultancy based in Delhi. In the north, rice might be sold in open sacks so consumers can inspect the goods. But in some parts of the south, rice is a common staple sold in sealed packets. Store lay-outs will also vary according to region. In big groceries in Klakata, eastern India and other coastal cities, fish is a staple sold in the vegetable section, whereas it is categorised with meat in inland areas.

Because of these distinct regional tastes, retailers 'don't look at India as India', says Mr Sahni. 'They pick a region or market or city . . . The first two years might be in one city.' He says that most do not have ambitions to open pan-Indian stores: 'Many start in one part of India and just stick to that.'

The Future Group has found another way of capitalising on regional variations: it has 72 annual promotions linked to local festivals. The company says the Big Bazaar store in Bhubaneswar, capital of the backwater eastern state of Orissa, took the group record for a single day's turnover after promoting a sale linked to a festival.

William Bissell, managing director of Fabindia, a chain of upscale boutiques that sells clothing and housewares, says 'Every store has to offer a different mix. That's why retailing in India is so complicated.' Mr Bissell notes that Fabindia, founded in 1960, has an inventory of 200,000 items to cater to consumer tastes that vary dramatically across regions. 'Any retailer will say that is crazy,' says Mr Bissell. To manage its enormous inventory, Fabindia has installed an IT system to track the flow of goods at nearly 100 stores in India. Capacious Western-style malls are also cropping up, especially for luxury goods. But when catering to the mass consumer, 'it makes sense to have smaller stores with more workers', says Mr Mukhedkar of Restore

Solutions. He points out that India's cities command some of the highest real estate prices in the world but labour costs are among the lowest. Packed shelves are also preferable to give the consumer a sense of abundance and choice. 'If a shelf can take 50 things, try to fit in 75,' Mr Mukhedkar advises. 'Density per square foot has to be as high as possible.'

For practical reasons, Mr Bissell favours smaller stores. He dismisses the notion of a 100,000 sq ft Ikea-style store in India, except where 'enormous' volumes might justify high maintenance costs. 'At 40 to 44 degrees in the summer I'm going to have to air-condition the whole thing. That would be an environmental disaster.' And it would be too expensive, he adds, in a country where electricity rates are high, and power cuts force many businesses to buy costly diesel-run generators.

The biggest misunderstanding about retail in India, says Mr Bissell, is that Indians consume as copiously as westerners. Instead, Indians are more selective, value-conscious and price-sensitive. Mr Sahni of Technopak agrees. In a grocery store, an Indian consumer will not fill up a trolley as is common practice in the west. 'Indians will shop with a basket. Below a certain income level, people won't want to spend so much with each transaction.' Smaller refrigerators and limited storage space at home are also factors. 'People will buy more frequently and in smaller packets,' says Mr Sahni.

But some aspects of retail in India are more abstract. To stay attuned to India's pulse, Mr Biyani has a special unit devoted to tracking the country's social trends to incubate ideas for new store brands and strategies.

The 'Future Ideas' group includes sociologists, interior designers, graphic designers and other cultural experts. One of their biggest tasks is analysing the changing tastes of Indian youth. With more than half of India's population under the age of 25, understanding their consuming habits and aspirations is a priority for the Future Group. 'India is still family-centred, and young people influence purchases,' says Mr Biyani. But by far his biggest challenge as a retailer is managing the speed of change in India. 'How do you make an organisation that is not permanent in thought, structure or design?' asks Mr Biyani. 'Retail in the next five years will be different. Nothing is permanent.'

Source: Yee, A., 'Indian stores in search of drama', *Financial Times*, 30 December 2008.

Questions

1 What lessons does this case study suggest for multinational retailers seeking to increase their sales in the Indian marketplace?

2 What more general lessons can be learned from this case study by international marketers?

International marketing planning

The fifth and final phase of the international marketing approach, outlined in Figure 9.1, involves implementation, coordination and control.

Implementation does, of course, presume that there is an international marketing plan to implement! The nature of that plan will depend on some of the issues already discussed, for example, whether the product is standardised or differentiated, the stage of the product life cycle reached in different countries, the national regulatory environment, whether prices are to be uniform internationally or whether price discrimination is to be pursued, the nature of the distributional channels selected, and so on. Of course, such an international marketing plan must be consistent with the key corporate objectives.

Implementation of the international marketing plan, whatever its characteristics, will depend in part on the corporate structure of the firms in question. For example, when a firm grows from exports into international alliances such as those involving joint ventures, licensing or the establishment of subsidiaries it will often create an international division. This can be organised by geographical area or by product and can even take the form of an independent subsidiary. Such divisions usually specialise in international areas of marketing, manufacturing, finance, personnel and research, with responsibilities for the overall planning and control of these international activities. The degree of centralisation of the marketing function will usually depend on the strength of the particular brand. Strong brands need centralised marketing to preserve the integrity of the brand, but for weaker brands there will usually be a great deal of local adaptation so that marketing decisions will also tend to be localised.

International market planning, coordination and control faces a number of particular problems:

- despite technological advances, the market intelligence available for many international operations may be of poor quality and incomplete, especially in the developing/transitional economies;
- few tried and tested models of international marketing exist and those that do are often based on North American constructs which may have little relevance to many international markets.

Useful websites

Now try the self-check questions for this chapter on the website at www.pearsoned.co.uk/wall. You will also find further resources as well as useful weblinks.

Interesting information on product launches, modifications, etc. can be found at:
www.mad.co.uk

The Business Owners Toolkit has a section on pricing and elasticity:
www.toolkit.cch.com

www.bized.ac.uk has information on the marketing strategies of various companies.

Information on market issues including objectives can be found at:
www.brandrepublic.com
www.keynote.co.uk
www.euromonitor.com

Interesting material on global marketing and segmentation strategies can be obtained from:
www.globalweb.co.uk

The Market Research Society can be found at:
www.bmra.org.uk
www.marketresearch.org.uk

Useful key texts

Daniels, J., Radebaugh, L. and Sullivan, D. (2006) *International Business* (11th edn), Pearson Prentice Hall, especially Chapter 16.

Dicken, P. (2003) *Global Shift: Transforming the World Economy* (4th edn), Paul Chapman Publishing Ltd, especially Chapters 7 and 17.

Hill, C. (2006) *International Business: Competing in the Global Marketplace* (5th edn), McGraw-Hill Irwin, especially Chapter 17.

Rugman, A. and Collinson, R. (2009) *International Business* (5th edn), FT Prentice Hall, especially Chapter 11.

Tayeb, M. (2000) *International Business: Theories, Policies and Practices*, Financial Times Prentice Hall, especially Chapter 16.

Wild, J., Wild, K. and Han, J. (2006) *International Business: The Challenges of Globalization* (3rd edn), FT Prentice Hall, especially Chapter 14.

Other texts and sources

Corstjens, M. and Carpenter, M. (2000) 'From Managing Pills to Managing Brands', *Harvard Business Review*, March–April.

Healey, N. (2007) 'The Multinational Corporation', in *Applied Economics* (11th edn), Griffiths, A. and Wall, S. (eds), Financial Times Prentice Hall.

Hill, E. and O'Sullivan, T. (2003) *Marketing* (2nd edn), Longman.

Hollensen, S. (2000) 'International Marketing Planning', in *International Business*, Tayeb, M. (ed.), Financial Times Prentice Hall.

Incandela, D., McLaughlin, K. and Smith Shi, C. (1999) 'Retailers to the World', *McKinsey Quarterly*, no. 3.

Kotler, P. and Armstrong, G. (1994) *Principles of Marketing*, Prentice-Hall, Englewood Cliffs, NJ.

Maruca, R.F. (2000) 'Mapping the World of Customer Satisfaction', *Harvard Business Review*, May–June.

Shermach, K. (1995) 'Portrait of the World', *Marketing News*, 28 August.

United Nations Conference on Trade and Development (UNCTAD), *World Investment Report* (annual publication).

United Nations Development Programme (UNDP), *Human Development Report* (annual publication), OUP.

World Bank, *World Development Report* (annual publication).

Chapter 10

International finance: theory and practice

By the end of this chapter you should be able to:

■ examine the functions of the main international financial markets (including the foreign exchange market);

■ analyse the impacts of these international financial markets on international business;

■ identify and evaluate some of the financial instruments used in the finance of foreign trade;

■ examine some of the key issues facing the firm in the management of international finance and when operating under different financial and fiscal regimes;

■ discuss the background to accounting and financial information available to organisations, identify the main users of such information and the key financial statements;

■ outline (and understand the reasons for) the differences of accounting treatment followed by various countries;

■ assess the need for international harmonisation of accounting practices.

Introduction

The first part of this chapter looks at some of the key issues in international financial management and some of the instruments used in the finance of foreign trade. The operation of the international currency and money markets are reviewed. Particular attention is given to a key 'price', namely the *exchange rate*, which is determined on the foreign exchange market. The broader international institutional environment, such as the role of the International Monetary Fund, World Bank and other international financial institutions has already been considered in Chapter 3. Here we emphasise the interconnectedness of global financial markets, the emergence of new methods and financial instruments within financial intermediation, and the contribution of these to current international liquidity problems. We also review some possible strategic international financial responses available to global business organisations and national governments.

The second part of this chapter looks at the role and nature of international accounting – its main divisions, key financial statements and the regulatory frameworks which govern it. It also contrasts the differing accounting principles used within certain groups of countries, which might produce misleading results if used for comparative purposes. There is a growing trend towards international harmonisation and in particular more use of International Accounting Standards (IASs). Over time it is expected that 'national' accounting regulations will be of less importance than agreed worldwide frameworks, and there is continuing pressure from international stock markets and organisations such as the European Union for the introduction of more unified and cohesive financial reporting standards.

International financial markets

The international financial markets are usually regarded as those involved in trading foreign exchange and various types of paper assets such as equities (shares), government debt (bills, bonds, etc.) and financial derivatives (options, etc.). They are important to firms, individuals and governments in raising finance to support international production, trade and investment, in reducing risks and in providing a potentially income-generating repository for any surplus funds they might hold. Of course, in recent times any such 'certainties' as to the role of these international financial markets and their various financial instruments have been shaken by a global liquidity crisis. We return to this issue, its underlying causes, its impact on international business and proposed remedies at various points in the chapter.

■ The foreign exchange market

The foreign exchange market is the market on which international currencies are traded. It has no physical existence: it consists of traders, such as the dealing rooms of major banks, who are in continual communications with one another on a worldwide basis. Currencies are bought and sold on behalf of clients, who may be companies, private individuals or banks themselves. A distinction is made between the 'spot' rate for a currency, and the forward rate. The *spot rate* is the domestic currency price of a unit of foreign exchange when the transaction is to be completed within three days. The *forward rate* is the price of that unit when delivery is to take place at some future date – usually 30, 60 or 90 days hence. Both spot and forward rates are determined in today's market; the relationship between today's spot and today's forward rate will be determined largely by how the market *expects* the spot rate to move in the near future. The more efficient the market is at anticipating future spot rates, the closer will today's forward rate be to the future spot rate.

The spot market is used by those who wish to acquire foreign exchange immediately. Forward markets are used by three groups of people:

1 *hedgers* who wish to cover themselves (*hedge*) against the risk of exchange variation. For instance, suppose an importer orders goods to be paid for in three months' time in dollars. All his calculations will be upset if the price of dollars rises between now and payment date. He can cover himself by buying dollars today for delivery in three months' time; he thus locks himself into a rate which reduces the risk element in his transaction;

2 *arbitrageurs* who attempt to make a profit on the difference between interest rates in one country and another, and who buy or sell currency forward to ensure that the profit which they hope to make by moving their capital is not negated by adverse exchange rate movements;

3 *speculators* who use the forward markets to buy or sell in anticipation of exchange rate changes. For instance, if I think that today's forward rates do not adequately reflect the probability of the dollar increasing in value I will buy dollars forward, hoping to sell them at a profit when they are delivered to me at some future date.

London is the world's largest centre for foreign exchange trading, with an average daily turnover of over US$10,000 billion. The market is growing all the time; indeed, the average daily turnover in 2008 was more than five times the value recorded in 1992. Some 64% of transactions are 'spot' on any one day, 24% are forward for periods not exceeding one month, and 10% are forward for longer than one month. Increasingly, however, more sophisticated types of transactions are being done. For instance, there is a growth in the following types of transactions:

- *foreign currency futures*, which are standardised contracts to buy or sell on agreed terms on specific future dates (*see* p. 397);
- *foreign currency options*, which give the right (but do not impose an obligation) to buy or sell currencies at some future date and price (*see* p. 397);
- *foreign currency swaps* – rather than purchase the foreign currency, countries and firms swap agreed values of one currency for another, to be returned at a specified future date (*see* p. 398).

Foreign exchange market business in London is done in an increasingly wide variety of currencies with the £/$ business now accounting for only 11% of activity.

Supply and demand for a currency

Prices of currencies are determined, as on any other market, by demand for and supply of the various currencies. Tourists coming to the UK will sell their own currency in order to buy (demand) sterling. Businessmen wishing to import goods will often sell (supply) sterling in order to buy currency with which to pay the supplier in another country. Other types of transactions, too, will have exchange rate repercussions. For instance, if an American company wishes to buy an office or a factory in the UK, it will need to convert dollars into sterling. A similar demand for sterling will result from foreign banks who wish to make sterling deposits in London, or residents abroad who wish to buy UK government bonds.

Another way of presenting this is to say that in any given period of time the factors that determine the demand for and supply of foreign exchange are those which are represented in the balance of payments account. For example, demand for sterling results from the export of UK goods and services and inflows of foreign capital into the UK (short and long term), which are all + signs in the balance of payments accounts. Similarly, a supply of sterling results from imports of goods and services into the UK and outflows of capital from the UK (short and long term), which are all − signs in the balance of payments accounts.

Of course companies and individuals are not the only clients of foreign exchange market dealers. In the case of the UK the Bank of England buys and sells foreign currency, using the official reserves in the Exchange Equalisation Account. In order to reflect on why this might be the case, we have to remember that governments have an interest in the level of the exchange rate (*see* Chapter 4) and that they may on occasion wish to intervene in the workings of the foreign exchange market to affect the value of their currency. Indeed, it was estimated that on the day sterling was forced to withdraw from the Exchange Rate Mechanism (ERM) (16 September 1992), the Bank of England spent an estimated £7 billion, roughly a third of its foreign exchange reserves, in buying sterling. In particular, it bought sterling with deutschmarks in an unsuccessful attempt to preserve the sterling exchange rate within its permitted ERM band. A current criticism by the US administration is that the Chinese authorities are continually intervening in the foreign exchange market to keep the exchange rate between the yuan and the dollar artificially low.

> The worldwide demand for and supply of a currency will determine its price (the *exchange rate*) on the foreign exchange market.

The exchange rate

The exchange rate is the price of one currency in terms of another. The exchange rate for sterling is conventionally defined as the number of units of another currency, such as the dollar, that it takes to purchase one pound sterling on the foreign exchange market. In the market, however, it is usually quoted as the number of units of the domestic currency that it takes to purchase one unit of the foreign currency. In general terms the sterling exchange rate is perhaps the most important 'price' in the UK economic system. It affects the standard of living, because it determines how many goods we can get for what we sell abroad. It influences the price of UK exports and hence their sales, thereby determining output and jobs in the export industries. It structures the extent to which imports can compete with home-produced goods, and thereby affects the viability of UK companies. Because the price of imports enters into the retail price index (RPI) any variation in the exchange rate will also have an effect on the rate of inflation.

Figure 10.1 presents a stylised picture of how the sterling exchange rate is determined on the foreign exchange market. Suppose we start with the supply of sterling S and the demand for sterling D, giving an initial equilibrium exchange rate $0P$ with $0Q$ pounds sterling bought and sold on the foreign exchange market. Anything which shifts one or other of the curves will change the equilibrium price (exchange rate) on the foreign exchange market. Supply and demand curves for sterling can shift for a number of reasons:

- A shift (increase) in supply from S to S_1 might be due to a change in the tastes of UK residents in favour of foreign products. More expenditure by UK residents on imports will mean more sterling being supplied in order to buy the foreign currencies to pay for those imports (more investment overseas by UK residents will have the same effect). The same increase in supply from S to S_1 could be the result of a rise in *capital outflows* from sterling deposits to overseas currency deposits in different currencies.
- A shift (decrease) in demand from D to D_1 might be due to a change in the tastes of overseas residents away from UK products. Less expenditure by overseas residents on UK exports will mean less sterling being demanded in order to pay for those exports (less investment in the UK by overseas residents – firms and individuals – will have

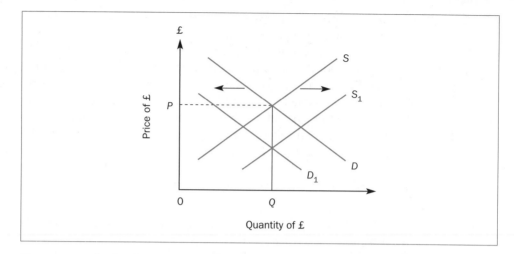

Figure 10.1 **The foreign exchange market**

the same effect). The same decrease in demand from D to D_1 could be the result of a fall in *capital inflows* into sterling deposits from overseas currency deposits in different countries.

Each of these changes (increase in supply or decrease in demand) will result in the pound falling in value (depreciating). We have already noted how a fall in the exchange rate makes exports cheaper abroad and imports dearer at home (*see* Chapter 3, p. 111).

pause for thought 1

In recent times the pound has been falling in value (depreciating against both the euro and the US dollar). Can you use Figure 10.1 to explain the factors that might cause the pound to fall below $0P$? Can you also use Figure 10.1 to suggest how the Chinese authorities might be attempting to prevent the yuan rising against the US dollar?

In actual fact there are different types of exchange rate, as is noted in Box 10.1.

Box 10.1 **Types of exchange rate**

In a foreign exchange market where exchange rates are allowed to 'float', every currency has a price against every other currency. In order to allow for measurability three different types of exchange rate may be used.

1 *The nominal rate of exchange*. This is the rate of exchange for any one currency as quoted against any other currency. The nominal exchange rate is therefore a bilateral (two country) exchange rate.

2 *The effective exchange rate (EER)*. This is a measure that takes into account the fact that each currency (e.g. sterling) varies in different ways against each of the other currencies, some of which are more important than others in the UK's trading relationships. It is calculated as a trade weighted average of the individual or bilateral rates, and is expressed as an index number relative to the base year. The EER is therefore a multilateral (many country) trade weighted exchange rate.

Box 10.1	Continued

3 *The real exchange rate (RER).* This concept is designed to measure the rate at which home goods exchange for goods from other countries, rather than the rate at which the currencies themselves are traded. It is thus essentially a measure of competitiveness. When we consider multilateral UK trade, it is defined as:

$$RER = EER \times \frac{P(UK)}{P(F)}$$

In other words, the real exchange rate is equal to the effective exchange rate multiplied by the price ratio of home, $P(UK)$, to foreign, $P(F)$, goods. If UK prices rise, the real exchange rate will rise unless the effective exchange rate falls.

In fact there was a sharp upward revision between 1996 and 1998 in nominal sterling exchange rates against individual countries and against the weighted average of 16 major industrial countries (i.e. the sterling effective exchange rate). This appreciation of sterling led to a sharp deterioration in the UK's international competitiveness between 1996 and 1998, making UK exports dearer overseas and imports into the UK cheaper. For example, the sterling effective exchange rate rose as an index from 86.3 to 105.3 (1990 = 100) between 1996 and 1998, a rise of over 22%. A lower price inflation in the UK than in its competitors did, however, help modify any loss of competitiveness, resulting in a smaller rise in terms of real sterling exchange rates.

Note, however, the dramatic fall in the sterling effective exchange rate in Table 10.1 since 2007. This downward revision of some 30% in sterling against the dollar, the euro and the broader basket of currencies is having a significant effect on the prices of UK exports (cheaper in the foreign currency) and UK imports (dearer in sterling).

Table 10.1 **Sterling nominal exchange rates 1997–2007**

Year	US dollar	Sterling effective exchange rate (2005 = 100)	Euro
2000	1.52	101.15	1.64
2001	1.44	99.49	1.61
2002	1.50	100.56	1.59
2003	1.64	96.88	1.45
2004	1.83	101.60	1.47
2005	1.82	100.00	1.46
2006	1.84	101.22	1.47
2007	2.00	103.53	1.46
2008	1.44	73.80	1.03

We consider the advantages and disadvantages of adopting the euro as a single currency in the on-line student resources for Chapter 10.

International debt financing

Firms can raise short and long-term loans on international as well as domestic financial markets. The term 'money markets' is usually applied to the buying and selling of short-term (less than one year to maturity) debt instruments, whereas the term 'bond markets' refers to trading longer-term (more than one year to maturity) debt instruments.

Here we select a number of important international financial markets by way of illustration. In doing so we examine the sources and impacts of the so-called 'credit crunch' and the new financial derivatives and instruments which have been widely traded across the world, and which underpin many of the contemporary issues that have arisen within global finance and trade. In fact, given the current volatility in international financial markets, it may be helpful to begin with the market in a wide range of structured investment vehicles (SIVs) and the origins of that market.

◼ Structured investment vehicles (SIVs) market

These are the financial instruments that have emerged in recent years and which consist of not one but a *variety* of securities, some of which involve mortgage debt (*see* Figure 10.2). Before reviewing the contribution of SIVs to current international financial developments, it will help to consider the so-called *sub-prime* market, and the impact this has had on the value of SIVs, many of which involve a mortgage-backed 'slice' of their overall portfolio.

Sub-prime market

The term 'sub-prime' is widely used to refer to excessive lending for mortgage purposes in the US to low income borrowers at high risk. When economic slowdown occurred in the US in 2006/07, many of these high risk borrowers lost their jobs and/or found themselves unable to pay the higher monthly repayments as US interest rates rose substantially in 2006/07 (by around 4% in little over one year). Nor did these low income/ high risk borrowers have assets to help cushion falls in their current income. As a result many have defaulted on their loans and the bad debt provision of the lenders have soared, putting huge pressure on themselves and on other financial firms worldwide which have invested in the mortgage related securities.

House prices fell by over 4% in the US in 2007 and a simulation by economists at the UBS Bank in 2007 suggested that a 10% drop in US house and share prices would

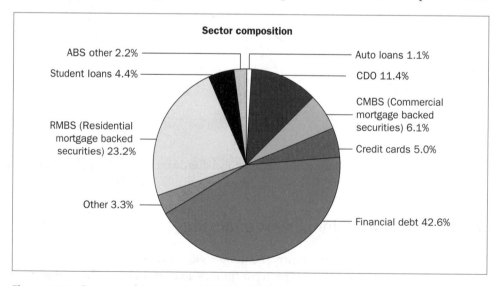

Figure 10.2 **Structured Investment Vehicle (SIV)**
Source: Davies, P., 'SIV managers dig out their manuals', *Financial Times*, 30 August 2007.

reduce US economic growth by as much as 2.6 percentage points. By early 2009 house prices in the US had fallen, on average, by over 30% since 2006, with the expectation that a further 10% decline was still possible. The negative impact on economic growth had indeed materialised, with the US economy officially in recession, having experienced two or more quarters of negative growth.

Box 10.2 takes a closer look at what exactly constitutes an SIV.

Box 10.2 The Structured Investment Vehicle (SIV)

1 A structured investment vehicle (SIV) exists to help those acquiring it make a profit from the difference between the low cost of short-term debt funding and the higher returns, or yields, of longer-term debt investments.

2 A SIV consists of a pool of debts of financial companies, such as banks and insurers, including asset-backed securities, or bonds, backed by mortgages, loans or other debt (*see* Figure 10.2).

3 The SIV funds these more profitable longer-term investments by issuing debt itself. A small portion of this debt (between 5 and 12%) is longer term and carries the first risk of losses if assets in the pool of investments start to go bad. This debt is also the last to be repaid, but it shares some of the profits made by the vehicle. This is the *junior debt*, otherwise known as the capital notes.

4 The lion's share of debt issued by the SIV is very low cost short-term commercial paper, which has a life span of days or weeks, and medium-term notes, which have a life span of three to six months. This is the *senior debt*.

Problems in this market for SIVs and associated financial instruments such as collateralised debt obligations (CDOs) have played a key role in the events unfolding globally over recent years. Case Study 10.1 provides some useful insights into the problems which subsequently materialised.

CASE 10.1 SIV managers dig out their manuals FT

One by one, some of the off-balance sheet vehicles run by banks and asset managers that buy bonds backed by mortgage and other debt are beginning to breach their investment rules and that could force them into a fire-sale of their assets. Asked recently what such a vehicle's next step was, one manager forced to begin selling assets responded with grim humour: 'I don't know – I'll have to read the instructions.'

The manager is unlikely to be alone among his peers in reaching for the chapter of an operating manual they hoped never to consult. While it might sound a bit like trying to learn the workings of a parachute after already having jumped from the plane, the comment illustrates the mechanical nature of a group of investors who hold nearly $400 billion worth of assets. Once 'triggers' are breached, managers have no room for manoeuvre and, for a group of investors looking at declining values in the assets they hold, the last thing their markets need is another wave of forced sales.

The vehicles that live and die by such tight rules are *Structured Investment Vehicles* (SIVs) and their near cousins, SIV-lites, which focus exclusively on mortgage-backed bonds and collateralised debt obligations (CDOs). CDOs are packages of debt that split into slices with different risk [see Case Study 10.2 on page 391].

▶

These SIVs have been laid low by two factors. First, they have recently faced difficulties in raising funding since the short-term debt markets they rely on heavily have seized up. Second, the market values for some types of the assets they hold have been falling as investors have deserted asset-backed securities over fears of contagion from the US subprime mortgage markets.

As Sachsen Funding 1, a SIV-lite run by the troubled German bank Sachsen LG, put it in a note to investors through the Irish stock exchange: 'Any vehicle which relies on the [short term debt] market for funding and has market value triggers is under pressure.' Analysts at Royal Bank of Scotland estimate that forced asset sales from two struggling SIVs and four troubled SIV-lites mean assets with a face value of up to $43 billion worth are already at risk of flooding on to the markets.

One vehicle to hit trouble was Cheyne Finance, an SIV with assets with a face value of roughly $6 billion run by Cheyne Capital Management, a London-based hedge fund. The firm announced that its SIV had hit an 'enforcement event', which is rating agency jargon for having to sell assets in order to pay back debt. Cheyne's SIV is thought to have a significant amount of cash at hand to cover debt repayments over a number of months while it attempts to work out a route to survival. But its chances of success depend heavily on a restoration of faith in the values of the kinds of assets it holds.

For many SIV and SIV-lite managers, the biggest frustration is that they do not believe the intrinsic value of their highly rated assets is as low as the current fear-stricken market prices them. They argue that many of the assets they hold have not suffered any significant downgrades in their credit worthiness from the ratings agencies.

But while the market lacks faith that an AAA rating on certain kinds of mortgage-backed securities or collateralised debt obligations really means these products are safe, managers' hands are tied by the market value rules of their vehicles. Ganesh Rajendra, head of securitisation research at Deutsche Bank has argued that the 'securities arbitrage' models of SIVs – the aim of profiting from the difference between cheap short-term debt funding and higher long-term investment returns were likely to be under increasing pressure. 'SIV capital requirements may already be under pressure, particularly we think for the newer vehicles that are less likely to benefit from lower leverage or cash and other reserve cushions,' he said.

Standard & Poor's, the rating agency, estimates SIVs that issued more than $23 billion worth of senior debt began operations between March and May of 2007 alone. Two of the largest launches ever seen came in 2007. Axon Financial Funding, run by TPG-Axon Capital, the hedge fund of former Goldman Sachs banker Dinakar Singh, had issued more than $11 billion in senior debt by mid-July 2007 after launching only in March, according to S&P. The health of these and other vehicles depends on their exposure to US sub-prime mortgages through mortgage-backed securities and CDOs, which can vary wildly. However, few managers have come out to clarify their exposures.

Source: Davies, P., 'SIV managers dig out their manuals', *Financial Times*, 30 August 2007.

Questions

1 What factors are suggested as having contributed to problems for SIVs?

2 To what extent have events subsequent to August 2007, when the article was written, justified the issues raised in the article?

'Contagion' is a word much feared by analysts of the sub-prime market. Many innovative financial instruments which were developed and used ('securitisation') to stimulate extra lending and borrowing are now viewed with much greater suspicion by the financial markets. Lending between financial intermediaries themselves has also diminished, as they have become more unsure of the true creditworthiness of the borrowers, given that there is now serious concern over the value of many of these new financial instruments in their portfolio. This reluctance of financial intermediaries to lend to each other was a key factor in the problems experienced in 2007/08 by Northern Rock in the UK, whose business model depended on regular inter-bank loans which were no longer forthcoming. The share price of Northern Rock collapsed in late 2007, forcing the Bank of England to step in as 'lender of last resort' and to avoid a systemic banking failure in the UK.

Collateralised debt obligations (CDOs) are themselves bundles of other securities and have been traded on international financial markets singly, or as part of broader SIVs. The linkage of slices of these securities to the falling value of mortgages and to other assets of diminishing value, has been a major element in the declining portfolio and capital values of many international organisations.

CASE 10.2   Seniority brings a false sense of security   FT

When Martin Sullivan met investors in AIG in December 2007, the man who succeeded Hank Greenberg as chief executive spent much of the time discussing the esoteric topic of 'super-senior' debt.

No wonder. One of the most bitter ironies of the AIG saga is that it was not gambles on ultra-risky assets that brought down the mighty insurance group. Instead, the main cause was an instrument previously considered so secure that bankers dubbed it 'more than triple A' debt – implying that this product was safer even than, say, US Treasury bonds.

The 'super-senior' concept evolved on Wall Street almost a decade ago, when banks such as JPMorgan and Credit Suisse started creating complex bundles of derivatives and bonds, known as collateralised debt obligations (CDOs) and then sold investors pieces of this debt, ranked according to different levels of risk.

The instruments at the top of the capital structure were called 'super-senior' notes, since they would suffer losses only if every other type of investor had been wiped out first – a scenario that seemed extremely unlikely. Indeed, in 2001 Alan Greenspan, then chairman of the US Federal Reserve, even suggested that 'nearly riskless' products such as super-senior could replace Treasuries in asset managers' portfolios.

Hence groups such as AIG happily accumulated large volumes of them, collecting returns of 4–11 basis points over Treasury yields. AIG also earned fees by insuring triple A securities held by banks. This it considered to be extremely low-risk. In the case of US mortgage debt, AIG calculated that super-senior paper would suffer losses only if 40% of homeowners defaulted on their debt and about half the value of those homes was destroyed.

But the past two years have shattered these assumptions, for two reasons. First, it has emerged that the assets inside many CDOs are not representative of the housing market as a whole, but are skewed towards the worst types of loan. The second mistake centres on prices. Super-senior instruments, which had traded near face value, collapsed last autumn to between 40 and 80% of that.

Initially, bankers thought this slide was temporary. However, that hope may be wrong. Apart from defaults, another factor dragging down prices is that banks created these products (and wrote insurance on them) to exploit regulatory loopholes. But regulators are scrambling to plug those. That could also depress the price of super-senior debt, and associated insurance, for a long time. Hence the writedowns at banks and at AIG.

Source: Tett, G., 'Seniority brings a false sense of security', *Financial Times*, 7 October 2008.

Question

Examine the contribution of CDOs to current problems in the international financial system.

Box 10.3 identifies some of the other, more conventional instruments, used in the finance of international trade.

Box 10.3 Financial instruments and international trade

The following is a brief review of some of the more traditional financial instruments associated with the finance of international trade.

- *Bills of exchange*. An exporter may send this to an importer ordering the importer to pay a certain sum of money to the exporter on receipt of the bill or at a specified date in the future (often three months). The exporter (seller) is the '*drawer*' of the bill and the importer (buyer) the '*drawee*', the exporter's bank is the '*remitting bank*' and the importer's bank the '*collecting bank*'. The bill of exchange must be '*accepted*' (endorsed) by the foreign importer (*drawee)* before it becomes a 'negotiable instrument' – i.e. once accepted the bill can be sold to a third party for less than the face value (i.e. discounted) if the exporter needs immediate cash or held for the full three months, etc.

- An '*avalised bill of exchange*' carries a guarantee from the importer's bank that the bill will definitely be honoured. If the bill is not avalised, then the exporter's bank will expect the exporting company to repay the loan itself should the importer default. '*With recourse financing*' is a term used whenever a bank can demand compensation from an exporter should the importer default.

- *Forfaiting*. For large-scale (and often long-term) finance a company may issue a bundle of bills of exchange, each one maturing on a different date (e.g. six months, 12 months, 18 months, 24 months, etc.) up to the completion of the project. Once 'accepted', these bills can be sold in their entirety to the company's own banker should immediate cash be required.

- *Letters of credit*. These may be required by exporters who wish to have proof that they will be paid before they send their products abroad. Such letters are an order from one bank to a bank abroad authorising payment to a person named in the letter of a particular sum of money or up to a limit of a certain sum. Letters of credit are not negotiable but can be cashed at the specified bank. A 'confirmed' letter of credit is one which has been guaranteed by a bank in the exporter's own country; the confirming bank has no claim on the

> **Box 10.3 Continued**
>
> exporter should there be any default. Normally the exporter is paid by the confirming bank which then collects the money from the foreign bank issuing the credit. Almost all letters of credit are 'irrevocable', i.e. they cannot be cancelled at any time by the customer (importer).
>
> - *Factoring.* Here the debt is sold on to another company for a price (usually well below the face value of the debt), with the new company now responsible for collecting the original debt.
> - *Invoice discounting.* Similar to factoring, except that the exporter retains responsibility for debt collection and for an agreed proportion of bad debts. However, the exporter does receive a cash payment (loan) from the invoice discounter issued to customers.
> - *Securitisation.* The process of converting any existing (non-tradable) loan into a security which is tradable. The seller of the asset (security) guarantees payment of interest in the new bundled security, which now becomes more liquid than the assets it replaces.
> - *Options, futures and swaps* pp. 397–8.

The relevance of the availability, as well as cost, of international debt financing to global trade is well illustrated by Case Study 10.3. There is a distinct lack of trust between financial intermediaries themselves, given that no party knows the extent to which the other has CDOs or other mortgage backed securities in their portfolios or SIVs. As a result there is a reluctance to lend even to other financial institutions, given the uncertainty arising from this information asymmetry. Case Study 10.3 amply illustrates the adverse impacts of these liquidity shortages on the global supply chain.

CASE 10.3 Sum of the parts   FT

The idea of a 'crisis cell' might suggest counter-terrorism more than it does corporate risk management. But at Safran, the French aerospace and defence company, it is the name of a team charged with responding to the ever-increasing pressure on its global supply chain.

Safran's crisis cell monitors the group's 4000 suppliers, which receive €5.3 billion ($6.7 billion, £4.5 billion) in total a year in return for products and equipment. Xavier Dessemond, Safran's purchasing director, says the aim is to deal with the problem in 'a preventative manner'. He adds that while no supplier has yet experienced great difficulties, 'We know there is a crisis and we know our industry will be probably affected.'

It is a growing concern for manufacturers worldwide. Companies' supply chains have become far more global in the past decade, with the consequence that stress from the financial crisis is spreading quickly to suppliers large and small. It is testing the global supply chain to an extent rarely seen and spurring companies in industries from aerospace to retailing to take extraordinary measures.

VT Group, a leading British defence group, is a good example. The former Vosper Thornycroft has a solid business, as many of its orders come from the UK government. But in late 2008 it summoned its leading 100 suppliers – which account for about 70% of its £500 million ($740 million, €580 million) annual supply budget – to a meeting. The message from Paul Lester, chief executive, was stark: 'If you get into financial difficulties, don't delay but come and talk to us. You are probably better talking to us than banks, because banks aren't really doing their jobs right now and we can help.' Possibilities for help include paying suppliers in cash earlier, giving them longer orders or even lending them workers, says Mr Lester. At Safran, Mr Dessemond says his company could put capital into its suppliers, help them obtain aid from government agencies or change payment terms – but all only in 'exceptional cases'.

Mr Lester says simply: 'We want a good supply base. And we are just nervous that, particularly among SMEs [small and mid-sized enterprises], somebody will get into difficulties.' A small software supplier to VT did go bust recently – the latest in a number of European supplier collapses, from Stankiewicz, the German car parts supplier, to several manufacturers that serve UK retailers.

All this marks a huge shift for many large industrial groups. Previously much of the talk focused on whether their suppliers had the capacity to keep up with demand. 'It is amazing how the conversation has changed in the last few months,' says Aaron Davis, the marketing manager of Schneider Electric, the French energy management company. Now, many suppliers are more likely to be calling to ask for bailouts. The culprit is obvious, according to manufacturers: it is the banks. DVA, the Germany carmakers' association, accuses some banks of 'making credit lines more expensive, withdrawing them or making credit due in the short term'. Ratings agencies, such as Moody's and Fitch point to the increased difficulties small and medium-sized companies face in securing credit from banks.

But the big companies may also be partly to blame. Many have squeezed suppliers mercilessly for years. The car industry is renowned for manufacturers suddenly imposing demands for 10% across-the-board cuts in component prices. Likewise, UK retailers led by Tesco have succeeded in pushing payment terms with suppliers increasingly in their favour. Tesco has increased the time it takes to pay for some goods from 30 days up to 60 days.

Bart Becht, chief executive of Reckitt Benckiser, the consumer goods group, recently criticised such moves as making no sense. Julie Metelko, a business improvement specialists at PA Consulting, says that such an approach risks backfiring on large companies: 'If suppliers aren't getting cash, then you risk taking them out.'

That is why companies such as Daimler, the German luxury carmaker, and some of its rivals are looking at giving cash straight to suppliers in difficulties. Three hundred thousand jobs are at risk in this industry – due to a crisis that was not caused by small and mid-sized companies but [which] is making them suffer massively,' says Dieter Zetsche, Daimler's chief executive. Volkswagen, Europe's largest carmaker, has set up a special team to stop suppliers from collapsing.

Counterparty risk is well-known in the financial world, where it refers to the chance one side of an agreement will default. As it becomes a concept to be reckoned with in the real economy, manufacturers are checking their exposure. 'We have got to look at risk in the supply chain much more closely. Is your Chinese supplier financially sound? Are they capable of maintaining your supply?' asks Tim Lawrence, a supply chain expert at PA Consulting.

Many counter that they have double or triple sourcing with suppliers for the same part or component spread across the world. 'In tough times like these, you need as much as possible to keep two suppliers. Globalisation helps here,' says Pierre-Jean Sivignon, chief financial officer at Philips, the Dutch electronics group. Don Gogel, chief executive of Clayton, Dubilier & Rice, the US private equity firms, says: 'Globalisation is a big positive, as it has led to multiple suppliers around the world.'

But doubts remain. One is over how quickly a supplier can respond to take over the capacity if one of its rivals collapses. Another is the fact that some components are so complex they are manufactured only by one supplier. Additionally, companies such as carmakers often use one supplier for each model or project, meaning changing component makers could take months.

Just-in-time delivery – long the mantra of many manufacturers worldwide – is also turning into a possible weakness in the supply chain. A problem with just one supplier can throw the entire system into chaos, as can shipping difficulties. Manufacturing experts say that for these and other reasons they are starting to see western companies bring back operations or suppliers from far-off countries in Asia to closer to home: eastern Europe or Mexico.

'We are hearing about it more and more – that companies that went to China and elsewhere in Asia for the low costs are facing rising energy and labour costs. So they are bringing production back closer to home either to the UK or more likely to eastern Europe,' says Jane Lodge, head of the manufacturing industry team at Deloitte in London.

One factor driving the cuts in stock is the approach of the end of the year for accounting purposes. Many companies are keen to have as much cash on their balance sheets as possible by year-end. Ms Metelko says: 'Everybody is being much more aggressive this year, especially as they're looking at weaker demand.'

Daniel Corsten, a professor at the IE Business School at Madrid, says these are desperate times for some otherwise solid suppliers: 'Supply chains are generally in good shape . . . But what we see now is very worrying. Previously robust suppliers in terms of quality and reliability cannot finance their production cycle any more. Shrinking demand means that customers pay late, less, or default, and as a consequence suppliers receive less revenue and later revenue. Counterparty risk has reached the real economy.'

Source: Milne, R., 'Sum of the parts', *Financial Times*, 17 November 2008, p. 12.

Question

Examine the relevance of the 'credit crunch' to supply chain strategies.

We now review some of the other important international financial markets.

■ Eurocurrency market

Eurocurrency is currency held on deposit with a bank outside the country from which that currency originates. For example, loans made in dollars by banks in the UK are known as Eurodollar loans. The Eurocurrency market is a wholesale market and has its origins in the growing holdings of US dollars outside the USA in the 1960s. Since that time, Eurocurrency markets have grown rapidly to include dealing in all the major currencies, and have become particularly important when oil price rises have created huge world surpluses and deficits, resulting in large shifts in demand for and supply of the major world currencies.

The major participants are banks, who use the Euromarkets for a variety of reasons: for short-term inter-bank lending and borrowing, to match the currency composition of assets and liabilities, and for global liquidity transformation between branches. However, the market is also extensively used by companies and by governmental and international organisations. Lending which is longer term is usually done on a variable-rate basis, where the interest is calculated periodically in line with changing market rates.

There are two important factors which make Eurocurrency business attractive. The first is that the market is unregulated, so that banks which are subject to reserve requirements or interest rate restrictions in the home country, for instance, can do business more freely abroad. The other factor is that the margin between the lending and borrowing rates is narrower on this market than on the home market, primarily because banks can operate at lower cost when all business is wholesale and when they are not subject to reserve requirements.

◼ Euro-paper and Euro-note markets

The Eurocurrency markets have led to the issue of various types of *Euro-paper* and *Euro-note* debt instruments.

- *Euro-commercial papers* (ECPs) are short-term debt instruments usually denominated in dollars. They can be issued by multinational companies with excellent credit ratings, and holders obtain a return by purchasing them at a discount (i.e. paying less than face value at issue and receiving face value on maturity).
- *Euro notes* are short to medium-term debt instruments (up to five years to maturity) which again can be issued by multinational companies, but with an interest return (rather than discount) to those holding them to maturity. Euro medium-term notes (Euro MTNs) have been growing rapidly in recent years, often being seen as much more flexible than more conventional debt instruments (e.g. more choice in terms of value, maturity date, currency, fixed/variable interest, etc.).

◼ Eurobond markets

Longer-term bonds typically have maturity dates ranging up to 30 years. A *Eurobond* is underwritten by an investment bank and can be sold only outside the country from which the bond originates. Eurobonds are usually issued by large multinational firms (of high credit standing), governments and international institutions. The interest paid may be fixed or variable; in the latter case a linkage is made with other interest rates (e.g. the London Interbank Offer Rate – LIBOR). Some Eurobonds are 'convertible' in the sense that holders can convert the bond at a set price ('warrant' price) prior to the maturity date. The Eurobond market has grown substantially, partly because there is less regulation and fewer disclosure requirements than in other bond markets and various tax advantages (e.g. interest on Eurobonds has been exempt from the EU income-withholding tax).

Futures and options markets

Exchange rates became highly volatile in the early 1970s as countries moved away from the system of pegging their exchange rates to the dollar. Futures and options markets have therefore developed as a means of reducing the risks of companies requiring foreign currencies for international transactions. Both of these instruments are referred to as 'financial derivatives'. Attempts to avoid future risks of this kind are sometimes referred to as 'hedging'.

Futures markets

A foreign currency futures contract is an agreement to deliver or receive a fixed amount of foreign currency at a future specified time and price. The 'margin requirement' refers to the price the purchaser of the future foreign currency must pay for others taking the risk of exchange rate volatility. Typically such margin requirements are 5% or less. The International Monetary Market (IMM) on the Chicago Mercantile Exchange is the main US market for foreign currency futures. Eurex is the German equivalent and LIFFE (London International Finance and Futures Exchange) the UK equivalent.

- *Holder* is the purchaser of the option.
- *Writer (or grantee)* is the seller of the option.
- *European options* are those which can only be exercised on the specified expiration date.
- *American options* are those which can be exercised at any time before the expiration date.
- *Premium* is the initially agreed difference between the selling and buying price of the currencies (i.e. the cost of the option to the purchaser).

Clearly those involved in buying and selling options must negotiate the premium. However, the other avenue for gain/loss is the difference between the exercise (strike) price agreed at the outset and the spot (current) price at the time at which the option is exercised.

Such options can be traded on formal exchanges or on less formal, over-the-counter (OTC) markets. Important formal exchanges include LIFFE in the UK, Chicago Mercantile Exchange and Philadelphia Stock Exchange in the USA, the European Options Exchange in Amsterdam and the Montreal Stock Exchange.

Options markets

There are obvious similarities between the futures and option markets. The main difference, however, is that the forward and future contracts markets involve a legal obligation to buy or sell a fixed amount of foreign currency at a specified point in time (expiration date), whereas the options markets only involve a right to such a transaction.

- A *call option* purchaser has the right to buy foreign currency (sell domestic currency).
- A *put option* purchaser has the right to sell foreign currency (buy domestic currency).

Currency and interest rate swaps

The IMF introduced (in 1961) the idea of 'currency swaps' by which a country in need of specific foreign exchange could avoid the obvious disadvantage of having to purchase it with its own currency by simply agreeing to 'swap' a certain amount through the Bank for International Settlements. The swap contract would state a rate of exchange which would also apply to the 'repayment' at the end of the contract.

Multinational firms as well as governments are now making use of swap facilities, with the swaps arranged by dealers located in various international financial centres. These can involve both currency swaps and interest rate swaps. For example, one multinational may borrow funds in its own financial market in which it has low interest access to funds and swap these loans with those similarly obtained by another multinational located overseas. As well as removing the exchange risk on low-cost borrowings, such swap transactions have the further advantages of not appearing on the firm's balance sheet! Interest rate swaps can also involve changing the maturity structure of the debt. Here one party to the swap typically exchanges a floating-rate obligation for a fixed-rate obligation.

International equity markets

As well as raising international finance by trading in various types of debt instruments, business can raise funds by issuing share capital (equity) in financial centres throughout the world. Equities (or shares) are non-redeemable assets issued by companies, and investors are actually buying part-ownership (a share) of a company. Investors in ordinary shares receive dividends if companies are able to pay them, but their major advantage as an asset lies in the possibility of capital appreciation if strong profits growth is anticipated. In the case of *preference shares* the company pays a fixed annual sum to the shareholder, and there is also the possibility of capital appreciation when the share is sold. *Ordinary shareholders* bear the largest risks since if the company goes out of business, the 'preferred' shareholders are entitled to a share of the money raised by selling assets first (although only after the Revenue and Customs and secured bank borrowers are paid). However, in good times, the ordinary shareholder will earn the greatest returns as dividend payments may be much greater than the fixed return received by preference shareholders. As always in the financial markets, those who bear most risk have highest potential for returns.

A high proportion of equities are traded on the stock exchanges throughout the world. Strictly speaking, 'stock' refers to the issued capital of a company other than that in the form of shares (equities). In more recent times the term 'stock' has become synonymous with the issue of securities of any type (bonds, shares, etc.). The stock exchanges we consider below are markets for all these securities though our main concern here is with equities.

■ London Stock Exchange (LSE)

The London Stock Exchange (LSE) is the second largest market for equities in the world. The largest is in the hands of Euronext, the company that controls the Paris exchange. In recent times the securities markets in Germany, France and Italy have all become 'integrated', i.e. with cash and derivatives trading, settlement and clearing all done under one roof. In contrast the UK securities market on the London Stock Exchange remains fragmented, with different institutions responsible for settlement, clearing and trading.

Individual share prices may move for a whole host of reasons: stockbrokers' reports; bid rumours; executive departures; adverse press reports; results which beat, or fall short of, market expectations. This last factor is one of the most important. Outsiders are often puzzled when a company which reports a 30% rise in profits sees its shares fall.

Markets indulge in what one might call the 'White Queen syndrome', after the character in *Through the Looking Glass*. The White Queen screamed before she pricked her finger and when the injury actually occurred, made only a small sigh, as she had got all her screaming over with in advance. Similarly, stock markets are forever looking to the future and anticipating what will happen. Expectations are built into the market, thus, if a company is expected to increase profits by 40% and only reports a rise of 30%, its shares will fall.

■ FTSE

Because there are so many quoted shares, investors use 'benchmarks', in the form of baskets of representative stocks, to track the market's overall movements. The most commonly used in the UK is the FTSE 100, which stands for the *Financial Times/ Stock Exchange 100 index* and is designed to show the UK's 100 largest companies. Broader indices, such as the *FTSE All-Share*, which includes around 800 stocks and the *FTSE SmallCap*, which covers shares in smaller companies, are also used. Companies drop in and out of these indices as their shares rise and fall, or are subject to takeover.

The indices are also used to monitor the performance of fund managers who look after other people's money, whether it be pension funds, charities, or the portfolios of private investors. Experience has found that it is very difficult to beat these benchmarks. In part, this is because the index will inevitably represent the average performance of all shares, and thus all investors; by definition, therefore, half of all investors should not beat the index. On top of that factor is the burden of administrative and dealing costs, which investors have to pay, but the index does not reflect. More fundamentally, it seems as if very few people have the ability to pick successful shares. Academics have argued that this is because markets are efficient; share prices reflect all the available knowledge about a company. What will affect the price, therefore, is future news, which by definition cannot be known.

The main factors which cause the market to rise and fall include the following:

- *Interest rates*. Broadly speaking, rising interest rates are bad news for share prices and falling rates are good. Rising rates increase the cost of corporate borrowing and thereby reduce profits. Higher interest rates also increase the attraction of selling shares to hold funds on deposit. Factors which are likely to lead the government to raise interest rates – rising inflation, strong economic growth – are therefore often bad news for the markets.
- *Profits growth*. Equities represent a share of the assets and profits of a company. The faster profits grow, therefore, the better for the markets. Tax changes which eat into profits hit the market.
- *Supply and demand*. Flotations and rights issues increase the supply of shares in the market and drive prices down (other things being equal); high dividends, share buybacks and takeovers for cash, increase the demand for shares and push prices up.
- *International influences*. Increasingly, stock markets are being dominated by global influences as investors move money round in search of the most attractive havens.

There is a tendency for share prices to move up and down together; London, in particular, is heavily influenced by Wall Street and a sharp fall in the US market usually has a knock-on effect in the UK.

Strategic financial risk management

A number of issues involving international financial management have already been discussed. These are:

- *sources of international finance*, including the use of various international money, bond and equity markets as sources of funds and the various financial instruments associated with these markets;
- *the management of foreign exchange risk*, including the use of options, swaps and futures markets to 'hedge' against unpredictable changes in exchange rates.

Risk assessment is often influenced, for international business, by the decisions taken by the credit rating agencies. It will be useful, at this point, to review their contribution to the perception of risk by many international businesses.

Risk assessment and the credit rating agencies

Before issuing bonds in the public markets, an issuer will often seek a rating from one or more private credit ratings agencies. The selected agencies investigate the issuer's ability to pay interest on the bonds and to repay the full initial loan when the bonds 'mature' (fall due for repayment). The credit agencies look in particular at such matters as financial strength, the intended use of the funds, the political and regulatory environment in which the issuer is operating and any potential economic changes in that environment. After conducting these investigations, the agency will make its estimate of the 'default risk', i.e. the likelihood that the issuer will fail to service the bonds as required. The expense involved in making this rating is normally paid for by the issuer, although in some cases an agency will issue such ratings on its own initiative.

The well-known companies, Moody's Investors Service and Standard & Poor's, both based in New York, dominate the ratings industry. Two smaller firms, Fitch IBCA and Duff & Phelps Credit Rating Co., also issue ratings for many types of bonds internationally. The firms' ratings of a particular issue are not always in agreement, as each uses a different methodology. Table 10.2 interprets the default ratings of the four major international firms.

There are also many other ratings agencies that operate in a single country, and several that specialise in a particular industry, such as banking.

A downgrading of the credit ratings of either private company or government bonds can have serious implications for the issuer. Lenders will insist on higher interest rates on any future loans to that company or government in order to cover the increased risks of making such loans. This can be important for both individual businesses and for the macroenvironment in which they operate since higher interest rates are likely to depress aggregate demand (both consumption and investment) in the country and increase the prospects of economic recession.

Table 10.2 **Credit risk assessments**

	Moody's	Standard & Poor's	Fitch IBCA	Duff & Phelps
Highest credit quality; issuer has strong ability to meet obligations	Aaa	AAA	AAA	AAA
Very high credit quality; low risk of default	Aa1 Aa2 Aa3	AA+ AA AA−	AA	AA+ AA AA−
High credit quality, but more vulnerable to changes in economy or business	A1 A2 A3	AA+ AA AA−	AA	AA+ AA AA−
Adequate credit quality for now, but more likely to be impaired if conditions worsen	Baa1 Baa2 Baa3	BBB+ BBB BBB−	BBB	BBB+ BBB BBB−
Below investment grade, but good chance that issuer can meet commitments	Ba1 Ba2 Ba3	BB+ BB BB−	BB	BB+ BB BB−
Significant credit risk, but issuer is presently able to meet obligations	B1 B2 B3	B+ B B−	B	B+ B B−
High default risk	Caa1 Caa2 Caa3	CCC+ CCC CCC−	CCC CC C	CCC
Issuer failed to meet scheduled interest or principal payments	C	D	DDD DD D	DD

Case Study 10.4 looks in more detail at the impacts of a downgrading of national credit ratings in early 2009.

CASE 10.4 Spate of downgrades raises fears FT

A sudden spate of sovereign downgrades in early 2009 has added to the all-too palpable sense of nervousness gripping global financial markets. The downgrades of Spain, Portugal and Greece and a warning for Ireland have immediate implications for all four economies as their borrowing costs relative to Germany, Europe's biggest country, have risen.

But the action by Standard & Poor's also has wider implications: will one of the four countries default? Will the euro zone collapse? Is this just the start of a series of downgrades that could affect countries not just on the euro zone periphery but some of the worlds' biggest economies – such as the US, UK, France and Germany?

Such a scenario would have big repercussions as it would immediately reduce the value of these countries' assets, including government and corporate bonds. The US dollar is the reserve currency of the world, so a downgrade would shave billions off the holdings of every large central bank. This week sterling has fallen sharply because of increasing worries over the risk that the UK government is taking on with its new financial rescue package, although Moody's eased the pressure yesterday by ruling clearly something within the rating that you could call 'political' if you want. We have seen this back in 2003 to 2005 when Germany was on the line for a downgrade and neither of the rating agencies did actually follow through. With the UK there are similar problems. If they downgraded the UK, there could potentially be massive problems because the pound is a reserve currency.

S&P strongly denies politics played a part in its decisions. It said: 'We have explained in detail the rationale for our sovereign rating actions in recent days, both affirmations and downgrades. Our role is, and always has been, to provide an independent opinion of credit-worthiness as we see it, regardless of the interests of other parties and regardless of the potential market impact. Other people are free, as they always have been, to agree or disagree with our analysis.'

Certainly S&P's rival agency, Fitch, disagrees. The contrast between the two agencies over Spain was dramatic, when on Monday S&P took away the country's triple A status, while Fitch reaffirmed its top-notch rating.

S&P said: 'The downgrade of Spain reflects our expectations that public finances will suffer in tandem with the expected decline in Spain's growth prospects. Spain's current account deficit is unsustainably high at 10% of GDP in 2008.'

Fitch said: 'The government's relatively moderate debt-to-GDP ratio – estimated at 39.4% of GDP at the end of 2008 – is expected to rise to around 60% of GDP by the end of 2010. With this debt ratio, Spain will still rank well below other large triple A countries, including France, Germany and the UK.'

These differences are important. German banks have taken a big hit from the Spanish downgrade. Analysts say these banks are large holders of Spanish securities, which have all fallen in value because of the lower credit rating. Central banks are also big buyers of sovereign bonds. The combined value of Spanish, Portuguese, Greek and Irish bonds circulating in the market is €600 billion, according to Dalogic, so a weakening in sentiment in any one of these countries can reduce the value of central bank holdings sharply.

Many analysts think S&P was wrong to lower Spain's ratings, while others attack it for being 'behind the curve' as the markets have been pricing in the chance of a downgrade of many of the peripheral economies since the start of 2008. This has been reflected in the massive widening of bond yields between these economies and Germany, which have risen fivefold in the past year.

Meyrick Chapman, fixed income strategist at UBS, said: 'I don't think Spain should have been downgraded. Moreover, if S&P was consistent in the reasons given, they could have downgraded four or five years ago. When you look at the country's current account deficit, one of the most important indicators because of the difficulties of getting foreign credit, it has been above the critical 5% threshold since around 2004. It is actually improving now.'

Source: Johnson, M. and Oakley, D., 'Spate of downgrades raises fears that a big economy could be next', *Financial Times*, 23 January 2009.

Table 10.3 Revised S&P credit ratings of four countries and their performances

Greece	Portugal	Spain	Ireland
Sovereign credit rating (S&P)			
A−	A+	AA+	AAA
Current account deficit (% of GDP)			
14.5	10.9	9.7	6.2
Budget deficit (% of GDP)			
2.8	2.2	1.5	5.6
Government debt (% of GDP)			
93.0	64.5	37.8	29.7

Source: Various

Table 10.3 captures the downgrades made by S&P of the credit rating of three of these four countries (Ireland was merely 'warned').

Questions

1 What factors might influence country ratings of credit risk?

2 Examine the impacts of a downgrade in a country's credit risk rating.

3 How justified is S&P in downgrading on the basis of the data in Table 10.3?

We now look in rather more detail at some further aspects of international financial management, with our main concern being to review strategic issues in risk management, and especially the new possibilities of 'integrated' or 'enterprise' risk management. The suggestion here is that, via the identification and assessment of all the collective risks, the company can then implement a company-wide strategy to manage them. As we shall see, the early discussion on new financial instruments and associated derivatives markets will be relevant here.

■ Methods of integration

Lisa Meulbroek (2000) suggests that there are three ways of implementing integrated risk management objectives: modifying the company's operations, adjusting its capital structure and employing targeted financial instruments. Managers assess the advantages and disadvantages of each method before identifying the most appropriate mix for their particular enterprise.

1 *Modifying the company's operations.* The strategy adopted here will depend on the nature of the company's operations. Microsoft has chosen to use a higher ratio of temporary to permanent staff than is typical for activity within its sector. By reducing the fixed overhead of a more permanent workforce, it seeks to reduce the risks to its permanent workforce of unexpected and adverse shifts in demand, technology or regulation in an intrinsically volatile industry.

2 *Adjusting the company's capital structure.* Managers cannot always predict the magnitude of a particular operational risk or indeed any specific risk. However,

they can adjust the company's capital structure to give a general reduction in risk exposure, as for example by reducing the debt to equity ratio. Such low levels of leverage policies are practised by Microsoft, which in early 2000 has no outstanding debt, thereby using equity as a risk cushion.

3 *Employing targeted financial instruments.* Here companies seek to focus on a specific risk and to hedge against it at the lowest feasible cost. This method is, of course, only feasible where financial instruments exist for the specific risk the company seeks to target. The development of liquid markets for a broad set of financial instruments has greatly helped this method in recent years. Although its figures are now in doubt, Enron, the Houston-based power and industrial group, bought and sold options and forwards (*see* p. 397) in the electricity and gas markets to reduce its risk exposure. In contrast, Microsoft will, arguably, find that few of its major risks are correlated with existing financial instruments and must depend on the other two methods of risk management control.

Finding the appropriate mix

The essence of an integrated approach is to combine elements of these three methods to minimise the aggregate net exposure to risk from all sources. By aggregating risk, some individual risks within the company will partially or completely offset each other. Thus by concentrating on covering the (lower) aggregate net risk instead of each risk separately, an integrated approach to risk management can add value to the company by reducing costs. The technology products group Honeywell purchased an insurance contract in 1997 that for the first time covered a company's aggregate losses. By aggregating individual risks and then insuring the total net risk, Honeywell was able to make a 15% saving on its previous contract. Since such an integrated approach to risk management clearly requires a thorough understanding of the company's operations and financial policies, it must be implemented by senior management only. It cannot be delegated to managers of functional areas.

Alternative risk transfer (ART)

Traditionally companies have used the capital and money markets to raise much of their finance and the *insurance markets* to cover many of the individual risks to which they are exposed, with the two market types being quite distinct. However, a vast array of new financial products are now available from both market types which, together with the impact of the Internet, is causing considerable convergence between these previously separate markets. This broad trend is often referred to as 'alternative risk transfer' (ART) and is reflected in Figure 10.3.

One driving force behind ART has involved the provision of financial instruments which can now be broken down into their smallest constituents, giving opportunities to price different bundles of risks in entirely new ways. The ability to identify and strip out individual risks and devise specific financial instruments to cover even the most complex bundle of such risks, is arguably a revolutionary development. So much so that the term *'nuclear financial economics'* has been applied to this process of stripping down any complex situation into its constituent 'risk particles' which can then be priced. Many insurance companies are now able to diversify into providing financial instruments to cover foreign exchange and other contracts that were previously only available from the more traditional capital and money markets.

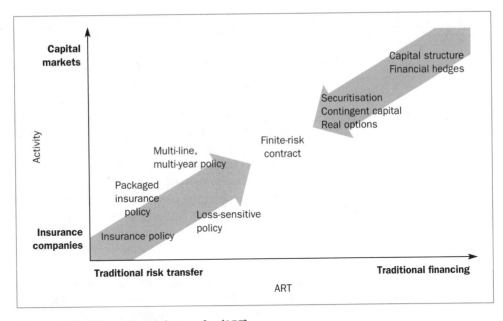

Figure 10.3 **Alternative risk transfer (ART)**

As can be seen from Figure 10.3, just as some insurance companies are developing financial instruments, which were once the preserve of the capital markets, the capital markets are themselves developing a variety of risk-related financial instruments, involving options, futures markets and swaps. The net result is a vast array of traditional and non-traditional instruments from all market sources able to meet the particular circumstances ('finite risk contract') of almost any corporate client. For example, since September 1999 the Chicago Mercantile Exchange has traded weather-linked securities (derivatives) whose value varies with the temperature, measured by an index of warmth in four large cities in the USA.

Such financial instruments can be the basis of 'contracts' to cover situations which previously would be regarded as entirely unpredictable and beyond mankind's control. Of course, the fears of such haphazard future contingencies often deterred firms from entering into a project, especially so the more risk-averse the firm's senior management. Now firms can take such risks explicitly into account and insure against them. For example, British Aerospace paid some $70 million in 1999 for an insurance policy that helped take £3 billion of aircraft-leasing risks off its balance sheet. Within six weeks of taking out the policy British Aerospace shares had outperformed the market by some 15%, the argument being that its future profitability now depended on its skill in operating its core business of building aircraft rather than on haphazard events (involving leasing issues) outside its direct control.

A second driver behind ART has been the rapid development in telecommunication and computer-related technologies. Clearly the Internet has reduced search costs and times close to zero as regards finding the lowest price for various products. Intelligent automated asset managers are progressively able to seek out the financial instruments that best fit an investor's particular risk-profile. The availability of these technologies is clearly aiding the unbundling process, enabling providers to parcel risks into different classes of security on which prices can be readily quoted.

Case Study 10.5 looks at the impact of these automated risk valuation models in rather more detail.

CASE 10.5 Risk needs a human touch **FT**

In extraordinary and treacherous conditions, aircraft passengers would almost certainly prefer a human pilot to be at the controls than the autopilot – and for good reasons. No matter how powerful and sophisticated our computers are, there are always subtleties and nuances of experience that we cannot yet program them to judge. A computer would never have pulled off that emergency landing on New York's Hudson river in January 2009.

Investigators into the global financial crash landing are already producing remedies even as the disaster continues. A major realisation has been that banks and their supervisors trusted too much in the risk management autopilot. Lord Turner, chairman of the US's Financial Services Authority, has highlighted attempts by the Basel Committee to overhaul the use of 'value at risk' (VaR) models, which predict how much a bank can lose on a given day. These models have allowed the systematic underestimation of risk, which in turn has meant that only very small capital cushions were required in banks' trading operations. VaR models used unduly short historical data sets to predict future developments and discounted the worth of incorporating rare, but extremely painful outcomes. VaR, he said, 'fails to allow for the fact that historically low volatility may actually be an indication of irrationally low risk-aversion and therefore increased systemic risk'. Lord Turner gave an example of a bank whose trading assets made up 57% of its total book, but which set its market risk capital requirement at just 0.1% of trading assets. This is extreme, but others in the sample chose 0.4% and 1.1% – better, but hardly a paradigm of prudence.

The Basel Committee, unsurprisingly, wants to raise these capital charges as swiftly and comprehensively as possible. The key driver for its action is the mind-boggling losses suffered in 2008 in the trading books of banks such as UBS, Merrill Lynch and Citigroup. Institutions exploited the low capital demands of VaR models to keep very large and long-term complex structured bond positions in a book really meant only for temporary asset positions.

The Basel Committee is cracking down hard on this area and their changes look likely to handicap seriously the potential for any recovery in securitisation. It will prohibit banks from recognising any capital benefits from securitisations, even as hedging tools. This is because the Committee believes that 'the state of risk modelling in this area is not sufficiently reliable as to warrant recognising hedging or diversification benefits attributable to securitisation positions'.

For the most part, banks seem only too willing to accept these changes. Many bankers with global responsibility for credit trading are seeking different kinds of risk managers in their businesses. The new risk manager's human judgement would be the final arbiter rather than the strict letter of the VaR law, which could only act as a guide.

Most important would be 'intent'. People in risk management should not be allowed to work for themselves, embattled and concerned mainly with their own job security. 'They need to be close to the action, but not so close that they lose their perspective. In volatile, liquidity-strained times, traders need to be given more freedom around risk limits, but everyone needs to have a rounded view, across asset classes, markets and the full trading room'. What is needed, it is suggested, is a greater spirit of collectivism – an attitude of solving for the greater good.

Fine words, but markets are social phenomena riddled with dysfunction. They pursue bad leads and develop sustained distortions. As the lending drought shows, there are conflicts between what is rational for the individual and what is rational for the whole. And as investors have felt repeatedly in this crisis, markets can stay insane longer than they can stay solvent.

But the biggest difficulty and the reason VaR dominates is the business case. It is very difficult to turn human, qualitative judgement into numbers in the boardroom. Banks more than most demand quantitative assessment and as long as bonuses need to be calculated, this will not change.

Source: Davies, P., 'Insight: Risk needs a human touch but models hold the whip hand', *Financial Times*, 23 January 2009.

Question

Consider the advantages and disadvantages of the use of automated risk management models.

■ Centralised versus decentralised financial decisions

The financial decisions taken by MNEs reflect a variety of influences, such as choosing the types and sources of financing, the need for foreign exchange management, the short- versus long-term goal orientation of the company, the financial reporting requirements of different nations, tax, interest rate, inflationary and other financial considerations, and so on. Nevertheless, an important issue is whether the MNE seeks to take such decisions centrally or to direct many of these decisions to the management of affiliates in host countries. The facts would suggest a tendency towards centralisation: for example around 57% of fund raising by MNE affiliates took place in host country financial markets in 1989, but this figure had fallen to below 45% by the late 1990s.

We might usefully review some of the arguments for and against such centralisation.

Centralised financial management

A number of arguments support this approach.

1 *Minimising cost/maximising return*. The rapid growth in type and source of financial instrument already considered suggests a global rather than local approach to financing. Specialist financial managers with a global perspective can help the MNE borrow funds wherever in the world they are cheapest and invest them wherever the expected returns are highest.

2 *Flexibility*. Only centralised control can permit a rapid corporate response to changed conditions. For example, moving cash away from nations with high projected rates of inflation/currency depreciation and towards nations with high projected rates of economic growth/currency appreciation, etc.

3 *Scale economies*. Large-scale centralised borrowings can secure lower interest rates from lenders and reduce transaction costs per pound/dollar borrowed. Similarly, large-scale centralised deposits of cash surpluses can secure higher interest rates from borrowers.

4 *Professional expertise*. Higher paid and more expert financial managers can be expected to better appraise the vast array of financial alternatives open to the MNE. Specialisation in such operations can be expected to further develop these skills.

5 *Synchronisation*. Centralised control permits a more uniform approach across all affiliates with regard to financial matters, one more likely to be consistent with stated corporate objectives.

Decentralised financial management

A number of counterarguments can be used to support a more decentralised approach.

1 *Generality*. The financing requirement of particular foreign affiliates may be overlooked by managers at headquarters who focus on more global needs. Pump-priming and other longer-term objectives of foreign affiliates may be sacrificed if funds are unavailable for new developments. Headquarter financial management may be unaware of the particular circumstance of local financial markets, so that low-cost sources of funds are overlooked.

2 *Motivation and morale*. These may be diminished among employees within the foreign affiliate as they perceive a lack of control over their own financial destiny.

3 *Conflicts*. Headquarter policy may conflict with policy deemed appropriate by host countries to firms operating there. For example rationalisation of production involving unemployment in foreign affiliates where host governments are seeking to expand output and employment. Similarly, only affiliate financial managers may be able to appraise which financial reporting, control and cash management systems are appropriate to accurately reflect their local operations.

4 *Inflexibility*. Local financial managers may experience delays in receiving the go-ahead for new initiatives from an overburdened and bureaucratised headquarters.

In practice most MNEs centralise some of the financial management decisions and decentralise others, the extent of such decentralisation sometimes depending on the host country in which the affiliate operates.

Accounting and financial decision making

It will be useful, at this point, to reflect on the accounting information which so often provides a basis for financial and other decision making, especially in so many aspects of international business.

Accounting is split into two key branches: financial accounting and management accounting.

Financial accounting is that part of accounting which records and summarises financial transactions to satisfy the information needs of the various user groups such as investors, lenders, creditors and employees. It is sometimes referred to as meeting the *external* accounting needs of the organisation.

Management accounting is sometimes referred to as meeting the *internal* accounting needs of the organisation, and is designed to help managers with decision making and planning. As such it often involves estimates and forecasts, and is not subject to the same regulatory framework as financial accounting. One professional body, the Chartered Institute of Management Accountants (CIMA), defines management accounting as follows:

> The application of the principles of accounting and financial management to create, protect, preserve and increase value for the stakeholders of for-profit and not-for-profit enterprises in the public and private sectors. Management accounting is an integral part of management. It requires the identification, generation, presentation, interpretation and use of the relevant information to:
>
> - Inform strategic decisions and formulate business strategy
> - Plan long, medium and short-run operations
> - Determine capital structure and fund that structure
> - Designed reward strategies for executives and shareholders
> - Inform operational decisions
> - Control operations and ensure the efficient use of resources
> - Measure and record financial and non-financial performance to management and other stakeholders
> - Safeguard tangible and intangible assets
> - Implement corporate governance procedures, risk management and internal controls.
>
> (CIMA 2005)

The CIMA definition is deliberately all-embracing, and there are some obvious infringements on what financial accountants might see as their 'territory'. It reinforces the notion that there are overlaps between financial and management accounting, particularly in the recording, interpreting and communicating aspects.

■ Users of accounting information

The International Accounting Standards Board (IASB) was formed in 2000 with the aim of developing accounting standards that 'require high quality, transparent and comparable information in financial statements and other financial reporting to help participants in the world's capital markets and other users make economic decisions'. In 2001 the IASB adopted a *Framework for the Preparation and Presentation of Financial Statements* which set out certain concepts that underlie the preparation and presentation of financial statements. The Framework (IASB 2001) also identifies the following seven groups of users (*see* Table 10.4) together with the information which they need from the financial statements:

Table 10.4 **User groups and information needs**

User group	Information needs
Investors	Investors need to assess the financial performance of the organisation they have invested in to consider the risk inherent in, and return provided by, their investments
Lenders	Lenders need to be aware of the ability of the organisation to repay loans and interest. Potential lenders need to decide whether to lend, and on what terms
Suppliers and other trade creditors	Suppliers need to take commercial decisions as to whether or not they should sell to the organisation, and if they do, whether they will be paid
Employees	People will be interested in their employer's stability and profitability, in particular that part of the organisation (such as a branch) in which they work. They will also be interested in the ability of their employer to pay their wages and pensions
Customers	Customers who are dependent on a particular supplier or are considering placing a long-term contract will need to know if the organisation will continue to exist
Governments and their agencies	Reliable financial data helps governments to assemble national economic statistics which are used for a variety of purposes in controlling the economy. Specific financial information from an organisation also enables tax to be assessed
The public	Financial statements often include information relevant to local communities and pressure groups such as attitudes to environmental matters, plans to expand or shut down factories, policies on employment of disabled persons, etc.

Source: International Accounting Standards Board (IASB) (2001) *Framework for the Preparation and Presentation of Financial Statements*, IASB.

Major financial accounting statements

In addition to the day-to-day recording of financial information, a number of critical financial summaries are also the responsibility of financial accountants, including the:

- income statement
- balance sheet
- statement of changes in equity
- cash flow statement.

The income statement

This is the statement which summarises the revenue and expenditure of a specified period, disclosing whether the organisation has made a profit or loss. Under accounting conventions, all income and expenses for the specified period are included, whether or not cash has been received or paid. This is an important principle as otherwise the summary would fail to reflect the impact of all relevant transactions and financial events. For example, the decline in value (depreciation) over the lifetime of the organisation's non-current assets (e.g. buildings, machinery and computers) is estimated and included as an expense, even though no related cash outflow results in the period. 'Accruals and prepayments' are calculated – these are adjustments to ensure that all relevant expenses are included, not just the cash paid in the period – and adjustments for unsold inventory are also made.

The organisation's operating profit or loss is adjusted for taxation charges and dividend distributions in order to arrive at a retained profit (or loss) which increases (or decreases) the accumulated reserves of the company.

Table 10.5 **Tesco plc: group income statement**

Year ended 23 February 2008	2008 £m	2007 £m
Revenue (Sales excluding VAT)	47,298	42,641
Cost of sales	(43,668)	(39,401)
Pension adjustment – Finance Act 2006	–	258
Impairment of the Gerrards Cross site		(35)
Gross profit	3,630	3,463
Administrative expenses	(1,027)	(907)
Profit arising on property-related items	188	92
Operating profit	2,791	2,648
Share of post-tax profits of joint ventures and associates	75	106
Profit on sale of investments in associates		25
Finance income	187	90
Finance costs	(250)	(216)
Profit before tax	2,803	2,653
Taxation	(673)	(772)
Profit for the period from continuing operations	2,130	1,881
Discontinued operation	(10)	(6)
Profit for the year	2,120	1,875

Source: Tesco plc Annual Report 2008 (adapted).

Table 10.5 is an example of an income statement for Tesco plc.

pause for thought 2 Comment on the data in the table and possible implications for strategic choices.

The balance sheet

This statement summarises the assets, liabilities and shareholders' equity of the organisation at the end of a company's reporting period (e.g. for Tesco plc, at 23 February 2008). Assets are usually divided between:

- *non-current assets*, which are significant items likely to be owned by the organisation for at least a year, such as land, buildings, machinery and computers. These examples are all *tangible* non-current assets, meaning they are 'physical' assets, but organisations may also own *intangible* non-current assets such as patents, trademarks and also the price paid for 'goodwill' (the value of a reputation) when buying other businesses; and
- *current assets*, which are items which tend to change value rapidly during a financial period, being used in day-to-day trading. These include inventory, trade receivables (debtors) and bank and cash balances.

Liabilities are divided between:

- *current liabilities*, such as trade payables (creditors), taxation and short-term indebtedness such as bank overdrafts; and
- *non-current liabilities*, such as loans due for repayment after more than one year from the balance sheet date.

Table 10.6 is an example of a balance sheet for Tesco plc.

Table 10.6 **Tesco plc: group balance sheet**

23 February 2008	2008 £m	2007 £m
Non-current assets		
Goodwill and intangible assets	2,336	2,045
Property, plant and equipment	19,787	16,976
Investment property	1,112	856
Other investments	4	8
Derivative financial instruments	216	–
Deferred tax assets	104	32
	23,864	20,231
Current assets		
Inventories	2,430	1,931
Trade and other receivables	1,311	1,079
Derivative financial instruments	97	108
Current tax assets	6	8
Short term investments	360	–
Cash and cash equivalents	1,788	1,042
	5,992	4,168
Other assets held for sale	308	408
	6,300	4,576
Current liabilities		
Trade and other payables	(7,277)	(6,046)
Financial liabilities		
Borrowings	(2,084)	(1,554)
Derivative financial instruments and other liabilities	(443)	(87)
Current tax liabilities	(455)	(461)
Provisions	(4)	(4)
	(10,263)	(8,152)
Net current liabilities	(3,963)	(3,576)
Non-current liabilities	(7,999)	(6,084)
Net assets	11,902	10,571
Equity		
Share capital	393	387
Share premium account	4,511	4,378
Other reserves	40	40
Retained earnings	6,871	5,693
Equity attributable to equity holders of the parent	11,815	10,506
Minority interests	87	65
Total equity	11,902	10,571

Source: Tesco plc Annual Report 2008 (adapted).

pause for thought 3   Comment on the data in the table and possible implications for strategic choice.

Statement of changes in equity

This gives an overview of the various reasons (including the payment of dividends) for the changes in the *total equity* as shown in the opening and closing balance sheets, and cuts through much of the fine detail presented elsewhere in the annual report to

Table 10.7 **Tesco plc: statement of changes in equity**

	Issued share capital £m	Share premium £m	Other reserves	Retained earnings £m	Total equity attributable to equity holders of the parent £m	Minority interests £m	Total £m
At 24 February 2007	397	4,376	(182)	5,914	10,506	65	10,571
Foreign currency translation differences	–	–	33	–	33	5	38
Actuarial gain on defined benefit schemes	–	–	1	186	187	–	187
Tax on items taken directly to or transferred from equity	–	–	250	(127)	123	–	123
Decrease in fair value of available for sale financial assets	–	–	–	(4)	(4)	–	(4)
Gains on cash flow hedges	–	–	37	–	37	–	37
Purchase of treasury shares	–	–	(118)	–	(118)	–	(118)
Share-based payments	–	–	68	131	199	–	199
Issue of shares	3	135	–	–	138	–	138
Share buy-back	(7)		7	47	47	(27)	20
Purchase of minority interest				47	47	(27)	20
Minority interest on acquisitions of subsidiaries						38	38
Profit for the year	–	–	–	2,124	2,124	6	2,130
Equity dividends authorised in the year	–	–	–	(792)	(792)	–	(792)
At 23 February 2008	393	4,511	97	6,814	11,815	87	11,902

present a clear picture of the reasons why shareholder value has changed over the period. Table 10.7 shows Tesco plc's statement, which, for the year ended 23 February 2008, indicates that the company's total equity increased from £10,571 million to £11,902 million, mainly as a result of the year's profit of £2124 million less dividends of £792 million and the cost of a share buy-back of £665 million. A 'buy-back' occurs usually where a company buys its own shares on the stock market and then cancels them, in order to maintain share values (fewer shares in issue), and reduce future dividend payments.

The cash flow statement

Even profitable business can fail due to their inability to find enough cash to pay their creditors, so a third statement is produced which concentrates on changes in the *liquidity* of the company during the financial period. *Liquidity* is the ability of a company to access enough cash and 'cash equivalents' (e.g. asset balances in bank current accounts) to meet liabilities as they fall due, and the statement focuses on the overall change in cash and cash equivalent balances during the financial period. The cash flow statement usually breaks down information into cash flows from operating activities (e.g. net cash inflows through trading) adjusted for interest and tax payments, investing activities (e.g. buying and selling non-current assets, interest received and dividends received) and financing activities (e.g. issue of shares, raising or repaying loans and paying dividends).

Table 10.8 is an example of a cash flow statement for Tesco plc.

Table 10.8 Tesco plc: group cash flow statement

Year ended 23 February 2008	2008 £m	2007 £m
Cash flows from operating activities	4,099	3,532
Interest paid	(410)	(376)
Corporation tax paid	(346)	(5445)
Net cash flow from operating activities	3,343	2,611
Cash flows from investing activities		
Acquisition of subsidiaries, net of cash acquired	(169)	(325)
Proceeds from sale of subsidiaries, net of cash disposed	–	22
Proceeds from sale of joint ventures and associates	–	41
Purchase of property, plant and equipment and investment properties	(3,442)	(2,852)
Proceeds from sale of property, plant and equipment	1,056	809
Purchase of intangible assets	(158)	(174)
Increase in loans to joint ventures	(36)	(21)
Invested in joint ventures and associates	(61)	(49)
Invested in short term investments	(360)	–
Dividends received	88	124
Interest received	128	82
Net cash used in investing activities	(2,954)	(2,343)
Cash flows from financing activities		
Proceeds from issue of ordinary share capital	138	156
Proceeds from issue of ordinary share capital	16	156
Repayments of borrowings	9,333	4,743
New finance leases	119	99
Repayments of obligations under finance leases	(32)	(15)
Dividends paid	(792)	(467)
Dividends paid to minority interests	(2)	–
Own shares purchased	(775)	(490)
Net cash from (used in) financing activities	412	(533)
Net increase in cash and cash equivalents	801	(265)
Cash and cash equivalents at beginning of year	1,042	1,325
Effect of foreign exchange rate changes	(55)	(18)
Cash and cash equivalents at end of year	1,788	1,042

Source: Tesco plc Annual Report 2008 (adapted).

pause for thought 4 Comment on the data in Table 10.8 and possible implications for strategic choice.

Published accounts

All commercial corporations will publish financial information, often as a requirement of a specific stock exchange or due to national legislation. For example, in the UK, Acts of Parliament require *all* limited companies to publish financial statements. Although there is no equivalent in the USA of the UK's Companies Acts, major US companies will be registered with the Securities and Exchange Commission (SEC), which sets out detailed requirements for audit and the rules of financial reporting. For smaller UK companies, only a brief summary of their finances is required, but for the largest companies, including all plcs (public limited companies), an 'annual report' must be prepared (often at great expense) which is sent (either electronically, or, if requested, as a paper copy) to all shareholders and Companies House, which is the UK government's 'storehouse' of company information. The public have a right of access to the information (see www.companies-house.gov.uk for details). Other countries have equivalent access to information, for example, Euridile at www.euridile.inpi.fr is France's official company register.

Many corporations regard their annual report as an opportunity to show off the best of their company, in effect treating it as a public relations exercise. The glossy photographs of the company's products and exotic locations of major contracts can give some reports the style of a travel brochure. Many large multi-national companies based in non-English speaking countries not only produce corporate reports in their 'home' language but also produce English-language versions for wider circulation. An example is Ericsson, a Swedish company. Its financial reports can be found at www.ericsson.com (click on 'investors', then 'financial reports').

An important feature of annual reports published within the EU is that they have to follow specific formats of presentation for the key summaries. These formats were devised to ensure a degree of uniformity, as they apply to all member countries. There is a small amount of flexibility allowed, for example a company can produce statements in either a 'vertical' or 'horizontal' format. The Tesco plc income statement and balance sheet shown earlier are presented in a 'vertical' format.

The *Financial Times* on 10 April 2007 stated that the annual report of the global bank HSBC had weighed in at 1.47kg and 454 pages, due mainly to increasing corporate reporting requirements and regulations. The UK's postal service, the Royal Mail, had to limit the number its postmen could carry in order to prevent back injuries.

Differences of reporting and accounting approach in different countries

The practical implications of countries adopting differing accounting procedures can be seen in the two extracts below which appeared on the same day in an accounting magazine. Whilst somewhat historical, the extracts usefully indicate the reason many advocate common international standards in accounting practice.

■ Extract 1: 'Rover trouble was avoidable'

'Sacked BMW chairman Bernd Pischetsrieder might have retained his job if he had persuaded colleagues not to impose harsh German accounting policies on Rover when the company bought the British car maker in 1994, analysis by *Accountancy Age* has shown. Though the British company is now widely blamed as jeopardising BMW's future as an independent business, Rover's results compiled under British accounting standards, quietly filed at Companies House, paint a picture quite different from the enduring story of huge losses that ultimately led to Pischetsrieder's downfall.

As shown in the table below, figures reveal that Rover made a profit of £147m between 1994 and 1997. Headline figures from consolidated accounts published by BMW, which took the company over in March 1994, however, show Rover making a loss of £363m in the same period. It is these figures that the press, analysts and indeed BMW's board have pounced on as proof of the British car maker's inefficiency.

(Losses in brackets)	Rover net profit using British accounting rules £m	Rover net profit using German accounting rules £m	Difference £m
1994	279	Unpublished	–
1995	(51)	(163)	−112
1996	(100)	(109)	−9
1997	19	(91)	−72
Total	**147**	**(363)**	**−216**

German accounting policies are notoriously harsh. Investments are depreciated faster; there are more possibilities for making provisions and different rules for valuing stocks. All these have the effect of depressing profits.'

Source: Accountancy Age, 18 February 1999.

■ Extract 2: 'UK standards add £200m to British Airways results'

'Differing international accounting systems are affecting airlines' reported profit levels by hundreds of millions of pounds each year, according to an aviation industry expert. Using an analysis of the results of British Airways, Richard Shaylor, a financial analysis lecturer with Signal Training, says the differences are confusing investors. The airline publishes its results according to UK standards and has no plans to move to an international standard. But, because it has shares listed on both the London and New York Stock Exchanges, it also includes a revised profit and loss account constructed according to US generally accepted accounting practice in its annual report. As the table below shows, one of the larger distortions arises from BA's 1996 figures. Under UK rules, it made a profit of £473m, whereas using US rules the figure was £267m.'

	BA net profit using British accounting rules (£m)	BA net profit using US accounting rules (£m)	Difference (£m)
1994	274	145	−129
1995	250	297	+47
1996	473	267	−206
1997	553	548	−5
1998	460	654	+194
Totals	2,010	1,911	−99

Source: Accountancy Age, 18 February 1999.

pause for thought 5 Comment briefly on how the issues raised in these two extracts have implications for international business.

As seen in the extracts above, major industrialised nations have developed their own specific accounting regulations. This rarely has a major impact when applied to domestic companies within those countries, but may have dramatic implications when international investment decisions have to be made. There are many reasons why countries developed dissimilar procedures, including those summarised in Table 10.9.

Table 10.9 Reasons for different accounting standards

The legal system	Some countries (e.g. France and Germany) have all-embracing sets of rules and regulations which apply to businesses, whereas countries such as the UK and the USA have more general statute laws backed up by case law, allowing more flexibility for individual companies. For example, in the USA, individual companies decide the rates at which assets depreciate, but in Germany the government decides what are appropriate.
Types of ownership patterns	Countries with wide share ownership (e.g. UK, USA) have developed strong independent professional accountancy associations to provide reliable financial data to shareholders. Those countries with predominantly small, family-run businesses (e.g. France) or with banks owning most shares of large companies (e.g. Germany), have had less need for providers of independent financial information.
The accounting profession	Strong independent professional associations of accountants developed in those countries (e.g. UK, USA) with the most liberal company laws and widest share ownership. Countries with restricted patterns of business ownership and rigid company statutes (e.g. France, Germany) had weak groupings of accountants, and sometimes the governments themselves controlled the profession.
Conservatism	Financial statements produced by independent accountants should ideally show a 'true and fair view'. This is open to many interpretations, not least being the problem of asset valuation. Should assets be valued at original cost, what they might be sold at today, what it would cost to replace them or a depreciated value based on usage, wear and tear, etc.? US practice is conservative – don't revalue, but depreciate on a reasonable basis over the asset's lifetime. German practice is also conservative – don't revalue, but depreciate on a basis decreed by the government. UK practice is liberal – allowing companies either to revalue at intervals or show assets at cost, and depreciate on a reasonable basis.

Global accounting standards

For many years there has been an increasing trend towards the implementation of an internationally recognised single set of accounting standards and practice which ultimately would allow meaningful comparisons to be made between companies, wherever they are based. Cost savings would also be made by companies who otherwise would have to produce detailed reconciliations between the results reported by differing sets of standards. For example, until recently, European companies listed on US stock markets presented two sets of results, one based on US GAAP, the other based on the standards required within the EU.

The International Accounting Standards Board (IASB) has been seeking a global convergence on an agreed standard for accounting for pensions – and is modelling its proposals largely on rules recently introduced in the UK. Sir David Tweedie, IASB chairman, wrote FRS 17, as the UK rule is known, when he was head of the UK Accounting Standards Board and some companies have blamed it for forcing the closure of their relatively generous defined benefit pension schemes. Like the IASB's standard on financial instruments, the new role on pensions puts a heavy emphasis on 'fair value' accounting. Under FRS 17, the measurement of the assets in a defined benefit pension scheme should reflect their fair or market value. FRS 17 also tells accountants how to arrive at the present value for future liabilities; it adds them up and discounts back at an interest rate equal to that on AA-rated corporate bonds. Credit ratings agencies are responding to FRS 17 by downgrading the debt of companies such as BAE Systems, the defence group, where they have concerns about pension deficits. Many UK employers, however, argue that FRS 17 is misleading: although a pension shortfall is presented as a liability, it is not one about to come due in full any time soon.

The International Financial Reporting Standards issued by the IASB have now been adopted by more than 100 countries, on all five continents, with some countries requiring their exclusive use whilst others permitting their use as an alternative to existing 'national' standards. Even the United States, which has traditionally tended to adopt a negative view towards non-US standards, has accepted the trend and is now not only accepting IFRS based company reports, but has also indicated a firm timetable to harmonise US reporting with the international benchmark – with the possibility of complete convergence by 2014.

Case Study 10.6 explores potential sources of criticism of the convergence process.

CASE 10.6 'To converge to a single set of standards is now crucial' **FT**

'The success of an accounting framework comes from widespread acceptance that it provides a reasonable basis to assess past performance and forecast future returns. That also requires the accounting framework to contribute to an understanding of the variability of return: risk, in other words.

'How much more difficult would that task be if every nation still clung to its own language for defining commerce? How much simpler would it be if everyone could understand each other perfectly? The current crisis has increased focus on what has worked well and what has not. It reinforces the need to move together to make things better and we are seeing real momentum towards achieving a shared universal language of accounting. That's why to converge to one set of accounting standards has never been more important and the current financial market crisis is acting as a catalyst to accelerate that path.

'Unfortunately, just as great strides have been taken towards the formation of global accounting standards, some commentators look to shoot the messenger (the International Accounting Standards Board). They point to unintended consequences and asymmetric outcomes to question the accounting framework. They complain when the rules don't change to suit their position and they claim lack of governance when changes, with which they disagree, are made quickly to respond to calls for clarification or correction.

'Within an independent standard-setting process, it is inevitable there will be differing views. That some stakeholders feel aggrieved at the outcome of the debate is evidence of the integrity and independence of the consultation process.'

Source: Flint, D., 'To converge to a single set of standards is now crucial', *Financial Times*, 6 November 2008 (abridged).

Questions

1 What is meant by an 'accounting framework'?

2 Why do some commentators regard changes made to correct and clarify global accounting standards as indicating a 'lack of governance'?

3 To what extent do you agree with the comment 'That some stakeholders feel aggrieved at the outcome of the debate is evidence of the integrity and independence of the consultation process.'

Corporate governance and international business

A number of major corporate failures in the US occurred in 2000–02 linked to alleged accounting irregularities, such as those involving Enron and WorldCom. As a result the Sarbanes-Oxley Act came into US law in late 2002 under which a variety of corporate activities would now be subject to criminal law. Executives who breach the accounts certification measures (*see* Box 10.4) face up to 20 years in prison and a $5 million fine. However in a global economy, these US laws will also affect international business worldwide.

| Box 10.4 | The Sarbanes-Oxley Act 2002 |

Which companies does the act apply to?

Any that have securities registered in America. About half the FTSE 100 companies, for example, have a secondary listing for their shares in the US, while hundreds of other British companies have issued American Depositary Receipts (ADRs) and corporate bonds.

Do chief executives have to swear to the truth of their company accounts?

Yes, and finance directors. But the consensus of legal opinion is that for non-American companies, only annual reports will have to be certified. American companies have to

▶

> ### Box 10.4 Continued
>
> provide a sworn statement even with quarterly accounts. Some British companies may, however, choose to certify their quarterly reports to show American investors that they are 'whiter than white'.
>
> #### What if the accounts are later proven to be wrong?
>
> If officers of the company are proven to have intentionally filed false accounts, they can be sent to jail for up to 20 years and fined $5 million.
>
> #### When does the act come into force?
>
> The requirement to swear the truth of accounts came into effect on 29 July 2002. A second, more onerous, requirement, which will ask companies to prove they have the correct processes in place to guarantee the accuracy of reports, came into effect at the end of November 2002.
>
> #### What will it mean for more junior executives?
>
> Some American companies have already started pushing responsibility further down the corporate ladder. Chief executives are asking divisional heads to sign similar statements pledging that the figures from their areas are accurate.
>
> #### What else should companies look out for?
>
> Sarbanes-Oxley contains a number of other corporate governance requirements. These include:
>
> - executives will have to forfeit bonuses if their accounts have to be restated;
> - a ban on company loans to its directors and executives;
> - protection for corporate whistleblowers;
> - audit committees made up entirely of independent people;
> - disclosure of all off-balance-sheet transactions.
>
> #### Is there any chance UK and other businesses may escape these provisions?
>
> Possibly. In some cases Congress has given the Securities and Exchange Commission (SEC) discretion to grant exemptions, and some legal experts think this will be used to spare companies from outside America some of the Act's more draconian demands.

In the UK the Higgs Committee in 2002 sought to improve corporate governance in the wake of the bitter experiences for shareholders and investors from the collapse of Enron, WorldCom and other high-profile companies. The Higgs proposals included the following.

- at least 50% of a company's board should consist of independent non-executive directors;
- rigorous, formal and transparent procedures should be adopted when recruiting new directors to a board;
- roles of Chairman and Chief Executive of a company should be separate;
- no individual should be appointed to a second chairmanship of a FTSE 100 company.

Useful websites

Now try the self-check questions for this chapter on the website at www.pearsoned.co.uk/wall. You will also find further resources as well as useful weblinks.

International Accountings Standards Board:
www.iasb.org.uk

Accounting Standards Board (UK):
www.asb.org.uk

An excellent site giving many accounting related links:
www.icaew.co.uk

Company websites include:
www.pearson.com/investor/ar2002
www.tesco.com/corporateinfo/

A site giving information on Alternative Risk Transfer:
www.artemis.bm/artemis.htm

A site giving information on Transfer Pricing:
www.transferpricing.com

Useful key texts

Daniels, J., Radebaugh, L. and Sullivan, D. (2006) *International Business* (11th edn), Pearson Prentice Hall, especially Chapter 19.

Hill, C. (2006) *International Business: Competing in the Global Marketplace* (5th edn), McGraw-Hill Irwin, especially Chapters 19 and 20.

International Accounting Standards Board (IASB) (2001) *Framework for the Preparation and Presentation of Financial Statements*, IASB.

Rugman, A. and Collinson, R. (2009) *International Business* (5th edn), FT Prentice Hall, especially Chapter 14.

Other texts and sources

Accounting Standards Board (1999) Statement of Principles for Financial Reporting, London.

American Accounting Association (1966) Statement of Basic Accounting Theory, AAA, New York.

Black, G. (2004) *Introduction to Accounting*, Financial Times Prentice Hall.

Choi, F., Frost, C. and Meek, G. (2001) *International Accounting*, Financial Times Prentice Hall.

CIMA (2005) *Management Accounting: Official Terminology*, London.

Healey, N. (2007) 'The Multinational Corporation', in *Applied Economics* (11th edn), Griffiths, A. and Wall, S. (eds), Financial Times Prentice Hall.

Meulbroek, L. (2000) 'Total Strategies for Risk Control', *Financial Times*, 9 May.

Nobes, C. and Parker, R. (2002) *Comparative International Accounting*, Financial Times Prentice Hall.

Answers and responses

Answers and responses to the 'pause for thought' sections are outlined below. Answers and responses to the Case Study questions have been placed in the Instructor's Manual to accompany this book.

Chapter 1

■ Pause for thought 1

There are many possible examples here. Case Study 1.1 (p. 10) shows Dyson, the vacuum-cleaner firm relocating production from the UK to Malaysia. Case Study 1.5 (p. 25) shows Hyundai outsourcing car production from South Korea to China. BT and other companies have relocated call centre and other back-office functions to India.

■ Pause for thought 2

'Losers' might include airlines, travel- and tourist-related activities (hotels, restaurants, theatres, etc.), among others; 'beneficiaries' might include providers of security equipment and security personnel, among others.

■ Pause for thought 3

France has total labour costs per hour some 32.7 points less than in Germany (based on UK = 100) but a productivity of labour some 8.4 points (based on UK = 100) higher than Germany. On this evidence France would seem the most attractive. However quality of output, transport and distributive infrastructure, host government incentives and many other factors might also be important in determining production location.

■ Pause for thought 4

While there is an ageing demographic profile in many advanced industrialising economies, in many developing economies the demographic profile is becoming progressively younger – with implications for labour supply and consumption patterns. The scourge of HIV in some countries may have important implications for MNEs, reducing labour supply, impoverishing the country (lower increases or even falls in real income per capita) and reducing demand, and so on. There are many possibilities here.

■ Pause for thought 5

Certainly there is greater interconnectedness – with terrorism, real or threatened, in one part of the world having an impact elsewhere. So shrinking space and time and disappearing borders would seem to be implied, which are related to the idea of globalisation as a new phenomenon. We noted earlier that global GDP is projected to be growing around 1% per annum less than estimated before 9/11.

■ Pause for thought 6

There are many possibilities here. For example the brands Kit Kat, Yorkie, After Eight Mints, Polo and Quality Street within the product group *confectionary* are all owned by Nestlé. The brands Ariel and Daz Automatic within the product group *washing powders* are owned by Procter & Gamble, and so on.

Chapter 2

■ Pause for thought 1

Many possibilities. Saturation of demand in domestic market; overseas customers may help extend the product life cycle (if in maturity or decline phase at home); extra output may yield scale economies (lower average cost), to the benefit of both domestic and overseas markets; having consumers in different geographical areas is a useful risk-reduction method; overseas markets may be higher income/growing more rapidly/have less competition than the domestic market, etc.

■ Pause for thought 2

Services are increasingly important globally and most patents refer to industrial applications. Copyright, trademarks and other more service-related means of protecting intellectual property rights are increasingly important.

■ Pause for thought 3

Pressure for greater transparency and compliance with WTO rules should help non-Chinese businesses to operate in China, as it becomes more open and 'rules based'. Entry into the WTO should further stimulate the Chinese economy, making it a still more attractive market for overseas firms.

■ Pause for thought 4

(a) Conglomerates have a diversified portfolio of products: many examples could be used, such as Virgin with its interests in transport (airlines, railways), entertainment (records, etc.), electronic products (e.g. mobile phones), foodstuffs (cola) and many other product groupings.

(b) Benefits include risk-reduction since not all product areas are likely to experience adverse conditions at the same time. Other benefits include enterprise scale economies, e.g. being able to raise capital more cheaply because of the high valuation of the whole enterprise.

(c) In recent times there has been a trend towards focusing on core competencies: the belief being that management can become overstretched by having to deal with too diversified a portfolio of products (i.e. 'sticking to the knitting'). Many recent de-mergers (e.g. Hanson group, ICI) point to this changing perspective.

◼ Pause for thought 5

There are many possibilities here. Reuters has outsourced its own back-office activities to separate service providers in India (as has BT) and many other MNEs. General Motors has set up its own financial arm to lend money to customers buying cars. Ford, Daimler-Chrysler and others have done the same. Ford, the world's second biggest car-maker, earns more from lending money than selling vehicles.

Chapter 3

◼ Pause for thought 1

(a) An export of 250 videos by A would now only give imports of 500 CDs instead of the previous 750 CDs. The new 'post-specialisation and trade' consumption point of 550 videos and 500 CDs is now inside A's production possibility frontier. In other words it could do better by being self-sufficient than by engaging in specialisation and trade according to comparative advantages.

(b) An export of 750 CDs by B would now only give imports of 75 videos instead of the previous 250 videos. The new 'post-specialisation and trade' consumption point of 250 CDs and 75 videos is now inside B's production possibility frontier. In other words, it could do better by being self-sufficient than by engaging in specialisation and trade according to comparative advantages.

(c) 1 CD : 0.2 videos equals 1 video : 5 CDs.

(d) Neither would be better or worse off by specialisation and trade according to comparative advantages. They would be in exactly the same situation as they would be had they chosen to be self-sufficient.

◼ Pause for thought 2

When there was complete protection, this area was *producer surplus* to domestic suppliers with the domestic price P_D. Now there is free trade, the world price for the product P_W is the same as the domestic price and this area is now *consumer surplus* to domestic purchasers. In other words, this area is neither gained nor lost as a result of free trade: it simply *transfers* from being producer surplus to being consumer surplus.

◼ Pause for thought 3

There are many possibilities here. *Architecture*: The Body Shop, PizzaHut, McDonald's and many other MNEs are well known for using contractual relationships (e.g. franchising) to further their businesses. *Innovation*: Microsoft has a well-established reputation for innovative approaches to home and business uses of its software systems. *Incumbency advantages*: BP has acquired interests in oil fields all over the world, some dating back to the early twentieth century and the easy access then available to the oil fields in the Middle East via British colonialism.

■ Pause for thought 4

From a *national* perspective, the major reductions in global GDP noted in Chapter 1 (some 1% lower growth per annum) means that for most countries 'demand conditions' will be less favourable, with possible adverse consequences for 'factor conditions' and 'related and supporting industries'. Of course nations with competitive advantages in particular sectors (e.g. defence, security industries) may be relatively better placed than others.

■ Pause for thought 5

Export prices of the UK products in the euro-zone would fall in terms of the euro and import prices in the UK (from euro-zone countries) would rise in terms of sterling. For example, an item priced at £1000 in the UK would have a euro-zone equivalent price of €1400 before the sterling depreciation but only €1000 after. An item priced at €1400 in the euro-zone would have a sterling equivalent price of £1000 before the sterling depreciation but £1400 after.

■ Pause for thought 6

For localisation: supports local output and employment; protects smaller firms and nations from the pressures of the larger (multinational) firms and nations; avoids allegedly unfair current rules of world trade; supports national sovereignty; etc.

Against localisation: lose any gains from global specialisation and trade; consumers may face higher prices since loss of scale economies (therefore lower real incomes); may be a reduction in global output and employment; involves imposing regulations on national governments; etc.

■ Pause for thought 7

We have seen that quotas, which form the basis of borrowing rights (e.g. reserve and credit tranches) are allocated in proportion to a member country's share of world trade. As a result, the richer countries get the higher quotas and borrowing rights when arguably they need them least. This same allocation principle also applies to Special Drawing Rights (SDRs) with most going to the richer countries. However, the many borrowing facilities (*see* p. 123) have been used to help the disadvantaged countries, as have many of the various stabilisation programmes, though many recipient countries have complained that the conditions required for such help have been too strict and too deflationary.

Chapter 4

■ Pause for thought 1

Mandatory labour benefits legislation (e.g. EU Social Chapter directives) and currency appreciation might figure highly. Other future possibilities include future risks of inflation, increased taxation and campaigns against foreign goods and perhaps violence (e.g. if the Northern Ireland peace process is disrupted, etc.). Expropriation/confiscation and civil wars are highly implausible.

▪ Pause for thought 2

Many possibilities here. Be careful in interpreting individual factors – for example, once established in a country, import restrictions (item 20 in Table 4.2) may benefit the MNE in excluding competitors rather than hinder it in excluding part of its supply chain.

Remember that political risk is only one of the relevant perspectives. Even if there is greater political risk, the MNE may choose that location if the potential economic or strategic benefits are deemed overwhelming. The decision also depends on how 'risk averse' the MNE management is.

▪ Pause for thought 3

Imperfect information: some buyers or sellers know more than others, and knowledge is power in a marketplace. *Non-competitive market structures*: monopoly power may give undue influence to some firms in setting higher prices (exploit consumers) or offering lower wages (exploit workers); etc. *Externalities*: negative externalities imply that social cost is higher than private cost, e.g. firms polluting the environment and not having to pay for it – tends to result in more output than society might want.

▪ Pause for thought 4

A weaker euro against the US dollar means that euro-zone exports become cheaper in the US and US exports to the euro-zone become more expensive. The same will be true for China, which should find it more difficult to penetrate the EU market now that its (low cost) exports are more expensive in the euro-zone. On the other hand, EU exports to China should be cheaper in the Chinese currency.

Chapter 5

▪ Pause for thought 1

Australia and Denmark both score relatively highly for 'individualism' but relatively lowly for 'power distance'. This suggests that managers and employees will tend to focus on their own and other individuals' interests and to be somewhat critical of those in authority. Both (especially Denmark) are towards the weak end of the spectrum for 'uncertainty avoidance', suggesting that change will be viewed rather positively. However, Australia scores much higher in terms of 'masculinity' than Denmark, suggesting that socially-orientated goals are more acceptable in Denmark than Australia where a more acquisitive and assertive outlook is usually adopted (at least vis-à-vis Denmark).

Japan and Singapore are both towards the 'collectivist' end of the spectrum with more focus on group interests. They both more readily accept authority (larger power distance) than Australia and Denmark. However, whereas Japan strongly favours structure and a consistent routine (strong 'uncertainty avoidance'), Singapore will more readily accept change and look for new opportunities (weak 'uncertainty avoidance'). Japan more readily accepts values associated with material possessions (high 'masculinity') than Singapore with its more socially-orientated values (weak masculinity/high femininity).

These different national characteristics clearly have important implications for many aspects of management including organisational structures, methods of incentivisation, human resource management issues and so on, many of which are considered in Chapters 7–10 of this book.

■ Pause for thought 2

Individualism. The more individualist approach may result in greater focus on outcomes and individual contributions to these outcomes rather than team and group 'success'. Relationships may be neglected, causing confusion and a lack of goal-congruence between the collaborating companies.

Long-term orientation. The company placing more emphasis on this aspect may be looking at longer-term goals (e.g. market share) rather than shorter-term goals (e.g. profits, shareholder value). Again, there may be problems in establishing goal congruence.

■ Pause for thought 3

Many possibilities here. For example the founders of some companies (e.g. The Body Shop, Virgin) can have a major influence on their values and culture.

■ Pause for thought 4

Many possibilities here. The 'individualism' versus 'collectivism' dimension of Hofstede is quite closely captured in the scores for the related dimensions of Trompenaars. Similarly, the 'power-distance' dimension of Hofstede is, again, quite similar in national scores to the 'achieved' versus 'ascribed' dimension of Trompenaars, with countries having a large power-distance for Hofstede tending to have a high 'ascribed status' for Trompenaars.

■ Pause for thought 5

You can apply the four strategies to any organisation with which you are familiar or work situations in which you have found yourself.

Chapter 6

■ Pause for thought 1

Various possibilities exist. For example, MNEs from western nations may resist various types of hospitality/gift-giving as akin to bribery, when in *guanxi* relationships of MNEs from East and South-East Asian nations it is an accepted way of doing business (*see* Chapter 5).

■ **Pause for thought 2**

What is deemed unethical under one set of national cultural values may be deemed acceptable under others. The *guanxi* relationships of giving which are part of a complex set of social networking in many Asian countries may be viewed as bribery in western-orientated countries, etc.

■ **Pause for thought 3**

There are many possibilities here, e.g. the *Forest Stewardship Council* sets the standards for sustainable forestry.

■ **Pause for thought 4**

There are many possibilities here, for example Nestlé introduced an 'ombudsman system', allowing its employees to blow the whistle on any unethical marketing of baby milk formula to mothers in developing countries.

Chapter 7

■ **Pause for thought 1**

Horizontal diversification involves new products in new markets, where those new products broadly correspond to the *existing stage of production* in which the initiating company currently operates and which have some relationship to the current product range. For example, a clothing manufacturer introducing a new range of clothing into, say, the niche, higher priced/quality designer market having previously operated in the mass, low price/quality standardised garment market.

Vertical diversification involves *different stages of production*. This can be 'backward' towards the source of supply (e.g. a retail outlet starting to make some of the products it sells) or 'forward' towards the retail outlet (e.g. a manufacturer starting to retail some of its products).

All the above types of diversification were regarded by Ansoff as 'related'. *Conglomerate diversification*, however, is 'unrelated', involving new products which have little or no relationship to the existing product range. Virgin moving into car retailing might arguably be an example here.

■ **Pause for thought 2**

Many possibilities here. For example, in terms of supermarkets ('multiple grocers'), Safeway prior to being taken over by Somerfield might have been regarded as a 'marginal' firm and Tesco is certainly a market leader. Tesco has developed competitive advantage over its rivals in terms of 'incumbency advantages' (scale economies, reputation, etc.), 'innovation' with new kinds of club cards, new services (e.g. financial) and 'operational efficiencies' (check-out facilities, just-in-time delivery techniques), etc.

Pause for thought 3

Firm A: low price; best outcome for A is firm B adopting high price (£3000).
Firm A: high price; best outcome for A is firm B adopting low price (£2000).
Mini-max for A is high price (worst of best possible outcomes).
Firm B: low price; best outcome for B is firm A adopting high price (£3000).
Firm B: high price; best outcome for B is firm A adopting low price (£2000).
Mini-max for B is high price (worst of best possible outcomes).
Mini-max outcome is high price: high price – both disappointed.

Pause for thought 4

Substantial economies of scale available, reducing average production costs substantially. When the minimum efficient size (MES) of the production unit is very high, the only way to be competitive with rivals may be to use these processes.

Chapter 8

Pause for thought 1

(a) There is considerable 'cultural distance' between Great Britain and Japan in terms of the four cultural dimensions shown in Table 5.3. To bridge this cultural distance, a more decentralised and polycentric approach is perhaps more likely than an integrated and ethnocentric approach.

(b) With Canada there is much less 'cultural distance' with Great Britain so that any of the IHRM approaches would appear feasible, depending on the MNE's needs and objectives. Certainly there is more likely to be an integrated and ethnocentric approach to IHRM for Canada as compared to Japan.

Chapter 9

Pause for thought 1

- *Benefit segmentation* looks at the benefits consumers want from the product. Thus, toothpaste may be bought to obtain white teeth or a fresh-mouth taste. A drink may be bought because it has a great taste or less calories.
- *Behaviour segmentation* is based on individuals' behaviour patterns and consumption habits. Thus some people will only buy clothing from speciality men's or women's shops, while others will use departmental stores or discount stores. These shopping habits may be used as the basis for segmentation.
- *Geodemographic segmentation* is used where there are noticeable differences in peoples habits based upon geography. For example, urban versus rural, hot versus cold or North versus South.
- *Lifestyle segmentation* is based upon how individuals spend their time and money. Many magazines segment their market by lifestyle. These magazines provide other firms who wish to reach the same segment with the opportunity to advertise to, and reach that target market.

■ Pause for thought 2

Some of the following points might be listed.

Domestic marketing	International marketing
Main language	Many languages
Dominant culture	Multi-culture
Research relatively straightforward	Research complex
Relatively stable environment	Frequently unstable environment
Single currency	Exchange rate problems
Business conventions understood	Conventions diverse and unclear

■ Pause for thought 3

- For price falls along a unit elastic demand curve (PED = 1) or segment of a demand curve, there will be no change in total revenue (Area 2 = Area 3).
- For price falls along a relatively elastic demand curve (PED > 1) or segment of a demand curve, total revenue will increase as there is a more than proportionate response of extra consumers to the now lower price (Area 3 > Area 2).
- For price falls along a relatively inelastic demand curve (PED < 1) or segment of a demand curve, total revenue will decrease as there is a less than proportionate response of extra consumers to the now lower price (Area 3 < Area 2).

■ Pause for thought 4

There are many possibilities here. Differences in costs of materials used in the Big Mac, in infrastructure costs such as leasing of premises, differences in income per head, differences in competitive environment, etc.

■ Pause for thought 5

This should result in an increase in demand for your product, i.e. shift of the demand curve to the right. At any given price, more consumers may switch to your product from other products now that they are aware that your product exists at a lower price.

■ Pause for thought 6

In Slovakia there may be more emphasis on reaching consumers with promotional campaigns on satellite television than in South Korea. However telephone campaigns would be more appropriate as a 'route to market' in South Korea than in Slovakia, as would computer-based advertising.

Chapter 10

■ Pause for thought 1

- Shift (decrease) in demand to the left of D. This might be caused by fewer overseas residents wanting to buy the UK's exports, demanding less sterling to pay for them. Alternatively, fewer overseas firms (or individuals) might want to invest in the UK, demanding less sterling to finance this investment.

- With the yuan as the currency vis-à-vis the dollar, the Chinese authority would try to *prevent* the demand for the yuan increasing against the US dollar and/or increase the supply of yuan against the US dollar. The latter is the more likely policy, with purchases by the Chinese authorities (and businesses) of the UK dollar or dollar denominated assets on the various foreign exchange and securities markets.

Pause for thought 2

Many possibilities here.

Pause for thought 3

Many possibilities here.

Pause for thought 4

Many possibilities here.

Pause for thought 5

A standardised international approach to accounting practice would certainly help investors interpret reported data. In some cases it would also help senior executives and management avoid damaging and selective reporting in the press. Under British accounting standards, Rover's trading situation was much healthier than it appeared under German accounting standards. In the case of British Airways, the reported net profit varied upwards or downwards due to the fluctuating effects of UK or US accounting standards in specific periods.

Index